Japan Encounters the Barbarian

Japan

Encounters the Barbarian

JAPANESE TRAVELLERS IN AMERICA AND EUROPE

W. G. Beasley

Yale University Press
New Haven & London   1995

Set in Meridien by Best-set Typesetter Ltd, Hong Kong
Printed and bound in Great Britain by Biddles Ltd, Guildford and Kings Lynn

Library of Congress Cataloging-in-Publication Data

Beasley, W. G. (William G.), 1919–
    Japan encounters the barbarian: Japanese travellers in America
and Europe/W. G. Beasley.
        p. cm.
    Includes bibliographical references and index.
    ISBN 0–300–06324–5
    1. Japan—Relations—Foreign countries. 2. Japan—Civilization—
Western influences. I. Title.
DS882.6.B43 1995
327.52′009′034—dc20   95–7979
                                                                       CIP

A catalogue record for this book is available from the British Library.

Contents

List of Illustrations   vii
Preface   ix
Note on Japanese words, names and dates   xi

1 *Prologue: Japan and China*   1
   TRADE AND TRIBUTE MISSIONS 2
   CULTURAL BORROWING 8

2 *Barbarian Books*   17
   THE REJECTION OF CHRISTIANITY 18
   DUTCH STUDIES 22
   THE MILITARY DIMENSION 29

3 *Unequal Treaties*   37
   THE FOREIGN POLICY DEBATE 38
   WESTERN STUDIES AND MILITARY REFORM 45

4 *The Mission to America, 1860*   56
   DIPLOMATIC TRAVELS 57
   THE VOYAGE OF THE KANRIN MARU 67

5 *The Mission to Europe, 1862*   71
   THE MISSION'S INSTRUCTIONS 72
   EUROPE OBSERVED 76
   INVESTIGATING AND REPORTING 88

6 *Envoys and Industry, 1865–1867*   95
   EDO AND FRANCE 96
   SATSUMA AND ECONOMIC OPPORTUNITY 105
   THE PARIS EXPOSITION 114

7 *The First Japanese Students Overseas, 1862–1868*   119
   BAKUFU STUDENTS 121
   DOMAIN STUDENTS 129

Contents

8 *From Tokugawa to Meiji*   139
   WESTERN ADVICE AND JAPANESE BUREAUCRATS   *140*
   STUDENTS AND OTHER TRAVELLERS   *147*

9 *The Iwakura Embassy, 1871–1873*   157
   PLANS   *157*
   TRAVELS   *162*
   REPORTS   *171*

10 *The Fruits of Experience: I. Later Careers*   178
    TOKUGAWA ENVOYS AND STUDENTS   *179*
    TRAVELLERS FROM THE DOMAINS BEFORE 1868   *188*
    EARLY MEIJI TRAVELLERS   *192*

11 *The Fruits of Experience: II. Policies and Ideas*   200
    WEALTH AND STRENGTH   *201*
    THE NATURE OF SOCIETY   *207*

12 *Conclusion: Japan and the West*   217

    Notes   224
    Bibliography   231
    Index   242

Illustrations

1. American telegraph, demonstrated at Yokohama, 1854. (Courtesy of Mr Matsudaira Yasushi of Tokyo and the Shiryō Hensanjo, Tokyo University)   46

2. Diagram of a Colt revolver, 1854. (Courtesy of Shiryō Hensanjo, Tokyo University)   47

3. Japanese sketch of a gas chandelier in the White House, 1860. Included with Yanagawa Masakiyo's diary, ed. M. G. Mori, Kobe, 1937.   60

4. The Japanese envoys received at the White House, May 1860. From *Harper's Weekly*, 26 May 1860. (British Library)   62

5. Members of the 1862 mission study a map of London on arrival. From *Le Monde Illustré*, 17 May 1862. (British Library)   82

6. The Japanese envoys visit the International Exhibition in London, 1862. From the *Illustrated London News*, 24 May 1862. (British Library)   83

7. Godai Tomoatsu and colleagues in London, 1865. From the biography of Godai Tomoatsu, ed. Godai Ryūsaku, Tokyo, 1933.   110

8. Tokugawa Akitake at Portsmouth Dockyard, 1867. From the *Illustrated London News*, 21 Dec. 1867, (British Library)   118

Preface

Japan is the outstanding example of a non-western country which has adopted a wide range of western institutions and ideas in the nineteenth and twentieth centuries. The results have been far-reaching. In the first place, the infusion of western knowledge and ideas — something much more complex and fundamental than mere 'copying', though that was part of it — contributed to the shaping of a society which proved able not only to fend off the imperialism of the nineteenth-century West, but also, within a generation or two, to build an empire of its own. This process culminated in the Greater East Asia Co-prosperity Sphere; and when the last of the wars associated with that process ended in defeat in 1945, the same borrowed skills were put to the creation of Japan's 'economic miracle'.

This, however, is not the whole of the story. Some of Japan's early students of the West, following a path which had begun to emerge in the eighteenth century, had concentrated their attention not so much on the practical merits of western civilization, in the form of contributions to 'wealth and strength', as on what they perceived to be its essential character. The studies they undertook of western laws and social structures, of western doctrines and behaviour, led them to identify alternatives to the Sino-Japanese tradition to which Japan belonged — especially to the authoritarian politics and social backwardness which in their view Japanese governments endorsed — and thus to lay a foundation for the American-inspired democracy of the occupation years (1945–51). They led, or provided arguments for, the demands for a parliamentary constitution, for political parties, for trade unions and more liberal labour laws, for equality for women, for everything, in fact, that comprised Enlightenment, as they saw it.

Historians often make the point that none of Japan's modern achievements, whether good or bad, would have been feasible without the political, social and economic framework which had been put into place under Tokugawa rule. That is, the modern has premodern roots, which are indigenous. This is true enough. Yet it is also true that a great deal of what occurred by way of change in Japan after the Meiji Restoration of 1868 rested on the efforts of several hundred Japanese travellers, who set out, soon after the ports were opened to international trade in 1859, to see the West for themselves and learn what it could teach. It is with these that most of this book will deal: their motives, where they went and what they studied, the knowledge and ideas they took home with them, the ways in which they contributed in later life to the moulding of their country's future.

In writing such a book I have incurred, as all western students of Japan must do, an enormous debt to the many Japanese scholars whose books, articles and published texts provide the bulk of the material on which it depends. They are, I hope, sufficiently identified in the bibliography. I would like in particular, however, to record here my special gratitude to the late Professor Numata Jirō, not only because of his many valuable publications in this field, but also because he contributed so much personally to the growth of my knowledge, first in teaching me to read late Tokugawa documents during 1950 and 1951, then by the help and advice he continued to give me in the following forty years.

In addition, I would like to express my thanks to Mr Matsudaira Yasushi for permission to reproduce the sketch of the telegraph equipment brought by Perry, which is part of his family records now on loan to the Shiryō Hensanjo, Tokyo University; to the Director of the Shiryō Hensanjo for allowing me access to the manuscripts in the Hensanjo collection and for authorising the publication of photographs from it; and to Professor Miyachi Masato of the Shiryō Hensanjo for his help in making these arrangements.

W. G. B.

Note on Japanese words, names and dates

Because the Japanese language is written in a combination of ideographs and syllabic script, there are a number of ways in which it can be rendered alphabetically. The one used in this book is the modified Hepburn system, which comes fairly close to being phonetic. There is a problem about distinguishing between long and short vowel sounds. The former are here identified by the use of a macron (kō, kū), the latter by its omission (ko, ku). For the sake of typographical simplicity, macrons are in all cases omitted in geographical names (e.g. Tokyo, not Tōkyō), as well as in words which are thought likely to be familiar to readers (e.g. Shogun, not Shōgun; daimyo, not daimyō). In Japanese nouns the singular and plural are identical.

Japanese personal names are given in the usual Japanese word order, that is, family name, followed by given name (e.g. Itō Hirobumi, where Itō is the family name). In the period studied in this book an unusually large proportion of men changed their names, either through adoption, or for some other reason. Cross-references are given in the index, but not always in the text.

Until 1 January 1873 Japan officially used a lunar calendar. Dates in this book have been converted to the western (Gregorian) equivalent, or some approximation to it (e.g. 'late June 1864' is Gregorian, and derives from a date which would have been given in Japanese as falling within the fifth lunar month of the first year of Ganji).

1

Prologue: Japan and China

In the nineteenth century European imperialism spread across Asia to reach the coasts of China and Japan, where in pursuit of markets for their trade the maritime powers concluded what are known as 'unequal treaties'. Imposed by the threat or use of force, these caused enormous resentment. In the case of Japan, paradoxically, they also prompted a programme of cultural borrowing from the West, designed to make possible a level of 'national wealth and strength' that might in due course secure revision of the treaties on equal terms. The policy was sometimes described as 'using the barbarian to control the barbarian'. In effect this was to give a new gloss to a Chinese phrase which had traditionally referred to the tactic of playing off one non-Chinese ruler beyond the frontier against another, but was now taken to signify the importation of western military organization and technology, financed by western-style commerce and industry. This book is about those who first set out for the countries of the West, either as students or as members of diplomatic missions, to acquire the knowledge which would make that policy feasible.

This was not the first time in Japanese history that cultural borrowing had taken place on a massive scale. During the seventh and eighth centuries, when the Japanese state was still in its infancy, its rulers had made considerable efforts to seek out for themselves and their subjects the skills and knowledge which were thought to be the secrets of China's power. The parallel did not escape the notice of men in late Tokugawa Japan. Sakuma Shōzan, then the most famous advocate of study of the West, writing to a friend in 1858, pointed out that by working to bring about the adoption in Japan of 'the strong points of China' in contexts ranging from etiquette, music, government and law to weapons, tactics, the calendar and arithmetic, the early emperors had taken just the kind of steps which he himself was urging to meet Japan's new needs.[1]

In the phrase 'use the barbarian', westerners were described as *i*, a term by which both Chinese and Japanese identified those who were outside the bounds of Confucian society. This reflected the fact that most members of Japan's ruling class were brought up, at least to a degree, in the tenets of Confucian thought. They believed, like their Chinese counterparts, that there was only one truly superior civilization, and that it derived from China. To them, being civilized depended on observing Confucian ethical rules. Since these rules were alien to the West, it followed that to undertake any kind of borrowing from the West which involved values, not merely techniques, was to turn one's back on what was best in the human condition and look for guidance to the barbarian.

Seen in this light, Japan's cultural debt to China over the centuries had significant consequences for the country's modern dealings with the West. On the one hand, it helped to make cultural borrowing as such respectable. On the other, it had introduced a number of beliefs which were obstacles to the acceptance of what non-Confucian societies had to teach. This being so, it seems sensible to start by taking a closer look at it.

TRADE AND TRIBUTE MISSIONS

Japan came under the influence of the nearby Asian mainland even before there were Japanese histories to record the fact. Rice and sericulture, bronze and iron, the skills of weaving and metalworking, the techniques of irrigation, all these entered Japan from the continent, apparently from or via Korea. At a later stage, beginning in the fourth century of the Christian era, came the ox and the ox-drawn plough, the horse and horse-trappings for mounted warriors, the Chinese written language, with which to keep records and accounts, and the Buddhist religion. Most of these imports were linked with the arrival of immigrants, some of whom were refugees from warfare in the Korean peninsula, or prisoners taken on Japanese forays there, while others were experts of various kinds, invited to Japan for the sake of their knowledge. As a result, by the early part of the seventh century men and women from abroad were present in Japan in considerable numbers. As scribes and interpreters at court, as Buddhist priests and monks and nuns, as craftsmen making weapons and tools or engaged in the building and decoration of Buddhist temples, they helped to raise Japanese culture to a level which even educated Chinese might have found acceptable, at least in the capital. A fair proportion reached positions of rank. A document of 815 described about one in three of the 1,200 noble families listed in it as being Chinese or Korean by descent.

Towards the end of the sixth century Japan's rulers began to make overtures to China on their own account, a decision they took as much from motives of fear as admiration. In 589 the Sui dynasty had brought all China under its control after a long interval of disunity. In 618 it was followed by the T'ang, whose imperial line was to rule for another three hundred years from its splendid capital of Ch'ang-an. One consequence was that being suitably 'Chinese' became an ambition of China's semi-barbarian neighbours along the northern frontier, partly for the sake of acquiring prestige at home, partly as a form of insurance against what was perceived to be the danger of Chinese attack. This insurance was princi-pally achieved through the so-called 'tribute system', that is, by sending envoys to China on a regular basis to present gifts and acknowledge a form of Chinese suzerainty, while receiving in return political protection and certain privileges of trade. Such missions had the additional merit of affording access to a knowledge of things Chinese, through which one might achieve self-strengthening.

Japan, like the states of Paekche and Silla in southern Korea, decided to adopt this course. Between 607 and 838–9 there were seventeen full-scale Japanese missions to China, in each of which the envoy and his deputy — men of high rank, chosen in part for their literary reputation, in order to sustain the claim that Japan was civilized — were accompa-nied by several councillors of diplomatic standing, together with interpreters in Chinese and Korean, supercargoes in charge of the tribute goods, priests, diviners, doctors, a painter, scribes, musicians, a military escort and various attendants. The duty of the painter was to copy religious pictures and images, that of the priests and diviners to conduct the appropriate ceremonies to ensure a safe voyage. It is not clear what the musicians were for, unless it was to demonstrate that in Japan, too, rites and music were held to be adjuncts to government in the Confucian manner. In addition to all these there were students and student-priests, who were not part of the official entourage, but whose studies were government-sponsored. They brought the total numbers, including ships' officers and crews, to about 250 in the early days, when two ships were usually sent, rising to 600 or more, carried in four ships, during much of the eighth century.

Their travels were difficult and dangerous. It was at first possible to use the safer route up the west coast of Korea and across the Yellow Sea, since much of it was controlled by the kingdom of Paekche, with which Japan was in alliance, but after 660 Paekche's defeat by Silla — hostile to Japan — increased the risks of such a journey. In 698 Japan sent a party to explore an alternative route via the Ryukyu islands, several of which were annexed, opening up a way across the East China Sea to ports near the mouth of the Yangtze. In the ninth century a variant on this emerged, by which ships sailed to China from Hakata via the Goto islands off northwest Kyushu. Both these southern routes involved a long and often stormy passage by the open sea.

3

The Japanese were a good deal less well equipped than Chinese or Koreans to undertake such voyages. Their ships were flat-bottomed and had no pointed bow. Sail-handling qualities were poor, making it possible to use sails only when running before the wind. This meant relying frequently on the use of oars or sweeps. Moreover, their commanders seem to have had only a minimal understanding of the seas they crossed. As European navigators were to find in the sixteenth century, the voyage from Japan to China under sail is best undertaken during the northerly monsoon, that is, in winter, and the return by the southerly monsoon in summer. To judge by their sailing dates, early Japanese ships' masters were not aware of this. Delays and disasters were therefore not uncommon: it has been estimated that almost a third of those who set out from Japan in the Nara period (710–84) never returned. It is not surprising in these circumstances that some of the men appointed to the missions declined to go, while others, having made the passage to China, preferred to remain there, or to come home in Korean ships, which were rightly thought to be better-found and better manned.

About the mission of 838–9, which was to be the last of the series, we know more than we do about the rest, because it was accompanied by the monk Ennin, whose diary has been published and translated.[2] Its members were appointed in 834. Building the ships, assembling the official gifts, and attending farewell banquets in the capital — at which most of those present became drunk, as custom seems to have required — took until the early summer of 836. The expedition then sailed from Naniwa (modern Osaka) as far as Kyushu, but when it left there two months later in the teeth of the monsoon, the four ships comprising it encountered a storm, by which one was sunk and the other three forced back to Japan's west coast. While they were being repaired, which took a year, the envoys returned to the capital. In the summer of 837 they tried again, only to be driven back once more by the weather; and before a third attempt could be made in 838 the vice-envoy and four others pleaded illness as grounds for withdrawing from their duties. They were punished by exile from the court, but their fears proved not to be unfounded. When the ill-starred venture at last reached China, two of the three remaining ships ran aground and had to be abandoned. The third, attempting the return crossing from the Shantung peninsula in 839, was driven south by contrary winds and wrecked on an island, possibly Taiwan. Its thirty survivors made their way to southern Kyushu in the spring of 840, rejoining the rest of their party, who, showing greater circumspection, had travelled via the Yellow Sea and the coastal route in chartered Korean ships.

Most of those who succeeded in reaching China on the various missions were required to remain at their port of arrival until the voyage home, but the ambassadors and their immediate entourage travelled at

China's expense to Ch'ang-an, using the facilities provided for Chinese officials. It was at this stage that difficulties of protocol were likely to occur. The mission of 607, for example, carried a letter described as being from the emperor (*tenshi*, or Son of Heaven) of the land of the Rising Sun to the emperor of the land of the Setting Sun. Such a claim to equality, or even superiority, can only be described as ill-advised. The Sui court's reply may well have contained a sharp rebuke: the Japanese envoy took care to lose it on his way home. Certainly in 608 Japan tried something less provocative. 'The emperor (*tennō*) of the East', its greeting read, 'respectfully addresses the emperor (*huang-ti*) of the West'.[3] Since the Chinese did not perceive Tennō to be the equal of Huang-ti, this was allowed to pass, but letters were not brought at all in the next two hundred years, so far as the records show. Nor does Japan's imperial house appear to have used a royal title bestowed by the Chinese emperor, as would have been normal practice in tribute relationships with other countries (though the absence of any mention of such a title may simply reflect caution on the part of the scribes).

There were also susceptibilities of a different kind. Chinese histories had from very early times described Japan by the name Wo (Wa in Japanese), meaning dwarf. This had derogatory and perhaps Korean connotations. However, sometime after the middle of the seventh century Japan began officially to use the name Nihon, or Nippon, meaning Sun-origin. Chinese chroniclers duly followed suit (their reading of the written characters, Jih-pen, giving us — through Marco Polo — the western usage, Japan). A little more controversial at times were the diplomatic niceties to be observed in the Chinese capital. For example, in 753 a Japanese mission was in Ch'ang-an on the occasion of a New Year reception for foreign representatives. When the Japanese ambassador discovered that he was to be accorded a place below that of his counterpart from Silla, he protested — successfully — on the grounds that Silla itself was in the habit of sending tribute to Japan.

Despite these assertions of monarchical dignity, the reality was that the Japanese came to China as supplicants, much to their profit. The gifts they brought, where we have knowledge of them, included silver, pearls, agate, several types of crude silk and hempen cloth, together with silk floss, that is, natural products of Japan and rudimentary textiles. Individual members of the missions brought gold dust, apparently for personal expenditure: Ennin tells us of a man who spent what seems the staggering sum of two hundred ounces of gold dust for lessons on the lute (*biwa*) from a famous Chinese teacher. Return presents from the Chinese court, which as a matter of course were more valuable than those it received, took the form of rich silks, damasks and brocades, perfumes, medicines, musical instruments, and weapons. To these were added books, many of them requested by the Japanese. A catalogue of

891, which listed Chinese books available in Japan, includes over 1,700 titles, dealing with such subjects as the Confucian classics, court ceremonial, legal codes, medicine, Chinese history, poetry, calendars and divination.

Acquiring these books was probably in the long run more important than the other information-gathering activities of the missions, since there is little reason to believe that the Japanese who went to China were able to learn very much through conversation. Ennin, for example, though a Chinese scholar of repute, had to conduct his initial investigations of Buddhist doctrine by exchanging written questions and answers with Chinese abbots. The Chinese histories also tell us of other Japanese who had similar problems. From this one must conclude that when Japanese envoys were given permission to consult Confucian teachers and Buddhist priests, they did so through their interpreters. In any event, what they learnt in China does not often seem to have helped their subsequent careers, to judge from the study made by Charlotte von Verschuer.[4] The doctors did better than the diplomats in this respect: the superior medical knowledge they acquired stood them in good stead professionally on their return. Some of the students did better still, coming home after several years as 'China experts' in the fullest sense, a qualification which promised academic and even, perhaps, political recognition. Kibi no Mabiki, who went to China in 717 and stayed for seventeen years, later became head of the university in Nara and lecturer to the court on the Chinese classics; was sent to China again in 752 as vice-ambassador; and ended his career — exceptionally — as a senior minister.

Japan occasionally received return embassies from China, though these were little more than a formal response to the tribute relationship. Of more practical value were those which came China's other tribute states, such as Silla and Parhae (a kingdom in northeast Korea). While ostensibly for the exchange of diplomatic gifts, these visits had trade as their prime object, at least as much so as those of Japanese to China, and Japan came to rely on them for a number of luxury items. Custom required that the imperial house and its courtiers should have first choice of these, but on at least one occasion a market was set up outside the palace gates at which the surplus was sold to the rest of the capital's population. It is a testimony to the value of this thinly-disguised commercial activity that during the ninth century, when official missions came to an end, it was continued by Chinese and Korean merchants coming to northern Kyushu. The goods for which they found the readiest demand were the same as those which embassies had brought as presents: silks, damasks, brocades, perfumes and medicines from China, plus books, together with metalwork (including bronze mirrors), skins, cosmetics, ginseng and honey from Korea. Japan offered in return mostly silk floss and low-grade textiles.

Missions to China came to an end after that of 838, partly because of a breakdown of political order in the region as the power of the T'ang declined, putting in question the benefits of Chinese patronage, partly because of the increasing value of the non-tribute trade which Japan enjoyed, since this ensured that most of the profits of the China connection could be had without the expense of sending and receiving envoys. These considerations were reinforced by increasing Japanese self-confidence with respect to culture. For the next few hundred years, trade, carried on by Chinese and Korean merchants, whenever political turbulence did not prevent it, was the main form of Sino-Japanese contact. It brought to Japan goods from the outside world, including books and other cultural objects, and it provided the ships by which Buddhist monks could travel at need to the continental centres of their religion.

The commercial link, always tenuous and often threatened by violence, continued intermittently until the fifteenth century. Tribute missions were then resumed, though on a different footing. Effective power in Japan had by that time passed from the hands of the imperial court into those of feudal overlords, holding office as Shogun; and the most recent of these, drawn from the Ashikaga house, which had established its power during the fourteenth century, saw enough advantage in trying to bolster their authority at home through recognition by the Ming to accept some loss of dignity to secure it. In the letters they began to send to China in 1401 they regularly signed themselves 'King of Japan, a subject of the Ming Emperor'. China's rulers hoped for their part that by renewing official relations with Japan they could persuade the Ashikaga to suppress the pirates, based in western Japan and nearby islands, whose raids on the Chinese coast had grown in scale and frequency in the previous hundred years.

In the event, neither side achieved its political objectives. Piracy continued. The Ashikaga, for all that they sent a selection of supposedly pirate heads to China from time to time, were too weak to control the lords of west Japan, several of whom gave the pirates protection. As a result, the envoys Japan sent to the Ming court — there were nineteen missions between 1401 and 1549 — met an increasingly cool reception. Nor did they show the same readiness to study China's institutions and ideas as those who had gone in earlier centuries. The shift to feudal patterns of government in Japan meant that China's established form of imperial rule no longer seemed entirely relevant as a model; and while educated Japanese still expressed an admiration for Chinese art, literature and religion — indeed, more so under the Ashikaga than for a long time past — a knowledge of these no longer depended on diplomatic missions. The

7

true nexus of the relationship, in fact, remained seaborne trade, now carried once more in tribute ships. Shogun and feudal lords gave their patronage to voyages for the sake of a share in the proceeds. Merchants brought Chinese books and paintings to Japan as a commercial venture. Even the shrines and monasteries, whose priests, travelling as envoys, interpreters and students, were the principal agents in bringing the culture of Sung and Ming to Japan, won political influence as a reward for their services. What had chiefly changed was that these things were now being done by Japanese on Japanese initiative.

The benefits to China were less apparent. There was no reduction in pirate attacks on the China coast; rival Japanese missions, sponsored by different political authorities, came to blows in Chinese ports; and disputes emerged about the nature of official presents and the prices to be paid for other goods. At last, in 1549 the Ming withdrew permission for Japanese ships to come to Ningpo, thus breaking off official relations. This did not in itself put an end to trade — for the next ninety years the Portuguese, newly arrived in Chinese waters, carried cargoes between Macao and Japan, while Spanish, Dutch and English merchants, joined later by Japanese, all of whom lacked access to the China coast, acquired Chinese goods for Japan through Chinese junks, voyaging to Southeast Asia — but it did for a time restrict cultural contacts. It was only in the seventeenth century, when the European links, except those with the Dutch, were severed by the actions of the Tokugawa Shogun (see Chapter 2), that Japan's older Asian trade was reestablished. For the next two hundred years or more, junks from China, Korea and Ryukyu made their way once again to ports in west Japan. Tribute missions arrived in the Japanese capital. In other words, the channels were reopened by which Chinese culture could reach those Japanese who were eager for it, whether clerical or lay.

CULTURAL BORROWING

If one allows for certain changes in circumstance and technology, the methods by which Japan acquired a knowledge of China in and after the seventh century were not so very different from those that were used to study the West in modern times. The same cannot be said of what was learnt. Seventh-century Japan was primitive in every respect when compared with China: in political structures and ideas, weaponry, economic techniques, religion, science, art and literature. Late Tokugawa Japan, by contrast, although 'backward' by western standards, implying an absence of certain beliefs and skills, was in some contexts — poetry, painting, music, religion, for example — essentially the product of a different, but not necessarily inferior, cultural tradition, owing much of its character to

China. As a consequence, the second phase of Japanese cultural borrowing was much more selective than the first.

One motive which led the Japanese to turn to China was the wish to understand Buddhism better. The Buddhist priests they had encountered, whether Chinese or Korean, were learned in many things Chinese. They brought with them to Japan a religion which in the refinement of its thought, the decoration of its temples and the magificence of its ceremonial far outshone anything already to be found there. They were organized hieratically and expounded doctrines founded on scripture. All these were characteristics that seemed attractive to Japan's early rulers, seeking to build an orderly society.

In 552 (or possibly 538) the Korean king of Paekche sent to Japan a Buddhist monk, who brought with him a Buddha image and copies of holy works (sutras). This marked the formal introduction of the religion to the Japanese court, though it was a century more before it was established in any strength. In 639 an emperor for the first time ordered the endowment of a Buddhist house. In 651 Buddhist ceremonies took place in the palace. In 652 lectures on Buddhism were held there. The emperor Kōtoku, who succeeded to the throne in 645, was even said in the chronicles to have 'honoured the religion of Buddha and despised the Way of the Gods', that is, despised the indigenous Japanese deities (*kami*).[5] By 741, when orders were issued that at each provincial capital there was to be a state-supported Buddhist temple, it is fair to describe Buddhism as a state religion in Japan. Under the administrative code of 701 its clerics had been made subject to the civil law, not only for lay offences, like bribery, brawling and drunkenness, but also for a religious one, propagating false doctrines.

Japanese Buddhism was in its early days greatly dependent on links with China. Its scriptures were Chinese translations of the Indian originals. Its senior figures were at first men and women from China or Korea, then Japanese who had studied abroad (though foreign priests were still invited to settle in Japan from time to time in later centuries). Even its sects were mostly Chinese by origin and designation. Those of the Nara period were wholly of this kind — their proceedings must have been well-nigh unintelligible to all but a tiny fraction of the capital's inhabitants — and while some adjustments were made when the court moved to Heian (modern Kyoto) in 794, the tone remained very Chinese. In 804 the monk Saichō received permission to travel to China with one of the Japanese diplomatic missions, studying at the famous religious centre of T'ient'ai (Tendai in Japanese). When he returned in 805 he founded a sect of that name in Japan, the chief temple of which, Enryakuji, grew into a vast complex on Mount Hiei, dominating the capital's northern outskirts. Saichō's contemporary, Kūkai, also went to China in 804, staying until 806. He brought back the Shingon (True Word) teaching, whose followers built their headquarters on Mount Koya, south of the Nara plain. Kūkai himself acquired a well-deserved reputation as Chinese scholar and poet, completing a major survey of Indian and Chinese religious thought, plus a detailed and systematic account of the rules for composing Chinese verse.

As the authority of the imperial court weakened in and after the twelfth century, opening the way to feudal rule, Buddhism in Japan lost some of its aristocratic qualities and became more widely diffused through the population. In some respects it also became less Chinese. Neither Jōdo (Pure Land) nor Jōdo Shinshū (True Pure Land), the sects which were the most popular of those emerging in the middle ages, felt the same compulsion to maintain a connection with China. On the other hand, Zen (Ch'an in Chinese), which came into prominence in the thirteenth century, made such a link central to its religious practices: its followers held that enlightenment was achieved through contemplation under the guidance of a master, which led them to put a high value on contact with those centres in China where the greatest teachers were to be found. For this reason Zen monks played an important part in missions to China under the Ashikaga Shogun. This in turn enabled them to introduce into Japan aspects of Chinese culture that were not directly related to religion.

The other principal Chinese contribution to the life of ancient Japan was in political institutions. Chinese government, as it existed under the T'ang, was enormously impressive to China's neighbours: centralized, authoritarian and bureaucratic, it afforded a model of power which many of them tried to emulate. The Japanese were no exception. The imperial house set out to create a Chinese-style court as early as the beginning of the seventh century. After Kōtoku came to the throne in 645 the process was greatly extended, taking in most features of administration. Boards and ministries were established in the capital. Provinces were designated and put under officials appointed by the court. Registers of population were ordered to be kept. New rates of tax and labour dues were announced, payable to the court and its representatives. In 701–2 these piecemeal innovations were brought together in a Chinese-style set of legal and administrative regulations, known as the Taihō Code. It specified the staff and functions of the two councils, eight ministries and various independent bureaus which comprised the central government; provided in much the same way for administration in the provinces, though on a smaller scale; set out a veritable maze of requirements about paperwork, office hours, precedents and ceremonial; and prescribed rules for the selection and promotion of the capital's numerous officials. Annual reports were to be submitted in order to assess — in numerical categories — the efficiency, diligence and probity of all the system's functionaries, from state councillors at the top, through the grades of guards officer, historian and court musician to scribes, diviners, cooks, coastguards, and even those who manned the checkpoints on the roads.

Though the system was in principle Chinese and bureaucratic, the Japanese did not in practice adhere to Chinese models in every particular. This was true above all in matters which concerned the monarchy. In China, the source of imperial authority and the limitations on it were expressed in the concept of the Mandate of Heaven (*t'ien-ming*). As mediator between Heaven and Earth, it was held, the emperor ruled by Heaven's will. This, however, would cease to uphold him if he failed to provide just and stable government in Confucian terms: divine displeasure would be revealed, either in heavenly portents and natural calamities, or in rebellion and unrest among his subjects. All these could be taken as evidence that he had lost the right to rule. Such a doctrine was never fully accepted in Japan. Japanese emperors, after all, based their claim to legitimacy and succession, not on specific heavenly approval of this kind, but on their supposed descent from the sun-goddess, Amaterasu. If they had a mandate at all, it was an irrevocable one. Indeed, had they adopted, along with the methods of government of China, all the philosophical propositions on which these rested, they would have been in danger of denying the very beliefs from which their own authority derived.

Certain practical implications for monarchical rituals and institutions followed from this. So did a measure of ambiguity in official documents, notably on those occasions when the court wished to call in aid the support of both Chinese and Japanese beliefs. In 683 an emperor issued a decree which first stated that he ruled 'as a God Incarnate' (a Japanese concept), then went on to announce rewards for service on the altogether Chinese argument that 'auspicious signs' had been observed, demonstrating that 'the principles of administering the government are in harmony with the laws of Heaven'.[6]

The position of the Japanese nobility involved similar equivocations. Despite the trappings of imperial bureaucracy, Japan's hereditary grandees had never been brought as firmly under royal control as those of China had been, with the result that the regime which emerged in the Nara period took the form of a sharing of power between the imperial house and a rising class of officials of aristocratic birth. The Japanese Council of State, which both proposed and executed the policies the emperor approved, was dominated by six or seven great office-holders. These did not reach their positions of eminence solely by virtue of their merit. Parallel to the hierarchy of office in the capital was one of numbered ranks, linked to the processes of government by a rule which made the holding of appropriate rank a condition of appointment to each office: only those who held ranks one to three qualified to be ministers in the Council of State; ranks four and five gave entry to other senior posts, filled on direct imperial nomination; and ranks six to eight opened the way to the more humdrum levels of the central bureaucracy. Since the very highest ranks were in practice held by descendants of the old aristo-cracy and of the imperial house, whose children and grandchildren entered the structure as of right at privileged points, the posts which carried the greatest responsibility became the near-monopoly of an inner circle which ability alone did not enable a man to penetrate. Between 701 and 764 the offices of Minister of the Left and Minister of the Right, which were in normal times the senior posts at court, were shared by members of only five families. Nor did the narrowing of recruitment end there. Of the eleven senior officials of the Council of State in 772, no less than eight were Fujiwara, that is, relatives or descendants of the noble who had masterminded the coup d'état by which Kōtoku had come to the throne in 645. By the tenth and eleventh centuries the senior members of that house had risen to a position of almost unchallenged power at court, maintained through intermarriage with the imperial line. As a result, the elaborate paraphernalia of central ministries, though it continued to exist, was regularly bypassed in favour of Fujiwara household organs. This was very far from being Chinese practice. In fact, no matter how Chinese in other respects the government of Japan appeared to be, it did not aban-don its commitment to the claims of lineage at the highest levels. When in the course of time the power of the Fujiwara was destroyed, they were replaced, not by other office-holders of the court, but by an emerging feudal class, whose position depended on land rights and armed force. At all levels — that of Shogun, or national hegemon; that of feudal lord, or local despot; that of samurai retainer to one of these — the status of its members was hereditary.

Even so, Confucianism, whose tenets had penetrated every aspect of political life in Nara and Heian, did not entirely lose its importance in these later years. During what is usually called the Fujiwara period, most male members of the ruling class received the rudiments of an education in Confucian thought. Emperors habitually asserted that their rule was in accord with Confucian benevolence; aristocratic officials proclaimed loy-alty and filial piety to be the highest human virtues; and legal codes continued to provide for the punishment of those who offended against Confucian precepts. Some of these things even survived the transfer of power to feudal leaders after 1185, if only because the latter sought respectability in terms already familiar to their rivals. In other words, Confucianism, though not in itself a source of authority, as it was in China, continued to set rules of conduct for men of standing in Japanese society.

Under the Tokugawa, who held office as Shogun from 1603 to 1867, Confucianism emerged once more as something close to a governing ideology in Japan. It did so in the form in which it had been restated by

Chu Hsi under the Sung, that is, one which identified the relationship between Heaven and Earth as the model for that which should obtain between human beings. The effect was to justify the inequalities between ruler and subject, parent and child, husband and wife, elder brother and younger brother, placing an emphasis on the maintenance of order in society. Such a doctrine appealed greatly to Japanese feudal lords in the sixteenth century, seeking to turn their lands into principalities. The Tokugawa Shogun, as they strived after 1600 to impose their will on feudal lords, found it equally attractive. Thus Confucianism became once more a philosophy favoured by the state, though no longer for the benefit of a court and its aristocracy.

Some problems from the past repeated themselves. No head of the Tokugawa house was genuinely willing to rest his claim to office on Confucian virtue, any more than emperors had been. No more so were the feudal lords and their samurai, whose status derived from the prowess which they or their ancestors had shown on the field of battle. This made it necessary for scholars to adjust Confucian reason to feudal circumstance, in much the same way as it had been reconciled with the privileges of the nobility in Nara and Heian. And if this involved a degree of intellectual dishonesty, at least it left room for samurai to receive a Confucian education, which might 'civilize' their martial code. From this vantage point the Confucian ethic, albeit in simplified form, spread downward through the rest of the population. By the nineteenth century a growth in basic literacy, especially through the emergence of so-called temple schools (*tera-koya*) and private academies, coupled with the widespread use of printing, made possible an upsurge in popular fiction and drama, incorporating Confucian dilemmas into plots which reached into every level of the people's consciousness.

By the time of Japan's modern encounter with the West, in fact, most segments of the Japanese people were committed to the fundamentals of Chinese thought as expressed in Buddhist and Confucian doctrine, a circumstance which proved a barrier to their acceptance, not only of Christianity, but also of many western secular ideas. Nevertheless, it would be wrong to claim that Chinese religion, at least, went wholly unchallenged. Shinto, as the earliest Japanese beliefs and rituals came later to be called, although it quite soon entered into a symbiotic relationship with Buddhism, never lost its identity entirely or released its hold on the popular imagination, especially where shamanism, magic and fertility rites were concerned. The Buddhist monk Ennin, for example, facing the prospect of a dangerous voyage home from China in 839, called on a diviner to pray to Shinto deities for protection. At court, Shinto ceremony continued to play its part in matters concerning the imperial succession. In 749 the great Nara Buddhist temple, Tōdaiji, welcomed Hachiman, a Shinto deity brought from Kyushu, as guardian of its precinct, a practice which became widespread in later centuries; and while the Buddhist argument, familiar elsewhere in Asia, that local gods were manifestations of the Buddha, made its appearance in Japan as well, the contrary contention also emerged in time, asserting that Buddhas and Bodhisattvas were reincarnations of Shinto *kami*.

A similar persistence of non-Chinese influence can be recognized in other aspects of Japanese culture, though more in the later than the earlier periods. Chinese itself became at an early date the language of government and serious scholarship in Japan. There were, for example, six chronicles in Chinese, which together purported to provide a narrative of Japanese history and legend from the creation of the universe to AD 887. The Japanese also showed a taste for massive compilations in the Chinese manner — of laws and commentaries, of works on politics and history, of Buddhist exegesis — while many Japanese officials, as men of culture in the Chinese style, spent their leisure hours in writing Chinese poetry. Some visitors to Europe and America between 1860 and 1873 continued the tradition.

Chinese remains the classical language of Japan and has provided one of the two main elements of the country's writing system. It has also left its mark on everyday Japanese, though the primitive Japanese spoken language did not at all provide a suitable partner for it. Perhaps for this reason, Japan has over the centuries borrowed very large numbers of Chinese loan-words, or even phrases, which are given a pronunciation as close as possible to that of the Chinese — bearing in mind that Chinese is monosyllabic and tonal, but Japanese is not — with the result that most forms of oral and written expression in Japan have become in effect a Sino-Japanese agglomeration. Duality exists in literature as well. A taste for classical Chinese as a literary medium has continued to characterize many intellectuals even in modern times, though the most popular writing, both in poetry and prose, has always been in the language known as Japanese.

An almost equally strong strand of Chineseness is to be found in Japanese art and architecture. In the seventh and eighth centuries, buildings, sculpture and paintings were clearly continental (and Buddhist) in their themes and style. Many, after all, were the work of immigrants. Only slowly did this phase give way to one in which art became secular and more recognizably Japanese, in treatment as well as subject-matter. Even then, a classical Chinese school (Kara-e) continued to exist alongside that which was called Japanese (Yamato-e), both highly regarded, both exercising a pervasive influence on design and taste. At a later stage, for example, Sung landscape painting became a model for some outstanding Japanese artists, while even so 'Japanese' an art form as the woodblock print can be traced to origins in China under the Ming.

In language, literature and art, as in religion, there developed over the centuries not only a level of Japanese expertise which rivalled that of the country's Chinese mentors, but also a certain fusion between the Chinese and the Japanese traditions. In architecture, neither the Japanese model of the Ise shrines nor the Chinese one of the Heian palaces proved completely dominant. Many religious and aristocratic buildings came to show the influence of both. Some Japanese writers used both languages at different times. Artists became eclectic in matters of style. Japan's high culture, in fact, became more properly 'Sino-Japanese'.

The situation with respect to science and technology, however, was very different. In almost every field Japanese failed to match or master Chinese knowledge and achievements. For example, their grasp of calendrical science left much to be desired, despite its important role in government. It was a convention of the tribute system that states sending missions to China should employ the Chinese calendar in all official communications between the two. Japan adopted it in 645. From that time on, irregularly in the seventh century, but without interruption thereafter until the present day, Japanese identified years in the way the Chinese did, that is, in accordance with their consecutive place in short spans of time, each of which was labelled with an era-name (*nengō*). Thus the western year 1868 was year one of Meiji (meaning Enlightened Government), 1869 was year two, and so on, just as 645 had been the first year of Taika (Great Reform). In modern practice *nengō* have been made to coincide with imperial reigns, as they had done in China very much earlier; but for much of history the changes were arbitrary, prompted by the desire to bring about good fortune, or to mark some notable event. Years themselves consisted of twelve lunar months, except when it was necessary to insert a thirteenth 'intercalary' month to keep the calendar in step with the seasons, that is, about every third year.

Some aspects of calendar-making depended on decisions by authority. It was the court which decided what the era-name should be, when it should start, how long it should last, at what point in the year an intercalary month could conveniently be inserted. This accounts for some of the discrepancies between Chinese and Japanese calendars, since no attempt was made to coordinate such matters. Nevertheless, there were also errors of calculation. In China, because of the belief that heavenly portents were a comment on the monarch's virtue, and hence his right to rule, calendrical astronomy was handled with the greatest care, being entrusted to a large and generally competent government department. A similar office was incorporated by Japan into the Taihō state system of 701, but it was smaller and less effective than its Chinese counterpart, no doubt because it was not seen to have the same concern with the emperor's standing. In addition, Japan introduced modifications into Chinese practice, which were of a kind to imply a less 'scientific' approach. Whereas in China the study of astronomy and calendars was kept administratively apart from divination and astrology, in Japan it was not. Nor did members of the Japanese bureau acquire a sufficient grasp of the relevant mathematics to make corrections of their own to the lunar calendar — its adjustment to solar time, in particular — once the official connection with China came to an end. As a result, the Chinese calendar which had been introduced in 862 continued in use in Japan without amendment until 1684, despite its growing inaccuracy. Meanwhile the astronomical bureau came to devote itself more and more to the preparation of an annual almanac, containing information about the times of sunrise and sunset, plus significant dates — the summer and winter solstice, spring and autumn equinox, eclipses of the sun and moon — with a note on personal fortune-telling for each day, as well as on geomancy and taboos.

What was true of astronomy held good in most other scientific fields: premodern Japan was as much behind China as China proved to be behind the nineteenth-century West. An exception was medicine, which had greater practical importance. A knowledge of it, as understood in China, was brought to Japan in the sixth and seventh centuries by Korean and Chinese doctors; was supplemented by the physicians who visited China with the tribute missions; and was put under the supervision of one of the more effective departments of the Taihō official machine. Drugs were imported from China and Korea, comprising a valuable item of trade. When substitutes for some of them were eventually found in Japan, they were listed in publications on *materia medica*. In fact, Japanese doctors became in many respects less dependent on China and more professionally skilled with the passage of time, with the result that by the end of the Tokugawa period they were able to play an important part in the investigation of the West's science and technology across a broad spectrum.

One object of that investigation, as we shall see, was to study western 'strengths' in order to remedy Japanese 'weaknesses'. To contemporaries the primary definition of these terms was military, but it is also possible to set them in the context of what Japan had learnt or failed to learn of Chinese culture over the years. Science was an obvious example of a weakness that had to be repaired. So were the political institutions of the Edo state, for in turning away from Chinese-style imperial rule towards a feudalism much like that of medieval Europe, Japanese had not only offended against Neo-Confucian loyalty, but also committed themselves to a form of social structure which was notably uncompetitive when challenged by the modern West.

2

Barbarian Books

Japan's encounter with Europe in the sixteenth century was quite different from the earlier relationship with China. There was one important similarity, in that Europe's power was viewed with suspicion, as China's had been, but Europe was not at all regarded as the home of a superior civilization, which it might be right for Japan to emulate. Of the goods which Europe's merchants brought, those most coveted, apart from guns, were Chinese; the religion which its missionaries preached was in the end rejected, then persecuted; and its culture in any wider sense had a negligible impact, even among those Japanese who knew anything of it.

This phase lasted until about 1640, by which time Japan's rulers had taken steps to insulate their people from what they believed to be the dangers of the European connection. During the next two hundred years, while direct contact was slight, there was nevertheless a gradual development of Japanese interest in the skills and knowledge Europe had to offer, comparable, if on a smaller scale, with that which had been shown towards China in the middle ages, when no official relations existed between the two. There emerged in Japan an embryo study of the West that owed its existence to the trade the Dutch were allowed to carry on at Nagasaki — the books they provided were its main source of information — and was therefore called 'Dutch studies' (Rangaku). By the nineteenth century it had given a small number of Japanese scholars an understanding of some aspects of European art, science and technology.

Dutch studies might well have remained one of the fascinating but inconsiderable byways of Japanese history, had it not been for the renewal of European expansion in Asia after 1750, when the British and the French joined the Dutch as territorial powers in India and beyond, opening up trade with the China coast. The Japanese were told about these events — in pejorative terms — by both the Dutch and Chinese, slowly becoming aware that they might as a result find their own independence threatened. In this context, Dutch studies, renamed 'Western studies' (Yōgaku), took on an altogether more political character. Men began to argue that study of the West might provide the skills, especially military skills, with which to save Japan. Others, more traditional in outlook, claimed with even greater vehemence that an attempt to use it in this way would be bound to destroy Japan's own society and civilization, because it would undermine them from within. The debate was to continue in various forms throughout the country's modern history.

THE REJECTION OF CHRISTIANITY

The first Europeans to reach Japan were Portuguese, who came by Chinese junk in 1543. Their timing was fortunate. Since most of the country had for over eighty years been involved in sporadic but large-scale civil war, the firearms they brought attracted eager attention. Guns were soon not only being used, but also manufactured in Japan. What is more, the merchants who followed, this time in western ships, fell heir to a carrying trade between China and Japan. When China banned Japanese missions from its ports in 1549, the Portuguese were in a position to make voyages from Macao to Kyushu and other points in west Japan, bringing the Chinese silks and medicines of which the Japanese had no wish to be deprived. In return they took items for which there was an established demand in China, such as camphor, copper and lacquerware, plus large amounts of silver, which the Japanese were just beginning to produce on a substantial scale by imported methods of Chinese engineering. Some of this silver was invested in future ventures from Macao. Some of it was sent home via Goa to Lisbon, repatriating profits.

Reports of these profits attracted competitors. Spaniards came from the Philippines after 1571, the Dutch in 1600, the English in 1613; but as none of the latecomers was able to secure a footing on the China coast itself, they found it necessary to obtain Chinese goods for the Japanese market by dealing with Chinese merchants who travelled to Southeast Asia. The Japanese did the same, once their government gave approval for voyages in 1592. All, in fact, conducted what was in essence an indirect Sino-Japanese trade, supplemented by a number of Southeast Asian products. Clearly, neither this, nor the kind of direct trade carried on by the Portuguese, seemed likely to promote a flow of cultural influence from Europe to Japan.

By contrast, the Christian missionaries who came in Portuguese and Spanish ships — Jesuits under Portuguese patronage, starting in 1549; Franciscans,Dominicans and Augustinians under the patronage of Spain from 1592 — were as capable of spreading the knowledge of an alien civilization in Japan as Buddhist monks from China and Korea had been a thousand years earlier. Japanese feudal lords, anxious for gold and guns, seeing that foreign merchants and seamen treated missionaries with deference, thought it politic to receive them well. Some lords were themselves converted, ordering the whole population of their lands to receive the Catholic faith. As a result, by 1600 there were as many as 300,000 Christian converts, mostly in central and west Japan.

However, conditions were already changing to the disadvantage of the missionaries. Since the arrival of the Portuguese, Japan's domestic conflicts had entered a new phase. Between 1560 and 1600 three successive feudal leaders tried to achieve a national hegemony: Oda Nobunaga, who by 1580 had brought all the central provinces under his control; Toyotomi Hideyoshi, his vassal and successor, who conquered the rest of the country before extending his ambitions towards the Asian mainland; and Tokugawa Ieyasu, who seized power after Hideyoshi's death by a victory at Sekigahara in 1600. Ieyasu, unlike the other two, contrived to bequeath his gains to his descendants, eating the cake, as traditional teaching has it, which Nobunaga mixed and Hideyoshi baked.

In the course of their campaigns all three had found occasion to subdue not only rival lords, but also armed Buddhist sects; and although Christians were accepted as potential allies while these operations were in train, they began to look like subversives on their own account as soon as the campaigns came to an end. In the summer of 1587,having had an opportunity to note the considerable strength of the Christians in Kyushu, Hideyoshi issued two decrees.[1] The first ordered Christian priests to leave 'the land of the Gods', on the grounds that they had illegally stirred up 'the lower classes' to attack shrines and temples. The second prohibited mass conversion at the order of feudal lords, on the grounds that it was harmful to the state. Future conversions, Hideyoshi said, were to be subject to the approval of his own officials or of the individual's household head.

The decree requiring Jesuits and friars to leave was not immediately enforced. It was another ten years before Hideyoshi executed a group of priests and converts who had ignored it. Tokugawa Ieyasu, too, for a long time did not act on it; but in 1614, faced by what he conceived to be a threat from Hideyoshi's heir, to whom many Christians rallied, he in turn proscribed their religion. All Japanese were required to register as members of Buddhist communities. Before long there followed a savage persecution of Christians, initiated by Ieyasu's son after his father's death in 1616, then carried on with even greater relish by his grandson, Iemitsu. Mass executions took place at Nagasaki in 1622 and at the Tokugawa capital of Edo (modern Tokyo) in 1623. Torture was everywhere used to induce recantation. Some 3,000 Christians suffered martyrdom in all; and while a few pockets of 'hidden Christians' survived until the nineteenth century, preserving their faith by oral tradition, Christianity had in effect been destroyed in Japan by 1640. A system of regulations, informers and loyalty tests was put in place to prevent its revival.

Most of the foreign merchants had meanwhile lost their rights to trade. Spanish ships were banned from 1624. The English had withdrawn for reasons of commercial failure in the previous year. In 1639 Iemitsu severed the Macao link, citing as his reason a Kyushu peasant rising in which Christians were involved. When a Portuguese mission was sent to appeal against the decision in 1640 its senior members were put to death. This left the Dutch as the only Europeans with access to Japan; and despite the fact that as Protestants they did not count as 'Christian' in Japanese eyes, the Dutch were confined to an island trading post in Nagasaki harbour, called Deshima.

The most convincing explanation advanced for the restrictions which were placed on foreigners in Japan is that Christianity was seen as a threat to domestic order. In a letter sent to the Portuguese Viceroy at Goa in 1591, Hideyoshi observed that although he had been able to put 'the unity of the nation . . . on a firm foundation', the task of maintaining it for the future would involve support for Confucian doctrine, by which 'our relationships between sovereign and minister, parent and child, and husband and wife are established'.[2] Christian priests implicitly challenged this, he wrote, expounding 'in ignorance of right and wrong, unreasonable and wanton doctrines', which were likely 'to bewitch our men and women, both of the laity and clergy'.

Japanese of many different shades of opinion subscribed to this view during the Tokugawa period. The former Japanese Jesuit, Fabian Fucan, having renounced his Catholic faith and returned to Buddhism, wrote in an anti-Christian tract in 1620 that the Christian, by elevating obedience to God above obedience to ruler, was thinking in a way that might 'subvert and usurp the country'. The Confucian scholar Arai Hakuseki, though less hostile than many of his contemporaries, argued in 1710 that since the Christian god required all the believer's love and reverence, nothing was left for the loyalty and filial piety on which the fabric of society relied. As a consequence, 'once that doctrine begins to flourish, rebellious subjects *ipso facto* arise in the land'. In the early nineteenth century another Confucian, Aizawa Seishisai, described Christianity as an arm of imperialism. First came trade, he wrote, through which the foreigners learnt about the country's geography and defences. If the defences were weak, 'they dispatch troops to invade the nation'; if strong, 'they propagate Christianity to subvert it from within'. For when 'our people's hearts and minds are captivated by Christianity, they will greet the barbarian host with open arms'.[3]

Leaving aside their specific origins in anti-Christian sentiment, such statements reflect the enhanced importance given to Neo-Confucian thought in Tokugawa Japan. Although Japanese society remained feudal, in the sense that power and status were determined by birth and vassal-age, it became sufficiently bureaucratic under Tokugawa rule to provide once more a ready welcome for ideas which assumed the need for a centralized state machine. The head of the Tokugawa house, as Shogun, ruled through an administration, known as the Bakufu, staffed by his vassals. Offices in it were filled in every case by lords or samurai of stated rank. The offices themselves were numerous and often specialized; there were more candidates qualified by birth than there were places to be filled, which made necessary a system of selection for appointment and promotion; and there were detailed regulations governing administrative procedures. Given that each of the major feudal lords maintained a similar organization on a smaller scale, it is clear that a large proportion of Japan's supposedly warrior ruling class spent its time on office work, much as court nobles had done in Nara and Heian. It is not surprising that the vocabulary of government tended to be Confucian in these circumstances. Samurai received the elements of a Confucian education at official schools, to which admission was by rank. A minority even became full-fledged Confucian scholars, holding teaching posts and engaged in learned controversy. Since doctors, who were not quite samurai in status, were now more fully versed in the theory of Chinese medicine than in the past, while astronomers had at last achieved a level of knowledge which enabled them to comprehend and even modify the working of Chinese calendars, it is not unreasonable to conclude that under the Tokugawa 'for the first time in Japanese history, Chinese science and Confucianism were really understood as comprehensive systems'.[4]

The sense of civilized achievement which this state of affairs engendered brought about a change in Japanese views of China. Traditionally, China had been held to be 'civilized' (*ka*), whereas Japan, like other countries of East Asia, was 'barbarian' (*i*). This *ka-i* dichotomy, based on supposed observance or non-observance of Confucian principles, was at the heart of China's tribute system and its international inequalities. In the seventeenth century, however, it became possible to claim that a Confucian Japan should no longer be considered subordinate within such a framework. Japanese scholars began to justify what they saw as a new reality, claiming that Japan and China were equals in a world with 'two heavens', or that the centrality which had long entitled China to be called the Middle Kingdom, since it was a philosophical, not a geographical concept, could just as well be claimed by Japan, should her behaviour and institutions warrant it, or even that China's conquest by the barbarian Manchus had deprived her of the status of being 'civilized', which passed by default to an independent, Confucian Japan.

The nature of the country's relations with its Asian neighbours gave a measure of support to such pretensions. To call Tokugawa Japan a 'closed country' (*sakoku*) is to focus attention on the suppression of Christianity and the restrictions placed on European trade. This is misleading. There was a continuing network of relationships with nearby Asian states, similar to that which had existed in earlier centuries. Chinese junks resumed their voyages to Kyushu (Nagasaki) after 1600, eventually taking over the trade from which both Portuguese and Japanese were banned. They brought Chinese books and works of art, as they had in the past, as well as silk, and provided a means of travel between the two countries. Through the island of Tsushima trade was also carried on with Korea, while Ryukyu provided additional contacts with China and the south. What is more, Korea and Ryukyu sent occasional missions to Japan, which were treated as if they brought tribute and homage. The Dutch were required to act in a similar manner. In these ways the Tokugawa were able to maintain the illusion that Japan was the arbiter of a world of its own choosing, within which Edo and Kyoto held pride of place as centres of civilization.

Against such a background, the rejection of Europe in the seventeenth century appeared in retrospect to be something more than an act of *realpolitik*. On the one hand it became a matter of 'ancestral law': a decision taken by the founders of the Tokugawa line, which filial piety required their descendants to continue to observe. On the other it was assimilated to the distinction between 'civilized' and 'barbarian', hitherto applied to Asians. A Japan which had turned back culturally and diplomatically to an inherited Sino-Japanese tradition found it natural in the nineteenth century to designate westerners as barbarian (i), implying that Japanese were civilized (*ka*).

DUTCH STUDIES

Japan learnt little of lasting consequence about European civilization during the century of early contacts (1540–1640), despite the fact that the priests who were sent there were often men of education. In addition to bringing in hand-held firearms, the Portuguese, followed by both the English and the Dutch, made larger guns available, some of which were manufactured in Japan; but the use made of these by the Tokugawa in the civil wars, together with subsequent requests for instruction in the handling of mortars, suggests a lack of confidence in Japanese expertise. In any case, as peace became the norm in Japan after the middle of the seventeenth century, gunnery skills became less esteemed.

The same was true of the science of navigation, once Japanese ships had been forbidden to voyage overseas in 1633–5. Before this both Portuguese and Dutch pilots — and one Englishman, Will Adams — had served regularly under Japanese command, helping to spread a knowledge of European cartography and celestial navigation. Thereafter, for the next two hundred years, Japanese captains could only use such knowledge in the coastal trade, with the result that the import of European maps and atlases through Deshima, though it continued, had little maritime utility.

For the rest, some aspects of the West's techniques of civil engineering, applied to land surveys and mining, seem to have survived, perhaps because they were not seen to be conspicuously 'western'. It was only in medicine, however, that the Japanese set out to acquire an understanding of an alien science as such. It originated with the Jesuits, one of whom, forced by torture to apostatize in 1623, subsequently made known his knowledge of European surgery through several books in Japanese. The skills which became available in this way were subsequently handed down among the official interpreters in Nagasaki, sometimes with the help of the physicians who were sent to Deshima by the Dutch.

Surgery was relatively neglected in the Chinese-style medical training available in Japan. This made the European contribution welcome. It could also be understood — at the level at which Dutch barber-surgeons were able to teach it — without the need to read a European language. This was fortunate, since communication between the Dutch and Japanese was almost entirely oral, at first in Portuguese, later in Dutch. The Dutch were not allowed by the Tokugawa Bakufu to learn Japanese, while Japanese interpreters did not read Dutch in the seventeenth century, or not well enough, at least, to understand works of scholarship. It is significant that the official censors, seeking to keep out the malevolent doctrines of Christianity, prohibited the import of any Chinese books that might make reference to them, but apparently felt no need to take such action with respect to books in Dutch. This was not so much because the Dutch were Protestant, as because the language had no reading public in Japan. Even though some 'useful' Dutch publications on military science and medicine (including botany and zoology) were allowed into the country for officials and senior members of the feudal class, the Dutch merchants, taken annually to Edo for a kind of tribute ceremonial, often found themselves asked to explain the illustrations.

A change began to take place in the middle of the eighteenth century. The Shogun Yoshimune, who held office from 1716 to 1744, was a reformer with a special interest in agriculture, medicine and astronomy. He invited Chinese doctors and veterinary surgeons to Japan; ordered horses, seeds and plants from the Dutch at Deshima; established a medicinal garden in Edo; interrogated the Dutch representatives when they came to his capital about the contents of Dutch books in the Bakufu collection; and sponsored a revision of the calendar. Two of his decisions were of particular importance for European studies in the longer term. In 1720 he relaxed the ban on the import of 'Christian' books from China to

23

the extent of admitting works on calendrical science, prepared by the Jesuits in Peking. This was to recognize the superiority of western achievements in astronomy (though the Jesuits had not in fact accepted the Galilean description of the universe). Then in 1740 Yoshimune was persuaded by two of his advisers, one a physician, the other a Confucian scholar, that further scientific progress could not be made without a knowledge of Dutch, since this would give access to the relevant European literature. Both were ordered to pursue the study of it with the assistance of the Nagasaki interpreters. As a result, Dutch studies acquired a measure of respectability, becoming steadily more varied, more expert and more popular in the course of the next hundred years.

It was not easy to make headway in the language without textbooks and works of reference. Oral instruction, often at Nagasaki, and the compilation of word-lists, soon proved inadequate for the study of serious topics. The first attempt to systematize the learning process was Ōtsuki Gentaku's guide to Dutch studies (*Rangaku Kaitei*), which appeared in 1788. It did not discuss grammar, but included sections on conversation, pronunciation, reading and writing, together with lists of words and sentences, showing Japanese equivalents. In the following year Ōtsuki opened a private school in Edo for the teaching of Dutch and western medicine. The first Dutch-Japanese dictionary of any importance was a cooperative undertaking, based on François Halma's Dutch-French dictionary of 1717, and was completed in Edo in 1796. A smaller, more convenient dictionary, having less than half as many entries, was published in 1810. The earliest grammars appeared at about the same time.

Acquiring new kinds of knowledge required not only basic language skills, but also an ability to understand a technical terminology for which there existed no equivalent in Japanese. During 1770 Sugita Gempaku, a doctor who had already begun to study and practise western medicine in Edo, succeeded in obtaining — at a price which suggests that the marketing of scientific books was a profitable sideline for members of the Deshima factory — a Dutch translation of a German set of anatomical tables, originally published by Johann Kulmus in 1722. He quickly realized that in some respects the information they provided was quite different from what he had been taught. Fortunately an opportunity came within a few months to put this conflict of conflict of evidence to the test. In the spring of 1771 Sugita, together with some others from his profession, was invited to witness at the Bakufu's execution ground the dissection of the corpse of a woman criminal after she was beheaded. The dissection itself, as was customary, would be carried out, not by the doctors present, but by an outcaste (the handling of dead flesh, both human and animal, was thought to be a source of ritual pollution). He was a very old man, able to confirm from his own experience that what they saw was not in any way unusual.

Taking his copy of Kulmus with him, and accompanied by a friend, Maeno Ryōtaku, who also turned out to have the Kulmus volume, Sugita proceeded, step by step, to compare its illustrations with what the dissection revealed of human organs. Both men were 'amazed at their perfect agreement'. The official Bakufu doctors present, who had apparently seen such things before, expressed no great surprise at the differences between what their Chinese textbooks told them and what they now observed — as far as Sugita could judge, they believed that 'the Chinese and the Japanese were different in their internal structures' — but to Sugita and Maeno it was 'a startling revelation'. They felt ashamed of themselves, Sugita later wrote, 'for having come this far in our lives without being aware of our own ignorance'.[5]

On their way home, prompted by these feelings, Sugita and Maeno decided to attempt a translation of the Kulmus tables, a task in which three others eventually asked to join them. Maeno had some slight understanding of Dutch, acquired during a three-month stay at Nagasaki. He also had a rudimentary word-list. With this as starting-point, the five men, working whenever they could find the time, struggled for nearly three years to apply their own medical vocabulary to the captions and the illustrations in the Kulmus text. Sometimes they used the terminology of Chinese medicine, sometimes invented new words, sometimes transcribed a Dutch word into Japanese script. When the result was published under the title *Kaitai Shinsho* (New Book of Dissection) in 1774, it was an immediate success, setting its compilers at the head of their profession. It also started what in modern terms has been called 'a dissection boom'.

One aspect of the affair which is of more than linguistic or professional importance is the willingness shown by Sugita and his colleagues to challenge received wisdom in the name of what might be called experimental data. Although Neo-Confucian thought acknowledged a need to 'investigate the nature of things' (*kakubutsu kyūri*), an expression which in the nineteenth century was more and more assimilated in Japan to what western scholars meant by science, the interpretation of it in orthodox thinking was much more akin to an examination (*kyū*), whether by contemplation or by observation, of the relationship between the normative or ideal form of things (*ri*) and their physical substance (*ki* or *butsu*). Since this involved cosmology and the place of human society in the universe, as well as explanations of physical phenomena, it was as much an ethical or a metaphysical exercise as a scientific one in the western sense. To relate it to an inductive, experimental method, as Japanese students who went abroad after 1860 had to do — the majority wished to pursue some aspect of science or technology — created difficulties. It was partly for this reason that most had to start their scientific education at the primary level, sometimes to their indignation.

Those who wished to be doctors proved to be best prepared, largely because of the prominent place which medicine assumed in Dutch studies after the publication of *Kaitai Shinsho*. As language skills improved, translations of more European books appeared, dealing with internal medicine (1793), ophthalmology (1816), obstetrics (1823), paediatrics (1843) and pathology (1849). Twelve private schools of western medicine were established between 1786 and 1846, four in Edo, three in Kyoto, four in Osaka and one in Nagasaki, of which Ogata Kōan's academy in Osaka was the largest and most famous. When the German physician Philipp Franz von Siebold arrived to work at Deshima in 1823 and was permitted to set up a teaching course of his own in Nagasaki, students flocked to it from the whole of west Japan. Nearly all of them were already in practice as doctors. Among other things, von Siebold introduced them to vaccination, though because his vaccine proved faulty it had to be done again in 1849.

This is not to say, however, that vaccination or other kinds of western medical treatment became familiar in these years to Japanese in general. In 1844 a group of Japanese seamen, who had been wrecked in the Pacific and rescued by an American ship, which took them to Baja California, made their way back to Japan via China. Interrogated at length by two Rangaku scholars, who later published an illustrated account of what the castaways had seen, they described many aspects of western life that were new to them. These included a description of how the inhabitants of California were able to get protection against smallpox through 'infected blood inserted by needle around their arm muscles in their infancy'. Their editors dismissed this as almost certainly a misunderstanding of what they had been told: the process of vaccination, they pointed out, which was already understood in Japan from translations of European books, was more complicated than the castaways implied.[6]

The welcome extended to European medicine owed something to the fact that senior members of the ruling class were the most likely beneficiaries. By the same token, astronomy, as applied to calendars, received official support on the grounds that it was of service to the state (that is, because of the belief, in origin Chinese, that there was a relationship between heavenly omens and political authority). The Jesuits had long been respected in Peking for their understanding of it. Yoshimune, as we have seen, permitted use of their work, though the calendar that was produced as a result showed little sign of their influence. Indeed, it was not until the preparation of another calendar in 1842, introduced in 1843, that Japan showed an awareness of heliocentric theory and a knowledge of instruments like the quadrant and the pendulum clock. Even then there was no departure from tradition in one respect: the almanac in which the calendar was published continued to provide the horoscopes and other quasi-magical embellishments which had long been customary in Japan.

Copernican theory had been made known in Japan by one of the Nagasaki interpreters, Motoki Ryōei, as early as 1774. Another scholar translated a Dutch book on Newton's ideas of astronomical dynamics in 1802. Yet neither had as much impact as the contributions made by the artist Shiba Kōkan between 1792 and 1816. At the beginning of that period Shiba brought out copperplate versions of a world map, accompanied by notes explaining heliocentric theory and its importance to navigation. It was reissued in 1805 with fuller notes, this time showing lines of latitude and longitude. With it went an illustrated text containing pictures of famous sights — the pyramids in Egypt were shown with a cross on the summit — and tracing the routes between Japan and Europe. Comments on European society were included, some of which, such as an admiring reference to the charitable institutions known to exist in France, may well have been meant as criticism of their absence in Japan, for Dutch scholars were often politically unsound, as Bakufu officials saw these things. At a more technical level, Shiba produced a celestial chart in 1796, apparently based on a seventeenth-century Dutch design, plus a set of ten etchings on astronomical subjects. The latter depicted in diagram form a celestial globe, the sun, the moon and the earth, heliocentric and geocentric universes, and an explanation of the working of the tides.

The Japanese also made progress in the practical application of western-style surveying and cartography. The most famous mapmaker of the late eighteenth and early nineteenth centuries was Inō Tadataka (Chūkei), who began life as a sake-brewer, studying surveying and mathematics in his spare time. At the age of fifty, having made enough money to retire, he enrolled as a student of the Shogun's official astronomer. From this connection there eventually came a commission to carry out a survey of the northern territory of Ezo (Hokkaido) in 1800, which his assistant, Mamiya Rinzō, later extended to the islands farther north. Inō himself turned his attention to the remainder of Japan, intending to produce a map of the whole of the country. His death in 1818 prevented him from finishing this, but his assistants completed it in his name in 1821, and it proved to be of such accuracy that a manuscript copy of it, now in Greenwich, became the basis of the first British hydrographical survey of Japan, carried out after the ports were opened to foreign trade in 1859.

It would not be difficult to expand this catalogue of western scientific knowledge available in 'closed' Japan. There were, for instance, books on botany (1822), physics (1827), and chemistry (1837). One reads of

Japanese who had some understanding of electricity. In addition, certain artistic techniques were introduced: painting in oils, copperplate etching, and the use of shading to show facial modelling. Some of these borrowings reached a fairly wide public, contributing to a fashion for what Aizawa Seishisai described in 1825 as 'curiosities and concoctions from abroad that dazzle the eye and entice our people to glorify foreign ways'.[7] Sugita Gempaku gave an account of how men swarmed about the lodgings where the Dutch stayed during their visits to Edo, vying with each other to acquire clocks, telescopes, barometers, thermometers, Leyden jars and camera obscura devices. Castaways returning from abroad — when they succeeded in doing so — were eagerly questioned about everything from umbrellas to musical instruments. Woodblock prints were sold, showing the Dutch playing billiards at Deshima. Ōtsuki Gentaku, apparently to promote his private academy in Edo, organized New Year parties at which the guests wore makeshift western costume and were expected to use knives and forks, sitting at table on chairs.

There were nevertheless considerations more serious than fashion. Honda Toshiaki, of whom we shall have more to say in the next section, saw utility even in western paintings. They were intended, he wrote, to 'resemble exactly the objects portrayed so that they will serve some useful function'.[8] Maeno Ryōtaku, in a book published in 1777, argued that the superiority of western science must be taken as evidence that western civilization, too, was superior, even in terms of morality. How else could one explain the fact that Christianity had been adopted by more of the world's population than Buddhism or Confucianism? Sugita Gempaku, less controversially, said only that to study Europe was to learn that Chinese civilization was not world civilization; but in 1849 Sakuma Shōzan, the samurai official to whom reference was made at the beginning of this book, claimed that China's defeat by Britain in the Opium War was due to the fact that 'foreign learning is rational and Chinese learning is not'.[9]

Inevitably there were also those who denied that what they called 'the Dutch disease' had any such claims to notice. Matsudaira Sadanobu, head of the Edo administration from 1787 to 1793, although he collected Dutch books on medicine, astronomy and geography, believed that they encouraged 'idle curiosity' and 'harmful ideas' if put in the wrong hands. They were best kept, he said, 'in a government library'. The Shinto publicist, Hirata Atsutane, himself a physician, agreed that Dutch learning should be studied alongside Japanese learning, in order to 'choose the good features of each and place them at the service of the nation', but for the Dutch as people he had only ridicule. They urinate the way that dogs do, he wrote; and 'apparently because the backs of their feet do not reach the ground, they fasten wooden heels to the backs of their shoes'.[10]

As one would expect, Confucian scholars were quick to come to the defence of what they held to be the epitome of civilization. Aizawa Seishisai, who was quoted earlier on this subject, warned that because of the danger of subversion by Christianity, European imports ought to be forbidden and the people encouraged 'to despise foreigners as they would despise dogs and goats'.[11] Another Confucian scholar, Ōhashi Totsuan, writing at about the time of the first American treaty, argued that western learning 'denied the fundamentally hierarchical order of the universe and human society'. Its science was therefore 'an irrelevant waste of time'.[12] Believing, as his training required, that ethics was incomparably more important than an understanding of the physical world — indeed, that the latter depended on the former — he could not accept that a society which denied Confucian principles could be valued simply for its technology. It was not safe, he said, to drink from the sidestreams of a river, if the mainstream itself was poisoned.

THE MILITARY DIMENSION

The threat posed by Russian expansion in the islands to the north of Japan was brought to the attention of Tokugawa officials in 1792. In that year Adam Laxman, acting on the orders of Catherine the Great, set sail from Okhotsk with the object of opening formal relations with Japan, taking with him several shipwrecked Japanese seamen, who were to be returned to their country as a gesture of Russian goodwill. He wintered in Hokkaido. He was refused permission to proceed to Edo by the Japanese officials there, on the grounds that this would be a breach of the seclusion laws, but they provided him with a written pass to go to Nagasaki on some subsequent occasion, which was used in 1804 by Nikolai Rezanov, who made the long voyage from Russia's Baltic ports to the Pacific Ocean and presented himself at Nagasaki with a letter from the Tsar, seeking rights of trade. Rezanov was churlishly treated, his request was refused, and there began in consequence a turbulent period in Russo-Japanese relations, lasting nearly twenty years.

During the Napoleonic wars the expansion of British naval power also touched Japan. In 1808 the frigate HMS *Phaeton*, seeking to intercept Dutch ships (at a time when Holland was occupied by France), entered Nagasaki flying the Dutch flag, took hostages to enforce compliance with a demand for water and supplies, then departed before any attack could be mounted against her. Samurai in charge of the local defences were subsequently punished for negligence, their lords put under house arrest. Three years later, when British forces seized Java from the Dutch, so taking over Batavia, the British lieutenant-governor, Thomas Stamford Raffles, tried to convert the Dutch connection between Batavia and Japan

29

into a British one. He sent chartered ships to Nagasaki in 1813 and 1814, again under the Dutch flag, but the plan was foiled by the Dutch factor, Hendrik Doeff, who threatened to reveal it to the Japanese, still smarting from the *Phaeton* episode.

In the years that followed there were occasional clashes on the Japanese coast, provoked by British and American whalers seeking water and other supplies. They did not amount to much, but they helped to keep Japanese fears alive. More important was what was happening on the China coast, where British disputes over trading conditions culminated at last in the Opium War (1839–42), during the course of which it became apparent that there might soon be not only a British foothold in China itself, but also an extension of British, French, Russian and American interest to other nearby countries, including Japan. Such a prospect was underlined by visits of British warships to Japan in 1845 and 1849, American ones in 1846 and 1849, and French ships on several occasions to the Ryukyu islands, starting in 1844. A Japanese scholar, Shionoya Tōin, writing in 1847, was prompted by these events to ask, 'How can we know whether the mist gathering over China will not come down as frost on Japan?'[13]

In this changing situation there occurred a shift of emphasis in Japanese studies of the outside world. In 1811 the Bakufu established its own translation office within the astronomy bureau, putting it under the supervision of two well-known Rangaku scholars. For the next twenty years the staff of the office devoted itself in large part to translating a Dutch version of a French encyclopaedia of 1778–86, which furnished information on a wide variety of 'useful' subjects (not least the secret of attaining a happy old age). It was the kind of book, in fact, which can in many ways be compared with those the Japanese had used in order to gain a knowledge of China in the seventh and eighth centuries; but although many items from it were summarized or translated, especially on medicine, botany and zoology, nothing had actually been published by 1846, when the project was abandoned.

Meanwhile at Nagasaki the range of Japan's linguistic studies had been increased. One of the castaways brought back by Laxman had acquired enough Russian to start teaching the language; Rezanov's visit in 1804 had prompted the teaching of French (by the Dutch at Deshima, initially), since it was used in the documents the Russians brought; and the *Phaeton* affair led to the study of English in 1809. Both French and English were later incorporated into the work of the Edo translation office. Yet progress was slow. While an English conversation primer appeared in 1811 and a small English-Japanese dictionary in 1814, it was not until 1840 — thanks to the Opium War, perhaps — that Edo compiled an English grammar.

Edo's view that Japan was part of a world growing rapidly more dangerous was reflected in an increase in the attention paid to western military science. In 1790 Maeno Ryōtaku translated part of a Dutch text on fortification at the request of Matsudaira Sadanobu. In the following years there were works from other scholars on firearms, gunnery and the conduct of war, extending to more specialized studies of topics like naval gunnery and the use of cavalry, as Japan became more aware of what was happening in China. By the time of the Opium War the Japanese knew enough to be able to question the Dutch on quite specific points: the relative value of mortars and howitzers, the susceptibility of steamers to attack, the effect of heavy seas on modern naval operations. They had also begun to put some of their knowledge to practical use. A Nagasaki official, Takashima Shūhan, studied gunnery under Dutch tuition between 1823 and 1827. Thereafter he trained several hundred Japanese pupils, importing a number of books and up-to-date weapons for this purpose. News of the Opium War brought him a measure of support from his seniors in the capital, but the high profile this gave him, coupled with the fact that he was not a full samurai by birth, incurred the hostility of conservatives, who got him imprisoned in 1842. He remained in prison until 1846, then in compulsory retirement for several more years, that is, until the arrival of Perry's squadron in 1853 brought a demand for his services once more.

Military science was not universally thought to be a proper study for non-samurai, as Takashima's experience shows. Yet the majority of those who became expert in various forms of western skills and learning after the middle of the eighteenth century had been at best on the lower fringes of the samurai class. Taking sixteen of the most prominent,[14] four had some claim to samurai rank at a very low level; three were Nagasaki interpreters, that is, hereditary minor functionaries; and four more were official doctors to feudal lords, men of rather indeterminate status, who were often required to wear Buddhist robes to distinguish them from samurai retainers. The other five were commoners: two of farmer stock, two of merchant or artisan origins, one from a family of non-samurai farming and mining specialists. These were men of some standing, to be sure, but they owed the respect in which they were held in Japanese society to their expertise, not inherited position.

In the early years, most of the students who attended the private academies at which Dutch studies and western medicine were taught were men of similar background. Often the sons of doctors, who planned to practise in their home localities, they cannot have been poor, because the fees were high, but they were certainly not men of rank. As time went by, however, this situation changed. Samurai, attracted by the career opportunities implicit in the mastery of western military science, enrolled as students of Dutch and medicine by way of initial training, Itō Gemboku's school, which was opened in 1833, is said to have drawn as many as forty per cent of its students from samurai families, most of them from Edo, Nagasaki or one of the domains with a reputation for military reform. Ogata Kōan's school in Osaka, founded in 1838, which included military subjects and chemistry in its curriculum, also had a significant number of samurai. Some of its commoner students later achieved samurai rank through holding posts connected with defence. In both schools there was a peak of enrolment in 1853–4, the years of the Perry crisis.

The link between knowledge of the West and 'maritime defence' (*kaibō*) made western studies, as they were now coming to be called, a part of politics. Advocating the use and manufacture of foreign weapons as a means of defending Japan against attack was patriotic, there is no doubt, but it was a step which blurred the line between advice and policy; and since policy was the jealously preserved prerogative of Bakufu officials, this could be dangerous. In a book published in 1787–91, Hayashi Shihei not only pointed out that for an island country like Japan western-style ships and coast batteries were of much greater value than traditional types of weaponry, but also proposed that samurai be reeducated to their use. For this he was put under house arrest and had the blocks of his book destroyed. His contemporary, Honda Toshiaki, took due note. In urging a range of solutions to the country's economic problems, including overseas colonization and foreign trade, he allowed his chief works, written in 1798, to circulate only in manuscript among those he thought he could trust.

Two later incidents confirm the wisdom of this decision. We have already noted that the German physician von Siebold was allowed to conduct medical classes in Nagasaki after his arrival in 1823. He did more than that, however, for he had come to Japan with the intention of collecting as much information as possible about the country and its people. Through his students he was able to acquire books and pictures, botanical specimens, examples of clothing and models of houses. When he accompanied the head of the factory to Edo in 1826 he took the opportunity to survey the Shimonoseki Straits. In the capital itself he extended his range of acquaintances to a number of Japanese scholars, including the head of the astronomy bureau, Takahashi Kageyasu, whom he presented with Krusenstern's account of his voyage round the world (1804–6) in return for a copy of Inō Tadataka's maps of Japan. In 1828, when von Siebold was preparing for his voyage back to Europe, all this was accidentally discovered by Japanese officials. The doctor's collection was loaded on a Dutch ship which was wrecked by a typhoon in Nagasaki harbour. This meant that its cargo had to be transshipped to another vessel; and in the course of the move, some of the boxes were examined and found to contain a number of 'illegal' items, especially maps. The outcome was punishment for all concerned. Takahashi was arrested and died in prison in the following year, his corpse being beheaded, in order that death should not save him from disgrace. Several scholars who had acted as messengers between the two men were arrested and in some cases tortured. Von Siebold was expelled from Japan, though he had enough warning to be able to make copies of some of his maps before they were seized by the authorities.

The next such affair came ten years later. In 1837 a group of American missionaries on the China coast chartered the ship *Morrison* to take several shipwrecked Japanese seamen back to their country, in the hope that this would enable Christianity to secure a footing there. The venture was a failure — the ship was fired on by Japanese batteries, first at Uraga, then at Kagoshima, in accordance with Bakufu instructions issued in 1825 — but a garbled account of what had taken place, confusing the *Morrison* with an English missionary of that name, became current among students of the West in Edo. It prompted one of them, Takano Nagahide (Chōei), to write a pamphlet on the subject. Because he had studied under von Siebold, Takano was already in some degree suspect. His pamphlet, *Yume monogatari* (The Story of a Dream), made him more so, since its essential message was that Japan ought not to risk offending Britain by actions of this kind.

The sequel came in 1839, when Takano, together with a well-known painter, Watanabe Kazan, became embroiled in another dispute concerning foreign affairs. Alarmed about the implications of events in China, Edo officials decided in that year to undertake a review of coast defences in the approaches to the capital, a task which they entrusted to Torii Takaaki, a senior inspector (*ōmetsuke*), and Egawa Tarōzaemon, steward of the Tokugawa estates in the Izu peninsula. Torii was a known enemy of Dutch studies. Egawa had already begun to study western military science. He asked his acquaintance, Watanabe, who had a wide circle of friends in Rangaku circles, including Takano, first to suggest some men with western-style training to work on the survey, then to provide documents to support a submission to the Bakufu. In response to the second of these requests Watanabe produced a memorandum, complete with maps, describing the seaward defences of major cities elsewhere in the world — England, France, Holland, Portugal, Russia, Turkey and China — together with a background essay on world conditions. The latter turned out to be the kind of document that aroused Torii's anger, prompting the arrest of both Takano and Watanabe.

There are three extant versions of Watanabe's essay.[15] Two were sent to Egawa and greatly toned down at his request, with the result that the final text read much like an entry in a gazetteer. That is, it set out information about the location, territory, climate, natural products and population of various countries, together with brief descriptions of their governments, religions, social structures and economic institutions. This might have been accepted as relatively uncontroversial. The other version, which apparently contained Watanabe's first thoughts on the subject, was found at his house when Torii sent men to arrest him. It set out much the same material, but used it to try to identify the sources of western strength. Its central theme, echoing such writers as Honda Toshiaki and Satō Nobuhiro (see below), was that strength was a product of political, social and economic factors: stable government and laws; education, especially in science and technology; the promotion of scientific knowledge by every means; and territorial expansion, achieved through foreign trade and the founding of colonies. The reader was left to infer that Japan's weakness sprang from having few or none of these things. A concluding statement underlines the point, expressing the hope that Edo would 'broaden the scope of its policies' to meet the western threat.

Even as a reasoned plea on behalf of studying the West this would have been enough to provoke traditionalists like Torii, but it was more than that. The main thrust of the argument was to question Edo's policies. This made punishment inevitable. Watanabe, a samurai of some rank, was sent to his lord for confinement. He committed suicide in 1841. Takano, who was also implicated, was confined to prison. He was freed temporarily when the prison building caught fire in 1844 — this was customary in such emergencies — but failed to surrender again once the fire was over, spending the next few years in hiding in various parts of the country. He died resisting arrest in 1850, when discovered by police on returning to the capital.

The most obvious crime of which these men stood accused was the bureaucratic one of meddling in matters which were not their business. Yet behind this were considerations of greater consequence. In the previous two hundred years the political and social structure of Tokugawa Japan had increasingly been undermined by economic change. Rising agricultural production had brought an expansion of commerce. Towns became larger and more numerous, merchants became wealthy, farmers began to raise crops for the market. Gradually a number of non-economic consequences flowed from this. Samurai, as town-dwellers, living in and around the castles of their lords, fell into debt to merchants, because the temptations of urban life could not always be paid for from incomes based on land. Many of their lords suffered the same misfortune, if more slowly. Both felt threatened. Peasant revolt occurred with greater frequency as harsher taxes and the vagaries of the market put pressure on farmers. As a result, officials began to talk of the need for 'reform', by which they meant steps to restore Japan to what they conceived to be its 'proper' condition, established in the seventeenth century. They also became more sensitive to critical comment.

In these circumstances the writings of students of the West, who meant something quite different by reform, invited trouble. Honda Toshiaki had been the first to reveal potentially revolutionary notions, though not in public. In part of what he wrote in 1798 he had compared Japan to England. In respect of natural resources, he said, the latter was essentially 'a wasteland', much like Kamchatka, so its wealth and strength clearly depended, 'not on the quality of its land, but on its institutions and teachings'. It followed that if Japan were to adopt something like them, there could soon emerge 'a great island of Japan in the East comparable with the island of England in the West'.[16] A generation later Satō Nobuhiro — expert in agriculture and mining, student of Dutch and western science, associate of Watanabe Kazan and Takano Nagahide — drafted in some detail a plan for the reorganization of Japanese government and society. Although it did not directly challenge the feudal basis of Tokugawa rule, it called for the creation of specialized departments to handle different aspects of administration, such as military forces, economic policy and education, and proposed the teaching to an elite of military science, geography and foreign languages. Once implemented, Satō claimed, these measures would make possible not only defence, but also expansion. China 'would crumble and fall like a house of sand within five to seven years'. Remoter countries of Asia would come 'with bowed heads and on hands and knees to serve us'.[17]

Given that they were aware of this strand in contemporary thought, it is not unreasonable that Edo officials should have treated Watanabe's essay of 1839 as seditious. His description of Christianity as one of the world's major religions, to be ranked with the doctrines of Buddha or Confucius, was in the strict sense illegal, in view of the ban on Christianity. As recently as 1827 a Rangaku scholar had been crucified for possessing Christian books. Some of the items which Watanabe listed as sources of western strength were directly contrary to recent Bakufu decisions: the development of foreign trade (which the council had again rejected in its discussion of the *Morrison* affair), together with the promotion of science and the gathering of scientific knowledge throughout the world (for which Edo had punished von Siebold and Takahashi). Even education was a sensitive subject if taken to imply — as Confucian thought certainly did — that it was the approved route to government office. It is hard to believe that many of Edo's feudal officials doubted the wisdom of punishing those who put forward such ideas.

Yet 1839 was to mark a turning-point. In the next few years there was news of British victories in China, then a Dutch diplomatic mission, calling on Japan to admit that seclusion was unsustainable in a changing world. This was followed by the visits of a number of foreign warships to Japan and Ryukyu, as we have seen. In these circumstances study of the West became more widely accepted as a necessary adjunct to defence. Egawa Tarōzaemon enrolled as a student at Takashima Shūhan's school of gunnery. Sakuma Shōzan, another samurai with similar interests, became an adviser on coast defence, first in his lord's domain, then in Edo. In 1842 he wrote a memorial urging that Japan manufacture modern guns, build new coast batteries, construct western-style ships, and train a navy. He also questioned the choice of men for office, especially military office, solely on the grounds that were feudal retainers of appropriate status. Appointment should depend on ability, he stated, as it did in western countries; and the fact that he was not immediately punished for these views hinted that things might be about to change.

3

Unequal Treaties

In July 1853 Commodore Matthew C. Perry brought four ships of the United States Pacific fleet into Uraga at the entrance to Edo Bay. His object, as stated in a letter he brought from President Millard Fillmore, was to ask for a relaxation of Japan's seclusion laws in America's favour, preferably one which permitted trade; and having delivered the President's letter with calculated ceremony, he withdrew to the China coast for a time, in order to give the Shogun's officials a chance to reflect on it. He returned in February 1854 — accompanied, as he had promised, by 'a much larger force' — to open talks with Japanese representatives. The latter had orders to refuse his demands, or at least procrastinate. Perry, however, brooked neither refusal nor delay. Anchoring his warships in a line offshore as a gesture of intimidation, he forced the signature of a treaty, signed in March, which made no formal provision for trade, but opened Nagasaki, Hakodate and Shimoda to American ships as ports of refuge and supply. The British and Russian naval commanders in the western Pacific found occasion in the next few months to win similar terms for their respective countries. The Dutch at Deshima obtained minor improvements in the conditions under which they traded there.

A further phase in Japan's foreign relations began in the winter of 1856–7. News of a fresh Anglo-Chinese war (the Arrow War), in which France also joined, persuaded Edo that the powers had both the will and the means to insist on having their way in Japan. After long deliberation, treaties were concluded with Holland and Russia in October 1857, increasing the total value of trade at Nagasaki, subject to a degree of continuing government control. With these arrangements as evidence of good intentions, it was hoped that a clash with France and Britain might be avoided. This proved to be a miscalculation. The American consul, Townsend Harris, who had been at Shimoda since September 1856, insisted that only the kind of agreement which had already been imposed on China and Siam would be acceptable to the West. Repeatedly reminding Edo of its inability to match the strength of a British fleet, he succeeded in getting Bakufu consent to a draft on the China model, that is, unrestricted freedom of trade at selected 'treaty ports'; low tariffs, also fixed by treaty; and consular courts, administering western law, to which alone foreigners would be subject in Japan. The text was ready for signature by the middle of February 1858.

At this point its main provisions were made known outside official circles in the capital. They caused uproar. The Bakufu sought to postpone signature of the agreement while it tried to damp the clamour down, but this had still not been accomplished when there came reports from Tientsin, announcing China's acceptance of Anglo-French terms in June. Fearing that China's defeat must herald the early arrival of an Anglo-French fleet in Japan — which, Harris pointed out, would pose much greater dangers than any domestic protest — the Tokugawa council decided at the end of July to sign the American treaty. Envoys from Britain, France, Holland and Russia obtained almost identical concessions shortly after.

As expected, this outcome did nothing to still the objections of indignant Japanese. Resentment of the treaty provisions was everywhere expressed. What is more, doubts began to emerge about the future of the Tokugawa house. Since the policy of seclusion had not only provided a framework for the country's dealings with the outside world, but also acted as a prop to the Shogun's authority at home, much as the tribute system had done for earlier rulers, international failure vis-à-vis the West could be said in Chinese terms to undermine the Shogun's 'mandate'. One result was that foreign policy became a strand in the disputes that were to bring the regime down in 1868. Another was that study of the West became more than ever a politically sensitive undertaking.

THE FOREIGN POLICY DEBATE

Perry's arrival at Uraga in 1853 had not been unexpected. Ever since the Opium War Japanese scholars had been warning of something of the kind, though for the most part they identified Britain as the source of danger. In addition, the news that an American expedition was on its way had been passed on by the Dutch to the Edo government. Despite this, no policy had ever been agreed by Tokugawa officials to deal with the crisis when it came, nor did they have any regular means of framing one. Trade at Nagasaki, or relations with Korea and Ryukyu, were routine matters, entrusted to officials at Nagasaki and the hereditary lords of Tsushima and Satsuma, respectively. There was no central government department whose task it was to deal with them.

Lacking any bureaucratic machinery to handle foreign affairs, the Bakufu had to set about creating one when western envoys arrived, a process which was bound to take some time. Meanwhile the importance of the issue meant that decisions had to come from members of the Tokugawa council, whose only recent military experience had been with the suppression of peasant revolt. Their doubts and hesitations in this situation led them to undertake unprecedented consultations, extending to a few of the more powerful feudal lords. It would be useful at this point to identify those who were most involved.

The senior member of the council in 1853 was Abe Masahiro, a Tokugawa vassal lord (*fudai daimyō*) who had first been appointed ten years earlier. His successor, taking office at the end of 1855, was Hotta Masayoshi, another vassal lord. Ii Naosuke, head of one of the two most senior vassal houses, whose castle was at Hikone, just to the east of Kyoto, was made Regent (Tairō) in June 1858, superseding Hotta and taking precedence over other councillors. These three were in effect successive heads of the Shogun's government.Outside officialdom, the most significant figures were Tokugawa Nariaki, head of the Tokugawa branch house of Mito; Matsudaira Yoshinaga (Kei'ei, also known as Shungaku), a Tokugawa collateral, whose castle town was Fukui in the province of Echizen; and Shimazu Nariakira, *tozama daimyō* (a feudal lord not vassal to the Tokugawa) of Satsuma, a vast domain, having its capital in Kagoshima and covering much of southern Kyushu. The Shimazu were related to the Tokugawa by marriage. Nariaki and Nariakira also had marriage ties with high-ranking nobles of the imperial court.

Tokugawa Nariaki had for some years before 1853 made himself spokesman for all those who demanded immediate steps to ward off foreign attack. Several of the samurai who served him, above all Aizawa Seishisai, were widely known for their warnings against the West. Their desire to create a kind of 'fortress Japan' — as Aizawa put it, 'we must now make our islands into a castle and think of the ocean as a moat'[1] — was often reflected in Nariaki's memoranda on the subject of the treaties. The best-known of these was sent to Abe on 14 August 1853, that is, about a month after Perry's first visit. It described American actions as 'insolent'; dismissed trade as no more than a source of 'useless foreign goods like woollens and satin', in return for which Japan provided much more valuable ores (that is, copper and silver); condemned 'the evils of Christianity'; and insisted that Edo must give the lead in resisting foreign demands. To do this might involve war, even some initial defeats, Nariaki recognized, but it would be better than a 'temporizing and time-serving policy', which would risk causing 'the lower orders' to lose respect for established authority.[2]

By implication this was to criticize Abe and some of his advisers, who held that Japan's best course, given the country's state of military unpreparedness, would be to temporize with the West as long as possible, while seeking to improve maritime defences. Ii Naosuke was equally impatient with attitudes of this kind, though from a different standpoint. He, too, found the American demands offensive, but he did not believe in the concept of fortress Japan: 'when one is besieged in a castle', he wrote, 'to raise the drawbridge is to imprison oneself and make it impossible to hold out indefinitely'.[3] Instead, he maintained, Japan should take the initiative in developing trade and building steamships — they might require Dutch masters at first, but would be a means of training Japanese in navigation and gunnery — in order to lay the foundations of a fleet. For such a purpose Edo should be ready to tolerate 'complete or partial change in the laws of our ancestors'.

Tokugawa Nariaki and Ii Naosuke represent, respectively, the negative and the positive Bakufu approaches to relations with the West in this period. Both saw western incursion into Japan as a threat to the established order of Japanese society, in which they had a privileged place. Both were willing to adopt western weapons and military methods to defend that order. But beyond that point they differed. Nariaki's attitude towards western skills was minimalist and instrumental. Naosuke, by contrast, was willing to seek out those skills and accept significant reform as a condition of adopting them. His position attracted increasing support among officials as they came to know more about international realities.

The main stimulus towards reexamining Abe's policy of caution was the war which Britain and France fought against China, starting in October 1856. By that time Hotta Masayoshi was head of the council with responsibility for foreign affairs. From his predecessor he had inherited as advisers on that subject a group of administrative officials of more than usual ability, who were emerging as Japan's first specialists in the diplomatic field. They were Tokugawa vassals just below daimyo rank who had held posts in finance and the inspectorate, or had been governors of the ports being opened to foreigners, and were to provide the majority of those who were appointed to the new office of Commissioner of Foreign Affairs (Gaikoku Bugyō) when it was created in 1858.

In August 1856 the Dutch representative at Nagasaki, Donker Curtius, had started a fresh round of negotiations by asking for a commercial treaty with Japan, pointing out that to have concluded such an arrangement with Holland would be an advantage at the time, which would surely come, when Britain demanded one. Some months later he increased the diplomatic pressure by informing Edo of the outbreak of the Arrow War in China, emphasizing that it arose from China's mishandling of relations with the West. Much the same kind of warning came from the American consul at Shimoda. As a result, Hotta appointed a number of his subordinates to study how far Japan should permit an expansion of foreign trade. 'Should there once be the sound of a single cannon-shot', he cautioned them, diplomatic action 'will already be too late'. The replies took their cue from this. Some officials followed closely what they took to be Hotta's line, dismissing 'fruitless debate of impracticable plans' and recommending that Japan's leaders take the initiative in opening ports to trade, instead of waiting to have this action forced upon them. This, it was argued, would be the best way of upholding both the country's prestige abroad and the Shogun's authority at home. Others, rather older and of higher rank, accepted trade with greater reluctance. The Bakufu's 'inner thoughts', they urged, should remain 'rooted in the former system'.[4]

The treaties signed with Holland and Russia in October 1857, which combined an increase in trade with continuing government control, reflected these disagreements. The compromise they represented, however, was not good enough for Townsend Harris at Shimoda. Putting forward his own proposals for a commercial treaty in the winter of 1857–8, he insisted that Edo accept as a basis for negotiation the same 'unequal' arrangements as Britain and France were seeking in China. Edo saw this as a setback; but its belief that Japan was on the point of being attacked by a foreign fleet, following the British capture of Canton at the beginning of 1858, eventually brought Hotta and his colleagues to accept such terms. They soon discovered that by doing so they had run well ahead of feudal opinion in Japan at large, not least that of the most powerful of the feudal lords.

In an attempt to bring order out of the confusion, Hotta sought the emperor's approval for the treaty he proposed, going in person to Kyoto to secure it. He failed, partly because of the emperor's own anti-foreign convictions, partly because a quite separate dispute concerning the succession to the Tokugawa house cost him the support of key feudal lords and their friends at the emperor's court. Failure in its turn brought crisis in Edo. Hotta was dismissed as head of the council. Ii Naosuke came to power as Regent, bent on reasserting discipline; but faced by news from China about the negotiations at Tientsin, he accepted the inevitable and signed the treaty (without the imperial consent), before settling the succession question in favour of the Kii branch of the Tokugawa family. The second of these decisions meant ignoring the claims, argued on grounds of maturity and ability, which had been advanced on behalf of one of Tokugawa Nariaki's sons, Hitotsubashi Keiki (Yoshinobu), a step that further divided political society. As a precaution, therefore, the Regent moved to deter opposition. Nariaki and his daimyo allies were put under house arrest; samurai who had acted as their agents in the dispute were executed or imprisoned; and some of Hotta's own subordinates, known adherents of the Hitotsubashi cause, were removed to less influential offices.

As a consequence of these events the treaties became the subject of public and heated controversy, focussed as much on the Regent's high-handedness as on the merits of the diplomatic case. Those of high rank who had been punished were deeply resentful. Their loyal samurai were angry on their behalf. Many others, who had had no part at all in what had taken place, were affronted by the apparent slights to both their emperor and their country. Since nearly all the protestors were samurai, who habitually went armed, the streets of Kyoto, in particular, soon became dangerous to those who were said to have behaved as traitors. Once the treaty ports were opened in 1859, foreign residents and visitors, too, came to share the risks.

In these circumstances Japanese who wished to learn about the West, however patriotic their motives, were always exposed to possible assassination or assault: study was all too often taken to mean political affirmation. Yet even conservative Confucian scholars, who had always maintained that western civilization was fundamentally flawed, could not wholly deny its practical utility in the current crisis. Shionoya Tōin, a man who described the western alphabet with vast distaste as 'confused and irregular, wriggling like snakes or larvae of mosquitos', admitted that the foreigners had in practice shown themselves to be better disciples of Sun Tzu than the Chinese. The foreign barbarians know both themselves and their opponents, he wrote, in a reference to Sun Tzu's dictum that this was the path to victory. The Chinese, by contrast, had become 'so convinced of their superiority that they think it unnecessary to study conditions among the foreign barbarians'. It followed that when it came to fighting, 'the Chinese prove to be absolutely no match for the foreigners'.[5]

This brand of realism made it possible to devise an entirely 'respectable' case for acquiring western skills without in any way relenting towards Ii Naosuke's policies. It was made forcefully by Yoshida Shōin, one of the key figures in the growth of radical anti-Tokugawa thought and the terrorist activity soon to be associated with it. Born in 1830 into a low-ranking samurai family in Choshu (Yamaguchi), Shōin had from an early age shown an interest in western military science. He studied first at Nagasaki, then in Edo, where he enrolled in Sakuma Shōzan's school. At the time of the Perry negotiations, encouraged by Sakuma, who gave him money for expenses and a poem expressing support for the venture, he decided to try to study abroad. He first went to Nagasaki, with the object of joining the Russian squadron under Putiatin, but arrived too late. Back in Edo in time for Perry's second visit at the beginning of 1854, he became involved in various activist designs to strengthen Japan's resistance in the impending crisis, including one to assassinate Perry, though that was eventually dropped. It was only after the treaty had been signed that he reverted to the idea of studying overseas. By that time, Perry had moved on to Shimoda. Nothing daunted, Shōin followed him there, together with a companion who wished to join him on his travels. They drew up a statement explaining what they wanted to do. This they managed to pass unobserved to an American officer at the Shimoda landing; but as no response was made from the squadron during the rest of the day, they made their way by boat after dark to Perry's flagship. To their disappointment, the commodore was not willing to put the results of his mission at risk by conniving at a breach of Bakufu law. Before dawn, therefore, in the hope that they might escape official notice, the prospective students were put ashore again. Unhappily, it transpired that their seamanship was less commendable than their persistence. During the night their boat, which contained their swords and papers, including Sakuma Shōzan's poem, had come adrift from its moorings, and since they were unable to find it, it fell into Bakufu hands. Inevitably, all hope of secrecy was then gone. Arrested, Shōin was taken to the main Edo prison. His mentor, Sakuma Shōzan, also betrayed by the affair, was installed in the next cell.

Some six months later, both teacher and pupil were sentenced to house arrest and turned over to their own domains for custody. In Shōin's case, this lasted until the beginning of 1856, when he was released and allowed to open a school on the outskirts of Hagi, the Choshu castle town. In a very short time he had acquired as students a remarkable cross-section of future leaders of Japan. Several of them became 'travellers', whose experiences are recounted later in this book. They did not have long to enjoy Shōin's teaching, however. Towards the end of 1858 he became the moving spirit in a plot to assassinate one of Ii Naosuke's colleagues on the Tokugawa council, the man who had been appointed to persuade or browbeat the court into approving the treaties signed earlier in the year. The plot was discovered, Shōin was once more arrested, and this time he was condemned to death. His execution took place in Edo in November 1859.

Such a fate did not carry any stigma. On the contrary, it made Yoshida Shōin a hero and exemplar to many of his young contemporaries. His writings, circulated surreptitiously, won enormous popularity, not least for their condemnation of the Shogun and feudal lords for failing to avenge the dishonour suffered by Japan. What was needed, he wrote on one occasion, was a new national leadership, marked by commitment, not inherited rank, and loyal to the emperor. Once this was in place, weakness would give way to strength. Instead of suffering indignity, Japan could expand: 'we will seize Manchuria, thus coming face to face with Russia; regaining Korea, we will keep watch on China; taking the islands of the South, we will advance on India'. Learning about the West also had its part in this scheme of things. While 'to adore and idolize the barbarians . . . must be rejected absolutely', he believed, their 'artillery and shipbuilding, their knowledge of medicine, and of physical sciences, can all be of use to us'.[6] This was to be the theme of many official and semi-official approaches to the West in the ten years after Shōin's death.

The origin of these approaches, which envisaged direct contact with foreigners and foreign countries, not just the reading of books, can be traced to the discussions surrounding negotiation of the treaties. The most significant initiative was that of Sakuma Shōzan, who recommended that envoys be sent abroad to purchase ships; that men of ability be chosen to go to foreign countries as students, in order to learn about the 'highly ingenious techniques and machinery' the West had developed; and that foreign experts be brought to Japan as teachers. His declared model was Peter the Great, under whose guidance, he said, 'Russia in the end caught up with Holland'. Using the same methods, Japan could reach parity the West at the present time.[7]

Some of these ideas struck a chord with powerful feudal lords. Kuroda Narihiro of Kumamoto, commenting on the Perry expedition in 1853, made two proposals. One was that Japan should offer concessions to America and Russia, then exploit their gratitude as a means of keeping Britain and France at bay. This would be 'to use foreign countries to control foreign countries' (in the original Chinese sense, it should be noted). The other was to strengthen Japan's defences by inviting foreign advisers to Japan — American, as well as Dutch — to provide instruction in the manufacture of cannon and warships. Tokugawa Nariaki made similar proposals, subject to the proviso that men trained in western military skills should not use foreign languages or wear western uniform: 'without abandoning Japanese ways', he wrote in a letter to Abe Masahiro, 'we should adopt the best of foreign methods and join them to the best of our own'.[8] Aizawa Seishisai had at one time envisaged a still wider marriage of western means to Japanese ends. Writing of Peter the Great in 1801, long before Sakuma Shōzan did so, he had commended him for 'enriching the nation' and for enhancing Russia's strength by establishing schools, sending students abroad, building a fleet, and using the profits from trade to buy essential books. Such steps would be right for Japan, too, he concluded, if the knowledge so acquired were put at the disposal of the state.[9]

The greatest of the lords, men like Tokugawa Nariaki and Shimazu Nariakira, had the resources and independence to seek western military and scientific skills on their own account, but to be fully effective the policy had to be undertaken on a national scale. After all, as contemporaries recognized, it was the Shogun who stood to profit most from what Japan might learn from the West, just as it was emperors who had found good cause to send missions to China from Nara and Heian. During talk of the proposed treaty with Holland in the spring of 1857, officials had suggested that Japan should not only maintain good relations with 'trustworthy' states, wherever they were to be found, but also send official representatives and students to friendly countries. Hotta himself envisaged advantages in a plan 'to copy the foreigners where they are at their best and so repair our own shortcomings'.[10] However, the promise that these developments might have held for Japan's future study of the West was checked by the political crisis of 1858. The fall of Hotta and the relegation of his closest advisers to the bureaucratic shadows, together with Ii Naosuke's purge and the rising tide of anti-foreign sentiment which followed the signing of the treaties, ensured that the opening of the ports in 1859 took place in a much more restrictive atmosphere. When missions and students were eventually sent abroad, the step had to be justified to much more hostile critics.

Western studies and military reform

When Perry's squadron came to Japan in 1853 and 1854 it caused widespread alarm. Troops were rushed to key points along the shore. Residents of Edo sought safety for themselves and their belongings in the expectation of an attack on the city. Yet there was curiosity, too, as there always had been when foreign ships arrived. The humbler sightseers were kept away by guard-boats, but official ones came to visit the flagship in considerable numbers on one pretext or another. They included those whom foreigners called 'spies', making notes and sketches of everything they saw. These sketches were sometimes made up into more elaborate paintings or picture-scrolls for the edification of their superiors and leading feudal lords, as were pictorial records of the presents Perry brought (notionally for 'the Emperor', which Edo took to mean the Shogun). Among the latter were a scaled-down steam train, complete with rolling-stock and a circular section of rails, telegraph equipment (in working order), and a variety of modern weapons.

Because of the Bakufu's bureaucratic habits, we have an extensive visual record of the occasion, seen through Japanese eyes. There are portraits of Perry's officers, diagrams of the anchorage, showing the disposition of guards and attendant officials on ceremonial occasions, a large picture of a paddle-steamer, a painting of the banquet which celebrated the conclusion of the treaty (the American officers, it seems, had difficulty with chopsticks). There are careful drawings of uniforms, of the bandsmen's instruments, of umbrellas, ships' figureheads, the tombstone of an American marine who died in Japan, even the labels on equipment. Extra care was obviously taken to secure accurate diagrams of technical devices and machinery, such as the steam engine and the telegraph. In particular, there is something very like a working drawing of a Colt revolver, showing its separate parts; and it is said that when Shimazu Nariakira saw the cavalry rifle which was one of the official gifts, he asked that he might take it back to his Edo residence to study it more closely, then kept it overnight, while his retainers made detailed drawings from which to manufacture a replica.

In official circles generally, it was weapons which aroused the greatest interest. After all, instruction in gunnery and navigation, and the drawing

1. Demonstration of American telegraph equipment at Yokohama, 1854. The equipment, brought by Perry as one of the U.S. government's official gifts, was set up between the Treaty House, where the treaty was signed, and another building about a mile away.

up of plans for the construction of western-style ships and the casting of cannon, were regular tasks of the departments of western studies which the Bakufu and several domains had added to their schools for samurai. Many of the teachers and students at these schools had some idea of the relevant technology. Fukuzawa Yukichi tells in his autobiography of experiments with tin-plating and the making of sulphuric acid at Ogata Kōan's academy in Osaka. Matsuki Kōan, while teaching at the Satsuma school, became proficient in handling the telegraph.

The Bakufu's contribution to the acquisition of knowledge about the West was made principally through the Bansho Shirabesho (literally, Office for the Investigation of Barbarian Books). As early as 1846 Tokugawa Nariaki had urged Abe Masahiro to improve Edo's facilities for translating and circulating western books on military science. In August 1853, just after Perry's arrival, a Tokugawa retainer, Katsu Awa, who was later to be one of Japan's senior naval officers, proposed that a new

46

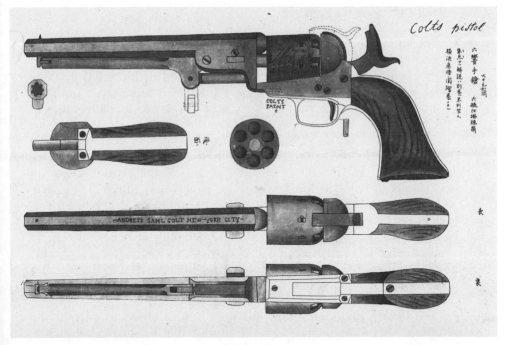

2. Diagram of a Colt revolver, another of the official gifts brought by Perry in 1854. This is probably a copy of an American diagram, annotated in Japanese.

institution be established for this purpose and provided with a library of books in Chinese, Japanese and Dutch. It should teach 'astronomy, geography, science, military science, gunnery, fortification, and mechanics', he recommended, its staff being recruited from domains if the Bakufu's own resources were inadequate. The plan was eventually approved by Abe. He entrusted its implementation to a group of his foreign affairs advisers, who produced a memorandum on the subject in July 1855. This envisaged the creation of an office to study 'truly useful things like the strength and weakness, the semblance and reality of each country, the state of its army and navy, the advantages and drawbacks of its machinery', all with a view to enabling Japan, by acquiring greater knowledge of foreign lands, to 'adopt their strong points and avoid their shortcomings'. Identified for early translation were 'books on bombardment, on the construction of batteries, on fortifications, books on building warships and manoeuvering them, books on sailing and navigation, books on training soldiers and sailors, on machinery . . . books on products'.[11] It was an ambitious programme. It was also broader in scope than many Confucian conservatives would have liked, which may explain the term *Bansho* ('barbarian books') in the institute's title: a reminder that all such departures from tradition had their origin in the need to 'know one's enemy'.

The Shirabesho, as it is usually called, opened in what is now the Kanda district of modern Tokyo early in 1856. It had at that time a staff of fifteen men, no less than six of whom had been trained as doctors. Only three were direct retainers of the Shogun, though four more came from the domains of vassal lords and two from those of Tokugawa relatives (one of them Echizen). Another three were from the 'outside' (*tozama*) domains of Satsuma, Choshu and Uwajima, which were to play a major part in the politics of the following decade. For all these men, translation duties took priority over teaching, because the opening of the ports brought an enormous increase in foreign-language paperwork, but students were admitted from February 1857 and some two hundred soon availed themselves of the opportunity. Three teachers of English were appointed in 1860, reflecting Japan's diplomatic and commercial needs, and there was a gradual extension of the curriculum thereafter to include French, German, science, geography and history. In 1863 the Shirabesho was renamed Kaiseisho (Development Institute) to mark its changing character.

The library of the institute has been reconstituted in part in the National Diet Library since 1954. It appears that existing collections of western books were transferred to it from the Astronomy Bureau and other Edo offices, as well as from some domains, bringing its total holdings to about 600 titles by 1859. From that time on it expanded rapidly, largely through purchases made on its behalf by Bakufu envoys who were sent abroad. Jansen concludes from what survives that there was a preponderance of works of 'direct and practical utility'. There was little on theory, or on scientific method, or on the ideals and values of the West as expressed in ethics and philosophy. In addition, some of the more difficult texts have uncut pages, while in a number of general works only the sections mentioning Japan show evidence of having been consulted, implying, perhaps, that the range of the material was greater than members of the staff had the skill or the time to master.

In the domains, western studies were widespread but patchy, depending a good deal on how narrowly men in authority concentrated on immediate military needs, and how far they were willing or able to meet the cost of what proved to be an expensive exercise. Geographical position gave some an advantage. Saga, for example, the castle town of Hizen, was only a hundred kilometres from Nagasaki. Partly for that reason Hizen had been chosen as one of the two domains to share the responsibility for Nagasaki defences, a duty which gave its scholars privileged access to the Dutch. Since Hizen's daimyo, Nabeshima Naomasa, gave western studies his full support, while financial reforms enabled him to do so with some generosity, Saga became a leading centre of western technology at an early date. Starting, as was often the case, with medicine, by 1850 its scholars had translated a Dutch book on reverberatory furnaces, the first step towards building iron guns (in place of bronze ones) for the Nagasaki batteries. After a successful casting in the summer of 1852, they produced guns in considerable numbers in the next three or four years, supplying as many as two hundred to the Bakufu. Meanwhile, when Edo raised its centuries-old ban on the building of oceangoing ships after the Perry crisis, Saga sent men to Nagasaki to study shipbuilding and navigation. Large-scale models of a steamship (and a railway engine) were produced. A complete shipyard plant was ordered from Holland in 1858. This, however, proved to be more than the domain could afford, so the equipment was handed over to Bakufu officials for use in their own planned dockyard.

Satsuma's activities were on a larger scale still. The domain's connection with Ryukyu had long enabled the Shimazu lords to conduct an indirect and illicit trade with China in the guise of Ryukyu tribute missions. It had also put Satsuma in the forefront of Japanese contacts with the West after the Opium War, since both French and British ships called at the islands on a number of occasions. Shimazu Nariakira, who succeeded as daimyo in March 1851, was well aware of the special opportunities this gave him. During a discussion of the proposed American treaty in 1857 he told a group of his retainers that since there appeared to be objections to some of the ports Townsend Harris wanted opened, it might be possible to put forward Ryukyu or a port in Satsuma as alternatives. Through these, he said, there would be a chance to expand the Ryukyu trade with Foochow, thereby creating a source of revenue to pay for the import of western guns and warships.[12]

This idea came to nothing because of Nariakira's death in 1858, though it contained the seeds of a not dissimilar plan for Satsuma trade with Europe in 1865 (see Chapter 6). In other respects, however, Nariakira did much to strengthen his domain on western lines. As a young man he had studied Rangaku in Edo under scholars like Takano Nagahide, acquiring a range of contacts which as daimyo he proceeded to exploit. He sent samurai to study under specialist teachers in Osaka, Nagasaki and Edo. He commissioned translations of Dutch books on steamships, steam engines, telegraphy, gas-lighting and photography, inviting some of those who carried out the translations to join a kind of science institute in the grounds of his Kagoshima castle, where they supervised production of the equipment their books described. Within a year or two gas-lighting had been installed and an experimental telegraph had been fitted between the gate and the castle keep. Nariakira himself, tutored by Kawamoto Kōmin, became an enthusiastic photographer, using a camera bought from Holland.

If these might be described as a rich man's technological toys, the same cannot be said of other processes carried out in Kagoshima. They included the making of gun-cotton, the manufacture of sulphuric acid and industrial alcohol, metal-plating, and the casting of coins, all carried out in the small industrial complex, known as the Shūseikan, which Nariakira ordered to be built on the shore of Kagoshima Bay in 1852. Its nucleus was a reverberatory furnace, completed in 1853 with the help of information acquired from Hizen (but not actually in operation until 1856 because of difficulties in making firebricks). A blast furnace was installed in 1854. Output was at first concentrated on the production of cannons and cannonballs, but facilities were later developed for the manufacture of rifles, agricultural implements, glass and pottery. The study of electricity through Dutch books made possible the electrical detonation of explosives for both mining and military use.

Work on building western-style steamships in Satsuma began with experiments on small steam-engines in the domain's Edo headquarters during 1851. This was followed by the production of a model paddle-steamer at Sakurajima (across the bay from Kagoshima) in 1851–2. Both these developments depended on translations from the Dutch, as had been true in Hizen, but Satsuma also received advice from a repatriated Japanese castaway, Nakahama Manjirō, who had spent some years in America. After Perry's arrival Nariakira came up with a more ambitious plan, that is, to build twelve western-style sailing vessels, armed with twelve to thirty-eight guns, plus three steamers with six to twelve guns. Abe Masahiro gave oral approval, on condition that some of the ships be made available to the Bakufu, and within a year the Sakurajima yard had launched the *Shōhei Maru*, a sailing ship originally designed for the Ryukyu trade, but now modified for use as a warship by the provision of four small and ten larger guns. It was brought to Shinagawa in the spring of 1855 to be shown to an admiring Edo. Members of the Bakufu council, including Abe, went to see it carry out practice firing; Tokugawa Nariaki paid it a visit; and even the Shogun viewed it, albeit safely from the shore. Nariakira then handed it over to the Shogun's officials, who sent it to Nagasaki to be used in naval training.

Steamers proved more difficult. A small one, the *Unkō Maru*, was launched at Sakurajima in the summer of 1855, but its fifteen-horse-power engines were never satisfactory and the project was abandoned. So were plans for a larger steamer, though this was apparently because of cost. In fact, although Sakurajima continued to produce sailing vessels, by 1858 Nariakira was turning his attention to the possibility of buying his steamers from abroad.

Like many of his contemporaries, Nariakira believed that the study of western military science and the adoption of western technology were matters of urgency for Japan. Yet he was not led on that account to deny the importance of Confucian values in politics and society. As a military reformer, he retained a commitment to traditional social structures, as was shown by his retention of forms of organization in Satsuma's 'modern' armed forces which did not significantly change their recruitment and composition. Artillery units were reorganized as battalions, each of eight guns. All the troops attached to them were required to have rifle training. The cavalry was to have platoons of twenty-four men, four platoons to a battalion (following the Dutch translation of a French cavalry manual). The domain's infantry began to drill in the western manner to commands which were given in Dutch. In all these cases the fighting men were samurai, or retainers of lower status (*ashigaru*), serving as a matter of feudal duty. It was not quite so easy to persuade such men to be sailors, but a number of samurai were sent to Nagasaki for training, with a view to becoming qualified in navigation and gunnery, while nearly two hundred others at various levels were recruited for less demanding duties by the offer of small supplementary stipends. Looking to the more distant future, Nariakira ordered one of his entourage to begin a study of the British navy. It was by having a strong navy, he said, that Britain had acquired world power and an empire in Asia. Japan must follow the same course if she was to defend herself successfully.

After Nariakira's death in 1858 these policies for strengthening the domain were soon resumed under the guidance of his brother, Hisamitsu, whose son became daimyo. There was a contrast here with Tokugawa Nariaki, whose efforts to adopt and manufacture western weapons in Mito showed little sign of being continued after his death in 1860. One reason was that the attitudes Nariaki bequeathed to his successors were more ambivalent towards western studies. Typically, when he ordered several of his retainers to take up these studies in 1855, he required of them an oath that the knowledge they acquired would be used for Japan's defence alone; and he never encouraged them in scientific or technological initiatives, preferring to rely on the Bakufu or on other domains for the necessary information. When he took the decision to build iron cannon, his first step was to send representatives to observe what Satsuma and Hizen were doing. Subsequent progress with the project depended heavily on the help of two 'outsiders', experts brought from Satsuma and from northeast Japan, respectively. Similarly, although he set up a shipyard at Ishikawajima in Edo in 1854, the first steam warship it produced (in 1866) owed more to Bakufu engineers than it did to Mito's. Nariaki was not at heart an innovator. Moreover, Japanese feudal lords, even the enthusiastic ones, like Nabeshima and Shimazu, possessed neither the technology nor the financial resources to build what Europeans and Americans of the time would have regarded as up-to-date ships of any kind, least of all steamers. Even the reverberatory furnaces of the various domains were sadly inferior by western standards. It could hardly have been otherwise, given the conditions in which they were produced.

51

On the face of it the Bakufu should have been in a much better position to profit from knowledge of the West, since it had revenue and access to technology on an altogether different scale. Yet in practice it did very little, at least in the early years. Notwithstanding the advice that came from Sakuma Shōzan and others, the task of producing iron cannon for coast defence, insofar as it was not undertaken by Hizen, was left largely to one man, Egawa Tarōzaemon, whom we have already encountered in connection with the disputes of 1839 (Chapter 2). After that incident, Egawa had studied gunnery under Takashima Shūhan. He had also founded a study group to consider defence-related topics at his official residence in Nirayama, where as hereditary steward (*daikan*) of large Tokugawa estates he was a person of consequence. He had the status to correspond regularly with Nabeshima Naomasa about what was being done in Saga and to keep in touch with the latest developments elsewhere. As a result, in 1849 the scholars in his service produced their own translation of the Dutch text on reverberatory furnaces that Hizen was using. In 1850 he sent men to Saga to see the installation there, then tried in the next year or two, though without success, to build a model furnace. Most of the problems he encountered at this stage were financial, like those faced by daimyo, since he was not able to draw on central government funds; but the arrival of Perry at last enabled him to persuade the Bakufu to finance his experiments more fully. The building of a reverberatory furnace was begun at nearby Shimoda, only to be moved almost at once to Nirayama, when its site was found to be within the area to which foreigners were to be allowed to travel once the port was open. At Nirayama success was finally achieved. With the help of technicians sent from Saga, the plant produced its first eighteen-pounder gun barrel in October 1857 (two years after Egawa himself had died).

In this context, the Bakufu, like Tokugawa Nariaki, had shown itself to be dependent on the expertise acquired by Hizen. In others, however, it had the advantage of being able with impunity to have dealings with the foreigners themselves. Several times during the debates about the treaties there had been suggestions about sending Japanese students abroad, or hiring foreigners to come to Japan, as a means of mastering the skills the country needed. In view of the seclusion laws it would have been politically unwise, to say the least, for one of the daimyo to have done this on his own account, but for Edo it was permissible, if controversial. As a means of creating a navy, which domains had found too great a task, it also made sense.

The first step in this direction came after Perry left for the China coast in 1853. In the latter part of that year the governor of Nagasaki was instructed to approach the Dutch representative, Donker Curtius, to enquire whether Holland might be willing to provide warships, guns and military textbooks to Japan, and to send a Dutch officer there to supervise naval training. Curtius replied in July 1854 (after the Perry treaty), explaining that the sale of warships would be difficult while a state of war existed in Europe (the Crimean War), but offering instead to arrange for the steam warship *Soembing* to visit Japan on a temporary basis to begin instruction in navigation and related subjects. In return he wanted a treaty like those completed with America and Russia. The *Soembing* duly arrived a few weeks later, staying until October. When she left, Curtius and the new Nagasaki governor, Mizuno Tadanori, reached a more formal agreement, by which Holland was to present the *Soembing* to the Bakufu, to serve as a training ship, and send a naval training mission to continue the work she had started. In addition, two ten-gun corvettes were to be built in Holland for sale to Japan, one for delivery in 1857, the other in 1858. The *Soembing* was accordingly handed over in the summer of 1855, when she was renamed *Kankō Maru*, and a naval party of twenty-two men under Commander Pels Rijcken began work at Nagasaki in September. The course they taught was to last two years. Among the students sent to it was Katsu Awa, one of its advocates (as he had been also of the founding of the Bansho Shirabesho). He was accompanied by a number of other Tokugawa retainers, plus men nominated by domains: forty-eight from Hizen, sixteen from Satsuma, and twenty-eight from Chikuzen (Fukuoka).

They were given instruction in certain basic skills, such as Dutch language and mathematics, together with navigation, seamanship, naval gunnery and aspects of ship construction. Language proved to be a particular problem. Apart from the minority with previous experience of Dutch — chiefly Katsu and the men from Saga — the students relied heavily on the official Nagasaki interpreters, whose vocabulary, they discovered, did not extend very far into the specialist naval terminology which the Dutch instructors used. Despite this handicap, the results were sufficiently encouraging for the Bakufu to remove some of the students in the spring of 1857, along with the *Kankō Maru*, in order to start its own training school at Tsukiji in Edo. At Nagasaki a further course began in the autumn of that year, when one of the ships built for Japan by the Dutch, later named *Kanrin Maru*, brought a second training mission to replace the first. The only important innovation was that on this occasion the *Kanrin Maru* carried out a voyage round the island of Kyushu in 1858, calling at Hakata (the port of Fukuoka) and Kagoshima. At both places the Dutch staff were closely questioned about possible 'improvements in their factories, especially concerning the manufacture of guns', and were asked for advice about fortifications.[13] Shimazu Nariakira spent most of a day on board in Kagoshima, inviting the Dutch officers ashore to visit his Shūseikan workshops.

Early in 1859 the Bakufu decided to transfer all naval training to Tsukiji and send most of the foreign instructors back to Holland. However, this did not end the Dutch naval presence in Nagasaki. Among those who had come with the second training mission was an engineer, called Hardes, who towards the end of 1857 took over the supervision of the shipbuilding and repair shops established by the Bakufu at the port, using the equipment bought from Holland by Hizen. During the next three years, according to the mission's medical officer, Pompe van Meerdervoort, Hardes brought into operation 'a machine shop where the Nasmith steam hammer operated, where a dozen large forges were in action with blacksmiths trained by him, where there was opportunity to do founding'. In addition, there were 'steam-powered lathes and drills where heavy pieces for steam engines and even new boilers were made', making it possible for 'all repairs needed by steamships' to be carried out.[14]

Pompe van Meerdervoort was himself the key figure in another development, providing western-style medical education and a hospital in Nagasaki. He, too, had come with the 1857 mission, but the course he devised was not part of its programme, nor attended only by its students. It was designed to give a medical education as that was understood in the West, including lectures on theory and elementary science, practical demonstrations, and diagnosis of patients. This was something new in Japan. It also encountered the same kind of interpreting problems as had occurred in naval training, exacerbated by the need for discussion between teacher and student. Even those who had previously studied Dutch, Pompe recorded, 'could not talk to me nor understand me'.[15] An additional obstacle was that many of those who came to study were older men, already practising as doctors, who sought profitable embellishments to their existing knowledge, not training *ab initio*. Impatient with theory, they stayed away from lectures on it, only to discover, when they came back to pick up what they wanted in some chosen field, that without the theory they could not understand what they were being told. Most of them soon stopped attending altogether, while not even the others, who lasted to the end, necessarily benefited as much as might have been hoped. Of the sixty-one who completed the course, over a third received diplomas which described them as having 'attended the classes without much result'.

After a time, Pompe managed to secure approval for a plan to open a hospital in Nagasaki at Bakufu expense. The building, completed in October 1861, provided 120 beds in eight wards, to which were added four single-bed rooms for surgical or isolation cases. Most of the patients came from the families of officials at first, because they took admittance to be their right, but Pompe eventually insisted — not without opposition — that the hospital should be open to the poor as well.

The Nagasaki medical school's most successful student, Matsumoto Ryōjun, became personal physician to the Shogun and head of the Bakufu medical school in Edo, then after 1868 the first Surgeon General of Japan's modern army. His career is a reminder that it was above all in the search for military expertise and personal advancement that Japan's feudal class had turned to the West for guidance. What had been demonstrated at Nagasaki was that in some matters of this kind government-to-government relations could achieve more than the efforts of individual scholars. It seemed to follow, too, that students taught by western teachers, whether in Japan or overseas, might well learn more, and faster, than those who were not. The lesson was not lost on those who were to be responsible for Japanese policy in the next ten years.

4

The Mission to America, 1860

Article XIV of the treaty which Townsend Harris signed in 1858 stipulated that ratifications were to be exchanged in Washington, a clause inserted on the initiative of those Japanese officials who not only recognized that Japan must review her relations with the outside world, but also hoped to play a leading part in carrying out the policy. One of them expressed an ambition to be ambassador to the United States. Another had his eyes on a similar post in London.

During the next twelve months the impetus behind this initiative weakened. The men who had promoted it found their influence on the wane, mostly because they shared Hotta Masayoshi's political eclipse. Their successors faced new problems, arising from the regular presence of foreigners in Japan. Samurai resentment of the treaties and the manner in which they had been agreed was manifested on several occasions after the summer of 1859 in attacks on foreigners in the newly-opened treaty ports and on Japanese who cooperated with them. A number of sailors were killed in Yokohama, as was Hendrik Heusken, Townsend Harris's secretary. A former Japanese castaway, employed as interpreter at the British legation, was murdered outside the legation's gates. In the atmosphere produced by these events, planning and taking part in what might seem to be a 'tribute mission' to America became a hazardous operation, to be approached with caution.

A further consideration was that coming to terms with the practical implications of the treaties was proving by no means easy. There were difficulties over currency, for example. The treaties provided that Japanese and foreign coins of similar character be exchanged weight-for-weight. Foreign merchants soon discovered, however, that because the gold-silver ratio customary in Japan differed from that in the rest of the world, they could make large profits by exchanging their silver dollars for Japanese gold coins, then exporting these to China. Edo's attempts to set things right by changing the face-value of the coins and restricting their availability threw the trade into disorder. Similarly, customs arrangements were a source of controversy. Since Japan had no bonded warehouses, there were disputes about the payment of duty on goods which were landed, but found no market. Nor was the valuation of imports straightforward, given the willingness of foreigners to put a much lower price on a customs return than they did when offering goods for sale. Finding acceptable solutions to problems of this kind soon came to loom larger in the minds of Japanese officials than did the wider question of studying the barbarian as a step towards reform.

As a consequence, when the mission to exchange ratifications in America at last took place in 1860, it was approached in a much more restrictive manner than had seemed likely a year or two before. The men chosen to go were cautious bureaucrats, not obviously smitten by 'the Dutch disease'; they were furnished with a staff of inspectors (*metsuke*), whose duty it was to ensure that the bounds of political wisdom were not exceeded; and insofar as the party included some members who were in a position to profit more generously from their travels — notably the interpreters and doctors — these were hampered by instructions which made the gathering of information, other than on matters related to trade and diplomacy, a secondary activity.

DIPLOMATIC TRAVELS

Townsend Harris had his own motives for supporting the idea of a mission to America. If Japanese of standing and ability were to go there, he considered, able to see and hear 'what might prove beneficial to the welfare of Japan', while observing 'the prosperity of cities, the wealth of citizens, the conditions of the army and navy, and the strength and greatness of the United States',[1] it would make his task of promoting American interests that much simpler. He would have preferred the mission to have been undertaken by one of the officials with whom he had established a relationship of trust when negotiating the treaty, but the political crisis of 1858 had ruled nearly all of them out of con-sideration. This left only lesser men, as Harris saw it. Nevertheless, by describing them in his letters home as 'Princes' and 'Governors', he encouraged Washington — perhaps deliberately — to treat them with more distinction than their status merited.

The senior envoy, whose appointment was announced on 8 October 1859, was Shimmi Masaoki, a man with some reputation as a Chinese scholar, but almost no diplomatic experience. His deputy was Muragaki Norimasa, who was better prepared, having served as governor at two treaty ports (Hakodate and Yokohama); but although this had given him some knowledge of foreign ways, it had done little to change an inherently cautious and conservative outlook. Only the third-ranking member of the group, Oguri Tadamasa, had the temperament to profit from foreign travel, but as he was one of the *metsuke* his chief responsibility was to see that everything was done in proper form, which did not encourage risk or innovation. These three came from the stratum of Edo officialdom that was to provide all the Tokugawa envoys to the West: men holding personal rank just below that of feudal lord (daimyo) and filling senior administrative posts in the government machine. Like most of their diplomatic successors, Shimmi and Muragaki were Gaikoku Bugyō, equivalent in modern terms to vice-minister of foreign affairs, though for the visit to America they were allowed to have an entourage appropriate to something higher.

The outcome was a mission totalling seventy-seven persons. They included eleven lesser officials, drawn from the departments of foreign affairs, finance and inspectorate; two interpreters, Namura Motonori and Tateishi Tokujirō, plus an apprentice interpreter, Tateishi Onojirō, who was Tokujirō's nephew; and three doctors, two from Edo, another from Hizen. Others went as attendants to the officials, including samurai from several non-Tokugawa domains — Choshu, Hizen, Kaga, Higo (Kumamoto), Tosa, Sendai and Morioka — sent by their lords, or travelling with their lords' permission, for the purpose of learning about conditions overseas. A remarkably high proportion of those who went kept diaries, which have since been published (two in English translation, the rest in Japanese); but it has to be said that most of these documents are more interesting for what they reveal of Japanese responses to an often bewildering world than as a compendium of knowledge about it.

Officially, as was demonstrated in the memoranda exchanged by the envoys and their superiors in the closing weeks of 1859,[2] study of the West had no part in the proceedings at all. The custom was for those undertaking negotiations on the Shogun's behalf to propose their own instructions. That is to say, before departure from the capital they consulted colleagues to determine appropriate aims and methods, then drafted a submission setting out their conclusions for the members of the council to approve. Once approved, the contents became binding on them. On this occasion the process was almost wholly concerned with matters of protocol. The papers examined the language in which the Shogun's letter to the President was to be written (Chinese, with a Dutch translation); the credentials the envoys were to carry (identical with those used for the treaty negotiations); the suite they were to take to their audience at the White House (just one or two persons, as had been the case when western representatives saw the Shogun); the clothes they were to wear for this ceremony (similar to those worn when receiving Korean envoys earlier in the century); and so on. The only points of substance raised were the answers they should give if asked whether Japan intended to send missions to other treaty powers, or instal resident ministers and consuls in foreign countries. To the first question, it was recommended, they should reply that no decision had been taken. To the second it would be enough to point out that Japan had as yet no trade overseas, carried on by Japanese subjects in Japanese ships. Until she had, there would be no need for legations and consulates.

In more general terms, the envoys were told to limit their activities to the bare essentials and return home as quickly as possible. This they did. In Honolulu they refused to enter into discussion of a possible treaty with Hawaii. When leaving Washington they showed a marked reluctance to go to Philadelphia and New York, though they complied with the arrangements already made for them. They refused outright to visit Boston and Niagara Falls. Whenever possible they avoided evening engagements. Muragaki in his diary gave a not very complimentary account of this decision: 'it was not our custom to go out at night, except where we had to oblige, or unless we saw some benefit of studying the superior characteristics of the nation in attending'.[3] It seems that he offered this explanation to his hosts.

Junior members of the mission showed much less reserve. Some went off to see a balloon ascent in Philadelphia, for example, while their superiors were employed more soberly at the National Mint. The youngest of them, the apprentice interpreter, Tateishi Onojirō, acquired a reputation as the darling of the ladies at official receptions and became famous in American newspapers under the name of 'Tommy'. His willingness to ride on railway engines, or to take over one of the hoses during firefighting demonstrations, was in marked contrast to the behaviour of Tamamushi Yasushige, a Confucian scholar. The latter, a samurai from Sendai, serving in Shimmi's personal entourage, wrote that any attempt he made to learn about 'the conditions and customs of the Americans' was apt to be frustrated by the rules imposed by the *metsuke*. These included a 6 p.m. curfew for embassy staff. In a final section of his diary, labelled 'secret' — the rest seems to have been written for private circulation, since it exists in over thirty copies — he observed that his efforts to visit such places as schools and orphanages had been hampered by a rule which required everyone who went off separately to be accompanied by one of the Bakufu officials. Officials, it appears, were not always available for this duty. His companions, he said, were not much troubled by the restriction: their principal interest was in shopping.[4]

Partly as a result of these constraints, much of the information provided in the mission's records, both public and personal, consists of descriptions of externals. At sea, meticulous notes were made about ships and their crews, their equipment, daily positions, the weather. On land we are given details about the size and facilities of hotels and public buildings, especially baths, toilets, gas fittings and the like. There is surprisingly little about machines and industrial plant, despite the opportunities made

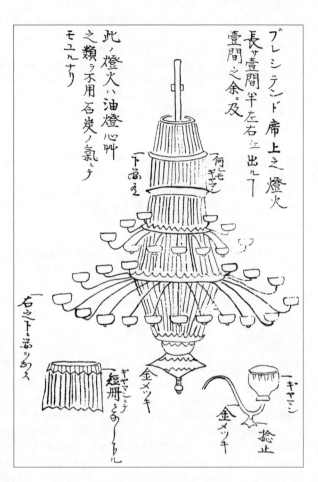

ブレシデンド席上之燈火
長サ壹間半左右ニ出ル了
壹間之余ニ及

此ノ燈火ハ油燈心卅
之類ヲ不用石炭ノ氣ミテ
モユルナリ

下ニモギヤ...

下ニ高ス

右之下ニ高シ...ス

金メッキ

ギヤマニテ
短冊とメ...

金メッキ

一ギヤミン

金メッキ

捻止

3. Sketch of a gas chandelier in the White House, made by a member of the 1860 mission (see fig. 4). The Japanese note at top right gives dimensions, the one on the left describes the chandelier as burning 'the vapour of coal'. Other notes identify the materials from which the chandelier is made.

available to inspect them; and while the sketches which survive include the obvious tourist mementos of places and ships and trains, as well as everyday items like beds, washstands, fireplaces, cutlery and 'foreign victuals', there is little sign of anything more consequential. Sometimes what was recorded was inaccurate as well. Yanagawa Masakiyo included in his diary a tolerably recognizable sketch of the balloon he saw in Philadelphia, but then described it, no doubt from hearsay, which he presumably misunderstood, as being equipped with a steam engine — not evident in his illustration — which would enable it to travel to New York in thirty minutes and to Japan in six days.

After a farewell banquet, much like those which had been enjoyed by missions to China in ancient times, complete with a competition in composing suitable farewell poems in Chinese and Japanese, Shimmi and his colleagues left Yokohama on 13 February 1860 aboard the steam frigate USS *Powhatan*, which had been put at their disposal for the Pacific crossing. To accommodate so large a party, together with their separate cookhouse and fifty tons of baggage, changes had to be made in the layout of the ship, including the removal of some guns. The three envoys were put in the captain's cabin, lesser men in staterooms erected on the upper deck. It was not a comfortable voyage, not least because the weather was bad. The Japanese, we are told in the *New York Times* (28 April 1860), occupied themselves making tea, smoking their tiny pipes, and 'reading books in their own language, whose pictures . . . were as grossly vulgar as the engravings were wretched'. The source of this comment, one suspects, was the ship's chaplain, Henry Wood, whose offer of an alternative occupation in the form of English lessons was not much taken up.

The party arrived at San Francisco on 29 March after a brief call at Honolulu for supplies. They stayed only a few days, but it was enough for Yanagawa to record his first impressions of the differences between America and Japan. The hotel in San Francisco was so large, he noted, that one could not get service by clapping the hands, as one did at home. One had to use a call-bell, fitted in one's room. The food, though ample, was greasy — this was a common Japanese complaint — and not very flavoursome. When there was a fire in the neighbourhood, only the firemen seemed concerned: those living nearby did not find it necessary to remove their possessions, as they would have done in Japan. This was because American houses were of stone or brick, which did not burn easily. A theatre which some of the travellers attended was notable for the fact that women played women's parts. Problems of language prevented any understanding of the plot. By contrast, those who went to a Chinese theatre 'enjoyed the play because it was like a Japanese play'.[5]

From San Francisco the envoys continued south to Panama, where they crossed the isthmus by train. It 'sped like an arrow', Yanagawa wrote, making a noise like 'a thousand peals of thunder over one's head' and rendering conversation impossible. Aspinwall (Colon) was linked to Panama by telegraph, he observed, though 'how it works I have not the faintest idea'. There followed a passage up the Atlantic coast in another American warship, USS *Roanoke*, which brought them at last to Hampton Roads (Muragaki was disparaging about its fortress in comparison with the new installation at his own former post, Hakodate). A smaller vessel took them on the final stage to the Washington Navy Yard.

Here on 14 May they had their first experience of large American crowds. Nearly 5,000 people are said to have witnessed their arrival, even Congress having adjourned to allow its members to attend. Another 20,000 lined the streets on the way to Willards Hotel, some of whom broke through the cordon of police on one occasion, so that the envoys'

4. The Japanese envoys are received by President Buchanan at the White House, 17 May 1860. (Note the chandeliers: fig. 3.)

carriage was mobbed by small boys, 'ragged, dirty, black and white, who insisted on shaking hands with them' (*New York Times*, 17 May 1860). There were similar demonstrations on a visit to the White House three days later, when a senator and three ladies were seen standing on a single chair to get a view of their arrival. Much the same enthusiasm was shown in Baltimore on 8 June. In Philadelphia on 9 June there was a military procession for the sixteen carriages taking them from the station. The streets were decorated with both countries' flags. New York did even better on 17 June: sixty-five carriages, several military bands, over 6,000 men from various volunteer regiments to provide an escort up Broadway. This was followed by a dinner for 10,000 ticket-holders at the Metropolitan Hotel. At all these cities there were civic receptions, fire displays, musical serenades outside the embassy's lodgings. The contrast with the restraint and measured dignity, or even ill-concealed hostility, which foreign envoys encountered in Japan, could hardly have been more striking.

This is not to say that the tumultuous welcome on America's east coast reflected an undiluted enthusiasm for Japan. Some of it stemmed from self-congratulation, because the mission had come to the United States, not Europe. Some was simply an excuse to escape from work for a while. Part was simple self-seeking, like the invitations from theatre managers, who hoped the presence of the Japanese would attract other customers to their shows. A good deal was dishonest. As the *Philadelphia Enquirer* noted on 15 June, the Japanese were 'shrewd enough to see that the public gratulations and ovations of which they are the heroes are insti-gated by . . . the singularities of their dress and customs'. Open flattery, it said, often concealed secret 'ridicule and burlesque'. On a different note, the *New York Ledger* (9 June) expressed doubts about whether there could be profits enough from the relationship to justify the costs of all this public entertainment. A few extra mines and mills at home, providing a market for farmers and employment for workers, would, it maintained, be 'of more national value than the trade with Japan will be for the next half-century'. These doubts were echoed by Tamamushi from a very nearly opposite point of view. If Japanese fell into the trap of pursuing trade for profit, he warned, foreigners would come to despise them, as they did the Chinese. What is more, raising Japanese production to the necessary levels would require unacceptable reforms to the national currency, as well as the introduction of steam machinery, by which one man 'can do the work of a hundred'.[6] He did not regard this as socially desirable.

Members of the mission found many aspects of American life bewil-dering. In their own country, as in China, foreigners were kept apart from the local population, living in 'foreign settlements' within the treaty ports. There was not even the regular exchange of diplomatic enter-taining between consuls and Japanese officials that would have been normal in the West. Accordingly, those who were sent to America in 1860 had had little or no opportunity to experience western food and drink, or other elements of western living. They were not very happy with knives and forks. One of them was observed at a banquet drinking the water from his finger-bowl. Beds they found comfortable, though in hotel rooms they preferred to dispense with chairs and sit on cushions on the floor. Food was a constant problem. They took with them large quantities of their own, but this either went bad, and had to be thrown away, or could not be prepared for lack of the proper facilities. They were much offended in Philadelphia to be offered rice cooked in butter, equally so when it was replaced by rice with sugar. They acquired a taste for ice cream and champagne, but not claret, which they likened to vinegar. In Muragaki's view, 'it is well beyond the power of my pen to describe what we, the Japanese, suffer on our journey to a foreign country'.[7]

Language was the greatest obstacle of all. Official communications were in Dutch, through their own interpreters and a Dutch-speaking Ameri-can, A. C. Portman, brought back from Edo for the purpose; but an arrangement in which questions put in Japanese-Dutch-English were answered in English-Dutch-Japanese was not only very clumsy, it was simply not available at all unless both sets of interpreters were present.

Muragaki noted that at one point during a reception by the Secretary of State 'I did not at all understand what was being said', because of this. A different kind of problem arose from certain national preconceptions. When taken to a session of Congress, he claimed to have refrained from asking questions, despite not understanding a word of the debate, on the grounds that 'we considered it as presumptuous to inquire into the state affairs of another nation'. Not all his countrymen would have agreed, however, as we shall see in later chapters. Nor was Muragaki himself wholly unwilling to criticize what he saw. The scene from the gallery of members shouting and 'gesticulating wildly' was, he thought, like nothing so much as 'our fishmarket at Nihombashi'. Earlier in his diary he had described the toasts and speeches at the mayor's dinner in San Francisco as being 'as noisy as the drinking bouts of workmen in Edo'.[8]

It is uncertain how far those of lower rank were able to communicate directly with Americans. The official interpreters had brought with them a Dutch-English dictionary from the library of the Bansho Shirabesho in the hope of doing so. One of them, Namura, was able to read the proofs of an article in English during a visit to the offices of the *Pacific Commercial Advertiser* in Hawaii. He was described in its pages (8 March) as being able to read and write English 'very readily'. Nothing was said about his conversation skills. At least one of the officials from the foreign affairs department could read and speak Dutch. Surprisingly, the three doctors had all been trained in Chinese medicine, not Dutch, and had made little headway in learning English on the voyage out. Tamamushi, the Confucian scholar, chose at Honolulu and San Francisco to exchange ideas in writing with local Chinese residents (as Japanese visitors to China had done for centuries past). All this suggests that the mission was not well equipped for collecting information, other than from official sources. All the same, one has to recognize that the doctors did succeed in meeting American scientists in Washington and witnessing surgery at a Philadelphia hospital; that Tamamushi did in the end visit an orphan school; and that some of the Japanese were able to inspect ships at the Philadelphia navy yard, apparently without the services of a specialist interpreter. For some things a limited range of language skills was enough.

This was true in particular where there were things to be seen, not just things to be heard. At the navy yard in Washington, having been escorted through the machine shops and smelting plant to watch weapons being made, Muragaki concluded that the introduction of such machinery into Japan 'would contribute greatly to the enhancement of our national interests'. At the observatory, despite difficulty in understanding the answers to his questions — 'the best we could do through our interpreters' — he commented that it would be 'most profitable for our nation' to send Japanese to study navigation and surveying in America. At the

Patent Office he would have liked to have made a closer examination of the models of machinery, but was prevented by the size of the crowd. Gas-lighting and the gasworks attracted his attention in Philadelphia. By contrast, neither there nor in New York did he choose to remark on the theatres, the Academy of Music, a sugar refinery, a spinning mill and a rubber factory, all of which were on the itinerary.[9]

Only in one or two instances did the visitors seek to modify the programme worked out for them by a protocol committee of the State Department. These were mostly of minor consequence — for example, the slightly puzzling desire to attend a private wedding in New York — but there was one which was clearly of official substance. During a visit to the National Mint in Philadelphia, Shimmi expressed a desire to have Japanese and American coins, whose exchange rate was to be determined by weight, according to the treaties, assayed accurately in his presence. The request occasioned some delay, because he wanted a comparison of specific whole coins, not of small samples, which was the Mint's usual manner of proceeding; and when he returned for the purpose next day, according to the *Philadelphia Inquirer* (15 June), after the relative fineness of a gold dollar and a gold cobang (*koban*) had been determined, the envoys then asked further questions about the kind and quantity of the alloys used. This required a further test. They waited patiently for it to be completed, partaking meanwhile of a midday meal sent from their hotel, and at the end were given a certificate showing the result. Throughout, both Shimmi and Muragaki paid close attention to what was being done; the *metsuke*, Oguri, made measurements and calculations of his own; and the attendant artist made 'faithful sketches of the bottles, furnaces, and other apparatus'. This was not sightseeing, but officials going about their business.

Of a quite different order were the occasions on which an assessment could be made of American society. They were, of course, relatively artificial situations: on board ship; at diplomatic or civic receptions, dinners and balls; on escorted tours to public and private institutions thought worthy of note; in hotel lobbies, or sometimes in the street. The Japanese were dazzled by the hospitality they received and by the warmth of the American greeting. On the other hand, observing the behaviour of American sailors towards their officers, the failure of the President to appear in uniform in public, his willingness to allow ladies to be present when he received the envoys formally, and the treatment of women and children everywhere, they could not fail to be struck by the contrast with how they behaved at home. Muragaki found it distasteful: 'there is no respect for order and ceremony [*rei*] or obligation [*gi*]'. Only Tamamushi, less moved by the absence of elaborate etiquette, despite his Confucian education, was prepared to concede that in the navy, at least, informality did not appear to produce indiscipline. He thought Japan might have something to learn from this, though 'I would not go so far as to esteem barbarian ways'.[10]

It seems that the senior Japanese, if not the rest, left for home with their prejudices intact. They came to no apparent understanding of America's political and judicial systems, no obvious awareness of American social problems, no usable knowledge of trade and industry as they operated in the West. Though they were in the country when Lincoln was nominated as a presidential candidate, their diaries contain no reference to the dispute between North and South. Such attempts as they made to describe how a president was elected are almost unintelligible. Comments about social issues — Yanagawa, for instance, wrote on one occasion that 'blacks are inferior as human beings and extremely stupid' — have the air of received wisdom, derived from statements by their hosts. True, such things may reflect nothing more than a reluctance to tread on delicate ground, on a par with the warning given to Tamamushi by his superiors not to include references to monarchy when writing Confucian tags as souvenirs, because Americans were republicans; but the more likely explanation is an inability to communicate freely with the people they met. What we have in the mission's records, in fact, is what could most readily be learnt: notes about the size and shape of buildings, an account of life in hotels, some practical information about material things like ships, fire engines, street lights, military technology. There is little about the abstract and the theoretical.

The voyage home, this time via the Atlantic and the Indian Oceans, added little of importance to the travellers' knowledge, as far as we can tell. Taking with them a collection of photographs and explanatory literature from the places they had visited, plus a variety of items received as gifts — it included howitzers and other modern weapons, a printing press, various seeds, a number of books (some useful, some improbable), a stereoscopic viewer, a sewing machine, several packs of playing cards, and a set of gold teeth — the party left New York aboard USS *Niagara* on 29 June. Making the minimum number of calls for fuel and supplies en route (a fact which occasioned complaints about boredom and shortage of water), they reached Batavia on 1 October. Muragaki had his first bath for over three months. It was disappointingly lukewarm. They paid a courtesy visit to the Dutch governor, inspected the navy yard (which attracted little interest, in view of what they had seen in America), and assembled some gazetteer-type information about the East Indies. After ten days they sailed again for Hong Kong, where Muragaki commented on the 'fearful lesson' for Japan in China's latest defeats by France and Britain in the north. Soon after, when passing the coast of Taiwan, he noted that if only Japan could annex and develop it, attracting to it Chinese 'who desire to escape the warfare on their mainland', the island could 'contribute greatly to our national strength'.[11]

Yokohama was reached on 9 November, filling the Japanese passengers 'with a joyous excitement'. It cannot have lasted long. Their reception, as described in the San Francisco *Daily Evening Bulletin* of 9 January 1861, quoting reports from Japan, was distinctly low-key. 'No notice whatever was taken of their arrival at Kanagawa by the Japanese', readers were told, the envoys being 'quietly landed in common Custom House boat in a remote part of the town'. Nor did the envoys receive official honours or promotion. To Edo, this was no more than proper caution, given the rising tide of anti-foreign feeling in Japan. Even Muragaki may have thought it appropriate. Summarizing his narrative of the mission, he described it as one which showed 'how I came to recognize the admirable traits of our country, after having travelled widely abroad'.[12]

THE VOYAGE OF THE *KANRIN MARU*

Linked with the diplomatic mission was another visit to America in 1860, which in the long run did rather more for Japanese knowledge of the West. This was the voyage made to San Francisco by the *Kanrin Maru*, a ship which had been built for the Tokugawa by the Dutch (see Chapter 3). At several points during discussion of the arrangements for exchange of ratifications it had been suggested by Japanese officials that it would enhance the country's prestige if the envoys travelled to America in a Japanese warship; and although the plan was dropped in the end — apparently for fear of national disgace should things go wrong — it was eventually agreed that when the official party departed aboard the USS *Powhatan*, the *Kanrin Maru* would be sent as well. She was to carry someone senior enough to replace one of the two chief envoys in the event of accident or illness. Kimura Yoshitake, a man of about the same rank as Shimmi and Muragaki, who was responsible for Edo's naval administration, and was usually known to Americans as 'the admiral', was chosen for this duty. The command of the ship itself was entrusted to Katsu Awa, said to be the most able of the graduates from the Nagasaki training school.

The *Kanrin Maru* carried a complement of ninety-six men. Most were naval trainees — navigators, engineers, seamen — but there were also two doctors, an interpreter (Nakahama Manjirō, the former castaway, who had at one time advised Shimazu Nariakira of Satsuma), and several samurai volunteers, serving as attendants to Kimura in much the same way as others did to the envoys who went to Washington. One of the volunteers was Fukuzawa Yukichi, a student of Dutch from Ogata Kōan's school in Osaka, who was at that time learning English at the Bansho Shirabesho. In addition to these, there was an eleven-man US naval party, taking passage home. It was led by a navigation specialist,

Lieutenant. John M. Brooke, commander of a schooner which had been destroyed by storm at Yokohama, while engaged in a survey of steamer routes from San Francisco to Hong Kong. He had offered to take some of his men back aboard the *Kanrin Maru*, while providing advice on navigation and seamanship to the Japanese crew. It was a proposal accepted with some alacrity by the Bakufu.

In the event, Brooke and his sailors did more than advise. The *Kanrin Maru* sailed from Uraga on 10 February 1860, three days before the *Powhatan*, and took the great circle route direct to San Francisco. Although recently built, steam-powered and propeller-driven, she could only carry a few days' supply of coal, which meant that she had to do most of the passage under sail. She also met with persistent bad weather. Such conditions soon revealed inadequacies among the Japanese ship's company. Kimura was seasick, Katsu ill. Both kept mostly to their cabins. The ship could never carry her full weight of sail, because — in Brooke's words — 'the Japanese are not competent to manage it '. The officers he thought 'very ignorant indeed'. The helm and watchkeeping were left almost entirely to the Americans, partly because they were least likely to be seasick, partly because among the Japanese there seemed not to be 'any such thing as order or discipline'. The situation was complicated by the fact that few of the seamen understood Dutch, the language in which commands were supposed to be given. Only gradually was Brooke able to overcome these problems. Crew members were taught to reef sail, an operation apparently omitted from their earlier training. Proper watches were organized, so that duties were no longer left to be performed 'incidentally by whoever felt a disposition to do something'. Indeed, by the time they reached San Francisco on 17 March, Brooke felt able to report to his superiors in Washington that the Japanese at last seemed 'fully competent to manage their vessel'.[13] The voyage had in effect been a shakedown cruise.

Fukuzawa Yukichi stated in his autobiography that the Pacific crossing was completed 'without help from foreign experts', a feat which 'Peter the Great of Russia, who went to Holland to study navigation, with all his attainments could not have equalled'.[14] In the light of Brooke's account one can only assume that Fukuzawa's choice of words was dictated as much by the nationalist euphoria of the 1890s, when he was writing, as by the realities of 1860. Even so, the voyage was a notable achievement. Brooke himself blamed the difficulties he encountered mostly on the fact that the Japanese 'had not been properly instructed by the Dutch', though this, too, may well have been a nationalist reaction. Kimura and Katsu he judged to be men of intelligence. For Nakahama Manjirō he had a very high regard indeed, both as seaman and interpreter. The chief engineer, Hida Hamagorō, he thought 'pretty good'. One of the other officers, Ono Tomogorō, was 'an excellent navigator'.

The *Kanrin Maru* remained in San Francisco until 9 May before setting out on the return passage to Uraga, this time via Honolulu and genuinely without any foreign help. Much of the interval was spent in repairing storm damage to the ship at the Mare Island naval dockyard. Her copper had to be checked and the packing round the propeller renewed. This required that she be drydocked, an operation carried out, according to the *Daily Alta California* (27 March), 'much to the gratification of the Japanese, who hardly imagined how easily a ship could be taken out of the water'. Katsu recorded the event in detail. Two new masts were fitted and a new set of sails provided to replace the existing ones, all at the expense of the US government. While this was going on, the Japanese officers were able to make a careful examination of the dockyard facilities, including machine shops, ammunition store and naval hospital. The care with which they did so can be gathered from a description in the *Daily Evening Bulletin* (19 March) of a visit they paid to one of the American ships in harbour: 'they fell to sketching her whole frame, drafting the form of the timbers, taking measurements of every part, so that . . . they had the materials for reconstructing at home her counterpart'.

This underlines one of the differences between the naval party and those who went with the diplomats to Washington. The former had not only more leisure to examine what they saw, but also a better technical training by which to understand it. Even Fukuzawa, though not a naval man, had dabbled enough in science at Ogata Kōan's school to be able to do without the explanations he was offered about ironworks and telegraphs and sugar refining: 'there was really nothing new, at least to me', he wrote.[15] What did impress him was the very widespread use of steam-powered machinery, not only in seagoing ships and the navy yard, but also in harbour ferries and tugs, metalworking of every kind, even the milling of grain. Less favourably, he noted the widespread waste, evident in the amount of discarded iron left lying around, plus the high prices of food, which were seven or eight times those in Japan. The latter he attributed to the presence of goldmines in the region.

Katsu, too, found nothing remarkable about ironworks, which were similar to those he had known at home. The items which he did think worthy of special care in description, apart from the drydocking of the *Kanrin Maru*, were the gas-lighting in the streets and private houses, the machinery at the local mint, and the printing plant at a newspaper he visited. His account of all these things was much more exact than anything produced by those who went to the east coast. Like them, however, and also Fukuzawa, he wrote a great deal about everyday sights and sounds: the appearance of buildings, the noise in the streets, American dress and food, fire stations and firefighting, local transport (he distinguished between carriages, which were something like Japanese ox-carts 'with a hut on top', and freight carriers, which had no hut on top). As a naval officer, he added to his compilation an assessment of American naval power, listing bases, ships, armament and personnel.

Because they stayed longer in one place and were accepted as part of a naval community, the Japanese who went to San Francisco formed closer relations with their hosts and enjoyed better opportunities to learn about American society than did the diplomats. Like their compatriots visiting the capital, however, they found American informality on official occasions very strange, as was the deference paid to women. Ballroom dancing seems to have caused them secret mirth. Katsu, at least, admired the decorum that was shown at receptions, which he contrasted with the heavy drinking and disorderliness witnessed at parties in Japan; but when he was taken to the theatre to see a minstrel show, which included girl dancers, he observed that although as a spectacle it was not obviously lewd — he would not have understood what was being said, of course — it was odd to be offered nothing to eat and drink. He rarely attempted anything more serious than this by way of social comment. He noted that the poorest local inhabitants worked in the mines, or as slaves and house servants to the more affluent; that the wealthy habitually rode in carriages; and that Chinese could easily be identified, because most of them retained their national dress and hairstyle. He could detect no sign of a parallel with the distinctions made in Edo Japan between samurai, farmers, artisans and merchants. American military men, for example, seemed to him more like 'country samurai' (*gōshi*), because they were allowed to mix freely with the rest of the population and engage in trade. Since they did not habitually wear swords, it was not easy to tell them apart from merchants.

In other words, while Katsu was better able than the diplomats to deal with western technology, he was still, like most of his fellows, too bound by Japanese social concepts to arrive at any real understanding of how western society worked. His superior, Kimura, seems to have come away with even less. His diary comments favourably and at length on the warm hospitality offered by the Americans, and on what he conceived to be their desire to establish friendly relations with Japan; it meticulously records all the gun salutes given and received, as well as a certain amount of navigational data when at sea; it notes with pride Japan's achievement in sending a ship across the Pacific; but it says not a word about anything technical and makes no attempt to draw any conclusions about what the party had seen of American life. The more senior the Japanese, it appears, the less useful were his observations. The pattern was to be repeated when a mission was sent to Europe in 1862.

5

The Mission to Europe, 1862

The mission Japan sent to Europe in 1862 differed in two respects from that which had gone to America two years earlier. In the first place, it had a diplomatic purpose which was more than a formality. Once the ports had been opened in 1859, Japanese resentment of the treaties showed itself in intermittent violence, partly directed against Bakufu policy-makers at the highest level (the Regent, Ii Naosuke, was assassinated in March 1860; another senior member of the Tokugawa council, Andō Nobumasa, was wounded in February 1862), partly against foreigners in the treaty ports. Townsend Harris's secretary, Hendrik Heusken, was killed in January 1861. In July, a band of samurai made a night attack on the British legation at Tozenji, killing some of the Japanese guards and wounding one of the British staff, Laurence Oliphant.

A leading motive for these actions on the part of anti-foreign extremists was the desire to undermine the treaties by embroiling the Edo authorities in disputes with the powers. The Bakufu's response, encouraged by advice from Townsend Harris, was to seek to pacify opinion by changes in the treaties. The agreements made in 1858 had provided that two ports, Hyogo (modern Kobe) and Niigata, together with the cities of Edo and Osaka, would not be opened to foreign trade until dates ranging from 1 January 1860 to 1 January 1863. The proposal now put forward was that the opening be postponed by several years. Since it was assumed that the United States, for whom Harris spoke, was likely to agree, but that the representatives in Japan of the European treaty powers would be much more difficult to persuade, a plan was worked out to send envoys to Europe to put Japan's case to their various governments.

The mission was also entrusted with a second task, which is more directly relevant to the subject of this book. There were still men in the middle ranks of Bakufu officialdom at this time who saw Japan's best chance of dealing successfully with the outside world as being an attempt to acquire wealth through trade, and military technology through an expanded knowledge of the West. They argued that sending missions overseas should be made the occasion for finding out how best this might be done; and in this objective they received a measure of support from foreign representatives in Japan, who believed that the more the Japanese became aware of the West's superiority, the less they would be inclined to resist the West's demands. A reluctant Edo gave way to these pressures. It issued appropriate instructions to the members of the mission; appointed to its staff a handful of scholars thought to be capable of carrying out the necessary studies; and then, when a substantial report on the nature of European institutions and society was prepared on the mission's return, buried it in the archives.

THE MISSION'S INSTRUCTIONS

Both the French and British ministers in Japan had been irritated by the Japanese decision to send the country's first overseas mission to the United States. They were also scornful of its achievements. Soon after it returned, Rutherford Alcock expressed the view that another mission, sent to European capitals, could 'open the eyes of the Japanese to the power and wealth of Great Britain', reveal to them 'the splendour of a Court in Europe', and remove some of the 'erroneous impressions' brought back from America. It might, he suggested, leave Japan in February or March 1862, so as to arrive in Europe in April or early May, 'when there might be some hope of fine weather'. The French minister, de Bellecourt, wrote to Paris in much the same terms. In talks on the subject with members of the Tokugawa council, Alcock emphasized that the men who were sent 'should see and learn as much . . . as possible'. They ought not to be put under the same restrictions as had apparently been imposed on their predecessors going to Washington, when the requirement that they behave as high-ranking feudal lords had meant that they 'went nowhere and saw scarcely anything'. 'It would be very provoking', he said, '. . . if a Japanese Embassy visited all the principal countries in Europe, and yet came away as ignorant as they went'.[1]

These ideas were received in Edo with courtesy, rather than enthusiasm, but Alcock won his point in the end. He and de Bellecourt agreed that Britain and France should provide suitable naval transport to and from Marseille, while giving notice that the party would need to be a good deal smaller than that of 1860, if only on grounds of cost. The total was eventually held down to thirty-six. Expenses in Europe, which were to be borne by the Bakufu — a decision later reversed by London and Paris for reasons of prestige — were to be met through credits arranged with the Rothschild house.

Alcock also tried to influence who went. He recommended that Sakai Takayuki, a junior councillor, should lead the mission, because he had got on well with him in recent talks, but the Bakufu demurred, apparently in the belief that this would give the affair too high a profile. The choice eventually fell on Takenouchi Yasunori, who as Gaikoku Bugyō (Foreign Affairs Commissioner) had a measure of diplomatic experience. A man of fifty-five, described by one of his colleagues as placid in appearance and of unshakeable gravity, he was no doubt thought to have a safe pair of hands. About his deputy there was some controversy. The first name put forward was that of Kuwahara Motoyasu, an elderly Gaikoku Bugyō with a cast in one eye, but Alcock objected privately that he was too old and too unprepossessing to be sent to represent Japan in the courts of Europe. Mizuno Tadanori, the next to be proposed, was held to have been discredited by the attacks on foreigners in Yokohama while he was governor there. In the end, Matsudaira Yasunao, one of the abler and younger men among the Tokugawa diplomatic specialists, was chosen. The addition of an inspector (*metsuke*), Kyōgoku Takaaki, made the leadership a triumvirate. As senior assistants these three were accompanied by officials from the foreign affairs office, including Shibata Takenaka, who had been concerned with the affairs of Yokohama in recent months, and some from the finance department. A small number of samurai were attached to the party on the nomination of leading feudal lords.

Altogether six of those who were chosen had travelled with Shimmi to America in 1860, or taken part in the voyage of the *Kanrin Maru*. Among them was Fukuzawa Yukichi, who was one of four interpreters (the others being Fukuchi Genichirō, Tachi Hirosaku and Ōta Genzaburō), all selected for their knowledge of English or French. Ōta, though he came from a family of Chinese interpreters in Nagasaki, had learnt English, then worked in the office of the Kanagawa governor, whose responsibilities included Yokohama. Fukuchi, also from Nagasaki, had studied Dutch at Deshima and English under Moriyama Takichirō in Edo, serving later in the Yokohama Customs. In addition, there were two translators from the Bansho Shirabesho: Mitsukuri Shūhei, member of a famous line of Dutch scholars, and Matsuki Kōan (later known as Terashima Munenori). Matsuki was a Satsuma man of lower samurai parentage, who had been adopted by one of the domain's doctors, specializing in Dutch medicine, then educated in Edo under some notable Rangaku scholars before being recalled to Kagoshima to be one of Shimazu Nariakira's advisers. After Nariakira's death in 1858 he worked for the Bakufu as translator at Yokohama for a time, before returning to the Bansho Shirabesho in 1860. Like Fukuchi, he appeared on the mission's list of personnel as a physician, as did Takashima Yūkei and Kawasaki Dōmin. These four were considered to be its scientific experts, able to comment on technology, as well as medicine.

In preparing a draft on which his own instructions would be based — other than those that concerned the postponement of the opening of the 'two ports and two cities', as they were usually called, since this issue was always treated separately — Takenouchi turned for advice to Dr Philipp Franz von Siebold. After his expulsion from Japan in 1829 (see Chapter 2), von Siebold had tried to return when the Perry expedition arrived, only to be frustrated by Donker Curtius, the Dutch representative at Deshima, who thought his presence would be an embarrassment. He finally succeeded in getting to Nagasaki in 1859 in the service of the Netherlands Trading Company of Amsterdam, successor to the Dutch East India Company; but a little under two years later, despite having been warned not to seek official standing, he entered Japanese service at Yokohama as an adviser. During the spring of 1861 he busied himself in several diplomatic matters, an activity which so annoyed the French and British ministers that they called on the Dutch — unsuccessfully — to have him removed from Japan as an illegal resident.

Takenouchi took this record as evidence of a welcome degree of independence from the major treaty powers. At the end of May, therefore, he consulted von Siebold about the European visit. The doctor strongly urged him not to limit its scope to France and Britain, but rather to continue from Paris and London to the Hague, Berlin and St Petersburg, taking in Lisbon on the way home. He should spend twenty or thirty days in each capital, he was advised, extending his investigations to military training and equipment, shipbuilding, mining, science, industry and agriculture. Not all von Siebold's proposals were acceptable — at one point, for example, he recommended that the mission engage in trading operations in partnership with the Netherlands Trading Company, in order to defray the cost of its travels and provide funds for purchasing arms and hiring foreign teachers; this suggestion seems to have been ignored — but the itinerary itself, as eventually followed, seems to have been pretty much of his devising.

On 30 November 1861 the three envoys submitted their conclusions to the Bakufu.[2] They began and ended their memorandum by stating a general intention to study any matter which would be 'to our country's benefit', including basic laws and political customs, the nature of fortifications, methods of production, and the manufacture of machines. On the other hand, when they passed to the specific items on which they envisaged a need for Japan to be informed, they concerned themselves only with points of diplomatic and commercial practice, related to disputes which had occurred in the treaty ports. It was important, they said, to examine the supposed right of warships to call at ports not opened by treaty; the level of rents to be paid by foreign residents in Japan, including legations and consulates; the nature of regulations in the West concerning the conduct of trade and the provision of pilots; the rules about goods imported by officials and merchants for their own use. In other words, having become aware in the course of their duties in Japan that they were still in large part ignorant of the conventions to which western consuls and merchants habitually appealed when discussing international trade, they identified these as the context in which Japan must first 'study the barbarian'.

On this occasion the Bakufu responded in writing to the recommendations, which was not a frequent occurrence. On 19 January 1862, just before their departure, it addressed a memorandum of instructions to the envoys, approving some of their proposals, but also adding others. It put emphasis on the difficulties that might be encountered if foreign warships were admitted to ports not officially open, especially where these were in the territories of leading feudal lords; authorized formal discussion with European governments of the rents and land tax that should be payable by foreigners in the treaty ports; and confirmed that a good deal more information was required about matters like pilotage and bonded warehouses. It then went on to add additional desiderata of a similar kind. For example, it would be useful to discuss with France the export of silk cocoons: since foreign demand, especially from France, was pushing up the price of silk at home, and this was an item of everyday use, there would be advantages in an agreement giving Edo power to limit export quantities. Again, the mission might explore the possibility of a ban on the firing of salutes by foreign ships in Japanese harbours, and seek to abort the rumoured plans for bringing in French and British troops to defend the foreign legations. The information to be gathered included the nature of taxes that might be levied on the sale of warships and merchant vessels to Japan, as well as the restrictions that might be imposed on the supply of military equipment in time of war. Western practice with respect to the entertainment of foreign diplomats also needed study.

It has to be said that none of this seems to open the door to a broad consideration of western society and the lessons Japan might learn from it. The memorandum, like that of the envoys, referred briefly to the study of the political and military systems of the West. It added education, but simply as a category of subject-matter. For the rest, it defined 'conditions in the West' in practical diplomatic and military terms. The products of industry were conceived almost entirely as weapons and the machines for making them (plus mints and coinage). 'Institutions' were those concerned with the workings of government. Law was international law. The word 'civilization' was not mentioned at all.

This was not at all what Alcock wanted. Having heard reports about the nature of these instructions, he resumed his pressure at the beginning of 1862 to ensure that the envoys were under orders to seize 'every opportunity of seeing all that was worthy of their attention'.[3] The result was a supplementary Bakufu statement, produced at the last minute, supposedly making good what he thought to be the defects of the earlier ones.

It was produced, in fact, too late to be given to the envoys before they sailed. Alcock therefore took charge of it, sending it under seal to London to be forwarded to Takenouchi via the British embassy in Paris. We know that it arrived. We do not know exactly what it said; but the fact that the members of the mission, above all those who were held to be 'experts', pursued their studies of life in the West with much greater assiduity after leaving France suggests that Alcock had gained his point.

EUROPE OBSERVED

The Takenouchi mission left Yokohama on 21 January 1862 aboard the British steam frigate HMS *Odin*, which was to carry it as far as Suez. There had been a last-minute flurry of preparations before departure. Alcock, belatedly realizing that Japanese official designations would not be familiar enough to European governments to permit them to rank the envoys in the customary manner, for the purpose of deciding the appropriate salutes and other ceremony, hurriedly arranged suitable translations. Takenouchi became an Envoy Extraordinary, Matsudaira and Kyōgoku Ministers Plenipotentiary. In addition, one of the British student interpreters, John Macdonald, who in Alcock's view knew enough Japanese to be 'in ordinary matters, agreeable and useful to the envoys', was attached to the party to ease their path at the mostly British ports of call. That left the problem of what to do about baggage. The members of the mission, despite advice from colleagues who had been to America in 1860, pointing out that it was not necessary to be self-sufficient on their travels, had assembled no less than two hundred pieces, including fifty charcoal heaters (*hibachi*) and five hundred champagne bottles filled with soya sauce. Some of it had in the end to be sent separately by sailing vessel via the Cape of Good Hope.

The *Odin* had been modified to accommodate the party in suitable style. The whole main deck was given over to the mission, plus a separate galley on the upper deck, in which their attendants could cook meals. Their cabins were stripped of all furniture, except bunks, and provided with low-level tables of the kind used in Japan. Japanese baths were installed. The ship's commanding officer, Lord John Hay, was much put out by these disruptions of routine. He expressed the hope to a friend that he would not find himself required to cope with the return voyage too. Nor were the Japanese entirely happy with their experience. Shibata Takenaka, writing from London to colleagues in Edo early in May, complained of the ban on smoking on board ship, of the tea-coloured water (carried in iron tanks), which was best drunk with the eyes shut, and of the heat, which made sleeping difficult. He was not much better pleased with some of the things encountered on arrival in Europe. Most of the food, he said, was 'animal meat', often greasy. In France they had been able to get sliced raw fish, which was an acceptable substitute for *sashimi* when served with soya sauce; but in London they read in a newspaper a report comparing the Japanese habit of eating raw fish with that of the natives of South America, so felt compelled to give it up for the sake of national dignity. This left them almost nothing to eat that was really to their taste.[4]

The voyage started with contrary winds, which forced a call at Nagasaki for extra coal, but Hong Kong was reached without further incident on 4 February. There the senior members of the party moved to a hotel ashore, where they had their first experience of shoreside living in the western manner. In addition to a round of visits to gun batteries, a gun foundry, the barracks and a hospital, there was a ball, given by the governor, at which they had an introduction to the rather shocking concept, ladies first; poked discreet secret fun at ballroom dancing; greatly enjoyed ice cream; and were much impressed by the brilliance of the lighting (though it derived from nothing more than the lavish use of candles). They admired the precision of troops, both British and Indian, marching on the parade-ground; asked many questions about government and municipal regulations; and in the course of an informal walk about the town were astonished when the American owner of a bar they entered greeted them effusively and claimed — mistakenly — to have met them before in Washington. Lesser persons also went sightseeing. Ichikawa Wataru, a retainer of one of the middle-ranking officials in Edo, travelling as attendant to Matsudaira, complained that he found the Chinese 'rude and deceitful', apparently because of his encounters with hawkers in the street.

The only excitement at Singapore, the next port of call, was a visit from a Japanese castaway of Opium War days, who had married a Chinese woman and settled there. Nor did much happen at Trincomalee, though Fukuzawa was impressed by the speed with which their arrival was reported in the local paper. Suez, however, which was reached on 20 March, provided the novel and slightly alarming experience of travelling by train, first across the isthmus to Cairo, then to Alexandria. Fukuzawa was interested to see paddy fields 'no different from those of our own country'. Ichikawa, whose diary is one of the more interesting documents relating to the mission, admired the railway tunnels. His impression of Cairo, however, was chiefly of dirt, smells and flies, the last 'intolerably vexatious'. Of Alexandria he said that the people were stupid and lazy, their city 'gradually going to ruin'. Takenouchi and some of his entourage were taken one day to the pyramids, but the expedition was not a success. The heat and dust made them irritable and thirsty. They had little opinion of Nile boats and donkeys as means of transportation. They refused point-blank to climb a pyramid or go inside it.

From Alexandria they travelled in a British troop transport, the *Himalaya*, which was not only more spacious than the *Odin*, but also served better food. There was a three-day break in Malta, once again under British jurisdiction, and back in the world of saluting batteries. Diaries and letters reveal a preoccupation with such matters almost everywhere. As Ichikawa noted, saluting was a subject which touched 'the dignity or meanness of a country'. This made it a point of satisfaction that the mission was welcomed to Marseille on 3 April by a salute of fifteen guns.

After only a brief stop in Marseille the party set out by train for Paris, a journey which usually involved a night in Lyon, but this time required two, because there were no trains on Sunday. It was at Lyon that they first came under the scrutiny of the European press. The *Salut Public* (quoted in the London *Times* of 10 April) observed, somewhat patronizingly, that the Japanese visitors 'have an intelligent physiognomy, although their countenances are not very prepossessing'. It added that they 'usually drink liqueurs and rice-water', for food 'prefer boiled poultry', and at meals 'sit at table, use knives and forks, and season everything they eat with pepper and spice'.

Paris, which was reached on 7 April, proved to be formal. Met at the station by a representative of the Foreign Ministry, the envoys had a military escort to the Hôtel du Louvre, where they were installed in considerable luxury. The junior members, at least, had ample time to examine the accommodation it provided, for they were not allowed out of the hotel until their superiors had paid their diplomatic calls. Even after that their liberty was restricted by orders of the *metsuke* to two periods a day, the second ending at six o'clock (as had been true for those who went to Washington in 1860).

The diplomatic business of the mission made little progress. After presenting their credentials to Napoleon III on 13 April — watched by large crowds when they were escorted by cavalry on a roundabout route to the Tuileries (which faced their hotel) — the envoys began a series of meetings with the Foreign Minister, Thouvenel. The latter proved uncooperative on the subject of postponement, leading Takenouchi to the conclusion that there was little point in remaining very long in Paris. It was Britain whose decision would matter, it appeared. He therefore decided to continue to London at the end of the month.

This left the travellers less than two weeks in which to see something of the city, then in the process of being rebuilt on the emperor's orders. Nearly all of them liked it, as did most of the Japanese who followed them in later years. A good deal of the time of the envoys themselves, usually accompanied by some other members of the party, was taken up by official sightseeing, arranged by the government: Napoleon's tomb, Versailles, a munitions factory, the military museum at the Invalides, industrial museums, the imperial printing-house. At the opposite end of the scale, those who enjoyed no such special consideration walked the boulevards, admiring the gas-lights and the glass-fronted shops, so different from the street scenes of Japan, and watching the bustle of the traffic. Some of those of middle rank were taken occasionally to the opera or the theatre (which they treated simply as spectacle), or to Longchamp racecourse (which they no doubt found more intelligible, since the foreign residents in Japan had one at Yokohama). The task of trying to come to terms with western civilization in any more intellectual sense was left pretty much to the medical men and the interpreters. Matsuki, Fukuzawa and their colleagues, sometimes together, sometimes separately, visited military and civil hospitals, a medical museum, the St Germain medical school, the Jardin des Plantes, the Conservatoire des Arts et Métiers, and the civil engineering library at quai Malaquais. By contrast, there is nothing to show that any member of the mission took an interest in art or music.

Fukuzawa's journal (much more than his autobiography) gives a good idea of the sort of things he thought it worth setting down at the time. The visits to hospitals produced a note, not only on size and the number of beds, but also on funding, which mostly derived, he explained, from fees and private donations. He was equally concerned with the financial arrangements for the building of railways, working out at one point the average cost per Japanese *ri* (just under four kilometres) for the line from Paris to Lyon, and describing how private capital was raised by the companies which undertook construction. In another entry he wrote about France's national assembly (which for some reason he called the 'House of Commons', transcribing the English words phonetically). He outlined its composition, its powers, the frequency of its sessions, the electoral law, that is, the basic information that might be needed to establish such an institution in Japan.

The mission's arrival in England on 29 April was distinctly low-key by comparison with its treatment in France. The British ambassador in Paris had warned the envoys, when they called on him to confirm the arrangements for the journey, that they must not expect to be received by Queen Victoria, who was still in mourning for her husband. They had not seemed entirely convinced, he reported to London, by his assurance that they would nevertheless be shown 'every attention'. If so, they must soon have felt that they were right. At Dover there was no military ceremonial to greet them. The official reception was provided by Macdonald, a mere student interpreter, who had travelled on ahead of the party after taking them to France. In addition, a former British consul at Hakodate, who was present in a private capacity, called on the crowd to give three cheers for the Japanese — Ichikawa observed that while the meaning of 'hip-hip-hooray' was not clear to him, it seemed to be 'a congratulatory expression' — but this was no real substitute for an honour guard. Nor was there one in London, where they were simply taken by carriage from the station to Claridge's Hotel. Some of the party, at least, thought it inferior to the Hôtel du Louvre, an opinion reinforced, no doubt, by finding Chinese translations of the Bible in their rooms.

Discussions at the Foreign Office in their first few days made it clear that Earl Russell had no intention of conducting serious diplomatic business until Alcock arrived home on leave, accompanied by Edo's chief interpreter, Moriyama, who had fresh instructions for the envoys on the subject of postponement, which proved to be on 30 May. Since the instructions left Takenouchi no option but to accept the terms already agreed by Alcock in Edo, it took only a week thereafter to draft and sign what was to be known as the London Protocol, which deferred the opening of the two ports and the two cities for another five years, subject to a promise from the Shogun that Japan would in all other respects 'strictly execute' the agreements of 1858. The envoys were left to attempt on the rest of their travels what seemed likely to be the fairly straightforward task of persuading other treaty powers to sign something similar. In pursuit of it — and departing with greater dignity than they came — they left London on 12 June by the royal train to board a Dutch warship at Greenwich.

Because of the delays, the mission had had six weeks in England, mostly free for the pursuit of non-diplomatic interests. These showed greater variety than had been evident in France. The official occasions in and around London were not so very different, if more numerous: the Tower of London, the Mint, Parliament, Windsor Castle (but no royal audience), Hampton Court, the Crystal Palace, the Royal Observatory at Greenwich, the British Museum, the Regent's Park Zoo, Derby Day at Epsom. There were receptions, dinners, even a ball. Fukuzawa, Matsuki and the other doctors went off to hospitals again, very much as they had done before, though on one visit to King's College Hospital they had the new experience of seeing an operation performed under chloroform. Their engagements also included a foundling home and schools for the dumb and the blind. Among more casual occasions was an inspection of the London Tunnel under the Thames at Wapping: twin tunnels, in fact, one for the railway, one for pedestrians, the latter lit by gas and complete with souvenir stalls.

Some of what was done comprised an organized approach to the study of the West, undertaken by several different groups, working separately. It involved *inter alia* a few days spent outside the capital, inspecting industrial centres in the Midlands and the north (Newcastle, Liverpool and Birmingham). Most of the arrangements on these and similar occasions were made by the Foreign Office, but as many of the requests for them came through Macdonald, they may well have been the result of a Japanese initiative, especially where they were couched in very general terms. On 7 May, for instance, the Foreign Office asked the Admiralty to arrange for the envoys to see 'the most important ironworks connected with ship-building', which is hardly a form of wording one would expect from those who knew which they were.[5]

In the letter he wrote to Edo on 9 May, Shibata had expressed doubts about the feasibility of preparing the kind of report the Bakufu now seemed to want in a stay of less than thirty or forty days. Western institutions, he said, were entirely different from those of Japan, 'like ice and charcoal'. In the event, because of the delays in negotiation, he had the time he needed, and his subordinates made good use of it. By dividing their efforts — there was a day when one group investigated machinery at the South Kensington exhibition, another visited the offices of the *Illustrated London News*, while a third went to Woolwich Arsenal — they were able to cover a remarkable amount of ground. *The Times* on several occasions commented on how assiduous they were. At the Zoo, one of them 'busied himself without intermission' in sketching birds and animals 'with great rapidity and fidelity' (3 May). At Woolwich Arsenal, because of the conditions under which they had to work, they exemplified 'the pursuit of knowledge under difficulties' (8 May). At a boiler and engine factory in Greenwich, 'they made copious notes and drawings' of every kind of machinery (14 May), as they did in Portsmouth too. The outcome was a quite detailed report on contemporary Europe and its civilization when they went home, especially on Britain. We shall examine it in the next section of this chapter.

Given the degree of Japanese preoccupation with international strength and weakness, it was to be expected that military establishments, plus the factories which armed and equipped them, came high on the list of things to be observed. At Woolwich Arsenal, for example, where Sir William Armstrong was superintendent of the ordnance works, the new rifled heavy guns named after him aroused particular interest. The envoys and suite went to see them on 7 May, while their subordinates returned more than once to expand their notes. Visits to shipyards and engineering plants on the Thames, sometimes by Admiralty steamer, gave more attention to naval than to mercantile shipping. At Liverpool on 28 May they saw a warship under construction and witnessed a practice firing of the latest breech-loading guns ('newly-invented guns which load from the back' was Ichikawa's description). Portsmouth dockyard was their destination on 2 June. Once again they made careful notes about ships and their armament.

Another major object of study, which their hosts constantly pressed upon them, was the non-military side of British industry. The most convenient introduction to it was the Fourth International Exposition at South Kensington, the opening of which the envoys attended on 1 May. Seated with the diplomatic corps — a rare experience — they proceeded

5. Members of the 1862 mission study a map of London on arrival, planning their exploration of the city.

to show a lively interest in everything around them, though their entrance was suitably solemn and restrained. Other members of the mission went later, some of them more than once. They were not much impressed by the quality of the objects which Alcock had sent from Edo to represent Japan, but there is no doubt about the impact of the exhibition as a demonstration of western technology and skills. This is Fukuzawa on the subject:

> Manufactures from all countries and newly-developed machines have been collected here to be shown to people . . . and in addition artisans have been sent to show how the machines are operated. Steam machines to make cloth from cotton and wool, chemicals to make ice in summer, steam-powered equipment for pumping water, all are here. There is fire-fighting apparatus, ingenious clocks, agricultural tools, horse trappings, kitchens, ship models, old books, and paintings without number.[6]

Ichikawa mentions many of these things too, though he also includes weapons, especially Armstrong guns. His comment on western art — one of the few — was that pictures were 'accurately drawn', so as to 'represent things as they really are', but lacked any element of 'the voices of

6. The Japanese envoys and suite visit the International Exhibition in London in 1862.

spirits and the manifestations of the gods'.[7] The only interest shown in music was the question put to Macdonald at the opening ceremony: why was the conductor of the orchestra waving his arms?

The study of industry was later extended to particular plants and establishments: at Newcastle on 26 and 27 May (the Armstrong works, a shipyard, a North Shields coalmine), at Birmingham on 29 and 30 May (the manufacture of glass and small-arms), in London on a number of dates (firms concerned with small-scale items, like watches, razors and surgical instruments). Commerce was represented by warehousing at the London Docks, the Customs House, the Telegraph Office.

A *Times* leader on 16 April, a week or two before the mission reached England, had said that the envoys ought to go back to Japan, not 'astounded at our magnificence', but 'musing, rather sadly perhaps, over our vast industry and our tremendous power'. This aim, though never acknowledged by the government, was a theme running through much of what the visitors were shown. There was certainly less 'magnificence' than there had been in France: a conducted tour of the state and private apartments at Windsor Castle, plus a call on Earl Russell at Pembroke Lodge, hardly matched the ceremony of the Tuileries. This may help to explain why the Japanese found London less to their taste than Paris. To

Shibata, whereas Paris was like a garden, 'the capital of England seems all smoke, so different are they'. The dirt in the streets and the prevalence of shops and other commercial buildings all made it less attractive than the Parisian boulevards. Matsuki made much the same point, likening Paris to Kyoto and London to Edo. What is more, he thought the crowds he saw in the London streets were evidence of depravity, as well as prosperity: many of them, he wrote, were beggars, brought to that state by the excessive drinking of brandy (though he may have meant gin).[8]

The visit to Holland made both a friendlier and a more flattering start than the one to England. Donker Curtius, the former Dutch minister in Japan, accompanied by a Leiden professor, Johan Joseph Hoffmann, who could read Japanese, came to London to escort the mission. A Dutch warship was provided for the North Sea crossing, the royal yacht for the final entry into Rotterdam. At Rotterdam on 14 June there were large crowds, placards written in the Japanese script, a military escort, a speech by the burgomaster, followed by a special train to the Hague and another official welcome. The crowds were to continue everywhere in the next few weeks. On 1 July there was a royal audience, described in the Japanese records, as that in Paris had been, with meticulous details of dress and ceremonial. A visit to the States General on 21 June was accompanied by the Navy Minister (for the upper house) and the Finance Minister (for the lower house).

During the month they were in Holland the staff of the embassy were as busy as they had been in Britain, and in much the same way (except that on two occasions they visited art collections, which was something new). They went to schools, including those for the blind and the dumb, hospitals, orphanages, shops, textile factories. In the shops they found to their surprise that they were able to replenish their stocks of soya sauce, though at a price they thought inordinately high. There was the mint at Utrecht, the university at Leiden, a printing works at which they were shown the colour illustrations for a new book on Japan. Most of all, as in England, there were the heavy industries. Accompanied at times by Captain Pels Rijcken, who had commanded the first Dutch training contingent at the Nagasaki naval school, they were taken to engineering works, producing equipment for both ships and railways, to dockyards, a gun foundry, a munitions factory. It was an itinerary decided at least in part by the fact that Takenouchi's supplementary orders, brought to London by Moriyama, authorized the purchase of more machinery for the Bakufu's facilities. In Amsterdam, where they stayed three days, starting on 25 June, they saw gem-polishing, a telegraph office, a sugar refinery and the customs house, in addition to an ironworks and the naval dockyard. Some of their days must have been exhausting. One in Rotterdam, for example, included a demonstration of a steam-hammer and other dockyard equipment in the morning, then visits to ships, a school, a hospital and a zoo, as well as a good deal of entertainment along the way.

Since more of the party were capable of speaking Dutch than other European languages, they found it easier in Holland to get about on their own and ask questions about what they saw. On the other hand, this did not necessarily give them a pro-Dutch bias. Matsuki, writing to his Satsuma colleague Kawamoto Kōmin on 13 July, expressed some disappointment with Holland, despite the warmth of the reception there. The country had neither the strength nor the level of civilization of France and Britain, he said, and had shown them nothing they had not seen elsewhere. As a language, Dutch was not widely used. Even in Holland the people bought mostly books in French and German, while scholars in France and England had expressed amazement when they heard that the Japanese relied on it in their studies. As a consequence, 'we have become ashamed of it and stopped telling people'. If the Bakufu planned to send students to Europe, as he had heard, then they must at all costs, he believed, go to France or Britain, not to Holland.[9]

The mission left Utrecht for Dusseldorf on 17 July and was met there by a representative of the Prussian Foreign Ministry, another former minister to Japan. There was a night stop in Cologne to see the cathedral and the Hohenzollern Bridge across the Rhine, then a train to Berlin next day. On 21 July the three envoys were received in audience by Wilhelm I — 'with great pomp', according to the British ambassador — when Takenouchi conveyed the Shogun's greetings in Japanese, Moriyama put them into Dutch, and a Prussian interpreter translated into German. Other official engagements had a predominantly military tone: a cavalry parade at the Potsdam academy, commanded personally by the king; a gunnery demonstration; a visit to a weapons museum; inspections of a gun factory at Spandau and a major arms works (several times by different groups). Various members of the party also found time to go to the opera, the observatory, Berlin University, the zoo, a foundling home, some hospitals, and a prison. Fukuzawa attended a debate in parliament.

These activities had to be fitted into a period of about two weeks, since there was no diplomatic business to justify a longer stay. The Prussian treaty with Japan had stated no dates for opening the two ports and two cities, so all that was needed was a note repairing this omission in the light of the London agreement and providing for minor changes in the regulation of trade. This was signed on 31 July. On 5 August Takenouchi and his companions set out for Russia, first in a special train as far as Stettin, then by sea to Kronstadt.

There had been little private or municipal entertainment in Prussia, or social contact with anyone but officials. The atmosphere in Russia proved to be much the same: stiff, formal, very grand. After a night spent in Kronstadt, an imperial yacht took the party into St Petersburg on

9 August, landing them at English Quay on the south bank of the Neva River. Their arrival was watched from the windows of the British embassy by the eighteen-year-old Prince Alfred, Queen Victoria's second son, who was making a private visit to the city. Once they were ashore, a military escort, comprising detachments of Cossacks, Lancers and the Finland Guards, took them to their quarters in one of the state buildings (the Marble Palace), which was used for distinguished visitors. A formal call was made on the Foreign Ministry on the 12th. Two days later Alexander II gave an audience to the envoys and the senior members of their staff. Bearing head-high the box containing the Shogun's letter, they were led through the galleries and state apartments of the Winter Palace from the Nicholas Hall to the Great Throne Room, where they were received by the Tsar and Tsarina. The Tsar was in military uniform. The Tsarina wore a dress in hollyhock pattern, made from material which was an earlier Tokugawa gift (a fact which was nowhere mentioned in the account of the occasion that appeared in the *Journal de St Petersbourg* next day).

In Russia there was more diplomatic discussion to be entered into than there had been in other countries, because of the recurrent problem of disputed boundaries in Sakhalin. General Nikolai Ignatiev, conducting the negotiations for the Russian Foreign Ministry, demanded for Russia the whole of Sakhalin in response to Japan's claim to the territory south of fifty degrees north; but when he then offered to compromise on a division at forty-eight degrees north, Takenouchi and Matsudaira, who showed signs of accepting this, were warned by the *metsuke*, Kyōgoku, that they had no power to vary the Bakufu's instructions. This brought deadlock. An agreement about postponement was signed on 17 September, but the Sakhalin issue was put on one side.

One result of the boundary dispute was that the mission had longer for study and sightseeing in Russia. There were escorted tours of the imperial palaces at Peterhof and Tsarskoye Selo, outside St Petersburg. Visits were made to inspect the Kronstadt naval base and various military installations, a gun foundry, a naval ironworks, the observatory, the engineering and mining schools. By way of entertainment there were boat races to watch on the Neva River and an expedition to see the countryside outside the city. Fukuzawa and others pursued their investigations at hospitals, the botanical gardens, the customs department, the telegraph office, technical and commercial schools, two government factories (glass and porcelain), and the imperial library (where only a tiny proportion of the books were in Russian). They do not seem to have found a great deal to impress them in all this. Matsuki, writing a discursive letter home on 14 September, described Russia as less advanced than France or Britain, though he admired the hospitals.[10] He also remarked that the encouragement of immigration had resulted in bringing large numbers of residents of German origin to the city. He thought the local Russian women 'extremely ugly'. The beautiful ones all seemed to come from other countries.

In one respect the Japanese found St Petersburg very different from Berlin. The Prussian ambassador in London had told his government that there was no reason to expect problems over food and accommodation, since all members of the mission could use a knife and fork and eat western food (with a preference for rice, fish, oranges and champagne). Accordingly, they had been installed in the Brandenburg Hotel on arrival in Berlin, the three envoys and Shibata each in bedrooms of their own, the rest sharing, three or four to a room. They all took meals in the hotel dining room, seated at three tables in order of rank. Things in St Petersburg were not at all like this. Their rooms at the Marble Palace turned out to have Japanese-style wooden pillows, sword-rests, writing-brushes and tobacco-pipes, much as they might have done at home. Japanese-style refreshments were served to them on arrival. A word-list was provided in each room, written in both Japanese and Cyrillic scripts. They owed all this, they discovered, to the efforts of one of their com-patriots, working for the Russian Foreign Ministry, though they were never able to meet him. His name, it is now known, was Masuda (for-merly Tachibana) Kōsai, a priest of lower samurai origins, who had given some assistance to the Russian admiral, Putiatin, when he was negotiat-ing a treaty with Japan in 1854–5. He had returned with Putiatin to Russia, become an official translator for the Russian government, and lived in St Petersburg under the name of Vladimir (or Dimitri) Yamatov.

By the time the mission reached St Petersburg, the cost of its travels was beginning to make its European hosts uneasy. The Prussian Foreign Minister wrote to his ambassador in the Russian capital, instructing him to ensure if at all possible that the journey back to Holland be made by sea, not via Berlin, since he had no desire to have to authorize further expenditure. The British chargé in St Petersburg reported to London at the end of August that while Takenouchi and his entourage had been 'received with almost regal honours and sumptuously lodged and enter-tained', they were showing signs of wearing out their welcome. Ignatiev had told him that 'their appetite for pâté de fois gras and champagne was extraordinary and the expense of their entertainment quite enormous'. Russia had no desire to quibble about postponement, in the hope of getting rid of them quickly.[11] Nor did the Dutch seem anxious to see them again, though there were still some points of detail to be decided after their earlier talks. They suggested that these could be settled well enough by the Dutch ambassador in Paris.

The outcome was that the envoys and their suite left St Petersburg by train on 17 September, stopped at Berlin, but only briefly, then continued to Paris, arriving late — and tired — on 22 September. Three days later an agreement about postponement was signed with the Dutch ambassador.

Donker Curtius also came to see them to discuss Japanese imports of machinery. Thouvenel, having failed to persuade Takenouchi to insert a clause expanding the silk trade and admitting French missionaries to Japan, followed the example of the other powers in signing a diplomatic note on 2 October about the opening of the ports. This done, the mission was encouraged to leave. On 5 October it entrained for Rochefort in the southwest, where its members were at once taken to their ship for Portugal, walking almost a mile from the station to the quay — carriages were not provided — through files of soldiers 'placed in glorious array on both sides of the road'. Fukuzawa, whose description this was, thought he detected a certain hostility, but in view of the earlier reactions of the Prussian, Russian and Dutch foreign ministries, it may have been no more than a belated attempt to economize.

The food and the accommodation aboard their ship, reinforcing this impression, were not at all satisfactory. Indeed, the voyage home was not a very happy one. In Lisbon, reached on 16 October, there was a royal audience, an agreement about the ports, little else of consequence, unless one counts a final set of souvenir photographs. They sailed again for Alexandria on 25 October, still in the same French ship. Even so, their problems were not quite at an end. At Singapore (29 December), the ship which had brought them from Suez was diverted to Indo-China, where it was needed to take part in a fresh French campaign, leaving them to continue their travels in something very much smaller. This brought them to Shinagawa on 29 January 1863. Like their predecessors of 1860, the envoys landed with little ceremony on the following day.

INVESTIGATING AND REPORTING

After their return to Edo the envoys submitted a brief report on the diplomatic aspects of their mission, while those members of their entourage who were thought to be experts on European civilization, principally the interpreters and translators, were set to the task of preparing more detailed documents about the countries they had visited. These were labelled *tansaku*, or 'investigations'. They still exist in manuscript in Tokyo, but only the section dealing with Britain has been published.

It is clear that the senior members of the mission did not know enough about Europe or European languages to play any effective part in the preparation of the *tansaku*. Fukuchi called them 'blind-deaf pilgrims'. Most of their attendants were similarly handicapped. Ichikawa recorded — with little sign of regret — that he had been unable to 'make enquiries and form opinions, or obtain a knowledge of these peoples, their customs, manufactures, and dispositions', since he had learnt neither their 'crab-writing' nor their 'shrike-tongued languages'.[12] He could only be an observer, or ask questions of his companions. One or two other members of the party bought dictionaries and learnt some phrases of English or French on their travels, but most, like their superiors, could see, but not speak or hear. The situation was made worse by the restrictions imposed on freedom of movement by their own officials. In Fukuzawa's words, it was 'like carrying the policy of seclusion all around Europe'.[13]

The interpreters themselves were less competent in French and English than in Dutch, the language in which the majority had received their early training. Alcock, travelling to Europe with Moriyama, described him as 'quite at home' in Dutch, but was more equivocal about his English.[14] Fukuzawa, who had the advantage of having been to San Francisco in 1860, spoke English better than most, as well as having published an English-Japanese dictionary. Fukuchi's linguistic experience was mostly in translating diplomatic correspondence, though he did his best to make good any deficiencies of vocabulary by reading widely when in Europe. Matsuki, too, was a translator, first for the Bansho Shirabesho, working in Dutch, then at the Bakufu office in Yokohama. He had begun to learn English when he joined the Shirabesho in 1856, but it is not clear how much he had used it. The other linguist of the group, Tachi, was described in a French newspaper as having some knowledge of written French. The implication is that he was not proficient in the spoken language.

In these circumstances the task of studying Europe at first hand came to depend in some degree on the cooperation of a handful of Europeans who could communicate, however imperfectly, in Japanese. One was Macdonald, Alcock's student interpreter, who travelled with the party to Marseille, and was in attendance upon them for the whole of their stay in England. He certainly organized many of the visits they made, and may have suggested some of them. In France the formal interpreting was done by Abbé Gérard, whom de Bellecourt had sent back from Yokohama for this purpose, but Gérard does not seem to have taken part in sightseeing or other similar occasions. More important in that context was Léon de Rosny, a young scholar, trained originally in Chinese, who was attached to the party by the French government. He had studied chiefly written Japanese — he was not always easy to understand in conversation, according to those Japanese who had dealings with him — and was eventually to become the first Professor of Japanese at the Collège de France. In 1862 he visited the members of the mission at their hotel as soon as they arrived in Paris; occasionally acted as interpreter on the various expeditions they made; and became particularly close to Fukuzawa, Matsuki and the other specialists in western studies, travelling to join them when they went to Holland, then appearing again in St Petersburg. It is doubtful whether they needed his help in Holland, but a knowledge of French, which was widely spoken by Russia's ruling class, would certainly have been an advantage in St Petersburg.

In Holland the Dutch government nominated as interpreter and major-domo Dr Johan Josef Hoffmann, formerly an associate of von Siebold, who was Professor of Japanology at Leiden. His age — he was sixty-six — was a constraint on what he could do for the party, while like de Rosny, he had a better command of written than spoken Japanese. Ichikawa, who tried to converse with him, described it as 'like scratching an itching place through one's shoe'.[15] Not surprisingly, most communication with him was in writing.

Setting the diaries and other records of the mission's travels against what is to be found in its later reports suggests that some of the contents of the latter derived, not from what the travellers saw, but from what they were told or read. About Britain, in particular, there were statements concerning politics and society which could have had no other source, unless our knowledge of the itinerary is defective. We know that no less than 369 volumes in various languages were taken back to Japan for the Bakufu collections. There are also references from time to time to members buying books on their own account. All these would have been available, one supposes, to those who later compiled the 'investigations'. In addition, there is evidence that they had an informant in London who provided social and political information. It has not been possible to identify him, beyond what is said about him in the Japanese texts: that he was a Dutch doctor, twelve years resident in London, called — transcribing the Japanese script — Shimmon Berihente (which might conceivably be Belinfante). No explanation is given of how contact was first made with him, but it appears that he met the Dutch speakers among the Japanese on more than one occasion, giving them written and oral statements in Dutch about various British institutions, then answering their questions. Towards the end of Fukuzawa's travel notebook — which is separate from his journal — there are several pages, written almost entirely in Dutch, which appear to be his notes on these occasions. They are much more coherent than his other jottings, and correspond to several sections of the report on Britain.

Not all the information that was collected found its way into the final drafts which were prepared in Edo. Matsuki, for example, was recalled to Kagoshima soon after the work of compilation began, so his notes, put together for a book which was never written, were presumably not available thereafter. They concerned, he tells us in a memoir written some years later,[16] chiefly hospitals and schools, which were his special responsibility; and since Fukuzawa covered much the same ground, they cannot have been an irreparable loss. Indeed, Matsuki also says that it was the custom of those of his colleagues who were engaged in studies of this kind, when they returned to their hotel in the evening, not only to write up their own notes, but also to compare them with those of others. This meant that knowledge was shared, at least in general terms.

Yet this cannot have been true of all the specialist detail that was gathered, because of its quantity. *The Times* (21 May 1862) describes how six of the party, not including the envoys themselves, made a visit to Woolwich Arsenal with a view to examining more carefully than they had done previously the processes by which Armstrong guns and certain explosives were made. They came equipped with diagrams provided by the War Office, acquiring more in the course of the day, to which they added the titles of relevant books and the suppliers of machinery. Their notebooks became 'filled with remarks and sketches, which they no doubt considered a sufficient model for their guidance in establishing the manufacture in their own country'. Fukuzawa was apparently one of them, for his notebook at one point sets down the formula for the rifling of Armstrong guns — one full turn in twenty-seven diameters of bore — a piece of knowledge which does not appear in the subsection on Armstrong guns in the Edo report. The latter, in fact, although it identifies various types of gun, giving dimensions and effective range for each, is not nearly long enough to have included everything six men could have set down in a day.

In putting their material together the compilers followed the pattern of the gazetteer or encyclopaedia, that is, the kind of work occasionally translated by the Bakufu's Dutch scholars earlier in the century. They may even have taken some of these older translations with them by way of guidance, for Ichikawa, when describing the visit to Russia, referred in passing to a translation of a text about that country, made previously by Mitsukuri, which they found to be a good deal out of date. His own notes, presumably correcting it, covered subjects as diverse as the population of St Petersburg, the Winter Palace, Russia's armed forces, the university, foundling homes, and military and naval hospitals.

The report as a whole was organized in six sections, one for each of the countries visited. Those on Britain and Russia were the longest — perhaps reflecting an estimation of their importance as threats to Japan — Holland came next, that on Portugal was much the shortest. The longer ones (Britain, Russia and Holland) included in each case subsections on political institutions, the armed forces and their equipment, aspects of law, trade, products and manufactures, financial institutions, schools and hospitals. To these were added a number of other headings particular to the country concerned. The section on France had very little on the armed forces or law, and not a great deal on industry, no doubt because the investigators only got down to serious business after they left for England. The one on Portugal was very slight indeed, being almost entirely about trade and related matters. Here and there in the text of most of the sections is evidence that description was not the only purpose of the exercise: there are attempts to distinguish what was seen from what was hearsay, and to record certain differences of interpretation.

One can take the section on Britain as the most convenient one for further analysis, since it is available in published form. It is divided into forty subsections, each with its own heading. The first contains general comment on government and society, some parts of which are expanded later. Next comes a description of the country's diplomatic structure, then an evaluation of British politics in the form of a comparison with France (specifically attributed to Berihente). There follow five subsections on naval and military matters, three more on aspects of society (including class differences and poor relief), and another three on regulations applying to foreign ships and citizens visiting Britain. The next subsection deals with London hospitals and schools. The remainder are still more varied, covering — in this order, though the list is selective — the Armstrong gun, reverberatory furnaces, steam trains, city rents, the establishment of legations and consulates, government finance, the port of Liverpool (in three parts), smuggling, bonded warehouses (under the heading 'entrepots'), national products, commodity prices, gas-lamps, commercial taxation, and the leasing of ships.

To give an idea of the content of what was said, it will be useful to summarize one or two of the subsections, translating passages from them. Terminology poses an unusual problem in such translating. In some cases the Japanese text includes English words in transcription, e.g. *royal, Peers, House of Commons*. These are given in italics in the translation. Elsewhere, some terms used in the Japanese leave one in doubt whether the topic being discussed had been properly understood. Where this is the case, to introduce the correct English term into the translation might be misleading. On the other hand, finding a sensible alternative can be difficult. For instance, what are likely from the context to be the counties of England and Wales, or possibly the parliamentary constituencies, are called *buraku* in the report, a word which has the modern meaning of hamlet or rural settlement. It has been translated here as 'localities', in order not to be too precise. Similarly, those whom one can take to be the elected members of the House of Commons are described as *tōdori*, a term which varies in meaning with the context in Japanese, but designates some kind of local dignitary, or foreman, or even company president. It has been rendered 'spokesman', for lack of any better equivalent. Finally, a good deal of what is said in the text about British government and society rests on an implicit comparison — or contrast — with feudal Japan. This has been borne in mind in the choice of terminology.

The account of British government starts with the statement that 'nothing can be done' unless king, lords and commons are in agreement. Business is first discussed in the House of Commons, sent to the Peers when agreed, then goes to the monarch for the royal consent. The House of Commons is described as follows:

The country is divided into fifty-two localities [*buraku*]. Men of esteem and outstanding talent in the localities are put forward from among the people and made spokesmen [*tōdori*] for their locality. Such spokesmen are sent from each locality to the *House of Commons*. When problems arise concerning institutions and customs, these are put forward for discussion in the *House of Commons* by any of the spokesmen, in order that a judgement may be reached for or against. This judgement is made by a *royal* office-holder [the Speaker], who presides over the discussion from beginning to end, though if he is in doubt which side has the better of the discussion, the matter is settled by majority count.[17]

This is tolerably recognizable to anyone with a knowledge of nineteenth-century Parliament. On social structure, however, we get into deeper waters. There is, for example, a statement that government ministers hold office only for life, their descendants then becoming commoners again, which betrays a misunderstanding of the relationship between office-holding and status in Victorian Britain, such as can only stem from assumptions based on Japanese feudal practice. Equally, the assertion that there are a number of hereditary lords, who derive their income from land, but 'have no authority', although they take part in politics, is only intelligible as an implied comparison between British peers and Japanese daimyo (who had almost absolute power over land and people within their domains). Of the men below this exalted level, who seem to have been thought of as the equivalent to samurai, both in rank and in access to office, the report has this to say:

Those with status as gentry-officials [*shikan*] have no hereditary stipends. Their status is only for life, their children are not included in the ranks of officialdom. One of them can be given the title *lord*, either for military prowess or for special services, such titles being retained by their families, which remain permanently in the official ranks. Despite this, their stipends are personal, held only for one generation. Their children have no stipend unless they take office (but usually enter the *House of Commons* and take part in its business).[18]

In other words, the Japanese observers found it difficult to understand and explain a society in which rank, office and income were not related in the way familiar to them in Japan.

As a final example let us take the passage on status differences.[19] Its very heading, 'The distinction between gentry [*samurai*], farmers and merchants in England', carries an echo of Tokugawa social structure. What was said on the subject, indeed, was in some respects a critique of that structure. In Britain, we are told, appointments to office are made by government on the basis of ability, even to the very highest levels. Tenure is not hereditary. The children of farmers and merchants can attain office by studying at schools of their choice, though children of poor families, studying at state-supported schools, cannot do so. Farmers do not have to hand over their crops to the government as tax. Nor does the government intervene in commercial activities, except that those who sell alcohol (*sakaya*) and coffee have to have permits. In fact, 'the government does not concern itself with persons who engage in agriculture and trade'. This, no doubt, was the closest the travellers could get to an explanation of economic *laissez-faire*. It was reinforced by references here and there in the document to the way in which the building of railways, the running of hospitals and the founding of schools all depended on private capital and donations.

This kind of statement came very close to the kind of 'dangerous thoughts' which had put some of Japan's earlier students of the West at risk (see Chapter 2), for it hinted at a different kind of society from Japan's, which might prove to be one of the secrets of western strength. This being so, it was probably fortunate for the authors of the report that few people had the chance to see it. The compilers were warned to be discreet about their work, even to do it at home, because of the dangers from anti-foreign fanatics. When completed, it was shown only to a handful of senior Bakufu officials. It is reasonable to assume that some of the information which had been acquired about international diplomacy and commerce was used to brief the members of the foreign department. It is possible, though there is no direct evidence for it, that what had been learnt about weapons and military technology had an impact on decisions about what Japan should buy. For the rest, it is difficult to identify any concrete results. What was said about western politics and society, after all, was far too unacceptable to the country's rulers to be taken as a model for contemporary Japan; and even those members of the mission, like Fukuzawa Yukichi, who were eventually to write about what they had seen and heard, were far too aware of the risks which this involved to make their knowledge public until the situation in Japan began to change.

6

Envoys and Industry, 1865–1867

An attack which was made by Satsuma samurai on a party of British residents and visitors at Namamugi, near Yokohama, in September 1862 was the beginning of a series of disputes between Japan and the treaty powers. Britain demanded compensation: from the Bakufu, as the responsible political authority; and from Satsuma, as overlord and protector of the 'criminals'. After wearisome and sometimes acrimonious discussions, lasting into the early summer of 1863, Edo agreed to pay. Kagoshima did not. In August, therefore, a British squadron was dispatched to Kagoshima to enforce compliance with the demand, carrying out a bombardment of the city and leaving much of it in flames before withdrawing to repair the damage inflicted on its ships by Satsuma batteries.

Meanwhile the crisis had spread to Choshu, the domain which controlled the westernmost part of Japan's main island. In the spring of 1863 Tokugawa officials approached the emperor's court, seeking imperial endorsement of a plan to negotiate the closing of Yokohama, a step which they hoped would conciliate anti-foreign opinion in Japan. The démarche failed. Choshu, prompted by its radical samurai, who had powerful friends in Kyoto, secured instead a call for expulsion of the foreigner in the emperor's name, set to take place on 25 June. On that day, without further reference to the Bakufu, Choshu guns opened fire on foreign ships passing through the Shimonoseki Straits, so closing the most direct route between Yokohama, Nagasaki and Shanghai. As a result, the powers — after some months of argument and consultation — decided to 'punish' Choshu, sending a joint naval squadron (British, French, Dutch and American) to capture and dismantle the batteries in the straits in September 1864.

These events had important implications for Japan's attempts to learn about the West. In the first place, they persuaded most samurai, including leaders of the anti-foreign movement, that what had been done in the past by way of naval and military reform had not by any means been enough. In the second, by precipitating a new phase in the struggle for power within Japan, in which the Tokugawa found themselves faced by feudal lords, capable of maintaining an army or a fleet, rather than by bands of disaffected samurai, they made western-style military organization and technology a factor in domestic as well as foreign politics. Once this became apparent, both sides entered into agreements with foreign countries in the attempt to secure better access to the relevant skills. The Bakufu developed a special relationship with France, seeking military instruction, weapons, and the means to manufacture them, in return for trade concessions. Shibata Takenaka was sent to Paris in 1865 to confirm the arrangements, provisionally agreed in Edo, for French military advisers to train the Shogun's army and French naval engineers to build a dockyard at Yokosuka. At almost the same time, Satsuma, too, sent a mission to Europe, partly to concert plans — in the event, with a Belgian entrepreneur — to develop the domain's trade and industry for the purpose of importing ships and guns. In both cases, the envoys were expected to carry out a task very different from the kind of generalized study of the West entrusted to Takenouchi and his staff in 1862.

EDO AND FRANCE

The coming together of the Bakufu and France had its origins in the negotiations over Shimonoseki in 1864. By the end of 1863 there were three outstanding issues between them: Choshu actions in the straits (one of the ships fired on had been French); Edo's attempts to negotiate the closing of Yokohama (which were thought to threaten the silk trade); and the murder of a French army officer on the outskirts of that port. In November the French minister in Japan, de Bellecourt, proposed a mission to Paris to settle them, a device, he reported to his government early in 1864, which would provide an opportunity 'to demonstrate to Japan the superiority of French culture', while laying a foundation for future trade advantages.[1] The Bakufu, believing that such a mission could be used to buy time in a moment of crisis, concurred. It announced that Ikeda Nagaaki (Chōhatsu), one of the Gaikoku Bugyō, would take on the duty, accompanied as usual by two associates of similar rank, as well as by Tanabe Taichi of the foreign department as secretary, and by Shioda Saburō as chief interpreter. Minor officials and personal attendants brought the size of the party up to thirty-three. No military experts or specialists in western studies were included, though several had asked to go.

The mission left Yokohama on 6 February 1864 aboard a French warship for Shanghai, where it transferred to the regular mail steamer for Suez and Marseille. Marseille was reached on 18 April. In Paris at the start of May there began a series of meetings with the Foreign Minister, Drouyn de Lhuys, at which a member of the French legation in Edo was principal interpreter, while Philipp Franz von Siebold, who had come from Germany to volunteer his services, acted as unofficial adviser and go-between. It quickly became clear that France, having consulted Britain, Holland and the United States, was wholly unwilling to accept the closing of Yokohama, no matter what inducements Ikeda offered. What is more, the threat was made that if the Bakufu did not act against Choshu, 'la France devra employer la force'. On 20 June, despairing of any better result, the Japanese delegation signed a convention in which it was promised that the Shimonoseki Straits would be opened within three months of their return; that force would be used to achieve this if all else failed; and that Edo would act if need be in concert with the French naval commander in Japan. There was no mention at all of Yokohama.

Ikeda and his colleagues were left in some difficulty. The convention to which they had put their names was quite contrary to the instructions they had received before leaving home. It seemed obvious from what had been said in Paris that the other treaty powers would be as obdurate on the subject of Yokohama as the French had been, so no useful purpose would be served by travelling to other capitals. This left them no obvious means of using up more time, as the Bakufu had clearly wanted them to do. They therefore decided to go straight home, risking the wrath of their superiors. When they reached Yokohama on 18 August and submitted their report — they were denied entry to the capital — their convention was promptly disavowed, those who had signed it were dismissed from office and put under house arrest, Ikeda was deprived of half his fief.

Nevertheless, the mission had not been quite as negative in its results as this might make it seem. Though it had contributed very little to Japanese understanding of the West in the wider sense, its members had come back with some shrewd observations to make about the situation in Europe and its relevance to Japan. The countries of Europe, they noted in their report, were held back from attacking Japan, first, by rivalries among themselves, which seemed likely soon to result in war, and second, by the difficulty of carrying on hostilities in so distant a region. Before these obstacles were removed, or reduced — the first by a peace settlement of some kind, the second by the building of the Suez canal — Japan had a year or two of relative safety in which to strengthen her position. One urgent need was to reinforce unity at home. Another was to station resident ministers overseas and conclude treaties with countries which might prove to be reliable allies. A third was to send students abroad, 'in order to avail ourselves of western skills in land and sea warfare'. Japanese, in fact, should be allowed to travel freely, 'both to trade and to make themselves familiar with conditions overseas'.[2]

During the talks in Paris two points had been taken up which had some bearing on a policy of this kind. Apparently at von Siebold's urging, Napoleon III had agreed to make a warship available for purchase by Japan, as well as other arms, in order to strengthen the Bakufu against its enemies at home. Ikeda for his part had proposed sending young Japanese to France to study the natural sciences and undergo naval training. Drouyn de Lhuys had agreed. Though there was nothing about this in the convention, the discussion of such matters at the highest level provided a foundation on which Léon Roches, the new French minister in Japan, was able to build.

Roches had taken up his post in April 1864. Helped by his Jesuit interpreter, Mermet de Cachon, he established a working relationship with Oguri Tadamasa and Kurimoto Jo'un, two middle-ranking officials of some influence in Edo, who became the nucleus of a pro-French party there. With their cooperation, he worked out a number of agreements during 1864 and 1865, by which the Tokugawa might enjoy the benefit of French industrial technology and military expertise, while France secured in return a favourable place in Japanese foreign trade. He anticipated that the result, as he told Drouyn de Lhuys in October 1865, would be to make Japan for France 'what China is for England'.[3]

His first move came in connection with Edo's plans for a new naval dockyard. The installation which existed at Nagasaki (Chapter 3) had begun to seem inadequate in size and perhaps too difficult to defend against a background of potential conflict with the lords of west Japan, prompting discussion about building something larger and more up to date near Edo. Hida Hamagorō, who had served as an engineer aboard the *Kanrin Maru*, was sent to Europe to see what might be done with the help of Holland; but Roches put a different proposal forward, under which technical supervision would be provided by François Verny, a French naval engineer from Toulon, who was then building gunboats for China at the port of Ningpo, while equipment would be purchased and the appropriate technicians hired from France. The plan was provisionally agreed by the Bakufu in November 1864. Verny came in January 1865 to survey possible sites, choosing Yokosuka at the entrance to Edo Bay; in February an agreement was signed for work to begin in 1867 and be completed in 1871.

Verny also recommended that machine shops and a small ironworks be established at Yokohama, using equipment already available in Japan. A plant of this kind would, he pointed out, be able to provide some of the machinery needed at Yokosuka, as well as train Japanese staff who would eventually have to take over from French technicians there. Quickly approved, it was ready by the end of 1865. Meanwhile Mermet de Cachon had founded a French-language school at Yokohama, intended to prepare interpreters for both establishments, and provide an elementary grounding in arithmetic and geography.

The pattern was rounded out in the autumn of 1865 by the founding of a company under official patronage to promote Franco-Japanese trade. One object was to ensure continued French access to Japanese raw silk and silkworm eggs, expanding French exports to Japan to pay for them. Another — in Edo's view, a crucial one — was to maintain a measure of government control over foreign trade. A scheme was worked out by Roches and Oguri Tadamasa in September, approved by Edo in October, by Paris in November. Implementing it was then entrusted to Paul Fleury-Hérard, Roches's banker in France, on whose initiative the Societé Générale d'Importation et d'Exportation dans l'Extrême Orient was formed with a capital of sixty million francs.

These arrangements made necessary another mission to Europe, a working one, less pretentious than that of 1862. In May 1865 Shibata Takenaka, who had been head of the mission secretariat in 1862, was appointed to lead it. He had two interpreters: Shioda Saburō, who had learnt French under Mermet de Cachon and been to Paris with Ikeda in 1864; and Fukuchi Genichirō, an English specialist, who had accompanied Takenouchi to Europe in 1862. Seven others made up the rest of the party. It was at first thought right that Shibata, now a Gaikoku Bugyō, should have diplomatic status, like his predecessors, but Roches argued that this would be inappropriate for what was really a purchasing commission. He was in the end made Special Commissioner. What is more, Roches told him, he should avoid 'affecting the pomp and seeking the reception of a special embassy, which the governments of Europe would be indisposed to consider adequately constituted, unless presided over by a daimyo'.[4] Fleury-Hérard and Verny were to be his mentors while in France.

In the event, Shibata's travels were not confined to France, nor his duties — at least on the face of it — to matters concerning Yokosuka and foreign trade. The British chargé, when he heard of the proposal, had warned that the Japanese 'would do well not to limit their enquiries to one country'. In June, when he was given formal notice of the mission, he had a meeting with Shibata, who tried to remove any doubts about the nature of the Bakufu's intentions by explaining that his principal object was to discuss the despatch of a French military training mission to Japan and to investigate 'useful appliances for the defence of the country'. He would not be purchasing ships, he said, but would have authority either to buy or to recommend for purchase any other item useful to Japan that came his way. More widely, he was 'to study foreign customs and report on them in order that the Japanese may be changed and improved accordingly'. For these reasons he hoped to visit England in

November. The statement was confirmed in substance by a letter from the Tokugawa council, expressing the hope that Shibata 'may obtain facilities for inspecting the military weapons and machinery which are daily invented in your country and . . . observe with his own eyes the constitution of your country, with a view to facilitate consideration of the state of our own'.[5]

The mission left Yokohama on 27 June and reached Marseille on 25 August. It was met there by Verny, who arranged visits to the naval base at Toulon and the shipyards at La Ciotat. The party then proceeded to Paris, arriving on 6 September. Contact was initially made with Fleury-Hérard, to whom Shibata delivered a letter of introduction from Roches. Next, Shibata, accompanied by Verny, went to the Foreign Ministry and saw Drouyn de Lhuys, who agreed that further discussions of detail should be carried on directly with the appropriate government departments. On 21 September there was a meeting at the Navy Ministry, which opened the talks about Yokosuka, and other meetings were held at intervals for the next two months. Between meetings, Shibata and his colleagues were taken to visit naval, military and industrial establishments, travelling as far afield as Brest and Angoulême.

We have three main sources of information about their activities.[6] One is Shibata's journal, kept for the whole period he was absent from Japan. It was a private record, but one would hardly think so when reading it, for there is nothing about it that is genuinely personal. It has more to say about administration than culture, and implies a greater concern with prisons than technology, except where the latter bore directly on his reason for coming to France. Nor did Shibata show any detectable enthusiasm for Paris or the French way of life, which was unusual among Japanese travellers. He did not like French food. Art and the theatre seem not to have appealed to him.

The diary of his attendant, Okada Setsuzō, a Kumamoto samurai who had studied in Nagasaki, then at Fukuzawa's school in Edo, has more to say, especially about the broader aspects of Japan's relationship with the outside world. Okada not only comments on the things he sees, but also records — how accurately we cannot tell — remarks made by the foreigners he met.

The memoirs of Fukuchi Genichirō, published in 1894, though brief, also throw light on the less official aspects of life in Paris. Attached to the mission as interpreter, Fukuchi did not have very much to do, since he knew no French and little spoken English. This left him a good deal of time to follow his own inclinations. These, apart from the theatre, were for various forms of self-improvement. He at one time had the idea of studying international law, but the scholars to whom Verny introduced him were adamant that neither his language skills nor his legal training was sufficient to make this possible. As an alternative, he turned to learning French and acquiring a wider range of information about western society and civilization. Not surprisingly, he found the rule which required members of the mission's staff to stay indoors in the evening, except on official occasions, an irksome one. For different reasons he was critical of Shibata's insistence that they all wear Japanese dress, to ensure that Japanese dignity be suitably maintained. Shibata he regarded as altogether too conservative and withdrawn.

The mission was at first lodged in Paris at the Hôtel du Louvre, where it was promptly visited by a number of Europeans, offering their services or seeking some profitable connection with Japan. The Comte des Cantons de Montblanc, a Belgian entrepreneur who had visited Yokohama in 1862, came with his Japanese assistant, Saitō Kenjirō, whom he had brought back to Europe on that occasion. He hoped to persuade Shibata to sign a treaty with Belgium, but was unsuccessful. Von Siebold, who had been waiting in Paris for several days before the mission arrived, bore plans for a trading company in Japan. These, too, were rejected. Another visitor was Léon de Rosny, who had spent so many hours with Matsuki and Fukuzawa in 1862. This time it was Fukuchi who saw him most, though he found him a difficult informant: de Rosny's spoken Japanese, he later wrote, was no more than 'thirty per cent understandable'.

On Verny's advice, the members of the mission eventually moved out of their hotel into a rented house. This was supposed to be in the interest of economy — Shibata's journal is full of notes about cost, even to recording the tips he gave — but it is not clear how much it saved, since the mission spent some of its time away from the city. Between 22 October and 6 November, for example, Shibata travelled in western France, visiting the naval dockyard and other facilities at Brest, the shipyard at L'Orient, an ironworks at Nantes, a small-arms factory in Chatellrault, and other such establishments in St Nazaire and Angoulême. He conscientiously recorded the facts about them in his journal, though one is sometimes left with the feeling that he lacked the technical knowledge to understand fully what he was shown.

On the question of trade, there were discussions with Fleury-Hérard about the possibility of including Japanese exhibits in the Paris Exposition of 1867. These gave rise to an embarrassing incident. There was by this time a Satsuma mission in Paris (see next section). Montblanc, who had found it more willing than that of the Bakufu to cooperate with his Belgian interests, made it his business to see the Shogun's representative, in order to persuade him that the Exposition should be open to exhibits sent by Satsuma, as well as Edo. Shibata, showing that this was offensive to him, at once broke off the discussion. Nor would he meet the Satsuma men, though some of his juniors did.

On 8 December the mission left Paris by a morning train and reached London the same evening. Installed in the new Langham Hotel, Shibata seems for the first time to have relaxed, perhaps because on this section of his travels his duties were to be less demanding. In the first few days, despite persistent fog, which made it necessary to keep the light on in his room whenever he wanted to work, he made time to revisit some of the places in London he had known in 1862. His official itinerary included many such places, too, possibly at his own suggestion: the offices of *The Times*, the Bank of England, the Royal Mint, Lloyds, the Royal Exchange, the Tower of London, Chelsea Hospital, the underground railway and the tunnel under the Thames, Westminster Abbey, the Houses of Parliament, and Millbank Penitentiary. No doubt these qualified as examples of western civilization, which he was supposed to study. At one point he noted in his diary the restrictions which Britain imposed on gypsies (part, no doubt, of what appears to have been a personal preoccupation with law and order). At the end of the mission's stay a day or two was devoted to the Horticultural Society and agricultural machinery.

The Foreign Office, having been told by the legation in Edo that the mission's main purpose was to inspect military and industrial installations, had arranged for Major F. Brine of the Royal Engineers to take charge of its programme. As a result, Brine took Shibata and his companions on a round of visits much like those already made in France: Woolwich Arsenal and Dockyard, the Ordnance Works at Greenwich, Portsmouth naval base — including the ironclad, HMS *Minotaur*, which, Shibata stated, was said by some to be a type of ship of questionable value — and Plymouth, including Devonport dockyard and the Saltash Bridge. Shibata and Okada both set down a plethora of statistics in their diaries, but do not seem to have made much effort beyond this to 'investigate'. One suspects that the whole operation was window-dressing in Japanese eyes, designed to obscure the fact that Edo was already committed to France for military and naval purchases.

In addition to the visits required by protocol, Brine took them one day to his club, the Army and Navy. Shibata wrote down a description of its various rooms, but admitted in his journal (18 December) that he was still 'not clear what a club is'. At Christmas, which was spent in Portsmouth, he declined the offer of tickets to the theatre or a ball, preferring to watch a party held for the servants in the hotel. The only other social occasion of note was the dinner he gave just before the mission departed, to thank all those who had entertained it or acted as escorts in London, Portsmouth and Plymouth. Fifty-three were invited, all men, of whom thirty-one came. The editor of *The Times*, though invited, was not one of those present.

Shibata no doubt improved his knowledge of the West by these proceedings, as did his companions, but their records give little indication of any conclusions that they may have drawn. Fukuchi learnt more about newspapers, which influenced his choice of future career. Okada became better informed about machines, including their application to agriculture. By contrast, on subjects like the operations of Parliament he offered no comment, beyond referring his readers to the writings of his teacher, Fukuzawa; while the general account of England, which he introduced into his text at the point of departure for France, was the familiar gazetteer-type entry, replete with facts, but unenlightening. His most interesting observations, which he put in an appendix, were attributed to foreigners. Their general tenor was that Japan could not trust western motives, even when countries like France and Britain vied with each other to offer military help; that promoting 'wealth and strength' was vital to Japan's survival, but would require better education for merchants and more respect for trade and industry on the part of government than had been evident so far; and that Satsuma's action in seeking independent relations with the powers was to be explained by Edo's own failure to act in the national interest. Such statements were so subversive by Tokugawa standards that Okada was plainly wise not to claim them as his own.

The return to Paris via Calais took place on 4 January 1866. It provided an opportunity to confirm the agreements made earlier and to give Verny power to hire staff for Yokosuka. Time was also made for a visit to the Bibliothèque Nationale, escorted by de Rosny and Montblanc. Two former Dutch representatives in Japan, Donker Curtius and De Wit, paid a call, offering their services, should the Tokugawa wish to make purchases in Holland. They left empty-handed. None of this took very long. On 15 January the mission set out for home, taken first by Verny to the great coal and iron complex at Le Creusot, then on to Lyon and Marseille. They reached Yokohama on 20 March, bringing with them the first engineers and machinery for Yokosuka.

As far as can be ascertained, no report was ever submitted about how Japan might be 'changed and improved' as a result of Shibata's travels, but unlike previous envoys to the West, he had the satisfaction of knowing that what he had done contributed to a series of innovations in Tokugawa policy. By July 1866 Verny was installed at Yokosuka with about forty French staff. He started building the first dock in the following May. Though still unfinished, the project was taken over by the Meiji government when the Tokugawa were overthrown at the beginning of 1868 and continued under Verny's supervision for another six years. The French connection with it continued intermittently until 1890.

The question of military training missions to Japan had also been raised by Shibata during his talks in Paris and London. London had reacted without enthusiasm. Paris eventually agreed — its hand was to some extent forced by the promises Roches had made to the Bakufu — but did not give the arrangements much priority. It was November 1866 before negotiations ended, early 1867 before a group of five officers and ten other ranks, commanded by Captain Charles Chanoine, arrived in Japan. By the end of that year they were engaged in training an infantry battalion, five artillery batteries, a company of sappers and a handful of cavalry. Although this operation, too, was brought to a halt by the political crisis in the winter of 1867 – 8, the relationship was resumed with the new regime after a suitable interval. Six army officers and ten other ranks arrived from France in May 1872, providing an element of French-style raining for the Meiji army, which continued at various levels until 1880.

The provision of naval training, which came up for discussion at about the same time, caused a degree of rivalry between France and Britain, or at least between their respective ministers in Japan. Early in 1866 French officers began to give instruction aboard a Japanese warship, newly purchased from America, but when Roches was made aware that this, coupled with the proposals he had already made for a French army mission, was likely to damage relations with Britain, he had the men withdrawn. At his suggestion, the Bakufu then sought British help. Sir Harry Parkes, the new British minister, who had arrived in June 1865, supported the idea, but London, like Paris, was not to be hurried, with the result that it was March 1867 before a naval party was despatched from England, October before it reached Japan. Instruction for seventy students began in late November at a naval school in Edo. Again, the venture was halted by the outbreak of civil war in 1868, only to be resumed at a later date, that is, on a small scale in 1870, on a larger one in 1873.

Although military reform was undoubtedly a Japanese priority, as Shibata's mission demonstrates, the parallel political proposals made by Roches held a promise of something more far-reaching, had they been acted on in full. He put them in person to the new Shogun, Keiki (Yoshinobu) — the former Hitotsubashi Keiki, Tokugawa Nariaki's son — who succeeded Iemochi at the end of 1866. In what seems very like the tradition of late-Tokugawa radical thought, stemming from such writers as Honda Toshiaki and Satō Nobuhiro, Roches recommended a package of measures designed to strengthen the Japanese government against its enemies at home and provide a better foundation for economic relations with the outside world: creating specialist departments of government; removing the status barriers which prevented the promotion of able men; making tax revenue less dependent on feudal dues; and introducing a realistic salary system for officials. In addition to all this, the money raised by the joint trading venture with France, he said, supplemented, perhaps, by a foreign loan, should be invested in economic development, which would involve railway-building (Edo to Yokohama), mining (especially in the northern island of Hokkaido), shipbuilding, and coastal shipping. In this way, a broader base could be established for 'wealth and strength'.

The Bakufu did not accept the whole of these ideas by any means. Leaving aside the fact that they were suspect, as coming from a foreigner, they were also unwelcome because, it was feared, they might do as much to undermine the loyalty of the Shogun's vassals as to strengthen the central power. Nor did those in high places in Edo, who had not themselves travelled overseas, have enough knowledge of the West to be aware of all the implications of this kind of 'wealth and strength'. It was therefore left to their successors to take up such policies once the Tokugawa had been overthrown; and that they were both able and willing to do so was in no small measure due to the Satsuma men who went to Europe in 1865.

SATSUMA AND ECONOMIC OPPORTUNITY

The Shibata mission had been a new kind of venture for Japan: modest in size and manner; headed by a single official; pursuing precise and limited objectives. It did not in the event, despite what Shibata and the council had told the British chargé, involve an attempt to assess the nature of 'western civilization'. There were to be others like it in the late Tokugawa years, one to Russia, one to the United States. Of these, only the second could be said to have added anything useful to Japanese knowledge of the West. It was headed by Ono Tomogorō, the naval engineer, who was sent to Washington in 1867 to settle the arrangements concerning payment and delivery for a warship Japan had ordered some years earlier; and although the American minister in Japan made it sound rather more like Shibata's mission — Ono and those who were to go with him, he told the State Department, counted on seeing 'navy yards, arsenals, foundries, machine shops, etc.' and 'learning as much as possible' on their three months' tour[7] — this proved over-optimistic. The naval officers attached to the party, it is true, visited various establishments of professional interest, but Ono did not raise his eyes very far from his financial brief. As far as we know, he only went beyond it in two respects: in permitting Fukuzawa Yukichi, one of his two interpreters, to study the public school system in Washington, and in contracting for a consignment of American school textbooks, dictionaries and similar works to be shipped to Japan for use in the country's English-language schools. The second of these steps, according to Fukuzawa — whose relations with Ono were far from good — was only taken in the belief that the Bakufu might turn a profit on the deal.

The mission which Satsuma sent to Europe in 1865 was of a different kind. For one thing, it was illegal. Tokugawa laws still at that time made travel overseas by Japanese subjects an offence, punishable by death, unless it was undertaken with the Bakufu's permission. A few men had defied them, usually with the connivance of foreign visitors — Masuda Kōsai, who had fled to Russia with Putiatin, and Saitō Kenjirō, Montblanc's assistant, for example — while others had been sent secretly as students by their lords (see Chapter 7); but what distinguishes Satsuma's action was that it was part of a calculated policy by the domain, aimed at securing weapons and industrial technology, perhaps foreign political support, as well as setting in train a more thorough study of the West.

In the aftermath of the Kagoshima bombardment there were two reactions to the event among Satsuma samurai. One was local pride, deriving from a belief that the domain had held its own in a contest with Britain (Japanese historians still call it the Anglo-Satsuma War). The other was a recognition that more needed to be done to develop Satsuma's military and naval strength before it could offer full-scale resistance to the West. As one step in that direction, an institute was founded in 1864, which was not unlike Edo's Kaiseisho, or Institute of Development, and was given the same name. Of its five departments of western studies, one dealt with naval and land artillery, military training, and fortifications; another with navigation and the associated fields of astronomy, mathematics and geography; a third with engineering and shipbuilding. The remaining two covered the natural sciences and medicine, both with a bias towards the practical. Students were given financial support by the domain. They were also encouraged to pursue their studies elsewhere in Japan, wherever better facilities could be found.

Underlying the policy was a belief that the Bakufu, having failed to come to the help of Satsuma and Choshu against the foreigner in 1863 and 1864, had surrendered its claim to lead Japan against the West. It followed, as men in Kagoshima saw it, that Satsuma must look to its own efforts for salvation, not only for itself, but for the country as a whole. The argument was given a particular slant in the summer of 1864 by Godai Tomoatsu, a samurai of modest rank, who had been sent to Nagasaki in 1857 at the age of twenty-two as one of the domain's nominees to the Bakufu naval training school, and had spent the greater part of the next six years there in various capacities before being recalled, like others, to take part in the action against the British squadron in 1863. At that time he tried, but failed, to persuade his superiors to compromise with Britain; was made prisoner, along with his colleague, Matsuki Kōan, in a cutting-out operation by the British forces; and was taken to Yokohama, where the two men were released. They felt it wiser at this point to go to earth for a while, for fear of reprisals from anti-foreign radicals. As a result, it was not until the beginning of 1864 that Godai made his way back to Nagasaki, travelling in secrecy, using a false name, and claiming to be a Bakufu retainer.

His experience in Nagasaki over the years undoubtedly helped to shape Godai's approach to Satsuma policy. In the early summer of 1862 he had contrived to ship as seaman in a vessel the Bakufu sent to investigate the prospects for Japanese trade with Shanghai, spending two months there. This chance to see at first hand the results of western encroachment in China convinced him of the immense importance of commerce as a factor in national power. It was reinforced by his contacts in Nagasaki with the Scottish merchant, Thomas Glover, in whose house he took refuge after he returned to that port in 1864. Glover's advice, in fact, can be detected at a number of points in the proposals which Godai put to his domain's officials later in the year.

They were incorporated in a long memorandum, which began by stating that in a world committed wholeheartedly to international trade the anti-foreign movement in Japan, by attacking the treaties, risked bringing down upon the country the same fate that India and China had already suffered.[8] To avert it, Godai recommended, Satsuma should take the initiative in opening direct trade with Shanghai. Japanese tea, silk and seafood products had long had a market there, deriving from centuries of contact through Chinese junks. The opportunity now existed, he believed, by selling Ryukyu sugar more actively in Japan, to raise the funds to buy Japanese rice and other goods for the China market, so expanding the range of these exports. Some of the proceeds of the sales would have to be used to set up a western-style sugar-refining plant in Ryukyu, if the plan was to be fully successful. Similarly, western machinery for cotton-spinning, mining and agricultural improvement should be introduced in the rest of Satsuma. On an economic base enlarged by measures of this kind, the domain could then go on to build up a dominant position in the Japanese coasting trade, using steamers bought from abroad.

This ambitious programme was carefully costed, which was presumably Glover's work. The figures showed that when all was done there would remain at Satsuma's disposal substantial annual sums, which could be used to acquire western military equipment: steam warships, complete with Armstrong guns; more heavy-calibre guns for coast defence; Minie rifles. The list no doubt reflects the knowledge brought back by Matsuki from Europe in 1862, since the two men had ample opportunity to discuss such things during the weeks they spent in captivity and in hiding in the second half of 1863. Matsuki may also have been the source of Godai's other proposal, that a mission be sent to Europe, spending several months there, during which it would investigate and, if possible, purchase the weapons and machinery Satsuma required. Its members would be able while on their travels to examine such institutions and technology as might be useful to Japan in the longer term: military affairs, geography and customs (which would require nine men, representing different ranks and opinions within the Satsuma samurai class); heavy artillery, rifles and fortifications (two of the domain's gunnery experts); agriculture (one local government official); schools, hospitals and poorhouses (one representative from the domain school). To these should be added three mechanics and draftsmen, who would prepare sketches of machinery and learn to handle it. In addition, the mission should take with it some twenty students, who could spend several years abroad, acquiring a more extensive knowledge of military and naval science, astronomy, geography and the manufacture of chemicals (including gunpowder) than a visiting mission as such could hope to obtain.

There were some changes of emphasis when these ideas were discussed by senior officials. The scope of the investigation of western society and civilization became narrower and the number of men to be engaged in it was reduced. A diplomatic component was added, designed to win British support for the proposition that Japan's great domains, like Satsuma, were entitled to a voice in the making of national policy, as well as to engage in foreign trade on their own account. Fewer students were to be sent than Godai had wished. Nevertheless, the substance of the scheme proved acceptable.

In the closing weeks of 1864 and the first few weeks of 1865 appointments were announced. Matsuki was ordered back from Edo to join Godai in Nagasaki, his role being that of investigator and interpreter, with a particular responsibility for diplomatic matters. Godai was to handle economic questions. Niiro Gyōbu, an upper samurai, holding one of the domain's highest offices, was put in command of the mission as a whole. Machida Hisanari, a man of similar standing, was given charge of a group of fourteen students, chosen partly from distinguished samurai families, partly from those enrolled at the Kagoshima Kaiseisho. Two others completed the party: Hori Takayuki, an interpreter from Nagasaki, and Ryle Holme, a young member of Glover's company, who was to escort them to Britain and provide introductions.

Because the operation was illegal, it had to be conducted with the utmost discretion. All those who were going took assumed names. If captured, they agreed, they would deny any official involvement by the domain. Once this was settled, Matsuki, Godai, Hori and Holme sailed secretly from Nagasaki on 15 April 1865 in one of the steamers for which Glover was agent; called at Hashima, a small port on the west coast of Satsuma, to pick up the rest of the party; then set out on the regular passenger route via Hong Kong and Singapore to Suez. From Alexandria they went by sea to Southampton, thence by train to London, which was reached on 21 June. At this point, members of the mission, except those who would be returning soon to Japan, had their hair cut short in the western manner.

Niiro, Godai and Hori took rooms at the Langham Hotel, while Machida and Matsuki settled in at another hotel in Queen's Gate Terrace, closer to the students, who were dispersed in private homes to begin their studies. Laurence Oliphant, once Elgin's secretary, now a Member of Parliament for a Scottish constituency, to whom they had a letter of introduction from Glover, took Niiro and his senior colleagues to see the permanent officials at the Foreign Office, to whom they explained their purpose in coming to England. Partly, they said — in what by this time must have been a familiar formula in Whitehall — it was 'to see the institutions, habits and manufactures' of Britain and other parts of Europe, in the hope that their own country 'in time may become like England'.[9] Partly it was to ask for British pressure to be put on the Bakufu, in order to enable the great lords to engage in foreign trade. The argument seems not to have been immediately persuasive. It was not until the death of Palmerston brought back Russell as Prime Minister and Clarendon as Foreign Secretary that their political aspirations found a more sympathetic hearing. In three meetings with Clarendon in March and April of 1866 Matsuki was allowed to develop the point that the Bakufu's 'selfish' policies with respect to trade, shutting out the domains, might well be thought to be in breach of treaty. This would justify the powers in lending their support to the demands being made by many Japanese for a restoration of the emperor's authority. Once that had been achieved, he claimed, the emperor would publicly approve the treaties and the clamour against them would die down. Clarendon was sufficiently impressed to ask his minister in Japan, Harry Parkes, to explore the possibilities.

More important for our present purposes is what Godai was doing in the intervening months. His programme, carried out as a rule in the company of Niiro and Hori, sometimes attended by a number of the students, began — under Foreign Office auspices — by taking in a selection of military and industrial establishments in Britain. In July, in response to a request from the Foreign Office that the Satsuma representatives be allowed to see 'the testing and practice of big guns and the manufacture of gunpowder', visits were arranged to Woolwich Arsenal, the artillery practice grounds at Shoeburyness, and the Royal Gunpowder Factory at Waltham Abbey. A few days later a group went to the Britannia Ironworks at Bedford, where steam-ploughs and reaping-machines were made. According to *The Times* (2 August), the Satsuma men took great delight in riding on the steam-ploughs. Two tours (August and December) were made to centres outside London, including Manchester and Birmingham. Nor was this mere sightseeing. Orders were placed for cotton-spinning machinery and for rifles and ammunition, books were bought for the Kagoshima library. All were shipped to Kagoshima under Glover's supervision.

In London Godai was approached by the Comte de Montblanc through

7. Godai Tomoatsu of Satsuma (*centre*), photographed in London in 1865 with his interpreter (Hori Takayuki) and his British escort (Ryle Holme of Thomas Glover's firm in Nagasaki). Unlike the Bakufu's representatives abroad, the Satsuma men adopted western dress (as did most Japanese students, when they were permitted to do so).

his Japanese assistant, Saitō Kenjirō, with the offer of a Belgian treaty and an economic partnership, much like that which had been made to Shibata in Paris earlier in the year. There is no evidence that any agreement was reached on this occasion, but when Niiro and Godai extended their travels to continental Europe in September, their first call was at Ostend. Montblanc met them and took them to his home at Ingelmunster for a day or two, after which there were talks with officials from the Foreign Ministry in Brussels. These led to an understanding (24 September) about a future treaty with Belgium and the first outline of a commercial agreement with Montblanc, which was embodied in a formal text and signed on 15 October. Saitō served as French translator. Two Belgians with unspecified government connections acted as witnesses.

Under this agreement Montblanc was to set up a company which would have a monopoly of Satsuma's European trade.[10] In return for rights to exploit local mineral deposits, it would act as an agent in procuring warships and guns, as well as the machinery required to develop a cotton-spinning industry and to improve existing methods of producing tea and wax. Accountants were to be appointed at each plant where the machinery was employed, in order to ensure proper control of receipts and expenditure; profit and loss were to be equally shared; and when the returns reached twice the amount of the initial capital investment, ownership of the plant would pass to Satsuma. In addition, while Satsuma undertook to open a port or ports in the Ryukyu islands, Montblanc promised that Japanese religious preferences would be respected — that is, that no attempt would be made to propagate Christianity — and that opium would not be brought to Japan.

Given the political risks which Satsuma ran in making such an arrangement, both from the Bakufu and from the powers, one is bound to ask, what did Godai see as its countervailing benefits? For an answer we can most usefully turn to the letters he sent home,[11] in which he spelt out a view of the relationship between 'wealth' (*fukoku*) and 'strength' (*kyōhei*) that was to become well-nigh axiomatic among Japanese officials after 1868. In Europe, he wrote in one of them, 'the power of the state rests on two foundations, industry and commerce'. By virtue of these a country could 'achieve military might'. Trade could be left to merchants. It was therefore to the growth of industry that Japan's leaders should give their minds: concluding treaties, setting up companies, sending exhibits to industrial expositions abroad, inviting foreign experts to Japan. Yet none of this would serve unless there was also a drive to consolidate national unity. A Japan which 'knows nothing of the world', like the frog in a well, and 'wastes time in domestic disputes', would inevitably be at risk from foreign powers. With Russia to the north, France and Britain to the west, America to the east, the country could not afford to ignore such dangers. The great lords must therefore be brought to work together — he envisaged something on the lines of the German Confederation — under the suzerainty of the emperor, so ensuring a sound political base. What is more, court nobles and feudal lords should travel abroad, that they might see for themselves the nature of the task before them. As in the case of some members of the Satsuma mission, who had been anti-foreign activists when they left Japan, experience would bring them round to his own understanding of things. There must also be changes to increase military and administrative competence by the promotion of men of ability, regardless of inherited status, and measures to create the kind of 'equitable and benevolent government' that would make the people prosperous and content. He saw a place for hospitals, poorhouses, orphanages, asylums, prisons and schools in such an undertaking, but he made no mention of parliaments.

Some of these statements, though probably not the economic ones, almost certainly reflected the influence of Matsuki Kōan. They also owed something to what Godai observed on his travels in Belgium, Holland,

Germany and France. In Liège he was taken to factories making munitions, railway locomotives, and paper; elsewhere in Belgium to a sugar
refinery, botanical gardens, the battlefield of Waterloo, a hospital, a
poorhouse and an orphanage (which he much admired). He was
impressed by the iron bridge over the Rhine at Cologne (22 October) and
the manifest efficiency of the Prussian army, took an interest in land
drainage and pumping equipment in Amsterdam (27 October), bought
books in the Hague. In Antwerp and Ghent he saw machines to polish
rice and make candles, both of which he thought would be useful in
Japan. During a long stay in Paris (12 November to 19 December) there
were visits to the theatre and a newspaper office with Montblanc, some
'idle conversation' with Léon de Rosny, a good deal of casual sightseeing,
often on foot. Industrial expeditions in France seem to have been few,
mostly to factories making porcelain and tobacco. In one of his letters,
however, there were comments on the French navy and French government, for which his diary offers no obvious foundation, so it may not
have recorded all he did in these five weeks. There was also some contact
with the junior members of Shibata's mission. Shibata's own refusal to
meet the Satsuma men, he thought, betrayed the low standards Edo
maintained in choosing the men it sent to represent it overseas. More
seriously, the task Shibata had been ordered to perform betrayed — in its
preoccupation with weaponry — a quite unsustainable belief that
'strength' could be achieved without 'wealth'.

Back in England again, where Godai expressed his delight that the
Langham Hotel flew the Japanese flag in the Satsuma mission's honour,
there was time for another two weeks in the industrial north and the
confirmation of several purchasing agreements before returning to Paris
in February 1866. Here there were further meetings with Montblanc,
tidying up a number of points about the joint company. Not least, Godai
expanded the list of things it might do. Montblanc was commissioned to
use Satsuma's share of the anticipated profits to buy a steam warship of
1,850 tons, armed with four large Armstrong guns, mounted in twin
turrets. It was described as being similar to those ordered from
Birkenhead by the South in the American Civil War. As if this were not
a sufficient drain on Satsuma resources, long-term plans were discussed
for such projects as a railway and telegraph linking Osaka with Kyoto, the
development of canals in Osaka, and a munitions plant in Kagoshima.

Niiro, Godai and Hori sailed from Marseille on 11 February 1866,
reaching Kagoshima on 25 April. Machida and Matsuki, who had briefly
joined them in Paris, returned to London, where Machida was to remain
in charge of the students until 1867. Early in May, having completed his
talks with Clarendon, Matsuki in his turn set off for home, taking with
him one of the students who had failed to settle down in London. They
left Marseille on 12 May for Shanghai, where they took passage in a

sailing ship for Nagasaki, reaching Kagoshima on 6 July. A few weeks later Matsuki changed his family name to Terashima, apparently to dissociate himself as far as possible from the days when he had served the Tokugawa in the Bansho Shirabesho.

In marked contrast to the way in which the Bakufu treated many of its envoys, Satsuma's representatives were all promoted for what they had done. Niiro became the senior official (Rōjū) in charge of foreign affairs. Godai was made a commissioner (Bugyō) with financial and trade responsibilities, covering not only the new Belgian company, but also trade with the rest of Japan. Matsuki/Terashima was appointed professor at the Satsuma Kaiseisho. The agreements Godai had made with Montblanc were approved and the plans for cotton-spinning and sugar-refining put into practice. The first party of technicians from Platt Brothers in Oldham arrived in December 1866, a second, together with the machinery, about two months later. By June 1867 the cotton mill had been completed and was beginning operations under its British technicians, employing two hundred workers. It continued in existence under various owners until 1897. The sugar-refining project was less successful, however. Four sites were chosen on one of the islands south of Satsuma; machinery, ordered both from Britain and Holland, was installed by the end of 1867; but opposition from the local population (the traditional sugar-producers), plus damage from a typhoon, prevented successful development. The plants were closed and the machinery sold towards the end of 1869.

Neither scheme, it must be said, made any great contribution to Satsuma's finances. Nor was there much by way of weaponry to show for it all, certainly not on the scale Godai had discussed in Paris. Indeed, during 1867 the Satsuma authorities began to draw aloof from Montblanc. One reason was that as its quarrels with Edo grew fiercer, the domain became less inclined to devote its funds to longer-term ambitions. Another was suspicion of Montblanc's apparent links with France, which was widely seen as an ally of the Tokugawa. To this the Satsuma students in London, perhaps prompted by Oliphant, added a warning about the international dangers inherent in the kind of agreements Godai had made. They had become convinced, they said, that 'the things to be learnt from the West are few in number, those to be avoided many'. Britain, it was clear, had 'cast off all morality in her pursuit of selfish interests', but Satsuma must also beware of France, for the danger always existed that a French fleet might be sent to intervene on Montblanc's behalf if disagreements arose.[12] It was unfortunate timing on the latter's part that he set out from Europe in August 1867, only a week or two after this letter was written, taking with him on his planned visit to Japan two army officers, two naval officers, two mining experts and two merchants, all of whom were French. The Kagoshima officials tried to head him off at Shanghai; and when he arrived, despite this, on 3 December, they refused to have anything to do with his plans, apart from accepting delivery of 5,000 rifles. It began to look as if Godai's arrangements with Montblanc, like the Bakufu's with France, were to have less immediate impact on events than their sponsors might have hoped.

THE PARIS EXPOSITION

When the possibility of Japanese participation in the Paris Exposition had been raised by the French with Shibata in 1865, he had made no firm commitment, but Niiro and Godai, to whom the matter was put shortly afterwards, said that Satsuma would wish to be included. This prompted Edo to circulate the other great domains to see whether any wished to take part as well. Only Hizen (Saga) replied in the affirmative. Satsuma, meanwhile, went ahead with the preparation of its exhibits. At the end of 1866 some four hundred cases of tea, sugar, porcelain, lacquerware and textiles, plus products from Ryukyu, were shipped from Nagasaki under the direction of the French consul there.

Kagoshima appointed one of its senior officials, Iwashita Masahira, to represent it at the exposition, partly because his status would underline the domain's claim to independence in the eyes of European powers, partly because he would have the authority to confirm orders of weapons through Montblanc. With nine others, including Ryle Holme, he arrived in Paris on 6 February 1867. His first step was to ask that the Satsuma exhibits, which he described as coming from the ruler of Ryukyu, be kept apart from those sent by the Bakufu and Hizen. This request the French commissioner, Baron Ferdinand de Lesseps, promptly granted, despite Bakufu protests. There followed a propaganda battle in the Paris press, conducted by Montblanc for Satsuma and Fleury-Hérard for Edo, concerning the political status of Shogun and daimyo, respectively.

Satsuma's actions persuaded Edo to take the exposition more seriously than it had at first seemed likely to do. On 25 January it announced that it would send a mission of its own, which was to be both larger and higher-ranking than that of Satsuma. It was headed — nominally — by the Shogun's younger brother, Tokugawa Akitake. Though only fourteen years old, he had the rank to be received as a full ambassador by Napoleon III, however little he might have by way of diplomatic duties. His entourage was to include several experienced officials, whose task it would be to cement the Bakufu's close relations with France on the foundations already laid by Roches. One of these, Mukōyama Ichiri, was not strictly part of Akitake's retinue at all, since he was to be Japan's resident minister in France. Another, Tanabe Taichi, a member of the foreign department of the Bakufu, had first been to France with Ikeda in 1864. A third was Shibusawa Ei'ichi, who was to be majordomo to the young prince, mostly on account of his financial expertise. A man of commoner origins, rewarded with samurai status for his services to the Tokugawa house, Shibusawa was to spend a good deal of his time with the banker Fleury-Hérard, acquiring some of the skills which were to make him Japan's outstanding entrepreneur in the later years of the century.

The Bakufu party, which was over twenty strong — in addition to the officials, their attendants, two interpreters and a doctor, Akitake had an escort of seven samurai from Mito, who seem to have been chosen for their unrelenting lack of enthusiasm for the West — left Yokohama on 16 February 1867 and reached Paris on 11 April. Once there, while the officials argued over Satsuma's standing, the prince-ambassador became involved in a round of entertainment and ceremonial. There was a formal audience at the Tuileries on 28 April. There was a race meeting at Longchamp, attended by Napoleon III, Tsar Alexander II, the King and Queen of Belgium, and the Prince Royal of Prussia. In such august company, according to the *Illustrated London News* (22 June), Akitake 'said nothing to anybody, and nobody said anything to him'. On other occasions he attended the opera, an imperial reception, a military review, saw the Arc de Triomphe and Versailles, and made several visits to the exposition.

There was a second motive for sending the Shogun's younger brother to France: to ensure that he obtained some experience of western ways and a western-style education. For this reason it was intended that Akitake make a tour of European countries once his duties at the opening of the exposition had been performed, then return to France for a further five years, undergoing instruction. This part of the plan caused a certain amount of friction. The Jesuit Mermet de Cachon, now back in Paris, was probably the only Frenchman well enough qualified in Japanese to play an active part in the prince's schooling. As Roches's former interpreter he was an obvious choice on political grounds. On the other hand, the Confucian-trained officials of Akitake's household, especially his tutor, Yamataka Nobuo, took exception to the idea that a boy who might be a future ruler of Japan should be subject to the influence of Christianity. Their objections were reinforced by the suspicions which the proposal aroused in London.

Our most detailed source of information about the ensuing arguments — not an unbiassed one — is the correspondence of Alexander von Siebold with Edmund Hammond of the British Foreign Office.[13] Alexander, the son of Philipp Franz von Siebold, had been employed since 1862 as an interpreter to the British legation in Japan, a post in which he had displayed much greater fluency in spoken Japanese than any of his fellows. He had also established good personal relations with a number of Bakufu officials, like his father before him. As a result, when the mission to Paris was being planned, he was asked whether he would be free to go with it as Akitake's interpreter. Sir Harry Parkes, anticipating diplomatic benefits, promptly gave him leave of absence for this purpose, thereby ensuring that Akitake and his entourage were accompanied on all their travels by a young man, speaking excellent Japanese, who reported regularly to London.

From Paris he wrote on 19 May that having established himself on terms of intimacy with Mukōyama and Yamataka, the two most influential members of the mission, he knew that they would oppose the introduction of any religious element into the boy's education. They were also troubled by French recognition of Satsuma's claims with regard to the exposition, as well as by the fact that Japan's allocation of space was unsatisfactory: 'a few spots here and there . . . divided by China and Siam'. All in all, their reception had not lived up to what Roches had led them to expect. They had found that 'little notice is taken of them by the French', while the army officer whom Napoleon III had appointed to be the prince's mentor had shown himself overbearing. Some months later Akitake, too, was moved to complain, saying he would much rather go to England, or back to Japan, than be 'sold to France'. Von Siebold was persuaded (letter of 19 November) that 'there is no longer any cause for apprehension that he will be made a Frenchman in ideas and inclinations'.

On 2 September most of the Bakufu party left Paris to begin a tour of Switzerland, Holland and Belgium, which was to include much state ceremony and many visits to military establishments. Akitake was shown the new breech-loading rifle which was to be issued to the Swiss army. The Dutch, von Siebold reported, 'took every means to flatter the Japanese vanity'. The Belgians behaved 'pretty well in the same manner'. There were royal audiences, dinners, receptions, opera performances. In Brussels there was a fireworks display, at which the tightrope-walker Blondin performed, while Antwerp and Liège showed off their military industries. It was all much more satisfying than France, where the presence of so many senior members of royalty had put the young Japanese prince — whose claim to such a title was in any case suspect — very much in the shade.

On 17 October, following another week in Paris, Akitake and his entourage set out for Italy. This proved to be an experience of a quite different kind. The royal invitations were mostly private ones, because of political unrest: a small ceremony to bestow orders and decorations, a shooting party in Milan, a battue of deer at the royal shooting grounds in Florence. Sightseeing included art galleries in Florence and the leaning tower of Pisa. Industry was represented by the making of mosaics.

Florence was as far south in Italy as they had planned to go, but at this point arrangements were completed for an extension of the tour to Malta under British auspices. Von Siebold had suggested the idea to Hammond on 11 October as 'a cheap and easy opportunity' to offer Akitake some civilities, in order to counteract 'the evil insinuations of the French'. Hammond had recommended it to the Colonial Office in similar terms, asking that the young man be treated as 'a quasi-royal personage' on political grounds, that is, because the French 'are seeking to make him think less of England and more of France than it is desirable for our interests in the East that he should do'.[14] The outcome was a British warship put at the Japanese party's disposal for the voyage from Livorno, full military honours on arrival in the island, military parades, inspections of the fortifications, ceremonial visits to warships in the harbour. Akitake and his suite were housed in a wing of the governor's palace. Altogether, von Siebold wrote (19 November), their reception 'entirely dispersed the unfavourable opinion which the Japanese had formed by French influence'.

Although there was not quite so much display for the visit to England itself, which began on 2 December, the mission was shown more public consideration than had seemed likely during early discussions. It was accommodated at Claridge's Hotel at government expense, and given a major of the Royal Engineers to act as escort, as Shibata had been. Hammond at one time expressed the hope that the Japanese might go to Manchester, Birmingham and Liverpool, because they would 'get more knowledge of the wealth and power of England by a visit to those places than any length of stay in London would give them',[15] but it soon became clear that this was not to Akitake's taste — as von Siebold put it, 'military matters and armaments' were 'the only thing he seems really to care for' (25 November) — so the industrial cities were omitted from the programme. The prince was received privately by Queen Victoria at Windsor on 4 December, but as a rule he avoided official receptions and dinners when he could. Major Bevan Edwards, his escort, told Hammond that he did not show any interest in 'many things that Asiatics generally like to see', such as theatres.[16] For all that, he was taken, like it or not, on the familiar round (Parliament, the Tower, Crystal Palace, the Bank of England, the Royal Mint, the offices of *The Times*), though the part of his itinerary which had a military flavour (Aldershot, Portsmouth and the establishments along the lower reaches of the Thames) clearly gave him more pleasure. Some of it, indeed, also had a political lesson to teach. After a practice firing of 300-pounder guns at Shoeburyness, von Siebold heard Mukōyama say to the prince that Japan 'must give up all idea of ever making war with these foreigners'.

The visit was a short one, lasting only two weeks. We shall never know what its long-term consequences might have been, for soon after the

8. Tokugawa Akitake at Portsmouth Dockyard, 1867.

mission returned to Paris came the news of the fall of the Tokugawa. Plans for visits to Prussia and Russia in the spring of 1868 had to be cancelled. Those for Akitake's education were abandoned. All this meant that a good deal of effort, both in France and Britain, had been wasted, but at least an example had been set in Japan of sending men of rank abroad to acquire a knowledge of the world. Japan's next government proved willing to follow it on a more liberal scale.

7

The First Japanese Students Overseas, 1862–1868

In the discussions about Japan's response to the West which took place during negotiation of the treaties, many of those who supported the idea of entering into trade relations with the powers also recognized the importance of sending men abroad to study. After all, if Japan was to succeed in maintaining her independence in the face of the threat the treaties posed, she would need both to know more about international relations, as the rest of the world conceived them, and to import western weapons and technology. The first of these objectives involved a knowledge of western law, government and commerce. The second, if military imports were to be put to effective use, required the possession of specialist skills, which Japan's own scholars were not in a position to teach. Neither kind of expertise could be acquired in the few weeks or months an envoy would be able to spend abroad.

The Shogun's government in Edo accepted the logic of these arguments. In 1862, seeking to extend the work begun by Dutch instructors at Nagasaki (Chapter 3), it sent a party of students to Holland, mostly for naval studies. In later years, others were sent to Russia, France and Britain. The emphasis was military; but as official awareness of the nature of western civilization grew, partly because of the experience gained by the Bakufu missions we have been discussing, so there came a recognition that this emphasis should not be a narrow one.

The practice of sending students overseas was also taken up by authorities other than the Bakufu. Twelve of the domains ordered or permitted men to go abroad before 1868. Two of them, Choshu and Satsuma, sent as many as thirty-seven between them.

The total number of those who went in these years remains uncertain. Early estimates put it as low as 92, but Ishizuki Minoru (1972) gave it as 153, whom he listed. The nature of the records, which makes it difficult to be sure in some cases about identities and dates, led Inuzuka Takaaki (1987) to eliminate some of those in Ishizuki's list, reducing his own to 128. This number will be taken as the basis for the present chapter. It includes 57 sent by the Bakufu, of whom 53 were Tokugawa retainers, directly or indirectly (the other 4 being samurai from domains, attached at the request of their lords). Of the 71 others, 2 who went without the permission of their feudal superiors count technically as 'private' students. The other 69 went on the orders of their lords, or at least with their approval. Most received some kind of official grant towards their expenses.

The destinations of these Japanese students were much more varied than those of Asian students from European colonies, who were expected to go to the appropriate metropolitan country. Britain, France and Holland received most of those from Japan in the early years, though the United States became more popular towards the end of the decade. All were samurai, apart from six artisans, whom Edo sent to Holland for technical training in 1862, but they differed widely in rank within the samurai class. Women do not appear in the lists at all before 1868.

Many of the men were older than one would nowadays expect from the use of the word 'student' to describe them (and are made to seem a little more so by the nature of the records, which, in accordance with Japanese custom, treat age as being one in the calendar year of birth, two from the following New Year, and so on, thereby adding anything from a few days to more than a year to a person's age by western standards). We have no information about age for a considerable number, but where it does exist it indicates that the first groups to go were older than the later ones: the Bakufu men sent in 1862–4 averaged about thirty years of age (and included two who were over forty), whereas those going in 1865–7 averaged no more than twenty (in a range which included four over thirty and one as young as twelve). The Choshu and Satsuma students who left Japan between 1863 and 1867 conform more closely to the second pattern than the first, that is, an average of a little more than twenty-two, with three over thirty and five under sixteen. Representatives from other domains were much the same.

It is not easy to generalize about how long students stayed abroad. One or two died on their travels, a few returned home after a year or less, either for personal reasons, or because they were unsuccessful in their studies, but a good many were away long enough to acquire a basic training in some specialist field, or even a formal qualification. Although the overthrow of the Tokugawa in 1867–8 distorts the figures in this respect, because it resulted in some students being recalled, or finding themselves too short of funds to continue, it remains true that in the period as a whole seventeen from the Bakufu and twenty-six others spent more than four years out of Japan. This is a third of the total. A further twenty-one, or one-sixth, were away between two and four years. What could be achieved in that time, of course, depended in part on the education they had had before setting out. In most cases this was minimal by western academic standards, so students usually had to have a spell of preliminary training in schools or from private teachers before they could enter college (if they ever got that far). Even so, when we come to consider their later careers (Chapter 10), it will be apparent that no matter what disadvantages this entailed, those who went before 1868 included a remarkable proportion of men who achieved distinction later in life.

BAKUFU STUDENTS

Proposals from various quarters within Japan for students to be sent overseas, made against the background of Perry's arrival, crystallized at the end of 1856 in a Bakufu plan to send twenty or thirty men to Holland, chiefly in order to learn naval skills. The idea temporarily dropped from sight during the foreign and domestic crises of 1858, but it surfaced again in 1860–1 in a modified form, that is, to send students to America, first, in connection with the 1860 mission (eventually set aside in favour of sending the *Kanrin Maru* on a training cruise to San Francisco), then as part of a package for the purchase of warships (frustrated by the outbreak of the American Civil War). When it became clear that none of this would serve, Edo turned once more to the Dutch. Discussions at Nagasaki with the new Dutch representative, De Wit, led to an order for three warships being given to the Netherlands Trading Company on 10 April 1862. Supplementary to it was an agreement for a party of naval officers and engineers to go to Holland to learn to handle them.

The first students were named next day. They included five graduates from the Nagasaki naval school, four of whom were to specialize in engineering, gunnery, navigation and shipbuilding, respectively, while one — the most senior, Uchida Masao, aged thirty-five — was to train for executive duties. Taguchi Yoshinao, a former student of medicine, now aged forty-five, was the oldest; Enomoto Takeaki, aged twenty-seven, was to prove the most famous. The two others were Sawa Sadatoki, who had studied gunnery under Egawa, and Akamatsu Noriyoshi, a prospective naval constructor. Both were in their twenties. When their training was completed, these officers were expected to bring back to Japan the first of the ships built to Bakufu order.

Joining them were two members of the Bansho Shirabesho, Nishi Amane, a samurai from Tsuwano, and Tsuda Mamichi, who came from Tsuyama, both aged thirty-three. As specialists in western studies they had the task of acquiring a knowledge of law, government and economics, so taking one step further the investigation of institutions begun by the 1862 mission. Itō Gempaku (aged thirty) and Hayashi Kenkai (aged eighteen), formerly of the Nagasaki medical school, were attached to the party with a view to extending their competence into the field of military medicine. Itō was the adopted son of Itō Gemboku, one of the best-known of Japan's Dutch scholars. Hayashi was the son of a Bakufu doctor and nephew to Matsumoto Ryōjun, Pompe van Meerdervoort's senior assistant (Chapter 3).

These higher-ranking members of the group were accompanied by six seamen and artisans, ranging in age from twenty-eight to forty-three, who were expected to become the first ship's petty officers. Two were seamanship ratings: Furukawa Shōya. who was in charge of the rest, and Yamashita Iwakichi. Both were fishermen from an island in Sanuki province. Of the others, Nakashima Kenkichi had had experience as a gunnery technician in Echigo; Ōno Yazaburō, son of an employee at the Bakufu observatory, had until recently been responsible for surveying instruments in a domain in Echizen; and Ueda Torakichi, whose family were shipwrights in the Izu peninsula, had turned his traditional skills to the building of western-style ships, first to help the Russians build a schooner in 1854, when Putiatin's flagship was wrecked by a tidal wave at Shimoda, then in the Bakufu's service at Nagasaki. About the sixth man, Ōkawa Kitarō, a blacksmith, little is known, except that he drank himself to death in Holland.

The students left Nagasaki in a Dutch ship at the beginning of November 1862, reaching Batavia on 9 December. There they had to wait two weeks for a passage to Holland, living meanwhile in a western-style hotel, which was a new experience. Like their compatriots in America two years earlier, they enthused about ice cream and the use of ice in drinks. The long voyage which followed — round the Cape of Good Hope and up the coast of Africa — gave them time to become accustomed to shipboard routine, plus some much-needed language practice, but very little else, as far as one can judge. Rotterdam was reached at the beginning of June 1863. Soon after, discussions at the Hague with the Navy Minister, Huyssen van Kattendijke, who had commanded the second Dutch naval training contingent at Nagasaki, decided how their studies were to be organized. The two doctors were put under the supervision of Pompe van Meerdervoort, now recalled from Japan, and later transferred to the navy's medical school; the five naval officers — wearing western dress on van Kattendijke's recommendation, despite Bakufu orders to the contrary — were established in the Hague with private instructors in their different specialist fields, all living separately in rented rooms, in order to discourage them from speaking Japanese; while Tsuda, Nishi and the six artisans settled down in Leiden, studying Dutch under Professor Hoffmann, who had earlier been in attendance on the Takenouchi mission.

Once this preliminary stage was over, Tsuda and Nishi began instruction under Simon Vissering, a teacher of economics at Leiden University (who was later to be Finance Minister). Every week for the next two years he gave them private tutorials on law, economics and statistics on Thursday and Friday evenings. The artisans scattered to various institutions appropriate to their needs: Furukawa and Yamashita to a seamanship school, where they shared a dormitory with Dutch trainees for a while; Ōkawa and Nakashima to an iron foundry; Ōno to a clockmakers where he worked on marine chronometers. In December 1863 Furukawa, Yamashita and the shipwright, Ueda, joined Akamatsu at Dordrecht, where he was gaining practical experience of ship construction at the yard building the first of the Bakufu's ships (later named *Kaiyō Maru*). Its keel had been laid two months earlier. Akamatsu was transferred to the naval dockyard at Amsterdam in the middle of 1864, followed by Ueda, Ōno and Nakashima, but the seamen, Furukawa and Yamashita, remained in Dordrecht until the *Kaiyō Maru* was completed. She sailed for Japan in December 1866. Nine of the Japanese (four officers and five petty officers) went with her as passengers, leaving the two doctors and Akamatsu in Holland. Nishi and Tsuda had been ordered home a year before, taking with them their notes of Vissering's lectures, which they later turned into books. They arrived in Yokohama on 13 February 1866. Akamatsu came back on his own in the spring of 1868.

Nishi and Tsuda seem to have led a frugal and rather narrow life in Leiden, pursuing their studies, but making no apparent effort to see anything more of Holland or the rest of Europe. On the other hand, though there is no indication that they enrolled in the university, they were certainly exposed to some of the main currents in contemporary European thought. Vissering explained to them the theories of Adam Smith, while the philosophy lectures of C. W. Opzoomer — attended at Nishi's insistence, because, as he said in a letter home, western philosophy could help 'to advance our civilization'[1] — gave them a knowledge of the positivism of Auguste Comte and the utilitarian ideas of Bentham and John Stuart Mill. This made them the first Japanese to understand the principal intellectual foundations of the industrial society which they and their compatriots had come to study.

The naval members of the group had a different kind of experience of the West. The artisans had great social difficulties, no doubt because their Dutch was never very good, but they all acquired skills which stood them in good stead later in life (see Chapter 10). Of the officers, Uchida is said to have taken his seniority too seriously to be popular. He held aloof from convivial drinking, spent much of his time painting and sketching, and eventually abandoned the navy as a career. Itō and Hayashi always lived apart from the rest because they were in medical school. Despite Pompe's training in Japan, they found professional competence a distant goal, remaining in the Hague until some months after the fall of the Tokugawa, then coming back to Europe later to continue their studies (in 1870 and 1873, repectively). Sawa, the gunnery specialist, qualified in addition as an explosives expert. Late in 1865 he was summoned to Paris for a few days to advise Shibata on Bakufu plans for a gunpowder factory. Back in Holland, he consulted one of his Dutch colleagues about the relative merits of French, British and German production methods; was referred to Belgium (with an introduction from van Kattendijke) to see the royal ordnance factory there; and after some discussion was allowed to spend several weeks, in November and December, living as a member of its staff. The outcome was an order for much of the equipment the Bakufu required, which was shipped to Japan towards the end of 1866.

Enomoto, as a naval engineer — though his subsequent career was to be more concerned with politics and diplomacy — was also used as a Bakufu consultant while in Europe. In June 1864 he was ordered to France with Uchida to inspect a steel warship, recently launched at Toulon, which Ikeda Nagaaki had been told could be made available to Japan. Later in that year he went to Britain for a month with Uchida and Akamatsu, visiting shipyards, mines and engineering factories. In much the same way, Akamatsu — who lived part of the time with a Dutch teacher's family in Dordrecht, where he became a member of a local officers' club — was adviser about Japanese ship purchases after the others left Holland in the *Kaiyō Maru*. For example, when Hizen sent a representative in 1867, in order to buy a ship like the *Kaiyō Maru*, Akamatsu, who had known him at the Nagasaki naval school, put him up in his own lodgings for several months and acted as his interpreter in talks with the Dordrecht yard.

There can be little doubt that these extracurricular activities, especially where they involved large expenditure in European countries, or the prospect of it, helped to ensure the Japanese students a friendly reception. So did their curiosity value. They were sometimes asked to wear Japanese dress and the two swords of the samurai at parties or receptions, because of the interest these aroused. On at least one occasion they had to leave a theatre because the audience showed itself more inclined to watch them than the play.

Being exotic also brought benefits in other ways, not least because of exaggerated western assumptions about their personal rank. For example, at the end of February 1864 Enomoto and Akamatsu arranged to travel with two Dutch officers to see what they could of the fighting in the Schleswig-Holstein war. Wearing Japanese dress and swords for the occasion, they had no difficulty in securing passports from the Prussian and Danish ministers at the Hague, then from the Austrian minister in Brussels. This done, they took train for Berlin. From Berlin they went to Hamburg, presenting their credentials to the Dutch consul, who helped them to secure a carriage for the short journey to Altona, crossing the Elbe on the ice. The Austrian military commander received them courteously, but as the fighting had already ended in his sector they moved on to see the Prussian operations along the Danish frontier (where they were invited to share the tent of Prinz Karl). Withdrawing to Hamburg again, they next took ship from Lübeck to Copenhagen. This time their introductions conjured up a Danish colonel to take them on a tour of the front on the Danish side. To the twentieth-century mind, all this seems a little more than the normal politeness to be extended to visiting officers. What is more, having seen Krupp's new breech-loading field gun in action, Enomoto and Akamatsu decided to visit the Krupp factory at Essen on their way back to Holland; and although, when they got there, it was explained to them that inspection of the plant was not permitted, because of security requirements in time of war, they were nevertheless invited to lunch with Alfred Krupp (conversing, we are told, in simple German).

In view of Japan's long-standing Dutch connection, it is not surprising that the students who went to Holland were singled out for special attention by their hosts. They also had the advantage of being able to complete several years of study before the Tokugawa were overthrown. Others were less fortunate in both respects. Certainly few can have been more dissatisfied with their lot than those who were sent to Russia in 1865. The proposal that they should go had come both from Shibata Takenaka, when governor at Hakodate, and from the Russian consul there, Iosif Goshkevich, a Chinese scholar, who was critical of the Russian language teaching he had observed in Edo. Their aims were modest: to ensure a supply of competent interpreters, in the hope of preventing avoidable conflicts in the north. The Bakufu agreed – with some reluctance — in the spring of 1865, but at the instigation of the Kaiseisho (the former Bansho Shirabesho) it elaborated the plan, requiring the students to seek a wider knowledge of European society and culture. To this end the Russian government was asked to arrange for them to enter university in St Petersburg.

As leader of the party Edo named Yamanouchi Sakuzaemon, aged thirty, a member of the Hakodate governor's staff. The five others to accompany him were students in the more conventional sense of the word: one, aged fifteen, from Hakodate; and four, aged from thirteen to twenty-two, from the Kaiseisho, where they had been learning Dutch, French, English or German. They embarked at Hakodate in a Russian warship in the late summer of 1865, accompanied by Goshkevich, who had been provided by the Bakufu with funds for their expenses; and they sailed directly to St Petersburg via the Cape of Good Hope, arriving there a little over six months later, while winter still had Russia in its grip. It was not a good beginning. The students themselves, encouraged by the Kaiseisho, wanted to study such subjects as chemistry, mining, mechanical engineering and medicine; but they did not know enough Russian for this, still less to qualify as interpreters, as Hakodate had in mind, so they were installed in a house where they could have private language lessons from a visiting teacher. Their pleas to be allowed to go to school, in order to improve their conversation skills, were ignored by Goshkevich, whom the Bakufu had put in charge of them. By the time Mori Arinori, a Satsuma student from London, met them in August 1866, they were thoroughly dissatisfied. No-one came to Russia to learn, they told him, because such knowledge as the Russians possessed was borrowed from somewhere else. The language was difficult and of no use outside Russia. The climate was intolerable.[2]

Yamanouchi, convinced that the whole operation was a waste of money, made illness an excuse to return to Japan at the end of 1866. The others stayed on, though we know nothing of their subsequent life in Russia, not even whether they ever attended school. They were ordered home, like other Bakufu students, at the beginning of 1868 (except one, Ichikawa Bunkichi, who managed to remain in St Petersburg for another ten years with Russian help).

Much the same complaints about the way their education was handled were made by Bakufu students in England in 1866 and 1867. After discussions with Roches and Parkes about military and naval missions for Japan in 1865–6 (Chapter 6), Edo had decided that it would be tactful to send students to England for naval training, in order to compensate for the choice of French officers to instruct the Tokugawa army. London, informed by Parkes early in 1866, approved in principle. It sent back for its representative's information a memorandum, dated 21 March, setting out the arrangements which had been made for Turkish and Egyptian students coming under official auspices. This was by implication to be a model for Japan. Parkes took it very seriously, including its concern that someone must take responsibility for the men's behaviour and education while they were in Britain (paid by the country sending them). In November, reporting to the Foreign Office that fourteen students were to be sent, he recommended that the Rev. William Lloyd, chaplain and naval instructor in HMS *Scylla*, who was being invalided home after three years in the China squadron, be appointed to undertake this duty.[3] The Bakufu, he said, had already agreed that Mr Lloyd be in charge of the students on their voyage to England. It was willing, subject to Foreign Office approval, that he should continue in that capacity after their arrival. The students would be 'entirely amenable' to his authority; the sum of £ 5,000 had been lodged with the Oriental Bank to take care of their initial expenses.

In an enclosure to this letter Lloyd set out his own ideas on what should be done. Eventually, he said, the students should be enrolled at London University, either at King's College or University College, as the Foreign Office might decide. First, however, they would need to matriculate in Latin, English and mathematics. For this reason it was desirable that they should begin by improving their English under the guidance of a private tutor, who would have them 'under his own eye and roof'. Then they could be entered at either King's College School or University College School, depending on which college was chosen for them, though they would still need to be provided with accommodation, preferably in the care of someone who would also arrange visits to 'the many military, naval, manufacturing and other institutions within easy reach of London'. Were Lloyd himself to take on this responsibility, as he was willing to do, he estimated that the cost of board and lodging in a convenient part of London, plus clothing, medical attention, books and paper, would probably amount to £250 per annum for each student. Travel expenses would be additional to this. A Foreign Office minute commented that the terms seemed high, but that the duties would no doubt be 'onerous'. It also recommended the choice of University College, rather than King's, because students from Satsuma were already there.

The two senior students, who were to exercise a measure of discipline over the rest, had already been selected by the Bakufu before Parkes wrote to London. One was Kawaji Tarō, aged twenty-three, grandson of Kawaji Toshiaki, who had been one of Hotta's foreign policy advisers in the 1850s. The other was Nakamura Masanao (Kei'u), aged thirty-five, a Confucian scholar who had taken up Dutch and English in order to study those aspects of western society which he thought had been too often neglected in Japan, because of a preoccupation with the military and the material. By this he meant ethics, politics and law, the things with which a Confucian should concern himself. He had volunteered to go to England to pursue these interests, though there is a hint that Edo's reasons for accepting him were rather that he might impose some restraint on Kawaji's westernizing enthusiasms, while putting up barriers against the corruption of the younger students by unsuitable western ideas. The twelve others who were to accompany these two men ranged in age from twelve to twenty-two. They were selected after a simple — and in the event not very reliable — test of their knowledge of English. Most were related to Bakufu officials or Kaiseisho scholars, as were Kawaji and Nakamura. There were, for example, two members of the Mitsukuri family, which had produced 'Dutch' experts for several generations. One of them, under his later name Kikuchi Dairoku, came back to England in 1874 to take a degree at Cambridge. Another was Fukuzawa Yukichi's younger brother, Einosuke.

The party gathered at Yokohama on 28 November 1866, staying at the French language school. On 1 December, accompanied by Lloyd, they sailed for Shanghai aboard an English ship, travelling first class; changed ships there for the passage to Hong Kong, then again in Hong Kong and in Ceylon on the way to Egypt (an unusually complicated journey). Four days in Cairo provided an opportunity to learn about the building of the

Suez Canal before they left Alexandria on 21 January 1867. Southampton was reached on 2 February . Lloyd had given English lessons while at sea, but he later reported that not much progress had been made as a result.

After a spell in a London hotel, which gave *The Times* (5 February) a chance to comment that in dress, manners and appearance the Japanese 'differ very little from Englishmen', Lloyd acquired a house in Lancaster Gate, to which they all moved on a snowy day in early March. Here they settled down to a routine: morning English lessons under a visiting teacher, followed on most days by walks for exercise in the afternoon. They had to be back by 5 p.m. Breaches of rules, including this one, were punished by fines. By the summer their English was good enough for physics and chemistry to be added to the curriculum, the working day being extended to include evening sessions; but like their compatriots in St Petersburg, the students became restless under this regime, arguing that they would make faster progress, especially in the spoken language, if they could live on their own. They were also impatient to get to grips with the subjects they had really come to study, which were mostly military and technological. Lloyd resisted the demand for separate lodgings on the grounds of cost, but eventually gave way to the extent of giving ten of them (excluding Kawaji, Nakamura and the two youngest) the funds to find somewhere to live for themselves, though he still required them to come to his house for lessons. At the same time, he asked the Foreign Office to get a formal ruling from Edo that decisions of this kind were for him alone to take. When this in due course was done, he promptly required all the students to come and live with him once again in Lancaster Gate.

His action provoked great indignation. Indeed, those affected by it appealed against the decision to the Foreign Secretary, Lord Stanley, on 11 November, attributing Lloyd's actions — not unreasonably, on the face of it — to the profit he made from feeding and housing them. They also complained about the arrangements for their education. From the beginning of the autumn term, except for Kawaji and Nakamura, who were presumably thought to be too old, they had been enrolled at University College School to prepare for university entrance. Here they found to their disappointment that they were still to receive no training in specialized subjects. This was not what they had come for, they told Lord Stanley: 'we want to master thoroughly particular arts and sciences', not 'to be called an educated man'.[4] Lloyd, when consulted, objected that they were not yet ready to specialize. Stanley opted out. A decision, he said, would have to be made by the senior Japanese officials in Europe, those who were in Paris with Tokugawa Akitake (Chapter 6). It had still not been received when news came of the political crisis in Japan, followed a few weeks later by orders for the students in London to make their way to Paris on the first stage of their journey home. Similar orders went to those in Russia and Holland.

In Paris there was another contingent of Bakufu students, whose studies were brief and not at all well documented. Five had accompanied Tokugawa Akitake when he left Japan in February 1867. A further nine had joined them six months later. Two of Akitake's entourage also remained with him to study in Paris, once his diplomatic duties were completed. Of the first five, two were Tokugawa retainers, two were from Aizu (the domain of a Tokugawa collateral house), and one was from the vassal domain of Karatsu (the son of its daimyo held high office in Edo). Most of the second batch were from families of some standing in Edo officialdom. They differed widely in age: three fourteen- or fifteen-year-olds, including Akitake; two who were over thirty; but seven whose ages are not recorded at all. In the last few months of 1867 they seem to have spent most of their time improving their French, either in Akitake's Paris household under the supervision of a visiting teacher, or at a school run by Mermet de Cachon.

When all Bakufu students in Europe were told to return to Japan after the Shogun's fall, no exceptions were made. An appeal to let Akitake stay longer was refused. A move by Harry Parkes, the British minister in Edo, to allow those in London to complete their training was also turned down. All were in any case soon running out of funds, forced to borrow money where they could to support themselves, so they had little choice but to do as they were told. Even so, it was not until August of 1868 that they reached Yokohama, via Paris and Marseille. By that time the regime they had served was history.

DOMAIN STUDENTS

The students sent to Europe by the Bakufu in the 1860s were expected to acquire the kind of knowledge which would be of value to Japan in its confrontation with the West. Those sent by feudal lords had similar objectives, except that in some cases their motives were partisan as well as patriotic. That is to say, distrusting Edo, or seeing themselves as rivals of the Tokugawa, daimyo chose to seek access to the sources of western strength on their own account, sending parties of students abroad from their domains. Despite the fact that this was at first an illegal activity, there was no shortage of loyal and ambitious samurai willing to undertake it, notably from Satsuma and Choshu. Later, after travel ceased to be illegal in 1866, growing numbers also came from other parts of Japan, including a few who set out on their own initiative. These went in large part to the United States, or combined a visit to America with their journey to or from Europe, a choice often made because Americans in the treaty ports were willing to provide advice and introductions, or because access to American education was more readily available. By contrast, most of those who went in earlier years had gone, unlike their contemporaries from the Bakufu, to Britain. None went to Russia.

The first group to go illegally was that which went from Choshu to Britain in 1863. Although anti-foreign feeling was very strong in Choshu, it was tempered in this particular context by the example which Yoshida Shōin had given, and by his teaching that study overseas was a way in which samurai might learn the skills required to defend their country. Inoue Kaoru, one of those who persuaded his lord to let him go to London in 1863, had been a student of Yoshida Shōin. His companion, Itō Hirobumi, expressed a sentiment Shōin would undoubtedly have approved when he described their purpose as being 'to become living weapons of war'.[5] Experience was to modify these attitudes, but there is no doubt that patriotism in this form was a bond widely shared by Japanese students who travelled abroad in the late Tokugawa years.

Several strands came together to bring the Choshu venture into being. The domain's officials, like those of Hizen, had already shown a willingness to encourage their samurai to study the West and its technology, attaching one to the mission to America in 1860, another to the mission to Europe in 1862. Two more were allowed to join a Bakufu voyage from Hakodate to Nikolaevsk in 1861, another, Takasugi Shinsaku, to serve in a Bakufu ship which went to Shanghai at that time (as did Godai Tomoatsu of Satsuma, it will be recalled). All this tended to create a favourable climate of opinion for Inoue Kaoru's proposal, made in December 1862, that he should go to Britain to study, with a view to laying the foundations of a modern navy for the domain. As the plan was at first conceived, it was envisaged that two others should go with him — Yamao Kenzō and Nomura Yakichi (later known as Inoue Masaru), both of whom had made the voyage to Nikolaevsk — but Itō Hirobumi and Endō Kinsuke were later added at their own request. After some hesitation the scheme was approved, the men were granted five years leave of absence from their duties, and funds were set aside for their expenses while overseas. This was in June 1863.

The detailed arrangements had to be secret, in order to keep them from the knowledge of the Bakufu, but they were nevertheless made in Edo and Yokohama — where the Shogun's spies were thickest on the ground — because this was where Choshu had contact with foreigners. As soon as Inoue and his colleagues gathered there, a cautious approach was made to James Gower, the Yokohama representative of the British firm Jardine Matheson, through whom the domain had bought a ship in 1862. Gower saw no objection in principle to the plan, but introduced a quite unexpected obstacle by estimating that the cost (for passage, maintenance and academic fees) would be perhaps five times as much as had been made available so far; and it was not until Choshu officials in Edo agreed to set aside funds, designated originally for the purchase of arms, to finance a merchant loan for overseas study, that the full amount could be paid. Departure was then as surreptitious as the discussions had been. On 27 June the students boarded a Jardine's steamer after dark in Yokohama, bound for Shanghai. They hid in the coal bunker until the ship was well at sea.

It soon became clear that in the matter of language skills, at least, the young men were not well equipped for their task, despite the fact that Nomura had studied English for a while at Hakodate. On arrival in Shanghai they were interviewed by William Keswick, the head of the Jardine's establishment there. Asked what they wanted to learn in England, Inoue Kaoru, using one of his few English words, replied 'navigation', a term which he understood in a naval context, like most of his fellow-countrymen.[6] Keswick, unfortunately, took him to mean that they wanted to be merchant navy officers, with the result that he arranged for their onward travel to London in two of Jardine's vessels (Inoue and Itō in one; Nomura, Endō and Yamao in another), serving as crew for the sake of gaining practical experience. Inoue's account of the voyage that followed is one of unremitting gloom.Their quarters were uncomfortable, the food unpalatable; they were required to perform hard manual labour in difficult weather conditions; they suffered from seasickness and diarrhoea, Itō so severely that Inoue had to tie him in place at the ship's side — the only toilet available to crew — because he was so weakened by it. Neither knew enough English to be able to insist that they had paid to travel as passengers. London, which they reached on 4 November — there being no intermediate ports of call — therefore came as a profound relief, even though the first thing Itō did was lose his way while trying to find them food in the neighbourhood of the docks, when the captain and the crew all vanished, leaving them to their own devices.

After that, things began to improve. A messenger appeared and took them to a small hotel in the City, where they found Nomura, Endō and Yamao already installed, having had a faster passage. Hugh Matheson, head of one of Jardine Matheson's parent companies, arranged for them to enter University College London, though not until they had improved their English (they had studied the language as best they could with the help of crew members while at sea, with results one hesitates to assess). To help them, they were installed in Gower Street in the houses of two teachers from the college, Inoue and Yamao in one, the rest in another, studying with the help of a dictionary they had brought from the Bansho Shirabesho, supplemented by questions to the families of their hosts. They made a series of visits to museums, factories and dockyards, while making themselves familiar with as much as possible of London life.

This was all that Inoue and Itō were to achieve. By the spring of 1864 they were able with occasional help to read the daily newspaper, from which they learnt one day of Choshu's dispute with the powers — the closing of the Shimonoseki Straits had been almost simultaneous with their own departure from Japan — and of the action which foreign governments were planning as a result. The information alarmed them greatly , for the one conclusion they had inescapably reached on their travels was that an armed conflict with the West in Japan's existing state of unpreparedness would be courting disaster. Indeed, Inoue had written a letter along these lines to his superiors in Choshu as early as their arrival in Shanghai. Together with Itō, he now decided to return at once to Japan to see if there was something they could do to avert calamity. Since a steamship fare, they found, would leave their colleagues in London short of funds, they had no choice but sail, so although they left London in the middle of April, it was July when they reached Yokohama (via the Cape of Good Hope and Shanghai). This was just in time for them to try to mediate — unsuccessfully — between their domain and the foreign representatives.

Their three companions who remained in London, believing, they said, that this was their greater obligation, were in due course able to take up the study of science and industry at University College under the supervision of Dr Alexander Williamson, Professor of Chemistry and Practical Chemistry. Endō returned to Japan in 1866, but the other two stayed until the summer of 1868, when Nomura received his course certificate (Yamao having moved to Glasgow in 1866, to work at Napier's shipyard during the day and take evening classes at the university). In the meantime these two had been joined by other students from Choshu. There were three who came in the summer of 1865, one of whom died in 1866, supposedly of undernourishment. Four more arrived in the summer of 1867. By then the programme was proving difficult to finance, so two of these, who belonged to high-ranking samurai families, travelled at their own expense. The youngest went to school in Aberdeen before starting his training in London. Apart from these, Choshu sent one student to Holland and two to the United States in 1867, all, like those sent to London in that year, ostensibly to pursue naval or military studies. The later arrivals did not go back to Japan until various dates between 1871 and 1874.

The students whom Satsuma sent to England in 1865 (see Chapter 6), though they, too, went illegally, did so in circumstances which had more in common with those enjoyed by Bakufu than Choshu samurai. That is to say, they were official nominees, rather than simple volunteers, travelled under the auspices of a quasi-diplomatic mission, and were at all times under the supervision of an official of the domain. The plan had a long history. In 1857 the then daimyo, Shimazu Nariakira, had considered sending Satsuma samurai overseas — described as 'Ryukyuans' — to study medicine, gunnery, shipbuilding and navigation, as well as foreign languages. The idea had lapsed because of his untimely death in 1858, but Godai Tomoatsu had revived it when putting forward his proposals for economic development in 1864, this time in a more elaborate form. For example, he wanted to add agriculture and education to the subjects to be studied. He also recommended that those who were chosen to go should comprise a cross-section of the domain's elite, including not only able students with appropriate previous training, but also men of good birth, whose future careers in office would benefit from knowing something of the West.

These recommendations were broadly followed when decisions were being made about the composition of the party in the winter of 1864–5. Matsuki and Godai, who were to have the main responsibility for negotiations in Europe, were men of modest samurai rank, but Niiro Gyōbu, who was in overall charge, and Machida Hisanari, who was to be left in England to supervise the students, both held senior posts in the domain administration and the personal status qualifying for them. Three others, Hatakeyama Yoshinari, Murahashi Nao'ei and Nagoshi Tokunari, all aged between twenty and twenty-five, were also upper samurai. Twelve more were selected from the Satsuma school of western studies (Kaiseisho), seven being students of Dutch and five of English. All but one were under twenty-five, the youngest only thirteen. Among them were three who were to hold important offices in Japan's central government after 1868: Mori Arinori, Samejima Hisanobu and Yoshida Kiyonari.

During the voyage to London in the spring of 1865 the students acquired a rudimentary knowledge of western-style living, which made things easier for them when they arrived in London on 21 June. They were met by Thomas Glover's brother, James, who put them in a house in Bayswater. The youngest, Nagasawa Kanaye, being too young to enter college, was soon sent off to school in Aberdeen, which was the Glover family's home. Two others went to Paris to study medicine early in 1866. The rest were expected to enter University College London in October of that year, having spent the interval improving their English and preparing to matriculate; but the arrangements for working as a group in Bayswater proved less than satisfactory for this purpose, so in August they were sent in pairs to live and study at the homes of several teachers from the college, much as the Choshu students had been. They spent quite a lot of time with the three remaining Choshu students, Nomura, Endō and Yamao, to whom James Glover and Ryle Holme introduced them.

At this stage decisions were taken about future subjects of specialization: military and naval studies for the higher-ranking; English language and literature for Samejima; various aspects of science and engineering for the rest. This was to take the long view, however. In the shorter term they had to concentrate on mathematics and general science, while acquiring a background knowledge of British industry and society. As long as Matsuki and Godai remained in England, pursuing their official business, this was done by taking part in their visits to hospitals and factories and military establishments. Later the students developed interests of their own. Yoshida, for example, devoted much of his attention to the workings of Parliament, becoming in the process an admirer of Gladstone.

Their explorations were not confined to Britain. In the summer of 1866 Laurence Oliphant, who had acted as go-between for Matsuki in his talks with the Foreign Office, took Yoshida and Samejima on a visit to the United States. One of Machida's younger brothers — there were two of them with the party — was a guest of the Comte de Montblanc in Belgium. Hatakeyama visited France. Mori and Matsumura Junzō, more adventurous, made their way to St Petersburg, shipping as apprentice deckhands on a collier from Newcastle to Kronstadt (though they took the regular mail-packet for their journey back). Despite their very modest form of outward travel, once in St Petersburg the two moved in more exalted circles: a courtesy call on the Foreign Ministry; a visit to the British ambassador's summer villa; a meeting with Putiatin. Some of their time they spent with the six Bakufu students in the city, by whom they were warned of all the disadvantages of studying in Russia. These presumably did not surprise them. According to one of Mori's letters to his brother in Kagoshima, they had been told before they left England (apparently by Oliphant) that Russia was 'just a cold country, not a powerful one'.[7]

The students did not stay in England as long as some of them would have wished. Those who remained in London — apart from the two who had gone to France, one went back to Japan with Matsuki in May 1866 — began to find it more and more difficult to support themselves, as Satsuma devoted the greater part of its resources to its rivalry with Edo, cutting its budget for education overseas. In May 1867 Machida decided to go home, taking with him his two brothers and four others. The other six, who included Mori, Yoshida and Samejima, were thrown a lifeline by Oliphant, who offered to pay for their travels as far as the eastern United States, where he was intending to join a religious community founded on Lake Erie by Thomas Lake Harris. They accepted, though not entirely from religious conviction. Oliphant resigned his seat in Parliament and left for America in July, the six Japanese following in August. All went at first to Lake Erie. Nagasawa was in fact to remain a member of the Harris community for the rest of his life, but the others had a number of disagreements with Harris early in 1868, as a result of which they broke away. Mori and Samejima went home, sailing from New York via Panama in June. Yoshida, Hatakeyama and Matsumura continued their education in the United States, the first at Wilbraham Academy, the second at Rutgers College, the third at Annapolis. They returned separately to Japan on various dates between the beginning of 1871 and the end of 1873. Like many other students from Japan, they were therefore out of the country in the months of political crisis and civil war.

Satsuma, like Choshu, continued to send students abroad in the Bakufu's last two years, though as a result of decisions taken at the end of 1865 most of these went to America, not Europe (perhaps for reasons of cost). Of a total of nine in 1866–7, eight went to America and one to Britain. In addition, two of those who accompanied Iwashita to the Paris Exposition in 1867 were listed as students, though they do not appear to have been financed by the domain (one of them was Iwashita's son, the other Niiro Gyōbu's).

Few other feudal lords were willing to evade or challenge the Shogun's regulations in the same way as Satsuma and Choshu. Two men from Hizen (Saga) and one from Aki (Hiroshima) were sent to Britain in 1865 to study naval engineering. Higo (Kumamoto) paid for two nephews of one of its samurai advisers to study in America in the first half of 1866, one of whom entered Rutgers, the other Annapolis. In reality, what Higo did was a matter of giving retrospective approval to action the two brothers had taken on their own account, helped by an American missionary, Guido Verbeck, who was teaching in Nagasaki. After the fall of the Tokugawa both were accepted as official students by the new central government, but only the one at Annapolis stayed long enough — over seven years — to complete his training.

The situation changed during the second half of 1866, when pressure from the powers, seeking to widen their range of contacts with Japan, brought a review of Bakufu policy. In May, Edo announced that freedom of travel would be permitted for visits to countries having treaties with Japan, subject to the receipt of applications, accompanied by a certificate of approval from the relevant daimyo or local official. It was to include details of purpose and destination. The concession was slightly extended when it was incorporated into the tariff convention signed on 25 June, which provided (Article X) that Japanese 'may travel to any foreign country for purposes of study or trade'. Once a form of passport had been worked out to give effect to this, several domains took advantage of the opportunity. Between the middle of 1866 and the end of 1867 Chikuzen (Fukuoka) sent six students to the United States and two (to undertake medical studies) to Holland and Germany; Sendai in northeast Japan sent four to America; Kaga (Kanazawa) on the Japan Sea coast sent three to Britain. In other words, the area of recruitment was extended to cover most regions of Japan, as well as domains which were less politically active, while the United States emerged as a favoured destination.

When such students went with the encouragement and support of their feudal superiors their experience did not differ greatly from that of the ones we have been describing. They usually had contacts with western merchants or missionaries, who were able to arrange facilities and educational advice; they had sufficient funds at their disposal to make life tolerable, if not comfortable; and they were likely to meet other Japanese in the cities to which they travelled, providing a measure of companionship. This did not apply to everyone, however. There were a minority who made their own way abroad, either without the approval of their domains, or under only nominal supervision by them. For these, both comfort and the opportunities for study were more likely to depend on luck.

Practical considerations of cost and access made it likely that men of this kind would find their way to the United States, as many shipwrecked seamen had done before them. Niijima Jō was one of the fortunate ones. Son of a low-ranking samurai in one of the smaller domains, he began his career as a clerk in the domain's Edo office at the time when the ports were being opened. Having learnt a little Dutch, he made up his mind to go abroad to study, travelling first by sea to Hakodate, where he managed to support himself by teaching Japanese to a priest of the Orthodox Church, then, in the summer of 1864, working his passage to Shanghai on an American ship. He found employment during the next nine months in various capacities on the China coast, before finding the captain of another American ship, *Wild Rover*, who was willing to take him to America as cabin boy. In Boston he found a job as a watchman in the docks. However, when he explained that he had come to America to seek an education, his employer, the *Wild Rover*'s owner, arranged for him to go to school. From this time on his path was relatively smooth. Able and industrious, he moved from school to Rutgers College, graduating in 1870. In the following year the new Japanese government accorded him official sponsorship, so making it possible for him to continue his training, this time at Andover Theological Seminary. By the time the Iwakura embassy arrived in America in 1872 (see Chapter 9) Niijima was enough of an expert on American education to be used as an adviser on that subject, working with Tanaka Fujimaro, the mission's education commissioner, and going with him to Europe. He returned to Andover thereafter, completed his course, and went back to Japan in November 1874.

Takahashi Korekiyo was not so fortunate. In 1867, when he was thirteen, so his autobiography tells us, he took the decision to go overseas to study. Having learnt a little English by working as a houseboy in Yokohama — a choice which may have been at the root of his later misadventures — he made plans to sail as cabin boy in an English whaler, only to discover at the last moment that since he was by adoption a

Sendai retainer, he might qualify to join a group of students being sent abroad by that domain. This he succeeded in doing, setting out in company with Suzuki Tomo'o, a boy of his own age, and Tomita Tetsunosuke, a man of thirty-two. Because Suzuki and Takahashi were so young, Sendai officials arranged for an American merchant in Yokohama to take charge of them, paying him for their transport and education. He promised to place them with his parents in San Francisco.

There were problems from the start. One was that Takahashi found it impossible to buy western clothes to fit him in the treaty port, with the result that he put together an inelegant collection of odds and ends, including a pair of women's shoes. Then, when they went on board the ship which was to take them to San Francisco (August 1867), he and Suzuki found themselves in the steerage class, together with Chinese emigrants to the United States. They were much offended. They also suffered some hardship, though it was mitigated by the efforts of Japanese in the better accommodation, who smuggled food to them. San Francisco, when they reached it, proved confusing — like Itō in London , they began by getting lost — and not at all what they expected. Having at last made contact with the Yokohama merchant's family, they were provided with rooms, but were fed none too well and found that they were expected to do work about the house. No opportunity was provided for education, supposedly because schools were still closed for the summer.

Takahashi, who was the more determined of the two, eventually got himself transferred to another household, this time in Oakland, only to discover that there, too, he was treated as a servant, having in ignorance signed a contract to work three years for his hosts. Though he was kindly treated, there was still no school. He appears to have made himself a nuisance about all this, for he was soon offered a place in the home of a local customs officer instead. He refused, having by this time become wary of all such offers. As an alternative, he found himself a manual job at a shop selling tea and other Japanese products (well enough paid, it seems, to enable him to save some money, part of which he must have spent on clothes, for there is a photograph of him in his autobiography, taken at this time in San Francisco, in which he looks remarkably smart).

News of political events in Japan during the first few months of 1868, as reported in the San Francisco newspapers, persuaded Takahashi and another Sendai student, Ichijō Jūjirō, who was at college, that they ought to go home. They extracted Suzuki from the Yokohama merchant's family, with whom he had remained; used what was left of Ichijō's travel funds to book a passage for all three to Japan; and embarked towards the end of 1868, this time in the upper class. The voyage was uneventful, apart from a feud with a Chinese gentleman who had been given the other berth in their cabin, much to their disgust. They did their best to make him uncomfortable, in the hope that he would ask to move.

However, as the ship approached Yokohama in January 1869, they lost some of their confidence. They even threw their Tokugawa travel permits overboard, for fear these might prove to be an embarrassment in the new and unknown Japan that awaited them.

8

From Tokugawa to Meiji

Early in the morning of 3 January 1868 contingents of samurai from five of the largest domains, led by Satsuma, seized control of the palace gates in Kyoto. In the name of the newly-succeeded boy-emperor, Mutsuhito, whose reign-title was to be Meiji, an imperial council was summoned, to which only supporters of the coup were admitted; the office of Shogun was abolished, reducing the Tokugawa to the same standing as the other great feudal lords; and the country's central administration was put into the hands of the emperor's nominees. This is what is meant in the narrow political sense by the term 'restoration of imperial rule' (*ōsei-fukko*), or Meiji Restoration. The transfer of authority was subsequently confirmed by victory in civil war. Tokugawa forces in the vicinity of the capital were defeated within two or three weeks. Their supporters in north-east Japan surrendered in November after heavy fighting. A remnant, which held out in Hakodate under Enomoto Takeaki, was overcome in June 1869.

During these months it gradually emerged that the men who wielded the greatest influence in the new regime were not the daimyo under whose patronage it had been established, but a small number of middle-ranking samurai from the domains of Satsuma, Choshu, Tosa and Hizen in south and west Japan, working with a handful of nobles from the imperial court. The governmental offices which they initially created took over much of the institutional terminology of the prefeudal·past, when emperors were expected to rule as well as reign; but while this served well enough to signal a rejection of the Bakufu and its allies, it soon became clear that an administrative structure with eighth-century proce-dures would not meet nineteenth-century needs, whether political or economic. The changes that were contemplated as a result included, as might have been expected after the events of recent years, elements of western practice.

Two factors, in particular, encouraged this. One was that the Meiji government was the recipient of much unsolicited advice from western diplomats and missionaries in Japan, who took it for granted that the only path to progress was that of convergence with the norms of western life. The other stemmed from the fact that several Japanese who had travelled and studied in America and Europe before 1868 were now in positions of some responsibility. In these circumstances, during the first part of the Meiji emperor's reign a knowledge of the West became not just an instrument by which Japan could deal with issues of diplomacy, or acquire military and technological skills, but also a qualification for the drafting of reforms, that is, a key to promotion and power. The change was foreshadowed in government policy from the start. In a general statement of intent, issued in April 1868, which is known as the Charter Oath, it was stated, first, that 'Knowledge shall be sought throughout the world', then that 'Base customs of former times shall be abandoned'.[1]

WESTERN ADVICE AND JAPANESE BUREAUCRATS

There has been occasion to remark in previous chapters that western diplomats in Japan consistently urged the Bakufu to learn about the West by sending envoys and students overseas. One of their motives was the national self-interest of the countries they represented, of course: a desire to make Japanese officials better informed about commerce and diplomacy, as the rest of the world conceived them, and more aware of the risks they ran in flouting international norms. There was more to it than this, however. Almost all the foreigners whose work brought them to the treaty ports, especially the consuls and missionaries, thought of themselves as belonging to a 'higher' civilization, which it would be in Japan's interest to adopt. They argued not only that trade would bring prosperity, contributing in the long run to an improvement in welfare and stability, but also that the West possessed, in addition to advanced scientific concepts and technology, a superior system of ethics and social principles, even of 'culture'. These, they argued, should be models for semi-civilized Japan.

As an example of this point of view we need look no further than the writings of Rutherford Alcock, British minister in Japan from 1859 to 1864. In a book, *The Capital of the Tycoon*, which he published in 1863, he claimed that while the Japanese population demonstrated no inconsiderable degree of intellectual achievement, and enjoyed 'perhaps a more general diffusion of education than most nations of European stock can boast', the fact remained that it lacked the Christian ethic. This circumstance placed it, like the peoples of pagan Greece and Rome, at a lower level of civilization than modern Europe. Art, in particular, exemplified this. It had, he maintained, 'small pretensions in Japan to be considered a valuable civilizing agency'. Indeed, in 'pandering to the lower classes' Japanese artists had produced works of 'coarseness and indelicacy' which were 'essentially barbarizing agencies'. In a more general sense, although the Japanese possessed 'a material civilization of a high order, in which all the industrial arts are brought to as great a perfection as could well be attainable without the aid of steampower and machinery', their 'intellectual and moral pretensions . . . compared with what has been achieved in the more civilized nations of the West during the last three centuries, must be placed very low'. For all that, he believed, they were improvable. Their capacity 'for a higher and better civilization than they have yet attained' ranked 'far before that of any other Eastern nation'.[2]

This kind of opinion was expressed widely by foreigners. Francis Hawks, Perry's chronicler, described the Japanese as 'a very imitative, adaptative, and compliant people', something which held the promise 'of the comparatively easy introduction of foreign customs and habits, if not of the nobler principles and better life of a higher civilization'.[3] American missionaries often showed themselves ready to act on such ideas. Prevented from working openly to spread the gospel by the laws against Christianity, which were not withdrawn until 1873, they concentrated, like their colleagues in other difficult mission fields, on seeking esteem by their contributions to medicine and education. Since the first had led the development of western studies in Japan, and the second had a central place in Confucian thought, the result was to win them influential friends. Guido Verbeck, for example, a Dutchman by birth, who had emigrated to America and become a minister in the Dutch Reformed Church, was sent to Nagasaki in 1859 as one of the first group of Protestant missionaries in the newly opened treaty ports. He had no more success in making converts than others of his kind — it has been said that in the early days there were more Protestant missionaries than Protestant converts in Japan — but his knowledge of Dutch made him welcome to Rangaku scholars, while his early training as an engineer matched the technological preferences of Japanese students of the West. What is more, his willingness to teach English (using the New Testament and the American Constitution as texts) ensured that ambitious young samurai, sent to Nagasaki for training by the Bakufu or their lords, were glad to approach him. The Bakufu asked him to take charge of a language school there. The Meiji government invited him to Tokyo after 1868 as the principal of part of its new university.

Two nephews of Yokoi Shōnan of Higo, a scholar who contributed to the framing of the Charter Oath, studied at Verbeck's school at Nagasaki. He helped them to go to America to study in 1866 (see Chapter 6). He also established links with some of the Satsuma leaders, as well as with Ōkuma Shigenobu of Hizen, through whom he was able to make representations about the nature and objectives of the Iwakura embassy (see Chapter 9). With political connections such as these, he was in a position to recommend other Americans to posts in Japan after the Tokugawa had been overthrown. In 1870, for example, when Matsudaira Yoshinaga of Echizen was seeking foreign teachers for a school of western studies in his domain, Verbeck was instrumental in securing the appointment of William Griffis as instructor in physics and chemistry. Griffis was later to be Verbeck's biographer.

The missionary impact, as Verbeck's career suggests, was most of all on education. This made missionaries crucial in the long run for Japanese knowledge of the West, but gave them a lower profile in the early Meiji period than the contribution of some of the western diplomats. Of these, the French had to some extent been discredited by Léon Roches's support for the Tokugawa; the Dutch did not seem to disillusioned Rangaku scholars to matter much in the world; and the Russians, who had never sought a 'civilizing' role, were no longer thought of as providing models for Japanese reform, despite the achievements of Peter the Great. American influence in East Asia had been temporarily undermined by the Civil War and its aftermath. That left the lead unmistakably to Britain; and in Sir Harry Parkes, Alcock's successor, Britain had a representative who gladly seized the opportunity this offered. He expressed himself regularly and forcefully on any and every issue relevant to reordering Japanese life. Even under the Tokugawa he had declared it his intention to divert the country 'from military glitter to industrial enterprise' (an oblique condemnation of the policies of Roches). After 1868 he set out to promote modern — that is, western-style — government enterprise of many kinds: a mint, using machinery from Hong Kong and drawing its senior staff from Britain under a contract with the Oriental Bank; a lighthouse service, directed by a British superintendent, Thomas Henry Brunton; and the first Japanese railway, a line between Tokyo and Yokohama, which opened in 1872, employing British capital, British engineers and British rolling-stock. The last of these projects was especially close to his heart. Not only did it serve Britain's economic interests as Japan's principal trading partner, he wrote to Edmund Hammond at the Foreign Office, but it would also 'do more to promote the work of progress in this country than any other measure'.[4]

Foreigners were not the only source of advice available to the Meiji government. There were, after all, men in the new administration who had been abroad before the restoration of imperial rule and had the self-confidence to judge for themselves what Japan needed from the West. One of them, Terashima Munenori (formerly Matsuki Kōan), became deputy head of the foreign affairs department in the spring of 1869. Godai Tomoatsu, who had accompanied him to Europe in 1865, also had a senior post in that department before turning his attention from government to commerce. Itō Hirobumi served in the Finance Ministry during

1869–70, then in practice took over (as vice-minister) the newly created Ministry of Public Works in 1871. When he became minister of that department in October 1873, he was succeeded as vice-minister by another former Choshu student in London, Yamao Kenzō. Inoue Kaoru was vice-minister in the Finance Ministry from 1871 to 1873.

Where the knowledge of these men was not sufficient for its needs, the Council of State adopted the Bakufu practice of sending officials abroad on special missions of enquiry, like those of Shibata and Ono in 1865 and 1867, though with the difference that their object was now more often economic. In July 1870 Ueno Kagenori and Maejima Hisoka were sent to London, partly to settle difficulties which had arisen in connection with the Tokyo-Yokohama railway loan, partly to find a suitable printing house for Japanese banknotes, which were being widely counterfeited in Japan. Travelling via San Francisco and New York, they spent the best part of a year in Britain, returning in September 1871. Maejima, who had served as a translator at the Edo Kaiseisho before 1868, but was on this occasion travelling for the first time outside Japan, took the opportunity of following up some of the work he had been doing in Tokyo on the organization of Japanese postal services, by carrying out an investigation of those in London. Since he had no instructions to this effect, he at first found it difficult to get himself taken seriously. Eventually, however, he broke down the official reserve of the local authorities to the point of being able to secure both explanations and publications in response to his enquiries, so that in the event he went home very well informed, even on such points as the contribution the Post Office made to government revenue and the use of postal savings by small depositors. He was to spend the next few years reorganizing the mail system of Japan along similar lines, securing as a result Japanese membership of the Universal Postal Union in 1877 and a convention with Britain for the withdrawal of foreign post offices from the treaty ports in 1879. In Maejima's view, this was as much a patriotic as a bureaucratic achievement. It had, he wrote, enabled his country to 'recover to the full our national rights in the field of communications, which had been so violated'.[5]

At about the time Ueno and Maejima left for London, the Finance Ministry was engaged in discussing the changes which would be required to give Japan a modern banking and currency system. It had already been agreed with Parkes that a mint would be established, using British equipment and technicians, but Itō Hirobumi, who was the responsible official, recommended that before anything further be done there should be a more detailed study of how the relevant institutions were organized in the United States. This was approved in November 1870 by his senior colleagues (including Ōkuma Shigenobu and Shibusawa Ei'ichi). On 23 December Itō therefore sailed from Yokohama, taking with him three assistants — one of them was Fukuchi Genichirō, another former Bakufu translator — and representatives from leading Japanese financial and commercial houses in Tokyo, Osaka and Yokohama.

At San Francisco, which they reached on 17 January 1871, the officials took a few days to visit banks, factories and the local mint — it is not recorded how the businessmen spent their time — before the party entrained for Washington. Once in the capital, there were formal meetings with the President and the Secretary of State, then a series of discussions at the Treasury Department and the Inland Revenue. These were followed by an expedition to the Mint in Philadelphia (visited five times) and to banks in New York, all involving the collection of copious printed material, which was translated by Itō's staff. The outcome was a recommendation to Tokyo, subject to further investigation of certain legal and administrative points, that Japan adopt a gold-based currency and perhaps a decimal system for notes and coins (that is, following American rather than British practice).

In May came word that the mission must return to Tokyo, since final decisions were about to be taken. Before they left, there was a farewell banquet, at which Itō made a speech, explaining to his hosts how he saw the context of what he and his colleagues had been doing. Since the opening of the ports, he said, the Japanese people, having come to realize some of the deficiencies of their society, had begun 'the investigation of what constituted European and American civilization'. Starting with 'the introduction of some of the most useful of the foreign arts, sciences, and mechanical inventions into their country', they had now reached the stage of needing a greater knowledge of foreign systems of finance. It had been his task to obtain it. While doing so, he had also been able to inform himself about 'other branches of civilized government', such as might be 'of benefit to us in our efforts to reach that high estate which you have already attained' (*New York Times*, 14 May 1871).

Other Japanese envoys took a more humdrum view of what they were about. In the autumn of 1870 Kuroda Kiyotaka, a Satsuma samurai who had studied gunnery under Egawa Tarōzaemon and had led the imperial forces against Hakodate in 1869, made a tour of northern Japan for the purpose of establishing defence and development guidelines for the region. Not unnaturally, his focus was on the threat from Russia; and having come to the conclusion that as things then stood it was necessary for Japan to husband its resources and concentrate its efforts, he recommended that claims to Karafuto (southern Sakhalin), which the Bakufu had pressed, should be abandoned, in order to remove an immediate cause of friction, and that a ten-year programme of economic development be implemented for Hokkaido. This, he believed, would strengthen Japan's defensive position. He envisaged carrying it out with the help of foreign experts, preferably American ones, since the terrain and climate were similar to those of parts of the United States.

Kuroda left Yokohama on 22 February 1871, accompanied by seven students, who had been nominated by the Hokkaido Development Commission (Kaitakushi), of which he was deputy Commissioner. The students were to study agriculture and mining in America. Kuroda was to seek advisers there, a task he accomplished with some success — though at considerable cost — since General Horace Capron, Commissioner of Agriculture in President Grant's administration, was persuaded to go to Japan on a short-term contract. After a brief visit to St Petersburg, Kuroda returned to Tokyo in the summer, taking with him Capron and three technical assistants of Capron's choosing. Five more American experts in agriculture and mining were added later, forming the nucleus of an advisory team which worked under Capron's supervision until 1875. By that time exploratory mining surveys had been carried out and a start made on introducing new crops.

Some of the work of recruiting foreign advisers was undertaken by the resident ministers whom Japan had decided to appoint to the major world capitals at the end of 1870. The first two were appointed in November of that year: Samejima Hisanobu, who was to be minister jointly to Britain, France and Prussia, with Shioda Saburō as chief of his secretariat; and Mori Arinori as minister in Washington. Mori took up his duties in February 1871. Samejima, having first visited London and established a temporary office there, moved to Paris a few months later. It soon became clear, however, that his responsibilities were too much for one man to carry. In June 1872 he was relieved of his London duties, which were transferred to Terashima Munenori (with the rank of Minister Plenipotentiary, as befitted his higher bureaucratic standing). In 1873 the Berlin post, too, was made a separate one, Aoki Shūzō, a Choshu student in Germany, being made Acting First Secretary in January, then First Secretary proper in October. At the end of 1874 he made a short visit to Japan before returning to Berlin as Minister Plenipotentiary. Meanwhile, Sano Tsunetani had been made Resident Minister in Vienna (April 1873) and Kawase Masataka Minister Plenipotentiary in Rome (February 1874). There was a delay about St Petersburg, because Tokyo's first choice died in London in September 1873 on his way to take up his post, so it was not until June 1874 that Enomoto Takeaki was installed as Minister Plenipotentiary.

As a result of these appointments, by the middle of 1874 Japan was represented abroad at the most senior level by men who had some experience of living in the West. Mori and Samejima had been students with the Satsuma mission which went to London in 1865, and had travelled home via America. Aoki and Kawase, both from Choshu, had studied in Berlin and London, respectively. Enomoto, an older man, had been a Bakufu naval student in Holland from 1862 to 1866. Sano, a samurai from Hizen, was to some degree an exception, in that he had never studied overseas, but he had been with Enomoto at the Nagasaki naval school, and had spent some months in France in 1867 as Hizen's representative at the Paris Exposition.

Such experience, both in their own opinion and that of their superiors, qualified Japan's representatives to take over from western diplomats the function of acting as a channel for knowledge of the West. A particular example was the choice of foreign advisers, which was a matter of some political sensitivity. Mori Arinori, while in the United States, was instrumental in finding someone to supervise the newly-formed state education system. Tokyo's original idea, the implementation of which was entrusted to the Iwakura embassy, was to have four commissioners, one each from America, Britain, France and Germany; but Mori, when the embassy reached Washington early in 1872, persuaded its members that it would be better to have only one — an American — in order to avoid the potential embarrassment of getting conflicting advice. Once this had been agreed, he set in train a series of enquiries which led eventually to the appointment of David Murray, Professor of Mathematics and Astronomy at Rutgers College. One of his qualifications was that he had already had dealings with Japanese students there. In much the same way, Samejima recruited Gustave Emile Boissonade, vice-rector of the University of Paris, first to give lectures on law to Japanese students in France during 1873, then to go to Tokyo as adviser to the Justice Ministry later in the year. In 1878 Aoki Shūzō in Berlin secured the services of Hermann Roesler of the University of Rostock to be legal adviser to the Foreign Ministry.

Advisers of this standing were to have an immense influence on Japan's development of western-style institutions: Murray in education, Boissonade in drafting codes of law, Roesler in the shaping of the 1889 constitution. On the other hand, not all foreign employees of the Meiji government (*o-yatoi*) operated at this level. Of the very large numbers of *o-yatoi* who were hired between 1868 and 1912 — possibly as many as two thousand — a majority were almost certainly artisans, or filled other low-level jobs. Some, for example, were western residents or visitors, recruited in the treaty ports to perform routine duties for which they needed minimal qualifications. In 1873 the *Japan Mail* said of the foreign teachers working in Tokyo that many 'were graduates of the dry-goods counter, the forecastle, the camp, and the shambles, or belonged to that vast array of unclassified humanity that floats like waifs in every seaport'.[6] Others, of course, were higher-ranking technical specialists, brought from abroad, like the advisers to central ministries. Of those who came from Britain, many were engineers, engaged in public works and railway-building, or teaching at the Tokyo engineering college. From France came a military mission (Chapter 6), as well as lawyers. Germany became the main source of senior teachers of science and medicine. Americans were conspicuous in agricultural colleges and in education generally.

The top men in any of these fields were well paid and highly regarded. Horace Capron had $10,000 a year for his work on Hokkaido development. William Griffis, when teaching in Echizen, received a salary of $300 a month, and was provided with a house, an interpreter, several secretaries (to help prepare his teaching), four guards, a cook and a number of household staff. Such a level of provision was not unusual. Even so, not all *o-yatoi* were satisfied with their lot. The Japanese were careful not to give foreigners untrammelled authority, a circumstance which annoyed those — mostly British — whose notion of their place in the order of things derived from what their compatriots enjoyed elsewhere in Asia. Others were irritated by the fact that they were treated as strictly temporary staff, expected to help in training the Japanese who might in time replace them. These restrictions were not just a reflection of Japanese suspicion of foreign motives. They were also a matter of cost. The revised plans for sending Japanese students overseas, which took effect after 1873, envisaged, as we shall see, both a reduction in numbers and an insistence on the best possible preliminary training in Japan. By this means, producing Japanese experts was made much cheaper than hiring foreign ones.

STUDENTS AND OTHER TRAVELLERS

In 1864, when recommending that Satsuma send a mission to Europe, Godai Tomoatsu had urged that those who went with it should include men of high enough birth to qualify later in life for senior office in the domain. It was important, he wrote, that they should have a knowledge of the world with which Japan had to deal. After 1868 the argument surfaced again, this time with reference to the well-born of the country as a whole. The most explicit and authoritative statement of it came in December 1871 in the form of a message addressed in the emperor's name to members of the aristocracy, both court nobles and former feudal lords. It was their duty, this affirmed, to set an example in the pursuit of national wealth and strength. In particular, like other Japanese, they ought 'to fix their eyes upon the aspect of the civilization of the world, to cultivate pursuits of actual utility, to go abroad for purposes of study in foreign countries'. Not all of them, it was recognized, would be able to stay overseas for any length of time. Nevertheless, they should at least make the effort to go on a foreign tour, so as 'to widen their circle of knowledge by seeing and hearing, thus to improve their understanding';

and they should take with them wives, daughters and sisters, who could in this way 'become acquainted with the right system of educating children'.[7]

No doubt as a result of this admonition, a number of aristocrats, often of the younger generation, are to be found among Japanese travellers in the next few years, engaged on what might be called a nineteenth-century version of the European Grand Tour (extended in this case to include America). There were even a few imperial princes among them. Some of the nobles paid for themselves, some were subsidized from official sources, some were named as government students, though they did not always study a great deal. The government also looked with favour on junior officials who sought to gain experience outside Japan, whether or not they did so for purposes of formal education.

Young men who had fought with the imperial army in the civil war and had ambitions for a military career were among the first to seize the opportunity. In the summer of 1869 Yamagata Aritomo of Choshu and Saigō Tsugumichi of Satsuma, who had served together in the northeast campaign, were given funds by their domains, with the express approval of the Council of State, to travel to Europe 'to investigate conditions'. Accompanied by a Satsuma interpreter, who was on his way to England, they left Nagasaki for Shanghai at the end of August, then joined the regular mail-steamer for Marseille. After a few weeks in Paris, Saigō decided to stay there for the winter. Yamagata moved on to London, where he shared the lodgings of Kawase Masataka, who was later to be minister in Rome. In the spring of 1870 he resumed his travels, taking in Brussels, Berlin and St Petersburg before rejoining Saigō in Paris. It was not a diplomatic journey, so there were no royal audiences or meetings with heads of government along the way; but with the help of Choshu students like Kawase in London and Aoki Shūzō in Berlin — Yamagata was no great linguist — he was able to assemble a considerable range of information. He also came to certain conclusions which were to stay with him for the rest of his life. The German army impressed him. The British Parliament did not.

In the early summer of 1870 the two men made their way back to Japan via New York and San Francisco. It was during the train journey coast-to-coast that they heard of the outbreak of the Franco-Prussian War (and predictably disagreed about the likely outcome, each taking the side of the country with which he was best acquainted). Only two weeks after they arrived in Yokohama (28 August), reporting personally to the emperor, it was decided to send two more such men, Ōyama Iwao of Satsuma and Shinagawa Yajirō of Choshu, to observe the war and see what military lessons Japan could learn from it. They travelled via America, which was the quicker route. It was not quick enough, however, for them to reach London before the outcome of the fighting had been decided at Sedan. They managed to get into Paris, by then under siege, but once the siege had ended they parted company, much as Yamagata and Saigō had done, Ōyama staying to study in France, Shinagawa leaving for Berlin. They presumably saw no pressing need to report their findings, for Ōyama stayed in France until 1876, while Shinagawa, having spent some months in Germany, studying the language, moved to Britain late in 1871, then joined the Iwakura embassy for the final stage of its travels to Germany and home.

During 1871 the Council of State had taken another initiative of a rather different kind. Anxious to ensure that central government policies had the support of local as well as national officials, it requested thirteen of the larger domains each to nominate two samurai, preferably office-holders, to go on an extensive study tour of America and Europe. It was expected to last a year. Only nine of the domains responded favourably, though one, Kaga (Kanazawa), offered to add a third nominee to the party at its own expense. Hikone, which had not been on the original list, was allowed to send a single volunteer of its own, when it asked to do so, with the result that the party which finally left Japan comprised twenty samurai. To these were added interpreters and a number of students, bringing the total to thirty-eight. One of the interpreters, who was also to have duties as escort and guide, was an American missionary, David Thompson, who had been teaching English in Yokohama and Tokyo since 1863.

Things did not work out in practice as tidily as the plan envisaged. The party sailed from Yokohama on 23 June and reached San Francisco without incident on 15 July. Visits were organized by David Thompson to the university, a girls' school, newspaper offices, the local mint and a textile factory — a well-trodden path — though greater interest was shown, as had been true on earlier occasions, in the military establishments that were also part of the programme. Much the same kind of itinerary was followed during the three weeks spent in New York in August. Brief stays thereafter in Philadelphia and Washington were devoted to simple sightseeing, as far as one can judge, but when the time came to leave for Britain early in September, one of the men from Tottori, objecting that this kind of travel left no time for proper study, chose to remain behind in order to pursue his interests more seriously. A similar incident occurred in London, where Kataoka Kenkichi of Tosa dropped out (he stayed until the end of 1872, studying privately). In October Yamanaka Ichirō opted to stay in Berlin to learn German (though he later went to Paris to study French as well).

While what was left of the mission was still in Germany, news came of the decision taken in Tokyo at the end of August to abolish the domains. Alarmed by this, several of the remaining travellers decided that it was their duty to go home at once, while the rest continued to Paris and

St Petersburg. In the event, nine of the original twenty returned to Japan in the winter of 1871–2, two in the following spring, three in the course of 1873, the remainder even later. This kind of fragmentation was not unusual among organized parties of Japanese travellers: compare what happened to those whom the Bakufu sent to Holland in 1862 and Satsuma sent to Britain in 1865.

From what has been said so far in this section it can be seen that deciding who should count as 'students' in the early years of the Meiji period is not straightforward. The situation was further complicated by the fact that there were still a number of Japanese overseas who had been sent by their domains before 1868. The Council of State therefore tried to bring some order into the arrangements. In May 1869 it set out the procedures to be observed by those wanting to go abroad, requiring applicants to explain how their proposed studies would benefit the country; to give an undertaking about their behaviour overseas, which would include a promise not to borrow money from foreigners, or quarrel with them, or attack them; and to accept that they must neither take foreign nationality nor adopt a foreign religion while away. These regulations were revised in February 1871, when the overall purpose of study overseas was defined as being to 'promote the prosperity of the nation by encouraging the people in the path of enlightenment'.[8] From this time on, students financed by the state or by domains were to have qualified themselves by previous study in Japan, including language study, and to be subject to the supervision of Japan's legations in America and Europe. Fewer restrictions were imposed on those who travelled privately, but all were told to avoid any behaviour which might damage their country's reputation. They were also to pay a formal visit to a Shinto shrine before departure.

According to members of the Iwakura embassy, when they returned in 1873, there remained, despite these precautions, a certain lack of assiduity and academic discipline among the students. The scheme was also proving very costly. A further review was therefore undertaken in the next two years, the effect of which was to reduce the numbers going at government expense — the sending of students by domains had ended with the latter's abolition in 1871 — and to ensure that before they went they had the best training Japan's own education system could provide. This meant in practice that after 1875 official funds were only available to selected high-flyers, seeking approved forms of training. Those whose ambitions were more modest had to pursue them at private expense, if they wished to do so abroad. Problems of cost and admission standards ensured that most of them chose to go to America.

For the years 1868 to 1873 Ishizuki (1972) identifies just over 500 students who went overseas (leaving aside a few whose year of departure is uncertain and those whose destination was China or Hong Kong).

About one in ten were members of the court and feudal nobility. Inuzuka (1987), covering only the period to the end of 1871, lists about 350, of whom some 150 were selected and financed by various agencies of the central government, another 120 were sent by domains, and the remainder are classified as 'private'. The great majority stayed abroad for more than two years. Average age was rather lower than it had been before 1868.

Those who left in 1870 and 1871 provide a useful sample for analysis:[9] they appear in both the Ishizuki and Inuzaka lists, while quite a large proportion of them achieved a sufficient reputation to become the subject of biographies, or of personal entries in works of reference. There were some 320 altogether in these years (Inuzuka). Among those who were sent by domains (just under ninety), relatively few came from Satsuma and Choshu, whose political influence no doubt enabled most of their candidates to travel at Tokyo's expense. The largest contingent came from Hizen, which had a well-established tradition of western studies, especially in technology. Nine came from Kaga (Kanazawa), traditionally the richest of the domains, seven from Tosa (Kochi), and six from the Tokugawa branch house of Owari (Nagoya). Others came mostly in ones and twos from areas throughout the country, including some which had supported the losing side in 1868.

Government students were also diverse in origin, though in a different way. Most were selected by one or other department of the administration, and financed from that department's budget. Thus thirty-four were nominated by the Defence Ministry, twenty-five by various sections of the University (which was in effect an organ of government), fourteen by the Hokkaido Development Commission, nine by the Finance Ministry, and six by the Justice Ministry. One or two other ministries contributed smaller numbers, while forty were appointed by the Council of State itself. The departmental nominees were commonly sent for very specific kinds of training. Apart from the army and navy cadets, who were Defence Ministry nominees, one can cite the example of the six students chosen by the Finance Ministry from its coinage bureau, who went to London to acquire the expertise which would enable them to replace the British employees at the Osaka mint. Eleven medical students sent to Germany by the University in 1870 had a not dissimilar role, since the decision to send them was the result of choosing the German model for medical education. On the other hand, the Hokkaido Development Commission — influenced by its American advisers, perhaps — not only sent students to the United States to be trained in agriculture and mining, but also paid for five girls, aged eight and fourteen, to go to school there. They left with the Iwakura embassy in December 1871.

Both domain and government students, where they had any choice, opted for subjects of study which gave an indication of their chosen careers (though a few changed their minds while overseas). Numerically, military and naval studies took first place, though only by a narrow margin. Next came medicine, science and non-military technology. Law, politics and economics, which were seen to be the proper educational concern of aspirant bureaucrats, were a close third. Britain (93 students) was still at this stage the most popular destination, followed by the United States (75). Germany (46) displaced France (37) from the third place it had held in earlier years.

It is more difficult to generalize about the so-called 'private' students (approximately ninety in number in 1870 and 1871), who are defined only in terms of the source of their funds. In this case, too, a proportion took up military studies, though these were often men of good birth, for whom the army was as much a family tradition as a career. At the opposite end of the spectrum were those who chose what was described as 'general education', especially in America, apparently for the sake of the knowledge of the world and the social cachet it could give. More narrowly vocational in their objectives were some of the men of merchant background: both the Mitsui and the Ono companies sent family members and employees to study abroad. Even the two largest Buddhist houses in Kyoto, the Nishi and Higashi Honganji, sent priests to Europe on a tour of investigation.

A few individual examples will serve to illustrate the wide range of experience and study to which these initiatives, both official and private, provided entry. One of the twelve young men sent to Britain for naval training in 1871 was Tōgō Heihachirō, who was to become Japan's most famous admiral as a result of his victory over the Russian fleet in 1905. A low-ranking Satsuma samurai, born in 1848, Tōgō had had his first experience of warfare during the British attack on Kagoshima in 1863, when only fifteen. It convinced him of the importance of naval defences. In 1866, therefore, together with his two elder brothers, he joined the Satsuma naval force, serving as a gunner in one of its warships in the civil war of 1868–9, when it took part in the campaign against Enomoto in the north. Victory opened the way for him to join the emperor's new navy, though he first spent some time learning English in Yokohama and Tokyo.

In March 1871, together with eleven others, Tōgō was selected from the cadets at the naval school in Yokohama to go to Britain for training; but despite the efforts of Harry Parkes and the Foreign Office, when the party reached London it transpired that the Admiralty was unwilling either to admit them to the Britannia naval college or to let them serve in warships. As a result, they were first established in lodgings in Portsmouth to improve their English, then transferred to a private school for prospective naval officers, whence in due course they entered the training ship *Worcester*. The *Worcester* was primarily intended for merchant marine cadets, but it had strong naval connections, so the course included gunnery, taught in the naval dockyard. In February 1875, having completed it, Tōgō joined another training ship, the *Hampshire*, this time to make a voyage round the world, sailing from the Thames to Melbourne via the Cape of Good Hope, spending two months in Australia, and coming back by way of Cape Horn.

On his return he was sent to Cambridge for extra mathematics to improve his navigation skills, then moved to Greenwich, where his orders were to take part in the supervision of one of three warships being built in Britain for Japan. He remained there until the beginning of 1878, when he was attached to another of the ships, the *Hiei*, to make the passage home. She left Milford Haven on 23 March and arrived at Yokohama (via Malta, Port Said, Aden and Singapore) on 22 May.

Not all Japan's future leaders enjoyed this kind of organized and disciplined instruction if they went overseas. Katsura Tarō, a Choshu samurai, had to depend much more on his own initiative and effort. A year older than Tōgō, he, too, served in the campaigns of the civil war, receiving an imperial stipend as reward. Once the fighting was over, making a similar choice to Tōgō's, he enrolled in the French language school at Yokohama (October 1868), with the intention of studying later at a military academy in France. The plan looked like being frustrated when he was ordered to the new Japanese army school at Osaka in May 1870, but Katsura, still determined to study in France, withdrew on pretext of illness, then applied to his domain for leave to go to Europe on his own, surrendering his stipend in return for funds. All this was agreed in time for him to join Ōyama Iwao and Shinagawa Yajirō on a ship leaving Yokohama for America in September.

The voyage across the Pacific and Atlantic Oceans brought them to England in time to learn that Paris was already under siege. Katsura saw little point in persisting with the idea of studying in France. He therefore travelled to Berlin, where he joined Aoki Shūzō, a Choshu student of law and politics, who had left Japan in 1868 and was already well established in Germany. The first hurdle was to learn German, since his knowledge of French would now be of little use to him; but after six months of intensive work on it he knew enough to be able to start on military science, studying under a major-general of the Prussian army reserve, who had commanded a regiment in the war with Austria. By the end of two years Katsura had a sound knowledge of military training and organization as they had developed in Germany during the nineteenth century. He was also beginning to run out of funds. Temporary relief was afforded in 1873 by the arrival of the Iwakura embassy, to which, like Aoki, he acted as adviser on German affairs, but once it had departed he felt that the time had come to go home himself and seek employment. He left Berlin in September, travelling this time via Paris and Marseille. In Tokyo it did not take him long to find an outlet for his energy and knowledge in the staff work of Japan's newly-formed conscript army.

It was at approximately this date that Dan Takuma was beginning to train as an engineer in the United States. In 1871, when members of the nobility were being encouraged to acquire an understanding of the outside world, Kuroda Nagatomo, the former daimyo of Fukuoka, whose father had been an early patron of western learning in Japan, decided to accompany the Iwakura embassy on at least part of its travels. As companions on the journey, who were to remain in America and go to college, he chose two young samurai of good family from the domain, Kaneko Kentarō, aged eighteen, and Dan Takuma, aged thirteen. They were given five years' leave of absence for their studies, which, they were told, could be extended to seven years, if need be.

The three remained in company with the embassy until it reached Chicago in February 1872, then proceeded to Boston, where two other Fukuoka students were already established. After that, Kuroda went his own way, leaving Kaneko and Dan to start their schooling. They lodged with a primary school teacher, who taught them English; entered a local grammar school in September 1872; and only then made up their minds about future studies. Kaneko chose to read law at Harvard. Dan, following out a boyhood interest, decided to become a mining engineer, despite Kaneko's advice that this was not a proper occupation for a samurai. In 1875 he joined the Boston technical college, soon to become the Massachusetts Institute of Technology, from which he received his degree in 1878. Kaneko graduated from Harvard the same summer, so the two travelled back to Japan together, taking the train to San Francisco, then a ship to Yokohama. They returned to Tokyo on the railway built since their departure.

Some of this generation of students proved a disappointment to their mentors. Nakae Chōmin, for example, came back from Europe a confirmed political activist. In 1871 he had won nomination as a student of the Justice Ministry to go to France to study law, leaving Japan with the Iwakura embassy, like Kaneko and Dan, then making his own way to France after it reached America. Once there, he seems to have been left very much on his own. Though information about him at this time is scarce, it appears that he entered primary school in Lyon, only to withdraw because his age caused problems — he was twenty-five — then moved to Paris in 1873, where he decided to study literature and philosophy, rather than law. Like other government students, he was recalled to Japan in 1874, when the decision was taken to review the rules for sending students overseas. He was not sent back to France again, perhaps because his attitudes were already suspect.

Before leaving Europe, Nakae had paid a visit to London, where he spent some time with another Tosa man, Baba Tatsui, one of Fukuzawa Yukichi's students. Baba had been sent by his domain to qualify in naval engineering, but like Nakae soon changed his mind. In order to improve his English, he lived for a time in a village outside London, but in 1871 he returned to the capital to enrol for a science course at University College, starting in October. It then turned out that his taste was less for science than for politics and law. By the time the Iwakura embassy arrived in the summer of 1872, he was well enough versed in British politics to be of service to its members as a political guide, with the result that he was able to persuade them to recommend a change in his status, from that of domain student reading science to central government student reading law. Baba, too, was recalled to Japan in 1874. Unlike Nakae, however — because of his political connections, one presumes — he was sent back to London as soon as the regulations had been revised. In theory, he continued his studies in law until 1878, though he never qualified. In practice, he seems to have spent less of his time in chambers than in reading about British history and political institutions in the British Museum.

One benefit accruing from his studies was that his English improved to the point where he found it as easy to write in English as in Japanese, if not more so (as happened to a number of other Japanese students in the Meiji period). In 1875, when he came back from Japan, he published a pamphlet in English. Entitled 'The English in Japan', it was an attempt to explain to his English friends, especially those of a radical frame of mind, such as the members of the National Association of Social Science — a body active in such causes as women's rights, penal reform, and public health — that the way of life enjoyed by liberal British citizens within their own society, where 'laws recognize no difference in the rank or social position of man', and 'justice is impartially administered to all', was no guide to what their compatriots took to be normal in the Japanese treaty ports.[10] Foreign behaviour in Japan, he said, was nothing less than a betrayal of the values he had learnt in London. It was at this time that Baba joined an association, formed by a number of his fellow-students, which existed to discuss political issues of this kind. It proved to be the predecessor of another, founded in Tokyo after their return, which took an active part in the popular rights movement of the 1880s, calling for an elected parliament.

Nakae and Baba, as known opponents of the Meiji government, inevitably had less material success in later life than Kaneko and Dan. All the same, they have an important place in this study, because they serve to remind us that Japanese students did not always learn from the West the 'useful' things they were sent to learn. A few of them, at least, once they had access to college or public libraries, and the language skills to use them fully, became aware that the optimistic view of industrial society, propagated in Japan by men like Rutherford Alcock and Harry Parkes, was not universally shared. The books of Marx and Engels were available in London, as well as those of Darwin or Herbert Spencer or Samuel Smiles.

9

The Iwakura Embassy, 1871–1873

The embassy which left Japan in December 1871 was led by men of higher standing and more authority than any of its predecessors. Its senior member was Iwakura Tomomi, who as Minister of the Left and former Foreign Minister was the second-ranking official of the emperor's government. He was accorded the status of ambassador plenipotentiary by the powers. With him were associated four vice-ambassadors: Kido Takayoshi, Choshu's chief representative on the Council of State; Ōkubo Toshimichi, Satsuma's most powerful samurai politician, who had become Finance Minister earlier in the year; Itō Hirobumi, vice-minister of Public Works; and Yamaguchi Naoyoshi, assistant vice-minister of Foreign Affairs. Several other senior officials accompanied them.

Their mission had three separate objects. The first was to secure international recognition for Japan's restored imperial regime at the highest level. The second was to enter into preliminary discussions for the revision of the five treaties of 1858 and the others which had subsequently been concluded along similar lines with Prussia, Belgium, Denmark and Italy. Since these are matters which are not directly relevant to the subject of this book, they will be given only cursory treatment in this chapter. The third object, which will be examined in more detail, was that entrusted to several Tokugawa envoys from 1862 onwards: to assess the civilization of the West, with a view to adopting those parts of it which would be of value to Japan. This time, however, the manner of doing this was to be more elaborate and more effectively organized than it had ever been before.

PLANS

Iwakura Tomomi had first put forward a proposal to send imperial envoys overseas in the context of plans to overthrow the Tokugawa in the spring of 1867. The purpose, as he then envisaged it, was political, that is, to assert a claim that foreign policy was properly the business of the Court, not of the Bakufu. To this he added the need to study the state of international relations and foreign trade, in order that the emperor's advisers might frame a policy acceptable in the contemporary world. It was an aim he set within the wider framework of 'changing our institutions and reforming the government, so that high and low may be united . . . and military preparations completed to guard against attack';[1] and although the pace of events in 1867–8 made it impossible to implement such a policy at once, Iwakura kept the idea in mind. In January 1869, for example, when thanking the British minister for his government's readiness to recognize the new regime, he sought advice about how far 'we may profitably adopt in Japan the institutions which obtain in Europe', explaining that while the country had inherited from the past its own culture and traditions, 'still we recognize, since our contact with foreign nations, that in many respects our civilization is inferior to theirs'.[2]

To this desire for international standing and practical knowledge were later added ambitions for treaty revision. In February 1868, when making public a promise to uphold the treaties, the Meiji government also made clear its intention to remedy the 'abuses' and 'faults' which they embodied. A year later western diplomatic representatives were told of Japan's wish to enter into talks on the subject before 1872, though without being given specific proposals. Indeed, Tokyo's approach to the question continued to be leisurely. In the winter of 1870–1 a special treaty revision bureau, established in the Foreign Ministry, was able to produce no more than some suggested changes of detail. This was because anything more drastic, it was recognized, would have to wait until the powers could be persuaded to cooperate, chiefly by reforms in Japanese law and commercial regulations. Itō Hirobumi, who was engaged in a study of currency and banking in the United States (see Chapter 8), wrote to confirm that view, emphasizing that any such step would first require a more extensive knowledge of western practice, such as he was in the process of acquiring. Ōkubo, as Finance Minister, supported him in this opinion. The upshot was an agreement that any embassy sent abroad must give consideration to these matters.

Formulating a programme of study for such an embassy owed something to foreign advice. Both the American minister, Charles De Long, and the British chargé, Francis Adams, were consulted in the later stages of planning, but it seems to have been the American missionary, Guido Verbeck, who was most influential, providing the kind of help which Philipp Franz von Siebold had offered to the Bakufu mission of 1862. Verbeck first set down his ideas on paper in 1869, when he heard rumours that an embassy was planned.[3] The document he produced found its way through Ōkuma Shigenobu into the hands of Iwakura, who took the opportunity to discuss it with Verbeck on several occasions in the autumn of 1871. Its principal recommendations were then incorporated into the formal instructions sent to Iwakura before his departure. In order to identify the measures which would make possible 'a perfect political equality with the states of the West', Verbeck's argument ran, Japan would need both to consult foreign governments about the reforms they would require before revising the treaties, and to make observations of its own about the nature of western society. The first of these tasks would fall to the ambassadors. The second could best be performed by attaching to the embassy a number of special commissions, each with a particular field of enquiry to pursue: western laws and constitutions; financial institutions, including taxation, customs duties, insurance, currency and banking; education at primary, secondary and higher levels; and arsenals, dockyards, military organization and training. The study of western religion ought in his view to be undertaken by all members of the mission.

A letter which Sanjō Sanetomi, the senior minister, transmitted to Iwakura in October 1871 incorporated most of these points, omitting only the references to religion. The language in which it referred to the treaties was rather stronger than Verbeck's: Japan, Sanjō said, having lost her equal rights, must now 'seek means to wipe out the insults and redress the wrongs'. This required in the long run a revision of the treaties with respect to legal jurisdiction and tariffs, but the government was in no position to insist on such changes immediately. In fact, 'to restore our country's rights we must remedy the faults in our laws and institutions', which would inevitably take time. As a first step a plenipotentiary must be sent abroad, carrying expressions of good will and investigating 'the polity [*kokutai*], laws and regulations of the most enlightened countries of Europe and America'. To this end, the embassy would be provided with appropriate staff, organized in three sections: the first to study, both in theory and practice, legal and political structures, including diplomatic services, parliaments and law courts; the second to concern itself with banking, currency, taxation, foreign trade, industry, railways, telegraph and postal arrangements, factories, and so on; the third to examine the administration, finance and curriculum of education at all levels, including commercial and technical schools, as well as hospitals and other such social institutions. All these were to be approached 'with a view to adopting them in Japan and establishing them there'. In addition, every member of staff, whatever his specialization, would be expected to examine the organization, equipment and training of western armies and navies, in order to identify 'anything which will be of benefit to our country'.[4]

When he responded to this letter later in the month, Iwakura accepted the general thrust of the argument, including the conclusion that negotiations for treaty revision should not be entered into at once, but expressed some reservations about the scope of the proposed investigation of western society. The essential subjects for study, he maintained, were law, finance and diplomacy, that is, those which had a direct bearing on the provisions of the treaties. Perhaps for this reason, the embassy's formal instructions, issued in December, were less specific about the detail of the studies to be undertaken than Sanjō had been. However, the idea of appointing special commissioners for the investigations was retained. So was their essential purpose. In addition to exchanging views on the subject of treaty revision, the powers were subsequently told, the embassy would undertake such studies as would enable Japan 'to select from the various institutions prevailing among enlightened nations such as are best suited to our present condition'.[5]

The study plans were given greater depth and detail by a series of memoranda from executive departments of the government. Only one, the Defence Ministry, stated its aims in the form of an overall national objective: it argued that international equality could only be achieved if Japan were to have a navy modelled on those of America and Britain, and an army on those of France and Prussia. Most departments did no more than add precise subheadings to what had already been stated in outline in earlier documents. The Finance Ministry wanted material on the encouragement of agriculture and the conduct of censuses; the Ministry of Public Works asked for enquiries about the manufacture of steam machinery and the financing of ironworks; the Education Ministry — in a longer paper than most, emphasizing the role of education in reducing the disparities between Japan and the West — identified for study such items as the pay structure in schools and the organization of an inspectorate, together with information about museums and libraries; the Justice Ministry listed prisons, methods of interrogation, the maintenance of public order, and the establishment of law schools. Two offices, however, raised issues that were significantly new. The Imperial Household Ministry wished to know more about European monarchies: how they differed from that of Japan; the nature of royal expenditures, including that on guards units; military and naval reviews and other types of ceremonial; and the upbringing of heirs to the throne. The Bureau of Ceremonial extended this kind of enquiry to the aristocracy, ceremonial dress, and honours and rewards. Altogether it was an enormous shopping list. The contrast in scope and prior knowledge with what was specified in 1862 is striking.

The choice of Iwakura to lead the mission was logical, given the part he had played in its origins. In addition, Kido and Ōkubo, who had both been responsible for sending fellow-samurai overseas before 1868, and now claimed the same experience for themselves, were difficult to refuse, despite the fact that there were some officials in Tokyo who doubted whether the government could do without them for any length of time. Itō Hirobumi was presumably chosen as an expert on the West, being a departmental vice-minister who could therefore advise the leaders of the mission on something like equal terms. Yamaguchi Naoyoshi, a Hizen samurai, represented the interests of the Foreign Ministry. All five appeared in the first list of appointments, published on 20 November 1871.

Itō's English was fluent, Ōkubo's very limited, while Iwakura, Kido and Yamaguchi apparently knew none at all. Francis Adams, who gave them dinner at the British legation, had this to say about them.[6] Yamaguchi he disliked. Ōkubo, who seemed 'not very communicative', was 'little known to foreigners'. Itō was thought to be 'a clever useful fellow, but easily got hold of by foreigners not always of the best class'. Kido was well known to Algernon Mitford, a former interpreter in Japan, now serving in St Petersburg — Adams suggested that London recall him to meet the embassy — and was 'one of the most zealous members of the party of progress': a quiet man, but 'of the most fearless courage'. About Iwakura he waxed enthusiastic. Not only was he 'the Mikado's most trusted counsellor', but also 'the type of a Japanese gentleman', who 'treats questions broadly, without that tendency to wander from the point which is a characteristic of so many Japanese'. Equally important, he was 'of a conservative turn of mind', which made him 'a wholesome check upon the almost republican tendencies of some of the ultra-progressive members of the government'.

On 4 December six special commissioners (*rijikan*) were added to these names, to supervise information-gathering on behalf of various ministries. Among them were Sasaki Takayuki of Tosa, who was vice-minister in the Justice Ministry, Tanaka Fujimaro of Owari from the Education Ministry, and Yamada Akiyoshi of Choshu, a ranking army officer, to represent the Defence Ministry. Others came from the Imperial Household Ministry (a court noble) and the Finance Ministry. Hida Hamagorō, who had sailed as an officer in the *Kanrin Maru* in 1860, was nominated by the Ministry of Public Works. They were given assistants from their own departments, sixteen in all. There were also four officials from the Education Ministry, chosen, because of their language qualifications, to examine the education systems of Britain, France and Germany.

The ambassadors themselves were given a staff of secretaries and interpreters, several of whom had had experience overseas in the service of the Tokugawa. Tanabe Taichi and Shioda Saburō had gone to France with Ikeda in 1864 and had joined the Meiji government's foreign department after the Restoration. Fukuchi Genichirō, a veteran of the 1862 mission, was included despite having been imprisoned for a time because of pro-Tokugawa articles in a newspaper he founded in 1868. There was also Kawaji Tarō, one of the two men in charge of Bakufu students in London in 1867; Hayashi Tadasu, a member of the student party Kawaji had supervised (who had been in prison after taking part in Enomoto's defence of Hakodate against the imperial forces in 1869); and Nagano Keijirō, who as Tateishi Onojirō ('Tommy') had achieved fame in America in 1860. Clearly the skills such men possessed were at too much of a premium to be outweighed by any consideration of past political loyalties. Apart from these, the ambassadors were able to call upon the services of Japan's diplomats in place — Mori in Washington, Samejima in Paris, Aoki in Berlin, and Terashima, who travelled with the embassy to take up his post in London — all of them competent to make suggestions about a local programme, as well as to contribute, where necessary, to the interpreting. So were some of the Japanese students resident in the countries to be visited.

The official party, when it left Yokohama in an American steamer on 23 December 1871, was forty-eight strong. Accompanying it were five former feudal lords, travelling to see the world, attended by several retainers; the American minister, Charles De Long, combining diplomatic escort duty with home leave; his wife, who had agreed to look after five Japanese girls on their way to school in America; and a number of Japanese students, bound for various destinations. This brought the total of Japanese on board to just over a hundred. It was expected that the mission would last about eleven months: thirty days to reach Washington, via San Francisco, and twenty days there; the same in London and Paris; fifteen days each in Berlin and St Petersburg; between eight and ten days in Stockholm, Copenhagen, The Hague, Brussels, Madrid, Lisbon and Florence; fifteen days in Vienna (for the International Exposition). Varying amounts of time would be spent travelling between these places and on the way home. If this, as seems likely, was as long as those members of the government staying behind in Tokyo thought it politically wise for their colleagues to be away, they were to be disappointed.

TRAVELS

The members of the ambassadorial party did not always travel together, or stay at the same hotels, or visit the same establishments. Kido, Ōkubo and Itō, for example, had interests of their own — mostly within the overall scope of the embassy's duties, but not necessarily — which led them at times to follow a different programme from Iwakura. Assistants were quite often dispersed to follow up particular items of investigation which required more time than was available to their seniors. The special commissioners and their staff had their own business to conduct, which could cause their itinerary to diverge quite substantially from that of the rest. In other words, to write of 'the embassy' being in a particular place at a particular time can be misleading. Kume Kunitake, Iwakura's secretary, when compiling a detailed narrative of the journey, overcame this difficulty by assuming that the embassy was where the ambassador was in person, no matter who was in company with him. The same convention will be adopted here.

Before departure there was a Shinto ceremonial, followed by an audience with the emperor, in the manner of envoys going to China many centuries before. Sanjō also followed ancient custom in giving a farewell party at his official residence. In accordance with the more recent requirements of western practice, there was then a dinner at Yokohama for the diplomatic corps and government ministers, marking a break with tradition which was to characterize the whole of the mission's social life in the coming months. Typical of it was the mayor's reception at San Francisco (reached on 15 January 1872), when Itō made a speech in English, explaining the embassy's aims in terms very similar to those he had used in Washington the previous year. Kido mostly spent his time there visiting schools, as he was to do in other cities, observing in his diary that it was vital for Japan 'to promote the enlightenment of the common people' if the country was 'to maintain our national sovereignty and prevent any infringement of our independence'.[7] Ōkubo went off to see industrial plants and various commercial establishments: the railway workshops at Sacramento, a vineyard, some of the California gold mines. This, too, was to become a regular pattern. There was also time for some shopping. As the *New York Times* reported on 17 January, the Japanese diplomats — except for Iwakura, who continued to wear Japanese dress — had arrived 'in the most outlandish English ready-made garments of all styles since the flood', but quickly provided themselves with 'the most fashionable clothing obtainable'.

The journey east by rail met with a setback at Ogden, because snow blocked the track. This gave the party an unplanned stay of more than two weeks in Salt Lake City (partly spent in Japanese fashion at a hot springs resort nearby), during which the only event of note was that Iwakura refused an invitation to call on Brigham Young, on the grounds that it would be politically improper to meet someone who was said to be under restraint by the federal authorities. Once travel became possible again, Chicago qualified for no more than a one-night stop. It was nevertheless 29 February before the ambassadors were in Washington, two months after leaving home, and in the capital there were to be more delays, which put them still further behind schedule. Mori Arinori, Japan's resident minister, supported by Itō, was able to persuade Iwakura that an opportunity existed, and should be taken, to enter into full negotiations on treaty revision. Iwakura had no formal authority for any such action, so on 20 March Ōkubo and Itō were sent off to Tokyo to get it, while the rest, including Mori, began exploratory talks at the State Department with Hamilton Fish.

It soon became clear that there was considerable divergence between the American and Japanese positions. The Japanese wanted a review of the tariff arrangements and a promise that consular jurisdiction would come to an end as soon as Japan had carried out reforms to law codes and legal procedures. They also expected the wording of any new treaty to be fully reciprocal. Washington sought concessions as its price for agreeing to this, chiefly the opening of more ports and the granting of access to the interior. Some progress was made in the next few weeks in reconciling these contradictions; but when Ōkubo and Itō came back on 22 July, bringing full powers for Iwakura to negotiate, obtained in the face of some opposition from the Foreign Ministry, it transpired that Tokyo insisted on further talks taking place at a conference of representatives of the treaty powers, to be held in Europe. Since Hamilton Fish was unwilling to send an American delegate to such a conference, the result was deadlock. Kido was angry and ashamed. Japan, he believed, had been tempted into an unwise initiative by 'uninformed young men' — he meant Itō and Mori — who 'aspired to a moment of fame'. He detected the same lack of judgement in many of the Japanese students he had met in America, who seemed to him to 'admire American customs without knowing the tradition on which they themselves stand'.[8]

The four-month delay occasioned by the diplomatic negotiations left more time for the study of America than had originally been planned. Much of it was inevitably spent sightseeing: a guided tour of the Capitol, a journey to the north which took in Niagara Falls, a drive in New York's Central Park, a visit to Independence Hall in Philadelphia. Kido contrived to go up in a balloon, supposedly the first Japanese to do so. Yet there were also more serious concerns. Kume Kunitake and one of the interpreters, Hatakeyama Yoshinari, who had been a Satsuma student in London before 1868, settled down to translate the American constitution into Japanese. This done, they extended their study more widely to American political institutions, using a school textbook as their guide. Kido joined them. The officials from the Justice Ministry were sent to pursue their enquiries in New York. Two of those from the Education Ministry departed for Europe to begin their investigations in France and Germany. Others made a round of American government offices, including the Patent Office and the Treasury in Washington and the Mint in Philadelphia. West Point was included in their travels in the north (where Kido thought the scenery much like parts of Choshu). A reception at Annapolis provided the ocasion for some comments on the place of women in American society, similar to those made by members of the 1860 mission. In addition, the list included the Smithsonian Institute and the Agricultural Hall in the capital, several schools and colleges, and the Springfield rifle factory; but it was only around Boston (after Ōkubo came back from Tokyo) that there were visits to factories making consumer goods (wool and cotton textiles, carpets, clothing and shoes). The *New York Times* (12 June), impressed by the busy schedule, commented that 'the Japanese are very shrewd observers in all military, commercial and mechanical matters, but they don't care much for scenery'.

Kume Kunitake, when compiling his narrative, closed the American section of it, as he was to do in the case of other countries, by providing a passage of generalizations. The United States, he said, was European in culture, independent in outlook, and rich in resources. It was 'a country newly established', unlike those of Asia, and drew much of its vigour from European immigrants, who had shown themselves by their decision to seek a new life in a foreign land to be 'those strongest in the spirit of self-reliance and independence' in their countries of origin.[9] It is the sort of observation that is most likely to have come from one of the American school-books which Kume and his colleagues are known to have taken home. Like many other comments of the kind, scattered here and there through his text, its purpose was to inform Japanese opinion, not provide original analysis.

The embassy arrived in Liverpool on 17 August to start what was to be a four-month stay in Britain, six times as long as had originally been planned. The Foreign Office had arranged for Major-General G. G. Alexander of the Royal Marines to act as escort to it. W. G. Aston of the Tokyo legation was provided as interpreter, while the overall supervision of arrangements was left to Sir Harry Parkes, now home on leave. In his relations with Iwakura, Parkes was told, he was to act 'with the view of . . . producing an impression which may prove serviceable hereafter to our intercourse with Japan'.[10] *The Times* (20 August) gave the visitors a warmer welcome, not only as representatives of what it called an 'Eastern Great Britain', which had demonstrated a capacity 'to effect the most sweeping revolution without shaking the stability of the social and political edifice', but also because their country, unlike China, had shown itself willing to learn from the West. Iwakura confirmed at least the second part of this assessment in the course of interviews with Granville, the Foreign Secretary, later in the year. He and his colleagues had come to England, he stated, 'to study her institutions, and observe all that constitutes English civilization, so as to adopt on their return to Japan whatever they may think suitable to their own country'. Granville did not believe this to be Foreign Office business, but he did comment that Britain would only be prepared to make concessions on the subject of the treaties, such as might put British citizens under the jurisdiction of Japanese, 'in precise proportion to their advancement in enlightenment and civilization'.[11]

Parkes, on the other hand, interpreted his instructions to mean educating the members of the embassy, as best he could, with respect to those features of British society which he hoped they would take as models. This did not preclude sightseeing and entertainment — Buckingham Palace, St Paul's Cathedral, the Crystal Palace, the Tower of London, Brighton Aquarium, opera at Covent Garden, a concert at the Albert Hall, the circus in Liverpool, a tour of the Scottish Highlands and a day's foxhunting were all on the programme — but it did ensure that a great part of what was done was designed to promote an understanding of modern industrial society. Alexander and sometimes Parkes himself provided running commentaries. Nor were the lessons lost on their listeners. In Kume's account, a visit to the Kensington science museum (19 August) became the occasion for a short essay on the importance of technology in the development of trade and industry, and the key role played by the steamship and the railway engine in both 'civilization' (*bunmei*) and 'national wealth and strength' (*fukoku-kyōhei*). Similarly, the British Museum (27 September) provided an opportunity to consider the nature of 'progress', emphasizing the need to study the past, in order to secure improvement by the process of 'casting aside the old and devising the new'.

Much of what was seen would have been familiar to previous Japanese envoys and to those members of the embassy's staff who had been to London before. The military and naval visits took in Woolwich Arsenal, Portsmouth dockyard and the Spithead forts, the Birmingham Small Arms factory and the Armstrong works in Newcastle. There was the customary expedition to Parliament, accompanied by Alexander; but more attention was paid than in the past to local government, notably in a number of cities in the north, where members of councils and chambers of commerce set out their own evaluation of the contribution such bodies made to the community and the nation. All this was of considerable interest to Japanese leaders, who still faced the task of devising something to replace domains. Equally so were the methods by which Britain preserved public order. On 12 December Kido and Ōkubo were taken to see the Bow Street magistrates court in session, then to a police station to watch how arrests were handled, and finally on a tour of London low-life after dark, which included dosshouses — 'the poor people here are still more destitute than ours', Kido noted in his diary — several music-halls — 'to which the poorest people go' — and opium dens in an East End alley.[12] Outside London there were visits to a circuit court and a prison in Manchester, to the High Court in Edinburgh, to a court martial in Portsmouth. A gasworks in the Thames estuary provided an opportunity to learn something about strikes. *The Times* (4 December) reported that the Japanese, when told that the strikers were aiming to improve on their existing pay of thirty shillings a week, 'expressed their astonishment at anyone quarrelling with such advantageous terms'. Many libraries, colleges and schools were also on the itinerary. Kido recorded with particular approval the existence of company schools, at which factory owners provided part-time education for the children they employed.

Despite these very varied activities, the attention paid to non-military industry remains the most striking feature of the embassy's investigations in Britain. The list of factories and other plants to which the visitors were taken is extraordinary for both its length and its variety: shipyards in Liverpool and Glasgow; iron and steel works in Glasgow and Sheffield (Kume appended a note on the Bessemer process); a colliery in Newcastle; the railway works at Crewe; textile factories of various kinds in Manchester, Bradford and Galashiels; producers of rubber in Edinburgh, cutlery in Sheffield, clocks and glass in Birmingham, porcelain in Stoke and Worcester, beer in Burton-on-Trent, biscuits in Reading (Kume described at length how they were made). At most of these places there were civic receptions and business lunches, which must have been an ordeal for those in the party who spoke no English. *The Times* on one such occasion commended their fortitude.

The sight of the industrial north seems to have had its greatest impact on Ōkubo. The factories and industrial plants they had seen, he wrote in a letter to Japan in December, were 'sufficient explanation of England's wealth and strength'. What is more, 'this great growth of trade and industry in the cities is something which has happened in the last fifty years', that is, since the invention of the steam-engine. This suggested that Japan, too, might achieve a comparable success after not too long an interval.[13] Kume, writing about a visit to the Agricultural Hall in London (11 December), put his emphasis instead on the importance of applying science to agriculture. What Japan had done so far, he said, seemed 'childlike', even laughable, by comparison with the West; and Britain would make a better model in this field than America, because Britain, like Japan, had only a limited area of cultivated land.

Although Kume was not much given to writing about ceremonial and the embassy's formal social life, there is not much doubt that the reception it received in England was less 'bombastic' — the word was used by *The Times* — than that which it had encountered in America, or was to encounter again in several other European countries. On arrival in Liverpool in August the ambassadors had lunch with the mayor and were then taken by train to London by Aston and Alexander. There was no military display. It was explained to them that they could not immediately be received by Queen Victoria, who was as usual spending the summer at Balmoral. In the event their royal audience was postponed until nearly the end of their stay, and when it did take place at Windsor on 5 December it was not particularly warm in tone. Kume devoted only one line of text to the occasion. A visit to the Prince of Wales at Sandringham a few days later got only half a line more. Iwakura himself was never received by the Prime Minister, Gladstone, though they met at a dinner given by the Foreign Secretary. Only the City went out of its way to be hospitable: lunch with the Lord Mayor on 11 September — Kido thought the Mansion House much more magnificent than the White House in Washington — and a Mercers' Company dinner, at which for the first time they drank from a loving cup.

Departure from Britain was attended by more ceremony than arrival had been, at least in its final moments. On 16 December the embassy left London by what *The Times* called 'the ordinary 9.40 a.m. train' for Dover, there to be met by the Admiral Superintendent and a guard of honour. A special steamer was provided for the crossing to Calais. A month was then spent in France, a week in Belgium, two weeks in Holland, with the result that Berlin was not reached until 9 March. At this point Iwakura received word of disputes within the Tokyo government, which requested as a matter of urgency that Kido and Ōkubo should return and attempt to resolve them. Ōkubo agreed, leaving for Paris and Marseille on 28 March, thence to Yokohama. Kido, less concerned at the news, decided to continue with Iwakura to St Petersburg. Thereafter he travelled independently to Vienna, Venice, Florence, Rome, Naples and Geneva, before calling at Koblenz, Cologne and Paris on his way to Marseill. He was back in Japan on 23 July, some two months later than Ōkubo. Itō and Yamaguchi were left to accompany Iwakura, first to Scandinavia and northern Germany, then along Kido's route to Italy, Austria and Switzerland — less quickly and not always in the same sequence — to depart from Europe in the middle of July. They arrived in Tokyo on 13 September. Although Spain and Portugal had been omitted from their travels, because of reports about political unrest, while Greece had never been envisaged as part of the itinerary, it was in all other respects a remarkably comprehensive tour.

Since no further progress had been made on the subject of treaty revision while in London, the only diplomatic justification for the later visits was the formal one of confirming the legitimacy of Japan's new regime in the eyes of the world. This involved a good deal of ceremonial — audiences with heads of state, usually conducted with some pomp, and elaborate dinners at Europe's most famous palaces — but most of it was routine in European eyes, if one is to judge by the reports of British ambassadors. The only event to occasion special note was a private audience with the Kaiser in Berlin, attended by Bismarck. In St Petersburg a senior official of the Foreign Ministry (which had undertaken to pay the embassy's expenses, unlike its British counterpart) complained to the British ambassador, in a manner recalling 1862, that 'Japanese embassies are more costly to the governments they visit than productive to them of advantageous results'.[14] Altogether one is left with the impression, when reading the diplomatic correspondence, that Japanese missions to Europe no longer had the same curiosity value as in the past.

From the Japanese point of view this part of their travels did not add much to their knowledge of industry or technology in general. In France, for example, they set down in their records a good deal about education and banking, but not very much about heavy industry. There was sightseeing at St Cloud, Notre Dame, Versailles and Fortainebleu, plus tours of the academy at St Cyr and several other military establishments, the Paris observatory, the high court and a prison. Visits were also made to a porcelain factory (Sèvres) and to others making objects in the precious metals, perfume, and chocolate (this prompted a note on the economic value of colonies), but not to Lille or other industrial centres. The balance was to some extent restored in Belgium, where Liège was part of the itinerary, and much attention was paid to railways, iron and steel. Holland contributed shipbuilding in Rotterdam and diamonds in Amsterdam, as well as canals, the construction of which was studied in some detail, plus von Siebold's collection of models, maps and pictures from Japan at Leiden. However, little comment was made about the historical connection between the Netherlands and Japan, perhaps because it was a link with the Tokugawa, not the new regime. On departure the party stayed overnight in Essen to see the Krupp arms factory before moving on to Berlin. There they spent three weeks, attending the opening of the national assembly (Kume appended an account of the German constitution) and inspecting industrial plants, hospitals, the university, and yet another prison. There was sightseeing at Potsdam and Sans Souci. Itō wrote to his wife that their reception had seemed more friendly than elsewhere; Kido was greatly taken by a horse show (and by contrast devoted only two lines to the Siemens electrical works); while Bismarck invited the envoys to dinner, giving them a lecture on *realpolitik* as it applied to Japan's international position.

In St Petersburg in early April Kido noted that Russian music had more of 'a plaintive air' than anything they had heard in other parts of Europe. Aoki thought it was more like that of Japan. Kume went in some detail into the processes used in the printing of Russian bank notes and provided a summary history of the Russian navy since the days of Peter the Great. He also described what he took to be a market for the purchase of female slaves or bondservants. For the rest, the use of water-wheels in industry attracted some attention, as did an exceptionally well-equipped bath-house. Mining and agriculture were the most serious subjects of study.

After St Petersburg Iwakura and his remaining companions spent the second half of April and the first week of May travelling to Hamburg (shipping, plus comment on the German Confederation), Copenhagen (shipyards) and Stockholm (glass, steel, schools). Next came the long rail journey south through Germany to Florence, Rome, Naples, Venice and other cities in northern Italy, three weeks being spent in viewing the sites of classical history, libraries, museums and various Italian crafts (mosaics, porcelain, glass). None of this had much to do with 'wealth and strength', though some of the travellers, at least, recognized its importance to the development of European civilization. Kido, who was now about two weeks ahead of Iwakura and Itō, produced a remarkably well-informed account of the ruins of Pompeii. He also went to the Vatican, which might have been thought a political risk for a Japanese official.

Italy was followed by two weeks in Vienna, chiefly to visit the international exposition, though there was also dinner with Franz Joseph at the Schönbrunn Palace. Kume, who gave no less than forty pages to the exposition objected to some of the Japanese exhibits, especially the pictures of actors and prostitutes, which Europeans, he said, regarded as shameful. He would have preferred nothing more than birds and flowers. Kido, who had been in Vienna in time for the opening on 1 May, was still more sweeping in his condemnation. The Japanese, he recorded in his diary, had shown themselves 'not yet able to distinguish between the purpose of an exposition and a museum'.[15]

The visit to Switzerland, starting on 19 June, took nearly a month. Much of it was spent sightseeing and shopping, apart from a visit to the clock and watch industry of Geneva; but there was also a good deal in Kume's book about Swiss schools, emphasizing, as he had done in the case of Britain, the inclusion of the country's history and geography in the curriculum, as well as subjects 'which are important to human life'. This led him to criticize what was done in 'the East' — meaning China and Japan — as paying too little attention to such everyday things as agriculture and commerce. This type of education, he said, unlike that of the West, was of little concern to most of the population.[16]

From Geneva it was only a short journey to Paris and thence to Lyon — a brief stop to look at the silk industry, which was important to Japanese exports — before departure by steamer from Marseille on the long voyage home. The places seen along the way — Suez, Aden, Bombay, Colombo, Malacca, Singapore, Saigon, Hong Kong — served as reminders to the Japanese, if any were needed, of their reasons for setting out on these travels. All were Asian, all were under western domination. The European settlements were for the most part clean and affluent, the native cities dirty and poor. Europeans were arrogant, Asians everywhere oppressed. This kind of imagery, brought back by many Japanese travellers, not only those who went with Iwakura, was to have an impact on the ideas which went to make up Japan's nationalism and imperialism in later decades.

At the point in his narrative at which he described the embassy's departure from Marseille, Kume inserted a number of essays summarizing what in his view it had learnt on its travels. Insofar as these are chiefly relevant to the wider subject of Japanese knowledge of the West, it will be convenient to consider them later in this book (Chapter 11), but there is one aspect of them which can appropriately be stated here, because it derives, not from the deliberate study of western civilization, but simply from the variety of conditions that had been encountered. The experience had produced an enhanced awareness of the differences in national strength between the countries visited. On one occasion, when in Rome, Iwakura had confessed to Itō that he sometimes despaired of Japan's being able to match the achievements of even second- and third-ranking European countries, still less those of the major powers. At the same time, what seemed to Japanese to be the West's striking lack of cultural uniformity seemed to hold out a measure of hope to Japan. As Kume pointed out, everywhere in the West there was an insistence on preserving national and even local customs: in language and dialect, costume, religion, types of housing, the teaching of history. The implication was that Japan, too, might be able to find a way forward towards 'wealth and strength' which did not require the sacrifice of inherited traditions.

The West's diversity also had some bearing on Japan's own need, several times expressed by the country's leaders in the previous fifteen years, to find western friends and allies who might provide support against the imperious treaty powers. What Bismarck had said to the ambassadors over dinner touched directly on this. He had learnt in his youth, he told them, when Prussia was small and weak, that he could not put his trust in international law. The strong could ignore it when it suited their purpose. Japan, therefore, like Prussia, would have to look for safety to her own patriotism and strength. Nevertheless, she could rely on the friendship of Germany in this situation. Unlike France and Britain, Germany did not have territorial ambitions in the East. Yet she was just as capable as those two countries of providing 'men of talent' to assist Japan in her development. Ōkubo, who has been described in the title of one biography as 'the Bismarck of the East', found all this persuasive. 'Bismarck', he wrote to friends in Tokyo, 'has inspired me with confidence.'[17]

Reports

It was made clear from the outset that the Iwakura embassy was not only to gather information about the West, but also to incorporate it into reports, recommending possible applications to Japan. This intention, like the programme itself, proved overambitious. One difficulty was that much of the material collected and sent home during 1872 was destroyed by a fire in the Council of State's offices in May 1873. Another was that

171

cost outran budget, causing some investigations to be curtailed. Two officials who were detached in February 1873 to carry out a study of the Dutch waterways, extending to methods of construction, the working of lock gates and problems of flood control, acquired so much information that when financial considerations forced their recall to the main party three months later they were still not in a position to write up their results. Iwakura had meanwhile ordered the special commissioners and their staff to return separately to Japan as soon as their own particular contributions were completed, in an attempt to make further savings. Most began to leave early in 1873, though Hida Hamagorō's study of British railways, together with another of the German military system, took several months more. Despite Iwakura's efforts to economize, the bulk of what was eventually brought back to Japan was more than officialdom could comfortably handle. Some reports were never finished. Others got no further than the collection of unedited documents, translated into Japanese, but coming to no conclusions and making no recommendations. Many still exist only in manuscript in government archives.

The attempt to impose some order on the material began in October 1873, shortly after Iwakura arrived back in Japan. It was supervised mostly by the Foreign Ministry. Of the small group of officials to whom the work was entrusted, the most important were Kume Kunitake, the ambassador's secretary, and Tanabe Taichi, who, with the help of a team of translators and clerks, compiled an account of the embassy running to twenty-seven manuscript volumes. This was completed in January 1877. Fifteen of the volumes comprised a diary of events. The rest contained official documents, concerning protocol, treaty revision, and places visited, put together without commentary, or even a table of contents. Another forty-one volumes held reports from the special commissioners and their assistants.

The material provided by the special commissioners, which was intended to be a basis for policy decisions, was not all suited to that purpose by any means. Some was very sketchy indeed, having been produced by hard-pressed bureaucrats whose other duties left them little time to spare once they were in Japan again. What is more, very few of the compilations were ever seen by the wider public, which limited their usefulness. One exception was the Education Ministry's report on western educational systems, produced in 1873–4 in three sections (dealing with the United States, Britain and Germany, respectively). It was published in June 1877. In addition, Yasukawa Shigenari, a former Dutch scholar, who had taught at Fukuzawa Yukichi's academy and had been sent with the embassy by the legislative division of the Council of State, wrote an account of the British constitution and British politics, published in February 1875. A Finance Ministry official compiled a volume on international private law, consisting mainly of translated texts. Most other reports were mere fragments, at least when compared with the plans made in 1871. For example, Fukuchi Genichirō, who was detached from the embassy while in Paris in February 1873, under orders to travel home via Egypt and Turkey to examine the system of 'mixed courts' then being proposed for use in Egypt (as a step towards ending extraterritoriality), produced a document on that topic which seems simply to have stayed in the files. Another such report dealt with the British consular system in China. Both had presumably been intended to be part of a larger treatment of international diplomacy.

One can illustrate the disparity between intention and result by looking at Yamada Akiyoshi's blueprint for a modern army.[18] Before the embassy left, the Defence Ministry had written in grandiloquent terms of its plans for Japan to have an army and navy comparable with the best in the world. When it came back, Yamada, now representing the Army Ministry alone — the two service ministries had been separated in the course of 1872 — wrote only of military organization and training. Even within this narrower field he declined to make comments about staff functions and supply, on the grounds that these were matters needing further investigation. True, he opened his statement with a reference to the role of the soldier in modern society, adding the unexceptionable observation that to be successful an army needed the backing of a stable state and a properly organized ministry, but most of what he had to say was at a much less elevated level. For example, he acknowledged that annual estimates should be prepared by the army and submitted to the Finance Ministry for approval, ruling out the idea that military expenditure might be outside the national budget in some way, then went on to argue that to operate such a procedure properly there would have to be specialist supply officers with professional training. Other such specialists would be required for the artillery branch and the medical corps, he believed. Setting up facilities for training in these skills was therefore a matter of priority. Officers for general service should be recruited from middle school graduates (once the state education system was in full operation) and sent to a military academy modelled on America's West Point. Non-commissioned officers should be trained by regional commands. There were also two general desiderata (which he apparently derived from von Scharnhorst's reforms in Prussia between 1808 and 1812): an element of military training for all pupils in state schools; and arrangements for officers to give lectures to local audiences on Sundays, in order to encourage a popular awareness of the army's importance to society.

Long delays in the completion of departmental reports, causing irritation in high places, prompted Kume, with Iwakura's blessing, to prepare his own account of the embassy. Based on the papers collected in his editorial office, as well as on consultation with colleagues and his own recollections, it was entitled *Tokumei Zenken Taishi Bei-Ō Kairan Jikki* (Record of the Tour of America and Europe by the Special Ambassador Plenipotentiary). It was published in five western-style volumes by the Council of State in 1878. For the most part the book was arranged chronologically. The first two volumes covered travels in the United States and Britain, respectively. Volumes 3 and 4 took the narrative from arrival at Calais to departure from Italy. The last one, starting with the Vienna Exposition, described the final stages in Europe and the journey back to Japan. To this were added a number of essays on Europe and the West in general, divided according to topic.

The scheme of organization which Kume adopted is similar in many respects to that of the manuscript report of the 1862 mission (see Chapter 5). There is a day-by-day record of the activities of the ambassador, that is, of Iwakura and his immediate entourage, but not a great deal about those of the special commissioners, or of officials whose duties took them away from the embassy's main body. At the point of arrival in each country there is inserted a gazetteer-type entry about it, covering such subjects as geography, climate, population, history, products, trade and industry, religion and customs. In some cases the same kind of information is provided more briefly for major cities. The state of the weather and distances travelled are recorded with great regularity.

Compared with the 1862 report there are also some significant differences. One is that Kume shows much less interest in ceremonial: references to guards of honour, royal audiences and state receptions are so brief as to be dismissive. Another is that he gives little space to descriptions of buildings and their contents, whether because they no longer seemed wondrous to the Japanese, or because Japanese envoys were now in a better position to collect information which they found of greater interest. That he was less preoccupied with military technology than his predecessors had been does no more than mirror the tone of the mission as a whole: its organization embodied an awareness that 'strength' did not just stem from the possession of armaments. The same approach is evident in the way in which much of the material is presented, in particular by the introduction into the narrative here and there of short essays or longer digressions on general topics, usually of a kind which carried a moral for Japan. In San Francisco, for example, when a vineyard was visited, the discovery that its bottles and corks were imported from Europe, because these were the best, produced a note on the need to establish a reputation for quality if exports were to thrive. Again, to the description of a farewell dinner for Parkes and Aston before leaving London in December 1872 was appended, perhaps as a response to the dinner-time conversation, a series of financial and trade statistics, together with the comment that these were matters in which Britain and

America were supreme. Japan, Kume observed, would do well to pay them greater attention. The stay in Belgium prompted a discussion of the relative merits of state and private railways, while the classical monuments of Rome brought a discourse on the ancient world's contribution to western culture. This in turn became a peg on which to hang a reference to Japan's debt to China and Korea, as a consequence of which, Kume pointed out, his country had achieved 'an advanced level of civilization'. By implication, it could do as much again in the contemporary context, by turning its attention to the West.

Many of these passages have the appearance of received wisdom, deriving from what members of the embassy were told, or from a reading of the books they took home with them. They were not obviously the result of observation. Thus the inspection of agricultural tools and implements at the Agricultural Hall in London became the occasion for a note on British agrarian history, making a reference to enclosures and emigration as factors in the substitution of machines for manpower. Similarly, a visit to the British Museum gave rise to a comparison — illustrating the theme of 'progress' — of how orientals and occidentals treated buildings. When Europeans built a house, Kume wrote, they constantly sought to improve it. Chinese put great effort into building it in the first place, but then did no more, no matter how dilapidated it became. Japanese came somewhere between the two: they took care about the original construction: they restored and renewed the building when the need arose; but they did not try to make the house better. This was one respect, he concluded, in which their education ought to be reformed.[19]

There was quite a lot about political institutions in various sections of the book. After a description of the Capitol in Washington came a summary of the functions of Congress, stemming, no doubt, from the studies made by Kume and Hatakeyama. An account of the opening ceremony of the national assembly in Berlin was followed by a statement about the German constitution. British parliamentary government was treated at some length. It is worth summarizing what Kume wrote about it, for the sake of comparing it with what was said on the subject in 1862.[20] This time the principal features were accurately recorded: the summoning of Parliament, voting rights, the bicameral legislature. Reference was made to the differences between the American Senate and the House of Lords. The distinction between the monarchical cabinet system of Britain, in which an administration might change if it lost a parliamentary vote, and the presidential one of the United States, was also noted. Peers were described as a relic of former aristocratic government, still owing their position mostly to landed wealth; members of the House of Commons as men from the ranks of the well-to-do, chosen by a limited electorate. The debates in the Commons, Kume said, reflected the varied age, outlook and experience of its members: 'a hundred flowers bloom'.

In other words, there were none of the feudal class assumptions or uncertainties about terminology which are found in the 1862 report. There was even a cautious recommendation. As Kume saw it, an elected legislature, such as existed in Britain and other countries in the West, could provide the 'unity of high and low' which Japan had to have in order to defend herself in a dangerous world. Yet it could only be effective if commerce enjoyed a greater importance in society than it did so far in Japan. It followed that as a first step 'we must give our attention to fostering our finances and securing wealth and strength'. Parliamentary rule would come in due course as a natural consequence.

As this entry demonstrates, Kume did not intend his book to be a mere assemblage of factual information. It was rather an attempt to convey to the Japanese reader the main features of modern society, as the West conceived them, together with illustrations from the embassy's own experience and comments on their relevance to Japan. This is seen most clearly in those sections of volume 5 — approximately 125 printed pages — in which he presents material on the subject of government and economy in the countries of Europe, while pulling together what had been said here and there in earlier parts of the text. Government, Kume wrote, had in the East an ethical base (*dōtoku-seiji*), manifested in Confucian paternalism.[21] In the West, by contrast, it provided a framework of law, designed to keep in check the greed and rivalries within the population, which arose from differences of social origins, economic interests, religion, customs and tradition. A polity in the West could take one of several forms: monarchy, aristocracy, republic. A state could be organized in several ways: despotic, constitutional, federal. In all these cases, however, rulers faced a people in whom the struggle for livelihood contributed to an assertion of individual rights and to claims for political independence. It was a situation far removed from that which obtained in Japan. Japan would therefore have to move with very great caution in adopting political institutions from the West.

On the subject of the economy, too, Kume began from first principles.[22] Volume 5 included separate sections on transport, climate, agriculture, industry and commerce, in each of which there was an elementary statement of economic theory, followed by information on such matters as types of energy, prices, markets, labour, the manufacture of particular products, and the trade conducted in them. All this contributed to the general theme that an industrial economy was one in which manpower and technology were applied to the manufacture of low-priced daily necessities for supply to mass markets (a concept which was new to most of his Japanese readers). Such an economy, he explained, involved a division of labour between entrepreneurs, working for profit, and labourers, working for wages, each having an interest in the success of the enterprise to which they belonged, but differing functions within it. It was the business of government to regulate disputes between them through industrial law. Trade played an important role in the system, since it moved manufactured goods from areas of production to higher-priced areas of daily use, as well as raw materials and food supplies in the reverse direction. In both cases transport had a critical part to play. So did colonies. 'The flesh of the weak is the food of the strong' are the opening words of a passage on European seizure of lands in Southeast Asia.[23]

To Kume these were the essential characteristics of the society he identified as 'enlightened' (*kaimei*) and 'civilized' (*bunmei*). It was a recent phenomenon, he said, dating from the beginning of the nineteenth century, and its emergence had opened up an unprecedented gulf between East and West. After all, the East had not yet begun to enter the industrial age. Because of this, Japan, seeking international security, faced a much greater task than had ever been envisaged by the men who first used the slogan 'wealth and strength'.

It is not clear how far these conclusions and the recommendations arising from them were Kume's own, how far they were those collectively of the embassy's leadership. Echoes of them are to be found in memoranda by Kido and Ōkubo, as we shall see (Chapter 11), but this is not conclusive on the point of authorship. Similarly, although Kume seems to write at times with the enthusiasm of a convert more than the dutifulness of a scribe, it does not follow that all his conclusions were his own. He was, after all, a Confucian-trained scholar from Hizen, not in any way expert in western studies before he left Japan. To that extent his travels as Iwakura's secretary comprised a voyage of cultural discovery. It seems likely, therefore, that what he wrote reflected a wide variety of influences, both Japanese and western: conversations with western officials and businessmen; lectures from western scholars, arranged for the Japanese visitors; the reading of books and published reports which the embassy took home; things he was told by Japan's diplomats and students abroad, as well as by his editorial colleagues in Tokyo. Kume's contribution, it is usually assumed, was more a matter of literary skill than of knowledge and analysis. Yet however this may be, one cannot deny him the credit for having organized a huge compendium of information; and because it was published, it became a rich seam for his contemporaries to mine.

10

The Fruits of Experience:
I. Later Careers

It is not easy to demonstrate with any certainty what influence foreign study or travel may have had on an individual's career. Ability, character, birth, family connections, political affiliations, all enter into any explanation, not only of success or failure, but also of opportunity. It is relevant, for example, that most of the Japanese who went to America and Europe between 1860 and 1873 came from the ruling class, if only from the lower levels of it, which was a significant advantage in a country where equality was not a universal principle in their lifetime. Then again, the mere fact of being allowed or chosen to go abroad implied that in the eyes of their superiors they possessed determination, or ability, or both. In other words, experience overseas cannot be readily isolated from other elements in the equation.

The most difficult factor to assess is that of political background. The overthrow of the Tokugawa at the beginning of 1868, to be succeeded by a regime which drew both its authority and its leadership from a different source, ensured that anyone whose career spanned both sides of this temporal divide was likely to encounter great changes of fortune. Very few of the men considered in this book held important office both before and after 1868. Those who qualified by feudal status for positions of responsibility under the Shogun mostly sank into obscurity, or died, sometimes by their own hands, when his power came to an end. By contrast, those who became prominent in Meiji Japan, drawn with relatively few exceptions from the territories of feudal lords whose followers had not been eligible to serve the Tokugawa house, enjoyed the benefit, both of association with successful revolution — however remote it may have been in practice for many of them as individuals — and of strong regional loyalties. Very rarely, as we shall see, could other qualifications override considerations as powerful as this. Nevertheless, it is worth making some attempt to assess how far the knowledge and reputation which derived from travel were able to balance or outweigh the effect of suspect origins or lack of powerful friends.

178

TOKUGAWA ENVOYS AND STUDENTS

The men who were sent as envoys to China from Nara and Heian, already officials of some consequence before they left Japan, did little to improve their prospects of promotion by going. Much the same is true of those who led the Bakufu missions to America and Europe between 1860 and 1867. As Tokugawa vassals of rank and responsibility they were undertaking a duty which carried more risk than prospects of reward, and none of them in fact rose to higher posts in the remaining years of Tokugawa rule than their personal status would have led one to expect. Shimmi Masaoki, who went to Washington in 1860, was transferred to an office in the Shogun's household soon after his return, retired owing to ill health in 1866, and died in 1869. His colleague, Muragaki Norimasa, also held no further diplomatic appointments, but survived in retirement after the Restoration until 1890. The *metsuke* who had accompanied them, Oguri Tadamasa, had a more active later career. He became one of Edo's chief advisers on military reform in the regime's closing years, closely linked with Léon Roches; and perhaps because of this, his end was not a peaceful one. As a well-known opponent of the imperial cause during the crisis at the end of 1867, he was seized and executed by loyalist troops in the spring of 1868.

Takenouchi Yasunori was rewarded with an increase in stipend when he came back from Europe in 1863, but was not promoted and withdrew into relative obscurity from the following year until his death in 1867. One of his fellow-envoys, Kyōgoku Takaaki, served in undistinguished posts until he died in 1864. The other, Matsudaira Yasunao, was made a member of the Tokugawa council (Rōjū) in January 1866, a promotion far beyond that of any other envoy, but this owed nothing to his travels: it was because he succeeded to the headship of the main branch of his family, becoming a vassal daimyo (*fudai*). As such he was able to live in some comfort for the rest of the century, despite the fall of the Tokugawa. One other senior member of the 1862 mission, Shibata Takenaka, who was head of its secretariat, does seem to have profited from what he did. He was promoted through a series of offices dealing with foreign affairs in the next few years, then appointed to lead a mission to France and Britain in 1865–6(Chapter 6). Though this proved to be the high point of his career, he at least survived the Restoration, living quietly in Tokyo, sometimes consulted privately by the government on diplomatic questions.

Of the major Bakufu missions, that leaves only Ikeda Nagaaki's to Paris in 1864. Since those who took part in it were punished and dismissed from office for their failure to carry out orders, it is no surprise that they left little mark on later bureaucratic history. Ikeda himself was pardoned in 1866, but was appointed to only minor office, from which he soon resigned. Like some other former servants of the Tokugawa, he withdrew discreetly to the provinces after 1868, staying in Okayama until his death in 1879.

Those who accompanied the missions in a less elevated capacity fared better in later years, probably because their functions were more specialist than political. Kimura Yoshitake, who was the 'admiral' aboard the *Kanrin Maru*, never attained that exalted rank in reality, but did serve in some important defence and diplomatic posts after 1860. He refused to join the Meiji administration after the Restoration, despite invitations to do so. The ship's captain, Katsu Kaishū (Awa), was much more prominent, both before and after 1868. He was for a time head of the Bakufu's naval training school at Kobe; negotiated the surrender of Edo to imperial forces in the civil war of 1868, largely thanks to his contacts with Saigō Takamori, their commander; joined the new government as an official of the foreign affairs department in 1869; then moved to the defence department, becoming a Councillor of State and Navy Minister in 1873. He was made a count in the Meiji peerage in 1887 and died in 1899. One of his subordinates on the *Kanrin Maru* was the engineer, Hida Hamagorō, who was later sent to France and Holland to advise on ship purchases. After the Restoration he joined the Ministry of Public Works, which appointed him to serve with the Iwakura embassy as special commissioner. Another, Akamatsu Noriyoshi, went as a naval student to Holland in 1862, and returned to Japan as a shipbuilding specialist after the fall of the Tokugawa. In 1870 he followed Katsu to the Defence Ministry, which employed him variously at the naval academy and afloat until 1876; but for the rest of his active career, that is, until he was posted to the reserve in 1892, he worked in naval dockyards, commanding in turn those at Sasebo and Yokosuka. By the time of his death in 1920 he was vice-admiral and baron. Ono Tomogorō, who was a navigator on the *Kanrin Maru*, was engaged for a time in supervising the Ishikawajima shipyard and other Bakufu construction ventures; went to Washington in 1867 to arrange for the purchase of the warship *Stonewall* by Japan; worked for the Ministry of Public Works after the Restoration as a surveyor in connection with railway building; and spent his last twenty years after 1878 teaching science and mathematics.

Of the diplomatic and secretarial staff who went to Washington in 1860, none achieved anything of note. Tamamushi Yasushige, the samurai from Sendai, whose journal is one of the mission's more interesting documents, returned to his domain in 1861 and spent his time in the next few years collecting political and foreign intelligence for his lord. One of his compilations, *Ihi nyūkō roku* (Records of Foreign Entry to the Ports), is still valuable as source material on the period. Like Oguri Tadamasa, he supported the Tokugawa cause in the fighting of 1868, with the result that he was required to commit ceremonial suicide when captured. A few others from this group found minor posts in the Meiji Foreign Ministry. One man, Nonomura Tadazane, made use of his experience to open a western-style clothing store after the Restoration, apparently with success.

Among those who went to Europe with Takenouchi in 1862, Fukuda Sakutarō, a finance official, had a varied but not outstanding career later in life. It included duties at Yokohama, service in the military force trained for the Bakufu by French officers after 1865, and a position in the telegraph section of the Meiji Home Ministry. Ichikawa Wataru, whose travel diary has been translated in part by Ernest Satow, was one of the many samurai who found it hard to make a living after 1868. His chief employment was editorial work for the newspaper *Nichi Nichi* under one of the mission's former interpreters, Fukuchi Genichirō (see below). Sugi Norisuke, composer of Chinese poems about what he saw in Europe, found life easier, at least partly because he came from Choshu. He returned to senior office in his domain, was appointed after the Restoration to the Imperial Household Ministry, and was later made governor of Akita, a member of the Privy Council, and viscount.

Of the administrative staff of subsequent missions, two are especially worthy of note. Tanabe Taichi, who travelled to France with Ikeda in 1864, then again with Tokugawa Akitake in 1867, discovered after the Restoration that his diplomatic expertise was as valuable to the new government as it had been to the old. A post was found for him in the foreign department in 1870. He went abroad again with the Iwakura embassy as chief of its secretariat, accompanied Ōkubo Toshimichi to China in 1874 to settle a dispute over Taiwan, and later served as minister in Peking. He died in 1915. One of his 1867 colleagues, Shibusawa Eiichi, won even greater recognition — and wealth — in the Meiji period. Despite close links with the household of the last Shogun, Yoshinobu, who had sent him to Europe as comptroller to Tokugawa Akitake, his financial skills were recognized by a place in the Finance Ministry as early as 1869. He resigned after a dispute over policy in 1873, in order to devote himself to private business, with the result that by the time he retired in 1916 he was Japan's leading modern entrepreneur, active in founding the First National Bank and such companies as Oji Paper, Osaka Spinning and Tokyo Gas. He was President of the Tokyo Chamber of Commerce for twenty-eight years.

The interpreters who went with the missions acquired incontrovertible qualifications as experts on the West, but they did not often find the means to exploit them as bureaucrats or businessmen. Two were aboard the *Kanrin Maru*: Nakahama Manjirō and Fukuzawa Yukichi. Nakahama, a former castaway, American-educated, was among the best of the Japanese linguists. This facility was his principal source of livelihood after he returned to Japan in 1860. He taught English in Kagoshima, went twice to Shanghai to help Tosa buy western-style ships, and taught English again in Tokyo after the Restoration, both privately and in the government university. He also went to Europe with Ōyama Iwao and Shinagawa Yajirō in 1870–1. Fukuzawa was a man of a quite different order: a samurai, though a low-ranking one; a Dutch scholar, trained at Ogata Kōan's school; a Bakufu translator at the Bansho Shirabesho. In addition to the 1860 voyage to San Francisco, he took part in the 1862 mission to Europe and that of Ono Tomogorō to America in 1867, bringing together what he had learnt on these travels in a book, *Seiyō Jijō* (Conditions in the West), which was enormously successful as a first-hand description of western institutions and behaviour. In the tradition of Tokugawa scholarship, he founded a private academy in Edo, to which he eventually gave the name Keio Gijuku, which is now a university, still under that name; but unlike many of his fellows he seems to have made no attempt to enter government service under Meiji, even in education. Instead, he became a well-known writer of books and articles on 'enlightenment' (*kaimei*), as well as the founder of a newspaper, *Jiji Shimpō* (1882). We shall revert to an examination of his ideas at a later point (Chapter 11).

The senior interpreter among those who went to Washington with Shimmi was Namura Motonori. He continued to serve in much the same capacity for the rest of the Tokugawa period, mostly at Hakodate, though he also went to Russia with Koide Hidezane in 1866. There is no record that he held any office after the Restoration. The young Tateishi Onojirō ('Tommy'), only an apprentice interpreter in 1860, later opened a school in Edo. After 1868 he secured a post in the Meiji foreign affairs department, going as interpreter with the Iwakura embassy — he had meantime changed his name to Nagano Keijirō — but worked thereafter for the Ministry of Public Works and Ministry of Justice (probably in connection with foreign employees and foreign residents in Japan, with whom these departments were much concerned). He left little trace of his passing.

Of the 1862 interpreters, Moriyama Takichirō remained the Bakufu's chief interpreter in Edo until he was appointed assistant to the governor of Hyogo in 1867, when preparations were being made to open that port to foreign trade. He retired after 1868 and lived in Tokyo. Mitsukuri Shūhei, who was older than most of his colleagues, continued on the staff of the Bansho Shirabesho, except for a visit to Russia with Koide in 1866–7. After the Restoration he devoted his time to scholarship and education. Tachi Hirosaku, the youngest of this group, studied French under Mermet de Cachon in Yokohama after he returned to Japan, then later made what it is tempting to call the routine transfer to the Meiji Foreign Ministry. He subsequently held office for a time in the Finance Ministry, before resigning to join one of the newly-formed national banks. He died in 1879 when only thirty-four. Ōta Genzaburō, who was about ten years his senior, lived until nearer the end of the century, holding modest positions in the Ministry of Public Works and performing some diplomatic duties.

Two others who went to Europe in 1862 became figures of much higher public profile in the Meiji period. One of them, Matsuki Kōan, it will be more convenient to consider in the next section of this chapter as a member of the Satsuma mission of 1865. The other, Fukuchi Genichirō, went abroad four times as interpreter: to Europe with Takenouchi, and later with Shibata; to America with Itō in 1870–1; then with the Iwakura embassy. In the intervals he worked in the office of the Bakufu's Gaikoku Bugyō and for the Meiji Ministry of Finance (leaving aside a spell without official employment in 1868 and 1869, partly filled by an unsuccessful attempt to found a newspaper). During his travels he had learnt a good deal about the western press; and in 1874, feeling that his work at Finance was undervalued, he accepted appointment as chief editor of Tokyo's first daily Japanese-language paper, the *Nichi Nichi,* which had been founded in 1872. He remained with the *Nichi Nichi* until 1888, exercising considerable influence of a broadly conservative kind on Japanese political opinion. The rest of his life, which lasted until 1906, was spent writing plays, novels and works of history.

The Bakufu's most accomplished interpreter in French was Shioda Saburō, another pupil of Mermet de Cachon. He first went to France with Ikeda Nagaaki in 1864, again with Shibata in 1865, then as secretary to Samejima Hisanobu, when Samejima established the Meiji government's legation in Paris in 1871. He was also appointed first secretary to the Iwakura embassy. As this appointment suggests, in early Meiji he moved from being an interpreter to being a diplomat, rising steadily within the Foreign Ministry after 1873 until he was made resident minister in Peking in December 1885.

The students whom Edo sent abroad in these years have much in common with the interpreters, in that they came home experts on an alien civilization, like those who went to China in earlier centuries. That reputation was to stand them in good stead after the Restoration, when they had to make their way in the world without the Bakufu's patronage. The naval officers who were sent to Holland in 1862 were building on educational foundations already laid at the Nagasaki naval school and aboard the *Kanrin Maru,* but it is nevertheless remarkable that out of a party of nine (including Tsuda and Nishi, but not the artisans), one became a viscount and four became barons in the Meiji peerage. The two doctors, Itō Gempaku and Hayashi Kenkai, became physician to the empress and Surgeon General of the Army, respectively. Both were made barons. Uchida Masao, who abandoned his naval career on return to Japan, became an academic, working in the Bakufu's western studies institute (Kaiseisho) before 1868 and in the government university

(Daigaku) afterwards. He died in 1876. Sawa Sadatoki, the gunnery specialist, having spent two years in prison for his part in defending Hakodate in the name of the Tokugawa in 1868–9, became a naval officer once more, supervising the construction of the Ishibashi explosives factory, then going on to be deputy director of the naval academy.

The outstanding record among the members of this group is that of Enomoto Takeaki, who was to be a viscount before his death in 1908. On his return from Holland in 1867 he was made deputy commander of the Bakufu's naval squadron, serving under Katsu Kaishū; and when Edo was surrendered to the imperial forces in the spring of 1868 he took his flagship, the *Kaiyō Maru*, together with six other ships, and seized Hakodate, apparently as a step towards establishing an independent territory in Hokkaido to be colonized by Tokugawa samurai. For this, it transpired, he did not have the military backing, but he held out against the Meiji government's attacks until June 1869. Fukuzawa Yukichi tells us in his autobiography that when Enomoto at last surrendered to the besiegers, led by Kuroda Kiyotaka, he sent Kuroda the notes on navigation he had made in Holland, expressing the hope that they would be of value to the country, whatever his own fate might be. His patriotism was in due course rewarded. Pardoned in January 1872, together with his followers, he was first given an appointment in Hokkaido, then sent to St Petersburg in 1874 as minister plenipotentiary with the rank of vice-admiral. In 1878 he returned to duties in the Foreign Ministry, followed by a series of posts of ministerial rank: Navy Minister (1880), Minister of Communications (1885), Education Minister (1889), Foreign Minister (1891). He was the only former Tokugawa official, other than Katsu, to reach this level of seniority in the Meiji government.

The later careers of Nishi Amane and Tsuda Mamichi, who studied law and economics at Leiden, had much in common. After their return to Japan both became teachers at the Kaiseisho and advisers to the Shogun on constitutional law, in which capacity they drew up a draft of a western-style constitution for Japan. If adopted, it would have enabled the Tokugawa to retain some of their dignities and power within a structure headed nominally by the emperor, but the great domains, headed by Satsuma and Choshu, acted quickly to prevent this coming about. As a result, in 1868 Nishi and Tsuda found themselves following the new head of the Tokugawa house into seclusion at Shizuoka, where he had a much-reduced domain. Both had teaching posts there, much less lucrative and influential than those they had lost; but in 1870 they were invited, like other former Bakufu experts on the West, to join the Tokyo bureaucracy. Nishi was appointed to the Defence Ministry, where he took part in drafting the conscription law, and Tsuda in turn to Education and Justice. This set a pattern which continued for the rest of their working lives. Nishi became a specialist on the subject of administrative structures and military regulations in the War Ministry, the General Staff, and the Imperial Household Ministry. Tsuda concentrated on the legal aspects of foreign relations in Justice and War, then became a member of the committee which drafted the civil code. Both were made barons. Both also continued to play a prominent part in scholarship, which brought them membership of the Japan Academy (Nishi became its President in 1879).

The five technicians who survived their training in Holland — one had died there — came home, as one would expect, to a different kind of life from that of their social superiors. Of the two whose expertise was seamanship, Furukawa Shōya served afloat for some years, rising to warrant rank and commanding a supply ship on the Hokkaido run. He is later recorded as being employed at the Yokosuka dockyard, then as head of a factory or workshop making ship's fitting in copper. In the wars against China in 1894–5 and Russia in 1904–5 he was engaged in salvage duties, partly on the Asian mainland. About the other seaman, Yamashita Iwakichi, much less is known. He, too, worked at Yokosuka, being at one time in charge of sailmaking there, but returned to his native village in Sanuki province in 1887. The shipwright, Ueda Torakichi, followed Akamatsu to Hakodate in 1868 and worked under him again at Yokosuka after 1870, retiring in 1886. The other two men eventually went into business for themselves. Nakashima Kenkichi was an artillery technician for a time in government establishments in Osaka and Tokyo, then set up an ironworks of his own. Ono Yazaburō worked in the mint before establishing a watch factory in 1880 in partnership with his son, whom he had sent to Switzerland for training. It appears not to have been a success.

The six young students sent to St Petersburg in 1865 found their stay neither enjoyable nor in the long run very advantageous. One opened a chemist's shop after the Restoration. Two more found jobs in education, another first in government, then in the hospital attached to Tokyo university. The others at least made use of their knowledge of Russian, one in the diplomatic service, another in the preparation of a Russo-Japanese dictionary and in work as a translator for the Hokkaido Development Commission. As is evident from this summary, none of them achieved any great distinction.

Fourteen more students went to London in the following year. Perhaps because they were more carefully chosen, perhaps because the training they received was more relevant to Japan's future needs, some of them were to be better known in later years. Times were hard for them at first, as they were for other Tokugawa retainers, but after 1870 things began to improve. Of the two senior students, Nakamura Masanao reverted to Confucian studies as a professor at Shizuoka for a while, was briefly a translator for the Finance Ministry in 1872, then began a career in education in Tokyo, teaching both Chinese and English. He was finally appointed to the imperial university in 1881. His main claim to fame was as a translator, however, notably of John Stuart Mill's *On Liberty* and Samuel Smiles's *Self-Help*, both published in 1871 (see Chapter 11). The other senior student in London, Kawaji Tarō, was a grandson of Hotta Masayoshi's adviser in the 1850s, Kawaji Toshiaki. Toshiaki committed suicide when the Tokugawa were overthrown, and Tarō succeeded to the headship of the family, but he does not seem to have had his grandfather's ability. Although he had a post in the Finance Ministry in 1871 and accompanied the Iwakura embassy as an interpreter, by the time of his retirement from public office in 1876 he had risen no higher than Foreign Ministry archivist. He subsequently failed in a business venture, after which he turned, like so many others, to education, ending his career as head of a girls' high school in Kobe. He stayed there until 1918.

Several of the other London students drop out of sight in later years. One, Mitsukuri Keigo, died in 1870. Significantly — because it was a career in which Tokugawa loyalists could keep a low profile — of those who achieved a measure of prominence, all but one did so in the field of education. Ichikawa Morisaburō, after working for a time in the Education Ministry, returned to England in 1877 at his own expense, in order to study science at Manchester. He was later a professor in the imperial university. Toyama Sutehachi, who had known Mori Arinori in London, accompanied him when he went as minister to Washington in 1870; studied chemistry at the University of Michigan (1872–6); and entered the imperial university in Tokyo on his return, becoming Dean (1881) and President (1899). Mitsukuri Dairoku, under his later name of Kikuchi Dairoku, had a not dissimilar career: he went back to England as an official student in 1876 to complete his education there, taking a degree in mathematics at Cambridge, then introduced that subject in its modern form at the imperial university. He became President of the university in 1898, Minister of Education in 1901, President of the Japan Academy in 1909.

The only senior diplomat to emerge from the London group was Hayashi Tadasu. Son of one of the Bakufu's official doctors, he was sufficiently committed to the Tokugawa cause to join Enomoto in Hakodate in 1868, a decision which cost him two years in prison, but gave him a valuable patron later in life. After his release he was employed by the new government because of his knowledge of English, joining the Iwakura embassy as second secretary. He served twice thereafter as a prefectural governor before Enomoto brought him back to the Foreign Ministry in 1891. From that time on his promotion was rapid: minister to China (1895), to Russia (1897), to Britain (1900), becoming the first ambassador in 1905, then two periods as Foreign Minister (1906–8 and 1911–12). His daughter married Fukuzawa Yukichi.

It is tempting to ignore the students who went to Paris in 1867 on the grounds that they were not there long enough to gain much experience or knowledge. Of the fifteen, we have no information about the careers of six. Two more died early, one in the civil war of 1868, the other in Italy in 1869. Of the rest, Tokugawa Akitake, whose education was the primary motive for their presence in France, was caught up on his return in the reshuffle of Tokugawa family positions consequent on the retirement of his brother, the Shogun, emerging as head of the Mito house. As such he became nominally governor of the former Mito domain between 1869 and 1871, but he held no other public offices. One of his companions became an infantry colonel and head of the military academy. Another was resident minister in Italy, then held a post in the imperial palace. The other four had modest positions in central and local government, which they probably owed more to their birth than to education overseas.

The Bakufu sent fifty-seven men abroad as students in the years from 1862 to 1867, for whom we have career information about forty-four. Five were artisans, whose careers seem to have benefited from their newly acquired skills without being adversely affected by the Bakufu's fall. Another was Tokugawa Akitake, who lost the chance of becoming Shogun, but was still able to lead the life of a man of affluence and dignity. Of the remainder, ten had quite distinguished careers in various fields, ten more had a measure of success as Meiji bureaucrats, while sixteen used their western-style skills in the armed forces, education and medicine. The other two became businessmen, though they did not rank among Japan's leading entrepreneurs.

Comparing this record with that of the men who went with the diplomatic missions, it is clear that the fact of having been a Tokugawa retainer senior enough to have been appointed envoy, or something close to it, was a barrier to holding government office after the Restoration, but that to have been a Tokugawa official at a less responsible level was no such disadvantage. Quite the reverse, in fact, for where a knowledge of western technological or military skills was combined with ability and reputation, there was actually a better prospect of high office under Meiji, because a particular level of feudal status was no longer an essential qualification for it. The examples of Katsu Kaishū and Enomoto Takeaki bear this out. Even for less outstanding men such skills — as well as linguistic ones — might bring a respectable place in the scheme of things, usually in the army, navy or diplomatic posts.

The translators and interpreters, it seems, had fewer opportunities open to them, though their position under Meiji was not obviously worse in this respect than it had been under the Tokugawa. Interpreters were needed in many departments, while posts in education were increasingly available to men who knew something of the West. All the same, the men from this group who won the greatest public recognition were those who made a break with officialdom altogether, like Fukuzawa Yukichi and Fukuchi Genichirō. This was also true of Shibusawa Eiichi: though he was not an interpreter, his official position before 1868 was not dissimilar.

TRAVELLERS FROM THE DOMAINS BEFORE 1868

Men who went abroad from domains in the last few years of Tokugawa rule did not usually face the same uncertainties about employment after the Restoration as those sent by the Bakufu. If they were from Satsuma or Choshu, as more then half were, the transfer of power in 1868 improved their prospects, since their feudal superiors became key figures in the Meiji government. For others the change was at worst politically neutral. It is therefore reasonable to expect that the majority would to better than their Bakufu-sponsored counterparts.

Satsuma, like the Bakufu, did not only send students overseas. In 1865 it sent a mission to Europe, led by Niiro Gyōbu, an upper samurai and senior domain official. Despite this experience, his importance in the Meiji era was arguably less than it had been before: he served as a judge, then as a local administrator in the island of Oshima, which had been part of Satsuma territory before 1871. Machida Hisanari, who went with him in charge of the Satsuma students in 1865, had a similar feudal background and a Meiji career that was not much more distinguished. He entered the central bureaucracy after 1868, but not the policy-making sections of it, holding posts concerned with the preparation of Japanese exhibits for the international exhibitions in Austria (1873) and the United States (1876), then with plans for a Japanese national museum in Ueno. In 1885 he retired to a Buddhist temple, where he spent his time collecting antiquities. Iwashita Masahira, who was Satsuma's representative at the Paris Exposition of 1867, was another well-born samurai, holder at one time of the domain's highest office, that of Karō. He was a junior councillor (Sanyo) in the Meiji government in 1868, served successively as governor of Osaka and governor of Kyoto thereafter, and was made viscount in 1887.

This modest level of achievement was not inappropriate for men who had mostly been figureheads during their travels: dignified and high-ranking, they had never been expected to contribute much to the domain's relations with the West even before the Restoration. Matsuki Kōan and Godai Tomoatsu, who were Niiro's principal subordinates in 1865, though lower-ranking, had always had more to offer. Matsuki, under his later name of Terashima Munenori, joined the Meiji foreign affairs department in 1868 as one of its principal officials; went to London as minister plenipotentiary in 1872; returned to become Foreign Minister in 1873, holding that office until 1879; was then briefly Minister of

Education; and was posted to Washington as minister plenipotentiary in 1882. He was later made count and President of the Privy Council (1891). Godai also began in the foreign affairs department in 1868, dealing with the trade of Osaka and Yokohama, but in 1869, like Shibusawa Ei'ichi, he decided to quit government service to pursue a business career. This he did with considerable success, becoming *inter alia* the founder of the Osaka Stock Exchange.

In addition to mission staff, Satsuma sent twenty-six students overseas before 1868, nearly half as many as the Bakufu. Of these, one stayed permanently in the United States, one committed suicide while at college, and two died soon after their return to Japan. Of the rest, seven had distinguished careers in the Meiji period. Three of these were diplomats: Mori Arinori, who went to Washington as acting minister in 1870 and was promoted to minister resident two years later; Samejima Hisanobu, who went to Paris at the same time and became minister plenipotentiary there in 1873; and Nakamura Hiroyoshi, who was interpreter to Saigō Tsugumichi and Yamagata Aritomo in Europe in 1869–70, then joined the St Petersburg legation in 1873 in a subordinate capacity. Mori returned to Japan to serve in the Foreign Ministry from 1873 to 1878, was minister plenipotentiary in London in 1880–4, then abandoned diplomacy for posts in education in Tokyo, which led to his appointment as Education Minister in 1885. He was responsible thereafter for a stream of western-style reforms, which sufficiently offended conservative opinion to bring about his assassination in 1889. Samejima, less controversially, was vice-minister of foreign affairs under Terashima in 1875–8, then returned to his former post in Paris, where he died in 1880. Nakamura, who took much longer to reach a position of seniority, held minor appointments in Marseille and Italy, then put in several years as Foreign Ministry archivist, and did not reach the rank of minister resident (jointly to Holland and Portugal) until 1885.

Another Satsuma student, Yoshida Kiyonari, emerged as a Tokyo bureaucrat of considerable consequence. After leaving London in 1867 he studied at Rutgers University and acquired some knowledge of banking in New York. This made it logical that he should join the Finance Ministry on his return to Japan in 1870. In 1871 he was attached to the Iwakura embassy with the particular task of arranging a foreign loan. Thereafter he specialized for several years in matters connected with treaty revision in the Finance and Foreign ministries, but eventually came into conflict with Inoue Kaoru on this subject and was transferred to the Ministry of Agriculture and Commerce (1885). He was made a member of the Privy Council and viscount before his death in 1891. One of his colleagues at the Finance Ministry after 1873 was Yoshihara Shigematsu, who had been sent to America by Satsuma in 1866 and entered law school at Yale in 1869. He became the first President of the Bank of Japan in 1882.

The Satsuma group in London also produced two senior naval officers. One was Matsumura Junzō (originally Ichiki Kanjurō), who left Britain for America with Mori and Samejima in 1867, remaining there to study at Rutgers and Annapolis when they returned to Japan. He graduated from Annapolis in May 1873 and later specialized in naval training (partly, it is said, because his American education made it hard for him to work with Japan-trained officers in operational commands). He was made baron and vice-admiral on being transferred to the reserve in 1887. By contrast, Nire Kagenori, who went to the United States in the same group as Yoshihara, but did not go to Annapolis, received his naval training in Japan. Like Matsumura, he reached the rank of vice-admiral, but then went on to become Navy Minister, as well as viscount.

Two other Satsuma students deserve some mention. Hatakeyama Yoshinari, whom we encountered as an interpreter with the Iwakura embassy, helping Kume to translate the American Constitution, later worked in the Education Ministry and in the imperial university. He died at sea on his way back from the Philadelphia Exposition in 1876. Asakura Moriaki, who studied in France as well as England after 1865, used his language knowledge after the Restoration to collaborate with a French mining engineer in the development of silver mines in the Kansai region. He was appointed director of the local mining office, which subsequently passed under the control of the central government, and only left that position when the mines became imperial holdings under the Imperial Household Ministry in 1889.

These men apart, the Satsuma students who went abroad before 1868 included several Meiji bureaucrats of middle rank, two army officers, and two academics of no great distinction. The one businessman among them became president of a horse-tramway company in Tokyo.

The only other domain to have an official representative overseas in this period was Hizen, which sent Sano Tsunetami to supervise its exhibits at the Paris Exposition. For Sano this was a quasi-diplomatic experience, which, added to his earlier training at the Nagasaki naval school, opened the way to a career in foreign affairs and politics: minister to Austria and Italy in 1873; Finance Minister (1880); Minister of Agriculture and Commerce (1889).

All the Choshu travellers to America and Europe left Japan as students, not officials: fifteen in all, of whom one died in London and another died too early to have made a career for himself. Of the other thirteen, five became distinguished diplomatic or political figures (one prince, one marquis, three viscounts), while six were senior Tokyo bureaucrats. Interestingly, they did not include any army or navy officers or academics. The most consistently successful were the five who made their way to London in 1863. Inoue Kaoru, for all that he was out of Japan no more than a year, became one of the outstanding Meiji modernizers, serving twice as Foreign Minister (1879 and 1885), but also as Minister of Agriculture and Commerce (1888), Home Minister (1892), and Finance Minister (1898). For the rest of his life — he died in 1915 — he was a major infuence in the spheres of finance and foreign affairs.

His younger companion from 1863, Itō Hirobumi, who also returned in 1864, won even greater fame. He twice went abroad again in an official capacity before 1873, first to America in 1870–1, then as vice-ambassador to Iwakura. He was Minister of Public Works (1873), Home Minister (1878), Prime Minister four times (1885, 1892, 1898, 1900), and President of the Privy Council twice (1885 and 1909). He became Prince and President of the House of Peers, while the decisions for which he was responsible in the many offices he filled involved almost all the major political and diplomatic events in Japan's development in the forty years after the Restoration. He took the lead in remodelling central government in the 1880s and in drafting the Meiji Constitution of 1889. His policies were crucial in both beginning and ending the war with China in 1894–5. As Japan's first Resident General in Korea after 1905 — a post which brought his assassination at Harbin in 1909 — he had a decisive influence in bringing that country under Japanese rule (though it was not annexed until 1910). Only Yamagata Aritomo, his principal rival, also from Choshu, played a comparable part in Meiji history.

The three students who remained in London when Itō and Inoue left – that is, those who continued their western-style training — all became technocrats rather than politicians. Inoue Masaru, who studied mining and railway engineering at University College London, joined the Ministry of Public Works and became the head of Japan's state railways. Yamao Kenzō, who left London in 1866 to study shipbuilding in Glasgow, also went to Public Works, first as deputy to Itō, then as minister (1880). Endō Kinsuke returned to Japan in 1866 because of failure in his studies, but this did not prevent him from joining the Ministry of Finance, where he was responsible for the Osaka Mint and later the currency division. He was, however, the only one of the five not to receive a peerage.

Three more Choshu students followed these five to London in 1865, and another four in 1867. Kawase Masataka was the most notable of them. He, too, joined Public Works when he went home, but later became a diplomat, going to Italy as minister plenipotentiary in 1873 and to London in the same capacity in 1884. He served in the interval in the Justice Ministry. Two others from London were also employed in Public Works, as was one of the three who went to the United States in 1867. The second student from this group found a place in the Ministry of Communications, while the third became Japanese minister to Korea.

The regularity with which mining, railways, communications and other technologically-based employment occurs in this record of the students from Choshu, especially for those who did not reach the governmental heights, can be accounted for, one suspects, not only by the patronage which Itō Hirobumi was able to offer as Minister of Public Works, but also by the kind of education which was most readily available in Britain and the United States to those without official sponsorship. This second consideration also held good in some degree for students from other domains, though they had a more varied spread of careers. Those who left Japan in 1865–7 totalled twenty-eight, drawn from thirteen different feudal territories. Two died early, one of them in the United States, and we have no information about the later lives of another four. Of the rest, three can be described as men of some distinction. One of these, Takahashi Korekiyo of Sendai, worked in various central government departments (Finance, Education, Agriculture and Commerce) before moving to the Bank of Japan (1892), of which he later became President. He was Finance Minister for the first of several times in 1913, served briefly as Prime Minister in 1921, and was killed in February 1936, when army officers attempted a coup d'état in Tokyo. Another Sendai student, Fukuda Tetsunosuke, was also President of the Bank of Japan, in addition to being at one time governor of Tokyo. Hanabusa Yoshitomo of Bizen had a diplomatic career, first as chargé in St Petersburg in 1873, then as minister in Korea (1876), before becoming Chaiman of the Japanese Red Cross.

At a lower level, these domains produced five senior bureaucrats (three in Finance, one each in Justice and railways) and eleven other officials of low to middle rank in War, Navy, Justice, Education, Agriculture and Commerce, and Home Affairs. There were two academics of modest standing and one businessman (a former samurai from Sakura, Hotta Masayoshi's fief, who worked in a department store, though it is not known in what capacity). To these one ought probably to add Niijima Jō, though he does not count in the strict sense as a student from his domain, since he made his way abroad in 1864 without its knowledge or permission. After completing his education at Amherst and Andover, he returned to Japan in 1874 and founded his own college, which is now Doshisha University in Kyoto. He devoted the remaining sixteen years of his life to running it and raising funds for its continued growth. His case is *sui generis*, however. Most students from domains other than Satsuma, Choshu and Hizen did not begin to make their mark in Japan until some years after the political events which brought about the fall of the Tokugawa.

EARLY MEIJI TRAVELLERS

Defining early Meiji travellers for discussion here is not as simple as it might seem, because a good many Japanese who went abroad in one capacity or another before 1868 went again, sometimes more than once, thereafter. That is evident from the previous sections of this chapter. Out of fifty-seven students sent to Europe and America by Choshu, Satsuma and other domains between 1863 and 1867 — omitting others about whose later careers we have no information — no less than forty-seven held government posts in the Meiji period, if one includes officers of the armed forces and the staff of the Bank of Japan. Experience overseas, in other words, led more often than not to official employment. The reason is clear enough. These men were the possessors of what were seen to be useful skills, whether technological or linguistic — Takahashi Korekiyo's progress in financial office, for example, must have owed more to his knowledge of English than to what he learnt as a houseboy and storekeeper in San Francisco — and these were skills which the Meiji government was likely to need in its dealings with the West, sometimes outside Japan. Nevertheless, there were also many other Japanese, who were travelling for the first time. Some were men of birth or bureaucratic promise, who it was thought desirable should have a knowledge of the world. Others were those, already in office, who were sent to gather specific kinds of information. Others, again, were official students, believed — not always rightly — to be the seed-corn of the country's future.

Outstanding examples of the first of these categories were four men who visited Europe just before or during the Franco-Prussian War: Saigō Tsugumichi, Yamagata Aritomo, Shinagawa Yajirō and Ōyama Iwao. Significantly, they travelled in pairs, in each case one from Satsuma and one from Choshu, the domains whose alliance had made the overthrow of the Tokugawa possible. Saigō, whose brother, Takamori, was the *beau idéal* of Satsuma samurai, resumed his military career on return to Japan, rising to the rank of lieutenant-general in 1874. Having demonstrated his loyalty to the Meiji government by refusing to join his brother in rebellion in 1877, he moved on to ministerial posts in the departments of war, education, and agriculture and commerce in the next few years, before transferring to the navy and taking office as Navy Minister in 1885. With only brief intervals (as War Minister and Home Minister) he remained in that post until the end of the century. His travelling companion, Yamagata, rose faster and higher. He was lieutenant-general by 1872, War Minister in 1873, Chief of the Army General Staff in 1878. These posts provided the means to mould Japan's army in both ethos and organization, with the result that its officers gave him loyal support for the rest of his life. A long spell as Home Minister for much of the 1880s, during which he exercised his patronage with care, achieved much the same result in the civil bureaucracy. From that time on, he wielded an influence to rival that of Itō Hirobumi, despite Itō's higher public profile: Prime Minister twice (1889 and 1898); President of the Privy Council

(1893); commander of the First Army in the Sino-Japanese War in 1894, until recalled to become War Minister once again; commander-in-chief of land forces in the Russo-Japanese War of 1904–5. The appropriate honours followed: Field Marshal in 1898, Prince in 1907.

The other two were not quite of this level of distinction. Ōyama Iwao of Satsuma followed Saigō and Yamagata into the army, becoming in the course of time War Minister (under six cabinets between 1885 and 1896) and Chief of the Army General Staff (1882 and 1899). He was made Field Marshal in 1898, like Yamagata, and took command of the armies in Manchuria in the Russo-Japanese War. Shinagawa Yajirō, by contrast, who had been one of Yoshida Shōin's students, devoted himself to domestic politics, apart from a spell in Germany as minister plenipotentiary in 1885–7. He held senior posts in the Home ministry (1877) and in Agriculture and Commerce (1882), as well as in the imperial palace; became a member of the Privy Council; and ended his career as Home Minister (1891), an office he was forced to resign, when he tried to rig a general election on behalf of Matsukata Masayoshi, making extensive use of bibery and police intimidation.

Tokyo bureaucrats who went abroad to perform specific missions were also likely to be successful in later life. Kuroda Kiyotaka, one of Satsuma's military commanders, who visited the United States in 1871 to recruit foreign experts to assist in the development of Hokkaido, emerged in the 1870s as a leading figure in the affairs of the north. Then, following the assassination of Ōkubo Toshimichi in 1878, he became Satsuma's senior representative in the Meiji government, a status which guaranteed him a succession of cabinet posts, including briefly that of Prime Minister in 1888–9. He was made President of the Privy Council in 1895. At a slightly lower level was Maejima Hisoka, investigator of postal services in London in 1870–1. He continued his interest in mail and related subjects for ten years after his return, while working in the Finance and Home Ministries, but left the bureaucracy in 1882, following Ōkuma Shigenobu's resignation over plans for a constitution. He was for a time president of Ōkuma's Semmon Gakkō (now Waseda University); returned to office as vice-minister of Communications, setting up a government telephone system; and served as president of various companies, including two of the regional private railways.

The men who led the Iwakura embassy were already in 1871 the most powerful men in Japan and could hardly become more so by virtue of foreign travel. Until his death in 1883 Iwakura himself continued to fill the highest-ranking offices as the emperor's trusted aide. Ōkubo Toshimichi was acknowledged after his return to be the strong man of the regime, as well as its chief advocate of industrialization. Kido Takayoshi lost some of his influence after 1873, partly because of disputes with Ōkubo, but also because of ill health, which led to his death in 1877.

On Itō Hirobumi we have already commented in the previous section of this chapter.

Of the special commissioners attached to the embassy, Sasaki Takayuki from the Justice Ministry later became a palace adviser and Minister of Public Works; Tanaka Fujimaro from Education had a career largely in that department and in Justice, becoming Justice Minister in 1891, while Yamada Akiyoshi, sent to represent Defence, was later Justice Minister in four consecutive cabinets (1885–91). Kume Kunitake, Iwakura's secretary, did not remain in government employment once he had completed his account of the embassy's travels. Instead, he became a professor of history at the imperial university, though he was forced to resign in 1891 because an article he published was held to be critical of Shinto. He lived for another forty years, teaching, but avoiding public notice.

The group of twenty local government officers who were sent on a world tour in 1871–3, one step ahead of the Iwakura embassy most of the way, produced no individual with a record comparable to these. It is true that several members of the group became what it seems to have been intended they should be, loyal provincial supporters of central government's reforms, but no less than ten of them did not. One joined Etō Shimpei's rebellion in Hizen in 1874. Four others became supporters of the movement for popular rights, calling on the Meiji government to surrender some of its power to an elected assembly. Another five abandoned their official careers to take up new ones in commerce and industry. Perhaps it had not been wise to give them an American as interpreter and guide.

It is worth pausing at this point to consider some of the differences between the later careers of the Tokugawa envoys and those of the officials the early Meiji government sent abroad. The former, but not as a rule their subordinates, were shut out from positions of influence after 1868 by their status as Bakufu servants of some seniority. This one would expect. On the other hand, it would be difficult to show that by going overseas they had earned any promotion even while the Tokugawa were still in power. There was no parallel in this respect where the Meiji bureaucrats were concerned. In 1885 Japan adopted a western-style cabinet system. Between then and 1900 ten cabinets were formed, of which seven were headed by men who had been to Europe or America or both: Itō Hirobumi (four), Kuroda Kiyotaka (one), and Yamagata Aritomo (two). Of the next ten cabinets, taking the sequence down to 1921, six were headed by 'travellers', though this time all had been students when overseas: Katsura Tarō (three), Saionji Kinmochi (two), and Takahashi Korekiyo (one).

This brings us to a consideration of those who went as students in the Meiji period. There were far too many of them to make individual examination feasible, but the existence of Inuzuka Takaaki's list does make it possible to undertake a simple analysis of a substantial sample, that is, those who left Japan in the lunar years approximately equivalent to 1870 and 1871. There were 319 altogether. Of these, 28 died abroad or soon after coming home, while no information is available about the later careers of another 112 (presumably because they did not make enough of a mark to become well known). This leaves 179 whom we can consider: 88 sent by the central government or one of its departments; 37 from domains; and 54 who were privately financed.

Taking first the government students, these include four of the five girls who travelled to America with the Iwakura embassy (there is no record of what happened to the fifth). Three of them made successful careers in women's education. The fourth, who was trained in nursing, married Ōyama Iwao and was active in the nursing section of the Japan Red Cross. Of the eighty-four men in this category, fifteen took positions in life that might be described as honorific: members of the imperial house, or of the families of court nobles and former feudal lords, who held posts in the palace, the Imperial Household Ministry and the army. Nearly all had hereditary peerages after 1884. Another eleven had distinguished careers in government (eight), the armed forces (two), and education (one). They included Saionji Kinmochi, a court noble, who after he returned from studying law in France in 1880 was minister to Austria (1885) and Germany (1887), served on two occasions in Itō cabinets as Minister of Education, then twice became Prime Minister as leader of the political party which Itō founded (1906 and 1911). He was Japan's chief delegate to the Versailles conference in 1919. There was also Admiral Tōgō Heihachirō, victor over the Russian fleet at the battle of Tsushima in 1905, as well as Yamakawa Kenjirō, a science graduate from Yale, who worked his way up through the imperial university's science faculty to become president in 1901.

As one would expect, a large proportion of the official students came home to jobs in the bureaucracy, often in the departments which had financed their studies: fifty-three in all, of whom more than half reached senior positions. Only two are known to have entered business, though another, who was counted under 'government' above, was president of the semi-official Industrial Bank of Japan. Of the three who were not in any of these categories, one was a priest, another worked in the Russian consulate in Kobe, and the third, Nakae Chōmin, was a writer and political activist. Nakae, a Tosa samurai, returned from France in 1874 and opened a school to teach French in Tokyo. In 1881 he cooperated with Saionji, whom he had known in Paris, to found a radical newspaper, but it was suppressed in the following year. Thereafter, while Saionji overcame his radical inclinations to become a member of officialdom, Nakae took the path of opposition in support of popular rights. He was banished from Tokyo for a time under the Peace Preservation Law, but was elected to the lower house of the Diet in 1890 and continued to write political pamphlets and articles until his death in 1901. In 1882 he had also published a translation — in classical Chinese — of Rousseau's *Contrat social*.

Of the domain students sent abroad in this period, only thirty-seven can usefully be considered (out of a total of eighty-seven), because nothing relevant is known about the rest. One of those from Choshu is recorded only as having entered the House of Peers in due course. Two others from western Japan had distinguished careers, one in business, one in the army and politics. The first was Hara Rokurō of Tottori, who spent nearly six years in Britain and America studying economics, then worked in the Yokohama Specie Bank before becoming head of the Fuji Paper company. The second was Katsura Tarō, whose life was spent almost entirely in the army for many years after his return from Germany: major-general, 1885; vice-minister of war, 1886; a divisional command in Korea in 1894–5; Governor General of Taiwan, 1895; War Minister, 1900. The last of these appointments brought him into political life under Yamagata's patronage, which helped to make him Prime Minister three times in the next thirteen years.

Five of the men sent by domains became businessmen of some consequence, while another six were technical experts in various fields. Only six of the rest held posts of some seniority in government service, of whom three were in the navy. Nine more were officials at more modest levels. That leaves five engaged in education and medicine, one artist, and two politicians, both opposed to the regime. One of these was Baba Tatsui, who returned from Britain in 1878 and at once became prominent in the radical wing of the popular rights movement. He wrote articles for the press; was put in prison for a while on suspicion of trying to buy dynamite for terrorist purposes; and left Japan again after his release, this time for America, where he died in poverty in 1888.

Bearing in mind that very few of these students came from Satsuma or Choshu — Katsura was the outstanding exception — the figures suggest that many of those who came from other domains, perhaps believing that their feudal background was not of a kind to give them special consideration in bureaucratic posts, looked for opportunities in the armed forces, business or technology, where specific western-style qualifications might carry greater weight. Much the same pattern is to be found among those whose travels were privately financed. There were ninety-one of these in 1870–1, of whom thirty-seven have to be disregarded for lack of information or because of early death. The remaining fifty-four include sixteen whose later place in the scheme of things was largely honorific, so only thirty-eight can usefully be considered here. Of the four who achieved distinction, either in government or business, one was Makino Nobuaki, second son of Ōkubo Toshimichi (he changed his name as a result of adoption). Having held a variety of diplomatic and bureaucratic posts before 1906, Makino then became Minister of Education in a Saionji cabinet; was subsequently Foreign Minister and Imperial Household Minister; but is best known as Keeper of the Privy Seal between 1925 and 1935, in which capacity he was Saionji's ally in seeking to exercise a degree of restraint over the ambitions of Japanese army leaders. The postwar prime minister, Yoshida Shigeru, was his son-in-law. Kaneko Kentarō of Fukuoka, who studied law at Harvard, also had a political career. He was one of Itō's advisers in the drafting of the 1889 constitution and was made Minister of Justice in 1898, though for the rest of his life — he died in 1942 — he was influential chiefly behind the scenes. His fellow-student from Fukuoka, Dan Takuma, who had studied engineering at MIT, became one of Japan's most powerful industrialists. He made his reputation at the Miike coalmines near Nagasaki when they were under the supervision of the Ministry of Public Works, but when they passed to the Mitsui company in 1887, so did Dan, rising steadily through it to become chief director in 1914. In 1932 he was shot outside Mitsui's Tokyo head office by a member of one of Japan's so-called 'patriotic' societies.

The rest of the private students can be dismissed more briefly. Of ten who can be described as just short of distinguished, six were in the bureaucracy, four in education and technology. Another four held positions of some responsibility in business. Those of more modest standing comprised ten officials, of whom three were in the armed forces, and five educators. The other five took up a variety of occupations, ranging from religion and art to the press.

It is worth repeating that a very high proportion of the Japanese who travelled and studied overseas, even those who went privately, later pursued careers in government. Yet it does not follow that their success was directly related to their American or European experience. Government, after all, is precisely the context in which political affiliations and political patronage had their greatest effect. It can therefore be very difficult to decide how much weight should be given to family origins — especially to the fact of being a samurai from Satsuma, Choshu, Hizen or Tosa, the domains whose members provided most of the 'Meiji oligarchs' — and how much to knowledge of the West. Some of those who became famous, such as Itō Hirobumi and Inoue Kaoru of Choshu, spent time outside Japan as students; but there were also men, whose later standing was not so very different, like Matsukata Masayoshi of Satsuma, the Meiji government's most notable Minister of Finance, and Ōkuma Shigenobu of Hizen, Foreign Minister, Prime Minister and founder of a university, who spent no part of their youth abroad. In such cases it is difficult to see an unequivocal link between success and travel.

Leaving political posts aside, it is worth noting that seventy-four of the 179 students from 1870 and 1871, whose careers we examined above, spent much of their lives in occupations to which their new-found western knowledge was directly relevant, that is, education (thirty-one); technology, including the engineering branches of the armed forces (twenty); and other forms of naval and military service (twenty-three). Another fifteen went into business and banking, to which, too, experience overseas could be expected to contribute. To these one should add the lower-ranking diplomats and other officials, for whom a knowledge of foreign languages, or of law and economics, made the expense and effort of study abroad worthwhile. For all such persons, although travel might not have guaranteed an inevitable progress to the political or bureaucratic heights, it brought positions of profit and esteem.

To summarize, one can state the following broad conclusions: that firsthand experience or knowledge of the West, acquired during studies abroad, was a career advantage in the conditions which obtained in Japan after 1870, provided it was not coupled with senior status in the former Tokugawa establishment; that it did not necessarily lead to a senior position in the state unless reinforced by political patronage, or exceptional ability, or both; and that where neither of these additional qualifications was present, the skills obtained in the course of a training overseas were most likely to bring employment — not necessarily at the highest level — in the bureaucracy, education, or some technical field. With few exceptions, the men who urged the importance of commerce and industry did not themselves become businessmen.

11

The Fruits of Experience:
II. Policies and Ideas

Japan's approach to the West in the nineteenth century was an attempt to 'adopt the best of foreign methods and join them to the best of our own', as Tokugawa Nariaki had put it (Chapter 3). It was occasioned by a recognition of Japanese weakness in the face of western strength. In this very general sense, the decision in principle to adopt western weapons, technology and perhaps institutions was taken at arm's length, that is, before there was any significant personal contact between Japanese and foreigners, beyond that which took place in Japan on a limited number of occasions in the course of negotiating treaties. The envoys and students sent to America and Europe thereafter were expected to put flesh on the bones of a policy which had already been determined. Once the serious study of the West began, however, it became evident, at least to those engaged in it, that the process was likely to prove much more complex than had originally been envisaged. The superficialities of western strength could not readily be detached from the fundamentals of western civilization.

For this reason, the activity in which Japanese travellers engaged during the years we have been studying in this book cannot be described as exclusively instrumental. In addition to finding out how to do what their superiors had decided must be done, they were discovering additional desiderata, hitherto unsuspected, which, it seemed, would have to be met if Japan was to be strong in western terms. Some of these concerned modern industry and its relationship to science and technology. Others had reference to the nature of the modern state and its social, as well as political, structures. Still others involved the theories underlying these things. In this sense, the framing of policy came to depend in the longer term as much upon newly acquired knowledge as it did upon the leadership's initial purposes.

Equally important was the discovery that 'the West' was not in all respects an entity. In the first place, substantial differences existed between western countries — that is, between western nation-states — in

200

types of law, political structures, economic policies, cultural traditions, and religious allegiances. Japan could not take them all as models. In addition, western societies were in a state of flux. Japan encountered Europe and America at a time when many former axioms were being challenged there: in politics, by populist movements in the aftermath of the French Revolution and the doctrines associated with them; in religion, by a questioning of divine revelation in the name of science; in secular thought, by the application of the positivism of Auguste Comte and the utilitarian principles of Jeremy Bentham to the study of human society. In this situation Japanese found that they could not just acquire from the West a tidy package of universally held beliefs. Depending on where they went and how long they stayed, they were also likely to take home a selection of 'new' ideas, some of which were of a kind that kept the West divided. In time, they were to divide Japan as well.

WEALTH AND STRENGTH

In sending envoys and students overseas after 1860, the Tokugawa government had it in mind to acquire the information on which policy might be based, while training a number of men to assist in its implementation. The Meiji government followed this example in due course. For both, the immediate object, as has several times been said, was to enhance the country's ability to defend itself in any confrontation with the powers, a purpose expressed from time to time — and more frequently after 1868 — in the slogan *fukoku-kyōhei*. It is commonly translated 'national wealth and strength', as it has been on occasions in this book; but a more accurate rendering of the original Chinese would be 'enrich the country and strengthen its military [force]', implying that the first of these actions would contribute to achieving the second. In other words, strength was the objective, wealth a means.

The first duty of the travellers was that of finding out how to do what needed to be done. In terms of strength, narrowly defined, this prompted a concern with weapons and their manufacture — Armstrong guns, Minié rifles, turret mounts for ships' armament, steel plate for their protection — and the study of related skills, such as gunnery, shipbuilding and navigation. The heavily naval emphasis in the list reflected not only the expectation of naval attack on Japan, but also the absence of a tradition of naval warfare there, factors which made the task of establishing a navy both an urgent and a technically difficult one. Yet it did not pose the same political problems as reforms related to warfare on land. One of the lessons learnt by Japanese visitors to Europe and America — the opportunity to learn it in East Asia was lacking, since the West did not undertake large-scale land operations in the region after 1860, apart from

201

those of the French in Indo-China — was that a national army, to be effective, should not depend for its leadership and manpower on feudal units, each owing its duty to a different lord. Acceptance of this conclusion imposed severe limitations on what could be done by way of military reform while the Tokugawa ruled Japan. Even after 1868, when the emperor had been made once more the country's temporal monarch, something of this difficulty remained, since the imperial regime depended on a coalition of domains for several more years.

The main impetus towards changing this state of affairs in the early Meiji period came from the leaders of Choshu, whose contribution to the struggle against the Tokugawa had included a land campaign, fought in 1866, as well as the civil war of 1868. The fighting on both occasions had revealed the limitations of samurai troops. Studies then undertaken in Europe by Yamagata Aritomo, Katsura Tarō and Yamada Akiyoshi, all of whom had taken part in these operations, provided both a rationale for reform and a knowledge of how it might be carried out. Yamagata came back convinced that army units must be detached from their feudal allegiances, as well as 'trained and drilled in western tactics'. The conscription law of 1872, drafted under his supervision, was accompanied by an announcement which called for samurai and commoners to be 'equal in the empire and without distinction in their duty to serve the nation'.[1] Katsura acquired an admiration for von Scharnhorst's reforms of the Prussian army, which guided him in much of his staff work on return to Japan, while Yamada's travels with the Iwakura embassy made him aware of the need for specialist officers with professional skills in the supply, medical and artillery branches. Some of the implications were set out by Nishi Amane, a former Tokugawa 'traveller', writing as a military bureaucrat in 1878. Japan's feudal armies, he said, had been held together by a shared moral code, based on differences of inherited status. A modern one must rely on discipline, instilled by regulations and drill. Central to it was a code of obedience: 'no one has equal rights in a military society'; 'we must always obey orders, even when we disagree'.[2]

In 1873, introducing the proposals based on his travels, Yamada had commented that in Japan, as elsewhere, a modern army required a stable society as its base. In doing so he was addressing in his own particular sphere a conclusion of which Japanese reformers had been made aware both by recent experience and by the writings of Rangaku scholars like Satō Nobuhiro: that the nature of the organization of the state was itself an ingredient in national strength. Unhappily, they found in Europe and America no simple answer to the question of what might properly comprise it. By the time Kume wrote his narrative of the Iwakura embassy, many had become aware that the powers having treaties with Japan, all immensely strong in Japanese eyes, could variously be described as republican and monarchical, federal and unitary, absolutist and parliamentary. Nor was the range of possible models immutable. Between 1860 and 1873 Japanese visitors were in a position to observe the United States seeking to resolve the constitutional problems left by civil war; Britain moving with some speed towards a late Victorian world of more intrusive social legislation; France precipitated by defeat from the Second Empire to the Third Republic, surviving the Paris Commune on the way; Prussia under Bismarck becoming Germany under the Hohenzollerns; and Italy in the course of unification after centuries of division. Even in Russia Alexander II freed the serfs.

The only constant to be observed was that the West believed in national unity, not feudal separatism, such as existed in Japan. This was already evident before 1868 to some of those who, because they were opponents of the Bakufu, thought it necessary to consider what to put in its place if they succeeded in overthrowing it. Godai Tomoatsu, writing from Europe at the end of 1865 to a senior Satsuma official, Komatsu Tatewaki, made a distinction between Britain, which, he said, came first in Europe 'in point of equitable and benevolent government', and states like France and Germany, where there was a greater emphasis on law; but he contrasted all of them with Japan, which was 'wasting time in domestic disputes'. What was needed, he argued, was to bring about cooperation between court nobles and feudal lords, then to assess the relative advantages of different European political systems, and finally to make appropriate changes in Japanese government, so as to afford a basis for 'wealth and strength'. This done, Japan would be able in ten years or so to 'advance in Asia'.[3] His colleague, Matsuki Kōan, expressed the view that Japan would only find safety within an international system guaranteed by law, as weak countries like Greece and Denmark and Portugal had done. A necessary step towards that end would be to create a political structure in Japan which would bring about domestic unity and be respectable in the eyes of the West, perhaps an administration acting in the emperor's name on the advice of a council which would represent both Bakufu and domains.[4]

These issues had to be faced more directly by the leaders of the Meiji government after the Restoration. By then several of the men who had spent some time abroad, including Matsuki (now Terashima) and Itō Hirobumi, were advocating the abolition of the domains themselves in the interests of national strength, partly to put an end to the fragmentation of authority, partly to ensure central direction of the country's military resources; and it was in the light of the implementation of this policy in August 1871 that the Iwakura embassy was instructed to undertake a more extended investigation of the nature of government in the West. Kume's book, it will be recalled, included summaries of the constitutions of the United States, Britain and Germany, as well as a general section on western concepts of politics.

This aspect of the embassy's work was under the general supervision of Kido Takayoshi, who wrote a long memorandum setting out the conclusions he had drawn from it when he returned to Japan.[5] What he had seen on his travels, he wrote, had convinced him that a country's strength depended heavily on its constitution, as manifested in its laws. Poland, for example, had brought about its own destruction (by partition between Prussia, Russia and Austria) because of political disorder at home, which its institutions did nothing to prevent. The moral: that unity must be the first aim of a country's constitutional arrangements. If a state is divided among 'a multitude of petty rulers', each seeking his own advantage, 'the national strength is dissipated'; but where 'one sovereign can exercise control . . . though his territory may not be large or his people numerous, they will be able to protect themselves against the insults of their neighbours'. In this fundamental sense, a constitution was that 'which sets on a firm basis the weal of the entire nation, which prevents officials from taking unauthorized steps merely on their own judgment . . . placing under one control all the business of administration'. Japan had already taken steps in that direction, starting with the Charter Oath.

In more 'enlightened countries', Kido continued, among which Japan could not so far be numbered, the sovereign 'does not hold sway in an arbitrary fashion'. Instead, institutions were so ordered as to make evident 'the wishes of the whole people', by which those in office were bound. Japan was not yet ready for this stage, which depended on 'the degree of civilization of the people', for too many Japanese did no more than 'mimic idly the arts of civilization', while the country's laws, 'promulgated without due consideration', were still in a state of flux. Yet given patience, appropriate laws could be established and the people raised 'from their present state of degradation', until Japan could be classed with the world's 'prosperous and enlightened states'.

Although Kido himself was to play little personal part in it, Japan's institutional history in the next ten to fifteen years was to follow very much the course he envisaged in this document: the elaboration of a structure of local government, firmly under the control of the Home Ministry; the adoption of a western-style cabinet system in 1885, with a Prime Minister at its head; the establishment of a Privy Council; the reorganization of the civil service by Itō Hirobumi in 1885–6, providing for recruitment and promotion by examination; the provision of a bicameral assembly. Some of the relevant documents reflect Japan's willingness to pick and choose among western models: a French criminal code, a German commercial code, a civil code which combined Anglo-Saxon elements with traditional Japanese ones, a written constitution of multifarious origins, but largely Prussian in its inspiration. All these were components of what Japanese students of the West had come to recognize as the modern state.

So was education. There has been occasion to note at several points in previous chapters that members of the missions sent to America and Europe before 1868 had shown great interest in schools of every kind, ranging from military academies and technical colleges to schools for the poor, the orphans, the blind, the dumb and the deaf. As Confucian-trained samurai, to whom education was of the first importance, they held this to be one of the keys to understanding western society. After the Restoration the purpose of such enquiries changed. Because the new government undertook a direct responsibility for organizing education on a national scale, announcing its first Education Code in September 1872, Japanese now examined the educational systems of western countries with a view to adopting some of their features, rather than learning more about the civilization that produced them. Two things in particular attracted the attention of the Iwakura embassy, as Kume described it. One was practicality, that is, the inclusion in the curriculum of subjects which would help those who studied them to earn a living. The other was patriotism: teaching which would reinforce awareness of the nation and the citizen's duties to it. Both had an obvious relevance to 'wealth and strength'. This apart, however, Japan's educational models were as diverse as its constitutional ones. State education had a pervasive American tone after the appointment of David Murray as superintendent of schools, but in administration it owed a good deal to France, in science and medicine to Germany, in engineering to Britain.

The process by which Japanese ideas about 'strength' became broader and more clearly based on western thinking, in part as a result of what envoys and students learnt on their travels, applied also to the 'wealth' half of the slogan, though more slowly. The first phase, lasting for several years after the opening of the ports, had witnessed a gradual acceptance of the argument that foreign trade was not merely something imposed on Japan by treaty, but also — contrary to the tenets of traditional Tokugawa thought — a potential source of profit and revenue. The earliest missions were much concerned with finding out about the practicalities of hand-ling it: customs arrangements, bonded warehouses, exchange rates, currency. Thereafter their interests expanded to take in finance and the working of markets. Fukuzawa Yukichi wrote about the way railways and hospitals were financed, Tsuda Mamichi and Nishi Amane studied economics and statistics at Leiden, Shibusawa learnt about banking from Fleury-Hérard in Paris. Nevertheless, none of these things had much perceptible impact on Tokugawa economic policy. Even industry was treated by Edo as the manufacturing arm of military technology, not as a factor in increasing prosperity; and while it is true that some of those who went overseas learnt to think differently about it in the course of their travels, it cannot be argued that this was the object of those who sent them.

Edo's political opponents, especially those from Satsuma and Choshu, had much more open minds on these matters. Satsuma had a long-standing concern with foreign trade because of its links with Ryukyu; and when it decided in the winter of 1864–5 to send a mission and a party of students to Europe, its intermediary was a British trading firm at Nagasaki, not western diplomats (Chapter 6). Godai Tomoatsu, who was put in charge of the commercial aspects of the mission, was then introduced to the mysteries of company formation by the Belgian entrepreneur, Montblanc, with the result that he entered into a scheme which brought together trade, transport and industrial production in the service of Satsuma finance. His experiences persuaded Godai, as he wrote in one of his letters home, that in Europe 'the power of the state rests on two foundations, industry and commerce'.[6] It is not surprising that Godai himself became an entrepreneur of some importance later in life, and that two of the Satsuma students in London, Yoshida Kiyonari and Yoshihara Shigematsu, had distinguished careers in the economic sector of Meiji government. Similarly, Inoue Kaoru and Itō Hirobumi of Choshu, whose introduction to London was by courtesy of Jardine Matheson and its affiliates, never wavered in their commitment to the development of Japanese commerce and industry for the rest of their lives. Other Choshu students in London at this time went home as civil engineers.

The knowledge and experience of these men were put at the disposal of the new government after 1868, first through the Finance Ministry, in which Itō, Inoue, Godai and Shibusawa all served, then the Ministry of Public Works. They contributed to a number of economic reforms of vital importance to the regime: land tax, for example, plus the development of railways, together with the creation of a system of national banks. Yet they did not blindly follow the conventional wisdom imparted to them by their foreign mentors. Itō, writing from America in the spring of 1871, dismissed British arguments in favour of Free Trade as mere self-seeking, justified by neither Britain's past nor America's present. Japan, he believed, should act in a manner appropriate to her stage of economic growth, that is, she should 'follow the example of the United States and establish a protective tariff to ensure the prosperity of domestic manu-facturers'. Ōkubo Toshimichi, both as Finance Minister and as Home Minister, found the argument persuasive. Godai still held to it as late as 1880. Britain, France and America, he then observed, 'prosper today because their governments . . . protected commerce and industry at the time when these had yet to flourish'.[7]

Both Itō and Godai were advisers to Ōkubo, whose own enthusiasm for industry was greatly stimulated by his travels in America and Europe in 1872 and 1873. He took part in many visits to non-military indus-trial plants, especially in Britain. He had the opportunity to discuss with businessmen and various economic dignitaries — albeit through interpreters — their assessment of the role of industry in modern life. He acquired a knowledge, if only at second hand, of the corpus of elementary economic theory assembled by the embassy's secretariat and incorporated by Kume in his book. The result was a new approach to the making of economic policy.

He set it out in a memorandum on the subject of promoting industry in Japan which he wrote as Home Minister in the early summer of 1874.[8] It began with the assertion that 'a country's strength depends on the wealth or poverty of its citizens'. This in turn rested on industry. Japan had not yet made progress in developing such wealth, largely because government, which ought to provide the 'guidance and encouragement' essential to it, had not fully played its part. In Britain, 'an island country, possessing . . . bays and ports and rich mineral resources', where officials had long considered it 'their greatest duty to take advantage of these natural blessings', shipping and domestic industries had been protected by navigation acts until industry was 'extremely prosperous' and other countries were in no position to compete with it. This was the example Japan should follow. The obstacles to doing so did not lie in geographical position or a lack of national resources — in these respects Japan was 'quite similar' to England — but in the fact that the Japanese people lacked the spirit of enterprise needed for the task. This was a deficiency that government could make good by leadership and education. It must 'carefully investigate which products are to be increased and what kind of industries are to be encouraged', then 'initiate industrial enterprises', 'setting a standard in accord with the people's temperament and their degree of knowledge', in order to ensure that 'the country will . . . grow rich and powerful'. Such a policy would make it possible for Japan 'to compete with other powerful countries'.

As the minister responsible, Ōkubo devoted himself to this task in the remaining four years of his life. His former advisers, Godai and Shibusawa, cooperated in the capacity of entrepreneurs, though it has to be said that the number of ex-samurai who thought it any part of their duty to find out how the West conducted business and engage in it themselves still remained small. It was not difficult to accept that industrial and financial skills were something the West could teach. It took longer for Japanese, both officially and privately, to come to the same conclusion about commerce.

THE NATURE OF SOCIETY

Policy decisions of the kind we have been discussing did not so much depend on detailed knowledge of the West, or a training in its skills, as on an awareness of problems and possible solutions to them. The 'experts', whether Japanese or foreign, had their place in advising on policy, or implementing it, but the men who decided it, at least in the first generation of the Meiji leadership, were the politicians, especially those who had travelled in the western world enough to form a view of its virtues and defects. They had not usually studied there in any larger sense.

Some of the experts belonged to that category of Japanese travellers whom one might call intellectuals (though several who were also bureaucrats can be found among them). They are distinguished by the fact that they approached the West in a different frame of mind, recognizing that the civilization they faced was perhaps superior to their own, not just a military threat. There was nothing new about this attitude, which had been evident in scholars ever since the eighteenth century; but for men of this kind to see for themselves the great cities of Europe and America, to travel by steamship and train, to visit factories and universities and museums, to stay in western-style hotels, was to learn how inconsiderable their country was in western eyes, how 'different', even 'quaint', they themselves seemed. The reactions of Dutch army officers, or American newspapermen, or boys who followed them in the street, helped to bring it home to them that Japan was not only weak, but also semi-civilized by the criteria then becoming fashionable in the West.

They arrived at a time when the West's view of itself, as well as of the rest of the world, was changing. Darwin's *On the Origin of Species* was published in 1859. The famous public debate about its implications for religion between Bishop Samuel Wilberforce and the scientist T. H. Huxley took place in 1860, the year of the first Bakufu mission overseas. J. S. Mill's *On Liberty*, the classic statement of English liberal thought, also appeared in 1859, as did Samuel Smiles's *Self-Help*. Herbert Spencer wrote several of his most influential books between 1860 and 1873, while by the last of those years the principal works of Marx were also in print, though not, perhaps, well known. Thus the first Japanese visitors, seeking to understand the West, found the values of western civilization to be the subject of critical debate. To many of them, especially the scholars and interpreters, brought up in the rather old-fashioned tradition of 'Dutch studies', the situation was bewildering. It also posed a challenge to the mainly Confucian beliefs in which most of them had been raised.

One can arrive at some appreciation of the variety of their responses by considering the journal of Japan's first modern learned society, the Meirokusha, founded in 1873 on the initiative of Mori Arinori. Mori became its first president. Its other founder members had mostly been employed at one time or another in the Bakufu's Bansho Shirabesho, or its successor, the Kaiseisho. They came together at regular meetings to discuss the adoption of western ideas and institutions in Japan, with the intention of providing an element of informed opinion to serve as background to government reforms; and the papers read at these meetings, together with a number of other contributions, were published in the society's journal, *Meiroku Zasshi*. It brought out forty-three issues in 1874 and 1875.[9] Of the fifteen members who wrote material for it, seven had visited the West, either as students or interpreters.

A total of 156 short articles appeared in the journal (counting serial parts on a single topic as separate items). Twenty-nine were by Tsuda Mamichi, twenty-five by his fellow Leiden student, Nishi Amane, and eleven each by Mori Arinori and Nakamura Masanao, who had studied in London under the auspices of Satsuma and the Bakufu, respectively. Fukuzawa Yukichi, though a member, produced no more than three fairly unimportant pieces, reserving most of his energies for books and articles published independently. A good many of the contributions were straightforward translations or summaries of western works, but some were opinion pieces, taking different sides in current controversies. For example, the question of the need for tariffs to protect Japan's infant industries elicited comment from Kanda Kōhei, Sugi Kōji, Nishimura Shigeki, Fukuzawa Yukichi and Tsuda Mamichi. Not all that was written supported government policy by any means. In fact, it was the anticipation of difficulties with the censorship officials that led the society to suspend publication of the journal towards the end of 1875.

Mori Arinori, the first president, was an ardent advocate of change in Japanese society. In 1869 he had incurred the hostility of many samurai by proposing that they no longer wear swords in public. Nearly twenty years later he outraged loyalist sentiment and Shinto susceptibilities by an incident at the Ise shrine, when he was alleged to have used his walking-stick to raise the curtain to an area which only members of the imperial house were allowed to enter. His assassin in 1889 claimed to be avenging this sacrilege. Between these two incidents he had come to public notice not infrequently as a critic of Confucianism, which he held to be authoritarian, hence a barrier to the growth of 'self-reliance' among Japanese.

To Mori, all these were aspects of the search for 'civilization and enlightenment' (*bunmei-kaika*), the slogan by which he and other members of the society described their efforts to understand the West. In an early number of the journal he attempted to define it. Enlightenment, he said, marked the stage of human progress at which men, having sufficiently developed their knowledge of the world they lived in, were able to 'construct machines, erect buildings, dig mines, build ships, open seaways, produce carriages, and improve highways'. Because of 'the liberal expansion of commerce' which these things brought about, society also underwent change, making it possible for 'the true value of civilization' to make itself felt.[10] Tsuda Mamichi, writing in the same issue, associated the concept rather with ideas than technology. He identified enlightenment with what he called 'practical studies' (*jitsugaku*), but included among them the more theoretical ones: astronomy, physics, chemistry, medicine, political economy and western philosophy. More surprisingly, although he set aside the 'empty studies' (*kyogaku*) of Buddhism and Confucianism, he welcomed the introduction of a moral element, derived from the more liberal brands of Protestant Christianity.

On this evidence, Mori and Tsuda shared a belief that enlightenment was not just a stage in human progress, but also something the West could teach Japan. Mori chose to make the point in terms of social behaviour. In a five-part discourse entitled 'Wives and Concubines'[11] he condemned marriage as it was practised in Japan because it treated the wife as 'no different from a chattel', having no legal rights against her husband and required to accept into the family any children he might have by a concubine. Such a system 'obstructs enlightenment', he claimed, and changing it was one of the most vital tasks of reform. The family, after all, was the foundation of the social order. He therefore put forward for discussion a draft marriage law on western lines, in the hope that Japan might, by adopting it, rid itself of the reputation of being in these respects 'the most immoral country in the world'.

Tsuda, as befitted an expert on constitutional law, offered a discursive five-part article on 'Government'.[12] In it he summarized the ways in which, as he saw it, the political institutions of Japan still fell short of western standards, citing the failure to dissociate government and religion, as exemplified in court ceremonial; the absence of any separation of the powers of legislature and executive, or of a clear distinction between the administrative and legal functions of the judiciary; and a lack of independent scrutiny of government finance. The one subject on which he showed less enthusiasm than might have been expected from a constitutional reformer was that of proposals for a parliament. A House of Peers, he argued, would be of doubtful benefit to Japan, because the former feudal lords, who would be the majority of its members, had had an upbringing which made them 'most deficient in understanding'. He expressed similar reservations about the competence of potential electors to a lower house, though he conceded that these might be overcome by a system of indirect election, or in other ways 'modifying the election laws of European countries to suit the cultural level of our people'.

Nishi Amane was another who was sceptical about constitutions, believing, like Tsuda, that Japan was not yet ready to adopt in full the laws and systems of government to which he had been introduced in Holland. He also objected to the Confucian insistence on a link between ethics and political authority. His longest contribution to *Meiroku Zasshi* was a piece on 'Religion',[13] consisting chiefly of a plea for freedom of religious conscience (no doubt Dutch in derivation). The proper role of government with respect to religion, he maintained, was to prevent 'religious disturbances', as required by its responsibility for law and order.

There was no obligation on the people to accept any belief which gave religious sanction to the actions of rulers — by asserting that the king or emperor was a god, for instance — and no attempt should be made to force it on them. Nor should such ideas have any part in state education. The state certainly had the right to express approval of what it deemed best in religion, but not to enforce particular propositions, any more than it was licensed to choose national aims, like the pursuit of strength, without reference to ethical principle. 'Let us take warning from the fate of Israel', he concluded, somewhat obscurely.

Setting aside for the moment Nakamura Masanao and Fukuzawa Yukichi, whose most important publications on western society were not in *Meiroku Zasshi*, it might be interesting to compare what we have been considering so far with items in the journal written by men who had not been abroad, either as students or as members of missions. One of these was the Confucian scholar Sakatani Shiroshi, who contributed no less than twenty pieces. He did not at all dissent from the view that changes were necessary in Japan, but the manner in which he presented the case for them owed much less to western intellectual models than did the writings of Mori, Nishi and Tsuda. He welcomed the conscription law, for example, not only because it would help Japan to modernize her military establishment, as Germany had done, but also as a means of restoring the country's martial spirit after the excesses of western-inspired 'frivolity and shallowness' in which it had recently indulged. On another occasion he made an extremely convoluted case for the respectability of the slogan 'honour the emperor, expel the barbarian' (*sonnō-jōi*). Before 1868, he reasoned, the expression had been compatible with the opening of the ports, despite its apparent hostility to the West, because the second half of it really meant 'expelling our barbaric customs in conformity with the virtuous and just path that extends through the whole world'. In the Meiji period, honouring the emperor had come to incorporate 'the methods for public discussion by high and low'.[14] In other words, neither term in his view contradicted the liberal tendencies of his fellow-members, or meant what on the surface it appeared to mean.

Another stay-at-home Confucian scholar, Nishimura Shigeki, who was also later to be counted a conservative, at least in matters concerning education, was much readier to take account of western thought. In a *Meiroku Zasshi* article on 'Three Types of Political System', he examined, first, autocracies, which he described as the traditional type of rule, surviving from ancient history; second, constitutional monarchy, which was autocracy modified by 'reason', as a result of demands by the people for a share in government; and third, republican democracy, in which reason was paramount.[15] The last of these was to be found in countries where enlightenment had already existed at the time of the state's foundation (by which he presumably meant the United States). He did not, however, claim that it was necessarily the best. Rather, the best political system for any given society was in his view that which was most appropriate to its degree of enlightenment. To go too far or too fast beyond it would be dangerous.

These two Confucians can be contrasted with the economist, Kanda Kōhei, another non-traveller, who in 1867 had translated into Japanese William Ellis's *Outlines of Political Economy*, which set out *inter alia* the argument in favour of Free Trade. As a Finance Ministry official in 1873 and 1874, Kanda wrote in the journal about subjects within his bureacratic competence: the reform of national finance, the opening of iron mines, and questions concerning currency. All this was as 'western' as anything put forward by those who had studied overseas. The one exception was a short article he contributed on music, denigrating its condition in Japan and urging reform in accordance with both Chinese and western models. To it he appended an entirely irrelevant comment on *sumō* wrestling, 'an ugly, barbarian custom', which caused men to watch other men 'perform like beasts'. It ought to be abolished, he wrote, though gradually, 'since its followers will be outraged if it is suddenly prohibited'.[16]

It is not possible from so few examples to draw a clear line between the kind of articles produced by those who had been overseas and those who had not. The former usually returned with greater fluency in foreign languages and better informed than their compatriots about sources of further knowledge, but once back in Japan again they, too, relied mostly on books, like those who had never travelled at all. Hence the import of western books, in much the same way as the import of Chinese books in earlier centuries, was the essential key to understanding. On the other hand, it must also be said that with the passage of time the greater availability of translations made it less and less necessary to read them in foreign languages. One of those who helped to bring about that change was Nakamura Masanao.

His seven-part article in *Meiroku Zasshi* under the title 'An Outline of Western Culture' was not, it must be said, the best of his productions.[17] We are never told the name of the work from which it derived, though on the evidence of Nakamura's version it must have been a short, elementary text, probably acquired when he was in London. Much of what it said can have been barely intelligible to Japanese readers because of its brevity, despite the interpolation of explanatory notes from time to time: into a very few pages it managed to crowd not only a brief introduction to classical culture and the later spread of Roman law, but also a series of sketches of European thought from the Renaissance to the seventeenth century, touching on Grotius, Luther, Copernicus, Brahe, Kepler, Galileo, Francis Bacon, Machiavelli (who 'greatly injured government and morals') and Hobbes (who 'is generally reviled in recent writing'). A passing reference to David Hume suggests that the survey might have been carried further, had not the journal ceased publication in 1875.

Of greater consequence — indeed, the true basis of Nakamura's reputation — were two book-length translations which he published in 1871. One was John Stuart Mill's *On Liberty*, the other Samuel Smiles's *Self-Help*. Both works posed considerable problems of terminology in Japanese. For example, Mill's argument in favour of the rights of the individual and his narrow interpretation of the restraints which society should place on them was not easy to convey in a language which neither possessed words for 'rights' and 'individualism', nor made any clear distinction between 'government' and 'society'. Similar problems arose when translating Smiles. His first page contains the statement that the spirit of self-help 'is the root of all genuine growth in the individual; and, exhibited in the lives of many, it constitutes the true source of national vigour and strength'.[18] Nakamura clearly found this difficult to translate. He produced one rendering in his draft, then a different one for his final published text, in which the spirit of self-help became the root of 'wisdom as a person' and the means of 'building up the country's energy and vitality'. This is not altogether inaccurate, but it is a little at a tangent to the original. There are other examples of difficulties of this kind. More often than not the translator chose to insert explanatory passages, rather than seek equivalent words.

It would be wrong nevertheless to imply that the translation as a whole is clumsy or unsatisfactory. The main burden of what Smiles had to say was that achievement in this life depended on the exercise of personal qualities — hard work, perseverance, integrity and truthfulness — which were not innate, nor a product of inherited rank and wealth, but could be acquired by self-cultivation. For statements of this kind Confucianism offered a tolerable vocabulary, though Nakamura tended to prefer expressions that were simpler than the truly classical ones, in order to reach a wider readership. The result was not unlike the writings of Japan's early nineteenth-century agrarian moralist, Ninomiya Sontoku.[19] It certainly owed less to Protestant Christianity than the writings of Smiles had done, for all that Nakamura himself became a convert. Thus, when he had to find a translation for 'gentleman' in chapter thirteen — the connotation in Smiles is 'Christian gentleman', though he does not use that phrase — Nakamura transcribed the word phonetically, then added in parentheses the Confucian term *kunshi*, or 'superior person', before inserting an explanatory sentence which was not in Smiles's text. Later in the same passage, where Smiles quoted from the Bible, 'the Psalmist' became 'an ancient poet'. In this way the ethics take on a Confucian rather than a Christian colouring, partly, no doubt, for the sake of intelligibility, but also, one suspects, because it was natural for Nakamura, as a Confucian scholar, to use terms which were familiar to him.

In Japanese the book was given a new title, *Saikoku risshi-hen*, which might be rendered 'A Treatise on Determination [or Ambition] in Western Countries'. Its key word, *risshi*, derives from the Confucian classics. A literal translation of 'Self-Help' appeared as a subtitle to each chapter; the text was pruned by the omission of some of Smiles's many examples (often of men whose claim to fame is obscure to modern western readers); and the chapters were broken down into short sections, averaging about a page of the English text. Since these sections were given separate titles, designed to summarize the argument, the book's main thrust is actually easier to follow in the Japanese than in the English version.

Fukuzawa Yukichi approached the question of reform in a very different manner. Although, like Nakamura, he wished to identify and introduce into Japan the 'spirit' of western civilization, he did not at all conceive of doing so in Confucian terms. Confucianism, he wrote on one occasion, produced the kind of scholars who were 'of no more use than rice-consuming dictionaries'.[20] What the country needed — and this is the authentic voice of Japan's students of the West — was 'practical studies' (*jitsugaku*), incorporating not only mechanical and scientific knowledge, as developed in the West, but also economics and law and politics, which had a positive relevance for society. He did not stress the need for an absolute, unchanging ethic, as Nakamura was inclined to do, since this had too much about it of the Confucianism he rejected. Nor was he willing to accept Christianity as an alternative, by way of partner to science. This left him, like many of his Japanese contemporaries, struggling to find a set of ideas that might be the basis for rules of good behaviour, in the importance of which he still believed. A rather mystical notion of the inevitability of Progress, which he conceived in moral as well as social and materialist terms, proved not to be altogether adequate in this context. His writings, therefore, were not always as convincing on the subject of ethics as he might have wished.

Fukuzawa made only three contributions to *Meiroku Zasshi*, two on foreign relations, the third a brief attack on concubinage (on the grounds that it was contrary to the percentage distribution of the sexes in the population). His more considered observations on Japanese society were published partly in a series of pamphlets issued between 1872 and 1876 under the title *Gakumon no Susume* (An Encouragement of Learning), which took up many of the topics discussed in the *Zasshi*, and partly in books such as *Bunmeiron no Gairyaku* (An Outline of a Theory of Civilization), which appeared in 1875. The Outline was the fullest statement of his case for reform in Japan in the period we are considering. Set in a framework of Social Darwinist ideas, it placed Japan, like China and Turkey, in the category of semi-civilized nations, inferior to the West, but superior to Africa and most of the rest of Asia; it emphasized the West's 'spirit' of civilization, the cultivation of which would be the key to the country's independence and international equality; and it pointed to feudalism and Confucianism as barriers to building the kind of society which would enable Japan to escape the fate which India and other countries now under western dominance had suffered. In this type of argument, 'civilization' was not so much an ideal as an instrument, making possible equality with the West. 'Western civilization', he wrote, 'is an incomparable means for both strengthening our national polity and increasing the prestige of our imperial line'.[21]

Like most of his contemporaries, when he wrote about western society and civilization, Fukuzawa meant that which existed in America and Europe in his day. In almost all cases the books which Japanese studied and translated were chosen with this in mind. Except for the natural and social scientists, whose subject-matter imposed a different discipline, there was little apparent attempt to arrive at an understanding of what western scholars themselves might have held to be fundamentals. Greek philosophy, Christian beliefs, art (other than the representational kind, which counted as 'useful'), music (though it attracted an occasional expression of distaste), poetry, or other forms of literature received little mention. The compliments paid to French law and German science did not lead to any wider interest in the culture of those two countries until a good deal later in the century. Italy, too, was hardly known. Russia had already lost much of the reputation it had previously enjoyed as a country for Japan to emulate (possibly because of the strictures passed on it by Japanese visitors, though it seems more likely to have been a result of comments made by other Europeans). Civilization, as manifested in industrial society, was therefore to be found above all in America and Britain.

At a different level, Japan's early travellers had contributed through their letters, diaries and reports, and also, no doubt, by word of mouth, to a gradual differentiation in Japanese eyes between types of foreigner. Instead of mere 'barbarians', to be uniformly condemned for their barbarity, admired for their weapons and machines, and feared for their rapacity, there was now seen to be a variety of nations and races which went to make up international society, each with its own character and culture. As early as 1860 Shimmi and his colleagues had learnt to perceive Americans as something other than Europeans in their attitudes and behaviour. The 1862 mission to Europe had at least begun to recognize some of the ways in which Europeans differed from each other. Matsuki discovered that the Japanese view of Holland was not widely held. Kume's report on the Iwakura embassy tried to summarize national characteristics in a more organized way, even to comparing the skills and tastes of Austrians with those of Prussians.

A great deal of this was hearsay, of course, rather than observation. So was the picture which the travellers took home with them of non-western peoples and societies. Starting with Yanagawa Masakiyo's comments on 'blacks' in 1860 and Ichikawa Wataru's distaste for Egyptian flies and dirt in 1862, the records contain a string of references to 'ugly' Africans and 'lazy' Asians, contrasting with vastly superior Americans and Europeans. All this might be described as an account of the world seen from the first-class cabins of a ship on the Far East run, or from the salons of the western capitals. If Indians and Arabs were poor and oppressed, the Japanese were told by their fellow-passengers in the Indian Ocean, it was because they lacked the qualities to be otherwise. The Pacific crossing for its part induced a ready contempt for Chinese emigrants, taking passage in the steerage class. That impression was in no way changed by a sight of conditions in Hong Kong and Shanghai. The Chinese, in fact, were commonly seen, not as the representatives of a civilization from which Japan had taken a superior culture in the past, but as decadents, justly made victims of the West's imperialism in the present. Ichikawa Wataru called them 'rude and deceitful'. To Kido Takayoshi they were 'exceedingly dirty'. Against such a background, many Japanese began to see themselves, in the phrase that was sometimes used to describe them in the twentieth century, as 'honorary whites'. This was one of the less attractive aspects of their voyaging.

12

Conclusion: Japan and the West

During the Nara and Heian periods Japan imported three main features of Chinese culture: institutions (*seido*), by which was meant laws and the organization of the state; religious and political ideas, mostly Buddhist and Confucian; and some aspects of science and technology, ranging from astronomy to medicine, from architecture to metalworking. All these owed something to the missions which periodically visited China, but the learning process was also indirect. A knowledge of institutions, for example, derived less from personal observation than from the books which the missions brought home. Ideas, though transmitted in part through the students who accompanied the missions, owed as least as much to the Chinese and Korean priests invited to Japan. Technology was acquired in a variety of ways: through immigrants (especially for irrigation and metalworking); through the craftsmen who accompanied Buddhist priests (sculpture and building skills); and through some of the interests which Japanese travellers pursued (medicine and music). Both writing and painting entered Japan in conjunction with religion.

There are parallels between this situation and that which obtained when Japan turned to the West in modern times. The means of acquiring information then were much the same: Japanese missions, students and other travellers; foreign residents in Japan (chiefly diplomats, missionaries, and 'hired foreigners' working for the Japanese government); and the import of books. Only immigrants were lacking. What is more, the categories of knowledge sought by Japanese were broadly similar, though they had a different order of priority. The modern West presented itself to East Asia as a civilization characterized by science and technology on the one hand, by commerce and industry on the other. To this many of its citizens — especially, but not only, missionaries — would have added Christianity and the system of ethics deriving from it. It was natural enough for Japanese to accept the West at this valuation, even if they viewed the last of these items, religion, with suspicion and hostility.

217

Japanese interest in the West in the second half of the eighteenth century was chiefly in those aspects of science, technology and technique — medicine, especially surgery; astronomy, navigation and gunnery; oil-painting and etching — which could be understood with a minimum dependence on the written word and only a superficial knowledge of the civilization which produced them. They were something more than Aizawa Seishisai's 'curiosities and concoctions from abroad', but still fell a long way short of a threat to overturn Japanese tradition. After 1840 a perceived danger of attack from the West quickly changed this state of affairs. Because western military skills were required for maritime defence, they became part of government policy, not private scholarship; and the attempt to put them to effective use increasingly involved not only handling weapons from abroad, but also manufacturing them, a process which expanded, as knowledge grew, to take in related industries, such as iron-founding, steel-making, shipbuilding and explosives. The final stage, signified by the slogan 'Wealth and Strength', involved almost every aspect of government and economic organization.

For the political and economic historian this is the most important strand in Japanese cultural borrowing, lasting into the twentieth century. It had a central role in the Meiji government's efforts to modernize the machinery of the state; it played a key part in the shift from commercial to industrial capitalism; the deep-seated emotions it evoked on the subject of Japan's international strength and weakness, which did not by any means disappear when formal equality was achieved by revision of the treaties in 1894, helped to shape an emerging nationalism; and by virtue of all these things it contributed to the growth of Japanese imperialism and the military expansion through which it was pursued.

The major reforms were concentrated in the decade of the 1880s, when there had been time for the lessons learnt by the Iwakura embassy to be digested and applied to Japanese conditions. In the field of political institutions, a western-style cabinet system was adopted in December 1885; regulations concerning the duties, pay, appointment and pro-motion of government bureaucrats, providing for the introduction of selection by examination, based on syllabuses which were largely western in content, were issued early in 1886; the Privy Council was established in April 1888; a written constitution, creating a bicameral legislature, modelled in large part on that of Germany, was announced in February 1889. In all this, Itō Hirobumi played a key part. He was the first Prime Minister under the new cabinet system, the first President of the Privy Council. The civil service regulations were issued in his name. The consti-tution was drafted under his supervision, following a study tour to Europe in 1882–3, specifically to seek advice about its nature. On his return he had two German advisers to help him in Japan, Alfred Mosse and Hermann Roesler.

Reforms in law were accomplished more slowly, because some of them proved controversial.Boissonade's draft of a French-style criminal code, completed in 1877, was not published until 1882. Roesler drafted a commercial code along German lines, which was ready in 1884, but issued in 1890, while Boissonade's civil code, prepared in 1886–8, which was also largely European in inspiration, was not approved until ten years later. Meantime, the state education system, which had begun with primary schools in 1872, was becoming more elaborate. Middle schools were added in 1881, high schools for boys in 1886, and high schools for girls in 1889. The state university of early Meiji became Tokyo Imperial University in 1886. In all cases the greater part of the curriculum — excluding those sections which touched on patriotism and ethics — had a great deal in common with that of similar establishments in the West.

The extent to which this programme depended on the travellers who have been the main subject of this book can be illustrated by the composition of the first Itō cabinet in 1885. Apart from Itō himself, three other cabinet ministers had been students overseas before 1868: Inoue Kaoru (Foreign Affairs), Mori Arinori (Education), and Enomoto Takeaki (Communications). The departments of Home Affairs (Yamagata Aritomo), Army (Ōyama Iwao) and Navy (Saigō Tsugumichi) were headed by men who had spent some months studying conditions in Europe in the first few years after the Restoration. The Minister of Justice was Yamada Akiyoshi, who had been attached to the Iwakura embassy. Only the Finance Minister (Matsukata Masayoshi), and the first of several Ministers of Agriculture and Commerce (Tani Kanjō), had no similar foreign experience.

In trade and industry, apart from the founding of a number of model government factories and the further development of the military or quasi-military industrial plants inherited from the previous regime, Japan's main period of growth did not begin until after 1890. Nor did it owe as much to travellers: not very many of the early entrepreneurs fell into that category. Nevertheless, because the state was so much involved in the building of an economic infrastructure, so were bureaucrats, many of whom had been trained abroad. Those in Public Works who were engaged in railway-building, for example, had provided a trunk line from Tokyo to Osaka by 1889. Maejima Hisoka contributed an efficient mail and telegraph service. Several travellers held senior posts in the Mint, the Bank of Japan (1882), and the main foreign exchange establishment, the Yokohama Specie Bank (founded in 1880, reorganized in 1887). Finally, Shibusawa Ei'ichi, whom the Bakufu had sent to Paris in 1867, not only became president of one of the earliest private banks (Dai Ichi), but also founded the Osaka Cotton Spinning Company in 1882. Its ability to pay a dividend of eighteen per cent in 1884 was a major stimulus to the

219

emergence of Japan's cotton textile industry, by encouraging other businessmen to enter into it.

There was another element in Japanese study of the West which forms part of a quite different story. Prompted at times by simple curiosity, at times by domestic politics, it was directed towards the investigation of a civilization, which was not only distant, but also in some respects taboo. Always at risk from official disapproval, both under the Tokugawa and under Meiji, this kind of enquiry, seeking to probe the customs and conditions under which people lived in the West, led not infrequently to a questioning of how they lived in Japan. On occasions it brought demands for social and political reform, providing later generations, especially intellectuals, with an 'alternative' view of society, which governments were regularly tempted to suppress. It rested at first on little more than a recognition that there were differences of some substance between the societies of Japan, China, Europe and America; but in the course of time it came to reflect, in addition, an awareness of some features of modern western thought which were critical, not so much of those of non-Western peoples, as of the western ideas and institutions Japan was choosing to adopt. This, too, has proved to be an enduring feature of modern Japanese life, giving western forms to Japanese discontents: demands for the promotion of 'men of talent' by those who were fully persuaded of their own ability; a search for personal recognition by members of society whose material success was not matched by what they thought to be an appropriate higher status; protests against the injustices suffered in a variety of ways by 'commoners'; the whole range of aspirations embodied in socialism. Study of the West not only provided these grievances with a western rationale; the reforms to which it led also provided outlets for their expression, whether through parliament, press or education.

Japan's adoption of western ways is often described as evidence of western 'influence', implying that they were imposed on a country little able to resist. The argument is not entirely tenable. It is true that the nature of western expansion in the nineteenth century gave a particular shape and direction to Japan's response, but the motives for what was done and the initiatives that were taken were essentially Japanese. The verb 'sent' has often been used in earlier chapters of this book to describe Japanese travellers going abroad. This is accurate, insofar as their departure from Japan was commonly at the orders of higher authority; but one must not overlook the fact that the great majority of those who went, whether on the staff of missions or as students, had in the first place put themselves forward for consideration. Nor did they always do so from the patriotic motives stated in their letters and autobiographies. As officials who believed the experience would enhance their prospects of promotion, as samurai who hoped to equip themselves for profitable employment, usually in government service, or as scholars who sought to increase their knowledge and reputation — and hence their rewards — they had a variety of personal ambitions to pursue. In many cases their ambitions were fulfilled.

This was not wholly because of experience overseas, it must be said. Some acquired a knowledge of the West in other ways, or succeeded without it. Yet travel was certainly one of the routes to influence and prestige, as an examination of the careers of those concerned (see Chapter 10) strongly suggests. It gave opinions a measure of authority. It opened up channels of information and advice, which were not available in Japan. In a more general sense, it enabled Japanese collectively to achieve an uncommon degree of diversity in the ideas and knowledge they were able to acquire.

Partly because of geographical remoteness, partly because India and China were more attractive targets of imperialist expansion than Japan, partly because the Japanese were better able to defend themselves, even without western technology, than most peoples of Asia, the country did not in the event become subject to any one western power. Decisions about what to learn and where to learn it could therefore be made with greater freedom than would have been possible under colonial rule, as is evident from the varied destinations of the travellers. The Japanese were fortunate, too, in their timing. The gulf between western science and Japan's, though very large, was not yet unbridgeable. Japan's economy, while backward by comparison with that of America and western Europe, was not much more so than those of other European states, in which industrialization was only just beginning. Moreover, the self-confidence which characterized western society in the second half of the nineteenth century ensured that Japanese visitors, students as well as envoys, were given ready access to most of what they wanted to know. One consequence was that men who were sent, whether by government or feudal lords — and in later years by firms and families — 'to select from the various institutions prevailing among enlightened nations such as are best suited to our present conditon',[1] often came back having learnt more than their sponsors had intended, or even knew about. Where this was 'useful' knowledge it was welcomed. Inevitably, however, it also included both 'frivolity and shallowness', to use the description favoured by Sakatani Shiroshi, and a number of novel concepts which were likely to prove disruptive of the social order.

Japan's response to the West remained a matter of controversy in this situation. In 1887 Nakae Chōmin, one of the more unorthodox of the travellers, published a book under the title *Sansuijin Keirin Mondō* (A Discourse by Three Drunkards on Government), in which he set out to summarize the disagreements that existed. It consisted of an exchange of lengthy statements about the course Japan ought to pursue with reference to the West between three drinking companions, described, respectively, as the Gentleman of Western Learning, the Champion of the East, and the Master (or Teacher). The Gentleman asserted the inevitability of Progress and envisaged the emergence of Japan as a model of equality and justice in the world, protected from attack by the righteousness of her political institutions: 'If we adopt liberty as our army and navy, equality as our fortress, and fraternity as our sword and cannon, who in the world would dare to attack us?' The Champion, by contrast, argued that only strength, achieved by means of armaments and territorial expansion, could defend both tradition and the independence on which social progress must depend: 'civilized nations are always strong'. He added that the process of catching up with the West, which involved sweeping changes in culture and customs, threatened to divide the nation into 'lovers of nostalgia' (the over-thirties) and 'lovers of novelty' (the under-thirties). The disputes between them would increase the country's danger. The Master, as chairman, agreed fully with neither, condemning both the impracticality of the Gentleman's views, and the danger of provoking the West, which he held to be inherent in the Champion's. He offered no clear-cut alternative of his own, however, beyond a form of gradualism, applied to both foreign and domestic problems.[2]

As Nakae demonstrates, much that was imported from the West encountered prejudice in Japan. Some of it was traditionalist: a resentment directed against any attack on established Buddhist, Confucian or Shinto thought, or any attempt to change the structure of the family, the place of women in society, or the duty owed by the individual to the community. Government policy was a good deal influenced by such sentiment in the Meiji period. Shinto received state funding and patronage; the Confucian ethic became a compulsory part of national education; and at Itō Hirobumi's insistence the notion of imperial divine descent was entrenched in the constitution. Some prejudice, on the other hand, is better described as nationalist. The adoption of western ideas and practices in the name of 'wealth and strength', necessary though it might be, was still perceived by some as 'national dishonour', a cause of shame that could only be wiped out by restoring Japan's 'proper' place in the world.

By the time the constitution was announced in 1889 there was already in evidence a change of mood with respect to western-style reform, giving fresh emphasis to the more limited purposes of cultural borrowing, as they had been understood in earlier years. An imperial rescript to the armed forces reminded them that both loyalty to the emperor and 'moral principle' were essential contributions to 'the might and dignity of Our Empire'. Another, on the subject of education, enjoined all citizens to observe the Confucian virtues of filial piety and benevolence, in accordance with 'the teaching bequeathed by Our Imperial Ancestors'. More directly, a new national newspaper, *Nihon* (Japan), published on the day the constitution was announced, had this to say:

> We recognize the excellence of Western civilization. We value the Western theories of rights, liberty, and equality; and we respect Western philosophy and morals. We have affection for some Western customs. Above all, we esteem Western science, economics and industry. These, however, ought not to be adopted simply because they are Western; they ought to be adopted only if they can contribute to Japan's welfare.[3]

This was to insist that what Japan sought from the West was not a civilization, treated as a coherent entity, but an assemblage of parts, chosen for their utility; and while the Japanese people proved willing to take this proposition further than some of them would have wished, the record does suggest that what they borrowed was chosen piecemeal, usually in such a way as to be compatible, if only loosely, with their traditions, or at least able to coexist with those segments of tradition they decided to retain.

Cultural borrowing has remained a feature of Japanese life, though the circumstances in which it has been carried on have changed. After about 1890 travel ceased to play so large a part in it, for example. There was better-informed teaching in Japanese schools; more detailed reports and articles about the outside world in newspapers and magazines; a much wider range of translations of western works, extending to the literature of all major countries; and finally, during the twentieth century, an increasing number of programmes on radio, film and television. Knowledge became more soundly based, and was diffused more widely through the population. At the same time, western ideas and institutions, even words, patriated in Japan, were undergoing a quasi-independent development within their new environment. In other words, cultural borrowing had entered a different phase, to which the kind of activities considered in this book were largely irrelevant.

Notes

F.O.   Foreign   Office   (London)
archives (see Bibliography, p. 231)

1   Prologue: Japan and China

1   Quoted in Richard T. Chang, *From Prejudice to Tolerance: A study of the Japanese image of the West, 1826–1864* (Tokyo, 1970), 172–3.
2   Edwin O. Reischauer, *Ennin's Diary: The record of a pilgrimage to China in search of the Law* (New York, 1955).
3   Yoshi S. Kuno, *Japanese Expansion on the Asiatic Continent* (2 vols, Berkeley, 1937, 1940), I, 229–30.
4   See Charlotte von Verschuer, *Les relations officielles du Japon avec la Chine aux VIIIe et IXe siècles* (Geneva, 1985), especially 188–203.
5   W. G. Aston, trans., *Nihongi: Chronicles of Japan from the earliest times to AD 697* (reprint, 2 vols in 1, London, 1956), II, 195.
6   Ibid., II, 359.

2   Barbarian Books

1   The decrees are translated in George Elison, *Deus Destroyed: The image of Christianity in early modern Japan* (Cambridge, Mass., 1973), 115–18.
2   Translated in Ryusaku Tsunoda et al., *Sources of Japanese Tradition* (New York, 1958), 325–7.
3   Fabian Fucan is quoted in Elison, *Deus Destroyed*, 170; Arai Hakuseki, ibid., 237–41; and the passage from Aizawa Seishisai in Bob Tadashi Wakabayashi, *Antiforeignism and Western Learning in Early Modern Japan* (Cambridge, Mass., 1986), at 200–1.
4   Sugimoto Masayoshi and David L. Swain, *Science and Culture in Traditional Japan* (Cambridge, Mass., and London, 1978), 224.
5   The quotations are from a translation of Sugita's account of the incident by Ryōzō Matsumoto and Eiichi Kiyooka, published as Sugita Gempaku, *Dawn of Western Science in Japan* (Tokyo, 1969), which originally appeared under the title *Rangaku Kotohajime* in 1815.
6   *Kaigai ibun* [Strange Tales from Overseas], compiled by Maekawa Bunzō and Sakai Junzō, trans. Richard Zumwinkle and Tadanobu Kawai (Los Angeles, 1970), 80–1.
7   Quoted in Wakabayashi, *Antiforeignism*, 169.
8   Quoted in Donald Keene, *The Japanese Discovery of Europe, 1720–1830* (rev. ed., Stanford, 1969), 65.
9   Quoted in G. B. Sansom, *The Western World and Japan* (New York

and London, 1950), 258.

10 The quotations from Matsudaira Sadanobu and Hirata Atsutane are in Keene, *Japanese Discovery*, 75–6, 170, and Tsunoda, *Sources*, 544, respectively.

11 Wakabayashi, *Anti-foreignism*, 273.

12 Carmen Blacker, 'Ōhashi Totsuan: A study in anti-western thought', *Trans. Asiatic Soc. Japan*, 3rd ser., VII (1959), 154, 161, 165.

13 Quoted in R. H. van Gulik, '*Kakkaron*, a Japanese echo of the Opium War', *Monumenta Serica*, IV (1939–40), 500.

14 Grouping them in the categories used here in the text, they were: Hayashi Shihei, Hiraga Gennai, Honda Toshiaki and Maeno Ryōtaku; Motoki Ryōei, Shizuki Tadao and Yoshio Kōsaku; Nakagawa Jun'an, Ōtsuki Gentaku, Sugita Gempaku and Udagawa Yōan; Mamiya Rinzō and Yamagata Bantō; Inō Tadakata and Shiba Kōkan; and Satō Nobuhiro (Shin'en).

15 All three texts are given in Satō Shōsuke, ed., *Kazan, Chōei ronshū* (Tokyo, 1978), 59–105.

16 Quoted in Masao Maruyama, *Studies in the Intellectual History of Tokugawa Japan* (Princeton and Tokyo, 1974), 287–8.

17 Tsunoda, *Sources*, 577–8.

ibid., 130–9.

5 Quoted in R. H. van Gulik, '*Kakkaron*, a Japanese echo of the Opium War', *Monumenta Serica*, IV, 518.

6 The passages quoted are from David Earl, *Emperor and Nation in Japan* (Seattle, 1964), 174, 147.

7 Richard T. Chang, *From Prejudice to Tolerance* (Tokyo, 1970), 181, 171.

8 Kuroda's memorandum, dated 21 Aug. 1853, is in *Dai Nihon Komonjo — Bakumatsu Gaikoku Kankei Monjo* (Tokyo, 1911 — in progress), I, 566–78. Tokugawa Nariaki is quoted in Akao Tōji, 'Perry torai zengo ni okeru kokumin shisō no kōsatsu', *Shirin*, XXII (1937), 774.

9 Wakabayashi, *Anti-foreignism*, 84–6.

10 Quoted in Beasley, *Select Documents*, 167.

11 The translations are from Marius B. Jansen, 'New materials for the intellectual history of nineteenth-century Japan', *Harvard Journal of Asiatic Studies*, XX (1957), 578–9.

12 *Shimazu Nariakira Genkōroku* (Tokyo, 1944), 100–4, 115–28.

13 Pompe van Meerdervoort, *Doctor on Desima* (Tokyo, 1970), 74.

14 Ibid., 75.

15 Ibid., 85.

3 Unequal Treaties

1 Quoted in Bob Tadashi Wakabayashi, *Anti-foreignism and Western Learning in Early Modern Japan* (Cambridge, Mass., 1986), 248.

2 The first half is translated in W. G. Beasley, *Select Documents on Japanese Foreign Policy 1853–1868* (London, 1955), 102–7.

3 Memorandum of 9 Sept. 1853, ibid., 114–17.

4 The documents which include these exchanges are translated

4 The Mission to America, 1860

1 Quoted in Masao Miyoshi, *As We Saw Them: The first Japanese embassy to the United States* (Berkeley and London, 1979), 20–1.

2 They have been published in *Bakumatsu Ishin Gaikō Shiryō Shūsei* (6 vols, Tokyo, 1942–4), IV, 12–19.

3 Muragaki Norimasa, *Kōkai Nikki: The diary of the first Japanese embassy to the United States of America* (Tokyo, 1958), 92.

4 Miyoshi, *As We Saw Them*, 35.

5 Yanagawa Masakiyo, *The First Japanese Mission to America, 1860* (Kobe, 1937), 22–8.

6 Tamamushi Yasushige's diary, printed in Numata Jirō and Matsuzawa Hiroaki, eds, *Seiyō Kembun-shū* (Tokyo, 1974), 242–3.

7 Muragaki, *Kōkai Nikki*, 114.

8 Miyoshi, *As We Saw Them*, 71; Muragaki, *Kōkai Nikki*, 43, 90–1.

9 Muragaki, *Kōkai Nikki*, especially 93–4, 99–100.

10 Miyoshi, *As We Saw Them*, 71; Numata and Matsuzawa, *Seiyō Kembun-shū*, 236–7.

11 Muragaki, *Kokai Nikki*, 170. I have slightly revised the published translation to accord with my own reading of the Japanese text in *Kengai Shisetsu Nikki Sanshū* (see Bibliography), I, 192.

12 Muragaki, *Kōkai Nikki*, 181.

13 Brooke's journal of the voyage, quoted several times here, is in *Manen Gannen Ken-Bei Shisetsu Shiryō Shūsei* (see Bibliography), V, 67–96; his report to the Secretary of the Navy, ibid., V, 108–10.

14 *The Autobiography of Fukuzawa Yukichi*, trans. Eiichi Kiyooka (reprint, New York and London, 1966), 110–11.

15 Ibid., 115.

5   *The Mission to Europe, 1862*

1 F.O.46/11, Alcock to Russell, no. 18, 18 Mar. 1861; F.O.46/12, same to same, no. 30, 2 Apr. 1861.

2 The text of their memorandum, together with that of the Bakufu response dated 19 Jan. 1862, is given in Numata Jirō and Matsuzawa Hiroaki, eds, *Seiyō Kembun-shū* (Tokyo, 1974), 595–8.

3 F.O.46/21, Alcock to Russell, no. 5B, 24 Jan. 1862.

4 Shibata Takenaka's letter of 9 May 1862, in *Ihi nyūkō roku* (2 vols,

Tokyo, 1930), at I, 222–4.

5 There are a number of such letters in F.O.46/28.

6 Fukuzawa's journal, 'Seikō-ki', printed in the edition of his complete works, *Fukuzawa Yukichi Zenshū*, vol. 19 (Tokyo, 1962), at pp. 27–8.

7 Ichikawa Wataru's diary, translated in part by Ernest Satow as 'Diary of a member of the Japanese embassy to Europe in 1862–1863', *Chinese and Japanese Repository*, vol. 3 (London, 1865), at p. 526.

8 Shibata's letter of 9 May 1862, in *Ihi nyūkō roku*, I, 224–5; Matsuki's letter of 10 June 1862, ibid., I, 237–40.

9 Matsuki to Kawamoto, 13 July 1862. There is a Japanese text in *Ihi nyūkō roku*, I, 244, 249–50, but Inuzuka Takaaki, *Meiji Ishin Taigai Kankei-shi Kenkyū* (Tokyo, 1987), 70–4, summarizes what he describes as a less corrupt version from Kagoshima sources.

10 Matsuki's letter of 14 Sept. 1862, in *Ihi nyūkō roku*, I, 245–50.

11 F.O.65/606, Lumley to Russell, no. 79, 27 Aug. 1862.

12 Satow, 'Diary', 305–6.

13 *The Autobiography of Fukuzawa Yukichi* (New York and London, 1966), 132.

14 Rutherford Alcock, *The Capital of the Tycoon* (2 vols, London, 1863), II, 401.

15 Satow, 'Diary', 465.

16 Printed in *Sappan Kaigun-shi* (3 vols, Kagoshima, 1928), II, 933–6.

17 Numata and Matsuzawa, *Seiyō Kembun-shū*, 479.

18 Ibid., 481.

19 Ibid., 504–6.

6   *Envoys and Industry, 1865–1867*

1 Quoted in Ardath W. Burks, 'A sub-leader in the emergence of the diplomatic function: Ikeda

Chōhatsu', in B. S. Silberman and
H. D. Harootunian, eds, *Modern
Japanese Leadership* (Tucson,
1966), 303.

2 The report is translated in W. G.
Beasley, *Select Documents on Japanese Foreign Policy, 1853–1868*
(London, 1955), 274–82.

3 Quoted in Meron Medzini, *French
Policy in Japan during the Closing
Years of the Tokugawa Regime* (Cambridge, Mass., 1971), 113.

4 Medzini, *French Policy*, 122, quoting a letter from Roches to the
British chargé, 24 May 1865.
Roches's note to Shibata is in
Numata Jirō and Matsuzawa
Hiroaki, eds, *Seiyō Kembun-shū*
(Tokyo, 1974), 575–7.

5 F.O.46/55, Winchester to Russell,
no. 95, 7 June 1865, and enclosure.

6 They are listed in the bibliography
to this chapter.

7 Van Valkenburgh to Seward, 19
Feb. 1867, in *U.S. Foreign Relations,
1867–68* (United States State
Dept), Part II, pp. 24–6.

8 The text of the memorandum is in
Sappan Kaigun-shi (3 vols,
Kagoshima, 1928), II, 867–90.

9 F.O.46/61, Foreign Office minute
of meeting, 28 July 1865.

10 The text is given in Inuzuka
Takaaki, *Meiji Ishin Taigai Kankei-shi Kenkyū* (Tokyo, 1987),
113–14.

11 Printed in *Sappan Kaigun-shi*, II,
944–56.

12 Memorial of 10 July 1867, quoted
in Ivan P. Hall, *Mori Arinori* (Cambridge, Mass., 1973), 100.

13 Von Siebold's correspondence
with Hammond and a number of
related papers are to be found in
F.O.46/85 and F.O.46/86. The
documents in these two volumes
are arranged in date order, which
makes it possible to trace letters
by the dates given here in
the text.

14 F.O.46/86 Hammond to Rogers,

17 Oct. 1867.

15 F.O.46/86, Hammond to von
Siebold, 23 Nov. 1867.

16 F.O.46/86, Edwards to Hammond,
16 Dec. 1867, enclosing a note of
Akitake's itinerary in England.

7 The First Japanese Students Overseas, 1862–1868

1 Quoted in Thomas Havens, *Nishi
Amane and Modern Japanese
Thought* (Princeton, 1970), 50.

2 Mori Arinori's journal, cited in
Ivan P. Hall, *Mori Arinori* (Cambridge, Mass., 1973), 78–9.

3 The Foreign Office memorandum
of 21 March 1866 is in F.O.
46/74. The recommendations by
Parkes and Lloyd are in F.O.46/72,
Parkes to Stanley, no. 194, 17
Nov. 1866, and no. 196, 30 Nov.
1866.

4 The memorandum sent by the students to Lord Stanley, dated 11
Nov. 1867, together with related
correspondence, is in F.O.46/86.

5 Quoted in *Itō Hirobumi den* (3 vols,
Tokyo, 1940), I, 95–6.

6 The incident is described in *Segai
Inoue Kō den* (5 vols, Tokyo, 1933–4), I, 92–6.

7 Quoted in Hall, *Mori Arinori*, 84.

8 From Tokugawa to Meiji

1 Translation in Ishii Ryosuke, *Japanese Legislation in the Meiji Era*
(reprint, Tokyo, 1969), 145.

2 Rutherford Alcock, *The Capital of
the Tycoon* (2 vols, London, 1863),
II, 301; the quotations earlier
in the paragraph come from II,
254–6.

3 Francis L. Hawks, *Narrative of an
Expedition of an American Squadron
to the China Seas and Japan* (3 vols,
Washington, 1856), I, 359.

4 Parkes's correspondence with
Hammond is in the Hammond

Papers at the Public Record Office, Kew (F.O.391/14). The letters quoted here are those of 14 June 1867 and 18 Dec. 1868.

5 Quoted in Janet Hunter, 'A study of the career of Maejima Hisoka, 1835–1919' (unpublished D. Phil. thesis, Oxford, 1976), 139–40.

6 Quoted in S. Lane-Poole and F. V. Dickins, *The Life of Sir Harry Parkes* (2 vols, London, 1894), II, 305–6.

7 There is a contemporary printed translation (quoted here), origin unspecified, but dated 24 Dec. 1871, in the Satow Papers at the Public Record Office, Kew (PRO 30/33, 1–4). It is not known how many wives, sisters and daughters went abroad as a result of this exhortation.

8 Quoted in Ishizuki Minoru, *Kindai Nihon no kaigai ryūgakushi* (Kyoto, 1972), 139.

9 Since Japan was still using the lunar calendar until the beginning of 1873, these students are actually listed in the records as leaving in the third and fourth years of Meiji, i.e. the period from 1 Feb. 1870 to 8 Feb. 1872.

10 Baba Tatsui, 'The English in Japan', 1875; copy in the pamphlets collection of the Library of the School of Oriental and African Studies, London.

9 *The Iwakura Embassy, 1871– 1873*

1 Letter of 29 May 1867, published in *Iwakura Kō Jikki* (3 vols, Tokyo, 1927), at II, 36–7.

2 F.O.46/106, Parkes to Stanley, Confidential, no. 5, 13 Jan. 1869.

3 See A. Altman, 'Guido Verbeck and the Iwakura Embassy', *Japan Quarterly*, XIII (1966), 54–62.

4 The Japanese text is in *Iwakura Kō Jikki*, II, 927–34.

5 Letter of credence to the President

of the United States, quoted in S. Lane-Poole and F. V. Dickins, *The Life of Sir Harry Parkes* (2 vols, London, 1894), II, 180.

6 F.O.46/143, Adams to Hammond, private, 8 Dec. 1871; F.O.46/151, Adams to Granville, no. 13, Confidential, 12 Jan. 1872.

7 *The Diary of Kido Takayoshi*, trans. Sidney D. Brown and Akiko Hirota (3 vols, Tokyo, 1983–6), II, 118.

8 Ibid., II, 180, 149.

9 Kume Kunitake, *Tokumei Zenken Taishi Bei-Ō Kairan Jikki* (5 vols, Tokyo, 1878), I, 395–6.

10 F.O.46/150, Foreign Office to Parkes, 28 May 1872.

11 F.O.262/224, Aston's notes on the meetings, enclosed in F. O. to Watson (Tokyo), no. 59 of 28 Nov. and no. 67 of 13 Dec. 1872.

12 Kido, *Diary*, II, 261–2.

13 Ōkubo to Ōyama Iwao, 20 Dec. 1872, printed in *Ōkubo Toshimichi monjo* (10 vols, Tokyo, 1927–9), IV, 467–70.

14 F.O.65/852, Loftus to Granville, Commercial no. 27, 30 Apr. 1873. The inclusion of this dispatch in the commercial series is no doubt an indication of where senior diplomats thought Japan 'belonged'.

15 Kido, *Diary*, II, 322.

16 Kume, *Tokumei Zenken Taishi*, V, 81–4.

17 Ōkubo to Saigō Takamori and Yoshii Tomozane, 21 Mar. 1873, in Shōda Magoya, *Ōkubo Toshimichi den* (3 vols, Tokyo, 1910–11), at III, 54. There are also accounts of what Bismarck said, differing in emphasis, in Kume, *Tokumei Zenken Taishi*, III, 369–72, and Kido, *Diary* II, 300.

18 The text is published in the original series of *Meiji Bunka Zenshū* (24 vols, Tokyo, 1928–30), XXIII, 13–24.

19 Kume, *Tokumei Zenken Taishi*, II, 111–12.

20 Ibid., II, 72–83. On 1862, see Chapter 5, pp. 92–4, above.

21 Ibid., V, 145–63.

22 Ibid., V, 165–270.

23 Ibid., V, 353.

11 The Fruits of Experience: II. Policies and Ideas

1 Quoted in Roger F. Hackett, *Yamagata Aritomo in the Rise of Modern Japan* (Cambridge, Mass., 1971), 62, 65–6.

2 Nishi's argument is summarized in Thomas Havens, *Nishi Amane and Modern Japanese Thought* (Princeton, 1970), 201–3.

3 Godai's letter, dated 29 Nov. 1865, is in *Sappan Kaigun-shi* (3 vols, Kagoshima, 1928), II, 944–7.

4 Matsuki Kōan's views are summarized in Inuzuka Takaaki, *Meiji Ishin Taigai Kankei-shi Kenkyū* (Tokyo, 1987), 104–7, 124–6.

5 A contemporary English translation, taken from the *Japan Weekly Mail* of 8 Nov, 1873, is printed in *Meiji Japan Through Contemporary Sources* (3 vols, Tokyo, 1969–72), II, 99–110. The Japanese text is in *Iwakura Kō Jikki* (3 vols, Tokyo, 1927), III, 239–46.

6 Letter to Nomura Sōshichi, 28 Dec. 1865, in *Sappan Kaigun-shi*, II, 948–9.

7 The quotations from Itō and Godai are to be found, respectively, in Marlene Mayo, 'Rationality in the Meiji Restoration: the Iwakura embassy', in B. S. Silberman and H. D. Harootunian, eds, *Modern Japanese Leadership* (Tucson, 1966), 344; and Byron K. Marshall, *Capitalism and Nationalism in Prewar Japan* (Stanford, 1967), 19.

8 English translation in *Meiji Japan Through Contemporary Sources*, III, 13–17. The Japanese text is in *Ōkubo Toshimichi monjo* (10 vols, Tokyo, 1927–9), V, 561–5.

9 Meiroku is a contraction of 'Meiji rokunen', that is, the sixth year of Meiji, or 1873. Meirokusha might therefore be translated as 'The 1873 Society', and *Meiroku Zasshi* as 'The 1873 Journal'. All the issues of *Meiroku Zasshi* have been translated into English by William R. Braisted under the title *Meiroku Zasshi: Journal of the Japanese Enlightenment* (Cambridge, Mass., 1976).

10 Braisted, *Meiroku Zasshi*, 30–1. Tsuda's note on the same topic appears ibid., 38–40.

11 Ibid., 104–5, 143–5, 189–91, 252–3, 331–3.

12 Ibid., 123–5, 139–43, 155–9, 197–8, 200–2.

13 Ibid., 50–2, 59–62, 73–5, 109–11, 119–22, 152–5.

14 Ibid., 524–31, at pp. 527, 531.

15 Ibid., 346–50.

16 The article on music, including the comment on *sumō*, appears ibid., 235–7.

17 Ibid., 132–5, 145–7, 159–62, 191–3, 204–8, 295–6, 483–5.

18 I have used the centenary reprint of the 1866 edition of *Self-Help* (London: John Murray, 1969). For the Japanese text I have relied on the 1876 edition of Nakamura's translation in the British Library, which is entitled *Saikoku Risshi-hen*. Ōkubo Toshiaki has published a very useful article on the translation, reprinted in *Ōkubo Toshiaki Rekishi Chosaku-shū*, 5, *Bakumatsu Ishin no yōgaku* (Tokyo, 1986), 224–60. It includes some sample comparisons between the draft (in Shizuoka) and the published version, including one for the first paragraph of Smiles's text, quoted here.

19 Compare Ninomiya's observations on hard work and thrift, translated in Ryusaku Tsunoda et al., *Sources of Japanese Tradition* (New York, 1958), 583.

20 Quoted in Carmen Blacker, *The Japanese Enlightenment: A study of the writings of Fukuzawa Yukichi* (Cambridge, 1964), 52.

21 Fukuzawa Yukichi, *An Outline of a Theory of Civilization*, trans. David A. Dilworth and G. Cameron Hurst (Tokyo. 1973), 28.

12   Conclusion: Japan and the West

1 The Meiji government's notification to the United States about the aims of the Iwakura embassy; see Chapter 9, p. 160.

2 Nakae Chōmin, *A Discourse by Three Drunkards on Government*, trans. Nobuko Tsukui (New York and Tokyo, 1984). The passages quted appear on pp. 51, 94.

3 *Nihon*, 11 Feb. 1889, translated in Kenneth B. Pyle, *The New Generation in Meiji Japan* (Stanford, 1969), 94. The two imperial rescripts referred to here are translated in Ryusaku Tsunoda et al., *Sources of Japanese Tradition* (New York, 1958), 646–7, 705–7.

Bibliography

The history of Japan between about 1840 and 1890 is the subject of an enormous literature in both Japanese and western languages. It seems unnecessary to try to give a survey of it here, or to list a representative selection of works concerning it. The reader is therefore referred to the relevant chapters in W. G. Beasley, *The Rise of Modern Japan* (London, 1990), and to that book's bibliography, for a general introduction to the subject. The best single volume in English dealing with Japan's cultural relations with the West before about 1890 is G. B. Sansom, *The Western World and Japan* (New York and London, 1950). In Japanese, works by Inuzuka Takaaki, Ishizuki Minoru and Numata Jirō have all proved of importance to large segments of this study, but it has been thought best to list them, like others, in those parts of the bibliography relating to separate chapters, below.

Reference is made from time to time in this book to documents from the Foreign Office archives, held at the Public Record Office in London (at Kew). The reader might find it convenient to have them listed here, together with the series numbers, by which they are usually cited:

F.O.17:   General Correspondence, *China*.
F.O.46:   General Correspondence, *Japan*.
F.O.65:   General Correspondence, *Russia*.
F.O.262: Embassy and Consular Archives, *Japan*.

Volume numbers are appended to the series number after an oblique stroke.

1   Prologue: Japan and China

Early Japanese missions to China and related topics are treated in some detail in Charlotte von Verschuer, *Les relations officielles du Japon avec la Chine aux VIIIe et IXe siècles* (Geneva, 1985). For Ennin's experiences in 838–9 (p. 4), see Edwin O. Reischauer's two volumes, both published in New York in 1955: *Ennin's Diary: The record of a pilgrimage to China in search of the Law;* and *Ennin's Travels in T'ang China*. The Ashikaga missions (pp. 7–8) are described in Wang Yi-t'ung, *Official Relations between China and Japan, 1368–1549* (Cambridge, Mass., 1953). In Japanese, vol. 1 of Mori Katsumi and Tanaka Takeo, eds,

Kaigai kōshō-shi no shiten [Viewpoints on the History of Overseas Relations] (3 vols, Tokyo, 1975), provides a useful recent survey, while the volume of articles edited by Naoki Kōjirō, *Nara* (*Kodai wo kangaeru* series, Tokyo, 1985), is especially valuable on the eighth century.

On early Japanese cultural borrowing from China the best introduction is still G. B. Sansom, *Japan: A short cultural history* (rev. ed., London, 1962), though it is outdated on some points. It can be supplemented by the material in Ryusaku Tsunoda et al., *Sources of Japanese Tradition* (New York, 1958; later published in paperback in 2 volumes), which gives extensive translations from and comments on contemporary Japanese texts from all periods of history; and W. G. Aston, trans., *Nihongi: Chronicles of Japan from earliest times to AD 697* (reprint, 2 vols in 1, London, 1956). On early Japanese art history (pp. 14–15), see Robert Treat Paine and Alexander Soper, *The Art and Architecture of Japan* (Harmondsworth, 1955). The development of calendrical and other sciences (pp. 15–16) is treated in Sugimoto Masayoshi and David L. Swain, *Science and Culture in Traditional Japan* (Cambridge, Mass., and London, 1978); see especially pp. 50–100.

2   Barbarian Books

The Japanese response to Christianity in the Tokugawa period (p. 20) is discussed in George Elison, *Deus Destroyed: The image of Christianity in early modern Japan* (Cambridge, Mass., 1973). For eighteenth- and nineteenth-century Japanese criticisms of the West, see Bob Tadashi Wakabayashi, *Anti-foreignism and Western Learning in Early Modern Japan* (Cambridge, Mass., 1986), and H. D. Harootunian, *Toward Restoration: The growth of political consciousness in Tokugawa Japan* (Berkeley and London, 1970). On the use of the terms 'civilized' and 'barbarian' in Confucian thought, as applied to Japan (pp. 21–2), see Ronald P. Toby, *State and Diplomacy in Early Modern Japan* (Princeton, 1984), 211–27, and H. D. Harootunian, 'The functions of China in Tokugawa thought', in Akira Iriye, ed., *The Chinese and the Japanese* (Princeton, 1980), 9–36.

Sugimoto and Swain, *Science and Culture* (see Chapter 1), examines most aspects of the Japanese study of both Chinese and western science in the Tokugawa period. The best general account in English of the 'Dutch' scholars and their work is Donald Keene, *The Japanese Discovery of Europe, 1720–1830* (rev. ed., Stanford, 1969); it includes an account of the von Siebold incident (pp. 32–3) at pp. 147–54. On medical studies, see John Z. Bowers, *Western Medical Pioneers in Feudal Japan* (Baltimore, 1970); the efforts to translate Kulmus's anatomical tables (pp. 24–5) are described at pp. 67–72. There is an illustrated biography of Shiba Kōkan (p. 27), showing examples of his cartographical and astronomical work: Calvin L. French, *Shiba Kōkan: Artist, Innovator and Pioneer in the Westernization of Japan* (New York and Tokyo, 1974). The use made of Inō Tadataka's maps by British hydrographers (p. 27) is recounted in Norman Pye and W. G. Beasley, 'An undescribed manuscript copy of Inō Chūkei's map of Japan', *Geographical Journal*, CXVII (1951), 178–87.

Japanese study of western military science in this period is treated in an article by Arima Seiho in *Monumenta Nipponica*, XIX, 3–4 (1964), 118–45. This is a special number of the journal, edited by Numata Jirō, comprising contributions (in English) by Japanese scholars on the acceptance of western culture in Tokugawa Japan. Much of it is of value for the subjects considered in this chapter. The questionnaire on military matters put to the Dutch at Deshima at the time of the Opium War (p. 31) is translated in C. R. Boxer, *Jan Compagnie in Japan 1600–1850* (rev. ed., The Hague, 1950), 185–7. On samurai as students in late-Tokugawa academies (pp. 31–2), see Richard Rubinger, *Private Academies of Tokugawa Japan* (Princeton, 1982), especially pp. 119–24, 127–50. The dispute over coast defence in 1839 (pp. 33–4), involving Egawa, Watanabe and Takano, is described in detail in Nakada Masayuki's Japanese-language biography of Egawa, *Egawa Tan'an* (Tokyo, 1985), 69–92. For the writings of Honda Toshiaki and Satō Nobuhiro (Shin'en), see Keene, *Japanese Discovery* (above), chapter 5 and Appendix, plus Ryusaku Tsunoda et al., *Sources of Japanese Tradition* (New York, 1958), 552–78.

3 Unequal Treaties

The political background to the treaties and the crisis of 1858 are treated more fully in the early chapters of W. G. Beasley, *The Meiji Restoration* (Stanford, 1972). A selection of Japanese memoranda concerning the negotiation of the treaties is translated in W. G. Beasley, *Select Documents on Japanese Foreign Policy, 1853–1868* (London, 1955). The largest collection of Japanese papers on foreign affairs is to be found in *Dai Nihon Komonjo — Bakumatsu Gaikoku Kankei Monjo* [Ancient Japanese Documents — Documents on Late Tokugawa Foreign Relations] (Tokyo, 1911 — in progress).

The response of Japanese Confucian scholars to the foreign crisis is examined in R. H. van Gulik, '*Kakkaron*, a Japanese echo of the Opium War', *Monumenta Serica*, IV (1939–40), 478–545. On Yoshida Shōin (pp. 42–3) there are a number of studies in English, one of the more perceptive being chapter 4 of H. D. Harootunian, *Toward Restoration* (Berkeley and London, 1970); the same book also has valuable chapters on several other late Tokugawa thinkers. David M. Earl, *Emperor and Nation in Japan: Political thinkers of the Tokugawa period* (Seattle, 1964), also treats Yoshida at some length, while Inobe Shigeo, 'Sakuma Shōzan no taigai iken', included in his *Bakumatsu-shi no kenkyū* [Studies of Late Tokugawa History] (Tokyo, 1927), 576–644, remains one of the most useful examinations of Sakuma's ideas on foreign relations. Aizawa Seishisai's best-known work, *Shinron*, which had much influence on samurai opposed to the treaties, is translated in Bob Tadashi Wakabayashi, *Anti-foreignism and Western Learning in Early Modern Japan* (Cambridge, Mass., 1986).

For Japanese pictures and sketches concerning the Perry expedition (p. 45) I have looked chiefly at the collection in Tokyo University's Historiographical Institute, but there are others. For example, several were on display at an Ii Naosuke exhibition at Hikone Castle in 1990; see the catalogue published by the Hikone Castle Museum, 1990. One record of this kind is reproduced in Oliver Statler, *The Black Ship Scroll* (San Francisco and New York, 1963).

On Fukuzawa Yukichi's studies at Osaka (p. 46), see *The Autobiography of Fukuzawa Yukichi*, trans. Eiichi Kiyooka (reprint, New York and London, 1966). Matsuki Kōan's experiences in Kagoshima (p. 46) are described in Inuzuka Takaaki's biography of him (under the name he took later in life), *Terashima Munenori* (Tokyo, 1990), 47–8. The best account of the Bansho Shirabesho (pp. 46–8) is Marius B. Jansen, 'New materials for the intellectual history of nineteenth-century Japan', *Harvard Journal of Asiatic Studies*, XX (1957), 567–97. There is an account of Hizen's experiments in western industrial technology (pp. 48–9) in an article by Egashira Tsuneharu, reprinted in Honjo Eijirō, ed., *Bakumatsu keizai-shi kenkyū* [Studies in Late Tokugawa Economic History] (Tokyo, 1935), 59–100. This and cognate material on other domains, including Mito and Satsuma, is summarized in T. C. Smith, *Political Change and Industrial Development in Japan* (Stanford, 1955), chapter 1. Volume III of *Kagoshima-ken shi* [History of Kagoshima Prefecture] (5 vols, Kagoshima, 1939–43) is a major source of information on the modernizing activities of Satsuma in general and Shimazu Nariakira in particular (as noted here on pp. 49–51). A more personal view of Nariakira's ideas on the subject can be obtained from *Shimazu Nariakira Genkōroku* (Tokyo, 1944), which is a collection of his 'conversations' with his samurai advisers, compiled by one of them, Ichiki Shirō, and first published in 1884. Egawa Tarōzaemon's contribution to Bakufu gun-founding at Nirayama (p. 52) is described in Nakada Masayuki, *Egawa Tan'an* (Tokyo, 1985), 218–30.

The fullest account of Dutch naval training and associated activities at Nagasaki (pp. 52–5) is in Numata Jirō, *Bakumatsu yōgaku-shi* [Western Studies in Late Tokugawa] (Tokyo, 1950), 82–145. Pompe van Meerdevoort's memoirs of his work there, originally published as *Vijf Jaren in Japan* (2 vols, Leiden, 1868), have been selectively translated by Elizabeth P. Wittermans and John Z. Bowers as *Doctor on Desima* (Tokyo, 1970).

4   The Mission to America, 1860

The most detailed account of the mission is in Masao Miyoshi, *As We Saw Them: The first Japanese embassy to the United States* (Berkeley and London, 1979), which includes many quotations from contemporary material, both western and Japanese. The Japanese texts of the diaries of members of the mission (except that of Tamamushi, see below) have been published in volume 1 of *Kengai Shisetsu Nikki Sanshū* [Collected Diaries of Envoys Sent Overseas] (3 vols, Tokyo, 1927; reprinted 1971), and in volumes 1–4 of *Manen Gannen Ken-Bei Shisetsu Shiryō Shūsei* [Collected Materials on the Mission Sent to America in 1860] (7 vols, Tokyo, 1961). A large selection of American press reports concerning the mission, some of which have been quoted in this chapter, appears in the latter work at VI, 1–327.

Two of the diaries have been translated into English. One is that of Muragaki Norimasa, deputy to Shimmi, which appeared as *Kōkai Nikki: The diary of the first Japanese embassy to the United States of America* (Tokyo, 1958).

The Japanese text is in *Kengai Shisetsu Nikki Sanshū* (above). The other is that of Yanagawa Masakiyo, published under the title *The First Japanese Mission to America, 1860*, trans. Junichi Fukuyama and Roderick H. Jackson (Kobe, 1937). The Japanese text of Tamamushi Yasushige's diary is in Numata Jirō and Matsuzawa Hiroaki, eds, *Seiyō Kembun-shū* [Collected Reports on the West] (Tokyo, 1974); the 'secret' section is at pp. 228–45. The same volume includes a full list of the mission's personnel, plus valuable editorial comment.

Turning to the voyage of the *Kanrin Maru*, Brooke's journal and various cognate papers, quoted here (p. 68), are in *Manen Gannen Ken-Bei Shisetsu Shiryō Shūsei* (above), V, 67–96, 108–10. An account of his experiences is also available in George M. Brooke, ed., *John M. Brooke's Pacific Cruise and Japanese Adventure, 1858–1860* (Honolulu, 1986). Katsu Awa's account of the voyage and his stay in San Francisco (pp. 69–70) was published in 1889 as Books 7, 8 and 9 of his *Kaigun Rekishi* [History of the Navy] (reprint, Tokyo, 1967). His diary for the period spent in San Francisco and Hawaii is in volume 2 of *Kengai Shisetsu Nikki Sanshū* (above), as is that of the 'admiral', Kimura Yoshitake. *The Autobiography of Fukuzawa Yukichi* (see under Chapter 3) has a chapter on the voyage; the Japanese original was written in 1897.

5   The Mission to Europe, 1862

The diplomatic background to the mission is discussed in chapter 4 of Beasley, *Select Documents* (see under Chapter 3, above), and Meron Medzini, *French Policy in Japan during the Closing Years of the Tokugawa Regime* (Cambridge, Mass., 1971). On von Siebold's part in the arrangements (p. 74), see J. MacLean, 'Philipp Franz von Siebold and the Opening of Japan 1843–1866', in *Philipp Franz von Siebold* (Leiden University, 1978), 71–94; the article summarizes several of his long letters to the Minister of the Colonies in the Hague.

Much the most detailed account of the mission's travels is in Miyanaga Takashi, *Bunkyū ni-nen no Yōroppa hōkoku* [Report on the Europe Mission of 1862] (Tokyo, 1989), which includes a complete list of members of the mission at pp. 13–20. The book is based on the narrative sections of the long report prepared after the mission's return, the manuscript of which is in Tokyo University's Historiographical Institute (Shiryō Hensanjo), where it forms part of the papers of Fukuda Sakutarō, a Bakufu official in the foreign affairs department. Miyanaga also makes use of the diaries and correspondence of the participants, quoting extensively from them. His account can usefully be supplemented by the material in Uchikawa Yoshimi and Miyachi Masato, eds, *Gaikoku Shimbun ni miru Nihon* [Japan Seen in Foreign Newspapers], vol. I, 1852–73 (Tokyo, 1989). Valuable comments and analysis are to be found in Inuzuka Takaaki, *Meiji Ishin Taigai Kankei-shi Kenkyū* [Study of Overseas Relations in the Meiji Restoration] (Tokyo, 1987), as well as in Numata and Matsuzawa, eds, *Seiyō Kembun-shū* (see under Chapter 4, above).

The diaries of several members of the mission are in *Kengai Shisetsu Nikki Sanshū* (see under Chapter 4, above), including that of Ichikawa Wataru (at

II, 249–562). The first part of Ichikawa's diary, covering the period until departure from London for Holland, translated by Ernest Satow, was published in several parts as 'Diary of a member of the Japanese embassy to Europe in 1862–1863', *Chinese and Japanese Repository*, III (London, 1865), 305–12, 361–80, 425–37, 465–72, 521–8, 569–76. John Macdonald wrote a memoir of the same period: 'From Yeddo to London with the Japanese ambassadors', *Cornhill Magazine*, 7 (1863), 603–20. Fukuzawa Yukichi devoted a chapter to the mission in his *Autobiography* (see under Chapter 3), but his most useful contributions are his travel journal, 'Seikō-ki', and the associated notebook, 'Seikō-techō', included in his collected works, *Fukuzawa Yukichi Zenshū*, vol. 19 (Tokyo, 1962), at pp. 7–65 and 66–145. Fukuchi Genichirō's autobiographical account, which is much less informative, is in his *Kai-Ō jidan* (Tokyo, 1894), 67–92. His experiences are described briefly in James L. Huffman, *Politics of the Meiji Press: The life of Fukuchi Genichirō* (Honolulu, 1980). There are letters from both Shibata Takenaka and Matsuki Kōan in volume 1 of *Ihi nyūkō roku* [Records of Foreign Entry to the Ports] (2 vols, Tokyo, 1930). On Matsuki, see also Inuzuka Takaaki, *Terashima Munenori* (Tokyo, 1990), 64–77.

Information on the mission's activities in St Petersburg, including a note on the Japanese employee in the Russian Foreign Ministry (p. 87), is given in George A. Lensen, *The Russian Push Toward Japan: Russo-Japanese relations, 1697–1875* (Princeton, 1959), 431–4; Lensen gives him his original patronymic, Tachibana. In Miyanaga, *Bunkyū ni-nen* (above), 180–2, he is called Masuda, which is apparently the name by which he was known later in life. The reports on the visit by the British chargé (in F.O.65/606) contain much of interest.

The 'investigations' (*tansaku*) compiled after the mission's return to Edo (pp. 90–4) are not specifically considered by Miyanaga, but there is a long and informative essay on them by Matsuzawa Hiroaki in Numata and Matsuzawa, eds, *Seiyō Kembun-shū*, 579–98; *inter alia* it compares the contents of the different geographical sections (at pp. 582–3). The text of the section on Britain (discussed here at pp. 92–4) appears at pp. 477–544.

6   Envoys and Industry, 1865–1867

A general account of Japan's relations with France in this period is given in Medzini, *French Policy*, chapters 7–13 (see under Chapter 5, above). French military missions (pp. 103–4) are described in Ernst L. Presseisen, *Before Aggression: Europeans prepare the Japanese Army* (Tucson, 1965), 2–59. For British naval missions (p. 104), see Grace Fox, *Britain and Japan, 1858–1883* (Oxford, 1969), 253–7, 263–70. Léon Roches's proposals for Bakufu reform (pp. 104–5) are discussed in some detail in Conrad Totman, *The Collapse of the Tokugawa Bakufu, 1862–1868* (Honolulu, 1980), chapter 11.

Contemporary material on Shibata Takenaka's mission to Europe (pp. 99–103) is to be found in Shibata's own diary, printed in Numata Jirō and Matsuzawa Hiroaki, eds, *Seiyō Kembun-shū* (Tokyo, 1974), 262–476, and that of Okada Setsuzō, included in *Kengai Shisetsu Nikki Sanshū* (3 vols, Tokyo, 1927), III, 481–533. Fukuchi Genichirō's brief autobiographical account is in his *Kai-Ō jidan* (Tokyo, 1894), 128–35.

The best summary of the Satsuma mission (pp. 105–13) is in Inuzuka Takaaki, *Meiji Ishin Taigai Kankei-shi Kenkyū* (Tokyo, 1987), chapter 3. There is also a good deal of information about it in Ivan P. Hall, *Mori Arinori* (Cambridge, Mass., 1973), chapter 2. Godai's diary of his European travels, together with useful comment on it, is to be found in Ōkubo Toshiaki, 'Godai Tomoatsu no Ō-kō to kare no Tai-Ō shuki *Kaikoku Nikki* ni tsuite', reprinted in *Ōkubo Toshiaki Rekishi Chosaku shū*, V, *Bakumatsu Ishin no yōgaku* (Tokyo, 1986), 281–316. The diary does not cover the period spent in Britain before Godai's departure for Ostend. A narrative and diary kept by one of the Satsuma students, Matsumura Junzō, is in *Sappan Kaigun-shi* [History of the Satsuma Navy] (3 vols, Kagoshima, 1928), II, 895–933; and a short memoir of the mission by Matsuki Kōan, ibid., II, 939–43.

There is an account of Ono Tomogorō's mission to the United States in 1867 (p. 105) in *The Autobiography of Fukuzawa Yukichi* (rev. ed., New York and London, 1966), chapter 9. Tanabe Taichi covers Tokugawa Akitake's visit to Europe (pp. 114–18) in his partly autobiographical *Bakumatsu gaikō-dan* [Talks on Late-Tokugawa Diplomacy] (Tokyo, 1898), 466–91. The official records of the mission, which are in *Tokugawa Akitake Tai-Ō Kiroku* (3 vols, Tokyo, 1932), need to be supplemented by the journals kept officially and privately by Shibusawa Ei'ichi while in Europe, printed as *Shibusawa Ei'ichi Tai-Futsu Nikki* (Tokyo, 1928); his personal diary is at pp. 1–203. British Foreign Office papers concerning the mission are in volumes F.O.46/85 and F.O.46/86 in the Public Record Office at Kew.

7   The First Japanese Students Overseas, 1862–1868

The most useful general studies of Japanese students overseas in this period are those of Ishizuki Minoru, *Kindai Nihon no kaigai ryūgakushi* [History of Modern Japanese Study Overseas] (Kyoto, 1972), and Watanabe Minoru, *Kindai Nihon kaigai ryūgakusei-shi* [History of Modern Japan's Students Overseas] (2 vols, Tokyo, 1983). Watanabe has summarized part of his material in an article in English, 'Japanese students abroad and the acquisition of scientific and technical knowledge', *Cahiers d'histoire mondiale*, IX (1965), 254–93. The most recent discussion in Japanese is in Inuzuka Takaaki, *Meiji Ishin Taigai Kankei-shi Kenkyū* (Tokyo, 1987); the book includes as an appendix at pp. 311–41 a nominal list of students for the years 1862–71, on which I have relied a good deal in writing this chapter.

There is a detailed study of the Bakufu students sent to Holland in 1862 (pp. 121–5): Miyanaga Takashi, *Bakufu Oranda ryūgakusei* [Bakufu Students in Holland] (Tokyo, 1982). Thomas Havens, *Nishi Amane and Modern Japanese Thought* (Princeton, 1970), chapter 3, gives an account of Nishi and Tsuda at Leiden, as well as some material on the student party in general. For the students sent to Russia (pp. 125–6), see chiefly Ishizuki, *Kindai Nihon* (above),

60–8. The Bakufu students in England in 1866–7 (pp. 126–9) are treated in Hara Heizō, 'Tokugawa Bakufu no Eikoku ryūgakusei', *Rekishi Chiri*, 79 (1942), 345–74.

On students sent by the domains (pp. 129–38), in addition to the relevant sections of the general studies by Ishizuki and Watanabe, cited above, there is a good deal of material in Inuzuka, *Meiji Ishin*, and in *Kagoshima-ken shi*, vol. III (see under Chapter 3). The most detailed treatment of the Satsuma students (pp. 132–5) is in Inuzuka Takaaki, *Satsuma-han Eikoku ryūgakusei* [Satsuma students in England] (Tokyo, 1974), but Ivan P. Hall, *Mori Arinori* (Cambridge, Mass., 1973), chapters 2 and 3, is also valuable, especially for its use of Mori's journal and letters home.

Additional information on some of the individuals concerned is to be found in biographies and autobiographies, especially the following: on Inoue Kaoru and Itō Hirobumi (pp. 130–2), *Segai Inoue Kō den* (5 vols, Tokyo, 1933–4), I, 82–103, and *Itō Hirobumi den* (3 vols, Tokyo, 1940), I, 84–112; on Takahashi Korekiyo (pp. 136–8), *Takahashi Korekiyo jiden* (Tokyo, 1936), 27–75. The account given here of Niijima Jō's experiences derives from a statement, apparently based on one by Niijima himself, given in Charles Lanman, *Leaders of the Meiji Restoration in America* (rev. reprint, Tokyo, 1931; originally published in 1873 under the title *The Japanese in America*), 59–60.

8 From Tokugawa to Meiji

For comments by British diplomats on the prospects of future 'progress' in Japan, see, in addition to Rutherford Alcock, *The Capital of the Tycoon* (2 vols, London, 1863), the material on Parkes in S. Lane-Poole and F. V. Dickins, *The Life of Sir Harry Parkes* (2 vols, London, 1894), vol. II. Grace Fox, *Britain and Japan 1858–1883* (Oxford, 1969), has a good deal on both men, as well as on the projects Parkes encouraged. Two books by W. E. Griffis, *The Mikado's Empire* (New York, 1876), in which he includes an account of his own experiences in Japan, and *Verbeck of Japan* (New York, 1900), illustrate the attitudes of American missionaries and teachers. On foreign employees more generally (pp. 145–7), see Ardath W. Burks, ed., *The Modernizers: Overseas students, foreign employees, and Meiji Japan* (Boulder and London, 1985), chapters 8, 9, 10; and Hazel Jones, *Live Machines: Hired foreigners and Meiji Japan* (Vancouver, 1980).

The first appointments of Japanese resident ministers overseas (pp. 145–6) are treated in *Gaimushō no Hyakunen* [A Hundred Years of the Foreign Ministry] (2 vols, Tokyo, 1969), I, 70–6. The account given here (pp. 143–5) of the various Japanese officials sent to America and Europe in 1868–73 (other than the Iwakura embassy) is based chiefly on the following: Janet Hunter, 'A study of the career of Maejima Hisoka, 1835–1919' (Oxford D. Phil. thesis, 1976), and her article on Maejima in Ian Nish, ed., *Britain and Japan: Biographical Portraits* (below), 54–66; *Itō Hirobumi den* (3 vols, Tokyo, 1940) and James L. Huffman, *Politics of the Meiji Press* (Honolulu, 1980), for Itō in America; and Iguro Yatarō, *Kuroda Kiyotaka* (Tokyo, 1977), for Kuroda and Capron. Other material on Capron is to be found in Burks, *The Modernizers* (above), passim. On the travels of Yamagata and Shinagawa in the early Meiji years (p. 148), see their respective biographies: *Kōshaku Yamagata Aritomo den* (3 vols, Tokyo, 1933), II, 7–44, and Murata Munejirō, *Shinagawa Shishaku den* (Tokyo, 1910), 381–2. The travels of the party of officials from domains in 1871–3 (pp. 149–50) are narrated in some detail in Inuzuka Takaaki, *Meiji Ishin Taigai Kankei-shi Kenkyū* (Tokyo, 1987), 244–82.

Japanese students overseas in this period (pp. 150–6) are considered in the two books by Ishizuki and Watanabe, cited under Chapter 7; see also Ishizuki's article in Burks, *The Modernizers* (above). Further information on them is in Inuzuka, *Meiji Ishin* (above), and Charles Lanman, *Leaders of the Meiji Restoration in America* (see under Chapter 7). Ian Nish, ed., *Britain and Japan: Biographical Portraits* (London, 1994), includes, in addition to Janet Hunter's article on Maejima (above), others on Japanese engineers in Britain (by Olive Checkland, pp. 45–53), and on Tōgō Heihachirō (by Ikeda Kiyoshi, pp. 106–20). For the examples given at the end of the chapter (pp. 152–6), see the following works in Japanese: Ogasawara Naganari, ed., *Tōgō Gensui shōden* (Tokyo, 1926), 48–62; *Kōshaku Katsura Tarō den* (2 vols, Tokyo, 1917), I, 299–325; *Danshaku Dan Takuma den* (2 vols, Tokyo, 1938), I, 47–107; Hagihara Nobutoshi, *Baba Tatsui* (Tokyo, 1967), 29–79. The last-named is also discussed by Helen Ballhatchet, 'Baba Tatsui (1850–1888) and Victorian Britain', in Hugh Cortazzi and Gordon Daniels, eds, *Britain and Japan, 1859–1991* (London and New York, 1991), 107–17.

9   *The Iwakura Embassy, 1871–1873*

On the preliminaries to the embassy and the manuscript materials concerning it, including the reports drawn up after it returned, the most useful work is the collection of articles by Ōkubo Toshiaki, entitled *Iwakura shisetsu no kenkyū* [Studies on the Iwakura Mission] (Tokyo, 1956). The instructions to Iwakura in 1871 (pp. 159–60), together with a number of other relevant documents, appear in *Iwakura Kō Jikki* [Records of Prince Iwakura] (3 vols, Tokyo, 1927), vol. II. Marlene Mayo, 'Rationality in the Meiji Restoration: the Iwakura embassy', in B. S. Silberman and H. D. Harootunian, eds, *Modern Japanese Leadership* (Tucson, 1966), pp. 323–69, is especially valuable on the embassy's origins. On Verbeck's part in it (pp. 158–9), see A. Altman, 'Guido Verbeck and the Iwakura Embassy', *Japan Quarterly*, XIII (1966), 54–62.

The most detailed account of the embassy's travels (pp. 162–70) is in Kume Kunitake, *Tokumei Zenken Taishi Bei-Ō Kairan Jikki* [Record of the Special Ambassador Plenipotentiary's Tour of America and Europe] (5 vols, Tokyo, 1878). It can be supplemented by *The Diary of Kido Takayoshi*, trans. S. D. Brown and Akiko Hirota (3 vols, Tokyo, 1983–6), vol. II, and by the biographies of Itō and Ōkubo: *Itō Hirobumi den* (3 vols, Tokyo, 1940), vol. I, and Shōda Magoya, *Ōkubo Toshimichi den* (3 vols, Tokyo, 1910–11), vol. III.

On the reports made by the embassy (pp. 171–7), see, in addition to Ōkubo Toshiaki's volume (above), Marlene Mayo, 'The Western Education of Kume Kunitake, 1871–6', *Monumenta Nipponica*, XXVIII (1973), 3–67, and Eugene Soviak, 'On the nature of western progress: the journal of the Iwakura embassy', in Donald Shively, ed., *Tradition and Modernization in Japanese Culture* (Princeton, 1971), 7–34.

10   The Fruits of Experience: I. Later Careers

A study of early Meiji office-holders, which examines both political background and knowledge of the West as factors in shaping their careers, but not specifically foreign travel, is Bernard S. Silberman, *Ministers of Modernization: Elite mobility in the Meiji Restoration, 1868–1873* (Tucson, 1964).

Information about many of the persons considered in this chapter can be found in standard biographical dictionaries and other reference works. In some cases there are published biographies. The list of students given in Inuzuka Takaaki, *Meiji Ishin Taigai Kankei-shi Kenkyū* (Tokyo, 1987), is particularly valuable, because it shows the principal position each person reached in later life, where this is known. The names of the students are listed under dates of departure from Japan. Ishizuki, who gives similar information, lists students alphabetically under chronological sections.

I have also relied on the works cited above under Chapters 4 to 9. Those which are the most useful on later careers are the following:

On the 1860 mission, Masao Miyoshi, *As We Saw Them: The first Japanese embassy to the United States, 1860* (Berkeley and London, 1979).

On the 1862 mission, Miyanaga Takashi, *Bunkyū ni-nen no Yōroppa hōkoku* (Tokyo, 1989).

On the Bakufu students in Holland, Miyanaga Takashi, *Bakufu Oranda Ryūgakusei* (Tokyo, 1982).

On the Satsuma students in Britain, Inuzuka Takaaki, *Satsuma-han Eikoku ryūgakusei* (Tokyo, 1974).

On the Bakufu students in Britain in 1866–7, Hara Heizō, 'Tokugawa Bakufu no Eikoku ryūgakusei', *Rekishi Chiri*, 79 (1942), 345–74.

On individuals, apart from the works cited under previous chapters, the following can usefully be consulted (they are arranged in alphabetical order of subject):

Koizumi Shinzō, *Fukuzawa Yukichi* (Tokyo, 1966); Godai Ryūsaku, *Godai Tomoatsu den* (Tokyo, 1933); Ian Nish, 'Hayashi Tadasu (1850–1913)', in Hugh Cortazzi and Gordon Daniels, eds, *Britain and Japan, 1859–1991* (London and New York, 1991); Ishii Takashi, *Katsu Awa* (Tokyo, 1974); *Shōkiku Kido Kō den* [Kido Takayoshi] (2 vols, Tokyo, 1926); Yamaguchi Osamu, *Maejima Hisoka* (Tokyo, 1990); Nakahama Akira, *Nakahama Manjirō no shōgai* (Tokyo, 1971); Takahashi Masao, *Nakamura Kei'u* (Tokyo, 1966); Lesley Connors, *The Emperor's Adviser: Saionji Kinmochi and pre-war Japanese politics* (London, 1987); Johannes Hirschmeier, 'Shibusawa Eiichi: industrial pioneer', in W. W. Lockwood, ed., *The State and Economic Enterprise in Japan* (Princeton, 1965); Tsuchiya Takao, *Shibusawa Ei'ichi* (Tokyo, 1989); Kanai Madoka, *Tomi to iū na no Nihonjin* [Tateishi Onojirō] (Tokyo, 1979); Roger F. Hackett, *Yamagata Aritomo in the Rise of Modern Japan, 1838–1922* (Cambridge, Mass., 1971).

11   *The Fruits of Experience: II. Policies and Ideas*

The first section of the chapter, dealing with the framing of Meiji government policies, is based largely on works cited under chapter 6 (the Satsuma mission), chapter 7 (Bakufu students in Holland; Choshu and Satsuma students in Britain), and chapter 9 (the Iwakura embassy). The most important ones are Ivan P. Hall, *Mori Arinori* (Cambridge, Mass., 1973); Thomas Havens, *Nishi Amane and Modern Japanese Thought* (Princeton, 1970); Inuzuka Takaaki, *Meiji Ishin Taigai Kankei-shi Kenkyū* (Tokyo, 1987); and Kume Kunitake, *Tokumei Zenken Taishi Bei-Ō Kairan Jikki* (5 vols, Tokyo, 1878). On aspects of Meiji policy not covered in these works, see Roger F. Hackett, *Yamagata Aritomo in the Rise of Modern Japan, 1838–1922* (Cambridge, Mass., 1971), and the documents in *Meiji Japan Through Contemporary Sources* (3 vols, Tokyo, 1969–72).

The second section also makes use of material cited under earlier chapters, but there are a number of other works dealing more specifically with early Meiji writing. William R. Braisted, ed., *Meiroku Zasshi: Journal of the Japanese Enlightenment* (Cambridge, Mass., 1976), provides a complete translation of all issues of the journal. On particular contributors, see Hall, *Mori*, and Havens, *Nishi* (above); Carmen Blacker, *The Japanese Enlightenment: A study of the writings of Fukuzawa Yukichi* (Cambridge, 1964); and Takahashi Masao, *Nakamura Kei'u* [Masanao] (Tokyo, 1966). There is a detailed study of Nakamura's translation of Samuel Smiles, *Self-Help*, in Ōkubo Toshiaki, 'Nakamura Kei'u no shoki yōgaku shisō to "Saikoku Risshi-hen" no yakujutsu oyobi hankō ni tsuite', reprinted in *Ōkubo Toshiaki Rekishi Chosaku-shū*, 5, *Bakumatsu Ishin no yōgaku* (Tokyo, 1986), 224–60. On Nakamura's translation of J. S. Mill, *On Liberty*, see Ishida Takeshi, *Nihon kindai shisō-shi ni okeru hō to seiji* [Law and Politics in the History of Modern Ideas in Japan] (Tokyo, 1976).

Index

Abe Masahiro, 39, 44, 46–7, 50
Aberdeen, 132, 133
Adams, Francis, 158, 161
Adams, Will, 22
Aizawa Seishisai, 20, 28, 29, 39, 44, 218
Akamatsu Noriyoshi, 121, 123, 124, 124–5, 180, 185
Aki, see Hiroshima
Alcock, Rutherford, 72–3, 75–6, 80, 82, 89, 140–41, 156
Alexander, Maj.-Gen. G. G., 165, 166, 167
Alexander II, 86, 115, 203
America, see United States
Amsterdam, 84, 112, 123, 169
Andō Nobumasa, 71
Annapolis, 135, 164, 190
anti-foreign attitudes, see under Japan, anti-foreign attitudes
Antwerp, 112, 116
Aoki Shūzō, 145–6, 148, 153, 162, 169
Arai Hakuseki, 20
aristocracy, 11, 147–8, 151, 160, 162, 196
armed forces, careers in, 180, 184, 185, 187, 190, 193, 196, 197, 198, 199
Armstrong, Sir William, 81, 83
Armstrong guns, 81, 82, 91, 107, 112, 201
Arrow War, 37–8, 40
art and architecture, 14–15, 17, 28, 79, 82–3, 84, 116, 215, 218
Asakura Moriaki, 190
Ashikaga Shogun, 7–8, 10

Asia, early trade and relations with, 1–8, 9, 16, 18, 22; Japanese observations on, 35, 77, 170, 215, 216
Aston, W. G., 165, 167
astronomy, 16, 23–4, 26–7, 218
Austria, 168, 170

Baba Tatsui, 155, 197
Bakufu, organization of, 20–21, 38, 39, 40; foreign policy of, 21–2, 32–4, 35, 37–8, 39–41, 71–2, 80, 96, 97; attitude to Western studies, 23–4, 30–31, 32–5, 52–3; western-style military reform by, 31, 52–4, 98, 103–4, 202; missions sent abroad by, 58, 67, 72–3, 96, 99, 105, 114; students sent abroad by, 115, 116, 118, 119, 121–9; later careers of travellers from, 179–83, 187–8, 195, 199; see also Japanese missions overseas, Japanese students overseas
balloon ascents, 59, 60, 164
Bank of Japan, 189, 192, 219
banking, 115, 143–4, 159, 182, 199, 205, 206
Bansho Shirabesho (Office for the Investigation of Barbarian Books), later named Kaiseisho (cf.), 46–8, 64, 67, 73, 89, 121, 182, 208
'barbarians' (i), 1–2, 20–21, 215
Batavia, 66, 122
Belgium, 101, 111–12, 116, 124, 157, 168, 169, 175; Satsuma relations with, 96, 110–11

Bentham, Jeremy, 123, 201
Berihente, Shimmon, 90, 92
Berlin, 85, 87, 148, 149, 162, 168, 169, 175
Birmingham, 80, 83, 109, 117, 166, 167
Bismarck, Otto von, 168, 169, 171, 203
Boissonade, Gustave Emile, 146, 219
books, brought to Japan, from China, 5–6, 7, 8, 22, 212, 217; from the West, 17, 23, 24, 48, 90, 105, 109, 112, 165, 212
Brest, 100, 101
Brine, Maj. F., 102
Britain (also England), relations with Japan, before 1860, 8, 18, 20, 22, 29–30, 37–8; after 1860, 71, 80, 95, 97, 104, 109, 142, 165; Japanese missions to, 72, 79–84, 99–100, 102–3, 108–9, 112, 117–18, 143, 165–8; Japanese students in, 109, 113, 119, 120, 124, 126–9, 130–32, 135, 148–9, 152, 152–3, 155, 185–6; Japanese observations on, 35, 38, 41, 91–4, 203, 207, 215
British Museum, 155, 166, 175
Brooke, Lt John M., 67–8
Brunton, Thomas Henry, 142
Brussels, 110, 116, 124, 162
Buddhism in Japan, 2, 6, 7, 8, 9–10, 19, 152; cultural influence of, 10, 13–14, 210, 217, 222
bunmei-kaika, *see* 'civilization and enlightenment'
Bunmeiron no Gairyaku (An Outline of a Theory of Civilization), 214–15
bureaucracy and government, travellers' careers in, 180, 181, 182, 183, 184–5, 186, 187, 188–9, 190–91, 192, 193, 193–5, 196, 197–8
business, travellers' careers in, 181, 185, 189, 190, 192, 195, 196, 197, 198, 199

calendars, Chinese, 15–16, 21; western, 23–4, 26–7
Cambridge, 153, 186
Capron, Gen. Horace, 145, 147
cartography, 27
castaways and shipwrecked seamen, 26, 28, 29, 33
Ch'ang-an, 3, 5
Chanoine, Capt. Charles, 104

Charter Oath, 140, 141, 204
Chicago, 154, 163
Chikuzen (Fukuoka), 53, 135, 154
China, relations with the West, 1, 30, 35, 37–8, 40; early relations with Japan, 1–8, 16, 18, 22; cultural influence in Japan, 1–2, 7–8, 8–16, 175, 217; Japanese missions to, 3–8, 9, 16, 217; Japanese observations on, 21, 35, 66, 137, 216
Choshu (Yamaguchi), 95, 97, 139; western studies and military reform in, 42–3, 48, 130, 202; students from, 130–32, 148–9, 151, 153–4; later careers of, 190–92, 193, 193–4, 197, 206
Christianity in Japan, introduction of, 13, 18–19; ban on, 17, 19–20, 22, 23, 35, 111; missionaries of, 18–19, 135, 140, 141–2, 217; Japanese attitudes to, 19–20, 29, 115–16, 210, 213–14, 217
La Ciotat, 100
'civilization and enlightenment' (*bunmei-kaika*), 177, 209–10
Clarendon, Lord, 109
commerce and industry, Japanese investigations of, before 1868, 56–7, 65, 69, 74–5, 81–3, 84–5, 92, 101, 102, 109, 112, 114–15; after 1868, 159, 160, 163, 165, 166, 167, 169, 174–5, 205–7; *see also* industry
Comte, Auguste, 123, 201
Confucianism in Japan, 2, 6, 11; influence of, 12–13, 20–21, 50–51, 205, 209–10, 211–12, 213–14; anti-foreign ideas of, 20, 29, 115, 222
constitutions, Japanese study of, before 1868, 64, 66, 79, 84, 85, 92–3, 100, 103, 134; after 1868, 146, 164, 166, 169, 172, 175–6, 203–4, 210, 218; *see also* government and politics
Le Creusot, 103
currency, 56, 65, 143, 143–4, 151, 159, 191, 205, 212
Curtius, Donker, 40, 52–3, 74, 84, 88, 103

daimyo, position of, 19, 21, 39, 93, 99,

114; *see also* domains; *fudai daimyō*; *tozama daimyō*

Dan Takuma, 154, 155, 198

Darwin, Charles, 156, 208

de Bellecourt, Duchesne, 72, 89, 96

de Cachon, Mermet, 98–9, 115, 129, 182, 183

de Lesseps, Baron Ferdinand, 114

de Lhuys, Drouyn, 97, 98, 100

De Long, Charles, 158, 162

de Rosny, Léon, 89, 101, 103, 112

Denmark, 157, 162, 169

Deshima, 20, 23, 24, 26, 28, 37; *see also* Nagasaki

Devonport dockyard, 102

De Wit, 103, 121

doctors, on missions to the West, 58, 64, 73, 79, 80, 86, 90

Doeff, Hendrik, 30

domains (daimyo territories), send missions overseas, 96, 106–12, 114, 119; send students overseas, 108, 109, 112, 119–20, 129–38, 148–52, 153–4, 155; later careers of travellers from, 188–92, 192–3, 196, 197, 198, 198–9; *see also* separately under geographical names (e.g. Choshu, Hizen, Satsuma)

Dordrecht, 123, 124

Doshisha University, 192

Dutch language, Japanese knowledge of, 23–4, 25, 53, 68, 85, 89, 122, 123

Dutch studies (Rangaku), 17, 23–9, 30; Japanese schools of, 24, 26, 28, 31–2; *see also* Western studies

Echizen, 39, 48, 142

economics, study of, 121, 122–3, 176–7, 199, 205, 212

Edinburgh, 166, 167

Edo (modern Tokyo), 19, 71; *see also* Bakufu

education, western influence on, 31–2, 45–8, 106, 141, 146, 147, 205, 219, 222; investigations of, 80, 84, 90, 94, 105, 159, 160, 163, 164, 167, 169, 170, 172; careers in, 180, 181–2, 183–4, 185, 185–6, 187, 190, 192, 195, 196, 197, 198, 199

Edwards, Maj. Bevan, 117

Egawa Tarōzaemon (Tan'an), 33, 36,

52, 121, 144

Egypt, 77, 216

Ellis, William, 212

emperors, *see* monarchy; also names of individuals

Endō Kinsuke, 130–32, 191

Engels, Frederick, 156

engineering, study of, 121, 124, 132, 133–4, 135, 146, 206

England, *see* Britain

English language, Japanese knowledge of, 30, 48, 61, 67, 89, 126–7, 128, 131, 133, 141, 155

'enlightenment' (*kaimei*), 177, 182; *see also* 'civilization and enlightenment'

Ennin, 4, 5, 6, 13

Enomoto Takeaki, 121, 124, 124–5, 139, 145–6, 162, 184, 186, 187, 219

envoys, to China, 3, 8; to the West, 58, 67, 72–3, 96, 99, 105, 108, 114, 143–6, 157, 160–61; later careers of, 6, 179–80, 187, 194–5

era-names (*nengō*), 15

ethics, and study of the West, 28, 29, 127, 140–41, 176, 213–14, 217, 219, 222

Europe, Japanese missions to, 71–94, 96–7, 99–103, 107–13, 114–18, 130, 162, 165–70; Japanese students in, 108–9, 119, 120, 121–35, 145, 146, 148–9, 152–4, 154–5; Japanese observations on, 170–71, 172–7, 215

exhibitions (expositions), international, 81–3, 101, 114–15, 116, 135, 162, 170, 188, 190

Fabian Fucan, 20

feudal lords, *see* daimyo

Fillmore, Pres. Millard, 39

Fish, Hamilton, 164

Fleury-Hérard, Paul, 99, 100, 101, 114, 115, 205

Florence, 116, 162, 168, 170

food and drink, Japanese preferences in, 63, 76–7, 87, 100, 122

foreign employees in Japan (*o-yatoi*), 44, 103, 145–7, 217; *see also* military and naval missions

France, relations with Japan, 30, 37–8, 78, 88, 96–101, 103–5, 114, 116; Japanese missions to, 72,

78–9, 83, 87–8, 96–8, 99–101, 103, 114–17, 164, 168; Japanese observations on, 78, 91, 100, 113, 203, 215; Japanese students in, 116, 119, 120, 129, 146, 148–9, 152, 154
Franco-Prussian War, 148–9, 153
Free Trade, 206, 209, 212
French, Japanese knowledge of, 30, 48, 89, 98–9, 129
fudai daimyō, 39
Fujiwara house, 12
fukoku-kyōhei, see 'national wealth and strength'
Fukuchi Genichirō, travels as interpreter, 73, 88, 89, 99, 100–101, 103, 143–4, 161, 173; later career, 181, 183, 188
Fukuda Sakutarō, 181
Fukuda Tetsunosuke, 192
Fukuoka (Chikuzen), 53, 135, 154
Fukuzawa Einosuke, 127
Fukuzawa Yukichi, 46, 100, 127, 155, 172, 182, 186, 188; travels of, 67–9, 73, 77, 80, 85, 86, 88, 105; observations on the West, 79, 90, 91, 205; writings about the West, 182, 209, 211, 214–15
Furukawa Shōya, 122, 123, 185

Gaikoku Bugyō, 40, 58
Gakumon no Susume, 214
Geneva, 168, 170
Gérard, Abbé, 89
German, Japanese knowledge of, 30, 48, 125, 149, 153
Germany (also Prussia), relations with Japan, 85, 157, 171; Japanese missions to, 85, 112, 118, 164, 168, 169; Japanese students in, 135, 145, 151, 152, 153–4; Japanese observations on, 203, 215
Gladstone, W. E., 168
Glasgow, 132, 167, 191
Glover, James, 133
Glover, Thomas, 107, 108, 109, 133
Godai Tomoatsu, 106–14 *passim*, 130, 133, 134, 147, 188, 189, 203, 206, 207
Goshkevich, Iosif, 125-6
government and politics, Japanese study of, before 1868, 75, 91–3, 100, 103, 121, 123, 127; after 1868,

144, 146, 155, 159, 164, 166, 176, 203–4, 210–11, 211–12, 218; *see also* constitutions
Gower, James, 130–31
Granville, Lord, 165
Griffis, William E., 142, 147
guns, import of, 18, 22, 107, 110, 114; manufacture of, 48–9, 50, 52, 53; Japanese investigations of, 81, 82, 85, 86, 91, 92, 201; *see also* military science and technology

Hague, 84, 112, 122, 162
Hakata, 3, 53
Hakodate, 37, 139, 144, 184, 185, 186
Halma, François, 24
Hamburg, 169
Hammond, Edmund, 115, 117, 142
Hanabusa Yoshitomo, 192
Hara Rokurō, 197
Hardes, Dutch engineer, 54
Harris, Thomas Lake, 134
Harris, Townsend, 37–8, 41, 49, 56, 57, 71
Harvard, 154
Hatakeyama Yoshinari, 133, 134, 135, 164, 175, 190
Hawks, Francis L., 141
Hay, Lord John, 76
Hayashi Kenkai, 121–2, 123, 183
Hayashi Shihei, 32
Hayashi Tadasu, 162, 186
Heian, 9, 12, 13, 21, 217
Heusken, Hendrik, 56, 71
Hida Hamagorō, 68, 98, 161, 172, 180
Hideyoshi, *see* Toyotomi Hideyoshi
Higo (Kumamoto), 135, 141
Hikone, 39, 149
Hirata Atsutane, 28
Hiroshima (Aki), 135
Hitotsubashi Keiki (Yoshinobu), later Tokugawa Keiki (Yoshinobu), 41, 104
Hizen (Saga), 114, 139, 190; western studies and technology in, 48–9, 51, 52, 124; students from, 53, 135, 151
Hobbes, Thomas, 212
Hoffmann, Johan Joseph, 84, 90, 122
Hokkaido, 29, 144–5

Hokkaido Development Commission (Kaitakushi), 145, 151, 185
Holland, relations with Japan, 8, 17, 20, 22, 35–6, 37–8, 40, 41, 87–8, 169; Japanese observations on, 28, 85, 91, 142, 172; Japanese missions to, 44, 84–5, 112, 116, 168, 169; Japanese students in, 44, 119, 120, 121–5, 129, 132, 135, 145, 183–5; science and technology from, 49, 54–5, 84, 88, 98; naval training mission from, 52–4, 84; *see also* Dutch studies
Holme, Ryle, 108, 114, 133
Honda Toshiaki, 28, 32, 34, 35, 104
Hong Kong, 66, 77, 216
Honolulu, 61, 69
Hori Takayuki, 108, 109, 112
Hotta Masayoshi, 39, 40–41, 44–5, 56, 186, 192
Huxley, T. H., 208
Hyogo (Kobe), 71, 182

Ichijō Jūjirō, 137–8
Ichikawa Bunkichi, 126
Ichikawa Morisaburō, 186
Ichikawa Wataru, 77, 78, 79–80, 82–3, 88–9, 90, 91, 181, 216
Iemitsu, *see* Tokugawa Iemitsu
Ieyasu, *see* Tokugawa Ieyasu
Ignatiev, Nikolai, 86, 87
Ii Naosuke, 39, 39–40, 41–2, 43, 45, 71
Ikeda Nagaaki (Chōhatsu), 96–8, 124, 161, 179–80
immigrants, and cultural borrowing, 2, 14, 217
industry (western-style) in Japan, 48–52, 54, 98, 107, 110–11, 113, 205, 207, 219–20
Inō Tadataka (Chūkei), 27, 32
Inoue Kaoru, 130–32, 143, 189, 190–91, 198, 206, 219
Inoue Masaru, *see* Nomura Yakichi
interpreters, on missions to the West, 58, 73, 79, 96, 99, 108, 161–2; later careers of, 181–3, 187–8
interpreting and translating, in Chinese, 3, 6; in western languages, 23, 24, 27, 30, 125; on missions to the West, 63–4, 85, 88–90, 97, 110, 115–16, 124, 206–7
Ishikawajima shipyard, 51, 180

Italy, 116–17, 157, 168, 170, 215
Itō Gemboku, 32, 122
Itō Gempaku, 121–2, 123, 183
Itō Hirobumi, travels of, 130–32, 137, 143–4, 157, 158, 161, 162, 163, 164, 169, 170, 171, 198, 219; Meiji career of, 142–3, 157, 191, 192, 193, 203, 204, 206, 218, 219, 222
Iwakura embassy, travels of, 136, 149, 153, 154, 155, 162–70; planning of, 141, 157–62, 203; reports of, 150, 165, 170–71, 171–7, 202, 203, 205, 218; personnel of, 157, 160–62, 194–5, 219
Iwakura Tomomi, 157–73 *passim*, 177, 194
Iwashita Masahira, 114, 135

Japan, early relations with China and Korea, 1–8, 9, 16; attitudes to China, 2–3, 7, 21; trade with Asia, 5–8, 16, 18, 22, 107; early relations with the West, 8, 17, 18–20, 21–2; treaty relations with the West, 1–2, 37–8, 40–41, 56, 66, 71, 74–5, 80, 86, 88, 109, 157, 158, 159–60, 164, 171; trade with the West, 8, 17, 18, 74–5, 98–9, 104, 109, 110–11; knowledge of the West before 1860, 17–18, 22–8, 30–32, 45–55; anti-foreign attitudes in, 20–21, 28–9, 33–4, 39, 41–2, 56, 67, 71, 94, 95, 115, 130; *see also* Japanese missions overseas; Japanese students overseas
Japan Academy, 185, 186
Japanese missions overseas, to China, 3–8, 9, 16; to the West, planning of, 44, 56–7, 67, 72–4, 99–100, 107–8, 114, 157–62, 205; personnel of, 58, 67, 72–3, 96, 99, 105, 114, 157, 160–62; instructions to, 58–9, 74–6, 105, 107–8, 159–60; travels of, 59–67, 68–9, 76–88, 96–7, 100–103, 105, 108–13, 114–18, 143–6, 162–70; reports and records of, 59–60, 66, 69–70, 88, 90–94, 97, 102–3, 170–77; later careers, 179–83, 187–8, 193–5, 198–9
Japanese students overseas, to China, 3, 6; to the West, proposals concerning, 25–6, 44, 85, 97, 98,

108, 121, 125, 130, 132–3, 135, 149, 150; studies and travels of, 108–9, 113, 115–18, 121–38, 148–56, 162, 164; background, numbers, ages, countries of destination, time spent abroad, 119–21, 122, 127, 129–30, 133, 148, 149, 150–52, 153, 154, 178; later careers of, 6, 183–7, 195–9
Jardine Matheson company, 130, 131, 206
Jesuits, 18, 23, 24, 26, 98, 115, 129
jitsugaku ('practical studies'), 209–10, 214

Kaga (Kanazawa), 135, 149, 151
Kagoshima, 33, 53; bombardment of, 95, 106, 152; western studies and technology in, 49–50, 106, 108, 113, 133; *see also* Satsuma
Kaiseisho (Development Institute), in Edo, 48, 125, 127, 143, 183, 208; in Kagoshima, 106, 108, 113, 133
Kaitai Shinsho, 25, 26
Kaiyō Maru, 123, 124
kakubutsu kyūri, 25
Kanda Kōhei, 209, 212
Kaneko Kentarō, 154, 155, 198
Kankō Maru, 53
Kanrin Maru, 53, 67–70, 73, 98, 121, 161, 180, 181, 183
Karafuto (southern Sakhalin), 86, 144
Kataoka Kenkichi, 149
Katsu Awa (Kaishū), 46–7, 53, 67–70, 180, 184, 187
Katsura Tarō, 153–4, 195, 197, 202
Kawaji Tarō, 127, 128, 161–2, 186
Kawaji Toshiaki, 186
Kawamoto Kōmin, 49, 85
Kawasaki Dōmin, 73
Kawase Masataka, 145, 148, 191
Keiō Gijuku, 182
Keswick, William, 131
Kibi no Mabiki, 6
Kido Takayoshi (Kōin), 157, 160–70 *passim*, 177, 194, 204, 216
Kikuchi Dairoku (earlier Mitsukuri Dairoku), 127, 186
Kimura Yoshitake, 67, 68, 70, 180
King's College London, 126–7
Kobe, *see* Hyogo
Koide Hidezane, 182
Komatsu Tatewaki, 203

Korea, early relations with Japan, 2–8 *passim*, 9, 16, 22, 38
Kōtoku, Emperor, 9, 10, 12
Krupp arms factory (Essen), 125, 169
Kūkai, 9–10
Kulmus, Johann, 24–5
Kumamoto, *see* Higo
Kume Kunitake, 163–77 *passim*, 190, 195, 202–3, 205, 207, 215–16
Kurimoto Jo'un, 98
Kuroda Kiyotaka, 144–5, 184, 194, 195
Kuroda Nagatomo, 154
Kuroda Narihiro, 44
Kuwahara Motoyasu, 73
Kyōgoku Takaaki, 73, 76, 86, 179

law, study of, 100, 121, 122–3, 127, 146, 154, 155, 159, 160, 166, 172–3, 196, 199
Laxman, Adam, 29, 30
Leiden, 84, 90, 122–3, 169, 184, 205, 209
Liége, 112, 116, 169
lighthouses, 142
Lisbon, 88, 162
Liverpool, 80, 81, 117, 167
Lloyd, Rev. William, 126, 127–8
London, official visitors to, 80–84, 102, 108–9, 112, 117, 162, 166, 168, 174–5, 188–9; Japanese students in, 109, 128–9, 133–4, 145, 148, 149, 185–6, 189–90, 190–91; university, 126–7, 128, 131, 132, 133
London Protocol (1862), 80
Lyon, 78, 154, 170

Macdonald, John, 76, 79, 80, 83, 89
Machiavelli, Niccolo, 212
Machida Hisanari, 108, 112, 133, 134, 188
machinery, purchases of, 49, 54, 84, 98, 99, 103, 109, 110–11, 113, 124
Maejima Hisoka, 143, 194, 219
Maeno Ryōtaku, 25, 28, 31
Makino Nobuaki, 197–8
Malta, 78, 117
Mamiya Rinzō, 27
Manchester, 109, 117, 166, 167
Marx, Karl, 156, 208
Massachusetts Institute of Technology, 154

Masuda (Tachibana) Kōsai, 87, 106
Matheson, Hugh, 131
Matsudaira Sadanobu, 28, 31
Matsudaira Yasunao, 73, 76, 86, 179
Matsudaira Yoshinaga (Kei'ei, also
  Shungaku), 39, 142
Matsukata Masayoshi, 194, 198, 219
Matsuki Kōan (later Terashima
  Munenori), western studies of, 46,
  73, 89, 113; travels of, 73, 80, 106,
  107, 108, 109, 111, 112–13, 133,
  134, 183; observations on the West,
  84, 85, 86–7, 90, 203, 215; career
  in Meiji government, 142, 145,
  162, 188–9
Matsumoto Ryōjun, 54–5, 122
Matsumura Junzō (earlier Ichiki
  Kanjurō), 134, 135, 190
medicine, Chinese, 6, 16, 21; western,
  23, 24–6, 54–5, 146–7, 218;
  students of, 31, 54, 121–2, 133,
  135, 151, 152; *see also* doctors
Meiji government, institutions of,
  139–40, 149, 166, 191, 202, 203–4,
  218–19, 222; envoys sent by, 143–
  6, 157, 160–62; students sent by,
  148–53, 154–6; later careers of
  Meiji official travellers, 193–7
Meiji period, 15, 139
Meiji Restoration, 139
Meiroku Zasshi, 208–13, 214
Meirokusha, 208–9
military and naval missions to Japan,
  52–4, 96, 99, 103–4, 126, 146, 181
military science and technology,
  western, Japanese study of, 31–2,
  36, 45–8, 49, 121, 132, 133, 135,
  152, 153–4, 159, 172, 173, 201–2;
  its adoption in Japan, 36, 48–52,
  96, 100, 121, 218; *see also* guns;
  warships
Mill, J. S., 123, 186, 208, 213
Ming dynasty, 7–8, 14
ministers resident, Japanese, 97, 145–
  6, 184, 189
Minotaur, 102
Mint (Osaka), 142, 143, 151, 185,
  191, 219
missions, *see* Christianity in Japan;
  Japanese missions overseas
Mitford, Algernon, 161
Mito, 51, 115; *see also* Tokugawa
  Nariaki

Mitsui company, 152, 198
Mitsukuri Dairoku, *see* Kikuchi
  Dairoku
Mitsukuri Keigo, 127, 186
Mitsukuri Shūhei, 73, 91, 182
Mizuno Tadanori, 53, 73
monarchy, 11, 160
Montblanc, Comte des Cantons de,
  101, 103, 106, 109–11, 112, 113–
  14, 134, 206
Mori Arinori, travels of, 126, 133,
  134–5, 190; Meiji career, 145–6,
  162, 163–4, 189, 219; and
  Meirokusha, 208, 209, 210
Moriyama Takichirō, 73, 80, 84, 85,
  89, 182
Morrison incident, 33
Mosse, Alfred, 218
Motoki Ryōei, 27
Mukōyama Ichiri, 114, 116, 117
Muragaki Norimasa, 57, 58, 59, 63,
  64, 65, 67, 179
Murray, David, 146, 205
music, 3, 79, 83, 169, 212, 215

Nabeshima Naomasa, 48, 51, 52
Nagano Keijirō, *see* Tateishi Onojirō
Nagasaki, 20, 22, 29–30, 37, 48–9;
  western studies at, 17, 23, 24, 30,
  31; naval training at, 50, 52–4,
  121, 124, 146, 183; medical
  training at, 26, 54–5, 121–2; *see
  also* Deshima
Nagasawa Kanaye, 133, 134
Nagoya (Owari), 151
Nakae Chōmin, 154–5, 196–7,
  221–2
Nakahama Manjirō, 50, 67, 68,
  181–2
Nakamura Hiroyoshi, 189
Nakamura Masanao (Kei'u), 127, 128,
  185–6, 209, 211, 212–14
Nakashima Kenkichi, 122, 123, 185
Namamugi incident, 95
Namura Motonori, 58, 64, 182
Naniwa, 8
Naples, 168, 170
Napoleon III, 78, 98, 114, 115
Nara, 4, 9, 12, 13, 21, 217
'national wealth and strength'
  (*fukoku-kyōhei*), 1, 103, 104–5,
  111, 166, 174, 176, 177, 201–7,
  218

naval training, 50, 51, 52–4, 68, 104, 121, 152–3
navigation, Japanese study of, 22–3, 45–6, 53, 64, 68, 121, 131, 201, 218
nengō (era-names), 15
Neo-Confucianism, *see* Confucianism
Netherlands Trading Company, 74, 121
Newcastle, 80, 83, 166
newspapers, 64, 69, 81, 102, 103, 181, 183, 222–3
New York, 62, 65, 144, 164
Nichi Nichi, 181, 183
Nihon, 222–3
Niigata, 71
Niijima Jō, 136, 192
Niiro Gyōbu, 108, 109, 112, 113, 114, 133, 135, 188
Nikolaevsk, 130
Ningpo, 8
Ninomiya Sontoku, 213
Nirayama, 52
Nire Kagenori, 190
Nishi Amane, 121, 122–3, 183, 184–5, 202, 205, 209, 210–11
Nishimura Shigeki, 209, 211–12
Nobunaga, *see* Oda Nobunaga
Nomura Yakichi (later Inoue Masaru), 130–32, 191
Nonomura Tadazane, 181

Oda Nobunaga, 19
Ogata Kōan, 26, 32, 46, 67, 69, 182
Oguri Tadamasa, 58, 65, 98, 99, 179
Ōhashi Totsuan, 29
Okada Setsuzō, 100, 102, 103
Ōkawa Kitarō, 122, 123
Ōkubo Toshimichi, and the Iwakura embassy, 157, 160–68 *passim*, 171, 206–7; as Meiji leader, 158, 168, 171, 181, 194, 198, 207
Ōkuma Shigenobu, 141, 143, 158, 194, 198
Oliphant, Laurence, 71, 109, 134
Ono company, 152
Ono Tomogorō, 68, 105, 143, 180, 182
Ōno Yazaburō, 122, 123, 185
Opium War, 30, 31
Opzoomer, C. W., 123
L'Orient, 101
Osaka, opening of, 71, 80
Ōta Genzaburō, 73, 182–3

Ōtsuki Gentaku, 24, 28
Owari (Nagoya), 151
Ōyama Iwao, 148–9, 153, 182, 194, 196, 219
O-yatoi, see foreign employees

Paekche, 3, 9
Parhae, 6
Paris, Japanese official visitors to, 78–9, 83–4, 87–8, 96–7, 100–101, 112, 114, 146, 149, 162; Japanese students in, 129, 133, 135, 148–9, 154
Parkes, Harry, 109, 116, 126, 129, 142, 143, 152, 156, 165, 166
parliaments, *see* constitutions
Perry, Cdre M. C., 31, 32, 37, 42–3, 45
Peter the Great, 44, 68, 142
Phaeton, 29–30
Philadelphia, Japanese travellers in, 59, 62, 63, 64, 65, 164; National Mint, visits to, 65, 144, 164
Platt Brothers (Oldham), 113
Portman, A. C., 63
Portsmouth, 81, 102, 117, 152–3, 166
Portugal, early relations with Japan, 8, 18, 20, 22; Japanese missions to, 88, 91, 162, 168
postal services, 143, 194
Powhatan, 60–61, 67, 68
prime ministers, 191, 192, 193, 194, 195, 219
Prussia, *see* Germany
Putiatin, E. V., 42, 106, 122, 134

Raffles, T. S., 29–30
railway-building, 104, 112, 142, 143, 146, 180, 206, 219
Rangaku, *see* Dutch studies
Reading, 167
Regent (Tairō), 39
religion, *see* Buddhism; Christianity; Shinto
reverberatory furnaces, 48–9, 50, 51, 52
Rezanov, Nikolai, 29, 30
Rijcken, Cdr Pels, 53, 84
Rochefort, 88
Roches, Léon, 98–9, 100, 103, 104–5, 114, 115, 116, 126, 142, 179
Roesler, Hermann, 146, 218, 219
Rome, 168, 170, 175
Rousseau, J.-J., *Le contrat social*, 197

249

Rotterdam, 84–5, 169
Russell, Earl, 80, 83, 109
Russia, relations with Japan, 29, 30,
37–8, 41, 86, 144; Japanese
observations on, 44, 91, 142, 215;
Japanese missions to, 85–7, 118,
168, 169, 182; Japanese students
in, 119, 125–6, 129, 185
Russian, Japanese knowledge of, 30,
125–6
Rutgers College, 135, 136, 146, 189,
190
Ryukyu, 3, 8, 30, 38, 49, 111, 114,
206

Saga, *see* Hizen
Saichō, 9
Saigō Takamori, 180, 193
Saigō Tsugumichi, 148, 189, 193, 219
Saikoku risshi-hen (Self-Help), 214
St Petersburg, 85–7, 89, 125–6, 134,
145, 149–50, 162, 168, 169, 185
Saionji Kinmochi, 195, 196, 198
Saitō Kenjirō, 101, 106, 110
Sakai Takayuki, 72–3
Sakatani Shiroshi, 211, 221
Sakhalin (Karafuto), 86, 144
sakoku, see under Japan, national
seclusion
Sakuma Shōzan, 1, 28, 36, 42, 43, 44,
52
Sakurajima, 50
Salt Lake City, 163
Samejima Hisanobu, 133, 134–5, 145,
146, 162, 183, 189, 190
San Francisco, 61, 69–70, 137–8,
144, 149, 162, 174
Sanjō Sanetomi, 159, 160, 163
Sano Tsunetani, 145–6, 190
Sasaki Takayuki, 161, 195
Satō Nobuhiro (Shin'en), 34, 35, 104,
202
Satsuma (Kagoshima), 39, 95, 139;
and foreign trade, 38, 49, 107, 108,
109, 110–11, 114; western studies
and technology in, 48, 49–50, 51,
106, 107, 113; military reform in,
50–51; students sent abroad by, 53,
108, 109, 113, 127, 132–5, 148–9,
151, 152–3; missions to Europe
from, 96, 101, 103, 105–13, 114,
188–9, 206; later careers of
travellers from, 188–90, 193,

193–4, 197; *see also* Shimazu
Nariakira
Sawa Sadatoki, 121, 123–4, 184
Scharnhorst, Gerhard von, 173, 202
Schleswig-Holstein war, 124–5
science and technology in Japan,
Chinese, 2, 15–16, 21, 217;
western, 17, 23–8, 46–52, 54, 217;
students of, 125, 128, 132, 133–4,
152, 154, 155, 196; careers in, 180,
183, 184, 185, 186, 191, 196, 198,
199; *see also* military science and
technology
Seiyō Jijō, 182
Self-Help, see Smiles, Samuel
Sendai, 135, 136–8
Shanghai, 107, 130, 131, 132, 216
Sheffield, 167
Shiba Kōkan, 27
Shibata Takenaka, 125, 179; and the
1862 mission, 73, 76–7, 81, 84, 87;
and the 1865 mission, 96, 99–103,
104, 114, 124, 143
Shibusawa Ei'ichi, 115, 143, 181, 189,
205, 206, 207, 219–20
Shimazu Hisamitsu, 51
Shimazu Nariakira, 39, 44, 45, 49–51,
53, 73, 132–3
Shimmi Masaoki, 57, 58, 65, 73, 179,
215
Shimoda, 37, 52, 122
Shimonoseki Straits, 95, 97, 132
Shinagawa Yajirō, 148–9, 153, 182,
194
Shinto, 13–14, 150, 163, 195, 209, 222
Shioda Saburō, 96, 99, 145, 161, 183
Shionoya Tōin, 30, 42
shipbuilding, 49, 50, 54, 104, 121,
123, 124, 180, 201, 218
Shoeburyness, 109, 117
Shogun, office of, 7, 12, 20–21, 114;
see also Tokugawa Shogun
Shōhei Maru, 50
Shūseikan (Kagoshima), 50, 53
Siebold, Alexander von, 115–17
Siebold, Philipp Franz von, 26, 32–3,
35, 74, 90, 97, 98, 101, 115, 158,
169
Siemens electrical works, 169
Silla, 3, 5, 6
Singapore, 77, 88
sketches and drawings, Japanese, 3,
45, 65, 69, 81, 91

Smiles, Samuel, 156, 186, 208, 213–14
Smith, Adam, 123
Social Darwinism, 214
Soembing, 53
sonnō-jōi, 211
Spain, 8, 18, 20, 162, 168
Spandau, 85
Spencer, Herbert, 156, 208
Stanley, Lord, 128
Stockholm, 170
Stoke, 167
students, *see* Japanese students overseas
Suez canal, 97, 127–8
Sugi Kōji, 209
Sugi Norisuke, 181
Sugita Gempaku, 24–5, 28
sumō, 212
Sung dynasty, 8, 13, 14
Suzuki Tomo'o, 137–8
Sweden, 162, 170
Switzerland, 116, 168, 170

Tachi Hirosaku, 73, 89, 182
Taguchi Yoshinao, 121
Taihō system, 10–11, 15, 16
Tairō, *see* Regent
Taiwan, 4, 66
Takahashi Kageyasu, 32–3, 35
Takahashi Korekiyo, 136–8, 192, 193, 195
Takano Nagahide (Chōei), 33, 35, 49
Takashima Shūhan, 31, 36, 52
Takashima Yūkei, 73
Takasugi Shinsaku, 130
Takenouchi Yasunori, 73–4, 76, 77, 78, 84, 85, 86, 96, 179
Tamamushi Yasushige, 59, 63, 64, 65, 66, 180
Tanabe Ta'ichi, 96, 114–15, 161, 172, 181
Tanaka Fujimaro, 136, 161, 195
T'ang dynasty, 3, 7, 10
Tani Kanjō, 219
tariffs, *see* commerce and industry; Free Trade; 'unequal treaties'
Tateishi Onojirō (later Nagano Keijirō), 58, 59, 162, 182
Tateishi Tokujirō, 58
technology, *see* science and technology

Terashima Munenori, *see* Matsuki Kōan
Thompson, David, 149
Thouvenel, Count, 78, 88
Tōgō Heihachirō, 152–3, 196
Tokugawa Akitake, 114–18, 128, 129, 181, 187
Tokugawa Iemitsu, 19
Tokugawa Ieyasu, 19, 20
Tokugawa Keiki (Yoshinobu), *see* Hitotsubashi Keiki
Tokugawa Nariaki, 39, 40, 41, 44, 46, 50, 51
Tokugawa Shogun, authority of, 12–13, 21, 22, 38, 41, 43, 109, 114; overthrow of, 118, 128–9, 139; *see also* Bakufu
Tokugawa Yoshimune, 23, 26
Tokyo Imperial University, 219
Tomita Tetsunosuke, 137
Torii Takaaki, 33–4
Tosa (Kochi), 139, 149, 151, 155
Tottori, 149
Toyama Sutehachi, 186
Toulon, 100
Toyotomi Hideyoshi, 19
tozama daimyō, 39
Tōzenji incident, 71
trade, *see under* Japan
translations, Tokugawa period, 24–6, 27, 30–31, 46–9, 51, 52, 88–9; Meiji period, 164, 197, 209, 212, 213–14, 223
treaty ports, 37–8
treaty revision, 157, 158, 159–60, 164, 165, 168, 218
tribute system, 3, 6, 7–8, 15, 21, 38
Tsuda Mamichi, 121, 122–3, 183, 184–5, 205, 209, 209–10
Tsukiji, 53
Tsushima, 22, 38

Uchida Masao, 121, 123, 183–4
Ueda Torakichi, 122, 123, 185
Ueno Kagenori, 143
'unequal treaties', 1, 37–8, 41–5
United States, relations with Japan, 30, 31, 37–8, 56–7, 97, 142; missions to, 56–70, 72, 105, 130, 143–5, 163–5; Japanese observations on, 65–6, 70, 165, 215; Japanese students in, 120, 121, 129–30, 132, 134–5,

136–8, 141, 149, 151, 152, 154, 164
University College London, 126–7, 128, 131, 132, 133–4, 191
Unkō Maru, 50
Uraga, 33
Uwajima, 48

vaccination, 26
van Kattendijke, Huyssen, 122, 124
van Meerdervoort, Pompe, 54–5, 122
Venice, 168, 170
Verbeck, Guido, 135, 141–2, 158–9
Verny, François, 98, 99, 100, 101, 103
Victoria, Queen, 79, 86, 117, 167
Vienna, 162, 168, 170
Vissering, Simon, 122–3

warships, purchase of, 53, 67, 98, 99, 105, 107, 110, 112, 121, 124
Waseda University, 194
Washington, 61–2, 64, 144, 162, 163–4, 175
Watanabe Kazan, 33–4, 35
'wealth and strength', *see* national wealth and strength
weapons, *see* guns; warships
West Point, 164, 173
Western studies (Yōgaku), 18, 30–36, 106; Japanese schools of, 31–2, 45–8, 106; *see also* Dutch studies
Wilberforce, Bishop Samuel, 208

Williamson, Alexander, 132
Woolwich Arsenal, 81, 91, 102, 109, 166

Yale, 189, 196
Yamada Akiyoshi, 161, 173, 195, 202, 219
Yamagata Aritomo, 148, 189, 191, 193–4, 195, 197, 202, 219
Yamaguchi Naoyoshi, 157, 161
Yamakawa Kenjirō, 196
Yamanaka Ichirō, 149
Yamanouchi Sakuzaemon, 125–6
Yamao Kenzō, 130–32, 143, 191
Yamashita Iwakichi, 122, 123, 185
Yamataka Nobuo, 115, 116
Yanagawa Masakiyo, 60, 61, 66, 216
Yasukawa Shigenari, 172
Yōgaku, *see* Western studies
Yokohama, French installations at, 98
Yokohama Specie Bank, 219
Yokoi Shōnan, 141
Yokosuka dockyard, 96, 98, 100, 103, 180, 185
Yoshida Kiyonari, 133, 134, 135, 189, 206
Yoshida Shigeru, 198
Yoshida Shōin, 42–3, 130, 194
Yoshihara Shigematsu, 189, 206
Yoshimune, *see* Tokugawa Yoshimune
Young, Brigham, 163
Yume monogatari, 33

The American Congress

Sixth Edition

Steven S. Smith
Washington University

Jason M. Roberts
University of North Carolina

Ryan J. Vander Wielen
Temple University

CAMBRIDGE
UNIVERSITY PRESS

CAMBRIDGE UNIVERSITY PRESS
Cambridge, New York, Melbourne, Madrid, Cape Town, Singapore, São Paulo, Delhi

Cambridge University Press
32 Avenue of the Americas, New York, NY 10013-2473, USA

www.cambridge.org
Information on this title: www.cambridge.org/9780521749060

First published 2009

Printed in the United States of America

A catalog record for this publication is available from the British Library.

Library of Congress Cataloging in Publication data
The American Congress / Steven S. Smith, Jason M. Roberts,
Ryan J. Vander Wielen. – 6th ed.
    p.   cm.
Includes bibliographical references and index.
ISBN 978-0-521-74906-0 (pbk.)
1. United States. Congress.   2. United States. Congress – Evaluation.   3. United
States – Politics and government – 21st century – Public opinion.   4. Public opinion –
United States.   I. Smith, Steven S., 1953–   II. Roberts, Jason M.   III. Vander Wielen,
Ryan J.   IV. Title.
JK1041.A617   2009
328.73 – dc22   2009010737

ISBN 978-0-521-74906-0 paperback

Contents

Preface   *page* vii

Acknowledgments   xi

 1 The American Congress: Modern Trends 1

 2 Representation and Lawmaking in Congress: The
     Constitutional and Historical Context 27

 3 Congressional Elections and Policy Alignments 53

 4 Members, Goals, Resources, and Strategies 87

 5 Parties and Leaders 121

 6 The Standing Committees 165

 7 The Rules of the Legislative Game 207

 8 The Floor and Voting 237

 9 Congress and the President 267

10 Congress and the Courts 307

11 Congress, Lobbyists, and Interest Groups 335

12 Congress and Budget Politics 363

Appendix: Introduction to the Spatial Theory of Legislating   389

Notes   401

Suggested Readings   405

Index   425

Preface

The American Congress has long been one of the most powerful legislative bodies in the world. Congress is now struggling with momentous issues such as health care and worldwide environmental problems, the stabilization of the world financial system, the rehabilitation of America's infrastructure, funding the U.S. system of retirement security, the war against terrorism, and the place of the United States in the post–Cold War world. These issues present a serious challenge. They affect the interests of all Americans, they are highly controversial, and they involve complex public policies.

Major Features of *The American Congress*

Understanding the Place of Congress in American Democracy. Our primary goal in writing this edition is to instill in students and general readers an appreciation for the importance of a strong legislature in the American democracy. Such an appreciation requires an understanding of the constitutional setting in which Congress operates, the basic rules of the electoral and legislative processes, and the resources and strategies of members of Congress and other key players. Each chapter is designed to contribute to the reader's understanding by introducing key concepts, describing essential details of the process, and outlining general principles for understanding the subject.

The Changing Congress. In our efforts to introduce you to congressional politics, we emphasize the evolving nature of Congress. In writing a textbook, it is easy to describe current arrangements and create the impression that the rules and processes described have long been as described and are likely to stay that way for some time. We do not want to create that impression. Congress is created by its members and frequently changed by its members. Consequently, we emphasize the factors that influence legislators' thinking about their institution. Party conflict, competition with the executive branch, the drive for reelection, and other forces in congressional politics are discussed.

Important Ideas About Congress. We also highlight important ideas in recent public commentary and political science research about Congress and its members. Although we do not organize our discussion around debates in the professional literature on Congress, we do not hesitate to observe differences of opinion among our colleagues in political science on important subjects. Political scientists have offered competing and insightful perspectives on the sources of the incumbency advantage, the importance and motivations of legislative parties, the power of committees, and other subjects. We provide an accessible and balanced discussion of the deserving perspectives.

A Starting Point for Your Research on Congress. We provide a starting point for most undergraduate research projects by including an extensive bibliography on congressional politics at the end of the book. The bibliography emphasizes both classic and recent books, includes major journal articles, and contains major Web sites that include useful information on Congress and related subjects. Because we have provided a lengthy bibliography, we have limited references to literature in the text.

We have not hidden our enthusiasm for congressional politics. To be sure, Congress is easy to dislike and often difficult to defend. The rough-and-tumble world of legislating is not orderly and civil, human frailties too often taint its membership, and legislative outcomes are often frustrating and ineffective. Still, we are not exaggerating when we say that Congress is essential to American democracy. We would not have survived as a nation without a Congress that represented the diverse interests of our society, conducted a public debate on the major issues, found compromises to resolve conflicts peacefully, and limited the power of our executive, military, and judicial institutions.

Organization of the Text

Chapter 1 begins with an overview of the condition of the modern Congress. The chapter gives the reader a look at the general trends in American politics that are shaping the character of congressional policy making. It also reviews recent developments that have changed partisan control of the institution and altered the distribution of power within the institution.

Chapters 2 and 7 survey both constitutional and internal legislative rules to give an integrated perspective on the legislative game. The special character of American national legislative politics is the product of the Constitution, which created three institutions – the House of Representatives, the Senate, and the president – and set rules governing their interaction in the process of enacting public laws. In addition, the House and the Senate have developed different rules and practices that have a substantial effect on public policy.

Chapter 3 focuses on congressional elections. It covers the fundamental rules that govern elections and details the advantages enjoyed by congressional incumbents in their efforts to stay in office. The chapter concludes by evaluating the importance of election outcomes for the policy choices made by Congress and the president.

Chapter 4 focuses on individual members. It begins by reviewing the variety of political goals that members pursue. It also considers the resources that members may mobilize in pursuit of their goals and the political actors who influence members' behavior. The chapter concludes by looking at the strategies that members pursue in the case of voting and policy leadership.

Chapters 5, 6, 7, and 8 concern the central components of the legislative process – parties, committees, and the chamber floors. Parties and committees are not mentioned in the Constitution, yet the interaction of parties and committees defines the decision-making process in the modern Congress. The emphasis is on both the development of congressional parties and committees and recent changes that have altered the character of congressional decision making in important ways. Chapter 8, while detailing the activity that takes place on the House and Senate floors, concludes with an overall perspective on how parties, committees, and the floors are related to each other.

Chapters 9, 10, and 11 consider the major institutions and organizations with which Congress interacts – the president and executive branch, the courts, and interest groups. In each case, the emphasis is on the way in which resources and strategies of the institution or organization affect its relations with Congress.

Budget politics and process are the concern of Chapter 12. Budget politics has become a nearly dominant feature of congressional politics, and many important procedural developments have occurred in recent years. This chapter emphasizes the importance of the evolving budget process for the distribution of power in Congress.

A Special Appendix

We have added an appendix on spatial theories of legislative politics. Spatial theory now plays a central role in the political science of legislative politics.

Students at all levels benefit from understanding the basic ideas in spatial theory. We suggest that you read the relevant sections of the appendix along with the core chapters. We think it will enrich your understanding of the political strategies pursued by legislators and presidents and give you some basis for understanding the determinants of legislative outcomes.

Acknowledgments

We are very pleased to be publishing this edition of *The American Congress* with Cambridge University Press. Cambridge editor Ed Parsons has championed this project, provided wise advice to us, and shepherded the review and editorial processes with great skill.

This edition would not have been possible without the support and motivation provided by the Weidenbaum Center at Washington University in St. Louis. Chris Moseley provided superb administrative assistance.

Over the years, members of Congress have been remarkably generous with their time. Smith is particularly indebted to the late Speaker Thomas P. "Tip" O'Neill, with whom he spent a year under the auspices of the Congressional Fellowship Program of the American Political Science Association. He learned a great deal about congressional politics from Speaker O'Neill and his top aides, Ari Weiss and the late Spencer Smith.

We thank our many colleagues who teach about Congress for their encouragement.

Steven S. Smith, Jason M. Roberts, and Ryan J. Vander Wielen

Above: Members of the Congressional Black Caucus participate in the CBC ceremonial swearing in event at the Capitol Visitors Center Congressional Auditorium on Tuesday, January, 6, 2009. **Below:** WASHINGTON, DC – Nov. 17: House Representatives-elect on the East Front steps of the U.S. Capitol for a freshman class photo. Democrats bolstered their majority with a gain of 20 seats in the House in national elections in November. (Photo by Scott J. Ferrell/Congressional Quarterly)

1

The American Congress: Modern Trends

C ONGRESS IS AN EXCITING PLACE. REAL POWER RESIDES IN ITS MEMBERS, real social conflicts are tamed or exacerbated by its actions, and thousands of people – most of them good public servants – walk its halls every day. Much good work is done there. In recent years, Congress has passed widely applauded bills that have, among other things, approved new security measures for airports and funding for the war against terrorism; granted important civil rights to women, minorities, and the disabled; given parents job protection so they can care for sick children; forced states to reduce barriers to voter registration and supported reforms of voting processes; expanded funding for college students; and limited what lobbyists can give to legislators.

Congress is a frustrating place as well. It is not easy to understand. Its sheer size – 535 members and more than 25,000 employees – is bewildering. Its system of parties, committees, and procedures, built up over 200 years, is remarkably complex and serves as an obstacle to public understanding. Perhaps most frustrating is that its work product, legislation, is the product of a process marked by controversy, partisanship, and bargaining. Even some members of Congress are uncomfortable with the sharp rhetoric and wheeling and dealing that are hallmarks of legislative politics.

But Congress is also important. No other national legislature has greater power than the Congress of the United States. Its daily actions affect the lives of all Americans and many people around the world. It checks the exercise of power by the president, the courts, and the bureaucracy. If you want to understand the forces influencing your welfare, you must understand Congress.

Congress is always changing. It changes because it is a remarkably permeable institution. New problems, whatever their source, invariably create new demands on Congress. Elections bring new members, who often alter the balance of opinion in the House and Senate. Elections also frequently bring a change in majority party control of Congress, which leads to a transfer of agenda control on the floor and in committees from one party to another. And each new president asks for support for his policy program. Members of Congress often respond to these demands by passing new legislation. But as lawmakers pursue their personal political goals, compete with one another for control over policy, and react to pressure from presidents, their constituents, and lobbyists, they sometimes seek to gain advantage or to remove impediments to action by altering the procedures and organization of Congress itself. The result is nearly continuous change within the institution.

Explaining the ongoing changes in Congress is the central focus of this text. We begin in this chapter by highlighting several developments in American politics that have changed congressional politics. These developments – including changes in the way Congress is covered by the media, evolving standards for public ethics, the rise of plebiscitary politics and new information technologies, new forms of organized efforts to influence Congress, new kinds of issues, and the war on terrorism – have altered the context of congressional policy making in basic ways.

Low Public Confidence

The popularity of Congress ebbs and flows with the public's confidence in government generally. When the president's ratings and trust in government improved after the tragic events of September 11, 2001, Congress's approval ratings improved too. Still, Congress's performance ratings are almost always below those of the president and the Supreme Court. The legislative process is easy to dislike – it often generates political posturing and grandstanding, it necessarily involves compromise, and it often leaves broken promises in its wake. Also, members of Congress often appear self-serving as they pursue their political careers and represent interests and reflect values that are controversial.

Scandals, even when they involve a single member, add to the public's frustration with Congress and have contributed to the institution's low ratings in opinion polls. Some of the highlights are provided in the box on page 3. A consequence is that Congress is a never-ending source of comic relief, like the joke about the senator who dozed off during a roll-call vote, was jerked awake when his name was called, and reflexively yelled out, "Not guilty." There also is the joke about the member who kept referring to the presiding officer as "Your Honor."[1] But seriously . . . it seems fair to say that a large majority of today's members behave ethically. It is even reasonable to argue

HIGHLIGHTS OF RECENT CONGRESSIONAL ETHICS SCANDALS

- In 1989, House Speaker James Wright (D-Texas) resigned after Republicans charged him with ethics violations for receiving extraordinarily large royalties on a book.

- In 1991, Senator David Durenburger (R-Minnesota) was condemned in a unanimously approved Senate resolution for a book deal and for seeking reimbursement for expenses for staying in a condo that he owned.

- The disclosure that many House members had repeatedly overdrawn their accounts at the House disbursement office led people to believe that members enjoyed special privileges.

- Questions about the propriety of campaign contributions were raised in the "Keating Five" affair, which concerned the relationship between five senators and a prominent savings-and-loan owner seeking to block an investigation of his financial dealings.

- In 1995, a long investigation of sexual harassment charges against Senator Robert Packwood (R-Oregon) led to his forced resignation from office.

- In 1995, Representative Dan Rostenkowski (D-Illinois), former chairman of the House Ways and Means Committee, was found guilty of illegally receiving cash for personal use from the House post office. He later served a prison term.

- In 1995, Representative Enid Waldholtze (R-Utah) retired after her husband was charged with felonies in conjunction with raising funds for her campaign.

- In 1997, Speaker Newt Gingrich (R-Georgia) agreed to pay $300,000 in fines based on charges that he used nonprofit organizations for political purposes and misled the House Committee on Standards of Official Conduct.

- In 1998, Representative Jay Kim (R-California) pleaded guilty to charges involving more than $250,000 in illegal campaign contributions.

- In 2002, Representative James A. Traficant, Jr. (D-Ohio), was convicted of receiving bribes in exchange for helping businesses get government contracts and of engaging in a pattern of racketeering since taking office in 1985.

- In 2004, House Majority Leader Tom Delay (R-Texas) was issued letters of admonition by the House ethics committee for improperly promising to endorse the son of Representative Nick Smith (R-Michigan) in exchange for Smith's vote on a bill and for attending a fundraising event with lobbyists for a company that was lobbying him on pending legislation.

- In 2005, Representative Duke Cunningham (R-California) resigned and pleaded guilty to taking more than $2.4 million in bribes and related tax evasion and fraud, the largest financial sum involving an individual member.

- In 2006, Representative Tom Delay (R-Texas) resigned after being indicted in Texas for laundering money through a national party committee in his effort to redistrict Texas congressional districts.

(continued)

HIGHLIGHTS OF RECENT CONGRESSIONAL ETHICS SCANDALS (*continued*)

• In 2006, Representative William Jefferson (D-Louisiana) won reelection to the House but was denied a Ways and Means Committee assignment after FBI agents videotaped him appearing to solicit a bribe and later found $90,000 of the marked cash in his freezer – making this the cold cash scandal. Jefferson was defeated for reelection in 2008. The prosecution continues at this writing.

• In 2006, Representative Mark Foley (R-Florida) resigned after it was disclosed that he sent sexually explicit email messages to underage House pages.

• In 2006, Representative Bob Ney (R-Ohio) pleaded guilty to making false statements and participating in a conspiracy, receiving thousands of dollars in gifts from lobbyist Jack Abramoff. A Ney aide pleaded guilty to receiving gifts. Separately, Abramoff pleaded guilty to charges of conspiracy, fraud, and tax evasion.

• In 2008, Senator Ted Stevens (R-Alaska) was convicted of seven counts of failing to disclose gifts related to the renovation of his Alaska home on his Senate financial disclosure forms. His conviction was later overturned due to prosecutorial misconduct.

• In 2008, Representative Tim Mahoney (D-Florida) confessed that he had had an extra-marital affair with a staff member. Shortly after, news reports indicated that Mahoney attempted to buy the staff member's silence, his wife filed for divorce, and he was defeated for reelection.

that today's cohort of members is at least as ethical as any past cohort. No doubt the ethical standards applied by the public, the media, and Congress itself are higher today than at any other time. Yet, there is no denying that the seemingly regular flow of scandals harms Congress's standing with the American people.

Congress suffers generally from low ratings, which some observers believe represents a long-term trend. Political scientist Norman Ornstein notes that changes in the electronic and print media have led to a greater emphasis on the negative and sensational side of Congress. He refers to this as the "tabloidization" of media coverage:

> The drive to emulate the *National Enquirer* and the *Star* has spread to the most respectable newspapers and magazines, while network news divisions have begun to compete with tabloids like "Inside Edition" and "Hard Copy" with their own tabloid shows like "Prime Time Live" and "Dateline: NBC," and with changed coverage on the nightly news.

Stories or rumors of scandal – both individual and institutional – have dominated news coverage of politics and politicians in recent decades more than at any time in modern history, and not just in terms of column inches or broadcast minutes, but in emphasis as well:

> The expansion of radio and cable television talk shows also seems to have increased the speed with which bad news about Congress is disseminated and the frequency with which bad news is repeated. On many of these programs, there is a premium on a quick wit and a good one-liner and little time for sober, balanced commentary.[2]

Groups supporting term limits for Congress and other reforms probably have influenced public opinion too. Term limits advocates argue that congressional incumbents are a privileged class. Incumbents, in this view, have created a system in which various benefits of office – including biased districting, free use of official resources, fundraising leverage, and cozy relations with lobbyists – give them an unfair advantage that can be overcome only through radical reform. The more extreme versions of this argument suggest that incumbents have been corrupted by their experience in Washington. Incumbents are said to have developed an "inside-the-beltway" mentality (the Beltway is the freeway that encircles the District of Columbia and its inner suburbs) or to suffer from "Potomac fever" (presumably a condition brought on by proximity to the famous river).

Politicians, of course, quickly latch on to themes that resonate with the public. As a result, running for Congress by running *against* Congress, an old art form in American politics, has gained an even more prominent place in recent campaigns. Indeed, many recent arrivals on Capitol Hill promised to end "business as usual" in Washington and to push through reforms to "fix" Congress – to end the system of congressional perks, to stop the influence of special interests, and so on. The repetition of anti-Congress themes undoubtedly contributes to the low ratings for Congress and its members in public opinion polls.

The public's generally low evaluations of Congress have been observed for years. The Gallup Poll has regularly asked the question, "Do you approve or disapprove of the way Congress is handling its job?" Figure 1.1 shows that less than a majority of the public approves of Congress's performance most of the time. In the last few decades, the only time Congress's approval rating reached significantly above 50 percent was in the months following the terrorist attacks of September 11, 2001, during which anti-terrorist legislation was quickly approved.

While Congress languishes with mediocre approval ratings, individual members of Congress continue to do quite well. Typically, Gallup finds that about 70 percent of the public approves of the way its own U.S.

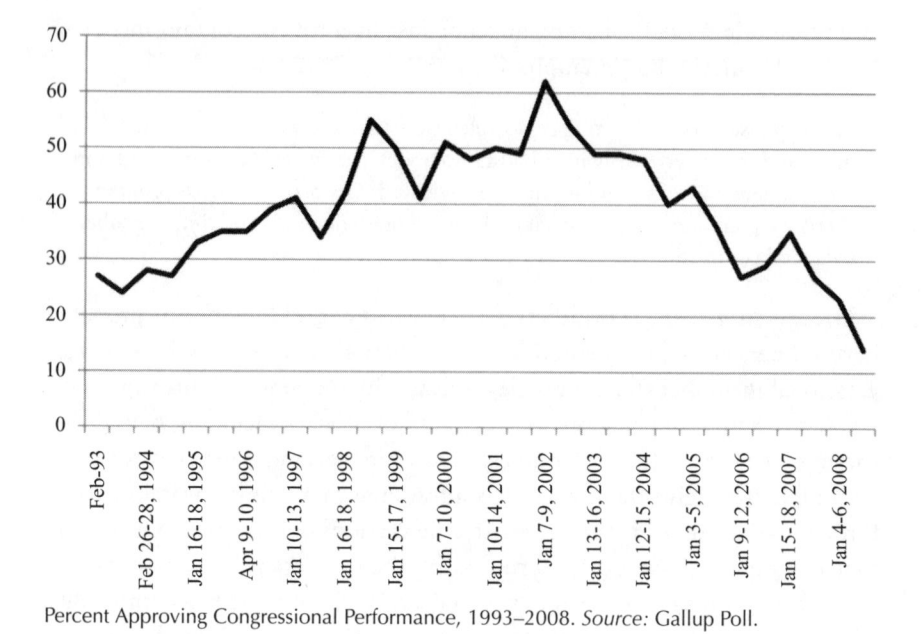

Percent Approving Congressional Performance, 1993–2008. *Source:* Gallup Poll.

representative is handling his or her job. Running *for* Congress by running *against* Congress works well.

Plebiscitary Politics

Political scientist Robert Dahl argues that Congress suffers from the increasingly plebiscitary nature of American politics. By a movement toward plebiscitary politics, Dahl is referring to the trend toward more direct communication between the public and elected officials and the demise of intermediaries – such as parties and membership organizations – that once served to represent or express public opinion to elected officials. Directly observed, rather than mediated, public views are more important than ever – which could not be further from Madison's aspirations for the national legislature.[3]

Plebiscitary politics is facilitated by new technologies. Advances in transportation allow most members of Congress to be back home in their districts or states most weekends. Public opinion polls, which allow the public's views to be registered with legislators, have become more affordable because of advancements in digital technology. Leaders and parties sponsor focus groups to learn about nuances and shadings in public attitudes. Radio and television call-in shows enable nearly every constituent to talk directly to a member of Congress from time to time. Satellite technology allows members to communicate easily and inexpensively with groups in their home state or district from Washington.

Members of Congress, and certainly candidates for Congress, find the new information technologies irresistible and contribute to the trend. Members love to demonstrate their commitment to keeping in touch with their constituents by being among the first to use a new innovation in communications. To be sure, members face real problems reaching constituents in districts and states with ever-growing populations. The average House district is approaching 700,000 people, up from about 300,000 in 1940 and 400,000 in 1960. Still, the political value of appearing to be connected to constituents drives elected officials to exploit new technologies.

On its face, plebiscitary politics might seem to be a good thing: It seems better to have public opinion influencing members' decisions than to have highly paid lobbyists representing organized interests swaying their votes. But as Dahl notes, the effects of direct communication between the people and their representatives on Capitol Hill may not be so desirable. For one thing, elected officials and special interests might manipulate direct communication to their advantage. If the politicians are the ones who choose the time and place for direct communication, the process may create nothing more than a deceiving appearance of responsiveness.

More important, plebiscitary politics may undermine both representation and deliberation in legislative policy making. With respect to representation, the "public" that is likely to communicate directly to members may not be representative of members' larger constituencies. They will be people who are intensely interested in politics, generally or in a single issue, and can afford and know how to use new information technologies. If so, then members' impressions of public opinion may be distorted by such communication.

With respect to deliberation, direct communication with more constituents could lead members to make premature public commitments on more issues and reduce their flexibility in negotiating compromises in the legislative arena. The possible result is that demagoguery and grandstanding would take precedence over resolving conflicts and solving problems. Public opinion may win out over the public interest, which is what Madison sought to avoid.

Governing as Campaigning

A close cousin to the rise of plebiscitary politics is the weakening distinction between governing and campaigning. Of course, we hope that there is a strong linkage between governing and campaigning. Elected officials' desire for reelection underpins our ability to hold them accountable. Broadly speaking, campaign promises are (and should be) related to governing, and election outcomes are (and should be) shaped by performance in office. Inevitably, then, the line between governing and campaigning becomes blurred.

In recent decades, campaigning has become more fully integrated with governing. No longer is governing done in Washington and campaigning done at home. The daily routines of members and top leaders are now geared to the demands of campaigning.

Few members retire from Congress without complaining about how much it costs to mount a campaign for reelection. Returning members may not have time to complain. In recent years, the average victor in a Senate race spent more than $8 million, and the average House victor spent more than a million dollars. Many races were far more expensive. For an incumbent seeking reelection, that is an average of more than $25,000 for each week served during a six-year Senate term and almost $10,000 for each week served during a two-year House term. These sums do not include additional millions spent by parties and independent groups on congressional campaigns. Competitive pressures, between incumbents and challengers and between the two parties, have produced a never-ending search for cash.

Congressional leaders have changed their ways, too. To assist their party colleagues, most party leaders spend many evenings and weekends at fundraising events. Many leaders have developed their own political action committees (leadership PACs, they have been called) to raise and distribute money. Leaders have formed public relations task forces within their parties, and the campaign committees of the congressional parties have greatly expanded their activities. Perhaps most important, congressional leaders now often use technology developed for campaigning in legislative battles. Professional consultants and pollsters help fashion legislative priorities and tactics. Opposition research – digging up dirt on your election opponent – is now conducted by the congressional campaign committees against congressional incumbents of the opposite party. Media campaigns are now planned for major legislative proposals with the assistance of television advertising specialists. Money, media, and partisanship feed on each other.

New Forms of Organized Influence

The number of interest groups in Washington and the rest of the country multiplied many times in the last half century. By one count, the number of groups increased from about 1,000 in the late 1940s to well more than

---

Congressionally Speaking . . .

Each Congress has a two-year life span. Federal law sets the date for federal elections, but the Constitution specifies the starting date for each Congress. Before 1935, congressional elections in November of an even-numbered year preceded the convening of a new Congress the following March. Since 1935, after the ratification of the Twentieth Amendment to the Constitution, a new Congress convenes on January 3 unless Congress otherwise provides by law, as it often does to avoid weekends. Each two-year Congress is given a number – the 111th Congress convened in January 2009 – and is divided into two one-year sessions. Congressional documents are often numbered 111–1 or 111–2 to combine the Congress and session numbers.

7,000 in the early 1980s.[4] Due to lobbying registration requirements that were enacted in 1995, we know that the number of registered lobbyists has more than doubled since 2000 to more than 35,000. This increase is primarily a by-product of the expanding scope of the federal government's activity – as more interests were affected by federal programs, tax policies, and regulation, more interests have sought representation in Washington. Technological developments in transportation, information management, and communications have enabled scattered people, corporations, and even state and local governments to easily organize, raise money, and set up offices and staff in Washington. The process feeds on itself, with new groups forming to counter the influence of other recently formed groups. The result has been a tremendous increase in the demands placed on members of Congress by lobbyists from organized groups.

Not only have interest groups proliferated, they have also become more diverse. Economic interests – corporations, trade associations, and labor groups – greatly outnumber other sectors among lobbyists. In addition, many groups represent new industries, and "citizens" groups sprouted in the 1960s and 1970s and continue to grow in number. These groups are often outgrowths of national movements – such as those for civil rights, women's rights, children's rights, the elimination of hunger, consumers' rights, welfare rights, gay rights, environmental protection, and the homeless. Many of these groups now enjoy memberships numbering in the hundreds of thousands.

Along with their increasing number and diversity, groups have become more skilled in camouflaging their true identity. For most major legislative battles, coalitions of interests form and take all-American names, pool their resources to fund mass media campaigns, and often dissolve as fast as they were created. Many of the coalitions are the handiwork of entrepreneurs in law firms, consulting outfits, and public relations shops who are paid to coordinate the activity of the coalitions they spearheaded.

The roots have been taken out of grassroots lobbying. New technologies provide the ability to make highly targeted, highly efficient appeals to stimulate constituency demands on Washington. By the late 1980s, computerized telephone messages allowed groups to communicate with many thousands of people within a few hours. Technology now allows a group to telephone its own members, a targeted group (such as one House member's constituency), or the general public; briefly interview the respondents about their views on a subject; and, for respondents who favor the group's position, provide a few more facts to reinforce their views, solicit them to write letters to members of Congress, and quickly transfer the calls to the appropriate Capitol Hill offices before the respondents hang up. Several groups have developed television programs – some shown on the many cable television channels that are available in most communities – as a way of reaching specific audiences. Lobbyists exploit email and interactive video technologies to motivate citizens to flood Congress with messages. As a result, for a group with money, the absence of a large membership is not much of an obstacle to generating public pressure on members of Congress.

New Issues

New issues – such as the war against terrorism and global warming – always present some difficulty for Congress. They often create problems for congressional committees, whose official jurisdictions were defined years earlier when the new issues were not anticipated. Committees scramble to assert jurisdiction, and party leaders sometimes are asked to referee. After some amount of infighting and delay, committees eventually manage to adjust. In the view of some observers, however, Congress's ability to adjust in a timely way is becoming more and more strained.

It is nearly hackneyed to say that the issues facing Congress are becoming more technical and complex, but it is true. Increasingly, expertise in science, engineering, economics, or other fields is required to understand policy problems and alternatives. Congress often solves this problem by setting broad policy goals and delegating the power to make the necessary technical decisions to experts in the executive branch.[5] In this way, Congress is able to respond to demands for action. However, it does so at the cost of enhancing the executive branch's power over the details of public policy.

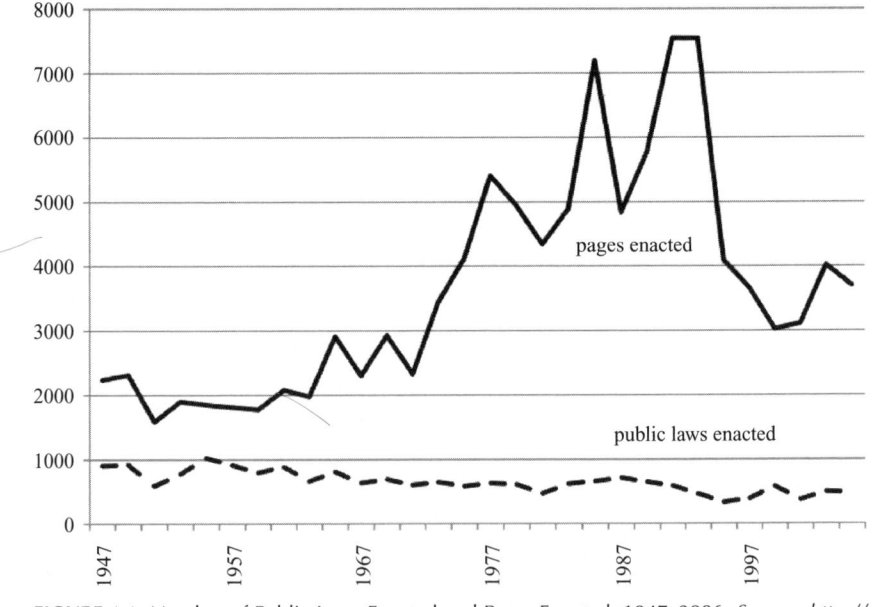

FIGURE 1.1. Number of Public Laws Enacted and Pages Enacted, 1947–2006. *Source: http://www.gpoaccess.gov/statutes/browse.html.*

At other times, Congress seeks to legislate the technical details. The cost then is that only a few members and staff assistants can understand the legislation and participate effectively in making important decisions. Scientific and medical research, defense programs, environmental protection, the regulation of financial institutions, international trade, and many other fields of public policy are no longer within the common experiences of elected officials. Thus, most members must look to competing interpretations of proposed legislation offered by staff specialists, lobbyists, and a wide array of outside experts.

The new policy challenges result from an increasingly complex American society coupled with the integration of international and domestic economies. Fewer major policies can be debated in isolation from other major policies. Health care reform, for example, concerns employer-employee relations, economic growth, welfare reform, and tax policy, among other things. This complexity leads Congress to craft unwieldy bills, often written by multiple committees, laden with technical language, and reaching several hundred pages in length. Figure 1.2 shows the increasing length of the average bill enacted by Congress in recent decades, at least until the Republicans gained congressional majorities in 1994. Between 1995 and 2006, the total number of bills and the number of pages enacted into law declined sharply, but the average length of a bill remained several times as long as for the 1950s. More than issue complexity underlies the increasing length of bills, as we will see in later chapters, but the length of bills presents a serious challenge to legislators who might want to understand the legislation on which they are asked to cast votes.

Political scientist Lawrence Dodd believes that Congress, at least as it now operates, cannot cope with the important issues of our time. In his view, the problem lies in the relationship between members and their constituents:

> The voters may see the decay of urban infrastructure, sense the declining educational and job opportunities of their children, acknowledge the ecological damage of industrial pollution, and worry about the long-term effects of a mounting deficit. But as they consider their vote for senator and representative, the citizens override any broad concerns they may have with collective issues and vote in accord with ensuring immediate benefits; they do so by voting for the powerful local incumbent who can assist with a desired local defense contract or who can help them with their veterans claim or Medicare benefits. They do so because of the immediate influence that a powerful incumbent legislator can have on their particularized interests... The emerging collective problems of the new era thus go unacknowledged and tear away at the fabric of society.[6]

If Dodd is right, then the public's ratings of congressional performance will continue to be low while incumbent legislators will continue to be routinely reelected.

Congress's tendency is to allow the president to define solutions to the nation's problems and then to criticize those solutions from narrow, often parochial perspectives. Unfortunately, plebiscitary politics, the proliferation of interest groups, and the new ways of influencing members of Congress of interest groups, and the new ways of influencing members of Congress reinforce this tendency. Modern politics puts more pressure than ever on members to explain themselves in terms that are readily understood by the folks back home. Scholar and congressman David Price (D-North Carolina) observes, "Members must constantly explain themselves and their actions in terms of ordinary knowledge. A decision that does not lend itself to such an explanation often has a heavy burden of proof against it. In the era of television journalism, of thirty-second ads and negative advertising, a defensive deference to ordinary knowledge has probably become more important in congressional behavior than it was before."[7] The gap between what legislators do and what they can explain seems to be widening.

Congressionally Speaking...

Every 10 years, the Census Bureau counts the number of people living in the United States. On the basis of that count, the Census Bureau allocates seats in the U.S. House of Representatives to each of the states according to a formula set in law. This allocation is called *apportionment*. States then draw the boundaries of districts for the House of Representatives, a process known as *districting*. Districting is controversial because it may advantage one of the parties or certain incumbent legislators. Districting was very controversial in Texas following the 2000 census. The original districting plan enacted by a Democratic majority in the state legislature was replaced by a plan enacted by a later Republican majority in the legislature. As the Republicans hoped, the new districting plan helped to elect more Republicans to the U.S. House of Representatives in 2004.

Changing Membership

Regional Shifts

In recent decades, demographic and social changes in American society have altered the composition of Congress in important ways. One important change has been in the allocation of House seats to the states. The 435 seats of the House are reapportioned every 10 years to reflect changes in the distribution of the nation's population across the states. A formula established by law guides the Census Bureau, which calculates the number of districts for each state every 10 years after the decennial census. Population shifts have allowed certain states in the South and West to gain seats in the House of Representatives at the expense of several eastern and midwestern states. The regional shifts are visible in Table 1.1. The South and West gained even more seats after the national census in the year 2000 – again at the expense of the industrial Northeast and Midwest.

The redistribution of seats away from the northern industrial states has reduced those states' political clout at a time when they could use it. The need for infrastructure repairs, worker retraining, low-income housing, and other government services is severe in the old industrial states, but the declining influence of these states is reducing their ability to acquire financial assistance from the federal government. Indeed, the shift of power to the more conservative regions of the country has undercut congressional

TABLE 1.1. Changes in the Apportionment of House Seats, by Region, After Census of 1960 and 2000.

Region	Post-1960 Seats	Post-2000 Seats	Difference
East	108	83	−25
Midwest	125	100	−25
South	133	154	21
West	69	98	29
Total	435	435	

Source: Census Bureau.

support for a major federal role in the rehabilitation of the industrial cities of the northern-tier states.

The population growth in the South and West is the result of that region's economic growth, an influx of workers from the older industrial states and other countries, and the expansion of the region's middle class. The most obvious consequence of these developments is that the South is no longer a one-party region, as it was just three decades ago. Republicans are now competitive in Senate races throughout the South and hold many House seats as well. As recently as 1960, Republicans held no Senate seats and only six of 104 House seats in the states of the old Confederacy. After the 1992 elections, Republicans held 13 of the 22 Senate seats and 48 of the 125 House seats in the region, with the largest numbers in Florida and Texas. The southern Senate seats were critical to Republicans between 1981 and 1986, when they controlled the Senate, and again after 1994.

Preliminary population estimates for 2010 promise a continuing shift of House seats away from the East and Midwest to the South and West. New York and Ohio may lose two seats each, while Illinois, Iowa, Michigan, Minnesota, and Pennsylvania may lose one each. Texas may gain four seats, Arizona may gain two seats, and Florida, Georgia, North Carolina, and South Carolina may gain one seat each.

Women and Minorities

Beyond the changes in regional representation and partisan composition in Congress, Capitol Hill has also acquired a sizable contingent of women and minorities. The growing strength of women's and minority groups, the acquisition of political experience by women and minority politicians in state and local government, and new voting laws have contributed to the

TABLE 1.2. Number of Women and Minorities in the House and Senate, 1971–2007.

Congress (first year)	Women		African Americans		Hispanic Americans	
	House	Senate	House	Senate	House	Senate
92d (1971)	12	1	12	1	5	1
93d (1973)	14	0	15	1	5	1
94th (1975)	18	0	16	1	5	1
95th (1977)	18	0	16	1	5	0
96th (1979)	16	1	16	0	6	0
97th (1981)	19	2	16	0	6	0
98th (1983)	21	2	20	0	10	0
99th (1985)	22	2	19	0	11	0
100th (1987)	23	2	22	0	11	0
101st (1989)	25	2	23	0	11	0
102d (1991)	29	2	25	0	10	0
103d (1993)	48	6	38	1	17	0
104th (1995)	49	8	39	1	18	0
105th (1997)	51	9	37	1	18	0
106th (1999)	58	9	39	0	19	0
107th (2001)	59	13	36	0	21	0
108th (2003)	62	14	39	0	21	0
109th (2005)	68	14	42	1	24	2
110th (2007)	67	16	40	1	24	3
111th (2009)	77	18	41	1	25	2

Source: *Vital Statistics on American Politics* (Washington, D.C.: Congressional Quarterly Press, 2000), p. 201; entries for the 107th–111th Congresses collected by the authors. Numbers reflect membership at the start of the Congress.

recent improvement in these groups' representation in Congress. In 1993, the Senate gained its first Native American, Ben Nighthorse Campbell (D-Colorado), who later switched parties, and its first black woman, Carol Moseley-Braun (D-Illinois). Table 1.2 shows the gains that women, African Americans, and Hispanics have made in Congress in recent years, and even more – many more – women and minorities have been running for Congress. More than 100 women have been major party candidates for Congress in each election since 1992. In 2006, 139 women ran for the House. Only three Native Americans have served in the Senate.

Women and minorities are still underrepresented in Congress relative to their proportions in the population, but few doubt that women and minority lawmakers have already had a substantial impact. Most obviously, the Congressional Caucus for Women's Issues, the Congressional Black Caucus, and, to a lesser extent, the Congressional Hispanic Caucus have become important factions within the House Democratic Party. Women and blacks comprise about 20 percent of the House Democratic Caucus. In 2009, the Senate began with 17 women and three Hispanics, and after he was appointed to replace President Barack Obama, one African American, Roland Burris (D-IL). In fact, in winning his 2004 bid for a Senate seat from Illinois, Democrat Barack Obama became only the third African American popularly elected to the Senate since the early twentieth century when the Seventeenth Amendment to the Constitution, providing for direct election to the Senate, was ratified. Only one Native American, Tom Cole (R-Oklahoma), a member of the Chickasaw Nation, remained in Congress in 2009. Cole was elected chair of the National Republican Congressional Committee, his party's campaign committee, in late 2006, which he gave up after the 2008 elections.

The presence of more women and minorities has changed the mix of voices heard in congressional debates. Social and economic problems seem to be more frequently discussed in the first person today – that is, more members refer to their personal experience when addressing their colleagues and constituents. In addition, more legislation reflecting the issues that are given greater emphasis by women and minorities is introduced. Generally, issues important to these groups have been given higher priority by party leaders, particularly Democratic leaders.

Only one woman, Rep. Nancy Pelosi (D-California), has been elected the top leader of a congressional party. Pelosi was elected Speaker in 2007 after the Democrats won a majority of House seats in the 2006 elections. She had been elected the Democrats' Minority Leader in late 2002 after serving in the number two position, Democratic Whip, for two years. The other women in party leadership are Representative Cathy McMorris Rogers (R-Washington), the House Republican Conference Vice Chair, Senator Patty Murray (D-Washington), the Senate Democratic Conference Secretary, Senator Debbie Stabenow (D-Michigan), the Senate Democratic Steering and Outreach Committee Chairwoman, and Senator Barbara Boxer (D-California), the Senate Democrats Chief Deputy Whip. Many women have gained sufficient seniority to chair important committees and subcommittees.

Only two African Americans have served in one of the top three leadership positions in a congressional party. J. C. Watts of Oklahoma served as House Republican Conference chair in 1998–2002, but he retired from Congress in

2002. James Clyburn of South Carolina was elected the House Democratic caucus vice chairman and chairman in 2002 and 2004, respectively, and then was elected Democratic Whip in 2006. When Rep. Robert Menendez of New Jersey became the House Democratic Caucus chair in 2002, he became the highest ranking Hispanic legislator in the history of Congress. Menendez was appointed to fill a Senate vacancy in late 2005 and was elected to the seat in 2006.

Previous Occupations

Notable changes have occurred in members' occupational profiles. Congress is still dominated by lawyers and business people, with over 200 lawyers and about 200 members with business backgrounds in the House and Senate in 2009. The number of farmers has declined – down from about 75 in the 1950s to just over two dozen in recent Congresses. Educators have become more numerous – over 90 in 2009. Overall, the occupational backgrounds of members are now somewhat more diverse than they were three or four decades ago.

These trends in the membership of Congress – the shift to the Sunbelt, the increasing numbers of women and minority members, and the greater diversity in members' previous experience – are likely to continue. The professions of law and business still dominate, but a wider range of experiences are reflected in the membership of Congress now than a generation ago.

Changing Party Control

Perhaps the most conspicuous changes in Congress in recent years were the changes in party control. During the 1955–1980 period, Democrats enjoyed majorities in both the House and Senate. In 1980, the Republicans gained a Senate majority but lost their majority in 1986. In 1994, Republicans won majorities in both houses, which they maintained until 2001 when Senator James Jeffords of Vermont gave up his Republican affiliation and created a short-lived Democratic majority. Republican victories in the 2002 elections produced Republican majorities in both chambers, which they retained and expanded in the 2004 elections. Democrats won narrow majorities in both houses in the 2006 elections, which they retained and expanded in 2008. With an evenly divided electorate, we have experienced a prolonged period of narrow majorities in both chambers of Congress in the last decade (see Figure 1.3).

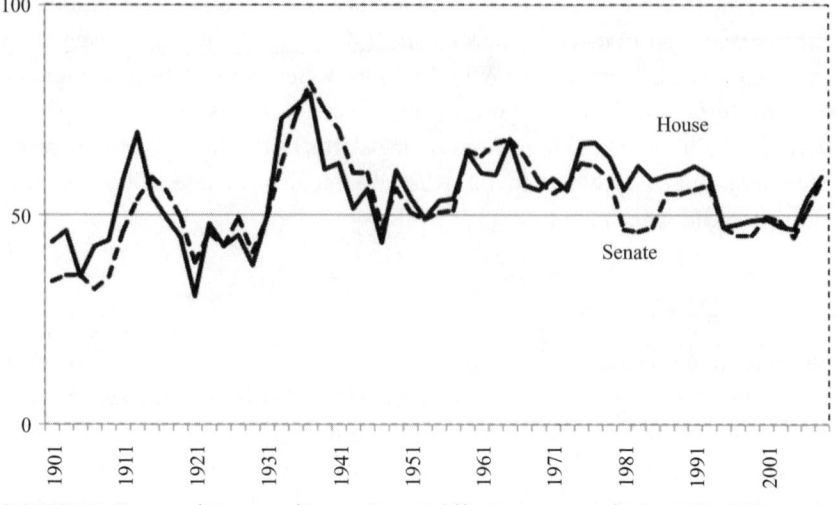

FIGURE 1.2. Percent of House and Senate Seats Held by Democrats at the Start of Each Congress, 1903–2009.

Political scientist Richard F. Fenno, Jr., argues that frequent changes in party control keep the arrogance of the majority party in check.[8] Fenno contends that the uncertainties created by frequent change in majority control reduce the temptation for a new majority to overreach itself once in office. According to Fenno, because the Democrats had dominated the House for 40 years, when the Republicans took over in 1994, they were both inexperienced and impatient. The Republicans overstated their mandate from the 1994 elections, translated that inflated mandate into rigid and ultimately unsuccessful legislative strategies, and perhaps contributed to the reelection of Democrat Bill Clinton to the presidency in 1996.

Fenno also observes that the long era of Democratic rule led the Republicans, prior to their 1994 takeover, to adopt radical measures to end it. The Republicans assumed an uncompromising stance in Congress, making legislating more difficult and intensifying partisanship. After the Republicans gained control, Speaker Gingrich led a rhetorical assault on the very institution his party had fought to control, contributing to a further loss of public support for Congress.

If Fenno is right, then alternating control of Congress produces greater flexibility in party policy positions, more pragmatic party strategies, greater civility in political discourse, and perhaps greater public support for the institution. Early evidence may have supported his argument. In late 1996, hoping to do well in the upcoming elections, a House Democratic leader was quoted as saying, "Our themes will be to make the institution look reasonable, to take moderate steps for average Americans and to make sure that the public understands what we are doing."[9] In 1997, after experiencing a lopsided defeat in the presidential election and a scare in the House elections of 1996, congressional Republicans proved considerably more willing to bargain with the president over the single most important matter before Congress, the budget (see Chapter 12). After the 2006 elections, leaders of both parties promised to turn down the level of partisanship. A political "uncertainty principle" – that an uncertain electoral future breeds political moderation – seems to contribute to these proclamations.

The moderating effect appears to have a very short half-life. By many accounts, the Congress has been more partisan since the turn of the new century than it had been for a hundred years. Poor personal relations among leaders of the two parties, the exclusion of minority party legislators from some conference committee meetings, minority obstructionism on judicial nominations, personal campaigning against incumbents of the opposite party, and other developments are cited by insiders as evidence of deteriorating relations across party lines. Moreover, after 10 years of Republican control of the House, many Democrats asserted that they need to follow the approach of the Republicans of the late 1980s and 1990s, that is, to better define differences between the parties, intensify public relations campaigns against the majority party, and gear legislative tactics to winning a majority in the next election. With new Democratic majorities in Congress, the Fenno hypothesis will get another test.

The War on Terrorism and Congressional Power

Perhaps the most serious challenge to Congress's role in the American constitutional system is secret government necessitated by national security. The war against terrorism has revived fears that secrecy in the national security agencies of government will threaten Americans' civil liberties and undermine Congress's ability to influence the direction of policy, to oversee the expenditure of public funds, and to hold executive officials accountable. Executive branch officials are hesitant to reveal certain information to members of Congress because they do not trust legislators to keep the information secret. For their part, legislators cannot know what information is being withheld from Congress, so secret government tends to breed distrust on Capitol Hill.

In the 1970s, in the aftermath of the Vietnam War and disclosures of misdeeds by intelligence agencies, Congress enacted a variety of laws to require notification of Congress, and sometimes to grant the power to approve or disapprove to Congress, for the commitment of armed forces abroad, arms sales, and covert operations. Congress also created intelligence committees and established other mechanisms for handling classified information. Presidents of both parties have not liked to be constrained by these laws, at times arguing that the laws unconstitutionally impinge on the president's powers. Many members of Congress, on the other hand, have been unwilling to assume some responsibility for national security policy by exploiting new laws or insisting on presidential cooperation. The result is continuing uncertainty about when congressional approval is required. Congressional participation in national security policy making varies from case to case, driven by political calculations as well as legal and national security considerations.

The fight against terrorism poses special challenges for members of Congress. More classified activity, more covert action, and a bewildering array of technologies are involved. More domestic police activity is conducted under the umbrella of national security. The need for quick, coordinated, multi-agency action is intensified. Congress is not capable of effectively checking such executive action. Congress is open and slow, its division of labor among committees is not well matched to the executive agencies involved, and its members are hesitant to challenge the executive branch on high-risk policies and in areas where the public is likely to defer to the president.

Congressional participation in policy making related to the war against terrorism tends to be limited to a few members. The president consults with top party leaders, while agency officials brief members of the intelligence and defense committees. Average members are not regularly informed about developments in the war. They are asked to support funding for the war without access to all relevant information.

With Republican majorities during much of the period since the 9/11 attack, Congress did not actively pursue oversight hearings and investigations of Republican administration's conduct of the war against terrorists or the war in Iraq. Democrats, after winning majorities in both houses in the 2006 elections, were more active.

Tempered Decentralization within Congress

The partisanship, concentration on budget, and national security issues have produced a Congress that behaves differently from what was predicted in the 1970s, when Congress last changed its organization and rules in major ways. Political scientists call this period the "post-reform" era. This term requires some explanation.

The House and Senate went through a period of reform in the early 1970s that led observers of the day to warn about the dangers of fragmentation in congressional policy making. In the House, new chamber and party rules were adopted to guarantee that committees operated more democratically and that subcommittee chairs were given greater independence from full committee chairs in setting their agendas and proposing legislation. Power appeared to be flowing away from central party and committee leaders and toward subcommittees and individual members. In the view of some members and outside observers, Congress seemed to be losing whatever ability it had to enact coherent policy. This occurred at a time when the pressures brought by new interest groups, new lobbying strategies, and new issues were mounting. Although Congress had become a more open and democratic institution, its capacity to manage the nation's affairs seemed diminished.

By the mid-1980s, however, Congress – particularly the House – had not turned out as many observers had expected. Individualism had moderated a little, the congressional agenda had become more focused, party leaders and party organizations showed signs of revitalization, and the decentralization of power to the subcommittees had been tempered. Although Congress did not revert to its old ways, it acquired a new mix of characteristics that justified a new label – the "post-reform Congress." A brief review of the characteristics of the post-reform Congress serves as an introduction to many of the topics addressed in later chapters.

Tempered Individualism

Whatever other changes occurred after the 1970s, the entrepreneurial spirit of individual members remained strong. In fact, it is almost a cliché to call members of today's Congress political entrepreneurs. The term is used to indicate members' relative independence from local and national parties. Candidates for congressional office now develop their own campaign organizations, raise their own money, and set their own campaign strategies. This independence from the political parties tends to carry over when the winners take office. Once in office, members use official resources and exploit their relationships with interest groups and political action committees for political advantage. Knowing that they are on their own when it comes to getting reelected, they take full advantage of taxpayer-supported travel opportunities and communications technologies to maintain a high profile at home. These topics are addressed in Chapters 3 and 4.

By the late 1970s, members had become weary of the surge in committee and floor activity that was the by-product of reforms and unchecked individualism. Part of the concern was that members were spending longer days on Capitol Hill, away from their families and their home states and districts. And part of the concern was political – members faced more numerous and more hazardous political choices as their colleagues forced recorded votes on more legislative proposals. In the House, some members, even some of those responsible for the reforms, began to ask committee and party leaders to assert more control. The most conspicuous response was to put more restrictions on floor amending activity in the House, a topic that is addressed in Chapters 7 and 8. But more generally, both representatives and senators now seem to appreciate leaders who are willing to set some direction, narrow the agenda, and reduce scheduling and political uncertainties. Individualism appears to have tempered somewhat.

Budget Constraints

A large federal budget deficit has a dominant force in legislative politics in most Congresses of recent decades. Other than in national security, few new federal programs were initiated, and much, if not most, of the period's important legislation consisted of large budget bills, particularly budget reconciliation bills. These bills, which are discussed in Chapter 12, are the handiwork of many congressional committees and affect the full range of federal programs over multiple years. This emphasis on large, all-encompassing budget bills further reduced the ability of committees and individual members to pursue policy initiatives.

In the late 1990s, it appeared that the federal budget would be in balance for the foreseeable future and that the politics of blame may be supplanted by a politics of claiming credit. At the start of 1998, the Congressional Budget Office, Congress's budget and economic forecasting agency projected no deficits and measurable surpluses to the year 2008. Predictably, new policy initiatives were proposed by Democratic president Bill Clinton, but few stood a chance of passage with the Republican majority in Congress. After George W. Bush was elected in 2000, Republicans enacted a tax cut bill was passed in 2001, one that seemed quite affordable to many observers until a recession settled in the economy and the terrorist acts of September 11, 2001, motivated large spending initiatives for New York, the war against terrorism, and the war in Iraq. Suddenly, the president and Congress were facing long-term deficits once again.

President Barack Obama and larger Democratic majorities elected in the 2008 elections occurred just after the Wall Street crisis of that fall and created budget challenges that were more serious than ever. The Democrats brought plans for a wide range of new domestic initiatives, all of which were expensive, just at the time the federal government was committing far more than a trillion dollars to bail out Wall Street and other corporations and hundreds of billions were being spent to address a deteriorating economy. The resulting budget constraints greatly limit the policy options of the president and Congress.

Revitalized Parties

In the post-reform era, parties and their leaders have taken on greater importance than was predicted in the 1970s. Frustrations with unrestrained individualism and an emphasis on balancing the budget – issues that had long divided the parties – also contributed to the assertiveness of top party leaders since the 1980s. The replacement of some conservative southern Democrats by conservative Republicans made the Democratic cohort in Congress more liberal on balance and reinforced the conservatism of congressional Republicans. Divided party control of Congress and the presidency seemed to intensify partisanship during much of the period since the 1970s, as each institution and party tried to avoid blame for ballooning deficits, unmet demands for action on social problems, and economic hard times. Top party leaders began to speak more authoritatively for their parties, and party regulars looked to their top leaders to aggressively promote party views in the media. For a year or so after the Republicans gained a majority of House seats in 1994, Speaker Gingrich came to be recognized as the most powerful Speaker since Joseph Cannon (R-Illinois) in the first decade of the twentieth century. Gingrich's successor, Speaker Dennis Hastert (R-Illinois) remained remarkably active in all major policy decisions and Speaker Nancy Pelosi (D-California) has proven to be even more pro-active in structuring the Democrats' legislative program. These developments are detailed in Chapter 5.

The heightened partisanship of recent decades is evident in the use of the Senate filibuster (Figure 1.4). Because the Senate lacks a general rule limiting debate, senators can refuse to stop talking in order to allow the Senate to vote on a pending motion or measure – a tactic called a filibuster. A filibus

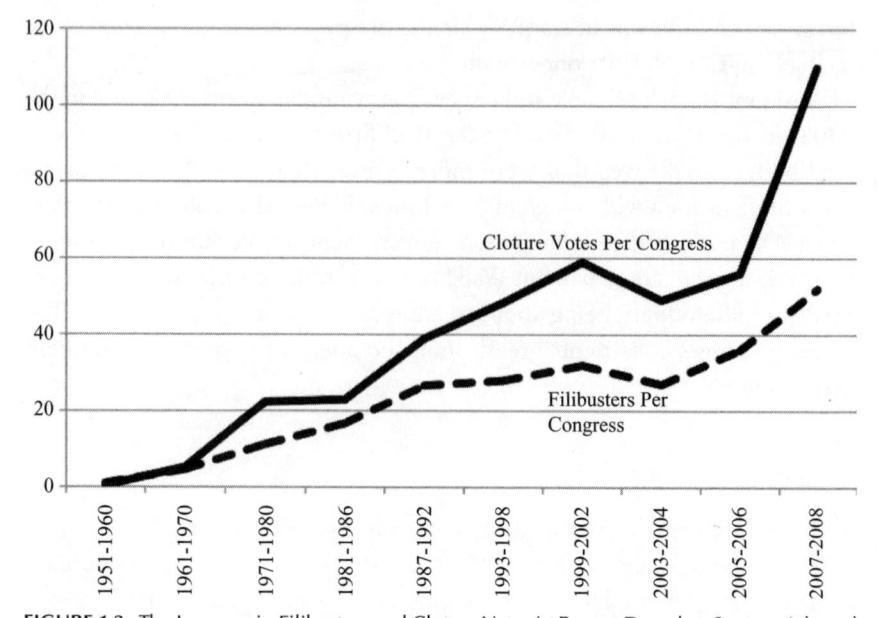

FIGURE 1.3. The Increase in Filibusters and Cloture Votes in Recent Decades. *Source:* Adapted from Barbara Sinclair, "The New World of U.S. Senators," in Lawrence C. Dodd and Bruce I. Oppenheimer, eds., *Congress Reconsidered*, 9th ed. (Washington, D.C.: CQ Press, 2009), p. 7.

obstructs Senate action and can be overcome only with a three-fifths majority of senators voting on most matters – a procedure called cloture. In the highly partisan Senate of recent Congresses, the minority party has more frequently attempted to block majority party legislation and the majority party responded with more cloture motions. This parliamentary arms race has contributed to sharper partisan rhetoric about which party is to blame for legislative outcomes.

Less Autonomous Committees

Chapter 6 details the substantial changes that have occurred in the role of the congressional committees in making law. Multiyear budget pacts, more ~~ertive party leaders, and less deferential parent chambers have altered the ~~ committees and their subcommittees in the policy-making process. ~~ees may act and the kinds of legislation they may propose ~~ighly constrained, and when they do act, committees are ~~ after receiving guidance from party leaders. Although ~~central features of congressional policy making, they do ~~ny that they once did.

The Changing Congress

The ways in which representation and lawmaking are pursued in Congress have evolved in important ways in recent decades. As this chapter has implied, not all of these developments have improved representation or lawmaking. In the chapters that follow, many of these developments are given a closer look. However serious we judge the problems of today's Congress to be, we should remember that Congress is a remarkably resilient institution. Its place in the political process is not threatened. It is rich in resources; critics even charge that it is too strong. Despite the attacks on Congress from many quarters, the legitimacy of its decisions is not seriously questioned by the chief executive, the courts, the states, or the American people.

POLITICAL PASSIONS LEAD TO VIOLENCE IN CONGRESS

Above: The caning of Charles Sumner (R-Massachusetts) by Preston Brooks (D-South Carolina). Brooks was upset by Sumner's speech against slavery.

Below: Cartoonist rendition of the first brawl on the House floor between Matthew Lyon (Democratic-Republican-Vermont) and Roger Griswold (Federalist-Connecticut). Lyon allegedly spit in Griswold's face after a heated debate, Griswold responded by attacking Lyon with a cane. Mayhem ensued as Lyon fought back with a fireplace poker as other House members looked on.

2

Representation and Lawmaking in Congress: The Constitutional and Historical Context

I N REPRESENTATION AND LAWMAKING, RULES MATTER. THE CONSTITUTION creates both a system of representation and a process for making law through two chambers of Congress and a president. One constitutional rule determines the official constituencies of representatives and senators; another determines how members of Congress are elected and how long they serve. Other constitutional rules outline the elements of the legislative process – generally the House, Senate, and president must agree on legislation before it can become law, unless a two-thirds majority of each chamber can override a presidential veto. More detailed rules about the electoral and legislative processes are left for federal statutes, state laws, and internal rules of the House and Senate.

Although the constitutional rules governing representation and lawmaking have changed in only a few ways since Congress first convened in 1789, other features of congressional politics have changed in many ways. The Constitution says nothing about congressional parties and committees, yet most legislation in the modern Congress is written in committees. Committees are appointed through the parties, and party leaders schedule legislation for consideration on the floor. In this chapter, we describe the basic elements of the representation and lawmaking processes and provide an overview of the development of the key components of the modern legislative process.

Representation and Lawmaking

Congress serves two, not always compatible, purposes – representation and lawmaking. Members of the House and Senate serve individual districts or states, yet they must act collectively to make laws for the nation as a whole. Collective action on divisive issues entails bargaining and compromise – among the members of each chamber, between the House and the Senate, and between Congress and the president. For compromise to be possible, members sometimes must retreat from their commitments to their individual states and districts. Determining who must compromise – and how to get them to do so – is the essence of legislative politics. The process can be messy, even distasteful, but, if it is to serve the nation, it is unavoidable.

Congress can be properly evaluated only by understanding our own conflicting expectations about the institution and about the politicians who work within it. To sort out the issues, we begin with a brief introduction explaining how representation and lawmaking occur in practice on Capitol Hill. As we shall see, achieving both perfect representation and perfect lawmaking, in the ways we desire each of them, is impossible.

Representation

REPRESENTATION BY INDIVIDUAL LAWMAKERS. Members of the House and Senate are expected to be *representatives* of their constituents back home. That is not a very precise job description. We might think that a representative's job is to faithfully present the views of his or her district or state in Congress – that is, to serve as a *delegate* for his or her constituents. But a delegate-legislator would not have an easy job because constituents often have conflicting or ambiguous views (or none at all) about the issues before Congress. Alternatively, a member of Congress might be considered a *trustee* – representing his or her constituents by exercising independent judgment about the interests of district, state, or nation. But it is impossible to be a both a faithful delegate and a true trustee.

A third possibility is to see the representative as a *politico* – one who behaves as a delegate on issues that are important to his or her constituents but on other issues has leeway in setting personal policy priorities and casting votes. Unfortunately, for many members of Congress, constituents are not likely to agree either about which issues are important or about when legislators should act as delegates and when they should exercise their own discretion. The challenge of the politician is to balance these legitimate, but often competing, expectations.

REPRESENTATION BY CONGRESS. Even if individual legislators can be considered good representatives for their own constituents, we might still wonder whether Congress can adequately represent the nation as a whole. Congress could be considered a delegate or trustee of the nation. As a delegate institution, Congress would be expected to enact policies reflecting nationwide public opinion, but public opinion often is conflicted,

TABLE 2.1. Two Forms of Aggregating Policy Preferences in the Public and in Congress.

District	District's policy position on a 5-point scale	Legislator's policy position on a 5-point scale	Difference between district and legislator
A	5	1	4
B	4	2	2
C	3	3	0
D	2	4	−2
E	1	5	−4
	3.0	3.0	0.0

Adapted from Robert S. Weissberg, "Collective vs. Dyadic Representation in Congress," *American Political Science Review* 72 (1978): 535–7.

ambiguous, or undeveloped. As a trustee institution, Congress would be expected to formulate policy in a manner consistent with its members' collective judgment about the nation's interests, whatever the state of public opinion. Members regularly invoke public opinion (a delegate perspective) or claim that Congress must do what is right (a trustee perspective) in their arguments for or against specific legislation.

COLLECTIVE VERSUS DYADIC REPRESENTATION. In practice, the correspondence between the quality of representation at the district or state level and that at the national level might be quite weak. To see this, imagine an issue on which five legislators from different districts take varying positions. As Table 2.1 illustrates, even if the legislators are not well matched to their districts, they can collectively represent the nation well. That is, *collective* representation can be good even when *dyadic* representation is not. Congruence between policy and public opinion may be poor at the state or district level but perfect at the national level. As a general rule, a legislative body will be at least as good a delegate for the nation as are individual members for their district or state.[1]

The logic of Table 2.1 does not guarantee that the House, the Senate, and the president will be able to agree on legislation. Indeed, James Madison, the chief architect of the Constitution, hoped not. Madison argued that policy should not necessarily reflect the majority's views. He justified the creation of an independent executive branch (the presidency) and a bicameral legislature (the two chambers of Congress) on the grounds that policy should not simply reflect majority public opinion. He gave the president and the members of the two chambers terms of different lengths, specified different means of selecting them, and gave the president the power to sign or veto legislation. Madison expected the two chambers and the president to reflect different interests, which would reduce the likelihood that a majority could capture all three institutions and impose its will on a minority.

PARTY AND GROUP REPRESENTATION. We often think of political parties and other groups as representing parts of the nation. Nearly all members of Congress are recognized as either Democrats or Republicans and often are identified with other groups based on their gender, race, occupation, age, and other personal characteristics. Legislators, presidents, and the public usually see Congress in terms of its party composition. We speak of a "Republican Congress" or a "Democratic Congress," reflecting the importance of party control of the institution. Although voters choose between congressional candidates only in a single district or state, and no one votes directly for a Republican or Democratic majority in Congress as a whole, the party of the candidates and voters' views about which party should control Congress influence many voters and election outcomes. In turn, legislators tend to join with others of their own party to enact or block legislation; to develop and maintain a good reputation with the public; and to seek or retain majority control. Plainly, a great deal of representation occurs through the party mechanisms.

Although we do not often speak of a white-male, lawyer-dominated Congress, many people are conscious of the composition of Congress beyond its partisan or ideological makeup. A farming background is important for candidates in many areas of the country, whereas a union background is important in other areas. Organized caucuses of women, blacks, Hispanics, and other groups have formed among members of Congress, and groups outside Congress have developed to aid the election of more members from one group or another. It is said that increasing the number of women and minorities in Congress is essential because legislators' personal experiences shape their policy agendas. Moreover, the presence of role models in Congress may help motivate other members of these groups to seek public office.

THE TRADEOFFS OF REPRESENTATION. We cannot hope for perfect representation in Congress. Our multiple expectations for representation can all be met only if Americans hold uniform views on questions of public policy. They do not. Tradeoffs and compromise between the different forms and levels of representation are unavoidable. Neither the individual legislators nor the institution as a whole can simultaneously be a perfect delegate and a perfect trustee. In practice, we muddle through with mixed and changing forms of representation.

Lawmaking

For Madison, representative government – also known as republican government – served two purposes. One was to make the law broadly responsive to the people. The other was to allow representatives, not the people themselves, to make law. This second purpose was, and still is, controversial. Madison explained in *Federalist No. 10* that he hoped representatives would rise above the inevitable influence of public *opinion* to make policy in the public *interest*.

THE UNITARY DEMOCRACY MODEL. Madison's argument assumes that the common or public interest can be discovered by an elected representative through deliberation. In this view, the purpose of the legislative process is to discover those common interests through a process in which legislators share information, offer policy alternatives, and move toward a consensus on action to be taken. Building a consensus, rather than resolving conflicts by force of majority vote, is the object of this process. The emphasis on a common interest has led scholars to label this decision-making process *unitary democracy*.[2]

THE ADVERSARIAL DEMOCRACY MODEL. Madison's view may not be reasonable. Inherently conflicting interests may lead legislators to articulate those interests and decide controversies by the power of a larger number of votes. From this perspective, deliberation is viewed as needless delay to a majority that has no interest in compromise and has the votes to impose policies of its choosing. The majority naturally emphasizes the importance of efficiency and majority rule. The presence of conflicting interests leads us to call this decision-making process *adversarial democracy*.

THE TRADEOFFS OF LAWMAKING. Congress cannot easily harmonize the ideals of both adversarial and unitary democracy. Deliberation and consensus building may seem to be the preferred model of decision making, but time and the compromise required will frustrate a majority eager to act. In practice, as for representation, Congress will make tradeoffs among the ideal forms of lawmaking. Congress sometimes looks quite deliberative but will be pushed by majorities to be more efficient and look, at least to outsiders, as quite adversarial and partisan. Moreover, the two chambers of Congress need not make the same tradeoffs. As we will see in later chapters, the smaller Senate continues to look more deliberative than the larger House, due in large part to significant differences in the rules that the two chambers have adopted over the decades to govern themselves.

The struggle to balance alternative models of representation and law-making never ends. Contending forces in American politics usually favor different models as they seek to define democratic processes that give them an advantage. An implication of our discussion is that most sides can find theoretical justification for their positions – to better represent Americans in Washington (usually meaning to increase the influence of one group or another) or to reform lawmaking processes (also usually meaning to increase the influence of one group or another). This is not to say that common interests do not sometimes exist or that the nation as a whole cannot be better represented at times. It is to argue that the history of Congress is not one of smooth progress toward "better" representation and lawmaking processes. Rather, it is a history of political conflict as parties and ambitious politicians sought to appeal for votes and determine policy choices.

The Predecessors of Congress

The First Congress convened on March 4, 1789, under the Constitution drafted in Philadelphia in the summer of 1787. Despite the newness of their institution, the members of the First Congress were not new to legislative politics. The American Congress shares the same roots as Great Britain's parliament. The colonists brought with them British parliamentary practices and quickly established legislatures that governed in conjunction with governors appointed by the British crown. Beginning with Virginia's House of Burgesses in 1619, the colonial legislatures became both elected representative bodies and important lawmaking institutions almost immediately. Most of the legislatures followed procedures similar to those used in Parliament. Representation and lawmaking were well-accepted features of self-governance long before the Constitutional Convention of 1787. Eventually, the usurpation of the powers of the colonial legislatures by British governors became a critical motivation for the Revolutionary War.

Besides their experience from the colonial era, the members of the First Congress had more recent legislative experience from participating in the Continental Congress and in their state legislatures in the years after independence. The first Continental Congress met in 1774, at the time of the

Boston Tea Party and British assertion of military and political control over Massachusetts, as a step toward jointly working out differences between the colonies and the British government. The Continental Congress was not intended to be a permanent body but rather a temporary convention of delegates from the colonies. The crisis with Britain extended its life into the Revolutionary War, and its role in the new nation was formalized in 1781 with the ratification of the Articles of Confederation.

The Continental Congress was severely handicapped by its own rules. Very open floor procedures and a weak presiding officer undermined efforts to coordinate the diverse interests of the states and encouraged factionalism.[3] The Articles of Confederation did nothing to change that. Although they legitimated the national government that the Continental Congress constituted, the articles gave the Congress little power. The Continental Congress could not regulate commerce or raise taxes, and without executive and judicial institutions to implement and enforce the laws it passed, it was wholly dependent on the willingness of state governments to carry out its policies.

In contrast to the weak Continental Congress, most state legislatures were very powerful. The state constitutions adopted after independence gave the legislatures the power to appoint the state governors, guaranteeing that these officers would serve at the pleasure of the egalitarian, popularly elected branch. The new governors were not granted the power to veto legislation, and most were denied the power to make executive branch appointments, which were left to the legislature. Governors, it was hoped, would be mere administrators.

Soon legislative tyranny came to be viewed as a major problem. In the 1780s, an economic depression led debtors to demand relief from their creditors, and because debtors greatly outnumbered creditors, the legislatures obliged them. This undermined financial institutions, creating instability. Thomas Jefferson referred to the situation in Virginia as "elective despotism." Majority rule itself came to be questioned, and people began to wonder whether republican government was viable.

The practice of having a bicameral, or two-house, legislature was well established in the states by the time the Constitution was written in 1787. Britain had evolved a bicameral parliament based on its social class system, with the different classes represented in the House of Commons and the House of Lords. All of the American colonies except for Pennsylvania and Georgia had bicameral legislatures in 1776. Even after the Revolutionary War, when the British model was called into question, most states continued with a bicameral legislature. Debate over the proper relationship between

Congressionally Speaking...

The terms *unicameral* and *bicameral* come from the Latin word *camera*, which means "chamber." Under the Articles of Confederation, the national Congress was unicameral – one chamber – but many state legislatures were bicameral. The Constitution, of course, provided for a bicameral Congress. Among today's American state legislatures, only Nebraska's legislature is unicameral. Nebraska adopted the unicameral form in 1934 after using the bicameral form until then.

the two chambers was frequent, and the states experimented with different means for electing their senates. Representing different classes in different institutions had lost its appeal, but the idea of preventing one house from becoming too powerful was widely discussed. By 1787, most political observers were keenly aware of the strengths and weaknesses of bicameral systems.

The Constitution's Rules of the Game

Against the backdrop of an ineffectual Continental Congress and often tyrannical state legislatures, the framers of the national Constitution sought a new balance in 1787. They constructed a stronger national government with a powerful Congress whose actions could be checked by the president and the Supreme Court.

For the making of public law, the Constitution establishes a specific process, involving three institutions of government, with a limited number of basic rules. The House of Representatives, the Senate, and the president must all agree to enact a new law, with the House and Senate expressing their agreement by simple majority vote. If the president vetoes the measure, two-thirds of the members of the House and of the Senate must agree to override the veto. If any of the three players withholds consent or if a presidential veto is upheld, the legislation dies.

The Constitution also provides for the election of members of Congress and the president, prohibits legislation of certain kinds, specifies the size of majority required in Congress for specific actions, and identifies the player who must make the first or last moves in certain circumstances. In addition, the Constitution allows the Supreme Court to determine whether Congress and the president abide by its rules.

The framers of the Constitution gave Congress tremendous political power. Article I, Section 8 of the Constitution grants to Congress broad discretion to "provide for the common defense and general welfare of the United States." It also specifies the basic powers of the national government and grants to Congress the authority to make laws to implement those powers. This general grant of power is supplemented by more specific provisions. Congress is given the power to tax, to regulate the economy, to create courts under the Supreme Court, to create and regulate military forces, and to declare war. Section 9 grants Congress control over government spending: "No money shall be drawn from the treasury, but in consequence of appropriations made by law."

The Constitution entrusts the Senate with the authority to ratify treaties and confirm presidential nominations to executive and judicial offices. Congress can regulate congressional and presidential elections and must approve agreements between individual states and between states and foreign governments. The breadth of Congress's powers is reinforced in the "elastic clause," which provides that Congress can "make all laws which shall be necessary and proper for carrying into execution" the powers enumerated in the Constitution.

To protect members of Congress from personal intimidation by executive, judicial, or local officials, the framers of the Constitution devised several important clauses. First, beyond the age and citizenship requirements, the Constitution leaves to each house of Congress the authority to judge the qualifications of its members, to rule on contested election outcomes, and to punish or expel members for inappropriate behavior. Second, the Constitution protects members from arrest during and en route to and from sessions of Congress. And third, no member may be questioned by prosecutors, a court, or others about any congressional speech or debate. Members may be arrested and tried for treason, felonies, and breach of the peace, but they cannot be held personally liable by other government officials for their official actions as members of Congress.

Legislative Procedures

With respect to the details of the legislative process, the Constitution offers little guidance, with a few important exceptions. First, the framers of the Constitution were careful to provide that each chamber keep a journal recording its actions (Article 1, Section 5). Further, they required that the votes of individual members on any matter be recorded in the journal upon the request of one-fifth of the members present. A successful request of one-fifth of the members is known as "ordering the yeas and nays." In the Senate, the yeas and nays are taken by having a clerk call out each member's

THE LEGACY OF 9–11 FOR THE CONSTITUTION, STATUTES, AND HOUSE RULES

The terrorist attacks of September 11, 2001, led members of Congress and other congressional observers to worry about how the institution would function if an attack on the Capitol complex killed a large number of legislators. In 2002, the resolution providing for the adjournment of the 107th Congress provided that representatives and senators designated by the Speaker and Senate majority leader be allowed to call Congress into session in the event that those two leaders were killed or incapacitated. Without the provision, only the president could have called the Congress into special session, as the Constitution provides, but legislators believed that Congress should be prepared to act as an independent branch of government. In 2003, the House adopted three rules to address such a possibility. One rule requires the Speaker to establish a list of members who, in order, could serve as Speaker Pro Tem if the Speaker died or was incapacitated. This provision would allow the House to convene to elect a new Speaker. A second rule allows the Speaker to recess the House if there is an imminent threat to members' safety. Previously, the Speaker was not allowed to recess the House if business was pending. A third rule allows the Speaker to lower the number of members counted for the purposes of a quorum when a member dies, resigns, or is expelled. Without the change, a majority of the 435 possible members would have to be present for the House to conduct business. The new rule allows the total possible to be reduced to the number of seats that are currently filled.

In the view of some observers, the measures taken to date are inadequate. Enacted legislation to require special House elections of substitute legislators within 45 days of a deadly attack is considered ineffective – no states have altered their laws to conform to the requirement. In 2005, the House adopted a rule that allows the House to act temporarily without a full quorum by empowering the Speaker (or his designee) to reduce the number required for a quorum after a series of lengthy quorum calls. Many observers doubt that this rule is constitutional because it appears to violate Article I, Section 5, of the Constitution, which provides that "a majority of each shall constitute a quorum to do business." A private study group recommended an amendment to the Constitution that would provide for quick and temporary appointment of replacements by state governors in the event of the death or incapacity of the incumbent, or by declaration of a national emergency by the House. The proposed amendment received only 63 votes in the House in 2004 and has not received a vote in the Senate.

The Senate is less of a problem. In nearly all states, governors are authorized by law to appoint replacement senators upon the death of the incumbents. Still, senators have expressed concern that the inability to gain a quorum in a national emergency would incapacitate the Senate. Legislation has been introduced to provide for temporary appointments if the majority and minority leaders jointly determine that the absence of a quorum to conduct business was caused by the inability of senators to discharge the duties of their office. States would determine how the temporary appointments would be made. No action has been taken on the proposal, which its sponsors recognized would have to be preceded by a constitutional amendment authorizing the process.

name and recording the response by hand. In the House, the yeas and nays have been recorded by an electronic system since 1973.

Second, the framers provided that tax bills originate in the House. Because the Senate was originally to be selected by state legislatures, with only the House directly elected by the people, it was thought that the initiative for imposing taxes should lie with the House. The Constitution provides that "all bills for raising revenue shall originate in the House of Representatives; but the Senate may propose or concur with amendments as on other bills." The Senate has used a variety of gimmicks to circumvent this restriction, but the House generally has jealously guarded its constitutional prerogatives and spurned Senate efforts to initiate tax bills.

Third, the Constitution requires that "a majority of each [house] shall constitute a quorum to do business" (Article 1, Section 5). In principle, a majority of the members of a chamber must be present at all times, but like many other rules, this one is not enforced unless a member raises a point of order – that is, unless a member asks the chair for a ruling that a quorum is not present. This is sometimes used as a dilatory tactic. In the Senate, quorum calls have become a routine way to take a time-out – while the clerk calls the roll of senators' names, senators can confer in private or wait for colleagues to arrive. The most important implication of this constitutional provision is that a majority of members must be present and vote on a measure for the vote to count. To prevent absence from being used as an obstructionist ploy, the Constitution further provides that each house "may be authorized to compel the attendance of absent members."

Finally, the framers outlined the process of presidential approval or disapproval of legislation (Article 1, Section 7). After each chamber has passed a bill, it must be presented to the president, whose options depend on whether Congress has adjourned in the meantime. Congress has an opportunity to override a president's veto only if Congress remains in session (see box, "Constitutional Procedures for Presidential Approval or Disapproval of Legislation"). If Congress adjourns, the president can kill a bill by either vetoing it or taking no action on it (which is known as a pocket veto). Congress may pass a new bill if the president successfully kills a bill.

Constraints on Congressional Power

Although the framers of the Constitution intended Congress to be a powerful policy-making body, they also feared the exercise of that power. This concern produced (1) explicit restrictions on the use of legislative power; (2) a system of three separate institutions that share legislative powers; (3) a system of direct and indirect representation of the people, in Congress and by the presidency; and (4) a Supreme Court that judges the constitutionality of legislation and interprets ambiguities in legislative outcomes. The result is a legislative process that cannot address certain subjects, is motivated by political considerations, is likely to involve bargaining, and is biased against enacting new legislation.

EXPLICIT RESTRICTIONS. A list of powers explicitly denied Congress is provided in Article I, Section 9 of the Constitution. For example, Congress may not tax state exports, pass bills of attainder (pronouncing guilt and sentencing someone without a trial), or adopt *ex post facto* laws (altering the legal standing of a past action). The list of explicit limitations was extended by the 1791 ratification of the first ten amendments to the Constitution – the Bill of Rights. Among other things, the Bill of Rights prohibits laws that abridge freedom of speech, freedom of the press, and the freedom to peaceably assemble (Amendment 1) and preserves the right to a jury trial in certain cases (Amendments 6 and 7). And the Bill of Rights reserves to the states, or to the people, powers not delegated to the national government by the Constitution (Amendment 10).

In practice, the boundary between allowed and disallowed legislative acts is often fuzzy. Efforts by Congress to exercise its powers have often conflicted with individual rights or with powers asserted by the president and the states. The Supreme Court has resolved many ambiguities about where the lines should be drawn around the powers of Congress, but many remain for future court consideration. In some cases, particularly in the foreign policy realm, the Supreme Court has left the ambiguities to be worked out between Congress and the president.

SEPARATE INSTITUTIONS SHARING POWER. Rather than creating a single legislature that represents the people and determines laws, the framers of the Constitution created three institutions – the House, the Senate, and the presidency – that share legislative powers. Formally, legislation may originate in either the House or the Senate, with the exception of bills raising revenue. The president may call Congress into special session and is required to

CONSTITUTIONAL PROCEDURES FOR PRESIDENTIAL APPROVAL OR DISAPPROVAL OF LEGISLATION

If Congress remains in session, the president may sign a bill into law, veto the bill and send it with a statement of his objections back to the house in which the bill originated, or do nothing. If the president vetoes the bill, two-thirds of both houses must vote to approve the bill (and thus override the veto) for it to become law. If the president does nothing by the end of 10 days (excluding Sundays), the bill becomes law.

If Congress adjourns before 10 days, the president may sign the bill into law, veto it, or do nothing. Because Congress has adjourned, it cannot consider overriding a veto, so a vetoed bill will die. Likewise, if the president takes no action by the end of 10 days (excluding Sundays), the bill will die. Killing a bill by failing to take action on it before Congress adjourns has come to be known as making a pocket veto.

There have been disputes between Congress and recent presidents about the meaning of a temporary congressional recess. Presidents have argued that they may pocket veto a measure while Congress is in recess for a holiday or another purpose, even though Congress has not adjourned *sine die* (formally adjourned at the end of a two-year Congress). Many members of Congress disagree. Lower courts have ruled against the presidents' position, but the Supreme Court has not written a definitive opinion on the issue.

recommend measures to Congress from time to time. The president's recommendations carry great weight, but the president cannot formally introduce legislation or compel Congress to act on his recommendations. Legislative measures are formally initiated in Congress, and once passed by both chambers, they must be sent to the president for approval or veto.

A special arrangement was established for treaties with foreign governments, which also have the force of law. The Constitution (Article II, Section 2) provides that the president "shall have power, by and with the advice and consent of the Senate to make treaties, provided two-thirds of the senators present concur." Thus, the president formally initiates legislative action on a treaty by submitting it to the Senate, and a two-thirds majority of the Senate must approve it for the treaty to be ratified. The House is excluded from formal participation. Nevertheless, the House participates in foreign policy making by sharing with the Senate the power to restrict the uses of the federal treasury, to declare war, and to regulate foreign commerce. The House also participates in foreign policy decisions that require congressional appropriations or changing in American domestic law, such as trade agreements.

Just as the president is an integral part of legislating, the Congress is central to implementing laws. The Constitution obligates the president to "take care that the laws be faithfully executed" and grants to the president the authority to appoint "officers" of the United States. But the Constitution requires that the president's appointees be confirmed by the Senate, allows Congress to establish executive departments by law and to establish means for appointing "inferior" officers of the executive branch, and grants Congress the authority to remove the president or other officers for "treason, bribery, or other high crimes and misdemeanors."

Interdependence, then, not exclusivity, characterizes the powers of the House, Senate, and president.

DIRECT AND INDIRECT REPRESENTATION. The framers of the Constitution wanted the government to be responsive to popular opinion, but they also wanted to limit the possibility that some faction could gain simultaneous control of the House, Senate, and presidency and then legislate to violate the rights of others. Only members of the House of Representatives were to be directly elected by the people. Senators were to be chosen by state legislatures, and the president was to be chosen by an electoral college composed of individuals chosen by the states. Furthermore, House, Senate, and presidential elections were put on different timetables: The entire House is elected every two years, senators serve six-year terms (with one-third of the seats up for election every two years), and presidents stand for election every four years.

The result was a mix of constraints and opportunities for the legislative players. By providing for direct or indirect election of members of Congress and the president, the framers of the Constitution increased the likelihood that electoral considerations would play an important part in shaping legislative outcomes. Political competition could be expected to motivate much legislative action. But the framers hoped that indirect election of senators and presidents, along with their longer terms of office, would desensitize them to narrow interests and rapid shifts in public opinion. This safeguard was considered particularly important in the case of treaties and major appointments to the executive agencies and the judiciary, which are left to the president and the Senate.

Concern about the responsiveness of senators to public opinion led to the adoption in 1913 of the Seventeenth Amendment to the Constitution, which provided for direct election of senators. Direct election of senators reduced the difference between the House and the Senate with respect to their link to the electorate. Nevertheless, because senators represent whole states and

representatives are selected from small districts regulated by size, along
the differences in term of office, it continues to be likely that the House
and Senate will have somewhat different preferences about public policy
and can frequently be controlled by different parties. The requirement that
both chambers approved legislation creates a bias against the enactment
of legislation and increases the probability that successful legislation will
represent a compromise among competing views.

JUDICIAL REVIEW AND STATUTORY INTERPRETATION. Since 1803, when
the Supreme Court issued its opinion in *Marbury v. Madison*, the federal
courts have assumed the power to review the acts of Congress and the president and to determine their constitutionality. This power of judicial review
gives the courts, and ultimately the Supreme Court, the final authority to
judge and interpret the meaning of the Constitution. The courts' interpretations of the Constitution serve to limit the policy options that can be considered by Congress and the president. For example, the Supreme Court's
interpretation of the freedom of speech provision of the First Amendment
bars policies restricting how much of her own money a candidate for elective
office can spend on her campaign.

In addition, the federal courts interpret the meaning of laws passed by
Congress – statutory interpretation. Individuals, organizations, and governments that are disadvantaged by executive branch interpretations of laws
often file suit in federal courts. The courts are asked to resolve ambiguities or
conflicting provisions in statutes. For guidance about congressional intentions, the courts rely on previous cases, congressional committee reports,
the records of floor debate, and other sources on the legislative history of
a statute. Court interpretations are often anticipated by legislative players
and subsequently shape the legislative language employed by these players. Legislators, in turn, often take court rulings into account when drafting
legislation.

The powers of judicial review and statutory interpretation are exercised by
federal judges who themselves are partially dependent on the legislative players. The Constitution provides that Congress may establish federal courts
below the Supreme Court and that the president nominate judges to the
federal courts with the consent of the Senate. Congress also has required
that lower court judges be nominated by the president and confirmed by
the Senate. But to protect federal judges from the influence of presidents
and members of Congress, the Constitution insulates them from potential
sources of presidential and congressional manipulation by granting them
life terms (although they may be removed by Congress for treason, bribery,

and misdemeanors) and preventing Congress and the ... cing their salaries. The effects of these provisions are ...er 10.

Development

Since the ratification of the Constitution, the United States has been transformed from a small, agrarian nation with little significance in international affairs to the world's largest industrial power and sole military and political superpower. The most rapid changes occurred during the industrial revolution of the late nineteenth century, when industry was transformed by new technologies, many new states were added to the union, modern political parties took form, and federal policies gained greater significance. These conditions changed public demands on members of Congress, who in turn changed their expectations of their institution. By the early twentieth century, many features of the modern Congress had taken form.

The Constitution provided only limited guidance to the House and Senate concerning how they should organize themselves. The House, according to the Constitution, shall elect a Speaker to preside, whereas the vice president shall serve as the Senate's president. The Senate is also authorized to elect a president pro tempore (or "pro tem") to preside in the absence of the vice president. And the Constitution requires that the House and Senate pass legislation by majority vote.

The Constitution says nothing about how legislation is to be prepared for a vote. Instead, it grants each chamber the authority to establish its own rules. Since their origin in 1789, the two chambers of Congress have each accumulated rules, procedural precedents, and informally accepted practices that add up to their own unique legislative process. The two chambers have developed similar legislative processes, but their parliamentary rules differ in important ways, which are detailed in Chapter 7.

The modern Congress has parties and committees that organize nearly all of its activities. Nearly all legislation passes through one or more committees in each house. Members of those committees take a leading role in writing the details of bills, dominate floor debate on those measures, and represent their house in conference committee negotiations with the other house. Parties appoint members to committees, give order to floor debate, and are given proportional representation on conference committees. The majority party in each chamber takes the lead in setting the agenda. But the Constitution is silent on the role of parties and committees in Congress. Both were created to meet the political needs of the members.

Congressionally Speaking . . .

In the context of the legislative process, *rules* can be a confusing term. While the Constitution outlines the basic features of the legislative process, each house of Congress has lengthy rules governing its internal affairs. In addition, Congress has placed rules governing its proceedings in many statutes, such as the Budget Act, which sets a timetable and special procedures for considering budget measures. Standing committees have their own rules, such as rules establishing subcommittees and providing procedures for committee meetings and hearings. Each of the four congressional party organizations (House Democrats and Republicans, Senate Democrats and Republicans) has its own rules to govern the election of party leaders, create party committees, and govern meetings. Chamber, committee, and party rules have been elaborated in many ways in recent decades as reformers have sought to reduce arbitrary rule by committee and party leaders.

Parties

We now assume that the presiding officer of the House, the Speaker, will be the leader of the majority party and will be responsible for setting the legislative agenda of the House. Similarly, we assume that the Senate's majority leader will set the agenda for that house. But in the early Congresses, no formally recognized party leaders existed. In fact, it took nearly a century for the House to develop something like its modern party-based leadership structure and the Senate took even longer. The Constitution, of course, is silent on the role of parties in Congress. Congressional parties developed only gradually, as parties outside Congress formed to compete in elections. Politicians and others seeking to get elected or to elect others have always taken the lead in forming political parties. Congressional party organizations have formed among newly elected members of the same party or, as has happened a few times, when sitting members form new parties to compete for reelection. They have varied in strength and influence as the degree of consensus about policy goals and political strategies has varied among their members.

EARLY FOUNDATIONS. Groups of legislators have collaborated to influence policy outcomes from the beginning. By the time of the Third Congress, shifting coalitions within the legislature had settled into polarized partisan groups, which began making organized efforts to get like-minded individuals elected. In the administration of George Washington, these groups were led by opposing cabinet officers (Jefferson and Madison versus Hamilton).

For a generation, the parties remained groups of elites, largely members of Congress and executive branch officials who shared party labels – at first, Republicans and Federalists. The congressional and presidential elections of 1800 initiated a period of Republican dominance that lasted until 1824. During that period, when the Federalist party faded away, members had clear party affiliations and gradually developed party caucuses to coordinate party activities. But there were still no formal party leadership posts in the House or Senate.

Speaker Henry Clay (R-Kentucky) was an effective leader, largely by force of personality, during his six nonconsecutive terms (the first starting in 1811). Remarkably, Clay gained the speakership during his first term in the House, which reflects as much on the weakness of the position as on Clay's popularity among his colleagues. But party factionalism, and sometimes assertive presidents, kept speakers relatively weak; indeed, small shifts in the balance of power among factions often led to the election of a new speaker. After Clay, strong personalities and factional leaders served as informally recognized leaders in both houses. Speakers enjoyed the power to make committee assignments, but this ability was insufficient to provide a foundation for party leadership because the most coveted committee assignments were promised in advance during the multicandidate contests for the speakership itself.

During the nineteenth century, the Senate did not have party leadership positions at all, except for caucus chairmen, whose duties and powers amounted to little more than presiding over caucus meetings. Strong regional leaders, like John C. Calhoun (D-South Carolina), Clay, and Daniel Webster (Whig-Massachusetts), tended to dominate Senate parties without holding formal leadership positions. But the first steps toward more party-based control of the chamber were taken in the middle of the nineteenth century. Conflict over control of standing committees led the parties in 1845 to rely on caucus meetings to prepare committee lists, and in 1847 the Democrats created a "committee on committees" to coordinate the task of making committee assignments for the party. In late 1859, the new Republican party formed its own committee on committees.

PARTY GOVERNMENT. The Civil War was an important turning point in the organization of the parties in Congress. Republicans became the dominant party during the war and began to use task forces and steering committees to coordinate the work of the House and Senate. After the war, the two major parties – now the Republicans and the Democrats – settled into broad regional divisions, with the Republicans powerful in the Northeast and the Midwest and the Democrats dominating the South. House Speakers during the 1860s and 1870s were not particularly strong, but they were the recognized leaders of their parties.

In the early 1890s, under Speaker Thomas Brackett Reed (R-Maine), rulings of the Speaker and new House rules gave the Speaker more power to prevent obstructionism and allowed House majorities to act. These changes, stimulated in part by intensifying partisanship on major issues, firmly established party-based governance in the House. For the next two decades, House decision making was highly centralized and under the control of the majority party's leader, the Speaker. Speakers Reed and "Uncle Joe" Cannon so firmly controlled the flow of legislative business that they were known as "czars." By the end of the first decade of the twentieth century, the press referred to Cannon's heavy-handed style as "Cannonism."

In the Senate, the presiding officer – the vice president – may not share the same party affiliation as the Senate majority and so was never granted powers similar to those of the House speaker. During most of the 1800s, the parties had caucus chairmen but they did not acquire genuine leadership duties until very late in the century. Arthur Pue Gorman (D-Maryland), the Democratic caucus chairman, emerged as his party's floor leader in the 1890s, but Republicans did not follow his example. Instead, by the late 1890s and into the new century, a group of four Republican senators, led by Finance Committee chairman Nelson Aldrich (R-Rhode Island) dominated the party.

"Aldrichism" was sometimes paired with Cannonism in the press, but the absence of rules limiting debate or amendments in the Senate prevented the majority party from changing rules to bolster the authority of its leaders. As a result, minority-party obstructionism was not overcome, as it was in the House. Any change in the rules that disadvantaged the minority party could be filibustered – that is, the minority could prevent a vote on a proposal to change the rules by refusing to conclude debate. Efforts by Aldrich and others to limit filibusters were themselves filibustered. Consequently the ability of even the strongest majority party leaders to bring legislation to a vote was severely constrained by the possibility of a filibuster (see Chapter 7).

THE TWENTIETH-CENTURY PATTERN. In the first decade of the twentieth century, a fragmenting Republican party altered congressional party politics for decades to come. Republican reformers in and out of Congress challenged Cannonism and Aldrichism. In 1910, a coalition of insurgent Republicans and minority-party Democrats forced changes in House rules that substantially reduced the power of the Speaker. The Speaker was stripped of the chairmanship of and power to make appointments to the Rules

which controlled resolutions that put important bills in order
In the next Congress, with a new Democratic majority, the
wer to make committee assignments was turned over to a party

in the Senate, with few formal chamber or party rules relating to leadership, the fading of Aldrichism was more gradual than was the revolt against Cannon. By the time the Democrats had gained a majority in 1913, no leader dominated either party, although Gorman and his successors as caucus chairs were known as the top party leaders. At a time when his party and the new president, Woodrow Wilson, wanted firmer Senate leadership, John Kern was elected Democratic caucus chairman and, in that capacity, also became known as majority leader, the first recognized majority leader in the Senate. Soon afterward, the Republicans created the position of minority leader, and both parties appointed "whips" to assist the top leaders in managing their parties' business on the floor.

For decades, neither House Speakers nor Senate majority leaders enjoyed the level of influence that Speaker Cannon and Senator Aldrich had possessed at the turn of the century. Committees became more important, as neither party, when in the majority, seriously challenged committee decisions. With a few short-lived exceptions, top party leaders fell into a pattern of supporting and serving the needs of committees more than trying to lead them. This pattern was maintained until the 1970s. Developments since that time are discussed in Chapter 5.

Committees

Members of the first Congresses were influenced by their experiences in the Continental Congress and in their colonial and state legislatures. They devised mechanisms to allow congressional majorities to express their will, while maintaining the equality of all legislators. They preferred that each chamber, as a whole, determine general policy through discussion before entrusting a subgroup of the membership with the responsibility of devising detailed legislation. Because legislators feared that committees with substantial policy discretion and permanence might distort the will of the majority, House committees in the first eight or nine Congresses usually took the form of special or select committees that dissolved when their tasks were completed.

EARLY FOUNDATIONS. The House took the lead in developing the foundations of a standing committee system. By 1810, the House had created 10 standing committees for routine policy areas and for several complex policy areas requiring regular investigation. The practice of referring legislation to a select committee gradually declined thereafter.

In its formative years, the Senate used select committees exclusively on legislative matters; it created only four standing committees to address internal housekeeping matters. A smaller membership, more flexible floor procedures, and a much lighter workload – with the Senate always waiting for the House to act first on legislation – permitted the Senate to use select committees in a wider variety of ways than did the House and still maintain full control over legislation. But beginning in 1806, the Senate adopted the practice of referring to the same committee all matters relating to the subject for which the committee had originally been formed, creating implicit jurisdictions for select committees.

In the decades leading up to the Civil War, the standing committee systems of both houses became institutional fixtures. Both houses of Congress began to rely on standing committees and regularly increased their number. In the House, the number of standing committees increased from 10 to 28 between 1810 and 1825 and to 39 by the beginning of the Civil War. The Senate established its first major standing committees in 1816, when it created 12. It added 10 more by the Civil War.

The expansion of the standing committee systems had roots in both chamber and party needs. A growing workload and regular congressional interaction with an increasing number of executive departments combined to induce committee growth. And the House began to outgrow a floor-centered, decision-making process. The House grew from 64 members in 1789 to 241 in 1833, which made open-ended floor debate quite chaotic.

In the House, partisan considerations also were important. Henry Clay transformed the speakership into a position of policy leadership and increased the partisan significance of committee activity. Rather than allowing the full House to conduct a preliminary debate, Clay preferred to have a reliable group of friendly committee members write legislation. The Speaker's control of committee appointments made this possible. During Clay's era, two procedural changes transformed committees' places in the sequence of the House bill process and further enhanced their value to the Speaker. First, the practice of allowing standing committees to report at their own discretion was codified into the rules of the House in 1822 for a few committees. Second, Clay made referral of legislation to a committee before floor debate the norm. By the late 1830s, after Clay had left the House, all House committees could introduce new legislation and report it to the floor at will. Preliminary debate by the House came to be viewed as a useless procedure. In fact, in 1880 the House adopted a formal rule that required newly introduced legislation to be referred to committee, which meant that the participation of the full membership was reserved for review of committee recommendations.

Changes to the Senate's committee system came at a slower pace. The Senate tended to wait for the House to act first on a bill before it took up a matter, so its workload was not as heavy as the House workload. Additionally, the Senate did not grow as quickly as the House. In 1835, the Senate had only 48 members, fewer members than the House had during the First Congress, and, in sharp contrast to the House, factionalism led senators and their weak party leaders to distrust committees and avoid referral to unfriendly committees. As a result, the Senate's standing committees, with one or two important exceptions, played a relatively insignificant role in the legislative process before the Civil War. The Senate retained a more floor-centered process.

PARTY CONTROL. In the half-century after the Civil War, the role of committees was strongly influenced by new issues associated with industrialization and the dramatic population growth, further development of American political parties, and the increasing careerism of members. Both houses had a strong tendency to respond to new issues by creating new committees rather than enlarging or reorganizing existing committee jurisdictions. When dealing with important issues, party leaders often liked the opportunity to appoint friendly members to a new committee within their jurisdiction. And committee chairs, who acquired offices and clerks when they were appointed, resisted efforts to eliminate committees. By 1918, the House had acquired nearly 60 committees and the Senate had 74. Nearly half of them had no legislative or investigative business, but allowed their chairmen to be assigned an office and hire a clerk.

The rapid growth in the number of committees in the late nineteenth century did not lead to a more decentralized Congress. Because of the stabilization of the two-party system and the cohesiveness of the majority-party Republicans in the late 1800s, majority-party leaders of both houses used the established committee systems as tools for asserting control over policy choices. In the House, the period between the Civil War and 1910 brought a series of activist Speakers who aggressively used committee appointments to stack important committees with friendly members, sought and received new bill referral powers, and gave the Rules Committee, which the Speaker chaired, the authority to report resolutions that set the floor agenda. With these powers, the Speaker gained the ability to grant a right-of-way to certain legislation and block other legislation.

Senate organization in the years after the Civil War was dictated by Republicans, who controlled that chamber for all but two Congresses between 1860 and 1913. The Republicans emerged from the war with no party leader or faction capable of controlling the Senate. Relatively independent committees and committee chairs became the dominant force in Senate deliberations. By the late 1890s, however, elections had made the Senate Republicans a smaller but more homogeneous group, with a coterie of like-minded members ascending to leadership positions. This group controlled the chamber's Committee on Committees, which made committee assignments, and the Steering Committee, which controlled floor scheduling. These developments made Senate committees agents of a small set of party leaders.

Party dominance did not last, however. After the revolt against Speaker Cannon in 1910, party cohesiveness and party leaders' ability to direct the legislative process declined substantially. With less central coordination and weaker party leaders, the bloated, fragmented committee systems became intolerable. Besides, the more independent members began to acquire small personal staffs in the 1920s and no longer needed the clerical assistance that came with a committee chair. As a result, both houses eliminated a large number of committees, most of which had been inactive for some time. Some formal links between party leaders and committees were broken as well. Because of reforms within the House Republican party organizations and similar policies adopted by the Democrats, the majority leader no longer chaired a major committee, chairs of major committees could not serve on the party's Steering Committee, and no committee chair could sit on the Rules Committee.

THE MODERN SYSTEM. The broad outline of the modern committee system was determined by the Legislative Reorganization Act of 1946. By 1945, most members shared concerns about the increasing size and expanding power of the executive branch that had come with the New Deal programs of the 1930s and then World War II. Critics noted that the large number of committees and their overlapping jurisdictions resulted in unequal distributions of work and participation among members, caused difficulties in coordination between the House and the Senate, and made oversight of executive agencies difficult. Committees also lacked adequate staff assistance to conduct studies of policy problems and executive branch activities.

The 1946 act reduced the number of standing committees to 19 in the House and 15 in the Senate, by consolidating the jurisdictions of several groups of committees. The standing committees in each house were made nearly equal in size, and the number of committee assignments was reduced to one for most House members and two for most senators. Provisions dealing with regular committee meetings, proxy voting, and committee reports constrained chairs in some ways. But the clear winners were the chairs of the standing committees who benefited from expanded committee jurisdictions and the addition of more committee staff, which they would direct. Chairs also continued to control their committees' agendas, subcommittee appointments, the referral of legislation to subcommittees, the management of committee legislation on the floor, and conference delegations.

Committees appeared to be quite autonomous in both chambers for the next decade and a half. Committee chairs exhibited great longevity. More than 60 percent of committee chairs serving between 1947 and 1964 held their position for more than five years, including approximately two dozen who served more than a decade. And, by virtue of southern Democrats' seniority, chairs were disproportionately conservative. Southern Democrats, along with most Republicans, constituted a conservative coalition that used committees to block legislation favored by congressional and administration liberals.

A set of strong, informal norms seemed to govern individual behavior in the 1940s and 1950s. Two norms directly affected committees. First, members were expected to specialize in matters that came before their committees. Second, new members were expected to serve an apprenticeship period, during which they would listen and learn from senior members and refrain from actively participating in committee or floor deliberations. These norms emphasized the development of expertise in the affairs of one's own committee and deference to the assumed expertise of other committees. The collective justification for these norms was that the development of, and deference to, expertise would promote quality legislation. By the mid-1960s, new cohorts of members, particularly liberals, proved unwilling to serve apprenticeships and to defer to conservative committee chairs. Many members began to demand major reforms in congressional operations.

A five-year effort yielded the Legislative Reorganization Act of 1970. It required committees to make public all recorded votes, limited proxy votes, allowed a majority of members to call meetings, and encouraged committees to hold open hearings and meetings. House floor procedures were also affected – primarily by permitting recorded teller votes during the amending process and by authorizing (rather than requiring) the use of electronic voting. These changes made it more difficult for House and Senate committee chairs to camouflage their power in legislative jargon and hide their domination behind closed doors. As we will see, however, the reform movement did not end with the 1970 act. Indeed, the act only set the stage for two decades of change in the role of committees in congressional policy making. The developments since the early 1970s are discussed in Chapter 6.

Conclusion

Congress's place in the constitutional scheme of representation and law making was shaped by the experience with the Continental Congress and the state governments in the years following the Revolutionary War. The Constitution made Congress more powerful than the Continental Congress had been, but it also limited its power by dividing the policy-making process among the two chambers and the presidency and by imposing explicit constraints on the kinds of law that can be made. The Constitution provided only the most rudimentary instructions on how the two houses of Congress were to organize themselves to make law. Gradually, as members struggled to control policy choices and to meet changing demands, legislators created the key features of the modern Congress:

- legislative parties, which gather legislators with common political interests;
- committees, which write the details of most legislation;
- leadership positions in both parties and committees, which are held by elected and appointed legislators who organize most legislative business; and
- rules, which are now very complex and govern the activities of individual legislators, parties, committees, and the parent chambers.

By the 1920s, Congress had taken its modern form, with a full complement of party leaders and standing committees.

Above: Democrat Kay Hagan, standing in front of her family, from left, daughter Carrie Hagan, son Tilden Hagan, and husband Chip Hagan, celebrates winning a U.S. Senate seat for North Carolina in a race against Elizabeth Dole at the Greensboro Coliseum in Greensboro, North Carolina, Tuesday, November 4, 2008. (Ted Richardson/Raleigh News & Observer/MCT)

Below: MINNEAPOLIS, MN - NOVEMBER 19: A ballot that was challenged during the election recount in the Senate race between Al Franken and Sen. Norm Coleman is seen at the Minneapolis Elections Warehouse in Minneapolis, Minnesota on November 19, 2008. Ballots circles are supposed to be filled in completely which is why this ballot was challenged. (Photo by Cory Ryan/Getty Images)

3

Congressional Elections and Policy Alignments

T HE YEAR 2008 MARKED THE SECOND CONSECUTIVE DIFFICULT ELECTION year for congressional Republicans. The 2006 midterm elections saw the Republicans lose control of both the House and Senate for the first time since 1994. This election continued a pattern of midterm elections being tough for the president's party in Congress – especially those occurring in a president's second term. Complicating matters further for Republicans going into 2008 was the declining popularity of President Bush, based in large part on the public's declining view of the war in Iraq. In contrast, national Democrats were excited about the possibility of winning back the White House and padding their congressional majorities. Republicans saw a number of incumbents retire rather than seek reelection, while Democrats had a seemingly unlimited supply of good challengers willing to target vulnerable Republicans. As the fall campaign shaped up, Republicans were forced to play defense in vulnerable states and districts, while leaving potentially vulnerable Democrats without seriously funded challengers. When the dust settled, Democrats had increased their majority by 21 seats in the House and at least 7 seats in the Senate. The 111th Congress thus began with large Democratic majorities in both chambers and a Democratic president, presenting Democrats with unified control of government for the first time since 1994.

The general policy preferences of the key players – the House, the Senate, and the president – are a product of elections. Elections are selection devices. They are intended to be competitive processes in which some candidates win and others lose. The winners arrive in Washington with certain personal policy views and an idea of what their supporters expect of them. Collectively, the winners give shape to the balance of policy preferences within the House and Senate and determine the broad contours of agreement and disagreement among the House, the Senate, and the president. Policy alignments change to some degree with each congressional and presidential election.

The connection between elections and policy is far from perfect. For one thing, election outcomes are influenced by factors other than the policy views of voters and candidates – such as personalities and scandals. For another, forces beyond constituency opinion and members' personal views are at work on most issues before Congress. Organized interest groups, expert and editorial opinion, and vote trading can influence policy choices. Moreover, most of the specific policy questions faced by Congress and the president do not arise in election campaigns, yet elections determine whether the same party controls the House, the Senate, and the White House, whether they lean in a liberal or conservative direction, and whether they are likely to agree on major policy questions.

Elections influence the legislative game beyond the party affiliations and policy positions of members of Congress and presidents. Most members seek reelection, and they seek legislative opportunities and resources that will further that goal. As we see in later chapters, the structure and function of virtually every major feature of Congress – committees, parties, rules, personal offices, and staffs – reflect the influence of electoral considerations. As political scientist David Mayhew wrote in 1974, and it is surely more true today, "[I]f a group of planners sat down and tried to design a pair of American national assemblies with the goal of serving members' reelection needs year in and year out, they would be hard pressed to improve on what exists."

Modern candidates for Congress face an electoral system that is highly decentralized and candidate-centered. The system is governed as much by state law as by federal law. Political parties endorse candidates for Congress, but they do not formally control the selection of candidates to run in the general election. Rather, any person who meets basic eligibility requirements may run in a primary election to gain a place on the general election ballot under a party's name. With few exceptions, candidates build their own campaign organizations, raise their own campaign money, and set their own campaign strategies. They do so in 435 different districts and 50 different states, each with a unique blend of economic, social, and political conditions. The winning candidates often emerge from their campaigns with strong individualistic tendencies, which they bring with them to the halls of Congress.

In this chapter we describe the formal rules and informal practices that shape congressional election outcomes. We then look at different types of candidates and at the advantages of incumbency. Next, we will consider national patterns in congressional elections, including the forces underlying divided party control of Congress and the presidency. Finally, we discuss the effect of elections on policy.

The Rules Governing Congressional Elections

More than 2,000 candidates run in congressional primary and general elections in any single election cycle. Their candidacies are governed by a web of rules provided by the Constitution, federal and state law, and, for incumbents, House and Senate rules. The rules have become increasingly complex as Congress and state legislatures, as well as the federal courts, have sought to prevent election fraud, to keep elections fair, and (on occasion) to tilt the rules in favor of one type of candidate or another. The rules concern eligibility for office, filing requirements, campaign finance restrictions, use of congressional staff, and many other matters. By shaping the strategies of candidates seeking election or reelection to Congress, these rules influence election outcomes and the political composition of the House and Senate.

The Constitution: Eligibility, Voting Rights, and Chamber Size

ELIGIBILITY. The Constitution requires that members of both chambers be citizens of the state from which they are elected, though this rule does not always prevent individuals from running to represent states that are not their primary residence. For example, Elizabeth Dole (R-North Carolina) had not lived in the state in decades before winning a Senate seat there in 2002. Members of the House must be 25 years old and must have been a citizen of the United States for seven years, while members of the Senate must be 30 years old and must have been a U.S. citizen for nine years. Candidates may be younger than the age requirements at the time they run for office, although they must have reached the required age before being sworn into office. Current Vice-President Joe Biden was only 29 when he first ran for the U.S. Senate. House members must reside in the state but not necessarily in the district they represent, though most do. Representatives serve two-year terms. Senators serve staggered, six-year terms, with one-third of the seats up for election every second year. Representatives' and senators' terms begin at noon on January 3 following each election or as soon thereafter as the House and Senate may determine by law.

VOTING RIGHTS. The Constitution leaves the "times, places, and manner of holding elections for senators and representatives" to the states, although Congress may enact (and has) certain federal regulations concerning

FILLING VACANT SENATE SEATS: VARIATIONS IN STATE LAW

The Seventeenth amendment gives state legislatures the option of allowing the governor to appoint a replacement or having a special election if Senate seats become vacant. The amendment reads in part, "When vacancies happen in the representation of any State in the Senate, the executive authority of each State shall issue writs of election to fill such vacancies: *Provided*, That the legislature of any State may empower the executive thereof to make temporary appointments until the people fill the vacancies by election as the legislature may direct." Recent events highlight the controversy that can arise with these appointments.

In Alaska, Senator Frank Murkowski (R-Alaska) resigned from the Senate upon winning the governorship of Alaska in 2002. He subsequently appointed his daughter, Lisa Murkowski, to fill the remaining two years of his term. Charges of nepotism surrounded Ms. Murkowski throughout the remainder of her father's term and her own campaign for the seat in 2004, but she was able to secure a full term for herself by narrowly defeating her Democratic opponent. Alaska law was subsequently changed to provide for a special election in lieu of gubernatorial appointments.

In Illinois, Senator Barack Obama (D-Illinois) resigned from the Senate upon winning the 2008 presidential election. By law, Illinois Governor Rod Blagojevich (D) was permitted to name a replacement. Controversy erupted however, when federal prosecutors arrested Blagojevich and charged him with numerous counts of corruption, including trying to trade the Senate seat for campaign contributions or a job for himself or his wife. Federal prosecutors released recordings from telephone wiretaps that included Blagojevich stating in relation to the Senate seat, "I've got this thing and it's [expletive] golden, and, uh, uh, I'm just not giving it up for [expletive] nothing." As Illinois legislators began to consider impeachment proceedings against Blagojevich he appointed Roland Burris, a longtime Chicago politician, to the seat. Senate Democrats initially indicated that they would refuse to seat Burris given the controversy surrounding the appointment, but he was eventually allowed to join the Senate.

elections. For example, in 1845 Congress fixed the date for congressional and presidential elections as the Tuesday following the first Monday in November, although this change was not fully implemented until 1880. Constitutional amendments have added several rules limiting the ability of states to regulate the right to vote in federal elections. The Fourteenth Amendment (ratified in 1868) bars restrictions based on race, color, or previous condition of servitude (slavery); the Nineteenth Amendment (ratified in 1920) bars restrictions based on gender; and the Twenty-fourth Amendment (ratified in 1964) prohibits poll taxes (a tax that must be paid before a person can vote). Most recently, the Twenty-sixth Amendment (ratified in 1971) guaranteed the right to vote to persons 18 years of age or older.

CHAMBER SIZE. By implication, the Constitution sets the size of the Senate – each state has two senators. Since the late 1950s, when Alaska and Hawaii joined the union, the Senate has had 100 members. The Constitution guarantees at least one representative for each state, but the specific size of the House is not dictated by the Constitution and instead is set by law. For more than a century, the House grew as the country's population grew and states were added to the union. Since 1911, federal law has left the House at 435 voting members. With the House's size fixed, a growing population has produced districts of growing size – most districts now contain more than 600,000 citizens, a far cry from the 30,000 originally provided by the Constitution. A House vacancy because of death or any other cause must be filled by a special election, which is called by the state's governor. A Senate vacancy, according to the Seventeenth Amendment, may be filled by election or appointment by the state's governor, as determined by state law (see box, "Filling Vacant Senate Seats"). Generally, state laws provide for a temporary appointment followed by an election at the time of the next regularly scheduled federal election to fill the remainder of the term. A bill to give the District of Columbia a House seat has been debated in recent years. The Senate passed a bill in early 2009 that would expand The House to 437, with D.C. receiving one seat and Utah the other. As of this writing, the House has not passed the bill.

Federal Law: Apportionment and Campaign Finance

APPORTIONMENT. After each decennial census, changes in the distribution of population among the states must be reflected in the allocation of House seats. Fifty seats are allocated automatically because of the requirement that each state have at least one representative. But the constitutional requirement that seats "be apportioned among the several states according to their respective numbers" leaves ambiguous how to handle fractions when allocating all other seats. Congress, by law, establishes the formula for apportioning the seats. Population shifts over the past half-century have resulted in a redistribution of power from the industrial Midwest and Northeast to the South and Southwest (see Chapter 1). In addition, since 1967 federal law has required that states with more than one House seat must create districts from which only one representative is elected (single-member districts).

CAMPAIGN FINANCE. The Federal Election Campaign Act (FECA) of 1971, and important amendments to it in 1974 and 1976 created the Federal Election Commission (FEC) and established limits and disclosure requirements for contributions to congressional campaigns. The regulations e a response to scandals involving secret contributions to presidential candidates of large sums of money from wealthy individuals and corporations, some of which was used for underhanded activity. FECA restricted the size of contributions that individuals, parties, and political action committees (PACs) could make to candidates for Congress. FECA created no restrictions on how much congressional candidates may spend, and the Supreme Court has barred limits on how much a candidate or family members may contribute to their own cause. The law required groups and candidates to report contributions and expenditures to the FEC.

Under the law, membership organizations, corporations, and labor unions may create PACs to collect money from organization employees or members in order to pad resources for campaign contributions. Because PACs may contribute more than individuals, there is a strong incentive to create PACs, which grew in number from 608 in late 1974 to more than 4,000 in the mid-1980s and was just over 4,000 in 2003. The largest growth was in PACs tied to corporations, which numbered 1,552 in mid-2003, but growth has occurred in all categories – labor union PACs, trade association PACs, PACs formed by cooperatives, and PACs not connected to any organization.

The limits on contributions reflect a judgment that contributions from the wealthy and corporations may be harmful to the system and that party participation is more desirable. The basic rules on contributions provide that

- individuals may contribute larger sums to candidates and parties than to PACs;
- parties may contribute larger sums directly to candidates than may PACs;
- parties may coordinate a certain amount of spending with candidates, while PACs cannot.

The law emphasizes public disclosure of contributions and expenditures by candidates, parties, and PACs. Full disclosure of all contributions must be made in reports to the FEC, all contributions of more than $50 must be individually recorded, and the identity of donors of $100 or more must be provided. Detailed reports on expenditures are required as well.

FECA has loopholes. Contributions may be bundled, for example, by gathering many individual or PAC contributions and offering them as a package to a candidate. Lobbyists and other interest-group leaders can use bundling, without violating the limits on the size of individual contributions, to make very conspicuous contributions to candidates who might not pay much attention to much smaller, separate contributions. The Honest Leadership and Open Government Act of 2007 did require disclosure of the identity of bundlers and the amount bundled. Furthermore, the law did not regulate "soft money" contributions, which by the late 1990s had taken on increasing importance in congressional and presidential campaigns. Soft money was contributed by wealthy individuals and corporations to political parties, to be used for television ads for the party (not specific candidates), party staff and office expenses, voter registration and GOTV efforts, and other purposes that are not directed by, but obviously benefit, the party's candidates. This loophole allowed individuals and PACs that had reached their limit in direct contributions to a candidate's campaign to contribute money to a party organization that can work on the candidate's behalf.

By the late 1990s, many had come to believe that the soft money loophole was allowing candidates, parties, and donors to circumvent the rules established by FECA. After almost a decade of bitter debate, proponents of campaign finance reform, including Senators John McCain (R-Arizona) and Russ Feingold (D-Wisconsin), succeeded in convincing Congress to ban most uses of "soft money" with the Bipartisan Campaign Reform Act of 2002 (BCRA) – sometimes known as "McCain-Feingold." In addition to the ban on soft money, the BCRA increased the amount of hard money that individuals could contribute to campaigns, created exceptions to the hard money limits for candidates facing self-financed candidates, and restricted "issue advocacy" by independent groups in the 60 days prior to an election (see Table 3.1).

A separate loophole was generated by a 1996 Supreme Court ruling that eliminated limits on how much parties could spend on congressional campaigns, as long as the spending was not coordinated with individual candidates' campaigns. The ruling paved the way for a sharp increase in fundraising and spending by the congressional campaign committees. The Senate Republicans immediately set up a special unit to raise funds for these "independent" expenditures. Total expenditures by the parties' congressional and senatorial campaign committees exceeded $900 million for the 2006 election cycle, which was up from slightly more than $500 million in 2004.

There are many legal obstacles for any new campaign finance reform law and the BCRA has been subject to many of them. The Supreme Court ruled in *Buckley v. Valeo* (1976) that the free speech clause of the First Amendment to the Constitution applies to campaign spending. The argument is that individuals and groups must be free to spend money to express themselves. Many observers thought that this interpretation of the First Amendment meant that the Court would not let stand the BCRA restrictions on when groups can spend money to advocate issues. However, the Court initially did just that in *McConnell v. FEC* (2003), on the grounds that the restriction of free speech was minimal and justified by the government's interest in curbing corrupt practices. However, the Court reversed itself in *FEC v. Wisconsin*

TABLE 3.1. Congressional Campaign Contribution Limits under the Bipartisan Campaign Reform Act of 2002, for the 2007–2008 Cycle.

Type of contributor	Limits	Additional provisions and explanations

Limits on Contributions from Individuals	• $2,300 per candidate for primaries
	• $2,300 per candidate for runoff
	• $2,300 per candidate for general election
	• $108,200 total per two-year election cycle
	  ○ $42,700 to candidates
	  ○ $65,500 to parties and PACs
	• unlimited independent
		The $2,300 limit on contributions to a candidate for the general election triples if a House candidate faces a self-financed opponent. A more complex formula raises the limit for Senate races.
		Independent spending is spending by an individual or political action committee for or against candidates without coordinating with a candidate

Limits on Contributions from Political Parties	• $10,000 per House Candidate (Combined National, State, Local) • $39,900 per Senate candidate • Parties can either spend independently or in coordination with a candidate, but not both • National party committees have no limits on donations to state & local party committees ○ 2 cents per voting-age person in the state in coordinated spending.	The Senate limit of $39,900 applies to House candidates in single-district states. Coordinated spending is party spending for services provided to a candidate without coordinating
Limits on Contributions from Political Action Committees (PACs)	• $5,000 per candidate for primaries • $5,000 per candidate for general election • $15,000 per calendar year to a political party ○ unlimited independent spending	Independent spending is spending by an individual or political action committee for or against candidates with a candidate

Source: Federal Election Commission, www.fec.gov.

Right to Life (2007). In a bitterly divided 5–4 opinion, a majority held that the restriction of so called "issue ads" in the weeks prior to an election amounted to unconstitutional censorship. This ruling is likely to increase the amount of corporate and union money used to indirectly campaign for or against candidates – which could effectively circumvent the soft money ban in the BCRA.

Even before the Court gutted many of the restrictions on advertising prior to a campaign, other loopholes in the BCRA had been exploited. Most notably, a number of so called "527" and "501(c)3" groups, named for the section of the tax code that permits their existence, formed during the 2004 election cycle. These groups, with names such as "MoveOn.org," "American Coming Together," and the "Media Fund" spent hundreds of millions of dollars seeking to influence the outcome of recent elections. In many ways, these groups filled in the void left by the soft money ban in the BCRA. 527 groups spent more than $200 million during the 2006 congressional elections.

THE "MILLIONAIRES' AMENDMENT". The Supreme Court's ruling in *Buckley v. Valeo* (1976) that money spent on gaining political office is protected speech invalidated restrictions on candidates' use of personal wealth that were contained in FECA. In recent years, many candidates for Congress and other offices have spent a considerable amount of their personal fortunes in their quests for office. Jon Corzine (D-New Jersey) is the most notable, having spent in excess of $60 million in his successful quest for the Senate. However, he is not alone. Maria Cantwell (D-Washington), Mark Dayton (D-Minnesota), and Peter Fitzgerald (R-Illinois) each spent in excess of $10 million from personal sources in their successful bids against Senate incumbents. Despite the fact that most self-financed candidates are not successful – Blair Hull spent more than $28 million in a losing effort to capture the Democratic Senate nomination from Illinois in 2004 – many observers have raised questions about the impact of self-financing on the electoral process. Critics argue that self-financing allows the wealthy to "buy elections," thus excluding citizens of more modest means from elective office. For their part, self-financed candidates often argue that by paying for their own campaigns they assure the public that they are not influenced by campaign contributions from organized interests.

The Bipartisan Campaign Reform Act of 2002 (BCRA) attempted to address the issue of self-financed candidates in the so called "millionaires' amendment." First, the act restricted the amount candidates can raise to repay themselves to $250,000 for loans to their campaign. Advocates of this restriction argued that candidates would be discouraged from self-financing more than that if they cannot repay themselves later. Second, the act allowed candidates running against self-financed candidates to raise additional hard money. Under the BCRA, candidates can only accept donations of $2,300 per election from an individual donor, yet if they were facing a self-financed candidate this limit tripled for House races and possibly more for Senate races. Advocates pointed out that this provision will "level the playing field" for candidates facing self-financed opponents. The Supreme Court ruled that this provision was unconstitutional in the case *Davis v. FEC* (2008). A narrowly divided court ruled that the unequal treatment given to candidates under this rule violated the first amendment to the Constitution. This continued a trend whereby the Supreme Court has continually chipped away at BCRA provisions, causing many to worry that the law will soon become ineffectual.

State Law: Redistricting and Primaries

State laws continue to regulate many aspects of congressional elections. They exhibit a bewildering array of provisions. Two sets of state laws – those governing the drawing of district lines and those governing the process of gaining a place on the ballot – are particularly important.

REDISTRICTING. Among the most sensitive issues governed by state laws is the drawing of district lines for House seats. Because the composition of House districts can make the difference between winning and losing, the two major parties and individual politicians, particularly incumbents, often fight fierce battles in state legislatures over the alignment of districts. These battles are renewed at least every 10 years, after the decennial census.

Following the 2000 census, the seven least populous states – Alaska, Delaware, Montana, North Dakota, South Dakota, Vermont, and Wyoming – were each allocated a single at-large House district, so redistricting was not an issue. Of the other states, 37 began by using the normal process of having the state legislature enact redistricting legislation. But in response to the controversial character of redistricting decisions, the other states adopted some special procedures – an independent commission, a combination of commission and legislative action, or some other special rules. Incumbent members of Congress often seek to influence state redistricting decisions, but their influence varies. Redistricting is likely to be most controversial when a state loses one or more seats and must pit incumbent members against one another in consolidated districts.

States face two significant constraints when drawing district lines. First, federal law – the Voting Rights Act – requires certain states to submit their plans to the U.S. Department of Justice or a federal district court for approval before implementing them. These are states where discriminatory barriers to voting were or now may be a problem – a total of 16 in 2001. Since 1982, the Voting Rights Act has barred districting plans that have the effect of diluting the voting power of racial minorities by splitting their vote among districts, even if there is no evidence of deliberate discrimination.

Second, the Supreme Court has moved to set standards to limit certain kinds of gerrymandering – the manipulation of district lines for political purposes – as well as some unintentional districting outcomes. The clearest court directive is that House districts must be equal in population – within a very narrow margin. In addition, the Court indicated in 1986 that districting plans designed to advantage one political group (such as a party) over another may be unconstitutional. But just what constitutes impermissible "political gerrymandering" remains unclear as of the Court's latest decision on the topic, *Vieth v. Jubelirer* (2004), in which the Court did not intervene in the case because it recognized that it could not offer a concise solution.

Racial gerrymandering is another matter. Following the 1990 census, the federal courts at first let stand very oddly shaped congressional districts created to give racial minorities a voting majority. These new districts were critical to the election of more African Americans and Hispanics to the House of Representatives in 1992. But between 1993 and 2001, the Court made a series of confusing rulings concerning the constitutionality of districts drawn with racial motives. The decisions have forced federal courts to determine whether other factors justified the redrawing of those districts' lines. By 2001, following the new Supreme Court rulings, courts had ordered "majority-minority" districts to be redrawn in Florida, Georgia, Louisiana, New York, North Carolina, Texas, and Virginia. In early 2009, a narrowly divided court ruled in *Barrett v. Strickland* that the Voting Rights Act only required protection against minority vote dilution in districts in which racial minorities make up a majority of the population. It is too early to know if this case will affect redistricting following the 2010 census, but if the past is any guide, more litigation over the composition of districts is likely.

Political and legal complications abound in redistricting. Failure to adopt a timely redistricting plan or to meet legal standards often leads a federal district court to design and impose a plan. After the 2000 census, federal courts became involved in redistricting in at least 10 states, and state courts became involved in several others. Several states did not have settled district lines until the summer of 2002, forcing some of them to extend the filing deadline for congressional candidates for the 2002 elections.

PRIMARIES. State laws that govern the placement of candidates on the November general election ballot are remarkably varied. All states provide for primary elections as the means for choosing candidates from the two major parties for the November ballot. In 2008, the earliest standard primary elections for House and Senate seats were in Illinois on February 5. The last standard primary was in Hawaii on September 20. But 10 states require that a candidate receive a specified percentage of the primary vote (more than 50 percent in most cases) before being placed on the November ballot; if no candidate wins the specified percentage, a run-off primary election is held soon thereafter.

Furthermore, states vary in the way they regulate voting in primary elections. Most states have closed primaries: Voters must register in advance as either a Republican or a Democrat and may vote only in that party's primary. Open primaries, used in nine states, allow voters to choose to vote in either party's primary at the polling place on election day.

Nearly all states have a system of plurality voting in the general election. That is, the candidate with the most votes wins, even if that candidate receives less than a majority of the total vote. Consequently, if more than two candidates are on the ballot (usually a candidate from each major party, plus minor party candidates), the winner may receive far less than half of the votes.

Louisiana has the most distinctive system. It puts all candidates for a House or Senate seat, regardless of party, in a single primary election. Prior to 1997 this primary occurred in October, and if a candidate received more than 50 percent of the vote, they were elected to office without a general election. If no candidate won a majority, the two candidates with the highest votes share, regardless of party, were placed on the ballot in the November general election. Because only two candidates would compete in the general election, if a general election were necessary, one candidate would win a majority (in the absence of a tie). In late 1997, the Supreme Court struck down the Louisiana primary election law. Because a candidate could be, and often was, elected in the October primary, the Court ruled that the Louisiana law conflicted with the federal law setting the date for congressional elections as the Tuesday following the first Monday of November. Following this ruling, Louisiana shifted the primary to the date for the general election with a runoff following if no candidate attains a majority.

THE CHANGING CONGRESS: REDISTRICTING EFFORTS HIGHLIGHT NEW PARTY STRATEGIES

Republicans in the Texas legislature found themselves in the majority for the first time in over 100 years when they convened in 2003. With some urging from then U. S. House Representative Tom DeLay (R-Texas), Texas Republicans began considering various plans to redraw the state's U.S. House districts to increase the number of districts likely to elect Republicans.

The drawing of House district lines is one of the most controversial and partisan issues faced by state legislatures, and the ensuing Texas episode was no exception. Aside from the requirements of equal population and certain restrictions found in the Voting Rights Act, states are free to draw their congressional district lines as they see fit. For much of the early part of the twentieth century, states redrew lines infrequently, if at all. Following the Supreme Court's decision requiring equal population in *Wesberry v. Sanders* (1964), redistricting became a decennial event in states, occurring prior to election years ending in "2." Nothing in federal law prohibits states from redrawing districts more frequently; in fact, in the late nineteenth century, states often redrew lines after each legislative election. Ohio, for example, once had six different sets of lines in six consecutive elections.

In the Texas case, Democrats fought the redistricting efforts for much of 2003. On two separate occasions, Senate Democrats fled the state to prevent the quorum necessary to enact the plan. After months of delay, a quorum was eventually attained after one of the Democratic senators relented and came back to Texas. After a skirmish among themselves, Texas Republicans eventually enacted a plan that significantly altered the partisan composition of many districts. The results were drastic for the Texas delegation. In the 108th Congress (2003–2004), Texas sent 17 Democrats and 15 Republicans to the House. Under the new districting system, the 109th Congress began with 20 Republicans and 12 Democrats, a net gain of five seats for the Republican Party.

In the wake of the Texas "re-redistricting" Colorado and Georgia enacted new districting plans. Colorado Republicans attempted to enact a plan that would have increased the proportion of Republicans in their U.S. House delegation, but were rebuffed when the Colorado Supreme Court ruled, and the U.S. Supreme Court affirmed, that Colorado law only permitted redistricting once per decade, while the new Georgia planned produced less net change in their congressional delegation.

ELECTION PRACTICE REFORM. In the wake of the 2000 presidential election controversy, Congress sought to expand the federal role in national elections by making it "easier to vote and harder to cheat." Congress enacted legislation in 2002, the Help America Vote Act (HAVA), which authorized almost $4 billion to aid states in improving the mechanics of the election process. Close to $1 billion of this authorization was to assist states in replacing the infamous "punch card" voting machines that were the source of controversy in Florida in 2000, as well as replacing other outdated voting technology. The law also required that states must allow voters to cast "provisional ballots" in federal elections if their registration status is unclear. Upon demonstrating that the voter is properly registered, these provisional ballots are then to be counted as actual votes. The law seeks to reduce voter fraud by requiring identification for first-time voters, and a state-issued identification is now required in order to register to vote.

House and Senate Rules: Office Accounts, Staff, and the Frank

The House and Senate have established rules to limit incumbents' use of their official offices, accounts, staffs, and other privileges for campaign purposes. Generally, incumbents may not use their offices or staffs for campaign purposes. For example, they may not accept campaign contributions in their official offices. Staff members are required to take leave without pay to work on their bosses' campaigns.

Dating back to the first Congress, members have been permitted free use of the mail by using their signatures in place of stamps. The use of their signature, called the frank, is now regulated by a 1973 law that prohibits the use of the frank for purposes "unrelated to the official business, activities, and duties of members" and for "mail matter which specifically solicits political support . . . or a vote or financial assistance for any candidate for any political office." In 1989, the House limited the number of district wide "postal-patron" mailings that could be sent. The rules forbid explicit partisan and campaign references and allow only a limited number of references to the member per page.

The rules also bar mass mailings within 60 days of a primary or general election in the Senate and within 90 days in the House. Many members still use the frank within the 60-day period for multiple batches of mailings of fewer than 500 pieces each to target certain groups within their districts or states, and members still use the frank more in election years than non-election years. However, the 1989 rule change combined with a further tightening of member allowances in 1995 have reduced the amount of money spent on franked mail from over $100 million in 1988 to less than $20 million in 1999.

Until 1992, House members could send mass mailings at taxpayer expense to individuals living outside their district. Responding to a court ruling of that year, the House banned all mailings to more than 500 persons outside a member's district. The restriction is a problem for members whose districts are redrawn in an election year and seek to quickly communicate with their new constituents. The restriction also constrains members who are contemplating running for a statewide office, such as a Senate seat or governorship, who want to reach a larger electorate.

The Candidates

Personal ambition, more than any other factor, seems to drive people to run for Congress in the modern era. In recent years, party organizations have become very active in recruiting candidates. Interest groups, ranging from environmental groups to women's groups to manufacturing associations, seek candidates who reflect their viewpoint to run for Congress as well. Nevertheless, the initiative for the vast majority of candidacies rests with the candidates themselves. They are self-starters – independent political entrepreneurs who personally assess the costs and benefits then assume the risks of running for Congress.

Conventional wisdom suggests that Congress is an ossified institution filled with well-entrenched incumbents. As usual, conventional wisdom is half right and half wrong. Incumbents are advantaged and usually win reelection when they seek it. But it does not take very many voluntary retirements and electoral defeats in each election for substantial change in the membership to occur over just a few elections. Despite the fact that 90 percent or more of incumbents seek reelection, it takes only a few years for substantial turnover in the membership to occur. In 2003, for example, 245 of the 435 members of the House had been first elected in 1994 or later. In the Senate, 45 of the 100 senators serving in the 107th Congress (2001–2002) had served less than one full six-year term.

Three types of congressional candidates should be distinguished: incumbents seeking reelection, challengers to incumbents, and candidates running in districts or states with an open seat (that is, where the incumbent chose not to run or was defeated in the primary). As Figure 3.1 illustrates, several clear patterns have emerged in recent decades:

- most incumbents run for reelection and win;
- House incumbents are more successful than Senate incumbents in the typical election;
- in the House, the percentage of incumbents who successfully seek reelection has reached new highs in recent elections.

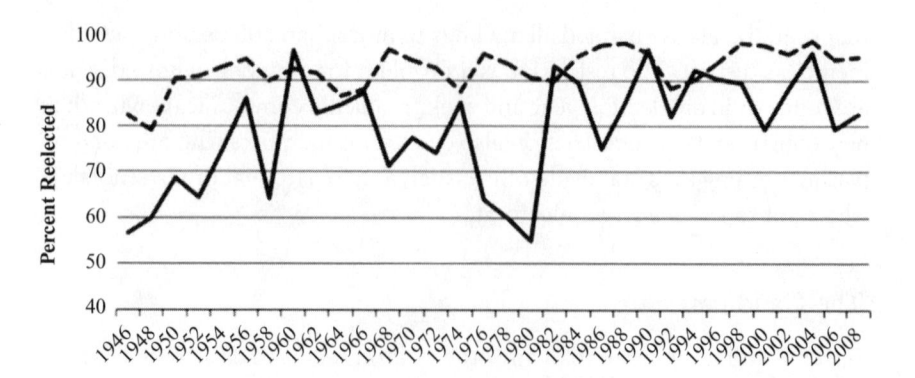

Year

FIGURE 3.1. House and Senate Reelection Rates, 1948–2008. *Sources:* Ornstein et al. Vital Statistics on Congress, 2001–2002; Abramson, Aldrich, and Rohde, Change and Continuity in the 2000 and 2002 Elections. 2004–2008 calculated by the authors. *Note:* The percentage includes only those seeking reelection.

Clearly, the odds are stacked against challengers, although challengers for Senate seats are more successful as a group than are challengers for House seats. The high rate of success for incumbents seeking reelection has led observers to note an incumbency advantage – something intrinsic to incumbent officeholders, their office and campaign resources, or the electorate that gives incumbents a built-in advantage over challengers.

One indicator of the strength of incumbents' advantage is the percentage of incumbents reelected with at least 60 percent of the vote. As Figure 3.2 indicates, this percentage was higher in the 1980s than in the previous three decades. The percentage dipped in the 1990s when incumbent Democrats suffered losses, but in 2002 and 2004, the percentage was back to levels seen in the late 1980s. This measure can be misleading. Any national shift in voter preferences favoring or hurting the majority party will affect most incumbents' margin of victory even if nothing associated with incumbency played a role – this appears to have been the case in 2006.

A better measure would provide a statistical adjustment for how well the candidate did in the last election and how advantaged or disadvantaged his or her party is nationwide. Such a measure indicates the advantage of incumbency corrected for the local and national advantages enjoyed by the incumbent and his or her party. Using a more refined measure, the House incumbency advantage shifted upward from 1964 to 1966. In the 1950s and early 1960s, the incumbency advantage was something less than five

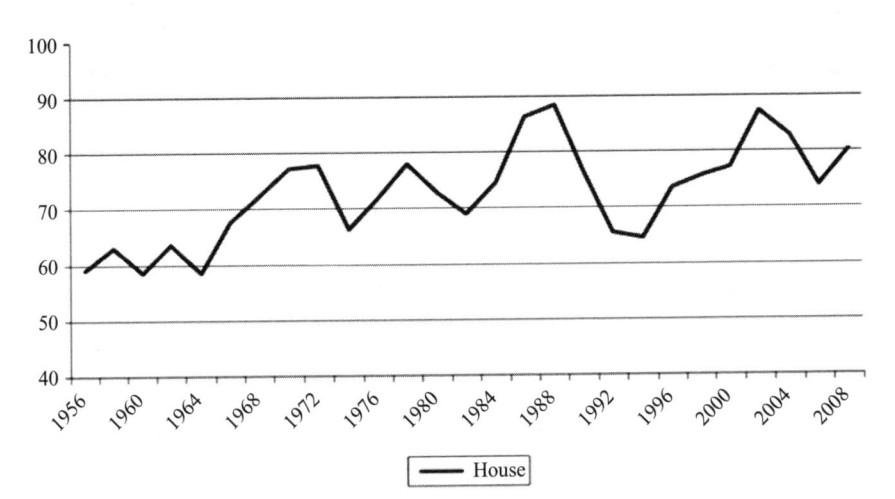

FIGURE 3.2. Percentage of House Incumbents Winning with At Least 60 Percent of the Major Party Vote, 1956–2008. *Source: Collected by authors.*

percentage points in most elections. Since then, the incumbency advantage has averaged close to 10 percentage points.

Senators' constituencies are often larger and more diverse than representatives' constituencies, and thus Senate races are often more competitive than House races. Incumbent senators find it more difficult than do incumbent House members to build a large base of support that will sustain them from election to election. The long six-year term may contribute to the inter-election variability in support for senators. Whatever the reason, Senate incumbents face a much higher probability of defeat than do their House counterparts.

In contrast to the pattern in elections involving incumbents, contests for open seats have become more competitive in recent decades. Between 1946 and 1964, only 20.3 percent of House open-seat contests produced a change in the party that controlled the seat; between 1966 and 2000, the percentage rose to close to 30. The trend is sharper in Senate open-seat races – 41.3 percent yielded party change between 1954 and 1964, and more than 50 percent did so between 1966 and 2000. In 2008, all three open Senate seats saw a change in party control.

Explaining the Incumbency Advantage

Political scientists have worked hard to identify the causes of the declining competition for seats held by incumbents and have discovered that many factors contribute to it. Influences include the declining importance of party identification in voting, an expanding incumbent advantage in campaign resources, more nonpartisan constituency service, imbalances in campaign funding, the quality of the candidates challenging incumbents, and more contact with voters.

The Decline of Party Identification

A major factor in incumbents' success is that their party holds the advantage in the district or state they represent. Democratic constituencies tend to elect and reelect Democrats; Republican constituencies tend to elect and reelect Republicans. For House districts, according to one estimate, the expected vote for incumbents, subtracting the vote attributable to their incumbency has varied from between 55 and 60 percent for most of the period since the late 1940s.

But party is a major element of the story of incumbency. The decline of party identification in the general electorate in the latter half of the twentieth century probably contributed to incumbents' advantage. As voters' psychological attachment to a major party weakened, the proportion of the electorate voting for congressional candidates in a reflexive, partisan way declined. This enlarged pool of "floating" voters and weak partisans produced more ticket splitting. The proportion of the electorate voting for the candidate of one party for one office and the candidate of the other party for another office – whether measured for House-Senate splits or House-president splits – nearly tripled from the 1950s through the 1980s, before declining in recent election cycles.

For congressional incumbents, weak partisanship and ticket splitting presented both danger and opportunity. The danger was that incumbents' natural base of support among fellow partisans was weakened, as there are fewer votes guaranteed for their party. This shift made the electorate more unpredictable. Indeed, for much of the 1960s–1980s there was more election-to-election volatility in incumbents' vote margins than there was in the 1950s – so much more that it nearly offsets the average incumbent's margin of victory. The increase in volatility accounts for the fact that incumbents were receiving a larger share of the vote but not actually winning at a much higher rate.

Expanded Perquisites of Office

The decline in party loyalty in the 1960s–1980s certainly contributed to the incumbency advantage, but incumbents have continued winning even in this era of renewed partisanship. Another important factor is that incumbents exploit their individual resources to combat electorate volatility and expand their base of support into the enlarged pool of independent voters. Their resources, which are discussed in Chapter 4, include a sizable personal staff distributed between their Washington and home offices, their committee staffs, office and stationery budgets, the use of the frank, a travel allowance, access to and influence over the White House and executive agencies, access to the media, and the expertise of the congressional support agencies.

All of these resources have grown since the 1960s and legislators can use them to attract favorable publicity at home. Staff members, often with the assistance of experts in support agencies, help members write legislation and timely amendments that are popular at home. Committee and subcommittee staffs assist their bosses in organizing hearings, some of which are held away from Washington and many of which attract media attention. Stationery allowances and the frank permit members to send mass mailings directly to their districts or states. Travel allowances make it easier for members to return home more frequently to appear before groups. And Congress's own radio and television facilities now permit members to make live and taped appearances on local television more frequently.

Expanded Constituency Service

Incumbents' official resources also can be used to improve their personal standing with their constituents. Additional staff and home offices have allowed members to provide personal services to constituents. Many of these services fall under the heading of "casework" – efforts to solve constituents' and local governments' problems with federal agencies. Perhaps the most common problem involves a constituent's eligibility for social security benefits. The expansion of federal programs since the mid-1960s has fostered this ombudsman role for members. Unlike legislating, which forces legislators to take sides on controversial issues, casework is a nonpartisan activity for which members can gain credit. The emphasis on personal service and de-emphasis on controversial issues facilitate more candidate-oriented and less party-oriented campaign.

Of course, the expansion of members' resources and the growth of constituency service have another side. In a large country with a large, complex federal bureaucracy, members perform a genuine service on behalf of constituents with real problems with government agencies. Legislators often justify their resources on the grounds that they are meeting the needs and

---

Congressionally Speaking . . .

Political scientists often use the *swing ratio* to gauge the bias of an electoral system. The swing ratio is the percentage change in seats won by a party for a 1 percent increase in its average nationwide vote. In a system of perfect proportional representation, the number of seats a party wins is proportional to the number of votes received, so the swing ratio is 1.0. A party winning 55 percent of the vote, for instance, would win 55 percent of the seats.

For single-member districts, a small percentage increase in the vote for a party may produce a large increase in the number of seats it wins (narrow defeats might be turned into narrow victories). The swing ratio for House elections has been about 2.0 in the twentieth century, indicating that a party gains two seats for each additional one percent of the nationwide vote it gains. The increasing incumbency advantage has reduced the House swing ratio in recent decades. Incumbents, who average more than 60 percent of the vote, can lose 5 or 10 percent of the vote and still retain their seats. This means that the system is less responsive – seat changes are smaller for the same change in nationwide vote.

---

expectations of their constituents. It is not surprising that members advertise their good works and get credit from voters for doing them.

Redistricting

One seemingly obvious explanation for the increase in the incumbency advantage is redistricting. With the Supreme Court ruling in *Wesberry v. Sanders* (1964) that districts had to approximate a "one person one vote" standard, many states had to redistrict for the first time in decades. In 1962, Michigan's largest district contained more than 800,000 residents, while the smallest contained less than 200,000. This massive wave of redistricting in the wake of *Wesberry*, is timed almost perfectly with the increase in the incumbency advantage.

For many years political scientists were unable to demonstrate that redistricting in the aftermath of *Wesberry v. Sanders* was responsible for the increased incumbency advantage. Recently, political scientists Gary Cox and Jonathan Katz have demonstrated that redistricting in the 1960s played a significant role. They point out that redistricting was dominated by Democrat-controlled state legislatures and federal courts staffed by Democratic judges. These authorities "packed" Republican voters into a few overwhelmingly Republican districts while spreading Democratic voters across more districts so as to increase the number of seats Democrats could be expected to win. This packing of Republicans produced a large number of seats that were virtually guaranteed to elect Republican members, but decreased competition in many other seats that were controlled by Democrats. Thus, they conclude that the increase in incumbency advantage was largely attributable to this increase in the number of safe Republican seats.

The post-2000 census redistricting has surely contributed to the lack of electoral competition in the 2002 and 2004 elections and helped prevent further Republican losses in 2006 and 2008. In addition to locking in more Republican seats, this round of redistricting considerably reduced the number of districts with a competitive party balance. By one count, 75 percent of the seats that had been competitive in 2000 were no longer competitive after redistricting. The most extreme of these "incumbency protection acts" was the new districting system in California, where all 53 districts had at least an eight percentage point registration advantage for one party.

Biased Campaign Funding

Changes in campaign finance laws and the introduction of PACs have been a mixed blessing for incumbents. The expanded resources and activities of party committees and PACs create a potential threat to incumbents. By recruiting, funding, and providing campaign services to challengers and even organizing mass mailings and media campaigns against incumbents, PACs and party committees can neutralize some of the advantages of incumbents. Republicans have proved to be especially adept at this strategy, but the Democratic party successfully used this strategy against them in 2006. Rep. Rahm Emmanuel (D-Illinois) and Sen. Charles Schumer (D-New York) successfully recruited and raised funds for many of the candidates who were key to the Democrats gaining a majority in the 2006 elections.

Of course, incumbents generally do not sit idly by as potential challengers are recruited and trained. In fact, by using their committee and subcommittee chairmanships, party posts, and other sources of influence, incumbents have done a good job of staying ahead of challengers. The incumbency advantage over challengers in PAC contributions, as well as in total contributions, is huge and has been growing since the 1970s.

Further, as the competition over majority control in Congress has intensified, the parties themselves have turned more attention to bolstering the resources of their own incumbents. Following the controversy surrounding the impeachment of President Clinton in 1998–99, House Majority Whip Tom DeLay (R-Texas) created a fundraising plan dubbed ROMP (Retain

Our Majority Program) in which incumbent Republicans donated over $1.5 million to the campaign funds of Republicans who were thought to be vulnerable during the 2000 election cycle. The stated goal of ROMP was to insure that vulnerable incumbents had enough money to "scare off potential challengers." Democrats instituted a similar program in 2004 called Frontline, which sought to funnel money from members in safe seats to endangered Democratic incumbents. In attempting to keep their newly expanded majority beyond the 111th Congress (2009–2010), the Democratic party had already identified 21 endangered incumbents for the Frontline program by February of 2009 – more than 19 months ahead of the 2010 election!

The flip side of contributions is expenditures. Figure 3.3 shows the historical record of spending by congressional candidates. The incumbent-challenger spending ratio increased from 1.5:1 in 1978 to 3.7:1 in 1990 for House races and from 1.9:1 to 2.1:1 in Senate races for the same years. By the year 2000, challengers improved their competitiveness, reducing the ratio to 2.2:1 in House contests and 1.6:1 in Senate contests, but in both 2004 and 2006 the ratios were over 4.5. In Senate campaigns, the gap between incumbents and challengers has grown, but generally it is not quite as large as the gap for House campaigns. Expenditures by open-seat candidates for the House show increases that parallel those of incumbents. In fact, open-seat candidate spending consistently runs ahead of incumbent spending. Without an incumbent to scare away candidates, open seat races tend to attract quality candidates and stimulate more spending on both sides.

The fundraising capacity of incumbents gives them a tremendous advantage over challengers. Indeed, incumbents now raise large sums early to deter potential opponents from entering the next race and to protect against unforeseen challenges. Incumbents' emphasis on deterrence and risk avoidance is evidenced in their efforts to raise far more money than they end up spending. These surpluses, along with fundraising efforts initiated just after an election, give the incumbents a huge – and growing – head start on any potential challengers for the next election. Figure 3.4 shows just how costly it has become to defeat a House incumbent. In 2000, the average winning House challenger spent approximately $750,000, but by 2006 that number had more than doubled to $1,800,000 – an increase of more than $1 million!

Candidate Quality

Congressional elections are primarily contests between local candidates, each of whom has a mix of personal and political attributes that influences voters' evaluations of them. If one party fails to field a quality candidate, or

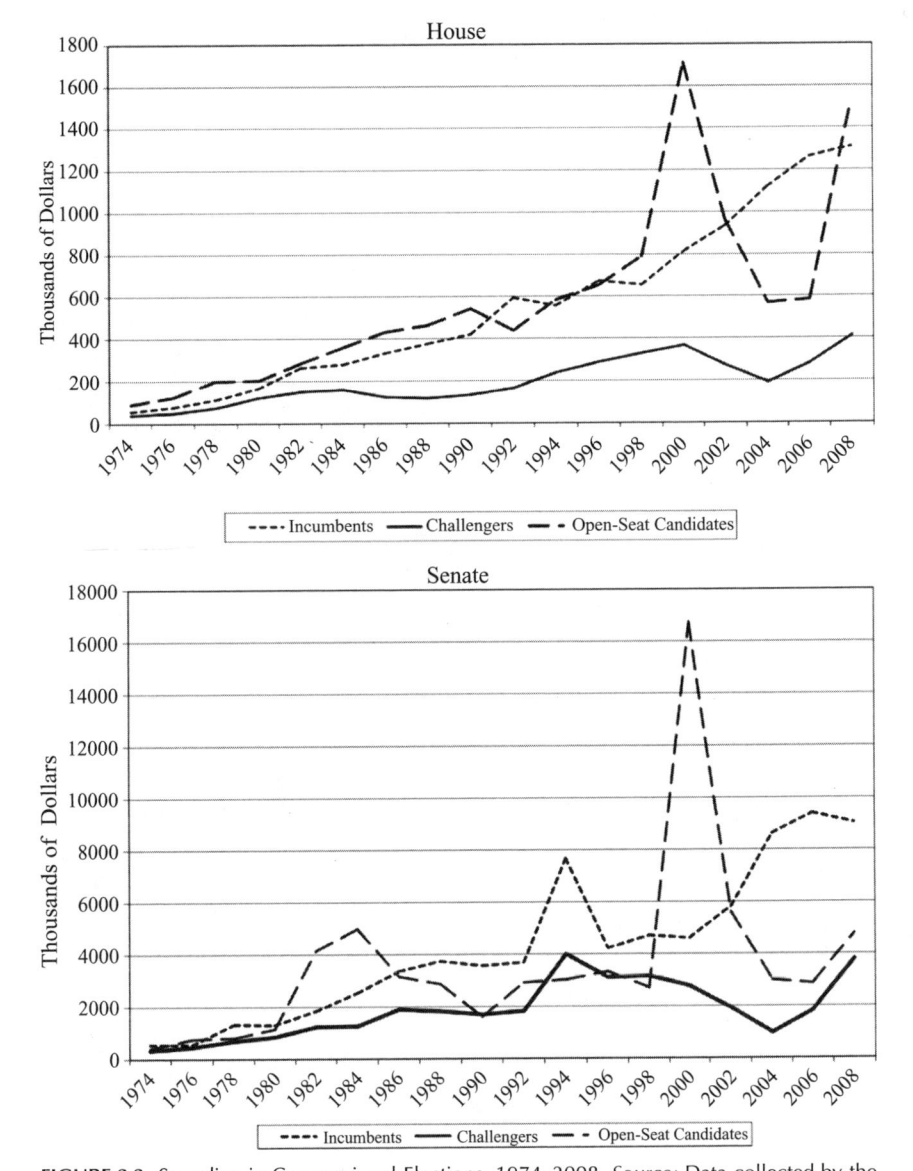

FIGURE 3.3. Spending in Congressional Elections, 1974–2008. *Source:* Data collected by the authors from FEC data and the Center for Responsive Politics.

perhaps any candidate at all, the other party is greatly advantaged. In fact, candidate quality, as measured by candidates' previous political experience, is strongly related to electoral success for both challengers and open-seat candidates. Members of Congress have always known this.

Declining quality among challengers may underpin incumbents' increasing margins of victory in recent decades. Over the past four decades, the

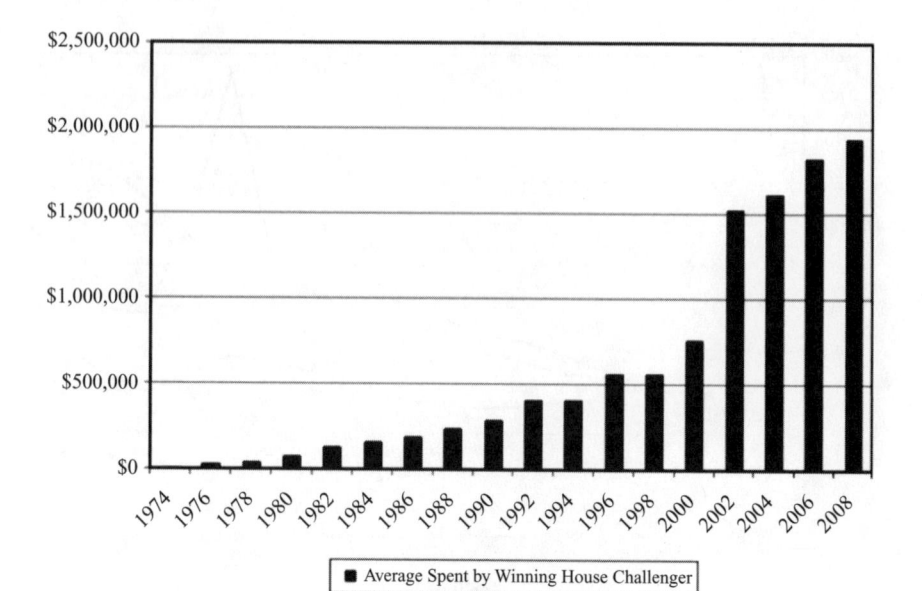

FIGURE 3.4. Average Spent by Winning Challenger, 1974–2008. *Source: Opensecrets.org.*

quality of challengers has declined, which may be a partial explanation for the growth of incumbent vote margins. Contributors, quite naturally, may have been less willing to give money to candidates who seemed unlikely to win. The party with the best set of challengers typically does a much better job of winning elections in the aggregate. Republicans attracted far more quality candidates to challenge Democratic incumbents in 1994, when they dislodged the Democrats as the majority party, but Democrats were able to turn the tables on them in the 2006 and 2008 election cycles.

The record in House open-seat contests, in which no incumbents are present to scare off potential opponents, is very different. In recent decades, the quality of open-seat candidates in general elections has improved. By one estimate, the number of high-quality, open-seat candidates (those with experience in elective office) has nearly doubled since the 1950s. This pattern, which contrasts sharply with the pattern for challengers, helps explain why open-seat races have become more competitive as races between incumbents and their challengers have become less competitive.

Contact with Voters

Incumbents' increasing advantage appears to be the product of several mutually reinforcing developments in the electorate's partisanship, incumbents' resources and behavior, campaign finance practices, and the decisions of potential candidates. Note also that scholars have eliminated several other possible explanations for incumbents' increasing vote margins.

The incumbency advantage, the competitiveness of open-seat elections, and House-Senate differences are all revealed by patterns in voters' contacts with candidates. Voters have somewhat more contact with small state Senate incumbents than with House incumbents, but the big difference lies between House and Senate challengers. Voters report far less contact with House challengers than with most Senate challengers, reflecting the vast difference in visibility and campaign resources for challengers at the two levels. In fact, Senate challengers do not lag much behind Senate incumbents in voter contact. One reason for this is the notoriety of many Senate challengers. People of wealth, celebrities, and well-known politicians make up a larger proportion of Senate challengers than House challengers. Many Senate challengers simply have a head start on their House counterparts.

The form of voter contact for which incumbents enjoy the biggest advantage over challengers is contact through the mail. This is true of both House and Senate incumbents, which suggests that incumbents' franking privilege and funding for mass mailings give them an important edge over the competition. Open-seat candidates have more contact with voters than do challengers, but have less contact than do incumbents. This is expected. After all, in comparison with challengers, open-seat candidates tend to be better qualified, more familiar to voters, and more successful at raising campaign funds. For the same reasons, Senate open-seat candidates are more successful than House open-seat candidates in reaching voters.

National Patterns in Congressional Elections

Although the local candidates and their personal and political characteristics are the major determinants of congressional election outcomes, national forces appear to be an influence worth at least several percentage points in some congressional races. Such a small effect may seem quite unimportant, but it is more than enough to determine the outcome in many close contests. The state of the national economy, the public's evaluation of the president's performance, and the public's tendency to be conservative are typically strongly related to which party is most successful in congressional elections. When the economy is weak, the president's performance ratings are low. When the public mood is out of sync with administration policy, candidates of the incumbent president's party are less successful. By influencing the outcome in at least a few races, such forces can shape the partisan and ideological balance in the House and Senate.

National forces may be felt in congressional elections in several ways. Voters and financial contributors sometimes reward or punish congressional candidates for national conditions. To the extent that they do, potential candidates have reason to assess the odds of winning. In any given year, potential candidates of one party may decide to stay out of congressional races when conditions do not seem favorable, reducing the pool of quality candidates that the party is able to field. Weak candidates, of course, attract few contributions, build ineffective campaigns, and are not likely to win. Thus, anticipated and actual choices made by voters, contributors, and potential and actual candidates combine to reward the candidacies of the party credited with good times and to punish the party blamed for bad times.

This description of the influence of national forces has one serious weakness: It cannot account for the frequency of divided party control between Congress and the presidency. The influence of national conditions generally pushes voters in the same direction for congressional and presidential elections. To be sure, idiosyncratic factors – a presidential scandal, for example – might occasionally produce a Congress and president of different parties. And yet, in 18 of the 29 two-year Congresses between 1952 and 2008, divided party control existed. All of the Republican presidents in that period served with a Democratic House and, usually, a Democratic Senate. In 1995–2000, Democratic president Clinton served with a Republican Congress.

It turns out that the effects of national forces, including presidential popularity, on congressional elections are not invariant. In fact, important changes have occurred in recent decades.

Presidential Election Years and the Coattail Effect

The "coattail effect" refers to the ability of popular candidates at the top of the ticket to attract voters to candidates of the same party for other offices. The coattail effect is thought by some to be generated by a spillover process – the popularity of the top candidate becomes associated with all candidates from the same party in the minds of voters. Such coattail effects may amount to rewarding all candidates of the same party for good times (or blaming all candidates of a party for bad times). Or perhaps the party of a strong top candidate, whose strength may come from favorable economic conditions, attracts better candidates for lower offices. Conversely, the pull might actually be in the other direction – popular congressional candidates draw support to their party's presidential candidate. Whatever the mechanism at work, coattails, when they exist, have an important consequence: They produce a change in voting in the same partisan direction for presidential and congressional elections, and they encourage the election of a president and congressional majorities of the same party. The best evidence mustered by political scientists indicates that the presidential coattail effect is irregular but has declined since the mid-twentieth century.

The weakened coattail effect is consistent with the expanded incumbency advantage. Incumbents may have been able to insulate themselves from negative public evaluations of presidents of their own party. They do so by working hard to associate themselves with the needs of their local district or state, distancing themselves from party labels, and advertising their personal attributes. How much they can divorce themselves from their party is limited, however, because they are listed with a party label on most state ballots, and challengers work hard to show the connection when it is advantageous to do so.

Midterm Elections

For congressional elections held in the middle of a presidential term – called midterm elections – there is no concurrent presidential contest. Yet for House midterm races, the number of congressional seats the two parties win is predicted well by the state of the economy and the public's evaluation of the president's performance. But candidates of the president's party are not credited or blamed for economic conditions in midterm contests as much as they are in presidential election years, when the choice of a presidential candidate is also on voters' minds. In Senate midterm elections, economic conditions are even more weakly related to partisan seat gains or losses than they are in the House.

Midterm elections are distinctive for two reasons. First, turnout among voters is lower in midterm elections than in presidential elections. Without the stimulus of a highly visible presidential contest, turnout is often 10 to 15 percentage points lower in a midterm election. In recent midterm elections, less than 40 percent of the nation's adult population has voted. Turnover varies widely among states and districts, however, and surges in midterm election turnout are related to the competitiveness of congressional races. Incumbents must be wary of challengers who can stimulate turnout and create uncertainties about the size and composition of the November electorate in midterm elections.

Second, for most of the twentieth century, political scientists could safely predict that the president's party would gain seats in Congress in presidential election years, but lose seats in midterm elections. This pattern held for House seats in every midterm election from 1938–1994 and for Senate seats in all but three midterm elections during the same period. In 1990, for example, the Republicans lost a net of eight House seats and one Senate seat. Between 1946 and 1996, the president's party suffered an average loss of about 24 seats in midterm elections, compared with an average gain of about nine seats in presidential election years.

The election outcomes in 1998 and 2002 bucked this familiar trend. In 1998, Democrats managed to win a net gain of five House seats and lost no Senate seats, whereas in 2002 Republicans gained seven House seats and three Senate seats. The common thread running through both of these elections is that both occurred while the president enjoyed extraordinarily high public approval ratings.

Furthermore, the president's party tends to lose more House seats in the midterm election of the president's second term than in the president's first term. By one estimate, which took into account other factors that influence House elections, the president's party does about twice as poorly in the second term as in the first term. The 2006 election is an excellent example of this as the Republicans, weighed down by an unpopular president, lost 30 seats in the House and 6 in the Senate.

A reasonable explanation of the difficulty confronted by the president's party in midterm elections is the exposure thesis. This thesis holds that the more a party gains in one election above its average or natural level for recent decades, the more seats it is likely to be holding in states and districts that generally favor the other party. The party that gains in a presidential election year becomes vulnerable to losing seats two years later in the midterm election. The number of seats won in the presidential election year that are above the party's average indicates how "exposed" the party will be to seat losses at the midterm. Actual results are influenced by national conditions and the president's popularity.

Congressional Elections and Policy Alignments

Assessing the effects of elections on public policy is tricky. We can never be sure what kinds of policies would have been enacted had the cast of players within Congress and the White House been different. Moreover, some of the factors that influence election outcomes, such as changing public attitudes, directly affect both old and new decision makers and might produce policy changes even if little turnover in Congress occurs. To complicate matters further, we usually cannot determine the policy preferences of members

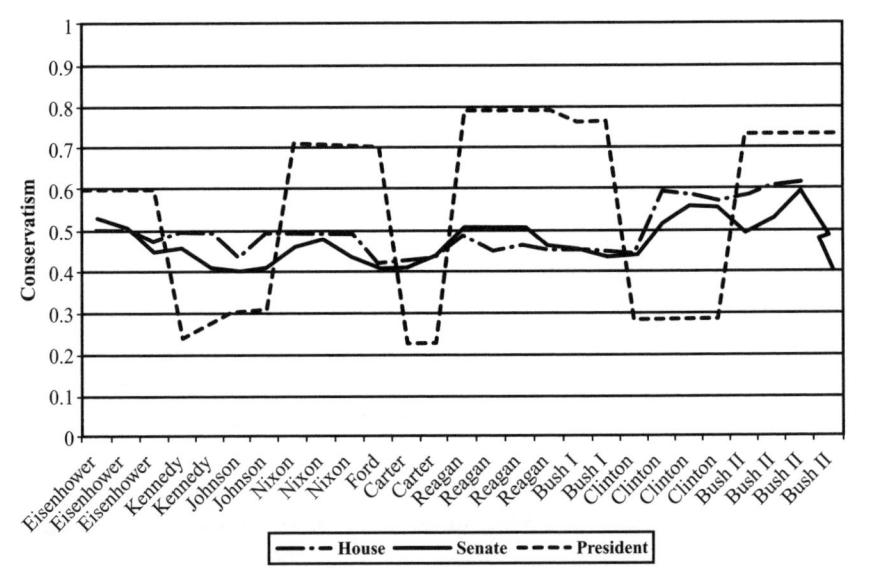

FIGURE 3.5. House, Senate, and Presidential Conservatism, 1955–2008. *Source: Data provided by Keith Poole and Howard Rosenthal,* http://www.pooleandrosenthal.com.

until they cast roll-call votes. This means that we usually cannot distinguish members' policy views immediately after an election from positions they take later on, which are influenced by new events, presidential demands, interest group lobbying, and other political forces.

Even when election results appear to predict future policy directions, there is no simple one-to-one correspondence between election outcomes, the ideological alignment of the three lawmaking institutions, and eventual policy outcomes. For example, the 1986 elections clearly produced a more liberal Senate – Republicans lost eight seats and gave up majority control. But the White House remained in the hands of Ronald Reagan, a conservative Republican president, whose concurrence was required to get liberal legislation favored by Congress enacted into law. Thus, although the Constitution provides the means (elections) for changing the policy views represented in Congress and the White House, it also established rules for the electoral and legislative systems that reduce the chances that changing views will be translated directly and immediately into new public policy.

Ideological Outlook

Figure 3.5 demonstrates the effect of elections on the changing ideological position of the House, the Senate, and the presidency in recent decades.

High scores indicate a conservative outlook, and low scores indicate a liberal outlook. Not surprisingly, the line for the presidency varies widely as it moves back and forth between Democratic and Republican control. Democratic presidents take a more liberal position than the typical member of the House or Senate, and Republican presidents take a more conservative position. In contrast, the ideological positions of the House and Senate are more stable, which reflects the tendency of single elections to produce only a small change in the overall membership of Congress.

The patterns revealed in Figure 3.5 are consistent with what might be expected. During most of the period since the 1950s, all presidents have faced challenges in gaining cooperation from the two chambers of Congress. As we might expect, Republican presidents Nixon (after his first two years), Ford, Reagan, and Bush differed from the Democratic houses of Congress by a larger margin than did Democratic presidents Kennedy, Johnson, and Carter. Republican President Eisenhower, however, did not differ a great deal from the Democratic Congresses that he faced in the late 1950s.

Moreover, the 1980 and 1986 elections, which produced a change in party control of the Senate, are associated with changes in the ideological placement of the Senate relative to the House and the presidency. The Senate became more like the Republican White House after the 1980 elections, although still not as conservative as the administration. After the 1986 elections, the Senate reverted to its usual place, close to the House, with Presidents Reagan and Bush taking far more conservative positions.

The patterns in Figure 3.5 are important because they show that elections shift the ideological alignment of the three institutional players. They indicate that the House and Senate are usually not too distant from each other, and the president is often the outlier. If left to their own devices, presidents probably would produce more radical shifts in policy than they are allowed to do in the three-player game. Nevertheless, important shifts do occur within Congress as well. For example, Congress moved considerably farther away from President Clinton following the 1994 election, leading to a conflict-ridden six years of divided government, while the 107th through 109th Congresses were very sympathetic to President Bush's legislative agenda, whereas the 110th Congress produced two years of acrimony between President Bush and congressional Democrats.

The extended period of divided party control of government under Presidents Ronald Reagan, George H. W. Bush, Bill Clinton, and George W. Bush have rekindled a debate about the policy consequences of divided control of government. Many observers have characterized the period as one of political deadlock: Conservative presidents have checked the initiatives of a liberal Congress, and the liberal Congress has blocked the proposals of conservative presidents (and, under Clinton, vice versa).

Partisan competition exacerbates the already difficult task of gaining agreement among the House, the Senate, and the president. This depiction of the state of American national government has led many critics to recommend radical reforms, so we must know whether it is accurate. Does divided party control of government make any difference?

The Divided-Government Debate

THE MAYHEW THESIS. Political scientist David Mayhew investigated the question of divided control in his book *Divided We Govern*. He examined the frequency of major congressional investigations of the executive branch and the enactment of major legislation for the period between 1947 and 1990. During that period, one party controlled both houses of Congress and the presidency for 18 years and neither party controlled both houses and the presidency for 26 years (including 1981 to 1986, when Republicans controlled the Senate and White House but not the House). He found that "unified as opposed to divided control has not made an important difference in recent times" with respect to either the undertaking of high-profile investigations or the rate at which important laws are enacted. Mayhew concluded that "it does not seem to make all that much difference whether party control of the American government happens to be unified or divided."

Mayhew's somewhat surprising findings call attention to the forces in American politics that lead to cooperation between the House, the Senate, and the president. All three institutions must respond to the same national problems, and they share many constituents. Furthermore, members of Congress and presidents both have strong electoral incentives to establish a positive record of accomplishment. And even if public opinion varies greatly among different congressional constituencies, shifts in public mood, which are produced by changing conditions and events, tend to propel all elected officials in the same direction.

OTHER EVIDENCE. Nevertheless, evidence seems to show that divided party control does make some difference. To make sense of patterns in the direction of public policy over time, we must take into account the ideological distance between the House, the Senate, and the president at specific points

TABLE 3.2. Presidential Success on Roll-Call Votes: The Effect of
Divided Government, 1953–2008.

Unified Government	76.6
	(16)
Divided Government	64.2
	(40)

Percentages reflect average success rates of presidents on roll-calls that they took
positions on. Data collected by the authors from *Congressional Quarterly Weekly
Report*. Number of years indicated in parentheses.

in time. After all, divided control may not always cause a large gap between
the policy positions of the president and the two chambers of Congress,
nor is it true that unified control insures ideological alignment between the
president and Congress. We have seen that ideological distance between the
House, the Senate, and the president is related to party control. In addition, we can examine direct measures of policy agreement and disagreement
among the three institutions. In fact, three such measures – the rate of success for presidential proposals, presidential success on congressional roll-call
votes (see Table 3.2), and presidential vetoes – show the expected differences
between unified and divided control. The president's recommendations are
adopted less frequently under divided party control, the president's position
on roll-call votes wins less frequently, and the president resorts to the veto
more frequently under divided control than under unified control.

Others have pointed out that differences between the president and
Congress are not the only causes of legislative gridlock. Factors such as
the level of consensus between the two chambers of Congress and within
each chamber of Congress, along with the strength of congressional parties
are also important determinates of legislative productivity. Scholars have also
pointed out that many institutional features of the lawmaking process, such
as the bicameral nature of Congress and the two-thirds majority required to
override presidential vetoes, impact the lawmaking process as much if not
more than partisan affiliation of the players.

A fair conclusion is that the party balance in Congress, a direct product of
elections, is an important force among the many different forces that shape
relations between the House, the Senate, and the president. Because party
control is related, albeit imperfectly, to ideological distance, it affects the
degree to which the president's policies are accepted by Congress and vice
versa. Other forces are at work as well, and many of them push the House,

Senate, and president in the same direction even when partisanship divides the three institutional players.

Conclusion

The electoral arena has changed in important ways in recent decades. New laws and court decisions have greatly complicated the rules governing congressional elections and are sure to continue to do so in the coming years. The power of the president's coattails has declined, PACs have blossomed and gained a critical role in financing campaigns, and parties have taken on a greater role in financing campaigns. Campaigns have become more candidate-centered and less party-oriented, with candidates often spending large sums of their own money to gain a seat. Perhaps most importantly, congressional incumbents, particularly House incumbents, have gained important advantages over challengers.

Although congressional elections are primarily contests between local candidates, they have had critical national consequences. Time and again, national conditions and elections have altered the ideological alignment between the House, the Senate, and the president. Since the mid-twentieth century, elections have regularly produced divided party control of government, which has increased conflict between the branches of government and has made it more difficult to assign credit and blame for government performance.

Above: Don Cravins, staff director for the Senate Small Business and Entrepreneurship Committee, speaks to Roll Call in his Russell Senate Office Building office on Thursday, Feb. 5, 2009.
Below: Administrative Assistant Art Estopianan talks with interns, from left, Ashley Hacker, Jenny Urizar and Sara Susnjar in the Washington D.C. office of Rep. Ileana Ros-Lehtinen (FL). (KRT) NC KD 2001 (Horiz) (Ide)

4

Members, Goals, Resources, and Strategies

I N TODAY'S WORLD, WE MAKE SEVERAL REASONABLE ASSUMPTIONS ABOUT
members of Congress. We assume that most of them will seek reelection,
and, if they do not, it is because they are seeking another elective office or
are retiring. We expect that legislators have the ability to get back to their
districts and states on most weekends to attend civic functions and meet
with constituents. We take for granted that legislators can answer the mail,
deal with the government problems of constituents, and address the policy
concerns of House districts that average about 675,000 people and states
that average nearly 6 million people.

These assumptions are fairly accurate, but Congress has not always been
this way. Only in the last few decades have nearly all legislators sought
reelection. In the late 1800s, it was common for two-thirds or less of House
members to run for reelection. Even in the 1940s, two out of 10 legislators
sat out the next election. But in recent Congresses, 90–95 percent of incumbents sought reelection. Moreover, the technology, resources, and staff
required to make frequent trips home and to be responsive to ever-expanding
constituencies are of recent vintage. Since the 1950s, office budgets have
quadrupled and personal staffs have doubled in size.

This chapter looks at Congress from the members' perspective. Legislators
exhibit a range of personal goals, but most modern legislators see politics as a
career and view reelection as essential to the achievement of their goals. Over
time, they have granted themselves the resources to pursue their electoral,
policy, and other objectives simultaneously. Still, legislators do not pursue
all goals all the time, but rather they exploit resources and opportunities
selectively. We will see that there are important patterns and generalizations
that can be made.

Setting Personal Priorities

Legislators have well-established policy attitudes by the time they arrive in Washington for the first time. For example, most of them can be characterized as liberals, moderates, or conservatives, with some variation on specific issues. Those attitudes are the product of many factors – personal experience, a track record in politics, the necessities of the campaign, and so on. In general, therefore, the voting behavior of most members is quite predictable. And yet members face many decisions for which their general ideological outlook offers little guidance – how to vote on hundreds of roll-call votes on narrow issues, which committee assignments to request, how to allocate staff, which issues to emphasize, and how much time to spend in Washington versus the home state or district. Members' choices about these matters mold their legislative careers.

Members have wide latitude in setting their personal priorities and choosing strategies for pursuing their goals. No party leader or president dictates how members vote, what issues members pursue, how much time members spend in their home districts and states, or how members organize their staffs. To be sure, members are subjected to pressure from leaders, presidents, and many other people and groups, but members of the modern Congress are remarkably free to shape their priorities and determine their own strategies.

There is a catch. Time, staff, and budgets are limited so members must exercise care in allocating their resources. New members face the most difficult choices. They must worry about organizing a staff, selecting and arranging new offices, requesting committee assignments, and responding to appeals from senior members competing for leadership posts – all while trying to find a place to live in a new city. Members do these things with incomplete information. In requesting committee assignments, for example, a member might like to know the career plans of committee and subcommittee leaders: Whether they plan to retire soon or to run for higher office will affect how quickly the member might rise to chair a committee or subcommittee. In hiring staff, a member might like to know what issues will be hot in the coming years so that he or she can appoint people with relevant expertise. In nearly every aspect of setting priorities, a member would like to know who future opponents are likely to be and whether economic and world conditions will favor his or her party. And most members would like to know if and when opportunities to run for higher office will arise. With the passage of time, members gradually resolve some uncertainties, acclimate themselves to others, and settle into routines that reflect their personal priorities, campaign experience, and style.

Members' Goals

Members of Congress tend to be quite purposeful in their professional activities as elected officials. Most of what they do as legislators is connected to some goal or goals – political scientists would label this *instrumental* behavior. They do not always articulate their goals, but they usually can explain how particular decisions affect their own political objectives. Moreover, they usually see connections between their goals and what they do every day. They try to use their limited resources effectively, if not always efficiently, and consciously move toward achieving their personal political goals. To be sure, not every move is calculated, but members generally think and act in ways that make it reasonable to characterize them as strategic politicians.

What are members' goals? For our purposes, focusing on the political goals that members mention when explaining their many decisions makes sense. Political scientist Richard Fenno, in studying differences among members sitting on different committees, found that three categories – reelection, good public policy, and influence – accounted for most of the goals expressed by members.

Reelection

Members of Congress are like the rest of us – most of them want to keep their jobs. They gain personal satisfaction from making contributions to public policy and serving the interests of people they care about, as well as from the prestige of holding high public office. Perhaps a few members like the income, have a craving for power, enjoy the attention given to them by lobbyists and others, or simply like to see themselves on television.

Members face a test for retaining their jobs that most of us do not. Periodically, at times fixed by law, they must seek the approval of a very large number of citizens they do not know personally. The opinion voters hold of their representatives and senators can turn on factors beyond the members' personal control. And campaigning, even for members who have won by wide margins in the past, involves a large commitment of time, money, and energy. Most of the rest of us do not face such an extraordinary test to retain our jobs once we have established a career.

We should not be surprised that many, if not most, members make obtaining reelection a high priority in their daily activities. In the view of critics, members care too much about reelection. Some critics assert that members ignore the general welfare of the country while pursuing the narrow interests of financial contributors, the special interests of organized groups, and the parochial interests of their home constituents. Furthermore, critics contend that the reelection drive has become more intense in recent years. Supporters of term limits, in particular, claim that members have become obsessed by reelection, have become excessively insular in their political outlook, and have built up staffs and perks – the resources that come with their office – that virtually ensure their reelection.

Even scholars often assume, at least for the sake of argument, that members are single-minded seekers of reelection. And for good reason: In recent decades nearly all members of Congress seek reelection, and much of what members do is best explained by the drive for reelection. Requesting assignment to committees with jurisdictions affecting their constituents, introducing popular legislation, winning federal funds for projects in their states and districts, solving constituents' problems with federal agencies, evaluating legislation for its impact on their constituencies, and soliciting media attention are common activities that members pursue to enhance their chances of reelection. Political scientist David Mayhew neatly summarized these activities as credit claiming, position taking, and advertising. And political scientist R. Douglas Arnold has shown how congressional leaders take into account the electoral calculations of members when designing strategies for building majority coalitions.

Still, great care must be exercised in declaring reelection to be the sole motivating force of congressional action. Reelection is probably better viewed as a means to an end rather than as an end in itself. As we see it, people seek election and reelection to Congress primarily because they value membership in Congress in some way. If other goals were not served by membership, or if running for office were too onerous, few people would make the effort. Those other goals, whatever they may be, surely influence members' daily activities as well.

Moreover, reelection plays little role in many decisions and activities of members of Congress. Many committee and floor votes have no consequences for reelection, and actively advocating legislation and building coalitions involves much activity that is unseen and unappreciated at home. David Price, a political scientist and a Democratic representative from North Carolina, explains that "most members of Congress, most of the time, have a great deal of latitude as to how they define their roles and what kind of job they wish to do. If they do not have the latitude, they can often create it, for they have a great deal of control over how their actions are perceived and interpreted."[1]

One way a member gains latitude is to earn the trust of constituents. Political scientist Richard Fenno observes that trust is earned only over time, as a member's constituents come to see him or her as qualified, as a person who

---

Congressionally Speaking . . .

The *pork barrel* is the term used in politics for local projects funded by Congress. The term is thought to originate in the pre-Civil War practice of serving slaves salted pork in large barrels. When the pork barrels were set out, slaves would rush to grab as much of the pork as possible. In the early twentieth century, journalists began to comment that members of Congress behaved similarly in an effort to distribute pet projects to their constituents.

Each year Congress approves funding for hundreds of local projects ranging from a university building to a youth center to a new dam or bridge. Legislators take credit for the projects by issuing press releases, including stories in their newsletters, and appearing at ground-breaking and opening ceremonies. As nonpartisan public works, almost everyone at home appreciates the "pork" projects and the legislators' efforts, a perfect combination for legislators eager to please voters.

Earmarks are provisions in bills or committee reports that direct funding to individual projects. In 2007, the House and Senate passed rules changes to reform earmark practices. As a result, both chambers now require committees and other sponsors of legislation to list earmarks and their sponsors in accompanying reports. Moreover, the chambers compel members to certify that they do not have a personal financial interest at stake in an earmark they sponsor. In 2009, the House also passed a rule prohibiting appropriations conference committees from inserting additional earmarks.

---

identifies and empathizes with them, and as someone who can defend his or her actions in Washington credibly. In seeking to develop such trust, members develop distinctive "home styles," tailored to their own personalities and skills as well as to the nature of their constituencies.

For one member of the House, Barney Frank (D-Massachusetts), wit has become a trademark. During his reelection campaign of 1992, a year in which a large number of members retired from office, Frank wrote a letter to supporters saying that

> I feel somewhat apologetic about what I am going to tell you: I do not plan to quit Congress. As I read the praise which the media lavishes on my colleagues who are retiring, I'm afraid my eagerness to keep working on a broad range of public policy issues may be taken as a character defect. So I hope that as character defects go, this one will be considered sufficiently minor for you tooverlook.[2]

Apparently, it was. Frank was reelected in 1992 with 72 percent of the vote and has been reelected every two years since then.

Nearly all members of Congress seek reelection, so it is reasonable to assume that concern about reelection plays a part in many, if not most, decisions that legislators make. Because it is a goal that must be achieved periodically if a legislator is to continue pursuing other goals in public office, it is not too surprising that reelection dominates all other considerations. Yet for most members, reelection does not explain everything.

Good Public Policy

Among the other goals members pursue is to make good public policy. The cynics are wrong: Most, if not all, members care about the country's future. Many members come to Congress with preexisting policy interests and often are deeply committed to certain policy views. These commitments influence members' committee preferences, staffing decisions, and legislative activities.

A good illustration of a legislator's background shaping his or her legislative interests is Representative Carolyn McCarthy (D-New York), who has developed a national reputation as a staunch advocate of gun control. In 1993, McCarthy's husband was killed and her son seriously injured by a gunman on the Long Island Railroad. When McCarthy's representative, Dan Frisa (R-New York), voted against a federal ban on assault weapons, she decided to run for office. Despite being a lifelong Republican, she ran under the Democratic label in 1996 and won by a decisive margin. Since her initial election to office, McCarthy has fought for stricter gun control laws. She has sponsored or cosponsored dozens of bills proposing more stringent regulation of guns and ammunition. She has won reelection six times – most recently with 64 percent of the vote in 2008.

Political scientists have shown that personal experience motivates involvement in the legislative process. For example, studies demonstrate that African American members of the House of Representatives devote more legislative effort to the issues that are particularly important to African Americans even when the composition of their home districts is taken into account. Similar findings are reported for women, although, on the whole, their behavior is not as distinctive as African Americans in Congress. More casual observations about other groups – farmers, veterans, business leaders, and so on – are made with some frequency, too.

Many legislators acquire policy interests, sometimes quite accidentally, while serving in Congress. It could hardly be otherwise. Members are introduced to many subjects in the process of listening to constituents, sitting through committee hearings, and discussing issues with colleagues, staff, and outside experts.

Political Influence

Many members also want political influence. Influence may be an end in itself, or it may be a means for pursuing certain policy goals, constituency interests, or even reelection. Most members try to develop a base of power within Congress so that they have more influence than other members do.

Influence can be acquired in many ways, but earning formal party and committee positions is particularly important in Congress. Party and committee leaders often enjoy certain procedural prerogatives and additional staff, both of which may give them an edge in influencing policy outcomes. Members striving for broad influence pursue party leadership posts by first seeking appointment or election to low-level party positions, in the hope of gaining a top post in the future. Holders of committee and subcommittee chairs also are advantaged, at least within the jurisdiction of their committees and subcommittees. Members also might try to gain a seat on committees with broad and important jurisdictions, such as House Appropriations and Ways and Means. Because the work of these types of committees is important to all members of Congress, and many special interests, a spot on one of them puts a member in a position to help fellow members. As Representative Norm Dicks (D-Washington) described the House Appropriations Committee, "It's where the money is. And money is where the clout is."[3]

Serving Constituents

Many members feel a strong obligation to look out for the interests of their home constituents, even when doing so has little effect on their reelection prospects or when there is little connection between their constituents' needs and their own policy interests. Political scientists have sometimes called the duty to behave in accordance with the wishes of constituents the delegate role. The delegate role is often contrasted with the trustee role, in which the member exercises independent judgment about questions of public policy. Of course, members seldom make a conscious philosophical judgment about whether to act as a delegate or as a trustee. For many members, behaving as a delegate comes naturally, at least on many issues. After all, most members grew up in the districts or states they serve. They often identify and empathize with their constituents, and believe that their constituents deserve good representation. But because their constituents have opinions about only a small fraction of the many policy questions Congress must confront, every member must behave like a trustee much of the time, no matter how committed he or she is to serving constituents' interests.

Political scientist Christopher Cooper and Representative Daniel Lipinski (D-Illinois), a former professor of political science, suggest that members strategically communicate their dedication to the delegate role. Using rhetoric, members signal to constituents the extent to which they are acting as a delegate or trustee, although the rhetoric may not be an accurate depiction of their legislative behavior. The use of this rhetoric for this purpose appears to be systematic. Members are more likely to emphasize the delegate role when they are in their first term or when they represent a district that contains a large percentage of blue-collar workers, senior citizens, or friendly partisan voters – groups that appear to prefer a more home-oriented form of representation.

Not all constituents are of equal importance to members. It goes without saying that virtually every member would prefer a happy constituent to an unhappy one, but members know that they are choosing which constituents to give priority to when they select their committee assignments, set their personal policy emphases, and cast votes on divisive issues. Members naturally give priority to constituents who supported them when they were forced to make tough choices, and this makes it difficult for the outside observer to distinguish between members who are genuinely committed to their constituents' interests and members who are motivated by reelection alone.

Higher Office

Higher office is on the minds of many members of Congress. They may not see their current position solely as a stepping-stone to higher office, but many members are clearly ambitious. In 2008, for example, 9 sitting House members left their seat to run for higher office. This number is particularly low in part because there were only 11 gubernatorial races, and only three of those races were open seats. Despite this, the number of House members that pursue higher office is quite large when we aggregate across several congresses. For instance, by one count, a total of 225 House members ran for the Senate between 1960 and 2008. Moreover, this surely understates the number of members with progressive ambition over this period of time. Counting only those that ran for higher office overlooks the potentially sizeable number of members who desired higher office but made the strategic decision not to run, at least for the time being. Table 4.1 details the political background of members of the 111th Congress (2009–10). Progressive ambition is quite apparent. In both chambers, the vast majority of members bring to their current positions experience in elective office. Nearly half of

TABLE 4.1. Highest Previous Elective Office of Representatives and Senators, 111th Congress (2009–2010).

	Previous Elective Office						
Current Office	U.S. Representative	U.S. Senator	Governor	State Legislator	Mayor	Other Elective Office	Percent with Previous Elective Office
House of Representatives[a]	–	0	1	214	15	54	65.6
Senate[b]	47	–	10	8	3	15	83.0

[a] At time of writing, Illinois district 5 and New York district 20 remain vacant.

[b] At time of writing, the Minnesota Senate seat is being contested.

Source: Congressional Biographical Directory. Coding done by authors.

all senators previously served in the House. And ambition does not stop with the Senate: For the general elections between 1960 and 2008, 29 of the 52 major-party candidates for president and vice president had served in the Senate.

Several factors contribute to a member's decision to run for higher office – comparative value of the higher seat to the current seat, probability of winning the higher seat, and cost of running for the higher seat. The relative value of seats is an important aspect in any member's decision to run for higher office, and it is often visible in Senators' determination whether to run for governor. Incumbent senators seldom run for small-state governorships but are more inclined to run for large-state governorships. The probability of winning is a factor that is frequently illustrated after the redistricting of House seats. House members who find their district lines changed radically anticipate that gaining reelection to their seat may be difficult and often choose to run for higher office.

Legislating

The work of legislating seems to have an intrinsic appeal to many legislators. The legislative game can be fun. Formulating strategies, mastering complicated issues, learning the complexities of the policy-making process, building majority coalitions against talented opponents, making a lasting contribution to public policy, and associating with other bright and energetic people appear to motivate many members. Former senator Dan Quayle (R-Indiana) is a case in point. A close observer of Quayle reports that "in recounting his first year's activities [as a senator] he exuded enthusiasm for legislative work in general. 'I had fun on all of them,' he said after canvassing his first-year interests. 'There was no one highlight. The highlight is getting involved and accomplishing a whole lot of things.'"[4]

Multiple Goals

Most members appear to be motivated by more than one goal. In fact, much of what they do is consistent with pursuing several goals. After all, the more goals served by a particular activity or decision, the more valuable it is likely to be. For example, using a committee hearing to draw attention to a policy problem and to oneself may simultaneously further a member's reelection chances, prospects for higher office, and public policy objectives. Furthermore, the media attention generated by a hearing may help influence colleagues' views about the member's intelligence and leadership ability as well as their views on the issue at hand.

Members can pursue a multifaceted strategy to avoid having to select among competing goals. For example, Senator Sherrod Brown (D-Ohio), an educator prior to entering politics, sought an assignment on the Agriculture Committee, which has jurisdiction over farm programs important to large parts of his state, but also gained a seat on the Health, Education, Labor, and Pensions Committee, where he can pursue issues of personal and national interest.

With limited time, money, and staff, members often face making tradeoffs among goals. Generally, representatives face more severe tradeoffs than senators do. With fewer committee assignments, a smaller staff and office budget, and a shorter term of office, representatives must carefully allocate resources among the various activities they would like to pursue. Fortunately for them, over the past few decades, all members have benefited from an expanding base of resources.

Members' Resources

Pursuing goals requires resources. A member's most important resource is the power to vote – in subcommittee, in committee, on the floor, or in conference. Members also have many nonprocedural resources. As managers of numerous offices – personal, committee, and perhaps even party offices – with their sizable staffs and budgets, members might even be thought of as heading small political enterprises.

Over the long term, a member's resources may expand. As a legislator takes on more important party or committee leadership positions, he or she will gain more influence and additional budget and staff support. Because many committee leadership posts are allocated on the basis of seniority, these additional resources are acquired by winning reelection repeatedly. In this way, the value of a House or Senate seat – to the member and to home constituents – increases with time.

Personal Office and Staff Allowances

For the first time in 1893, the House voted to permit the use of government funds to hire personal staff assistants. Until then, members either paid for assistants with their own funds or relied on family members, usually wives and daughters. Even committee aides were rare until the mid-nineteenth century. Only after office buildings were built adjacent to the Capitol early in the twentieth century did rank-and-file members acquire personal offices. Before then, only top party leaders and committee chairs were given separate rooms in the Capitol.

In the modern Congress, a spending bill for the legislative branch is passed each year. It specifies a certain amount of money for members' personal offices. In recent decades, members in both chambers have been given more discretion over the use of these funds. In 1987, the Senate adopted reforms that consolidated senators' office and staff allowances into a single, fungible account called the Senators' Official Personnel and Office Expense Account (SOPOEA). Whereas the previous system limited the portion of a senator's total personal budget that he or she could allocate to staff or office expenses, the reforms lifted those constraints. Senators now receive a single allowance from which they can determine the mix of resources that best suits their needs. In 1996, the House followed the Senate's lead by putting into place the Members' Representational Allowance (MRA) system. Prior to the MRA, members were required to pay for resources from three separate accounts – the clerk-hire allowance, the official expenses allowance, and the official mail allowance. The MRA puts these allowances under a single, flexible account, and permits members to interchange funds freely.

Although members in both chambers have a single account, the different needs of the members require that components of the accounts be calculated separately. In the House, members are allocated identical amounts for personnel, and are entitled to hire up to 22 employees – 18 full time and four part-time. That limit is up from eight in 1955, 10 in 1965, and 18 in 1975. Although there are a few restrictions on how office funds may be used, representatives are largely free to allocate staff as they see fit. Members adopt a wide range of strategies in choosing staff (see Table 4.2). The office and mailing expense components of the account vary from member to member depending on a variety factors, such as the cost of traveling to his or her district from Washington, long-distance phone costs to the district, and the cost of renting office space in the district. In calendar year 2008, the MRAs ranged from $1,299,292 to $1,637,766.

In the Senate, there is no explicit limit to the number of staff aides a senator can hire. Personal staff funding varies according to state population. Senators from large states have funding to hire many more staff assistants than do senators from small states. In addition, each senator receives an equal amount of funds above the clerk-hire allowance for the hire of three legislative assistants. Senators also have an official expense allowance to cover office, telephone, travel, and mailing costs. This allowance varies from

TABLE 4.2. Frequency of Staff Titles in Personal Staff Offices and Location of Staff, 2006.

Position title	Mean number per office	Typical location of staff member
Chief of Staff	1.00	Capitol Hill Office
Counsel	0.05	Capitol Hill Office
Legislative Director	0.78	Capitol Hill Office
Senior Legislative Aide	0.55	Capitol Hill Office
Legislative Assistant	1.28	Capitol Hill Office
Legislative Correspondent	0.55	Capitol Hill Office
Office Manager	0.33	Capitol Hill Office
Press Secretary	0.68	Capitol Hill Office
Executive Assistant	0.23	Capitol Hill Office
Scheduler (D.C.)	0.36	Capitol Hill Office
Systems Administrator	0.13	Capitol Hill Office
Staff Assistant (D.C.)	0.68	Capitol Hill Office
Staff Assistant (District)	0.60	District Office
Constituent Services Representative	1.80	District Office
District Director	0.56	District Office
District Scheduler	0.27	District Office
Field Representative	0.80	District Office
Grants and Projects Coordinator	0.14	District Office

Source: "2006 House Compensation Study," Chief Administrative Officer, U.S. House of Representatives, 2006.

one Senator to another, as it does in the House. In fiscal year 2008, these accounts ranged from to $2,757,743 to $4,416,993.

In addition to their personal staffs, many members enjoy sizable staffs in their capacity as committee leaders – chairs or ranking minority members. Committee staffs are particularly important to senators, nearly all of whom are committee or subcommittee leaders. From time to time, members shift staff between their committee and personal offices in response to changing priorities. The combined personal and committee staffs responsible to a member can be quite large. A large-state senator who chairs a committee can have more than 100 staff assistants reporting to him or her.

The total number of congressional staff workers grew steadily between the 1930s and the 1980s. The 1960s and 1970s marked a period of particularly rapid expansion of personal and committee staff in both chambers. The numbers have remained relatively stable since the early 1980s, as shown in Figure 4.1. The Senate, having a smaller membership, employs fewer total

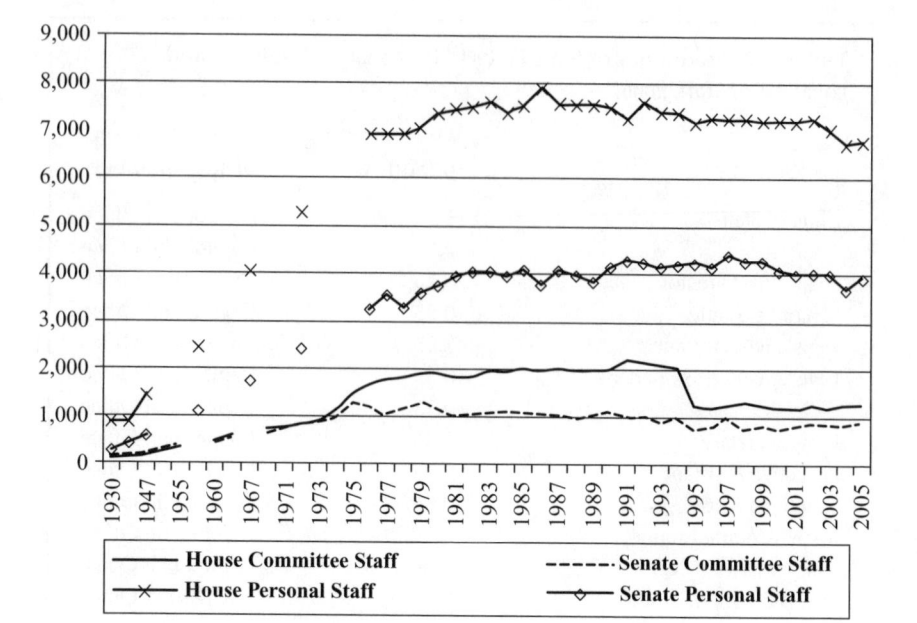

FIGURE 4.1. Number of Personal and Committee Staff in the House and Senate, 1930–2005. *Source:* Norman J. Ornstein, Thomas E. Mann, and Michael J. Malbin, Vital Statistics on Congress 2008. Washington, D.C.: Brookings Institution.

staff, although senators have more personal and committee staff per capita than representatives. In fact, the per capita advantage held by senators is substantial. In 2005, for example, the average senator had approximately 2.5 times more personal staff than the average representative. And the average senator's committee staff was more than three times as large as the average representative's.

One of the first decisions new members face is how to divide their staff between their home and Washington offices. Since the 1960s, as the size of lawmakers' personal staffs has increased, more members have placed staff aides in their home district or state. New members led the way in exploiting larger staff allocations to develop a more visible presence at home. As seen in Figure 4.2, the percentage of personal staff working in district or state offices has gradually increased since 1970. In recent years, approximately half of the personal staff of House members and over a third of the personal staff of senators have worked in district or state offices. Members have shifted more responsibility for constituency service to their home office staffs, allowing their Washington staffs to devote more time to legislative and policy work. Senators, with larger staffs, keep a larger percentage of their staff in Washington.

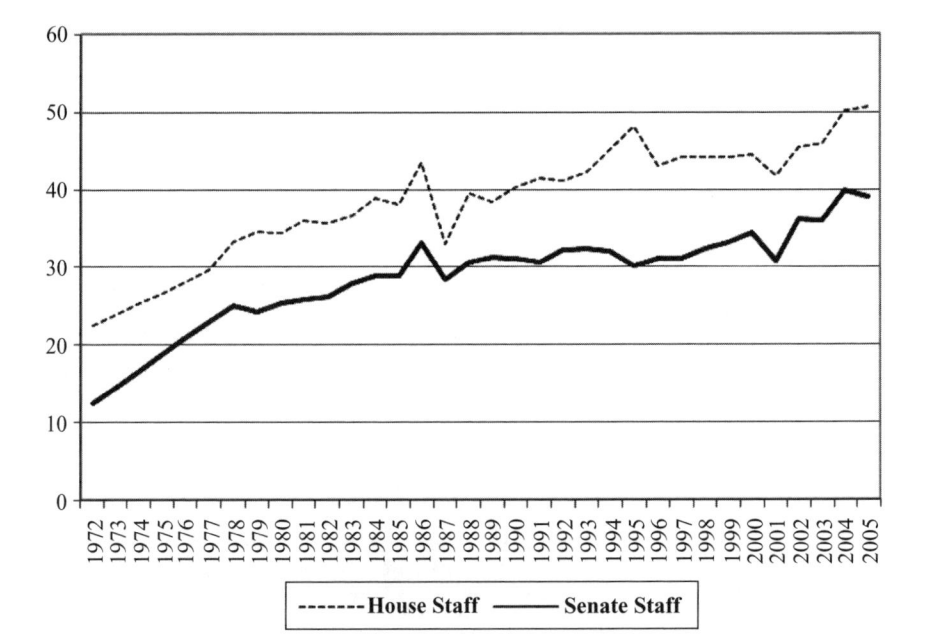

FIGURE 4.2. Percent of Personal Office Staff Located in District or State Offices, 1972–2005. *Source:* Norman J. Ornstein, Thomas E. Mann, and Michael J. Malbin, Vital Statistics on Congress 2008. Washington, D.C.: Brookings Institution.

Enlarged staffs have helped members meet increased demands for casework while at the same time more vigorously pursuing their legislative activities in Washington. Of course, members still differ in how they allocate their staff resources. First-term members seeking to solidify their hold on their seat often concentrate staff in their district. Senior members, who developed their staffing practices when members could not hire as many assistants and now have greater responsibilities in Washington, often are accustomed to having fewer local offices and tend to devote more staff resources to their Washington offices. In the House, a few committee and party leaders focus their personal staffs almost exclusively on constituency service and rely on committee or leadership staffs for their legislative work.

Travel and Recesses

Just as an increase in staff has reduced the severity of the tradeoffs members must make in setting priorities, expanded travel allowances and official recesses have enabled members to spend more time with constituents at home without fear of missing meetings or votes on Capitol Hill. Since the 1960s, the amount of time incumbents spend in their home districts and states has grown steadily. Before 1970, for example, House and Senate members averaged about two or three days per month at home. By 1980, House members were spending an average of about 10 days each month at home, and senators spent an average of six or seven days a month at home, a pace that they have maintained since then. In general, senior members spend less time in their districts, but members of both houses and at all levels of seniority make more trips home during an election year.

Both the House and the Senate have moved to accommodate members' need to travel to their home districts and states. The House, for example, rarely holds votes on Mondays or Fridays. Members are thus free to fly home on Thursday evenings and return to Washington in time for Tuesday votes. Members of the "Tuesday-Thursday club" can maximize their time at home among constituents without great cost to their performance in Washington. Many members of Congress do not even own or rent homes in the Washington area because they spend only two nights a week there. Several legislators have slept in their offices, sometimes for several years, before finding a residence in the D.C. area.

In both chambers, but particularly in the House, the number of official recess days increased significantly in the late 1960s and has remained high since then. In most years, official recesses now consume more than 100 days, not including weekends. The houses compensate for the increased number of recess days by concentrating their sessions into somewhat longer days. For instance, the 110th Congress (2007–08) was in session 52 fewer days than the 88th Congress (1963–64), yet was in session for 1,118 more hours, suggesting that the average workday was extended by approximately 4 hours and 40 minutes between these congresses. No committee markups or floor sessions are held during recesses so members know that they are free to go home.

Congressional Mail

Mail is a resource members use to remain visible in their districts between elections. By placing their signature where a stamp would go on an envelope (the "frank"), members of Congress may send mail through the Postal Service. Congressional offices are given budgets for this specific purpose. Members can maintain a presence at home by sending their constituents franked mail at the taxpayers' expense. Since World War II, the amount of mail sent by House and Senate members has grown steadily. Mail totals surge during election years and then drop in off years, a pattern that reflects members' efforts to advertise themselves as elections draw near.

THOSE NASTY LETTERS FROM CONSTITUENTS[5]

Most famous among the many witty responses that members and their staff have devised for constituents is the standard reply to critical letters of Ohio Representative Wayne Hays:

Dear Sir:
Today I received a letter from some crackpot who signed your name to it. I thought you ought to know about this before it went further.

Some of the increase in mail from Capitol Hill in recent decades is due to an increase in opinion letters from constituents and in requests for assistance from congressional offices (casework). As the population grows and constituencies become larger, legislators must respond by mail to a larger volume of demands. But that's only part of the story. Members more actively solicit opinions and casework in their newsletters and personal appearances – they are happy to be of service to voters. Moreover, most of the increase in outgoing mail is due to the vast increases in mass mailings from members' offices to their home districts and states. In fact, by one estimate, more than 90 percent of the mail sent by Congress consists of mass mailings of newsletters. Critics of the practice frequently cite the use of the frank for campaign-related publicity as an unfair incumbent advantage, and there is some evidence to support their view. Incumbents, on the other hand, argue that newsletters are essential for keeping their constituents informed about members' activities as their representatives. Despite lawsuits that have called into question the constitutionality of the franking privilege, the practice has withstood legal scrutiny.

Other Resources: Party Organizations and Support Agencies

The resources made available to legislators (at public expense) have expanded in many dimensions. A very conspicuous development is the expansion of House and Senate radio and television studios. Legislators use satellite up-link equipment to make appearances on local stations without leaving Capitol Hill. The congressional parties have their own facilities, too. These facilities are used heavily – nearly four out of five House members send regular radio programs to district stations. These programs are aired mostly, if not exclusively, by small-town stations with limited budgets and staff to purchase or produce their own programming. In addition, members sometimes can convince local television stations to use video news releases beamed in from Washington.

The addition and expansion of congressional support agencies (see box, "The Changing Congress") have made more expertise available to members seeking assistance and advice on policy questions. The assistance of policy analysts, scholars, lawyers, and other professionals in the support agencies makes it easier for rank-and-file members without large committee staffs to write bills and amendments, conduct studies, and meet constituents' requests for information.

Members are further aided by the computerization of Capitol Hill. Information networks give members and their staff instant electronic access to the text of bills and amendments, legislative summaries and analyses prepared by the Congressional Research Service, and a variety of databases on economic and social conditions and government programs. Computers also allow members to transmit large volumes of information among their Washington and home offices.

The tremendous expansion of the interest group community in Washington has also bolstered rank-and-file members' access to experts and information. By various counts, the number of lobbyists and others employed by interest groups doubled during the 1970s and 1980s, after having grown substantially in the preceding decades. Interest groups regularly distribute information favorable to their causes and make policy and legal expertise available to friendly members. Think tanks – non-profit organizations that produce studies and policy recommendations – also have expanded the availability of expert advice and assistance.

Influences on Members

Members act strategically. Their actions are not only a product of their own preferences and resources but also the actions and anticipated actions of others. Members care about other political actors – constituents, interest groups, party and committee leaders, presidents, and colleagues – because members rely on these actors to achieve their goals. Similarly, other actors place demands on members of Congress because members have something they want: influence over policy choices affecting them. The nature of the demands placed on members is the subject of this section.

Constituencies

Most members share the perspective of most constituents on important issues. This connection between legislators and their constituents is perhaps

THE CHANGING CONGRESS: CONGRESSIONAL SUPPORT AGENCIES

Congress has created a number of support agencies within the legislative branch to provide a variety of functions that are not conveniently provided by standing committees and their staffs. These units serve as nonpartisan servants of Congress and cost more than a half billion dollars each year.

Congressional Budget Office (CBO). Created in 1974, CBO provides economic forecasts, cost estimates for legislation, and other fiscal policy studies. CBO works most closely with the budget, appropriations, and tax committees and has more than 200 employees.

Congressional Research Service (CRS). Created in 1970 from the Legislative Reference Service, CRS provides policy research in nearly all policy areas and functions as a library reference service. CRS has nearly 700 employees. It responds to requests from committees and individual members and often lends policy experts to committees.

Government Accountability Office (GAO). Created in 1921 as the General Accounting Office, the GAO audits executive branch agencies, sets government accounting standards, settles certain claims against the government, gives legal opinions, and conducts policy studies as requested by formal acts of Congress, committees, and individual members. The GAO was renamed in 2004 (previously the Government Accounting Office) and has approximately 3,300 employees.

After the Republicans gained new House and Senate majorities in the 1994 elections, Congress closed the Office of Technology Assessment (OTA). OTA, with nearly 150 employees, was created in 1972 to provide analysis of scientific and technical issues.

the most important force in congressional politics. It originates in the process by which legislators are selected. Voters tend to favor candidates whose views are close to their own. Liberal, Democratic districts tend to elect liberal Democrats to Congress, just as conservative, Republican districts tend to elect conservative Republicans. As a result, legislators represent their constituencies' views fairly well simply by following their own political dispositions. In this way, legislators' personal views, the views of their constituents, and even partisanship tend to be mutually reinforcing influences on members' decisions.

Nonetheless, constituents' views are an important component of most members' decision-making process. Constituents, and more specifically voters, have something members want: votes in the next election. However, defining a member's constituency can be difficult. After all, the public rarely speaks with one voice and is rarely attuned to what is going on in Congress. Fenno proposes that members perceive constituents in four categories that

MEMBERS' PERCEIVED CONSTITUENCIES

Political scientist Richard F. Fenno, Jr., observes that many members view their constituencies as a set of concentric circles, ranging from their closest political confidants (the intimates) to their strongest supporters in the electorate (the primary constituency), to voters who vote for them (the reelection constituency), to their whole state or district (the geographic constituency). A great source of uncertainty for members is the variable composition of the primary and reelection constituencies.[6]

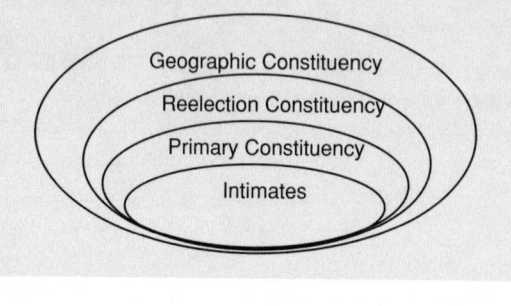

can be conceptualized as concentric circles (see box, "Members' Perceived Constituencies"). A member's strongest political friends (intimates) are at the center, and they are encircled by a larger group of constituents who support the member in primary elections. Next is an even larger group that supports the member in general elections, but whose support is more tenuous. The entire district population stands as the fourth, or geographic, constituency. Fenno observes that legislators develop styles – home styles, he calls them – for relating to each of these constituencies.

Concern about how activities in Washington will play at home often preoccupies legislators. Members have to anticipate whether a roll-call vote or other public action will come back to haunt them in a future campaign. Party and coalition leaders, lobbyists, and presidents seeking support from a member must consider how that member's vote will be regarded back home. All participants know that high-profile issues – abortion, tax increases, social security, and congressional pay raises – always attract a more attentive public, whose views must be considered. On some issues, only a narrow constituency takes an interest, but its interest may be so intense that members are compelled to pay attention to it. On other issues – perhaps, even on most matters that come before Congress – members need not be overly concerned about the electoral consequences of their decisions. Still, the uncertainty of electoral consequences may keep some members guessing about the political costs and benefits at home of their actions.

Representatives and senators have several ways to gauge constituents' opinions. When a particularly controversial issue comes up, a wave of letters, phone calls, and emails is likely to flood members' district and Washington offices. Much of the incoming post takes the form of preprinted letters or cards supplied by lobbying groups. Because it takes little effort to send that kind of mail, legislators may not put much stock in it. Still, members are attentive to groups of constituents with intensely held preferences. In such cases, members usually take note of where the letters are coming from and bear in mind the level of interest expressed.

Members also learn constituents' opinions from interacting with them at home and in Washington. Most members hold town meetings or other forums in their district to give constituents a way to express their views. While at home, attentive members are almost always asking questions of and listening to their constituents. And in Washington, many members schedule regular events, such as weekly coffee, to provide an additional outlet for constituents to voice their opinions. The internet has facilitated the interaction between members and constituents by reducing the need for the two to communicate in person (see box, "Changing Congress"). With increasing frequency, legislators commission public opinion polls with campaign funds, most often at campaign time.

Interest Groups and Lobbyists

For many people, lobbyists and interest groups represent the unseemly, even corrupt, side of congressional politics. "Money talks," "the best Congress money can buy," and "the golden rule of politics – whoever has the gold rules" – are among the clichés that capture common fears about who really runs Congress. Just where the line between legitimate representation and bribery falls is one of the ambiguities confronting every democratic system of government. On the one hand, lobbying is protected by constitutional guarantees of free speech, free association, and the right to petition the government for redress of grievances. Lobbying often involves building support for a position by bargaining, providing assistance to legislators, and even providing timely campaign contributions. On the other hand, lobbying can cross the line into bribery when cash or other material considerations are traded for certain official actions, such as introducing a bill or casting a particular vote. The whole business of lobbying seems tainted to many.

Perhaps the most important change in Washington in recent decades has been the great expansion and fragmentation of Washington's interest group community. The best study of the subject indicates that most interest groups were formed after World War II, that the formation of groups has accelerated in recent decades, and that more and more groups are locating in Washington, D.C. (see Chapter 11). Many single-issue groups have been

THE CHANGING CONGRESS: MEMBERS AND THE WORLD WIDE WEB

The Internet has become an invaluable resource to members of Congress, as it provides a relatively low cost means of interacting with constituents. In addition, it offers members another platform for disseminating an image or message. Member websites have proliferated over a reasonably short period of time. Today, every member of Congress has a website and many of them are quite sophisticated. While there is considerable variation in website features, a common feature is an email form for constituents to communicate with their member.

Not surprisingly, large volumes of e-mail pour into Capitol Hill computer networks every day. Each house receives more than 100 million e-mails directed to legislators' personal offices each year. When email became popular in the 1990s, congressional offices were not prepared to deal with it. Most offices sent automatic responses saying that they could not respond to email, and the writer should send a letter by regular mail. That has changed. According to a 2001 survey of House offices, more than a quarter of members' offices were responding to email with individualized email responses.

Members have even begun to capitalize on the proliferation of social networking websites, such as Facebook, Twitter, and YouTube. Until 2008, there had been a long-standing rule prohibiting members of Congress from posting official communication on websites outside of the house.gov and senate.gov domains, in part because third-party websites may contain advertising and politicking. Led by Representative John Culberson (R-Texas), who openly violated the rule during a 2008 debate over off-shore oil drilling by tweeting "I just learned the Dems are trying to censor Congressmen's ability to use Twitter QuikYouTubeUtterz etc – outrageous and I will fight them," the House and Senate changed their rules to allow members to post communication on external websites provided that the members and the websites themselves abide by certain guidelines. By one count, some 19 senators and 50 representatives post on Twitter. YouTube has also launched *House Hub* and *Senate Hub*, which allow members to create and manage their own channel.

created and nearly every industry group has professional representation in Congress. In the health care industry, for example, the older American Medical Association is joined by associations for hospitals, medical schools, medical equipment manufacturers, health insurance companies, and a variety of professional associations of nurses, dentists, and others.

Particularly noteworthy is the rise of "citizens' groups" or "public interest groups," organized around a general cause rather than a narrow economic interest. Good-government groups such as Common Cause, environmental groups such as the Sierra Club, and consumer product groups such as the Consumers' Union are examples. About one-fifth of all lobbying

groups counted in 1980 were citizens' groups. In addition, more corporations, state and local governments, universities, and other organizations have
established Washington offices for in-house lobbyists. By one estimate, the
number of corporations with Washington offices increased tenfold between
1961 and 1982. One consequence of this expansion in Washington-based
representation of organized interests is that the clout of individual lobbyists
and groups has actually declined. Often, large coalitions of lobbyists and
interest groups pool their resources to overcome the fragmentation in the
interest group community.

Party Leaders

Party pressures in congressional politics are weaker in the United States than
in most other national legislatures. Representatives and senators rarely are
dependent on party organizations – national or local – to secure reelection.
Moreover, party leaders in Congress have relatively few ways to compel
rank-and-file members to comply with their wishes. Indeed, party leaders
generally want their party colleagues to pursue legislative strategies that
will enhance their chances of reelection. When members of a congressional
party vote in unison, it is due more to their shared policy views and similar
constituency expectations than to pressure from party leaders.

Still, partisan pressures are ever-present in Congress. Many decisions
members make have no direct electoral consequences, so members are free
to meet the demands of party leaders. The high level of party loyalty on
procedural matters provides some evidence of this. Moreover, much of the
influence of party on legislators' behavior is indirect. For example, party
leaders set the floor agenda and, particularly in the House, shape the alternatives from which members must choose. But occasionally, particularly on
close votes, the direct pressure of party leaders can be critical. Even then,
the leaders target just a few members whose votes will make the difference
between winning and losing.

The President

Presidents need support from legislators for their own legislative programs,
and they can wield considerable influence in their efforts to gain it. Much
of the support presidents get from lawmakers comes from their partisan ties
to members. Because members' own electoral fortunes are affected by the
popularity of the president, members of the president's party have a stake in
the president's success and thus provide a natural base of support. The size

of that base of support depends on past congressional election outcomes, the diversity within party coalitions, and the president's popularity. Every member must decide when to stick with the president and when it is safe to ignore the president's wishes.

Presidents also influence members' choices by influencing the congressional agenda. By pushing major legislative proposals, presidents can help define the issues that dominate the congressional agenda and how the major alternatives are debated. A successful president draws the attention of the media, the public, and legislators away from issues that hurt him and toward issues that help him. An effective president also knows that his influence over the congressional agenda is tenuous. Presidents, after all, cannot require either house of Congress to vote on their proposals, or even to take their proposals seriously.

The task of presidents is primarily one of persuasion. Presidents have a variety of tools for influencing individual legislators (see Chapter 9). Presidents' primary source of influence is their formal power to sign or veto legislation, which gives them a source of leverage over members who want to see their own legislation enacted into law. Presidents' ease of access to the media gives them an advantage over members and other actors in shaping public opinion. In addition, their influence on agency decisions, which can have widespread implications for policy implementation, gives presidents more clout. That clout can be used to coax interest groups to work in support of presidents' legislative proposals or to prod legislators whose constituents are affected by executive branch decisions.

Staff

A popular theory is that members of Congress have been captured by their staffs. Michael Malbin's book, *Unelected Representatives*, lends credence to this view. Malbin, a political scientist who worked for many years as a Capitol Hill reporter and staff member, argues that "the staffs – individually well educated, hard working, and, in general, devoted to what they perceive to be the public good – collectively create a situation in which many of the elected members fear they are becoming insulated administrators in a bureaucratized organization that leaves them no better able to cope than they were when they did all the work themselves."[7] Malbin observes that staff assistants do a good job of representing their bosses, but, he continues, members delegate to their aides too much authority to initiate legislation, negotiate compromises, and narrow the range of policy choices offered to them. Staff assistants have created more work for members, distanced members from one another, and turned members into office managers. Staff influence is

TYPES OF CONGRESSIONAL STAFF

There are numerous types of congressional staff. Because legislators organize their own office staffs, there is tremendous variation in organization and titles. Some positions (e.g., legislative counsel) are quite rare in personal offices but quite common in committee staffs. Among the most common types of staff positions on Capitol Hill are chief of staff, legislative director (LD), legislative assistant (LA), constituent services representative or caseworker, and legislative correspondent (LC).

The top personal aide to a member is usually a chief of staff or administrative assistant (AA). This position oversees the entire operation and manages all staff. The legislative director supervises the policy staff and typically works closely with the member to devise legislative strategies. Legislative assistants are responsible for the legislator's work on specified policy areas and assist with committee work. Those charged with responding to constituent communications are often given the title of legislative correspondent.

All personal offices have constituent service representatives or caseworkers. These assistants are primarily dedicated to *casework*, the term used to describe constituents' problems that members are asked to solve. Casework ranges from getting a problem with social security checks solved to arranging for a leave for a soldier who just had a death in the family. These assistants usually are located in district or state offices where they can deal with constituents directly. They communicate electronically with federal agencies and the Capitol Hill office. Most legislators consider an effective caseworker essential to building a good reputation.

pervasive: It is felt both in the early stages of the legislative process, in the setting of members' and committees' agendas and at the late stages when the final details of legislation are worked out (see box "Types of Congressional Staff").

Choosing Strategies

Political scientists have no comprehensive theory to explain how members' goals, resources, and political environment combine to produce their strategies. Nevertheless, they have done a reasonably good job of describing and explaining members' behavior in one decision-making arena: roll-call voting on the floor. A newer area of research looks at policy leaders' coalition-building strategies, which focuses on how members solicit support from their colleagues. This section briefly reviews what we know about the typical member's approach to roll-call voting and coalition leadership and contrasts the strategies in these two areas of legislative activity.

Roll-Call Voting on the Floor

Casting roll-call votes is one activity members consider mandatory. Members want a good attendance record so that future opponents will not be able to charge that they are shirking their responsibilities. Maintaining a good attendance record is not easy, and maintaining a perfect record is nearly impossible. In recent Congresses, the average member voted on about 95 percent of the roll-call votes held, which have numbered between 500 and 1,000 per Congress. Plainly, members are forced to cast votes with such frequency that they cannot possibly study each issue with care. Yet, they are aware that they may have to explain a vote to some constituents, perhaps in response to a challenger's charges in some future campaign, or to some party or committee leader. Therefore, most members develop a general strategy for how to approach roll-call voting.

From time to time, members are confronted with particularly difficult choices. There is no question that the Emergency Economic Stabilization Act of 2008, more commonly known as the Wall Street Bailout Plan, put virtually every member of Congress in a very uncomfortable position, especially considering elections were right around the corner. The bill forced members to weigh the possibility of a financial crisis against a hastily constructed bill with a \$700 billion price tag. Voting on the wrong side – voting against a bill that proved necessary or supporting a bill that ultimately failed – would be a political liability. Weighing his options, Senator Judd Gregg (R-New Hampshire) saw little political advantage to being on the winning side of a successful bill, stating "If we do this and it works right, it's most likely that people will never appreciate how close we came to the brink." Despite this, Gregg eventually supported the bill, having assessed that the United States was "facing a crisis of proportions that are almost incomprehensible."[8] Given the grave economic circumstances, he presumably calculated the costs of obstructing the bill to be too great. Clearly Gregg was not alone in considering the electoral ramifications of this difficult vote, as vulnerable members and members representing conservative constituents from both parties were significantly more likely to oppose the legislation.

Political scientist John Kingdon conducted an ingenious study of the vote decision. Kingdon interviewed members about how they had made up their minds on a series of fairly important votes on controversial issues that had been the subject of substantial political activity. Kingdon asked a simple question about each vote: "How did you go about making up your mind?" He then noted whether the members mentioned their constituencies spontaneously, only in response to a follow-up question, or not at all. For

TABLE 4.3. The Frequency with which Legislators Mentioned Political Actors as Factors in Their Voting Decisions (Percent of Voting Decisions).

	Political actors involved in vote decision				
	Constituency	Fellow members	Interest groups	Administration	Party leaders
Mentioned Spontaneously	37	40	31	25	10
Mentioned in response to a question	50	35	35	14	28
Not Mentioned	13	25	35	60	62

Source: Kingdon, John. 1981. Congressmen's Voting Decisions, 2nd ed. New York: Harper & Row.

most members, the votes concerned issues that fell under the jurisdiction of committees on which they did not sit. Thus, most members interviewed by Kingdon had not had the benefit of listening to expert testimony in hearings.

Members' responses to Kingdon's questions show several important patterns (see Table 4.3). First, constituency considerations are frequently involved but are not always the most important factor. Members mentioned constituencies spontaneously 37 percent of the time. While members spontaneously mentioned fellow members more frequently than constituents, constituents ranked above every other group in this category. Members mentioned constituencies in response to probes 50 percent of the time and failed to mention constituencies altogether only 13 percent of the time.

Kingdon also found that the more salient the issue, the more likely members were to consider constituents' wishes to be of major importance in making their decisions. Consequently, they were more likely to vote in agreement with the constituency opinion they identified. Nevertheless, even on issues of low or medium salience, members were likely to give weight to, and vote in agreement with, constituency opinion. On most issues, members rely on trusted colleagues for cues about how to vote. In response to Kingdon's questions about their voting decisions, members mentioned their colleagues either spontaneously or after prompting 75 percent of the time (Table 4.3). As one member noted, "On a run-of-the-mill vote, on an obscure bill, you need some guidance. You don't know what's in it, and don't have time to find out."[9] Fellow members serve as informants who reduce uncertainty about the policy and political implications of a roll-call vote.

With so many staff assistants and lobbyists circulating on Capitol Hill, why do members rely so heavily on one another? Members turn to certain colleagues because they trust that their fellow representatives and senators, professional politicians with problems similar to their own, will make comparable calculations about which course of action to pursue. Indeed, members tend to rely on colleagues from the same party, state, and region – colleagues who can help them assess the political consequences of their votes – and committee members who know the issue well. Fellow legislators also are in the right place at the right time – on the floor as roll-call votes are being conducted.

Members obtain guidance from fellow members in many ways. One way is to read the "Dear Colleague" letters that are routinely sent to all members, explaining bills and soliciting support for amendments. These letters are usually concise arguments in favor of a bill, and they often explain how a bill's opponents plan to distort the bill's true intent. For more detailed information on a bill, members or their staffs are likely to turn to the written reports that accompany most bills when they are reported by committee.

After constituents and fellow members, interest groups and the administration rank as the most important influences on members' voting decisions. Most interest group influence, Kingdon found, came from groups connected to members' constituencies. For example, farm groups played an important role for members from agricultural districts. Presidential influence is greater for members of the president's party – members who are politically connected to the president and have the highest stakes in the president's success.

Finally, party leaders and staff aides appear to have influence only at the margins. In more recent years, party leaders probably have become more important than Kingdon found in the late 1960s, when he conducted his study (Chapter 5 describes the revitalization of party leadership in Congress). Similarly, as roll-call votes have become more numerous, other burdens on members' time have grown, and staffs have expanded in the decades since Kingdon's study. Thus, members may have become more dependent on staff assistants for guidance.

In summary, members adopt strategies in response to the unique character of individual voting decisions. Roll-call voting is repetitive, very public, consumes little time and few resources, is well documented, and is considered politically compulsory. Members rely on cues from colleagues to simplify their decision-making process and assess the political risks of specific votes. Members appear to be heavily influenced by constituency opinion and electoral considerations, which they assess by seeking advice from trusted colleagues and information from interest groups. At the same time, constituency considerations are seldom the sole or even the decisive influence on members' votes.

Coalition Leadership

Serving as a coalition leader on a legislative issue lies at the other end of the spectrum of legislative activities. In contrast to roll-call voting, assuming a leadership role on an issue may not be very visible to the general public, is difficult to document, consumes more time and resources, and is normally discretionary. Consequently, the strategies of policy leaders may be shaped by a different mix of considerations than are voting decisions.

Political scientist David Mayhew observes that the goal of reelection, although nearly universally held by members, motivates little leadership activity within Congress. The effort to mobilize colleagues for or against legislation is worthwhile for a reelection-oriented member only if constituents or important financial contributors are paying close attention to the member's behavior. On most matters, merely advertising one's position and token efforts – citing speeches made, legislation introduced, and amendments offered – may be all that is required to receive maximum electoral benefit from an issue. Certainly, members do not actually have to win legislative battles as long as the people who affect their reelection prospects – people with votes, money, or endorsements – believe they have put up a good fight.

If Mayhew is right, most genuine leadership is motivated by goals beyond reelection. A member aspiring to higher office may seek special distinction and media attention by championing a legislative cause. A committee chair, seeking to preserve a reputation for influence, may assume the lead in writing legislation and soliciting support simply to avoid being overshadowed by a rank-and-file member who would otherwise take over. That same rank-and-file member may pursue a policy leadership role because no one else seems equally committed to his or her policy views.

Senator Pete Domenici (R-New Mexico), who was a prominent legislator in budgeting and fiscal policy, is a good example of a policy leader motivated by objectives beyond reelection. Fenno, in his book about Domenici's rise as a Senate leader, explains:

> From the beginning of his Washington career, Pete Domenici's most transparent goal was to become a policy-making "player" inside the Senate. The chairmanship [of the Budget Committee] brought him that influence. His first two years in that position, he said later, "made me a senator." He wanted to keep or expand the policy influence he had gained. A second goal – institutional maintenance – has been imposed on him by this chairmanship. And Domenici adopted that one, too – to protect and to preserve the budget process itself. The two goals did not always lead to the same decision. . . . In the two years ahead, he would

often be forced to choose between his desire for inside policy influence and his desire to keep the budget process alive.[10]

Domenici's reelection prospects, Fenno recounts, were greatly enhanced by his prominence in the Senate. He won reelection easily in 1984, 1990, 1996, and again in 2002, with vote shares of at least 65 percent.

Domenici's story seems typical in many respects. Electoral concerns did not seem to drive his leadership activity in Washington, even though that activity paid dividends at home. Thus, partly by good fortune and partly by personal skill and dedication, Domenici's multiple goals of obtaining influence, making good public policy, and gaining reelection were served by his leadership activities. And yet his goal of reelection cannot account for the priority he gave to his chairmanship and the legislative tactics he pursued as chairman.

Some relevant evidence about members' goals in pursuing leadership responsibilities is available. In one study, a political scientist asked top legislative aides of a sample of 121 members of both houses to identify issues on which their boss had taken a central leadership role and to offer explanations for their boss's involvement in those issues.[11] All aides reported that their boss had taken a leading role on some issue, large or small. But few members had taken on more than two or three issues at one time. Senators' aides tended to mention more issues than did representatives' aides, reflecting important differences between the two chambers. In the Senate, members have more committee assignments and staff, and they receive more demands from larger, more diverse constituencies.

For each issue the aides mentioned, the researcher asked them, "Why did (Senator/Representative –) take the lead on this issue?" They often mentioned several reasons. For 52 percent of the issues mentioned, they noted the importance of the issue to the member's district or state, although for only 17 percent was reelection or some other constituency-related reason the sole motivation mentioned. For 72 percent of the instances of policy leadership described, the aides mentioned their boss's personal interest or policy commitments as a motivating factor. In addition, 28 percent of the issues pursued by members were related to their responsibilities as committee or subcommittee leaders. Only 3 percent of the instances of policy leadership were described as being connected to a member's pursuit of higher office.

We are led to this conjecture: Leaders – whether they are party, committee, or self-identified coalition leaders – are motivated by more than reelection, whereas their followers are motivated primarily by reelection. Followers, most of whom are not sufficiently motivated to assume a leadership role on most issues, allow their default goal – reelection – to orient their behavior. Of course, if members' reelection prospects seem unaffected by a particular issue, as they often are, they are free to pursue policy positions for other reasons. Nevertheless, it seems fair to say, coalition building on most important issues typically involves interaction between policy- or influence-oriented leaders and reelection-oriented followers.

Concluding that members ignore their reelection interests when they pursue other objectives would be a mistake. On the contrary, members often discover issues that fit them well – issues that allow them to pursue multiple goals simultaneously, including reelection. Indeed, 47 percent of the staff assistants in the study readily identified more than one goal served by their boss's policy leadership activities. Forty-eight percent reported that reelection in combination with some other goal, usually good public policy, motivated policy leadership activities.

A good example of a member who discovered an issue that fit is former senator Dan Quayle (R-Indiana), who was vice president under President George Bush (1989–1992). In the mid-1980s, congressional liberals were pushing legislation designed to reduce the effect of political influence on decisions about the acquisition of military equipment, to introduce more competition into the process of bidding for defense contracts, and to limit the ability of former Department of Defense officials to take jobs in defense industries. Quayle was chair of the Senate Armed Services Subcommittee on Defense Acquisition Policy, so the task of resisting the liberal onslaught and developing legislation acceptable to the Republican administration fell to him. Quayle had become the chair of the procurement subcommittee in 1983 because more senior Republicans had chosen other subcommittee chairmanships.

Two considerations appeared to motivate Quayle's initial eagerness to take on procurement reform. The first was his concern that bad publicity about procurement practices might undermine the nation's commitment to defense spending, which he had worked to increase in the early 1980s. The issue was getting some media attention because of a few highly publicized cases of wasteful defense spending (a $700 toilet seat for a military transport plane, for example). The second was his interest in reinforcing his developing reputation as an effective legislator. He saw an opportunity to assume a leading role on an emerging issue and he took it. Quayle asked the Armed Services Committee chairman, John Tower (R-Texas), to create a task force on procurement, which he then chaired and later turned into a regular subcommittee. Taking the lead and being reasonably successful were important to Quayle for reasons beyond his reelection prospects. He devoted considerable personal time, as well as the time and energy of his senior aides, to the issue.

Quayle soon saw new angles to the procurement reform issue. Developing his own reform legislation was a good way to score political points at home. Quayle also realized that Indiana had a number of defense contractors and subcontractors whose business might be affected by radical reforms. By working to protect Indiana businesses and jobs, Quayle was doing himself a favor. In a press release issued just before the 1986 election, Quayle's press secretary listed eight major accomplishments of Quayle's first term. The seventh was this:

> Senator Quayle had consistently supported the long-overdue strengthening of our national defense to meet the threat to our freedom. The help he has provided Indiana defense contractors and subcontractors in their dealings with Congress and the Pentagon has contributed substantially to the Hoosier State's economic development over the past six years; during that period, Indiana's share of defense procurement dollars has more than doubled – from $1.43 billion in FY 1980 to $3.16 billion in FY 1985. Quayle also succeeded in protecting the jobs of more than 800 federal workers in the drive to reform the Pentagon's purchasing practices to make sure our essential investment in national security is prudently managed.[12]

Pairing support for more defense spending with the procurement reform effort allowed Quayle to deflect Democratic criticism that he and other Republicans were throwing money at defense. The paired issues were mentioned in radio and television ads as well. The procurement issue was not given the highest priority in Quayle's advertising, but he obviously found a way to use his Washington activity effectively at home. In addition, taking the lead on more moderate reforms than those proposed by liberal Democrats yielded an influx of campaign contributions from defense contractors.

Just as important, Quayle developed a personal interest in procurement politics and policies. Mastering procurement procedures, mediating bureaucratic battles within the Department of Defense, and dealing with powerful defense contractors proved challenging. He appeared to develop a personal commitment to devising good reform legislation.

Assuming a policy leadership role, then, is far more discretionary than casting a roll-call vote. In addition, taking a leadership role on an issue requires an investment of resources far in excess of those involved in casting a vote. Members cannot afford to take on more than a handful of issues at a time. Because such efforts may have only small direct electoral benefits and take up time and resources that could be devoted to other activities, the potential value of the effort must be high in terms of policy objectives, personal influence or reputation, or other goals.

Conclusion

In this chapter, we have viewed the legislative process from the perspective of the individual member. Members' goals, resources, and strategies combine to shape their policy positions and political careers. We have seen how those goals, resources, and strategies evolve as a function of members' own choices, changes in members' institutional positions, and the evolution of Congress's political environment.

The roll-call voting and policy leadership examples in this chapter illustrate the two broad political purposes of members' strategies – avoiding blame and claiming credit. Avoiding blame seems to be the dominant situation in roll-call voting. The fact that roll-call voting is politically mandatory creates many hazards for members. Particularly in the House, where individual members have little control over the issues on which they must vote, members must frequently choose between groups of constituents in casting their votes. In contrast, claiming credit is the more dominant motivator in policy leadership. Senator Quayle's experience with procurement reform illustrates how goals, resources, and strategies can be combined opportunistically and give a member more control over the choices he or she confronts.

Since the late 1970s, members' opportunities for policy leadership have declined as budget constraints have limited new policy initiatives. Most members have not been as lucky as Senator Quayle. As a result, members have found that it is more difficult to counter the inevitable criticisms associated with voting by promoting one's own legislative successes. It certainly has contributed to the greater dissatisfaction with service in Congress that members have expressed in recent years and has intensified pressure on leaders to structure floor decision making more carefully.

Above: U.S. Senate Majority Leader Harry Reid (D-Nevada) answers questions from the news media as (L-R) incoming Minority Leader Mitch McConnell (R-Kentucky), Sen. John Ensign (R-Nevada), and Sen. Charles Schumer (D-New York) look on.

Below: Speaker of the House Nancy Pelosi (D-California) receives the Speaker's gavel from Minority Leader John Boehner (R-Ohio) after being elected as the first woman Speaker during a swearing-in ceremony in 2007.

5

Parties and Leaders

E LECTION OUTCOMES OFTEN MOTIVATE CHANGE IN THE ORGANIZATION and strategies of congressional parties. After the 2006 elections, in which Republicans lost seats in the House and Senate, there were important changes in their leadership. In the House, Speaker Dennis Hastert (R-Illinois), who was blamed for excessive partisanship and ineffectiveness in some quarters, quickly announced his retirement from leadership. In the Senate, Senator Bill Frist (R-Tennessee) had earlier announced his retirement from the Congress. Spirited leadership contests followed the elections in which candidates for the Republican leadership offered diagnoses of their party's failings and new approaches to legislating and public relations. The newly elected leaders of the two houses promised joint meetings, a unified communications strategy, and a common legislative program. Republican leaders promised to coordinate their efforts to reestablish an attractive "Republican brand," as one leader defined the task. At the same time, Senate Democratic leader Harry Reid (D-Nevada) created a new post, conference vice chairman, to reward Senator Charles Schumer (D-New York) for leading the Democratic Senatorial Campaign Committee during the 2006 campaign and to bring Schumer into the legislative leadership circle.

Republicans lost additional seats in the 2008 elections and discussion of replacing some leaders resurfaced. Two top House Republican leaders, the whip and conference chair, retired from their posts after it became clear that they would be challenged. Senate Republicans retained their top leaders. In both chambers, Republicans believed that an unpopular president, rather than ineffective congressional leadership, caused their losses in the 2008 elections. Nevertheless, the relatively new Republican leaders clearly were aware that their colleagues expected them to improve their party's image and win back seats in the 2010 elections.

The recent experiences of Republicans are typical of congressional parties throughout history. Unhappiness with the party's popularity, more than
anything else, motivates legislators to seek change in party strategy, organization, and even leadership. And when one party's innovations seem to
be successful, the other party tends to follow. Over time, the two parties in
each chamber of Congress have developed more elaborate organizations –
and they tend to look alike.

In recent years, congressional parties have become more important
avenues of participation for members and their leaders have been more
active in shaping policy outcomes. This chapter considers the nature of
congressional parties, outlines their organization, and describes the activities and resources of congressional party leaders and their organizations.
It concludes with a discussion of the factors contributing to the intensified
partisanship of recent years.

The Nature of Congressional Parties

Congressional parties exist to serve the interests of their members. The Constitution does not mention congressional parties. Just as candidates and their
supporters created electoral parties outside of Congress to effectively compete in elections, legislators created congressional parties to serve their ends.
The four congressional parties (House Democrats, House Republicans,
Senate Democrats, and Senate Republicans) convene separately before each
new Congress begins, and they meet with some frequency while Congress
is in session. No formal joint organization of House and Senate Democrats
or House and Senate Republicans exists, although party leaders of the two
chambers often discuss matters of mutual concern.

Congressional party organizations are independent of the national and
state political parties. Members of Congress have chaired and served in other
capacities on the parties' national committees, but the four congressional
parties have no formal relationship with the national party committees.
Moreover, members of Congress usually are considered important party
leaders in their home districts and states, but they are seldom officials of
their local party organizations. Members' candidacy for office usually is
endorsed by the local party organizations, but, as members know, winning
the party primary, not the endorsement, gets them on the general election
ballot in November. The bond between the local party and an incumbent
representative or senator can be weak. National committees, congressional
party organizations, and local party organizations do not directly control who
is nominated through primaries and eventually elected to Congress. Party

organizations may recruit candidates, contribute money, and offer campaign advice and expertise. They do not have the power to prevent someone from running in party primaries and gaining a seat in Congress.

A reasonable characterization of congressional parties is that they are relatively stable, but loose, coalitions of legislators that exist to serve the common interests of their members. Both electoral and policy interests appear to motivate party activity.

Common Electoral Interests

Members of each congressional party share a party label – a political "brand name." The party labels hold meaning for voters and influence their decisions at the polls, so members of the same party have an incentive to build and maintain a positive reputation for their party. This collective interest encourages legislators to develop party organizations and select party leaders who work to enhance the party's image. Leaders choose issues to emphasize, develop public relations strategies, and work with presidents and committee leaders to shape the content of legislation. They also work more directly to aid election campaigns by raising and contributing money, making appearances at fundraising and campaign events, disseminating information, and playing a role in recruiting candidates. In election years, top leaders spend several weeks traveling to support the electoral efforts of fellow partisans.

By building a favorable party reputation, leaders help their colleagues get reelected and help their party gain and maintain majority party status. A majority party controls committee and subcommittee chairmanships, which legislators covet, has more influence over the agenda, and, with more votes, is more likely to win legislative battles. Electoral failures have caused the defeat or led to the resignation of several party leaders (see box, "Electoral Trouble for Leaders").

Leaders are expected to promote their party's electoral interests, but tensions sometimes arise between leaders and rank-and-file members whose personal or political interests motivate them to vote differently than leaders and other party colleagues would like. Even congressional party leaders, whose job it is to rally support for their party's policy positions, are sensitive to the personal political needs of deviant colleagues. After all, most party leaders would prefer to give a deviant party member some leeway to vote as he or she chooses rather than lose that member's seat to the other party. Imperfect support for party positions is the typical pattern for most members. These differences in members' home constituencies are an important source of conflict over party strategy within all congressional parties.

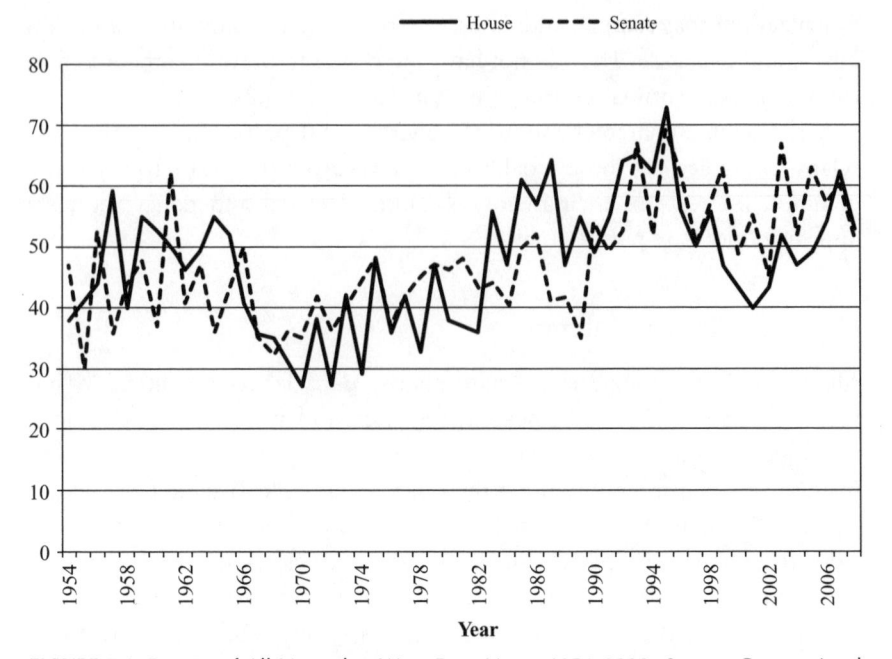

FIGURE 5.1. Percent of All Votes that Were Party Votes, 1954–2008. *Source:* Congressional Quarterly.

Shared Policy Preferences

Members of each party hold distinctive views on most important policy questions. The shared policy views among legislators of the same party are grounded in the similarities in the views of their home constituencies. Liberal-leaning districts tend to elect more Democrats than conservative-leaning districts, which elect more Republicans. Shared policy views create an incentive for members to choose leaders and coordinate their strategies.

Majorities of the parties have taken opposing positions on roll-call votes about half of the time in most recent Congresses. Figure 5.1 indicates the percentage of roll-call votes that were party votes – those on which a majority of Democrats voted against a majority of Republicans. In the recent past, party voting has tended to be higher in odd-numbered years than in even-numbered years, particularly in the House. This trend may reflect political pressures associated with the two-year electoral cycle of the House. In the odd-numbered years immediately after congressional elections, the winning side may feel emboldened to push a partisan agenda. But as another election approaches, members and party leaders may avoid issues that polarize the parties and create problems at home for some members.

ELECTORAL TROUBLE FOR LEADERS

Members of Congress expect their leaders to guide their parties to electoral success. Major failures, or even unexpected losses, as well as other embarrassing developments, can lead to the demise of a leader, as is evident in several episodes described in the following section.

After his party suffered unexpected losses in the 1998 elections, Speaker Newt Gingrich (R-Georgia) took the extraordinary step of resigning from the speakership and Congress. His party had lost five seats in the House of Representatives, narrowing the Republican advantage to 223, just five more than a majority of 218. Rarely does the party opposing the president lose seats in a midterm election. In fact, 1934 is the only other midterm election of the twentieth century in which the president's party won additional seats. Gingrich was blamed for failing to provide needed leadership.

In 2002, just after his party failed to win seats in the midterm election, Democratic Minority Leader Dick Gephardt chose not to seek reelection as the party leader. Gephardt soon announced his intention to run for president, but many viewed his decision to retire from the post a wise move. Gephardt had served as party leader since 1994, when House Democrats lost their majority for the first time since 1954, yet he had not managed to lead the party back to majority status.

After his party regained a majority of Senate seats in the 2002 elections, Senate Republican Minority Leader Trent Lott (R-Mississippi) was expecting to become the majority leader as soon as the new Congress convened in January 2003. However, in December a video recording of Lott's comments at a birthday party for retiring Senator Strom Thurmond (R-South Carolina) were aired on television. The recording showed Lott saying that the country would have been better off if Thurmond had won the presidency when he ran in 1948. Thurmond was the pro-segregationist candidate of the Dixiecrats in 1948. It was soon learned that Lott had made similar comments two decades earlier. The public uproar caused by these disclosures led many of Lott's colleagues to conclude that he had to step down as party leader. Lott stepped down as party leader but remained in the Senate.

In 2006, after his party lost its House majority, Speaker Dennis Hastert (R-Illinois) stepped down as his party's leader. In 2008, after his party lost additional seats, House Republican Whip Roy Blunt (R-Missouri) retired from his post.

The percentage of party votes was relatively high in the late 1980s and 1990s. We consider this trend later in this chapter. But why aren't more votes in Congress aligned along party lines? The primary reason is that Congress addresses many programs and issues that do not involve partisan considerations, such as the merchant marine, veterans' health programs, and flood

FACTIONALISM WITHIN CONGRESSIONAL PARTIES

Intra-party factionalism in Congress is reflected in the presence of named groups. In the Senate, owing to its smaller size, members appear to see less benefit and some cost in becoming associated with formally organized factions. In recent years, a handful of Senate Democratic liberals formed the Democratic Study Group, a bipartisan group of moderates formed the bipartisan Senate Centrist Coalition, and a group of Senate Democratic centrists and their staff met on a regular basis. Only the Steering Committee, the informal organization of Republican conservatives, has been in existence for long.

In the House, factions representing liberals, moderates, and conservatives have formed and reformed in both parties. Liberal Democrats comprise the Progressive Caucus, which had over 70 members in 2008 and is the largest of the Democratic member organizations. The New Democratic Coalition, organized in 1998 by a group of self-proclaimed centrists, had nearly 60 members in 2008. The Blue Dog Coalition is an organization of conservative or moderate Democrats with 51 members in 2009. In addition, the Congressional Black Caucus and Hispanic Caucus represent Democrats who generally are liberal.

On the Republican side in the House, the Republican Study Committee, which dates back to 1973, is the major faction and is comprised of about two-thirds of the party. In 1994, Republican moderates organized the Tuesday Group, which numbered about 35 in 2008. Both the Republican Study Committee and the Tuesday Group hired staff aides to assist the groups.

The one inter-chamber group of prominence is the Main Street Partnership, comprised of Republican moderates from both houses. In 2008, six senators and 46 representatives were members, along with two governors.

insurance. Congress considers a greater volume of legislation – and more detailed legislation – than do most other national legislatures. Most of the legislation enacted into law each year is routine or concerns matters of little political interest. The parties are not motivated to play a role in shaping such legislation.

Even on votes that generate partisan divisions, the two parties are seldom perfectly cohesive. In most recent Congresses, an average of 70 to 80 percent of members have voted with a majority of their party on party votes – meaning that a 20 to 30 percent rate of defection is common even when party majorities oppose each other. Indeed, nothing in the way that members are elected or reelected guarantees that members of the same party will agree with one another on important issues or that Democrats and

Republicans will take opposing views. To the contrary, variation in political views of members' constituencies promotes variation in the voting behavior of members of the same party. Factionalism often has made it difficult to use the party organizations to promote policy ideas and solicit support.

Party Identification

Most members, like most political activists and many citizens of the United States, identify with their parties and have a psychological and emotional attachment to their parties. This attachment reinforces a sense of group identification and enhances group cohesiveness. These bonds lead members to turn to party colleagues for cues on how to vote and for other forms of assistance and advice. Party leaders further strengthen party bonds by emphasizing common loyalties, policy commitments, and personal ties in their appeals for support from their colleagues. Furthermore, most members of Congress face another reality: Legislators are dependent on voters who, for the most part, share the same partisan affiliation and vote in party primaries. Members who vote against their party's position on major issues or, even worse, actively work to undermine their party's institutional position may face challenges from within their party in a primary. Few members are willing to take such a risk. In this way, the partisan connection between a member and his or her electoral base constrains members who might otherwise work to form inter-party coalitions within their chamber.

Most Common Coalitions

Although congressional parties are not perfectly cohesive, they have an important advantage over other groups that might seek to influence legislative outcomes: They are the most common basis for building majority coalitions. Because party-based coalitions are so common, members have an incentive to organize formal party organizations and identify leaders to work on behalf of their common interests. That is, over the long run, members believe that they are better off joining an enduring party organization than operating as freelance legislators. Once established, parties acquire important institutional advantages that make it difficult for other coalitions to establish formal organizations in Congress. By using their procedural and appointment powers, as well as by making a few concessions to dissident factions, majority party leaders have been able to defuse the few intra-party disputes that have threatened party control of their chambers.

Stable but Loose Coalitions

For all of these reasons, the House and Senate depend on party leaders to perform many basic organizational functions, but do not give them too much independent power. Members of the *majority* party choose the presiding officers of both chambers (the Speaker of the House and, to preside in the absence of the Vice President, the Senate President Pro Tempore), select committee leaders, and assume responsibility for scheduling activity at all stages of the legislative process. The parties assign members to standing committees and subcommittees as well as to all select, joint, and conference committees. The majority party in each house reserves for itself the majority of seats on nearly all committees. And within the committees, most activity is organized by party – the questioning of witnesses at hearings, the hiring of staff, even the arrangement of seats in committee rooms. Seating on the House and Senate floors is also arranged by party: The Democrats are on the left and the Republicans are on the right when facing the front desk. Partisan elements pervade the organization of the modern Congress and have done so since the first half of the nineteenth century.

Yet, American congressional parties are not as strong as parties in many other national legislatures. Congressional parties in the United States usually are not as cohesive on questions of public policy as are parties in other systems. U.S. congressional party leaders have little power over who is elected under their party's label and few resources to compel loyalty from members once they are in office. Equally important, state and national party leaders have no formal authority over legislators sharing their party label.

Congressional party leaders sometimes struggle to balance the diverse policy and electoral interests of their party colleagues. In their efforts to do so, they may delay action on a bill until the timing is more convenient for a legislator or urge their colleagues to be tolerant of a legislator whose political circumstances necessitate a vote against the party position. Still, there are situations when leaders seek the vote of every party member. Such situations usually involve legislation that is a high priority for a president of the same party, whose success or failure will reflect on the party, and for which there are not enough supportive members of the opposition party to muster a majority. Leaders may seek to accommodate some members by compromising provisions of the legislation or by promising certain actions on unrelated legislation. Explicit or implicit threats of retribution for disloyal behavior are sometimes issued, typically in the form of warnings about future committee chairmanship or appointment decisions made by party committees and leaders. These tradeoffs reflect the loose organization and

---

Congressionally Speaking...

Among the four congressional parties, only House Democrats call their organization a *caucus*. House Republicans, Senate Democrats, and Senate Republicans call their organizations *conferences*. The difference in labels dates to the 1910s, when the House Democrats used their caucus, the so-called King Caucus, to make policy decisions and required party members to support those positions. The Democrats' binding caucus was so distasteful to House Republicans that they chose an entirely different label for their organization. Senate parties followed suit and use the term conference.

---

discipline of congressional parties and the long-term importance of party affiliations to members.

Party Organizations

Each of the four congressional parties (two in each house) has three major organizational features: a caucus (or conference) comprised of all party members in the chamber, party committees, and elected and appointed leaders. All four party caucuses meet in late November or early December after each election to organize for the new Congress, which begins in January. They elect their leaders, may adopt and revise their rules, and begin to make assignments to standing committees. In recent Congresses, all four caucuses have met weekly or biweekly while Congress is in session. These meetings usually serve as forums for the discussion of party strategies. To facilitate candid discussion and avoid media reports of party infighting, caucus meetings are generally not open to the public or the press.

Each party has a set of committees (see Table 5.1). The policy committees discuss (and, infrequently, endorse) policy positions; the campaign committees provide advice and money to party incumbents and candidates; the committees on committees assign party members to standing committees. For several decades, the policy committees of the House and Senate Republicans have sponsored weekly luncheons that serve as forums on matters important to the party. Senate Democrats adopted the practice of weekly luncheons in 1990.

Party staffs provide a wide range of services to members. Services include timely reports on floor activity, briefing papers on major issues, media advice and technical assistance, newspaper-clipping services, recorded messages on current floor activity, personnel services, and limited research assistance.

TABLE 5.1. Party Committees, 111th Congress (January 2009).

House Democrats

Steering	Makes committee assignments; sometimes endorses policy positions; discusses party strategy
Democratic Congressional Campaign Committee	Provides money and other assistance to Democratic House candidates
Organization, Study, and Review	Recommends changes in party organization and rules

House Republicans

Steering	Makes committee assignments
Policy	Discusses and recommends policy proposals
National Republican Congressional Committee	Provides money and other assistance to Republican House candidates

Senate Democrats

Steering and Outreach	Makes committee assignments; formulates political strategy
Policy	Recommends policy priorities; provides a forum for conference discussion; staff provides research
Democratic Senatorial Campaign Committee	Provides money and other assistance to Democratic Senate candidates

Senate Republicans

Committee on Committees	Makes committee assignments
Policy	Discusses and recommends policy proposals; staff provides research
National Republican Senatorial Campaign	Provides money and other assistance to Republican Senate candidates

Source: Collected by authors.

The Senate parties operate closed-circuit television channels that provide senators and their staffs with informative details about floor action. They also provide radio and television studios that allow senators to appear live on home-state stations. Over the last two decades, most new party leaders have found additional services to promise and deliver to the membership. As a result, the party staffs have become large and expensive, with nearly all of the funding provided through appropriations.

TABLE 5.2. Top Party Leaders, 111th Congress (January 2009).

House Democrats

Speaker	Nancy Pelosi, California
Majority Leader	Steny Hoyer, Maryland
Majority Whip	James Clyburn, South Carolina
Caucus Chair	John Larson, Connecticut
Caucus Vice Chair	Xavier Becerra, California

House Republicans

Minority Leader	John Boehner, Ohio
Minority Whip	Eric Cantor, Virginia
Conference Chair	Mike Pence, Indiana
Conference Vice Chairman	Cathy McMorris Rodgers, Washington

Senate Democrats

Majority Leader (and Conference Chair)	Harry Reid, Nevada
Assistant Floor Leader (Whip)	Richard Durbin, Illinois
Conference Vice Chair	Charles Schumer, New York
Conference Secretary	Patty Murray, Washington
President Pro Tempore	Robert Byrd, West Virginia

Senate Republicans

Minority Leader	Mitch McConnell, Kentucky
Assistant Floor Leader (Whip)	Jon Kyl, Arizona
Conference Chairman	Lamar Alexander, Tennessee
Conference Vice Chairman	John Thune, South Dakota

Party Leaders

The Constitution provides for presiding officers in Congress but says nothing about parties or leaders. It provides that the members of the House "shall choose their Speaker," makes the vice president of the United States the president of the Senate, and requires that the Senate select a president pro tempore ("president for the time being") to preside over the Senate in the absence of the vice president. Although the Constitution does not explicitly require the Speaker or the Senate president pro tempore to be members of Congress, all have been.

Only in the House is the presiding officer, the Speaker, also the leader of the majority party (Table 5.2). At the start of each Congress, the majority and minority parties nominate their top leaders for Speaker. The majority party leader is then elected on a party-line vote. In the Senate, presiding over daily sessions is normally a routine activity, so the vice president is seldom present. Since the 1940s, the majority party has named its most senior member president pro tempore. The president pro tempore is usually busy as a committee chair and assigns the duty of presiding over the Senate to junior senators of the same party. All four parties choose a floor leader (known as a majority or minority leader), assistant floor leader (or whip), conference chair, and other leaders.

Major Responsibilities of Party Leaders

No specific statements about party leaders' jobs can be found in chamber or party rules. Rather, leaders' responsibilities have developed in response to their colleagues' expectations that leaders must promote the common electoral and policy interests of their parties. These responsibilities are primarily assigned to the top leader in each party, although the burden is shared among the top three or four leaders in each party.

BUILDING COALITIONS ON MAJOR LEGISLATION. Building coalitions in support of party policy positions is a large part of the job of leaders. Because the majority party is often divided to some degree on controversial issues, such majorities do not automatically materialize. Rather, leaders carefully count votes, craft legislation, and use various means of persuasion to try to unify their own party and attract votes from members of the opposition party to pass or block legislation. Leaders also work to build majority coalitions in committees and conference committees from time to time, but they tend to be deferential to committee leaders at those stages. Party leaders are most active on the floor.

Extra-large majorities must often be mustered as well. In the Senate, 60 votes must be secured to invoke cloture on a filibuster, unless the matter concerns the Senate's standing rules, in which case a two-thirds vote (67, if all senators vote) is required. On a few other occasions in the Senate, such as to waive a budget restriction, a 60-vote majority must be found. In both chambers, a two-thirds majority of members present and voting is required to override a presidential veto. In such cases, support from at least a few minority members is usually required for the majority party leaders to win.

MANAGING THE FLOOR. Managing floor activity is primarily the responsibility of the majority party leadership. This responsibility includes scheduling sessions of the chambers and arranging for the consideration of individual pieces of legislation. The stark differences between House and Senate floor scheduling practices are noted in Chapter 7. In the Senate, minority members' power to obstruct proceedings requires that the majority leader work closely with the minority leader. In fact, nearly continuous consultation between the two leaders and their staffs is typical in the Senate in mid-session. A much more distant relationship between the majority and minority party leaders is found in the House. As a result, the Senate majority leader has more difficulty gaining a tactical edge by careful scheduling than does the House Speaker.

SERVING AS INTERMEDIARY WITH THE PRESIDENT. Serving as intermediaries between the congressional party and the president has been a regular duty of party leaders since the early twentieth century. Leaders of the president's party normally meet with the president once a week while Congress is in session, and they often report on those meetings at party luncheons or caucuses. On matters central to the president's legislative agenda, the leaders work closely with executive branch officials to build majority support in Congress.

Congressional leaders of the president's party often have divided loyalties. Their most immediate obligation is to their congressional colleagues, who elected them, but they also feel an obligation to support the president. Tensions frequently arise as congressional leaders seek to balance the competing demands of the president and their congressional party colleagues.

Leaders of the out-party – the party that does not control the presidency – meet sporadically with the president, usually to be briefed on foreign policy matters. The relationship between a president and out-party leaders is not often one of genuine consultation, for obvious reasons. Occasionally, political circumstances or personal friendship may strengthen the bond. Senate Republican leader Everett Dirksen, for example, was a confidant of Democratic president Lyndon Johnson during the 1960s, and Dirksen's support for Johnson's civil rights and Vietnam War policies was crucial to the president's legislative success.

ENHANCING THE PARTY'S REPUTATION. Public relations is a central leadership responsibility in the modern Congress. Skillfully managing media relations is now considered an essential element of a good legislative strategy. The objectives are to win public support for legislative positions, to persuade undecided legislators of the political support for party positions, and to persuade voters that the party's legislative efforts deserve to be rewarded at election time.

REPLICATING SUCCESSFUL INNOVATIONS

In preparation for the 1994 elections, House Republican leaders prepared a 10-point legislative agenda – known as the "Contract With America" – that they promised to pass in the first 100 days of the new Congress if they gained a majority of seats. Republicans won a House majority in the 1994 elections for the first time since the 1952 elections and credited the new Speaker, Newt Gingrich, for enhancing the importance of national issues in House contests and ultimately for their success.

Ten years later in 2004, the House Democratic leader, Nancy Pelosi (D-California), organized a similar effort for her party. Drawing on the advice of outside consultants and citing the need for a clear message like the Contract With America, the Democratic leaders produced the "New Partnership for America's Future" in which they identified their party's six "core values." The effort did not lead to a new Democratic majority, at least not in the 2004 elections. In 2006, when the Democrats won back a House majority, Pelosi and the Democrats prepared a "Six for '06" agenda that included six legislative initiatives that were passed in the first 100 hours of legislative session in 2007.

Media skills were seldom a major consideration in leadership selection in the 1950s, 1960s, and early 1970s. Service to colleagues, mastery of the mechanics of the legislative game, and position among party factions were given greater weight. Perhaps because of their weak institutional position and lack of national media coverage, only House Republicans made media skills much of an issue in leadership contests. In general, party leaders took a back seat to committee leaders as opinion leaders on matters of policy. In fact, the leading studies on party leadership of the 1960s did not catalog service as party spokesperson or anything similar among the major functions or techniques of leaders.

Expectations have changed. The increasing importance of television as a medium of political communication, presidents' domination of television news, and the larger number of news programs seem to have intensified demand for telegenic leaders. Since the mid-1960s, out-party congressional leaders have sought and been granted time on the television networks to respond to presidential addresses. By the early 1980s, the role of party spokesperson had become so prominent as to warrant listing it among leaders' primary responsibilities.

Congressional party leaders realize that to compete with the president, television pundits, interest group leaders, radio talk show hosts, and other opinion leaders, all of whom actively court public opinion in an effort to

SWITCHING PARTIES, CHANGING PARTY CONTROL

In late May 2001, Senator Jim Jeffords (I-Vermont) announced that he was leaving the Republican Conference, becoming an Independent, and joining with the Democrats for the purpose of organizing the Senate. Since the 1880s, there have been 25 instances of party switching in the Senate, but Jeffords' move was the first time that such a switch caused a party to lose majority status in either chamber. The Senate had been divided 50–50 between Democrats and Republicans; the Republican Vice President Dick Cheney allowed the Republicans to be considered the majority party, for the Republican floor leader to be recognized by the presiding officer as the majority leader, and for the Republicans to control the committee chairmanships.

Republicans attempted to keep Jeffords in the party by offering more money for education programs, his favorite cause, giving him a seat in the leadership circle, and granting him an exemption to the party conference rule limiting the number of terms he could serve as chair of the Health, Education, Labor, and Pensions Committee. The new Democratic majority gave Jeffords a committee chairmanship. In the 2002 elections the Republicans gained additional seats and reassumed majority status. Jeffords lost his chairmanship. Jeffords did not seek reelection in 2006.

There have been 81 instances of party switching in the House since the 1880s.

generate pressure on legislators, they need media strategies of their own. All top leaders have daily contact with print, radio, and television reporters. The House Speaker and Senate leaders usually have brief press conferences before their chambers' daily sessions. They employ experienced press secretaries and speechwriters. They sometimes commission their own public opinion polls to gauge how well their party's message is being received. On a few major issues, they even create special party task forces charged with carrying out a media strategy.

CAMPAIGNING. Providing campaign support to colleagues is a regular part of leaders' activity. All modern leaders help their colleagues raise money and join them at campaign events. Leaders' efforts are not altruistic, of course. Party leaders want to see party colleagues reelected in order to maintain or gain a majority for their party, and they hope that their kindness will be repaid in loyalty. Even candidates for top leadership posts now spend time and money on their colleagues' campaign to attract support and demonstrate the kind of leaders they will be. All leaders, and most aspirants for leadership posts, form political action committees so they may receive contributions that they can donate to the campaigns of their colleagues.

MANAGING THE PARTY AND THE CHAMBER. Organizing the party and chamber is an important duty of party leaders. Obvious political aspects of this job include making committee assignments and appointments to various party positions. More administrative in character are the selection and supervision of chamber officers and other employees. For example, the majority party leaders in the two houses nominate and supervise the chief clerks and sergeants at arms, whose appointment must be approved by the houses, and they share responsibility for choosing a director for the Congressional Budget Office.

Selection of Leaders

The party caucuses elect their top leaders. The leaders are not chosen on the basis of seniority, although most recent leaders have been very experienced members. A candidate's place among factions and regional groups within the party, record of service to colleagues, personal friendships, intelligence and policy expertise, and other factors play a role in leadership contests. As noted, skill in managing relations with the media has become increasingly important. Members who have been serving in lower party posts may be advantaged because they have been in a position to demonstrate their skills and to perform favors for colleagues.

Only in the ascension to House Speaker is there much routine in leadership selection. A vacancy in the speakership is typically filled by the previous floor leader – the majority or minority leader – without opposition. The majority or minority leader generally has already won several leadership elections and has substantial support for the move to Speaker. Challenging the heir apparent would be pointless. Contests for the speakership have not occurred since the 1800s.

The election of Republican Speaker Dennis Hastert in early 1999 was a special case. After Speaker Gingrich announced his resignation shortly after the 1998 elections, in which the Republicans did unexpectedly poorly, the immediate favorite to replace Gingrich was Rep. Bob Livingston (R-Louisiana). But, after the media disclosed that Livingston had an extramarital affair years earlier, Livingston chose to resign from the House. Somewhat anxious to find a new leader, House Republicans asked Hastert, who had held only low appointive positions in the party and was not well known. Hastert was replaced by Nancy Pelosi, who had been the Democratic Minority Leader, after the Democrats won a House majority in 2006.

For other party offices, hotly contested races are common, usually to fill vacancies. As contests among fellow partisans, the races are often filled with intrigue. They involve intense campaigns as the candidates mak' _ sonal appeals to colleagues to solicit support. Organized factions sometimes choose a favorite; in fact, faction leaders often are the candidates. Wild speculation, personal grudges, and conspiracy are the standard fare. The behind-closed-doors campaigning and secret-ballot voting always generate a great deal of speculation and second-guessing among Washington insiders. A potentially close outcome heightens the suspense.

Challenges to incumbent leaders occur only occasionally. Most incumbent leaders do the kind of job their party colleagues expect. Challenges to an incumbent tend to be particularly divisive, and even disgruntled members usually try to avoid a fight within the party family. Of course, taking on an incumbent may be risky. Leadership contests are expensive in terms of time and effort. Running and losing may undermine future leadership hopes, to say nothing of incurring the wrath of the winner.

House Party Leaders

Today's House party leaders are much more visible and active than were their predecessors of the 1960s and 1970s. Personality is one reason, but more important are the power of television and demands of rank-and-file party members for aggressive, media-oriented leadership. Partly for those reasons, somewhat younger and more assertive members have been promoted to top leadership spots in recent years. Greater party cohesiveness has liberated leaders to be more pugnacious and partisan without alienating major factions within the party.

The Speaker of the House

The Speaker of the House possesses more formal authority than does any other member of Congress. House rules and precedents grant the Speaker important prerogatives concerning floor scheduling and procedures, bill referrals, and appointments to select and conference committees and to various commissions. One of the Speaker's newest prerogatives is the power to remove a member from a conference committee delegation and replace him or her without the approval of the House, a power that is intended to make majority party members of a conference delegation accountable to their party's top leader. In addition to the rules of the House, both parties' internal rules give their top leaders control over the party's appointments to the Rules Committee, extra influence over other committee assignments, and power to make appointments to party committees. It is the combination

TERM LIMITS FOR LEADERS

Since the early 1990s, term limits for party leaders and committee chairs have been a popular reform proposal. Congressional Republicans have moved farther in adopting limits than Democrats. The known limits on leaders' service in key positions appear to have stimulated ambitious legislators to announce their candidacy for leadership posts earlier.

House Republicans led the way among congressional parties to set limits on the number of terms a legislator could serve in a particular leadership post. Soon after they gained a majority in the 1994 elections, the House Republicans limited all party leaders to six-year terms in any given office, with the exception of the speakership for which an eight-year limit was established. House Republicans eliminated the limit on the Speaker in 2003 and Democrats did not reimpose a term for the Speaker when they gained a House majority in 2007.

Senate Republicans followed their House counterparts by setting a six-year limit for holding any leadership position with the exceptions of floor leader and President Pro Tempore for which no limit was set.

House Democrats limit their caucus chair, caucus vice chair, and elected regional whips to two consecutive terms, but do not set term limits for other party leaders.

Senate Democrats have not imposed term limits of any kind on party or committee leadership posts.

of powers granted under House and party rules that make the Speaker more powerful than the Senate's majority leader, who enjoys few special powers under Senate rules.

The Speaker's most important source of power is his or her control of the flow of business on the House floor. By precedent, the Speaker has the power to recognize members on the House floor without appeal. That means that the Speaker may choose to ignore members who seek recognition to call up legislation that the Speaker prefers to consider later or to block. Scheduling prerogatives give the Speaker control over the timing of floor action, which may affect the legislative outcomes and political impact of House votes. Among other things, the Speaker can keep from the floor legislation he or she opposes or wishes to delay. Also, the Speaker may use scheduling to reward or punish legislators.

As presiding officer and the majority party's top leader, the Speaker must exercise great discretion in making public appearances and statements. For example, Speakers make floor speeches on only a few occasions each year, for important issues and close votes. On the momentous occasions when a

Speaker does speak on the floor, nearly all members are in attendance and the galleries are packed. Speakers are granted the privilege of speaking last.

Recent Speakers – Thomas P. "Tip" O'Neill (1977–1986), James Wright (1987–1989), Thomas Foley (1989–1994), Newt Gingrich (1995–1998), Dennis Hastert (1999–2006), and Nancy Pelosi (2007–present) – have been more active in using their formal powers than were the Speakers of the middle decades of the twentieth century. The speakership gained particularly high visibility after the 1980 elections, in which Republican Ronald Reagan was elected to the White House and the Republicans gained a majority in the Senate. O'Neill, as the highest elected Democrat, became the chief strategist and spokesperson for his party. After Reagan's initial year of great legislative success, the Democrats united in opposition to the president's conservative agenda, with O'Neill taking the lead in challenging Reagan's program and presenting Democratic alternatives. In doing so, O'Neill was responding to the demands for leadership from the frustrated liberal rank-and-file members of his party.

O'Neill's activism paled in comparison with the boldness of his successor, James Wright. Upon gaining the speakership, Wright insisted that committees to act quickly on a range of domestic legislation, leading Republicans to complain about a new House dictatorship. In the foreign policy arena, Wright broke through unwritten limits on congressional involvement by negotiating directly with representatives of the contending governments and factions in Central America.

Wright resigned from the House in 1989 after the House Committee on Standards of Official Conduct charged him with several violations of House ethics rules. Thomas Foley, who succeeded Wright, had been caucus chair, whip, and majority leader. Compared with Wright, he was less assertive, more deferential to committees, and less inclined to make partisan attacks on Republican leaders. Like O'Neill, Wright was unlikely to take the lead on controversial issues unless a consensus had already crystallized within his party.

Republican Newt Gingrich became the most proactive Speaker since the first decade of the twentieth century after he was elected to the post in January 1995. A well-developed agenda, called the Contract With America, provided an unusually concise 10-point policy platform for Gingrich. Gingrich was given much of the credit for these developments – he had championed aggressive Republican strategies in the House, coauthored the Contract With America, raised money, and recruited candidates to challenge the incumbent Democratic majority. Gingrich, backed by his House Republican colleagues, became the leading spokesman for his party, dominated the selection of committee leaders and other committee appointments, directed the actions of committees, set the floor agenda, and pushed legislation associated with the Contract With America through the House in the first 100 days of the 104th Congress (1995–1996).

Gingrich's speakership was a lightning rod for partisanship and ended in political tragedy. Gingrich had leveled the initial charges against Jim Wright that eventually led to Wright's resignation and later, as Speaker, was at least as aggressive as Wright in leading the majority party. His political down-fall began with his 1995 strategy to hold hostage debt ceiling increases and funding for executive departments in order to get President Bill Clinton's approval of the Republican's budget plan. Clinton refused to budge and eventually the Republican Congress accepted Clinton's compromise leg-islation. The episode produced sharply weaker approval ratings in public opinion polls for Gingrich and much stronger ratings for Clinton. After that point, Gingrich became far less aggressive, setting aside his confrontational strategies. Following Clinton's reelection in 1996, Gingrich maintained a low public profile and appeared to be somewhat less heavy-handed in directing the work of the House, an approach that has received mixed reviews from his colleagues. In the summer of 1997 there was serious discussion among senior Republicans of replacing him. Gingrich continued to be subject to criticism for ineffective leadership, and he eventually resigned his post when challenged by Bob Livingston in the aftermath of the 1998 elections.

In 1995, the Republicans instituted a new House rule limiting the number of consecutive terms that a member could serve as Speaker. In December 1994, newly elected Republicans proposed a three-term limit for the Speaker, just as they proposed for committee chairs. At Gingrich's insistence, they approved a four-term limit instead, which was incorporated into the House rules in January 1995. Gingrich did not survive long enough for the rule to apply.

Hastert's style contrasted sharply with Gingrich's, at least at first. Hastert consulted more frequently with his fellow partisans and granted more inde-pendence to committee chairs. He successfully healed some of the rifts among Republicans left from the Gingrich years, and, for a while, he held regular meetings with the Democratic leader. He campaigned endlessly for his colleagues, earning their respect and indebtedness, and, in the view of some observers, used this support to gain the upper hand with other party and committee leaders.

However welcome Hastert's more accommodating style was initially, by late 2002 Hastert became more aggressive in his enforcement of party

loyalty. He denied committee chairmanships and choice committee assignments to several Republicans who had opposed the leadership position
on campaign finance reform, patients' bill of rights, and other issues.
He endorsed Majority Leader Tom Delay's (R-Texas) proclamation that a
Republican member of the party's organization who voted against the party
on any procedural matter be excused from service. In 2003, the Republicans' package of House rules changes dropped the eight-year term limit for
a Speaker. Democrats did not reimpose a term limit for the Speaker when
they gained a majority in 2007.

After the Democrats won a majority of House seats in the 2006 elections,
they elected their floor leader, Nancy Pelosi, the first woman Speaker. Pelosi,
a liberal Democrat from San Francisco, had worked hard as minority leader
to build support among moderate and conservative Democrats. During her
first few months in the speakership, she proved to be an aggressive leader
who set the agenda for her party and showed a willingness to work around
committee chairs who were not in sync with her agenda. While she worked
hard to win the support of fellow partisans on controversial issues, she created more opportunities for the minority party to offer alternatives and gave
her own partisans somewhat more freedom to vote as they chose. Nevertheless, Pelosi has proven quite willing to have the most important legislation
developed within her party with little minority party participation.

House Floor Leaders

Both House parties elect a floor leader – that is, a majority leader or a
minority leader – at the start of each Congress. As the label suggests, floor
leaders are the chief spokespersons for their parties on the House floor. The
majority leader is considered the second-ranking leader of the party, just
behind the Speaker. The minority leader is the minority party's top leader
and is always that party's (losing) nominee for Speaker at the beginning of
each Congress.

There are few duties formally assigned to the majority leader in party
rules. Recent Speakers have relied on the floor leader to receive and screen
requests to schedule legislation for floor consideration. The majority leader
consults with the Speaker (normally several times a day), works with the
Speaker and others to promote party unity, and increasingly serves as a party
spokesperson. Recent majority leaders have been loyal to the Speaker and
have seldom publicly disagreed with him or her. As the person who is next in
line to become Speaker, and an individual with a strong voice in scheduling

Congressionally Speaking . . .

The term *whip* originated in the British House of Commons. It is derived from the term whipper-in – the fellow who keeps the dogs in line during an English foxhunt. In the American Congress, the use of the term reflected the responsibility of the whip to get party members to the floor on time. Today the term is often used as a verb – as in "the undecided members were whipped" – to refer to the process of persuasion and arm-twisting.

and all other leadership decisions, the majority leader is considered very powerful.

The minority leader generally is the minority party's chief spokesperson and strategist. The minority leader sometimes consults with the majority leader about the floor schedule, although more often he or she is merely informed of the majority leadership's scheduling decisions. Keeping the minority party united and attracting majority party votes are the central tasks of the minority leader's job. The job is made easier when the minority leader's party controls the White House, and the president's resources can be drawn upon. The minority party can do little to obstruct a cohesive majority in the House, so the minority floor leader's job tends to be quite frustrating. The minority leader, like the Speaker, is an *ex officio* member of the Permanent Select Committee on Intelligence.

House Whips and Whip Organizations

The third-ranking majority party leader and second-ranking minority party leader in the House are the whips. Both whips are now elected, although the Democratic whip was appointed by the majority leader until late 1986 when the position was made elective. Both whips head large whip organizations, whose purpose is to collect information for the leadership and persuade colleagues to support party positions. To facilitate the communication process, the whip offices maintain systems of recorded messages and email about floor actions, issue whip notices about the upcoming schedule, and use automated telephone and paging systems to reach members about pending votes. Whips also try to keep track of the whereabouts of members, particularly on days when important, close floor votes are expected.

The Democratic whip organization has been large for many years. In recent Congresses, the House Democrats had as many as nine chief deputy

EVOLVING PARTY ORGANIZATIONS

Congressional party organizations have become much more elaborate in the past generation, a result of competitive pressures and the desire to include more members in party activities. A good example is the elaboration of the Senate Democratic leadership following the 2006 elections. Senator Charles Schumer (D-New York) was praised by his party colleagues for recruiting candidates, raising money, and aiding in the creation of a new Democratic majority. He was rewarded by Majority Leader Harry Reid (D-Nevada) with an appointment to a new party position, conference vice chairman, that Reid created for him. Reid said the position would be the third-ranking leadership post under the majority leader and assistant majority leader (whip). Schumer continued to hold the position in 2009.

whips, 12 deputy whips, and 70 at-large whips, all appointed by the party leader. In addition, there have been 24 regional whips elected by groups of Democrats from specific regions and one ex officio whip (the ranking Democrat on the Rules Committee), for a total of 88 whips. The whip system has grown rapidly as the top leaders have responded to demands for whip appointments from party factions and individual members.

The Democratic leaders often appoint task forces to collect information and generate support on specific issues. This approach has been called a "strategy of inclusion," because it gives a large number of members an opportunity to work closely with the leadership. By working hand-in-hand with the party rank-and-file, party leaders are able to persuade some members who otherwise might oppose the leadership to join the team.

The House Republicans have a more modest whip system, although it also has expanded in recent years. The Republican whip system has been comprised of a chief deputy whip and about 17 deputy whips – all appointed – and nearly 50 assistant whips elected by groups for regions of the country. The Republican whips meet irregularly. The Republicans maintain several subcommittees on their Policy Committee that serve purposes similar to Democratic caucus task forces.

Appointment or election as a whip, policy subcommittee, or task force member gives a member some prestige, an additional office to add to his or her letterhead, and access to informative weekly whip meetings. For some members, service in these party posts provides an opportunity to prove their leadership abilities to their colleagues, which can be important to a member who aspires to the top leadership posts. For all members, these posts provide an opportunity to learn more about the politics of key issues and of their party. Nearly all members advertise their assumption of these "leadership" positions at home.

Senate Party Leaders

Traditionally, the Senate's smaller party organizations have had fewer formal leadership posts, committees, and staff than have their House counterparts, although Senate party organizations have become more elaborate in recent years. The Senate's chief leaders are the majority leader and minority leader. These two leaders have historically been prominent politicians, frequently mentioned in the newspapers and seen on television.

Senate Floor Leaders

The majority leader is the principal leader of the Senate. The majority leader sets the Senate's schedule and plans the order of business for the Senate floor. Critical to that function is a procedural advantage granted to the majority leader by precedent: the right of first recognition. The presiding officer recognizes the majority leader to speak or to offer a motion before recognizing any other senator, a practice that dates back to the 1930s.

Like House Speakers, Senate majority leaders vary in their assertiveness. Lyndon Johnson (D-Texas), who served as Democratic leader from 1955 to 1960, set the modern standard for aggressive leadership. Recent majority leaders of both parties have played a more important role in enacting major legislation – negotiating the content of many important bills, pushing committees to bring legislation to the floor, and taking a leading role in managing controversial legislation on the floor.

A majority leader's ability to set the floor agenda depends on the cooperation of his or her Senate colleagues. To call up a measure for consideration on the floor, the majority leader normally must gain approval of a "motion to proceed." Although the motion requires only a simple majority for approval, it also may be debated and so may be subject to a filibuster. Thus, on a controversial measure, the majority leader may require 60 votes to invoke cloture on the motion to proceed and get a measure to the floor for debate and amendment. Once the motion to proceed is adopted, the measure itself or any amendment to it may be filibustered. Consequently, the Senate's schedule is often quite unpredictable.

The majority leader usually seeks to limit debate and often seeks to limit amendments without going as far as invoking cloture. But to do so, the

TIME FOR REFORM?

In 2009, Senator Robert C. Byrd (D-West Virginia), who turned 91 in late 2008, was reelected president pro tempore of the Senate. The 1947 presidential succession act provides that the Senate's president pro tempore is third in line to the presidency behind the vice president and speaker of the House. Because of the modern practice to give the position to the most senior member of the majority party, the president pro tempore often is quite old and may not be capable of managing the duties of the presidency. In 2001, Strom Thurmond served as president pro tempore at age 98 and surely would not have been an effective president. Concerns about an act of terrorism incapacitating national leadership have stimulated new questions about the age of presidents pro tempore, but there has been no serious effort to change the informal seniority practice or the 1947 law.

leader must receive unanimous consent – that is, the leader's request will be rejected if one senator objects. Objections are common from senators who want to protect their right to speak, do not want to give up opportunities to offer amendments, or simply do not want to be inconvenienced. Of course, leaders of both parties entertain requests from colleagues not to allow certain measures to be called up for consideration on the floor (see box, "Congressionally Speaking"). As a result, scheduling in the Senate is much less routine and more a process of negotiation than it is in the House.

The minority leader works closely with the majority leader on scheduling matters. The minority leader protects the parliamentary prerogatives of party members when the majority leader seeks unanimous consent to call up measures, schedule floor action, or limit debate and amendments. Like majority leaders, minority leaders differ in their aggressiveness, and their success depends on the size and cohesiveness of their parties. Unlike the House Speaker and floor leaders, the Senate floor leaders may retain committee assignments. Both Senate leaders are *ex officio* members of the Select Committee on Intelligence. Floor leaders do not hold full committee leadership positions, however.

In late 1996, Senate Republicans set a three-Congress term limit for party leadership positions except for the floor leader and President Pro Tempore. The term limit forced several leaders to give up their positions for the first time at the end of 2002. Senate Democrats are alone among the four congressional parties in not placing term limits on any leadership positions.

Congressionally Speaking...

The predicament of the Senate majority leader is illustrated in the practice of holds. A *hold* is an objection to considering a measure on the Senate floor. Senators usually communicate their objections by letter to their party's floor leader. For several decades, these communications were considered confidential so the name of the senator placing the hold often is not known to his or her colleagues. When senators place holds on measures, they sometimes merely want advance warning of floor action, but at other times they seek to change the bill or even prevent Senate action on the bill.

Working to remove holds is time consuming and involves bargaining with contending factions. Holds are not formally recognized in Senate or party rules, but rather are effective because they constitute notices to object to a unanimous consent request to move to the consideration of a bill or other measure. A leader may call the bluff of a colleague and seek to bring up a bill without clearing the hold, but leaders generally observe holds because they need the cooperation of their colleagues on other matters.

In 2007, a provision requiring public disclosure of the name of the senator placing a hold was included in the ethics reform legislation. The sponsors hoped that disclosure would limit the practice by allowing the public and fellow senators to hold accountable those senators who place holds. The rule proved toothless (requiring senators to disclose their hold *after* an objection to considering a bill was made), but holds did seem to become less frequent. Filibusters and gaining cloture proved to be far more serious problems for the majority leader in recent years.

Senate Whips and Whip Organizations

Both Senate parties call their whips assistant floor leaders to reflect their chief responsibility: standing in for the floor leader in his or her absence. The Senate whips conduct few head counts. One reason is that bill managers – committee leaders or others who take the lead in the floor debate – often do their own head counting, owing to the Senate's smaller size. Senate whips' specific duties depend on the needs of individual floor leaders. Senate party whips have sometimes named assistant or deputy whips to help with head counts and floor duties, but, as a general rule, the deputy whips have not played a regular or important role in the smaller Senate, where the top leaders, bill managers, and their staffs can manage most duties.

Party Leaders' Resources

The influence of the top congressional party leaders flows from their use of several important resources: (1) their parties' voting strength, (2) the procedural powers granted them by the formal rules of their chamber and party, (3) the tangible rewards that they can grant to members, (4) information, (5) their access to the media, and (6) their staffs. Generally, the combination of party strength and formal powers accorded to him or her makes the House Speaker the most powerful member of Congress, followed in descending order by the Senate majority leader, the Senate minority leader, and the House minority leader.

Party Strength

The relative size of the parties' delegations in Congress determines their majority or minority status and thus which party will enjoy the procedural advantages conferred to the majority. Figures 5.2 and 5.3 show the size of the two major parties in each house since 1900. But a party's ability to pass or block legislation involves more than its size. A majority party must also be fairly cohesive, or at least benefit from a fractured opposition, for its potential strength to be realized. Seldom are majority parties so large that they can afford to lose many votes from their own ranks and still win on the floor. Votes that require supermajorities, such as the two-thirds majority required to override presidential vetoes or the three-fifths majority required to overcome a Senate filibuster, are particularly troublesome for majority parties. As a general rule, there is uncertainty about a majority party's prospects of prevailing on important issues. Hard work is required to build winning coalitions on most important legislation. Not all party colleagues can be trusted to support their leadership, and ways of attracting support from members of the minority party often must be found.

Formal Rules

The standing rules of the House and Senate, as well as the written rules of the congressional parties, grant party leaders certain procedural advantages over other members. Of the four top leaders, the Speaker of the House is, by far, the most advantaged by standing rules and precedents. The Speaker enjoys powers that far exceed those of the most comparable Senate leader, the Senate majority leader.

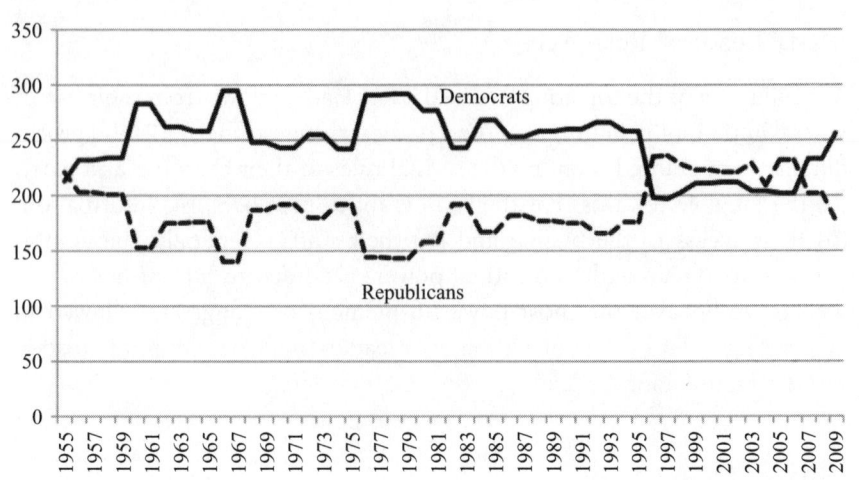

FIGURE 5.2. Number of Democrats and Republicans in the House of Representatives, 1955–2009.

The Senate majority leader, by virtue of the right of first recognition and a few other privileges, comes in second behind the Speaker in formal powers, but the Senate minority leader is not far behind. The Senate's cloture rule and its reliance on unanimous consent agreements to organize its business require the Senate majority leader to consult and gain the consent of the minority leader on most scheduling matters. No such consultation

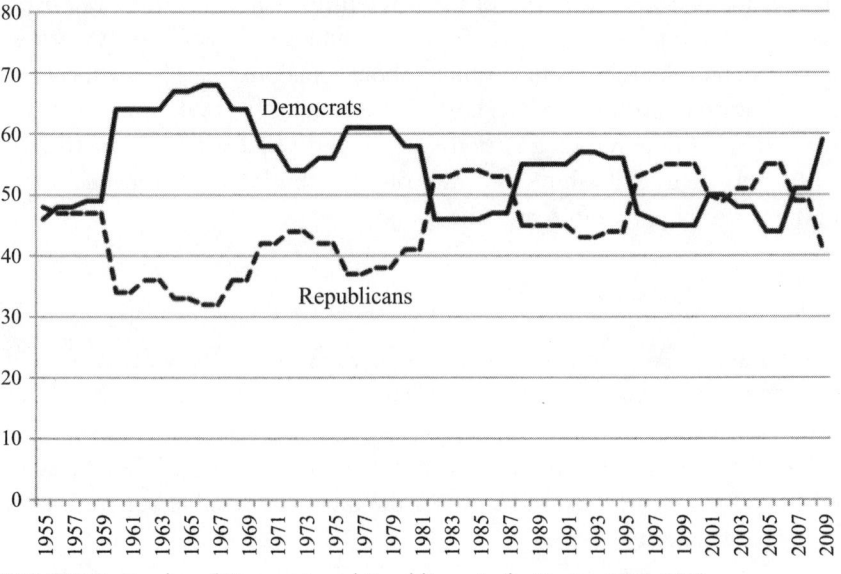

FIGURE 5.3. Number of Democrats and Republicans in the Senate, 1955–2009.

is necessary in the House if the Speaker has the backing of his or her party, making the House minority leader the weakest of the top congressional leaders.

In 1974, the formal power of the House Speaker was bolstered under House rules by granting the Speaker the ability to refer legislation to multiple committees or to propose the creation of an ad hoc or temporary committee. Previously, the Speaker was required to refer each measure to the single committee that had predominant jurisdiction over it. The Speaker now may send legislation to committees sequentially, with one committee identified as the primary committee, or can split legislation into parts to send to different committees. The Speaker may set time limits on committee action when more than one committee is involved. This flexible referral rule has substantially enhanced the Speaker's ability to control the flow of legislation in the House – even to direct legislation toward friendly committees and away from unfriendly committees. On only one occasion, for a large multi-faceted energy bill in 1977, whose content spanned the jurisdiction of many committees, has an ad hoc committee been used successfully.

The powers granted to the Speaker created the prospect of a more centralized, Speaker-driven, policy-making process in the House. That possibility certainly was not realized in the 1970s. Speakers Albert and O'Neill continued to defer to committees and did not attempt to manipulate committees by using their referral powers. To the contrary, the 1970s were a period of remarkably fragmented, decentralized policy making. This was the product of simultaneous reforms that diffused power from full committee chairs to subcommittee chairs (see Chapter 6). And it reflected the expectations of rank-and-file Democrats. Only in the last year or two of the 1970s did Speaker O'Neill begin to use his new referral powers with some vigor.

The power of the Speaker was enhanced in 1993 when the House, over the objections of minority party Republicans at the time, adopted a rule that allows the Speaker to remove members and appoint additional members to select and conference committees after initial appointments have been made. The new rule, which covers minority party appointees as well as majority party appointees, is aimed at majority party conferees who pursue positions that will obstruct outcomes favored by the leadership. Such conferees cannot be confident that their place on a prominent select committee or important conference committee will be protected once they have been appointed. Instead, the Speaker is free to correct errors in judgment made at the time of the initial appointments. In practice, the Speaker is likely to continue to defer to the minority leader on the appointment of minority party

ANOTHER STORY OF SWITCHING PARTIES

In 2004, with no advance notice, freshman Democrat Rodney Alexander (then
D-Louisiana) filed for reelection to his seat as a Republican. Not only were
House Democratic leaders surprised, they soon became upset when Alexander
did not promptly return approximately $70,000 in contributions that he had
received from the political action committees of several Democratic colleagues.
Democratic leaders threatened a lawsuit for fraud after failing to hear from
Alexander for a month. Alexander began to refund the contributions about two
months later, just a month before the November elections, which, at least one
Democrat complained, was so late that it limited the value of redirecting the
money to other campaigns. Alexander won the seat and was rewarded by his
new party with a seat on the prestigious Appropriations Committee, a move
up from the Committee on Agriculture and Committee on Transportation and
Infrastructure assignments he had as a Democrat. Alexander was reelected in
2006 as a Republican.

members to select and conference committees. The Republicans retained
the rule once they became the majority party after the 1994 elections and it
has remained in place since then.

With respect to intra-party rules and practices, the House parties give
their top leaders considerable power. They have a strong influence over their
party colleagues' committee assignments, appoint their parties' members of
the Rules Committee, and appoint members to a variety of party positions.
Through the Rules Committee, the Speaker, the majority party's leader,
controls the flow of major legislation to the floor. In combination, the powers granted under House and party rules make the Speaker exceptionally
influential.

Tangible Rewards

Party leaders have a few resources at their disposal that provide direct political benefits to their colleagues and can be used to reward friends and punish
enemies. Influence over committee assignments is the most prominent of
these resources. An assignment to a committee with jurisdiction over legislation important to a member's home constituency or to well-financed special
interests may be important to the member's electoral prospects. Other committees are coveted because of their jurisdiction over important legislation
and place their members in the middle of the most important legislative
battles. Because party leaders play a major role in their parties' committees

THE LIEBERMAN SAGA

Senator Joseph Lieberman (I-Connecticut), a lifelong Democrat and the Democratic candidate for vice president in 2000, lost his party's primary election in 2006, largely over the issue of his support for Bush administration policy on the war in Iraq. Nevertheless, he successfully won reelection as an Independent. After the election, he continued to caucus with Senate Democrats and, by virtue of his seniority, continued to hold his committee and subcommittee chairmanships as a Democrat. His relations with some people in his party were strained because they had advocated the election of the official Democratic nominee.

In 2008, Lieberman endorsed and campaigned for the Republican presidential candidate, Senator John McCain, a longtime friend. His active support for McCain upset many of his Democratic colleagues, some of whom advocated that Lieberman be excluded from the Senate Democratic Conference or at least be stripped of his committee chairmanship.

After the election, in which the Democratic Senator Barack Obama won the presidency, no serious consideration of excluding Lieberman from the party conference was contemplated. Although he lost a valued committee assignment (see Chapter 6), Lieberman found Democratic leaders eager to find a way to keep him in the party. Party leaders did not want to alienate Lieberman more than necessary to appease rank-and-file Democrats. Party leaders surely figured that it was better to have a larger party and that Lieberman's support might prove critical on many issues.

on committees, where committee assignments are made, they can offer or withhold favors from colleagues.

Tangible rewards come in many other forms, too. The expanded use of task forces by the congressional parties has increased the number of opportunities for leaders to bestow special status on party colleagues. Leaders can appoint members to special commissions and approve international travel plans.

Leaders can be supportive of their colleagues' campaign efforts. They can influence the allocation of funds from the party campaign committees. In recent decades, party leaders have created political action committees of their own and contributed to colleagues' campaigns. Even candidates for leadership posts seek to demonstrate their leadership abilities by raising money that is directed to their colleagues' campaigns. And in recent years, leaders have become very active in attending the fund-raising events of their colleagues, sometimes even choosing not to attend an event to make clear their dissatisfaction with a member's behavior. In a few cases, leaders have intervened to discourage primary challenges to an incumbent colleague.

Information

Information is critical to legislative success. Devising effective legislative strategies requires information about the specific policy issues and alternatives that will arise during the Congress, the policy preferences of the membership, the administration, the other key players, and how others plan to act. Advantages from chamber or party rules, or even party strength, remain only potential sources of leadership power if they are not matched by useful and timely information.

The top leaders navigate in a sea of information. With the help of their staff, leaders collect and absorb information about committee schedules and actions, floor scheduling, presidential requests, members' political circumstances, and interest group activity. The top leaders do not have a monopoly over most kinds of information, of course, but they are uniquely placed to assimilate information from many different sources. Requests are made of them on such matters as scheduling, committee assignments, and campaign assistance, and leaders can sometimes pry information from members, lobbyists, and others who want something from them. The whip systems and party task forces are often activated to gather and disseminate information. And the time they spend on or near their chamber floor gives leaders and their staffs opportunities for casual conversations and informal exchanges of information.

Because information flows to the top leaders so readily, few other members can compete with party leaders as coalition builders. To be sure, committee leaders and bill sponsors master information relevant to their own legislation. But from time to time even committee leaders turn to party leaders for assistance in gathering and distributing information. By exercising care in granting access to their information, party leaders can affect the strategies of other important players.

Leaders' informational advantage is stronger in the House than in the Senate, owing to the House's larger size. In the House, the seemingly simple task of counting members planning to vote for or against something is onerous. For the majority party, this means reaching more than 218 members, many of whom might be away from Washington when the information is needed. Consequently, House bill managers often must rely on the services of the party leadership – whip offices and task forces – for timely information. In contrast, Senate bill managers are more self-reliant because they need to count fewer heads. Thus, Senate whip organizations are not critical to the collection and dissemination of information on most important matters.

The overall trend in recent decades has been toward a diffusion of information across Capitol Hill. Junior members have benefited from the expansion of committee, personal, and support agency staffs and from the growth of the interest group community and informal members' caucuses. Party leaders now have more competition in the market for information than they did just a few decades ago.

Access to the Media

Although top party leaders cannot compete with the president for media attention, they enjoy far better access to the media than do most other members. The media often turn to top leaders for their reactions to events or to presidential decisions or statements. This phenomenon is natural: Leaders are presumed to represent their parties and to be in a position to act on their views. Even when there is no breaking story, leaders' routine press conferences attract reporters on the chance that the leaders will say something newsworthy. Few other members can count on such attention. Thus, leaders gain media attention because they are powerful, and, at least in part, they are powerful because they gain media attention.

Party leaders' media access serves as an important resource in the legislative game. Leaders can share their access with colleagues: They can mention a colleague's legislation, invite a colleague to join in a press conference, or refer reporters and television producers to a colleague. They can selectively divulge information about the plans of friendly and unfriendly factions. They also can increase the ease or difficulty of reaching compromises by intensifying or softening the rhetoric of claiming credit and avoiding blame.

Until recently, Senate leaders generally had an advantage over House leaders in their access to the media. The greater public prestige of the Senate and greater public interest in senators than in representatives encouraged the national media to pay more attention to Senate leaders. The advent of televised floor sessions in the House in 1979, about seven years before the Senate permitted television coverage of its sessions, seemed to make little difference.

Recent House Speakers have been as visible as the top Senate leaders on network news programs. In the 1950s through the mid-1970s, Senate leaders were far more visible on television news programs than were House leaders. The Speaker of the House has gained prominence since the 1970s. For a couple years in the mid-1990s, Speaker Gingrich was second only to the president in media visibility. The House minority leader generally lags

ONE NAME, TWO PARTIES

House and Senate Democrats and House and Senate Republicans have separate organizations and elect their own leaders, but there are still good reasons for fellow partisans in the two houses to coordinate their activities. In fact, periodically a party's House and Senate leaders, usually from the "out party" (the party that does not control the White House), promise to work together on an agenda and public relations. A president tends to dominate congressional leaders in defining the party's policy agenda and shaping the party's public image. Soon after the Republicans lost the White House in the 2008 elections, their congressional leaders promised greater coordination. Coordination tends to fade quickly as leaders in each house struggle to meet the expectations of their own party conference.

far behind other top leaders in media visibility, reflecting the relatively weak formal powers and informal influence of most House minority leaders. In contrast, the power of the Senate minority to obstruct bills, coupled with the Senate's prestige, gives the Senate minority leader a big advantage over his or her House counterpart in attracting media attention.

Recent party leaders in both houses have made a concerted effort to shape the message communicated through the media to the general public. They have expanded their press office operations, hired media specialists, consulted pollsters, created party committees or task forces to shape party messages, and sought new ways to communicate to the public. All recent top leaders have sought to fashion coherent policy programs, to advertise their programs, and to develop a common argument or theme for the parties on major issues.

Leadership Staffs

Top leaders' staffs have expanded as leaders have sought to meet colleagues' expectations and extend their own influence. These staffs now include policy specialists, public relations personnel, and experts in parliamentary procedures, as well as people who assist the leaders with daily chores. With the help of expanded staffs, leaders can more carefully follow committee deliberations, more rapidly respond to political events, and more frequently take a leading role in the negotiation of legislative details.

Organizational arrangements for the staff of the four top party leaders vary, reflecting both differences in the leaders' positions and historical accident. The House Speaker's leadership staff is spread between the Speaker's office and the Steering and Policy Committee. Similarly, the Senate

Democratic leader's staff is located primarily in the Policy Committee. The House and Senate Republican leaders' staffs are housed within their leadership offices. Both Senate leaders manage the activity of the party secretaries, who are staff members, and the secretaries' assistants.

An Era of Reinvigorated Parties

The role of parties and their leaders in Congress is not written in stone. Indeed, members of the early Congresses could not have envisioned modern congressional parties. The development of congressional parties has occurred in response to the changing needs and demands of members, who elect the top party leaders and are free to write and rewrite the rules of their chambers and party caucuses. New issues, turnover in the membership, new presidents, new political cleavages in American society, the nature of electoral parties, and changing rules sometimes alter members' calculations about the kind of legislative party organization and leadership that will best serve their interests.

In recent decades, stronger parties and leaders have emerged. This development would have surprised most observers of the mid-1960s. At that time, the House and Senate caucuses of the majority party Democrats were inactive; today, all four congressional party caucuses (or conferences) are active and meet regularly. In the mid-1960s, the top Democratic leaders were deferential to committee and subcommittee chairs; today, party leaders frequently name party task forces, composed of members both on and off the standing committees of jurisdiction, to devise policy and strategy on major issues. In the mid-1960s, party leaders assumed that committee leaders would speak for the party on policy matters; today, party leaders themselves are clearly expected to assume a prominent role in the media on nearly all important matters. In the 1970s, extreme individualism was the most common description of Congress; during the last 20 years, unrestrained partisanship has been the dominant theme.

These developments appear to be the products of change in the several basic elements of the legislative game –what the issues are, who the players are and what they want, and the rules. Each of these elements contributed to forming the parties' coalitions inside and outside of Congress and deserves brief consideration.

The Issues

Large federal deficits in the 1980s and early 1990s dominated the policy agenda of Congress and exacerbated long-standing differences between the parties over the appropriate size and function of the federal government. Such matters as tax hikes and cuts, the allocation of money between defense and domestic programs, and government commitments to entitlement programs for the elderly, the sick, and the poor stimulated pitched battles between the parties. Few issues were perceived to have as direct a connection to electoral fortunes as aggregate spending and tax choices, so the incentives for the parties to seek credit and avoid blame were high. The partisan electoral consequences of fiscal politics produced demands on the top leaders to be more assertive in public relations and to work harder to bolster their parties' public images. Partisan differences over fiscal policy reemerged as a central issue after the 2000 elections and remain important. Contributing to partisanship is the use of omnibus legislation for the federal budget. As a consequence of procedures authorized by the 1974 Budget Act, budget policy was wrapped into two major pieces of legislation each year – a budget resolution and a reconciliation bill. The stakes are particularly high for reconciliation bills, which typically package the proposals for spending cuts of more than a dozen committees. These high-stakes bills force party leaders into all negotiations and encourage members and outside observers to judge outcomes in terms of party winners and losers.

To make matters worse, this high-stakes contest, between a Congress controlled by one party and a president of the other party, tended toward stalemate. Blaming the other party – and the other institution – for the lack of action became the chief political strategy. Only top party leaders and the president could overcome the gridlock, but that only increased the stakes and enhanced the perceived partisan consequences of the outcome.

In this environment, party leaders were expected to be aggressive and outspoken. Some leaders were not especially comfortable or capable in that role. Only after Jim Wright assumed the speakership in 1987 did House Democrats have a Speaker who relished a prominent place in the media. When Senator George Mitchell took over after Byrd relinquished his leadership post, also in 1987, Senate Democrats had a leader who saw being a party spokesperson as a high-priority responsibility. Since then, leaders of both parties and in both houses have aggressively promoted their party's views.

Contributing to a stronger role for party leaders have been issues that cut across the jurisdictions of multiple standing committees. When party interests dictate action on issues such as global warming and energy that fall under the jurisdiction of many committees, their chairs cannot be expected to act promptly and effectively to coordinate legislative action. The majority party's interests dictate that central party leaders coordinate the development of legislation, take the lead in finding compromises among party colleagues, devise public relations strategies to sell the legislation to the public, and concentrate the resources required to build majorities on the floor.

Members' Demands

Former Senate parliamentarian Floyd Riddick once observed that "the position of the floor leader is not that of an army general over a multitude of soldiers. Unlike army officers, the floor leaders must maintain continued support. They are subject to periodic reelection by the same persons they have been leading."[1] That is, party leaders are appropriately viewed as agents of their party colleagues, and their success depends largely on the cooperation of those colleagues. Consequently, leaders' goals and strategies are shaped by the demands and expectations of their party colleagues, whose own political goals and needs change over time.

Many observers have commented on the individualism that has characterized members of Congress in recent decades. This "new breed" of lawmaker, as it is often called, is a product of the 1960s. New-breed members are anti-establishment, intolerant of traditional norms and authority, and more national, or even worldly, in their orientation. They are more independent, outward-looking, issue-oriented, media-oriented, and entrepreneurial. Their individualism is encouraged by expanded opportunities outside Congress – a swelling interest group community, broader single-issue constituencies facilitated by new forms of electronic communication and greater ease in cross-continental and intercontinental travel, and the growth of computerized mass mailings and telephone solicitation techniques. In addition, individualism among legislators is encouraged by the necessity of personally raising large sums of money to gain reelection.

In the late 1960s, the Senate's new breed began to produce presidential candidates. In the 1970s, new-breed members contributed to a redistribution of power within House committees from full committee chairs to subcommittee chairs (see Chapter 6), the distribution of more resources to rank-and-file members in both chambers, and a surge in floor amending activity. They also contributed to the demise of such waning norms as deference to committee recommendations and serving a quiet apprenticeship period to learn the ropes before actively seeking to influence policy choices.

Unrestrained individualism created several problems for party leaders. Surveying, coordinating, and scheduling chamber activities became more complicated. No longer could majority party leaders rely on consultations with a few senior committee leaders. Individualism meant that leaders were less certain about who wanted to participate and who expected to be consulted, that committee leaders could expect more challenges to committee bills, and that floor sessions would be longer and less predictable. Of course, many bill managers faced difficulties because of their inexperience. In the House, individualism also meant less restrained tactics on the part of minority party members.

As members struggled to adapt to the new conditions, many majority party members turned to their party leaders for assistance. More and more frequently, majority party leaders were called on to resolve intra-party conflicts that had once been negotiated or squelched by committee chairs. Even before legislation was ready for floor action, conflicts between committees and between committee members and nonmembers led some members to ask top leaders to intervene. And majority party frustration with minority party tactics – calls for votes, redundant amendments, and so on – resulted in calls for a crackdown on the minority by the majority party leadership. The Speaker responded with some rules changes and more creative use of special rules to limit floor amendments. Ironically, then, from the chaos of unrestrained individualism came demands for stronger central leadership.

Policy Alignments

At the same time that policy making was becoming further complicated by individualism, members' positions on major policy questions became more polarized by partisan affiliation. Electoral forces and changes in Congress's policy agenda contributed to greater partisanship in voting during the 1980s.

The budget-oriented agenda produced intensified conflict among legislators. Large deficits increased the difficulty of finding funds for new or expanded programs, and old programs became targets for budget cutters. Consequently, legislation that in the past had seemed to produce far more winners than losers, such as student aid and environmental protection measures, was evaluated less on its own merit and more on the basis of its impact on the deficit during the next few years. Attention shifted from individual programs, which often attract support across party lines, to the overall spending and taxation patterns of the federal government – just the kind of issue that taps deeply held ideological beliefs and most differentiates the two parties.

Electoral forces also contributed to party polarization. The largest changes appeared in the South, where the expansion of the African American voting

LEADERSHIP IN ANOTHER ERA

Sam Rayburn (D-Texas) was the most beloved twentieth-century Speaker of the House. He served as Speaker from 1940 to 1961, with the exception of four years when Republicans controlled the House. Rayburn listened well and was always kind to his colleagues, and because he was sheepish about his bald head, he shied away from cameras. He exercised his power quietly. A Rayburn biographer reported an incident on the floor of the House that was typical of the way he ruled:

"[W]hen a bill providing for a cooling-off period to stave off labor strikes came to the House floor, Rayburn wanted it debated fully. Experience and instinct told him that with feelings running high an attempt might be made to shut off debate and go directly to a vote. This proved correct when Jennings Randolph of West Virginia, a member of the Labor Committee, won recognition and started to make a motion to do this.

While he was still talking, Rayburn walked down from the dais and headed toward him. With each approaching step Randolph's voice grew weaker. Finally he stopped talking when Rayburn reached him and put a hand on his shoulder. For a short time, with his face set sternly, Rayburn spoke in a low, gruff tone to Randolph, whom he liked. Then still talking, he removed his hand, plunged it into his jacket pocket, and his body rocked back and forth from his heels to his toes. Then he turned suddenly and walked back to the rostrum.

Laughter swept the chamber as embarrassment crossed Randolph's face. When silence came, Randolph announced he was withdrawing his motion, and he added, 'As a legislative son I am always willing to follow the advice of my legislative elders.'"

Rayburn was special, to be sure, but no recent Speaker, in an age of televised floor sessions and independent-minded members, would have dared embarrass a colleague in that way.

base for Democrats and the suburban, white base for Republicans altered the electoral coalitions for the two parties. Southern Democrats became more moderate and sometimes quite liberal, making the Democratic contingents in the House and Senate more homogeneous. Southern Republicans, a scarce breed before the 1970s, fit the traditional conservative Republican mold, so they reinforced the homogeneity of the Republican party in Congress. Southern Republicans now hold many of their party's top leadership posts.

A change from less to more polarized parties has characterized developments in the House and Senate since the late 1970s. Increasing intra-party hesiveness, reinforced by increasing inter-party conflict, has altered the demands placed on party leaders. That partisanship has led members to insist that their leaders actively pursue party interests, and at the same time it has reduced resistance to strong central leaders from the remaining but shrinking minority factions within the parties.

Rules of the Game

The reinforcement of the Speaker's powers, beginning in the early 1970s, represents an important development in the distribution of power in the House. The House party leaders appoint the members of the Rules Committee, which, in the case of the majority party, gives the Speaker effective control over the content of special rules governing the consideration of major legislation on the floor. Furthermore, the Speaker now has the power to refer legislation to multiple committees and set deadlines for committee action. In the House, therefore, the majority party leader can exercise a good deal of control over the process by which legislation is brought to the floor, debated, and subject to amendment.

In many cases, the House Speaker's new powers have been exercised in routine ways. The Speaker does not seek to influence most committee assignments, for example, because many committees have little relevance to partisan concerns or few members are competing for the available seats. For more routine legislation going through the Rules Committee, the committee relies on past experience to guide the design of rules, without consulting with the Speaker. Similarly, the parliamentarian makes recommendations on multiple referral based on established precedent and inter-committee agreements and the advice usually is followed. The Speaker seldom gets personally involved. The development of such standard operating practices is a natural product of the gradual accumulation of precedents under new rules and the desire of members and their staff to lend predictability to the process.

The new powers become a political tool only when the Speaker deliberately calls them into play. In the 1970s, Speakers Albert and O'Neill generally let their procedural tools sit idle. But since the late 1970s, the nature of the policy agenda and members' demands led speakers to employ their powers more often and aggressively. In fact, the speaker's bill referral and special rules prerogatives are a regular part of strategic calculations by most members on important, controversial legislation. As a result, the speaker frequently is brought into discussions about strategy by other members at early stages in their planning so that the speaker has regular opportunities to influence the policy directions taken by House committees and subcommittees.

Strategies of Adaptation

Party organizations and leaders are much more important to congressional policy making now than they were three decades ago. Four aspects of party responses to the changing conditions deserve summary.

EXPANDED SERVICES. Since the 1970s, congressional party organizations and leaders have greatly expanded the services they provide their members. In doing so, party leaders seek to both gain or maintain majority status and earn the gratitude of party colleagues. Secondary leaders – whips, the chairs of the campaign, policy, and research committees, and conference chairs and secretaries – who, in their effort to demonstrate their fitness for even higher positions, have led the way by diversifying services. As members compete for votes to get elected to party posts, they solicit ideas for new services and move to expand services once elected. While doing so, secondary leaders expand party staffs that they control and extend their own reach to a broader range of issues.

Party staffs now provide quite varied services: publications on the chamber schedules, legislation, policy problems, and political matters; email communications; clearinghouses for job applicants; analyses of floor voting records; assistance in the production of newsletters and graphics material; and facilities and staff assistance for the production of radio and television messages and programs. In the Senate, the parties maintain in-house cable television systems to provide senators' offices with up-to-the-minute information on floor developments and satellite up-link equipment so that senators can make live appearances on local stations or at meetings away from Washington. On a personal basis, leaders work harder to meet the scheduling demands of party colleagues and to assist colleagues in fundraising, campaigning, and attracting media attention.

STRATEGY OF INCLUSION. All leaders want fellow party members to feel that they have influence on party policy stances and tactics – a strategy of inclusion. All four party caucuses (or conferences) and many of the party committees meet regularly. Whip organizations have grown and task forces have multiplied to give more members an opportunity to participate in policy making beyond the confines of their assigned standing committees. Leaders also call together informal groups of members to solicit their views and encourage their participation through party channels. These developments contribute to leaders' efforts to gather information, promote a party spirit, solicit support, and build majority coalitions.

PROCEDURAL STRATEGIES. Leaders have expanded their repertoire of procedural strategies. The standard committee-to-floor-to-conference process remains, but variations on that process are now more common. Discussions in party councils are more likely to occur before action is taken in standing committees. Leaders more frequently engage in negotiations with committee and faction leaders after committees have reported legislation but before floor action. Party task forces have added a layer of party members who influence both the content of legislation and coalition-building strategy. At times, task forces even initiate legislation, and their proposals are taken directly to the floor by party leaders. Flexibility, not rigidity, characterizes the legislative process in recent Congresses.

Majority party leaders, particularly in the House where their formal powers are the strongest, use their procedural tools to set the agenda in a way that favors their party. This happens at two levels. On the first level, leaders more actively seek to set detailed policy agendas for their chamber, including a general schedule for action on major legislation. On the second level, leaders work harder to control the specific alternatives that are considered on the floor once legislation gets there. In the House, this is done through special rules written by the Rules Committee. Controlling alternatives is more difficult in the Senate, where unanimous consent must be obtained to structure the consideration of alternatives, a requirement that severely limits the ability of the majority leader to manipulate the floor agenda. Nevertheless, pressure to lend some structure to the process comes from members of both parties, all of whom have busy schedules and an interest in avoiding embarrassing or repetitious votes. At times, negotiating unanimous consent agreements becomes a full-time job for the majority leader.

PUBLIC RELATIONS. Leaders work harder to influence the image of their party that is communicated through the mass media. Such efforts are aimed at creating a climate of public opinion favorable to the party, which makes it easier for party members to support their leaders and explain their votes at home. If successful, leaders' media strategies produce support for party positions from independent-minded members who are not readily pressured.

Congressionally Speaking...

In 2004, Senate Democrats created a "war room" to coordinate public relations and legislative strategy on a bill to extend unemployment benefits. Party leaders and staff met there to respond to the rapid flow of attacks from the other side by utilizing the full range of media outlets. The war room operation was made a regular part of the Senate Democrats' leadership structure after the 2004 elections, when Democrats lost four Senate seats, to improve the "message strategy" of the party. The term was used in a political context by the campaign strategists in the 1992 presidential campaign of Bill Clinton to describe their headquarters and was made famous as the title of a film documentary on the campaign. The official name for the Senate Democrats' operation is the Senate Democratic Communications Center. All four congressional parties now have some form of war room operation.

Conclusion

The environment of the late twentieth century and early twenty-first century pushed congressional party leaders to the forefront of policy making. Party leaders are now central strategists and coordinators of policy development in Congress. It has not always been so. In the mid-twentieth century, party leaders coordinated the floor schedule and worked closely with committee leaders on strategy, but, for the most part, they left the development of legislative details to the standing committees and their chairs.

Party leaders are not all-powerful. Far from it. Congressional parties still lack the capacity to deny nomination or election to Congress and so have limited influence over their members, far less influence than exists in most other national legislatures. To be sure, the parties elect leadership, organize the standing committees, and structure floor and conference action. Moreover, congressional parties' internal organizations and staffs have become more elaborate. And in the last two decades leaders have been prime movers in the legislative process on major issues. Nevertheless, diverse constituency interests across a large, heterogeneous country, the weakness of the parties in candidate selection, the fragmentation of American party organizations across several levels of government, and the difficulty of coordinating House and Senate activities stand in the way of party-directed policy making over the long term.

Above: Sen. Charles Schumer, D-NY, introduces Sen. Hillary Rodham Clinton, D-NY, prior to her testimony before the Senate Foreign Relations Committee regarding her nomination by President-elect Barack Obama to be Secretary of State on Capitol Hill in Washington on January 13, 2009. (UPI Photo/Roger L. Wollenberg)

Below: WASHINGTON, DC – Dec. 05: General Motors Chairman Richard Wagoner Jr.; Chrysler CEO Robert Nardelli; and Ford Motor Co. CEO Alan Mulally; during the House Financial Services hearing on potential financial aid legislation for the U.S. auto industry. (Photo by Scott J. Farrell/Congressional Quarterly)

6

The Standing Committees

ONE OF THE MOST VISIBLE AND ENDURING FEATURES OF CONGRESS IS its committee system. From hearings to investigations to legislative activity, committees are the congressional darlings of the mass media. And considering the central role that committees play in modern-day lawmaking and oversight, there is little wonder why they garner so much attention. Most important legislation originates in a standing committee, most of the details of legislation are approved in committee, and standing committee members usually dominate floor and conference action. When legislation dies, it usually does so in committee.

The significance of standing committees in the policy-making process varies over time. In the mid-twentieth century, committees were often described as nearly autonomous policy makers (see Chapter 2). The tremendous growth in government and power of the presidency that characterized the New Deal and World War II era of the 1930s and 1940s led Congress to reevaluate the way it did business. The Legislative Reorganization Act of 1946 reduced the number of standing committees, provided detailed, written committee jurisdictions, guaranteed a professional staff for each committee, and directed committees to conduct oversight of executive agencies. As a result of the 1946 act, most of the key features of the modern committee system were put into place. Moreover, the leadership of the internally divided Democratic majority usually preferred to defer to committees rather than risk open divisions on the House and Senate floor. In fact, prescriptive norms deference to committees and senior committee leaders – were articulated by leaders to bolster the power of committees.

In recent decades, committees have lost much of the autonomy they had gained in the middle of the twentieth century. A more assertive membership, increasingly polarized parties, stronger party leadership, and new checks on

165

committee leadership, among other factors, reduced the level of independence once held by committees and their leaders. Still, committees retain a
considerable amount of power within their issue domains; they process the
vast majority of legislation that is approved by the House and Senate. In
this chapter, we profile the House and Senate committee systems and then
examine the foundations of committee power and how these powers have
evolved over time.

Types of Committees

Modern congressional committees have two formal functions: (1) collecting information through hearings and investigations and (2) drafting and
reporting legislation. Committee hearings are Congress's primary means for
formally receiving the testimony of representatives of the executive branch,
organized interest groups, independent experts, the general public, and,
occasionally, movie stars. Congress usually relies on committees to investigate disasters (natural or human-made), scandals in government or elsewhere, or policy crises. Informally, congressional hearings provide opportunities for legislators to publicize causes and receive media attention. On the
legislative side, the vast majority of bills and other legislation introduced by
members are referred to the committee or committees with the appropriate jurisdiction. In committee meetings for considering legislation, called
markups, the details of legislation are reviewed or written.

The House and Senate have developed several types of committees to perform these informational and legislative functions. All committees can hold
hearings and investigate policy problems that fall within their jurisdiction.
However, not all committees have the right to receive and report legislation, and not all committees are considered to be standing or permanent
committees (Table 6.1).

Standing committees have legislative authority and permanent status (standing committee are listed in Table 6.2). Their legislative jurisdiction is specified in chamber rules and precedents, and they write and report legislation
on any matter within their jurisdictions. Committee members, and particularly chairs, are territorial about their committees' jurisdictions and resist
efforts to reduce or reallocate their jurisdictions. As a result, with a few
important exceptions, change in the committee systems of the House and
Senate has been incremental.

Ad hoc committees may be created and appointed to design and report legislation, but they are temporary and often dissolve either at a specified date
or after reporting the legislation for which they were created. Since 1975,

TABLE 6.1. Types of Committees.

Permanent Status?	May report legislation to the floor?	
	Yes	No
Yes	standing committees	some select committees
		joint committees
No	conference committees	
	most select committees	
	ad hoc committees	

the Speaker of the House has been permitted to appoint ad hoc committees with House approval, but this authority has been used infrequently.

Conference committees are temporary and have legislative responsibilities. They are appointed to resolve the differences between House and Senate versions of legislation. The Constitution requires that legislation be approved in identical form by both chambers before it is sent to the president. While the Constitution is silent as to how the two chambers are to resolve their differences, conference committees were an almost immediate solution to this problem. Although inter-chamber differences can be resolved in other ways, conference committees are formed for most important legislation. Conference committees have wide, but not unlimited, discretion to redesign legislation in their efforts to gain House and Senate approval. In theory, conference committees are bound to the differences between the House and Senate legislation. In practice, however, it is not uncommon for conference committees to insert provisions into legislation that did not appear in either chamber's final legislation and remove provisions that were agreed upon by both chambers. When a majority of House conferees and a majority of Senate conferees agree, a conference committee issues a report that must be approved by both houses for the bill to be sent to the president. Conference committees dissolve as soon as one house takes action on the conference report.

Joint committees are permanent but lack legislative authority. Joint committees are composed of members from both chambers, and the chairs alternate between the chambers from Congress to Congress. The Joint Economic Committee frequently conducts highly publicized hearings on economic affairs, and the Joint Committee on Taxation serves primarily as a holding company for a respected staff of economists whose economic forecasts and reports on fiscal policy matters are frequently cited. The Joint Committee on

TABLE 6.2. Standing Committees of the House and Senate, 2009–2010.

House of Representatives Name (Number of Subcommittees)	Dems[c]	Reps[c]	Ratio[d]
Agriculture (6)	28	18	1.56:1
Appropriations (12)	37	23	1.61:1
Armed Services (7)	37	25	1.48:1
Budget (0)	24	15	1.60:1
Education and Labor (5)	29	19	1.53:1
Energy and Commerce (5)	36	23	1.57:1
Financial Services (6)	42	29	1.45:1
Foreign Affairs (7)	28	19	1.47:1
Homeland Security (6)	21	13	1.62:1
House Administration (0)	6	3	2:1
Judiciary (5)	23	16	1.43:1
Natural Resources (5)	28	20	1.40:1
Oversight and Government Reform (5)	25	16	1.56:1
Rules (2)	9	4	2.25:1
Science and Technology (5)	27	17	1.59:1
Select Committee on Intelligence[a] (4)	12	9	1.33:1
Small Business (5)	17	12	1.42:1
Standards of Official Conduct[b] (0)	5	5	1:1
Transportation and Infrastructure (6)	45	30	1.50:1
Veterans' Affairs (4)	18	11	1.64:1
Ways and Means (6)	26	15	1.73:1

Senate Name (Number of Subcommittees)	Dems[e]	Reps	Ratio[d]
Agriculture, Nutrition, and Forestry (4)	12	9	1.33:1
Appropriations (12)	17	13	1.31:1
Armed Services (6)	15	11	1.36:1
Banking, Housing, and Urban Affairs (5)	13	10	1.3:1
Budget (0)	13	10	1.3:1
Commerce, Science, and Transportation (7)	14	11	1.27:1
Energy and Natural Resources (4)	13	10	1.3:1
Environment and Public Works (6)	11	8	1.38:1
Finance (5)	13	10	1.3:1
Foreign Relations (7)	11	8	1.38:1
Health, Education, Labor, and Pensions (3)	13	10	1.3:1
Homeland Security and Governmental Affairs (5)	10	7	1.43:1
Select Committee on Indian Affairs (0)	8	6	1.33:1
Judiciary (7)	11	8	1.3:1
Rules and Administration (0)	11	8	1.3:1
Select Committee on Intelligence[a] (0)	8	7	1.14:1
Select Committee on Ethics[b] (0)	3	3	1:1
Small Business and Entrepreneurship (0)	11	8	1.3:1
Veterans' Affairs (0)	9	6	1.5:1

a = The two intelligence committees are officially named select committees but have authority to report legislation. b = The House Committee on Standards of Official Conduct may report legislation; the Senate Ethics Committee does not have legislative authority. c = Numbers include only full members of the chamber and vacant seats allotted to the party. d = Party ratio is (Democrats: Republicans). Ratios in House and Senate chambers are 1.43:1 and 1.41:1, respectively (counting the independent senators among the Democrats). e = Independent Senators Bernie Sanders (I-VT) and Joseph Lieberman (I-CT) are counted among the Democrats. *Source:* www.house.gov; www.senate.gov.

Printing performs the more ministerial duty of overseeing the Government Printing Office; the Joint Committee on the Library oversees the Library of Congress. Bills are not referred to joint committees, and joint committees cannot report legislation to the floor. The Joint Committee on Atomic Energy (1946–1977) was the only joint committee to date with authority to report legislation.

Select, or special, committees are, in principle, temporary committees without legislative authority. They may be used to study problems that fall under the jurisdiction of several standing committees, to symbolize Congress's commitment to major constituency groups, or simply to reward particular legislators. Select committees have been used for seven prominent investigations since 1970, including the Senate's 1973 investigation of the Watergate break-in and cover-up and the 1987 House and Senate investigation of the Iran-Contra affair. Major reforms of congressional rules and organizations have originated in select committees.

Unfortunately, committee nomenclature can be misleading. For example, the House and Senate have each made their Select Intelligence Committee permanent and granted it the power to report legislation. Some select committees, such as the House Committee on Homeland Security, began as select committees and gained standing status later. In 1993, under pressure to streamline the legislative process and reduce spending, the House abolished its Select Committee on Aging, Hunger, Narcotics Abuse and Control and its Select Committee on Children, Youth and Families. The Senate maintains a Special Committee on Aging, which studies issues relevant to the elderly, in addition to the Select Committee on Ethics, which handles ethics violations of senators and staffs.

Standing committees are the primary concern of this chapter. In the modern Congress, standing committees originate most legislation, and their members manage the legislation on the floor and dominate conference committees. Unless otherwise indicated, the following discussion concerns standing committees.

The Nature of Congressional Committees

The Constitution makes no provision for committees. Yet, committees emerged early in congressional history. And across time the committee system has undergone considerable change. At different points in history the House and Senate have adopted rules to expand and reduce the number of committees, as well as to modify their structure and authority. Given the emergence and longevity of committees, it is clear that the division of labor that allows each chamber to pursue multiple hearings and legislative efforts simultaneously has proven useful.

To whom are committees responsible? What interests do committees serve? Such questions have motivated an important literature in political science. Three prominent perspectives offer rationale for the existence of committees – the information, distributive, and partisan perspectives.

Informational Politics: Committees Governed by Floor Majorities

One view of congressional committees is that they are designed to meet legislators' need for information about policy problems and solutions. Given Congress's large workload and the complexity of issues, it is unrealistic to expect members to have the capacity to make informed decisions on all matters. By focusing on the issues before their own committees, legislators gain expertise that is applied in a committee setting to improve the fit of policy solutions to policy problems. The expertise serves the interest of the larger membership by generating information that is useful to all legislators in evaluating the recommendations of committees.

In this view, committee experts serve the interest of a majority of the parent chamber. If committee recommendations diverge too much from the preferences of the floor majority or prove misleading, floor majorities will reject committee recommendations and may even reform the committee system. Under normal circumstances, the better-informed arguments of committee experts will guide the behavior of other legislators.

Distributive Politics: Autonomous Committees

A classic view of congressional committees is the distributive theory. This perspective suggests that committees exist to help members secure gains from trade of policy benefits across constituencies with diverse interests. Committees are created to address the legislative interests of constituencies who are important to legislators' reelection efforts. The multiple committees of each chamber allow legislators to gain membership on the committee or committees most relevant to their own constituencies.

By empowering committees, each chamber gives legislators with the strongest constituency interest in a policy area the most influence over legislative action. Because members represent diverse constituencies, the committee system institutionalizes a mutually beneficial arrangement for legislators who want to do favors for home audiences. Public policy is then

SOMETIMES A SENSE OF HUMOR IS REQUIRED

Senators do not always get their first choice of subcommittees. In an interview, Senator Amy Klobuchar (D-Minnesota) told a reporter about her first day on the Subcommittee on Oceans, Atmosphere, Fisheries, and Coast Guard:

Somehow I got placed on the Ocean Subcommittee. I didn't ask for that. But it does have jurisdiction over the Great Lakes, which is important, and so I can be a voice for the Great Lakes. But when I got there the first I realized all the other senators had an ocean. Olympia Snowe (R-Maine) was on there, John Kerry (D-Massachusetts) was on there. And I wrote a note to Frank Lautenberg (D-New Jersey) and I said, "I am the only senator on the Oceans Subcommittee without an ocean." And he wrote back, "Just come back next year and ask for one."

Source: http://blog.washingtonpost.com/sleuth/2007/06/post 1.html

the product of a giant "logroll" – each committee of legislators getting what it wants.

From the perspective of distributive politics, committees serve the interests of individual legislators and their home constituencies (see box "Sometimes a Sense of Humor Is Required"). Therefore, the committee system reflects the pluralism of American politics and permits legislators to focus on the political interests that matter most to them. The distributive perspective considers committees to be relatively autonomous units to which parties and the parent chambers defer. Each committee operates in a community of executive branch agencies and interest groups with similar interests. The larger public interest may suffer as the demands of the disparate constituencies are addressed by committees.

Partisan Politics: Committees Governed by the Majority Party

The partisan perspective posits that parties create committees to better ensure the success of party programs. On committees whose jurisdictions matter to the majority party, party leaders make committee assignments to enhance the party's policy prospects. This, along with expectations of loyalty, constrains the behavior of committee members. And since the majority party has a numerical advantage on committees, it ultimately dictates the policies that emerge.

From this perspective, committee members serve the interests of the parties. While each chamber approves committee membership lists, each party determines which of its members are on each committee list. Parties structure the internal organization of committees – the majority party assumes the chairmanships and controls most staff. And the majority party leadership schedules committee legislation for action on the floor.

In Practice: Committees Governed by Multiple Principals

In practice, committee members must balance conflicting demands placed on them by their parent chambers, parties, and constituencies. While seeking to satisfy the expectations of constituents, they must stay on good terms with party colleagues to retain important committee positions and must meet chamber majorities' expectations to get legislation passed. Fortunate legislators find that the demands of constituents, party leaders, and the chamber majority are aligned most of the time, but real-world politics require many committee members to take risks, balance interests, and struggle with difficult choices.

The extent of independent committee influence over policy outcomes varies over time and across committees. Three sets of factors stand out for their impact on the relationship between committees and their principals: The character of the policy agenda, party strength, and institutional context.

SIZE AND SALIENCE OF THE POLICY AGENDA. The size and salience of the congressional agenda affects the importance of committees to the parties and all chamber members. A large policy workload requires the division of labor that a system of committees provides, but only issues that are salient to a large number of legislators will attract the attention of party leaders or rank-and-file members on the floor. Committees with jurisdictions that affect narrow constituencies are unlikely to be supervised by party leaders or given serious problems on the floor.

MAJORITY PARTY STRENGTH. Political scientists have observed that when parties lack cohesiveness because of internal divisions over policy, less authority is extended to party leaders to pursue partisan objectives. Under these conditions, strong-arm tactics are not tolerated and will alienate large numbers of partisans. Committee delegations will recognize party leaders' weakness and operate with little fear of retribution. In contrast, a cohesive majority party will expect its leaders to work pro-actively for party positions and pressure committee chairs and members to support the party.

INSTITUTIONAL CONTEXT. The House and Senate operate under very different rules. The larger, more unwieldy House has a stronger presiding officer and relies more heavily on formal rules than the Senate does. Senate rules protect each senator's right, on most legislation, to offer amendments on any subject and to conduct extended debate. In doing so, Senate rules protect individual initiative and create more opportunities to resist committee- or party-imposed policy choices. As a result, senators have more bargaining leverage with committee and party leaders than do representatives.

The Power of Modern Committees

Committees' power is expressly or implicitly granted to them by the parent chambers and parties. Their continued existence and parliamentary privileges depend on the sufferance of the parent houses and parties. The parent chambers formally approve all committee assignments, but the parties construct the committee lists that are routinely ratified by the chambers. This function gives the parties a source of leverage with committee members and allows the parties – and, most important, the majority parties – to regulate the behavior of committee members through formal and informal rules. For the most part, committees must function procedurally and substantively in ways that are consistent with the expectations of their parent chambers and parties.

The Legislative Power of Committees

Evaluating the power of committees is difficult. It is very difficult to determine the influence of a committee on any given measure without knowing what the outcome would have been in the absence of committee involvement. Nevertheless, it is reasonable to infer that committees exercise real power in the modern Congress. Much of their power stems from the indifference of most members about the details of most legislation. Committees are extended considerable autonomy because most matters over which they have jurisdiction are of some importance to committee members and little, if any, importance to most other members. Parties and leaders focus on the few issues each year that are likely to affect the parties' reputations and electoral prospects. Members do not and cannot take an interest in the details of much, and probably even most, of the legislation that is considered on the floor.

Even when members are not indifferent, committees still have advantages that give their members disproportionate influence over policy outcomes. Mounting real challenges to their power can be difficult. Threats to strip a committee of jurisdiction, funding, or parliamentary privileges or to retract members' committee assignments usually are not credible, if for no other reason than such actions would set precedents that members of other committees would not like to see established (see box "Committee Leaders Complain About Declining Influence"). In this way an implicit, self-enforcing pact among members underpins committee power. The most practical means for keeping committees in check is to reject their policy recommendations.

It is convenient to consider two forms of committee power.

- Positive power is the ability of committees to gain the approval of legislation opposed by others.
- Negative power is the ability of committees to block legislation favored by others.

On both counts, committees have substantial advantages over other players.

POSITIVE POWER. At first glance, committees appear to have no positive power. Under the Constitution, legislation can be enacted only by the full House and Senate. Neither chamber has rules that permit a committee to act on the chamber's behalf with respect to final approval of legislation. Thus, positive power for committees must come from sources other than the explicit provisions of chamber rules.

Standing committees start with considerable discretion in writing and reporting legislation. They are free to act as they see fit on most legislation that is referred to them. They may simply refuse to act, hold hearings but take no legislative action, amend the legislation in any way, or accept the legislation without change. They may also write their own legislation, or they may vote to report legislation with a recommendation that it pass, with no recommendation, or with a recommendation that it be rejected.

Nevertheless, committees are not guaranteed that their legislation will receive favorable consideration on the House and Senate floors. To gain passage of legislation that might not otherwise pass, committees may exploit four sources of potential positive committee power: (1) *persuasion* on the basis of superior argument and information about the merits of legislation, (2) *leverage* acquired through threats of unfavorable action on members' bills if they fail to cooperate with a committee on its agenda, (3) *strategic packaging* of unpopular legislative provisions with more popular provisions to win floor majorities, and (4) *domination of conference committees* to gain chamber endorsement of policy provisions favored by the committee. Each of these deserves a brief mention.

COMMITTEE LEADERS COMPLAIN ABOUT DECLINING INFLUENCE

Early in 2009, Speaker Nancy Pelosi dealt with an open revolt from committee leaders who were upset about major bills, such as the economic stimulus package, being written in Pelosi's office rather than in committee. The stimulus bill was not subject to the "regular order" or committee hearings and markups before a floor vote. This angered top-ranking committee members who see their influence raining on key pieces of legislation. Bart Stupak (D-Michigan) chair of the Energy and Commerce subcommittee said, "The question is: Are we [committees] going to get a chance to legislate?"

Despite the fact that most Democrats supported the general outlines of the legislation crafted in Pelosi's office, many fear that committee power may erode permanently. Referring to the new top-down process, one unnamed Democrat remarked, "One of the problems is that I think the Speaker thinks this is the regular order." For her part, Pelosi urged patience and suggested that these steps were necessary to insure quick action on important legislation such as the stimulus bill.

Source: Jared Allen. "Panel Chairmen Fighting Mad over snubs by Pelosi." The Hill, January 15, 2009.

First, committees can usually gain a tactical edge by being better informed than their opponents. Committee members sit through hearings, participate in discussions with lobbyists and executive branch officials, and often have previous experience with the issues their committee deals with. Committees' large, expert staffs and their extensive networks of allies in the executive branch and interest group community further enhance their informational advantage over competitors. Traditional norms such as serving an apprenticeship before actively participating, developing expertise in the jurisdiction of one's committees, and deferring to committee specialists reflect the importance of informational advantages for committee power.

Second, the ability of committees to obstruct action on some legislation can be used to gain leverage with members whose support is needed on other legislation. Particularly in the House, where circumventing a committee is neither easy nor convenient, obstructing action on legislation can be used as a threat to win support for committee recommendations.

Third, within the bounds of their broad jurisdictions, committees may package provisions addressing multiple subjects in legislation. By doing so, they can combine the unpopular provisions with more popular provisions to win support for bills. In the House, this power is enhanced when a committee can acquire a special rule from the Rules Committee that limits amendments to the unpopular provisions when the legislation is considered on the floor.

Fourth, members of committees gain positive power through their domination of conference committees. Conference negotiations between the House and Senate give conferees considerable flexibility to alter chamber decisions. The conferees know that they are free to exercise such discretion provided that they can attract majority support for the conference report – which cannot be amended on the House or Senate floor – when it is returned to the two chambers for final approval. The ability of conferees to choose any policy outcome that is at least as preferred to no bill by the two chambers often renders opposition to the committee's preferences futile.

NEGATIVE POWER. The negative power of standing committees rests in their ability to control newly introduced legislation and to obstruct alternative routes to the floor. The ability to obstruct action is often called "gatekeeping" in theories of politics. Committees' negative power is much stronger in the House than the Senate.

In the House, negative power is supported by rules that give committees near-monopoly control over newly introduced legislation and make circumventing committees difficult. House Rule 10 requires that all legislation relating to a committee's jurisdiction be referred to that committee, a rule that has been in place since 1880. Before 1975, the single committee with the most relevant jurisdiction would receive the referral, a process that often involved direct conflicts between committees with related jurisdictions. Since 1975, the rule has provided for multiple referral by granting to the Speaker the authority to refer legislation to each committee with relevant jurisdiction. Monopoly control by single committees was broken by the new rule, but the practice of referring nearly all legislation to committee remains in place.

Committees' blocking power is enhanced by their domination of conference committees. The wide latitude extended to conferences to design the final form of legislation gives committee members another opportunity to wield negative powers. Committee members appointed to conference can, and frequently do, delete provisions they find objectionable. Because conference reports cannot be amended when sent to the House and Senate floors, it is difficult to reverse a conference committee's surgical removal of legislative provisions. Conferees also can take the more drastic step of refusing to file a conference report, thus blocking the legislation in its entirety, at least temporarily.

Circumventing House committees is difficult but not impossible under House rules. The House operates under a germaneness rule that requires a floor amendment to be relevant to the section of the bill or resolution it seeks to modify. Thus, it is difficult to bring to the floor as an amendment a policy proposal whose subject has not been addressed in legislation reported by a committee. The germaneness rule can be waived, but only if a special rule from the Rules Committee is approved by a majority on the House floor. The Speaker's control of the Rules Committee means that this approach is unlikely to work without the Speaker's cooperation.

House rules provide additional means for bringing legislation to the floor. At certain times, members may move to suspend the rules to consider a measure blocked by a committee. Going this route is usually not feasible without the consent of the relevant committee because the member must be recognized by the Speaker to make the motion and two-thirds of the House must support it.

A second route is to gain a special rule from the Rules Committee to discharge a measure from committee. This route requires Rules Committee support and majority support in the House for the special rule. The Speaker's cooperation is typically required to gain Rules Committee action on such a rule.

Alternatively, party leaders occasionally circumvent committees by drafting legislation themselves or by delegating this responsibility to task forces or special committees. Task forces are ad hoc panels typically created by party leaders to carry out legislative duties. Party leaders may use task forces if they are concerned that a committee with jurisdiction will perform unsatisfactorily. For example, they may fear that the committee will not reach an agreement in a timely fashion or that it will produce a bill that either cannot pass the chamber or will not satisfy majority party members. When legislation is drafted in a task force, party leaders determine which members are charged with drafting the legislation and, in the House, can and often do exclude minority party members from the process.

Finally, House members may seek to discharge a measure from a committee that fails to report it within thirty days of referral. Any member may file a discharge petition, which requires the signatures of 218 members. Once the petition receives the necessary number of signatures, it is placed on the Discharge Calendar for consideration on the second or fourth Monday of the month following a seven legislative day waiting period. Many members are hesitant to encourage the use of discharge petitions because doing so threatens the power of their own committees. Nevertheless, there has been

ɔre interest in discharge petitions since late 1993, when the House voted
make public the names of members who sign them. Public disclosure
makes it easier to generate public or interest group pressure on members to
sign petitions.

The discharge petition may appear to be the most promising route for
circumventing committees because it does not require the assistance of the
Rules Committee or the Speaker. In fact, between 1931 and 2002, 563 discharge petitions were filed, but the petitions gained the required number of
signatures only 48 times. Of the 48 instances in which discharge petitions
gained the necessary 218 signatures, only 19 times did the discharged measure go on to pass the House. However, the threatened use of discharge
petitions, special rules, and suspension of the rules occasionally has stimulated committees to act in accordance with the floor majority's preferences.
For example, between 1931 and 1994 there were 15 cases in which the
needed 218 signatures were acquired on a discharge petition, but the majority leadership called up the legislation for consideration by other means.

The Senate's rules create weaker blocking power for its committees. Senate
committees lack much of the negative power that House committees enjoy.
Although measures are routinely referred to Senate committees upon their
introduction, a senator can easily object to a referral and keep a measure
on the calendar for floor consideration. Furthermore, the Senate lacks a
germaneness rule for most measures, so senators are able to circumvent
committees by offering whole bills as amendments to unrelated legislation.
Senators often hesitate to support efforts to bypass a committee in this
way, but it is a procedural route that is used much more frequently than
are the more complicated House procedures for circumventing committees.
Moreover, most conference reports are potentially subject to filibusters in
the Senate, giving Senate minorities a source of bargaining leverage over
committee members at the conference stage that does not exist in the House.

Nevertheless, in practice, Senate committees do retain some blocking
power. Calling up a measure from the calendar requires the cooperation of
the majority leader, who usually sides with the committee chair on procedural matters. And if the majority leader cooperates, committee members,
like all senators, may filibuster or threaten to filibuster unfriendly legislation.
Consequently, successful circumvention of a committee on a controversial
matter often requires the support of at least 60 senators, the number needed
to invoke cloture.

Nongermane amendments are troublesome for Senate committees, but
they can often be set aside by a motion to table. A successful motion
to table kills the amendment. Because a tabling motion is not debatable

CIRCUMVENTING UNFRIENDLY COMMITTEES

For Senator Sam Brownback, a Republican from Kansas, banning human cloning became a key legislative objective. Twice in the 107th Congress (2001–2002), Brownback introduced legislation that fell into the unfriendly jurisdiction of the Judiciary Committee. Senator Orrin Hatch (R-Utah), chair of the Judiciary Committee, openly stated that he supported scientific endeavors that could lead to finding cures for diseases.

On his third attempt at passing the legislation calling for a ban on human cloning, however, Senator Brownback manipulated the legislation to circumvent the Judiciary Committee. Knowing that Senator Judd Gregg (R-New Hampshire), chair of the Health, Education, Labor, and Pension (HELP) Committee, was supportive of his legislation, as were other HELP Committee members, Brownback changed the legislation so that a different part of existing law would be modified. Instead of calling upon the U.S. penal code, which falls under the jurisdiction of Judiciary, Brownback altered the legislation so that the ban would be enacted under the Public Service Act, which is under the jurisdiction of the HELP Committee. In response to this maneuver, a GOP senior aide said with understatement, "There are parliamentary conventions that can be used or abused to ensure referral to a more friendly committee."

Source: Emily Pierce, "Leaders Circumvent Hatch," *Roll Call*, February 5, 2003.

(and therefore cannot be filibustered) and is a procedural question, it often attracts more votes than would be cast against the amendment itself. Moreover, the members of conference committees have an opportunity to drop adopted nongermane amendments in conference.

In short, under most circumstances committees in both chambers – but especially in the House – exercise considerable negative power. Circumventing committees requires special effort and is usually possible only with the cooperation of the majority party leadership.

Oversight and the Investigative Power of Modern Committees

Central to the legislative power of committees and vital to the power of Congress as an institution is the ability of committees to oversee and investigate governmental or private activity that is or might be the subject of public policy. Courts have ruled that Congress's power to compel cooperation with its investigations is implicit in its constitutional functions of legislating and appropriating funds. Without broad powers to investigate and compel cooperation, Congress would not be able to exercise its legislative powers effectively.

Congressionally Speaking...

As part of their oversight and investigative powers, committees and subcommittees are authorized by House and Senate rules to issue *subpoenas* – formal writs compelling a recipient to testify or produce documents (or both) to the committee or subcommittee from which they originated. Typically committees/subcommittees receive the information they need without forcing compliance. Should the President invoke executive privilege or an official simply refuse to cooperate, however, subpoenas help equip committees to carry out investigations.

The decision rules for issuing a subpoena vary across committees, as they are not codified by chamber rules and parent bodies extend considerable autonomy to committees in determining their internal proceedings. House rules only require that a quorum (majority) be present at the time that the subpoena is agreed to. House rules also allow the committee/subcommittee to delegate subpoena power to full committee chairs. Senate rules provide even less guidance. It is important to note, however, that federal courts have established basic requirements that subpoenas must satisfy in order to be recognized as legitimate.

Throughout the history of Congress, committees have been the vehicle for conducting congressional investigations. Select or special committees have been appointed for many important investigations. In the last three decades, important investigations of the Watergate break-in and cover-up, the involvement of the Central Intelligence Agency in assassinations, and the Iran-Contra affair were conducted by select committees.

Since the passage of the Legislative Reorganization Act of 1946, standing committees have been assigned the duty of maintaining "continuous watchfulness" over executive branch activities within their jurisdictions. The 1946 act also created two committees with governmentwide oversight duties, now called the House Committee on Oversight and Government Reform and the Senate Committee on Homeland Security and Governmental Affairs. Both committees attract members who want to participate in hearings on and investigations into a wide range of government activity.

The 1946 act was reinforced by stronger directives to committees in the Legislative Reorganization Act of 1970, which required most committees to write biennial reports on their oversight activities. Moreover, during the 1970s both chambers assigned oversight responsibility for several broad policy areas to multiple committees to encourage oversight. Furthermore, the

House instructed many committees to create oversight subcommittees and allowed them to add an oversight subcommittee beyond the limit for the number of subcommittees that would otherwise apply. With these developments, committee staffs devoted to oversight expanded greatly in the 1970s, which enabled committees and subcommittees to organize more hearings and more extensive investigations.

Oversight became an increasingly important part of committee activity. In 1961, less than 10 percent of committee meetings and hearings were devoted to oversight; by 1983, more than 25 percent were devoted to oversight. The biggest surge occurred in the 1970s and appears to have been the product of several factors: the new independence of subcommittee chairs to pursue oversight, the expanded capacity of larger committee and subcommittee staffs to conduct oversight activities, tensions between a Democratic Congress and a Republican administration, and a generally more assertive Congress. The proportion of meetings and hearings dedicated to oversight continued to rise throughout most of the 1990s, as congressional Republicans aggressively investigated the Clinton administration. By 1997, nearly 34 percent of all committee hearings and meetings were devoted to oversight.

Declining Committee Autonomy

Committee power has been under siege since the early 1970s. Although committees continue to draft the details of nearly all legislation and their members remain central players in nearly all policy decisions, they have become less autonomous as their parent houses and parties have exercised more control over their operations and policy choices. Change has been most dramatic in the House of Representatives, where committees appeared to have dominated policy making during the middle decades of the twentieth century. The forces producing change in the role of committees in recent decades are similar to the forces that have been active throughout Congress's history – the policy agenda, strength of congressional parties, and the institutional context.

Changing Policy Agenda

Changes in the policy agenda have led to a decline in the autonomy of committees in recent decades. Many new and salient issues arose in the 1960s and 1970s, such as consumer protection, civil rights, and numerous others. Some of the emerging issues, like energy and the environment, were

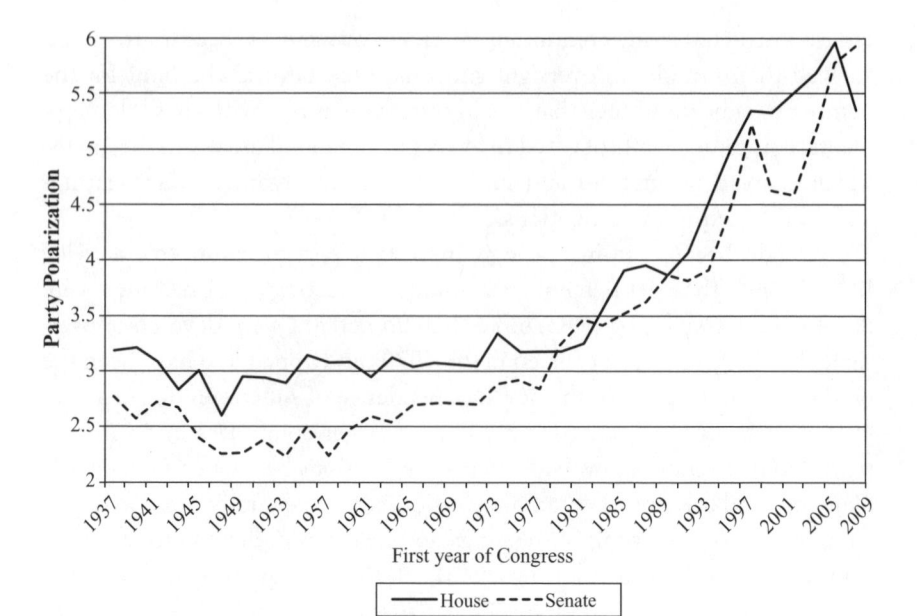

FIGURE 6.1. Party Polarization in the House and Senate, 1937–2008. *Source:* Common space scores from http://voteview.com/dwnl.htm. Calculations by the authors. Note: The measure of polarization is taken from Elizabeth Rybicki, Steven S. Smith, and Ryan Vander Wielen, "Congressional Committee Bias, 1963–2002." Paper presented at the 2003 meetings of the American Political Science Association.

interconnected, sparked controversy, and stimulated the growth of interest groups. They energized outsiders to seek influence over committees' policy choices and pitted powerful committees against one another. As a result, more controversy spilled out of the committee rooms and onto the chamber floors. Since the late 1970s, the struggle with budget deficits led Congress to adopt rules that limited the policy discretion of most congressional committees. As we report in Chapter 12, the effect of the budget rules was a shift in emphasis from authorizing to appropriating committees and increased control over committee action by party and budget leaders.

Changing Party Strength

The increasing polarization of congressional parties (see Figure 6.1) has generated demands for central leaders to become more assertive. Thus, party leaders have clamped down on committee autonomy. Furthermore, the rank-and-file members of the parties, particularly in the House, have become less tolerant of committee and subcommittee chairs' deviating from party policy positions. Following the Republican takeover of 1994, Republican and

Democratic majorities alike have been particularly aggressive in expressing their expectations of committee leaders.

The increase in activity by the party organizations and leaders during recent years is noted in Chapter 5. The party organizations now provide more opportunities for meaningful participation in policy making outside of members' assigned committees. The parties have provided forums, such as task forces, for those outside of committees to challenge the committees and their leaders and even to devise legislation for floor consideration. In the House, party leaders have frequently negotiated legislation after a committee has reported a bill and placed the negotiated provisions in the bill through use of a special rule from the Rules Committee.

Changing Institutional Context

Committee autonomy has been further undermined by rules changes that either directly regulated committee behavior or made it easier for members to challenge committee recommendations. These new rules were pursued by members who were unhappy with the nearly dictatorial control that some full committee chairs exercised over legislative proceedings. They reflected an effort to make committees – and especially committee leaders – more accountable to rank-and-file members of the parent chamber and to make members less dependent on committees for information and advice.

SUNSHINE RULES. Sunshine rules – rules that open congressional activity to public scrutiny – have contributed to the diminishing autonomy of standing committees. One such rule requires that roll-call votes cast in committee be recorded in documents that are open to the public. This rule was amended in 2007 to exclude votes taken in the Rules Committee. Another rule dictates that committee markups be held in public sessions (except for meetings concerned with national security matters) unless a majority of committee members cast a recorded vote in favor of closing a meeting. Even conference committees are required to hold their meetings in open sessions unless, as the House rule requires, a majority of the parent chamber approves the use of closed meetings. The rules were intended to make committee members more accountable, both to outside constituencies and to their colleagues. In recent Congresses, committees have voted more frequently to close meetings to the public, and they have become more creative in their efforts to sidestep the rules. In some cases, members appear to have allowed staff to negotiate legislative details to avoid holding official meetings subject to open-meeting rules. But party leaders have attempted to reinforce the sunshine rules by requiring that committees accommodate television and radio broadcasts and still photographers whenever a meeting is open to the public.

BILL REFERRAL RULES IN THE HOUSE. In 1974, the Speaker of the House was granted the authority to send legislation to committees jointly, sequentially, or in parts. Before 1974, the Speaker was required to assign legislation to the single committee that had the most relevant jurisdiction, a practice that guaranteed monopoly referral rights to a single committee in each policy area. Under the current rule, adopted in 1995, sending a bill jointly to more than one committee is no longer possible, but the Speaker may still establish a sequence of committees for consideration or split a bill into parts that are referred to different committees (sequential and split referral). In fact, in recent Congresses, about one-fourth of the workload for the average House committee has consisted of multiply referred legislation. In the Senate, all three forms of multiple referral are possible upon a joint motion of the majority and minority leaders. Multiple referral remains far less common in the Senate than in the House, perhaps because committees can more easily protect their jurisdictional interests by seeking to amend legislation on the floor.

Multiple referral in the House generates greater interdependence among committees and with the Speaker, reducing committee autonomy. Multiple referral creates more potential conflicts among committees and increases the number of legislators with some role in committee action on the affected bills. Sometimes the conflict among committees spills onto the House floor, where party leaders are asked to intercede. And, perhaps most important, multiple referral substantially strengthens the Speaker's influence over committee decisions. The Speaker determines, without appeal, the referral of legislation to multiple committees and may set deadlines for committee action in such cases. In designing such arrangements, the Speaker is in a position to advantage some committees, speed or delay committee action for strategic purposes, and send strong signals about his or her policy preferences.

VOTING RULES. Weakening committee autonomy and the demise of deference to committees are reflected in the record of floor-amending activity since the mid-1950s. In terms of both the absolute number of floor amendments, the number of amendments per measure, and the proportion of measures amended on the floor, floor-amending activity increased in both chambers during the 1950s and 1960s and surged upward in the 1970s. In the Senate, the number of floor amendments nearly tripled between the mid-1950s and late 1970s, with most of the increase occurring in the 1960s.

The number of House floor amendments more than quadrupled between the mid-1950s and the late 1970s, with most of the increase occurring in the early 1970s after the introduction of recorded electronic voting. Previously, recorded votes were not possible on most amendments, which made it difficult to bring public pressure to bear and enhanced the influence of powerful insiders, particularly committee chairs.

Floor-amending activity was perceived to be a more serious problem in the House and the House majority party could change its practices in response. The most important response was the expanded use of special rules to limit floor amendments. Most rules have not foreclosed floor amendments, but they have required that amendment sponsors notify the Rules Committee in advance, which permits the Rules Committee to arrange for their order of consideration and allows committee leaders to prepare against unfriendly amendments (see Chapters 7 and 8).

No effective constraints on floor-amending activity for the purpose of enhancing committee autonomy are possible in the Senate. The minority would prevent a vote on any reform that would put it at a disadvantage. In only two areas, budget measures and certain trade agreements, has the Senate moved to limit debate and amendments. In general, therefore, a majority of senators have no way to insulate committee bills from unfriendly or nongermane amendments whose sponsors are committed to offering them.

CONFERENCE RULES. The ability of committees to control conference negotiations on behalf of their chambers has long been a vital source of power. In the House of the 1970s and 1980s, challenges to committee autonomy were accompanied by challenges to committees' monopoly over appointments to conference delegations. New rules were adopted imploring the Speaker to appoint delegations that represented House preferences, to include members who had sponsored major components of the legislation in question, and to require conferences to hold their meetings in public sessions. The rules were targeted at senior committee members who had dominated conferences for decades. The Speaker's control over conference delegations was reinforced in 1993 when the House adopted a rule giving the Speaker the power to remove a member from a conference delegation at any time. In spite of these rules, few members not sitting on the standing committees originating legislation are appointed to conference committees.

RANK-AND-FILE RESOURCES. Individual members now have far more sources of information at their disposal than they once did in the mid-twentieth century, so the traditional advantage enjoyed by committee members over rank-and-file members – greater access to expertise and staff assistance – has been reduced. Over the years, changes in House and Senate rules have allowed members to expand their personal staffs. Much of a member's personal staff is devoted to nonlegislative duties such as answering the mail and handling constituents' problems with the federal agencies. Nevertheless, the great expansion in members' personal staffs has allowed legislators to draw on staff for assistance in developing legislative proposals, making arguments, and soliciting support – often in opposition to committee positions. Furthermore, members may draw on the congressional support agencies. These agencies often conduct studies for or delegate staff to congressional committees, but they also respond to requests for information from individual members and their staffs. As a result of the increased availability of these varied sources of information, an enterprising member can equip himself or herself to challenge committee members' arguments. Thus, seldom does a committee now command deference on the basis of policy expertise alone.

Committee Membership

At the start of each new Congress, members of the House and new members of the Senate seek committee assignments that will shape their daily schedules and perhaps their electoral and legislative futures. Returning members are routinely reappointed to their former committees, following the "property right" norm, unless they seek to improve their situation by transferring to other committees, as a few always do. State delegations, intra-party factions, and lobbyists work to maximize their influence over policy by getting friendly members onto the right committees.

Committee Size and Party Ratios

Majority and minority party leaders negotiate the number of Democratic and Republican seats on each committee, with the majority leaders having the upper hand because of their ability to win a floor vote on the resolutions that provide for the allocation of seats to each party. With important exceptions in the House, seats on most committees are allocated roughly in proportion to the size of each party. The exceptions are the House Appropriations, Budget, Rules, and Ways and Means Committees – which are particularly important committees so the majority party reserves a larger-than-proportionate number of seats for themselves (see Table 6.2). The House and Senate ethics committees are the only committees on which there is an equal number of majority and minority party members.

Committee Assignments

In each chamber, committee seats are filled on the basis of recommendations from each party. For example, the House rule states that "the House shall fill a vacancy on a standing committee by election on the nomination of the respective party caucus or conference." To accomplish this, each House and Senate party has its own committee on committees, which is responsible for making committee lists. Assignment decisions depend on the number of vacancies, the number of members competing for assignments, and rules on the number and type of assignments each member may hold. New members and returning members seeking new assignments must compete for support from the members of their party's committee on committees to gain assignment to the committees they want.

THE HOUSE. For the first time in 1995, as proposed by the new Republican majority that year, the House adopted a rule restricting the number of committee assignments its members may hold. The two parties had had internal rules, but the Republicans imposed the new rule and Democrats retained it after gaining a House majority in 2006. The rule prohibits a member from holding more than two standing committee assignments and more than four subcommittee assignments on standing committees. The two parties supplement this restriction by treating four committees (Appropriations, Energy and Commerce, Rules, and Ways and Means) as "exclusive" committees. Members serving on these committees are not permitted to hold seats on other committees. Both parties also identify "exempt" committees (Select Committee on Intelligence and Standards of Official Conduct) that do not count against a member's committee membership limit.

In recent years, both House parties have become less inclined to grant exemptions to their limits on assignments. Traditionally, members have received exemptions with relative ease and have been allowed to maintain them indefinitely. But leaders of both House parties grew frustrated with the number of members who expected to receive exemptions and retain coveted extra seats. Upon becoming leader of the House Democrats at the end of 2002, Nancy Pelosi (D-California) strictly applied party rules limiting committee assignments. In 2005, Pelosi decided against granting John Larson (D-Connecticut) a waiver that would have allowed him to keep his position as ranking member on the House Administration Committee after having been chosen to sit on the Ways and Means Committee. House Republicans approved a party rule in 2004 that requires members who have received a waiver to committee assignment limits to reapply every two years. Moreover,

HOW TO DISCIPLINE A WAYWARD MEMBER?

Senator Joseph Lieberman has had a strained relationship with Senate Democrats in the past few years. First, the former vice-presidential nominee filed and ran as an Independent in 2006 after losing the Democratic primary. He continued to caucus with Democrats after the 2006 election, but openly supported Republican Senator John McCain in the 2008 presidential election. Lieberman made a nationally televised speech at the Republican National Convention and suggested that Democratic nominee Barack Obama was not qualified to serve as president. After the 2008 elections, many Democrats wanted to punish Lieberman by stripping him of the chairmanship of the Senate Homeland Security and Governmental Affairs Committee. Following speculation that Lieberman might decide to caucus with Republicans if he lost his chairmanship, the Senate Democratic Caucus voted 42–13 to allow him to keep that post, but removed him from the Environment and Public Works committee.

the Republicans require members who wish to sit on multiple committees to receive the approval of the chairs of the committees involved in addition to the steering committee. For both parties, restricting exemptions allows party leaders to distribute desirable committee assignments to more members.

THE SENATE. Since the 1970s, Senate rules have restricted the number and type of committee assignments that senators may receive. A senator may sit on no more than two of the 12 most important committees ("A" committees) and is limited to an appointment to only one of five other standing committees, the Special Committee on Aging, or the Joint Economic Committee ("B" committees). There is no restriction for seats on the Select Committee on Ethics, the Committee on Indian Affairs, and the Joint Committee on Taxation ("C" committees). A senator may sit on no more than three subcommittees of any "A" committee (Appropriations members are exempt from this restriction) and no more than two subcommittees of any "B" committee. Both parties have adopted rules that further restrict membership on "A" committees. Senators are not permitted to sit on more than one of the "Super A" or "Big Four" committees, which include Appropriations, Armed Services, Finance, and Foreign Relations. The Senate occasionally grants exemptions to these assignment limitations at the request of the parties. Since the 1950s, both Senate parties have observed the practice of granting every senator a seat on one of the top four committees before any senator gets two such seats. The practice is called the "Johnson rule," after Lyndon Johnson (D-Texas), the Democratic leader who initiated the practice.

INFLUENCES ON ASSIGNMENTS. Many factors influence the committee assignment decisions of party leaders and the committees on committees. The legislators' political needs, claims by individual states or regions for representation on certain committees, geographic considerations, party loyalty, views on specific issues, and seniority are the most important factors. In the House, members supported by the largest state delegations are at a distinct advantage. For example, in 1992 New York's delegation lost all three of its members on House Appropriations through retirement or defeat, but it managed to regain all three seats (two Democratic and one Republican) for its members when new appointments were made. But there are few guarantees – New Jersey Democrats lost their representation on both Appropriations and Ways and Means (one seat each), but failed to gain a replacement.

Only for Senate Republicans has seniority historically been a decisive consideration. In fact, seniority has been the sole determinant in both the allocation of committee seats and the ascension of the committee hierarchy for Senate Republicans. In 2004, reflecting a desire to strengthen their leader's influence with party colleagues, Senate Republicans approved, by narrow margin, a change in party rules to grant the floor leader the authority to make influential committee appointments without regard to seniority. The rule permits the Republican leader to appoint at least half of the party's committee assignments on "A" committees. As a result, the leader has considerable say in the appointments to committees such as Agriculture, Appropriations, Armed Services, Finance, Foreign Relations, and Judiciary. For Senate Democrats, seniority has been an important, but less decisive, factor in committee assignment decisions.

Similar to the Senate Democrats, the House parties consider seniority along with many factors when making committee assignments. Having an established record of party loyalty, trustworthiness, and skill gives a more senior member an edge over newcomers. In recent Congresses, party leaders have increasingly taken into account members' contributions to party campaign efforts when distributing committee seats. Yet, particularly when a large class of new members enters Congress, party leaders make sure that a few freshmen are named to the top committees. The 104th Congress (1995–1996) was particularly unusual in having both a large class of new Republicans and a new Republican majority in the House. The change in party control gave the Republicans 31 new seats on the exclusive committees. The party allocated 19 of those seats to freshmen. In the years following the new Republican majority in 1995, it has become clear that the seniority norm has further weakened in the House.

LEADERSHIP PREROGATIVES. Assignments to the House Committee on Rules and the House Committee on House Administration are unique cases. The Rules Committee's primary function is to consider, devise, and report "special rules," resolutions that provide for the floor consideration of measures – usually reported by other committees – that would otherwise not receive timely consideration under the standing rules. In the 1960s and early 1970s, the independence of Rules Committee members was troubling to the majority party Democrats. Ultimately, both parties transferred the power to appoint Rules members to their top party leaders, making Rules Committee members agents of their party leadership.

In late 1994, both House parties also gave their top leaders similar power to name the members of the House Administration Committee. Because the House Administration Committee has jurisdiction over the internal administrative affairs of the House, including the way important resources are distributed to committees and members, the top leaders wanted to assert more control over it than they had in the past. The committee also has jurisdiction over election and campaign finance law – subjects of the highest partisan significance.

The Pecking Order

The appeal of committees to members varies. We can learn about the value of committees to members by examining the committees that members choose to leave and join. Because members have the ability to stay on the committee that they served on in the previous Congress (because of the norm of "property rights"), we can assume that members transfer to more desirable committees. This is especially likely to be true because of the costs members incur for leaving a committee on which they had accumulated seniority. Table 6.3 shows the ranking of committee values for the House and Senate derived from the study of members' transfers off and on committees.

House Ways and Means (taxes, social security, trade), Appropriations (spending authority), Commerce (health, regulation of interstate commerce), and Rules (special rules) have jurisdictions of exceptional breadth and importance and attract the interest of many members. Competition for assignment to these committees is intense. Because of these committees' importance, party leaders expect loyalty from members assigned to them. In late 1992, a House insider reported that the Democratic leadership was holding applicants to Appropriations and Ways and Means to a high standard of loyalty. Leaders were telling members, "There may be a time your

TABLE 6.3. Ranking of House and Senate Committee Values, 1979–2006.

Ranking	House Committees	Senate Committees
1	Ways and Means	Finance
2	Appropriations	Veterans Affairs
3	Energy and Commerce	Appropriations
4	Rules	Rules and Administration
5	International Relations	Armed Services
6	Armed Services	Foreign Relations
7	Intelligence	Intelligence
8	Judiciary	Judiciary
9	Homeland Security	Budget
10	Transportation and Infrastructure	Commerce, Science, and Transportation
11	District of Columbia	Indian Affairs
12	Government Reform and Oversight	Small Business and Entrepreneurship
13	Budget	Homeland Security and Governmental Affairs
14	Post Office and Civil Service	Agriculture, Nutrition, and Forestry
15	Financial Services	Health, Education, Labor, and Pensions
16	Science	Energy and Natural Resources
17	Resources	Environment and Natural Resources
18	House Administration	Banking, Housing, and Urban Affairs
19	Education and the Workplace	
20	Standards of Official Conduct	
21	Agriculture	
22	Veterans Affairs	
23	Merchant Marine and Fisheries	
24	Small Business	

Source: Keith M. Edwards and Charles Stewart III. "The Value of Committee Assignments in Congress Since 1994." Paper presented at the 2006 Annual Meeting of the Southern Political Science Association.

leader and your president will need your support. It may be difficult for you to vote for it. Will you be with us?"[1] Such anecdotal evidence illustrates the significant role of party as a cue to members on committees of prestige.

As a general rule, freshmen have difficulty gaining assignment to the top committees. Only when an extraordinary number of new members are elected does the leadership become eager to demonstrate a commitment to appointing a fair share of freshmen. And only when their numbers are large, are freshmen emboldened to demand their share of top assignments. At the start of the 103rd Congress (1993–1994), for example, the 63 Democratic freshmen and 47 Republican freshmen gained a total of 13 appointments to Appropriations, Ways and Means, and Commerce. Two years later, with an even larger class of Republican freshmen, 19 of the 31 available slots on the top four committees were given to freshmen by the Republican steering committee.

Beyond the common desire for assignment to one of the top committees, members vary widely in their preferences for committee assignments. Differences among members reflect their personal interests and political goals. As a consequence of these differences, many committees are not very representative of their parent house. Sometimes this imbalance is manifest in the policy preferences held by committee members. For example, the House Armed Services Committee, which attracts members disproportionately from districts with military bases, has been more conservative than the House as a whole for many years. But many committees are distinguished from the rest of their chamber less by their policy views than by their degree of interest in the subject matter. The House Agriculture Committee, for example, attracts legislators from rural farming districts.

Committee Bias?

Differences in the policy preferences of committees and their parent chambers are not easy to measure, but it does appear that the political balance on some committees is quite different from the balance in their parent chamber. Committee medians on a liberal/conservative scale (larger numbers = more conservative) for the Democratically controlled Congress of 2007–2008 are shown along with chamber medians in Figure 6.2. With Democratic majorities, we would expect to observe liberal-leaning committees and they were, but there still is substantial variation among committees. Among House committees, those with a larger proportion of Democrats are among the most liberal – House Administration, Appropriations, Budget, Rules, and Ways and Means.

The biases of congressional committees, as well as subcommittees, are evident in the character of the witnesses they call to their hearings. A study of congressional hearings between 1945 and 1986 on four issues – nuclear power, drug abuse, smoking, and pesticides – found large, predictable bias in the mix of industry and public-interest group representatives appearing before them. Committee majorities chose to listen to more witnesses that confirmed their views than opposed their views.

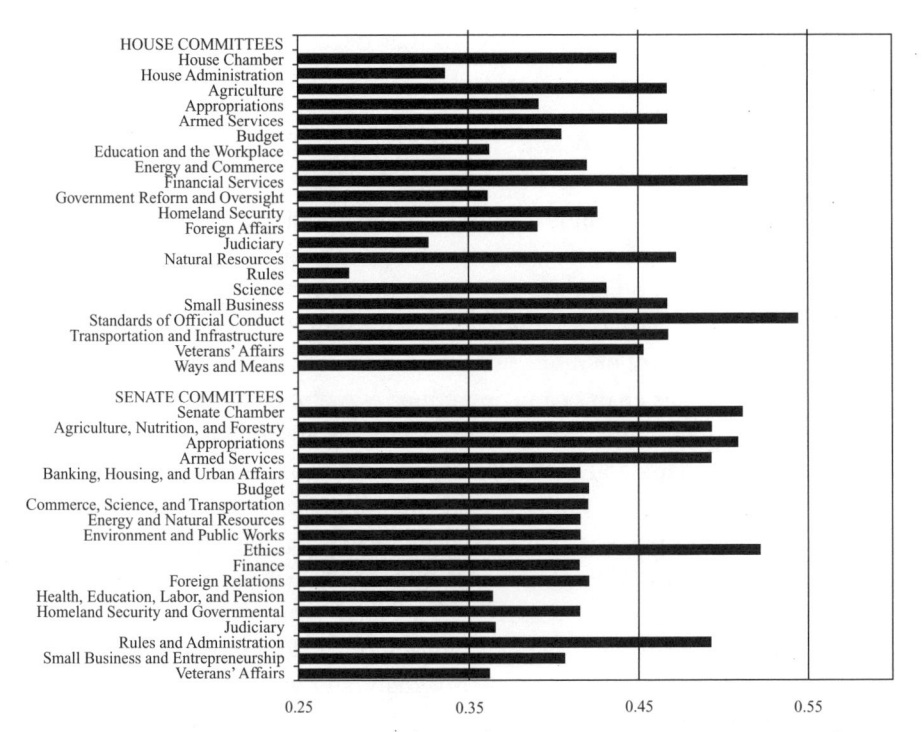

FIGURE 6.2. Median Conservative Score for Standing Committees, 2007–2008. *Source:* Common space scores from http://www.voteview.com. Committee medians calculated by authors.

Committee Leaders

The most powerful member on most committees is the full committee chair. The chair exercises considerable control over the agenda, schedules meetings and hearings of the full committee, and, in recent Congresses, approves the scheduling of subcommittees' meetings and hearings. Furthermore, the committee chair controls the committee budget, offers party leaders recommendations regarding the composition of conference committees for legislation falling under the committee's jurisdiction, supervises a sizable staff, and often serves as a spokesperson for the committee and party on issues under the committee's jurisdiction. The chair also reports legislation to the floor on behalf of the committee and makes requests of the majority leadership and, in the House, the Rules Committee to schedule the legislation for action on the floor. In exercising his or her formal powers, the chair benefits from years of experience in dealing with the policy problems and constituencies of the committee. Consequently, the support of the full committee chair can be critical to bill sponsors and opponents. However, full committee chairs no longer dominate their committees as they once did. Understanding why is important.

The Seniority System

Both the majority and minority parties designate a formal leader for each committee and subcommittee. The majority party names the chair of each committee and subcommittee, and the minority party appoints a ranking minority member for each committee and subcommittee. The seniority norm dictates that the party member with the longest continuous service on the committee serves as chair or ranking minority member, although there are limitations on the number and type of chairmanships a member may hold. Subcommittee chairs and ranking minority members are chosen, in most cases, on the basis of seniority within the committee. Accruing seniority toward leadership posts is one reason members are reluctant to transfer to other committees, where they must start at the bottom of the seniority ladder.

The seniority norm came to be recognized in the House in the late nineteenth century and was observed in both chambers, virtually without exception, in the middle decades of the twentieth century. The norm was weakened in the 1970s by party rules that required a secret ballot election of full committee chairs and ranking minority members. Senate Republicans led the way in 1973 by requiring that their ranking member on each committee be elected by the Republican members of the committee, although the full Republican conference retains the right to reconsider a committee contingent's decision. House Democrats followed by requiring that all committee chairs or ranking members and the chairs or ranking members of subcommittees on the Appropriations Committee stand for election in the Democratic caucus at the start of each Congress. They later required the chairs of Ways and Means subcommittees to stand for caucus election as well. The new rules had an impact. Three full committee chairs were deposed in 1974, an Appropriations subcommittee chair was replaced in 1977, and four more Democratic committee chairs were ousted later. The other two congressional parties, House Republicans and Senate Democrats, adopted rules in the mid-1970s allowing separate votes on the ranking committee members in their conferences.

The reforms have been extended. In 1992, House Republicans, then in the minority, adopted a new party rule to limit the tenure of their full committee and subcommittee leaders to three consecutive Congresses, forcing rotation in the top committee posts every six years. In 1995, the Republicans made this a House rule for committee and subcommittee chairmanships and Democrats retained it after winning a majority in 2006, but have since repealed the rule for the 111th Congress. A Republican conference rule applies the term limits to ranking committee and subcommittee leaders when the party is in the minority. Since the adoption of the term limits, only one exemption has been granted – for David Drier (R-California) to remain the Rules committee chair for the duration of the 109th Congress. Chairs are permitted to move from one chairmanship to another.

Predictions that term limits would lead to more frequent departures from the seniority norm in selecting committee chairs proved accurate. In the first Congress to have forced turnover in committee chairs, the 107th Congress (2001–2002), six of the 13 vacant chairs were won by members who were not the most senior of the remaining members on their committees. In the next two Congresses, there were five vacancies compelled by the term limits and only two were filled by the most senior remaining member of the committee. In one instance, five Republicans with more seniority were skipped over to elect a chair.

In 1996, Senate Republicans adopted a six-year limit on committee chairs. Because the Republican majority status was interrupted in the 107th Congress (2001–2002) following Senator Jim Jeffords' decision to leave the Republican Party, the term limits were enforced for the first time at the beginning of the 109th Congress (2005–2006). The resulting vacancies led to a game of musical chairs, as four term-limited chairs went on to chair other committees. The Senate Democrats have not adopted term limits on committee leaders. However, Senator Robert Byrd (D-West Virginia) agreed to give up the chairmanship of the Senate Appropriations committee prior to the 111th Congress at least in part based on concerns that his advanced age (92) left him unable to perform the duties of the job.

Senate Republicans also adopted a new rule governing the election of committee leaders. Rather than allowing the Republicans on each committee to elect their committee chair or ranking minority member, as they had been doing for many years, the new rule requires secret ballot votes within each committee and then by the full Republican conference, making the chairs and ranking members more accountable to the full conference. The first use of this rule, in early 1997, produced no changes in committee chairs. Nevertheless, two senators, Mark Hatfield (R-Oregon) and Arlen Specter (R-Pennsylvania), had to overcome substantial opposition from within their party conference to retain or gain chairmanships.

THE CHANGING CONGRESS: A HOUSE COMMITTEE CHAIR DEPOSED

The seniority system took a major hit in the 111th Congress as Henry Waxman (D-California) successfully challenged John Dingell (D-Michigan) for the chairmanship of the House Commerce Committee. Dingell, the longest serving House member in history had been either chair or ranking Democrat on Commerce since 1981. Waxman's challenge centered on the theme of "change" and argued that Dingell's policies on energy and the environment were out of touch with the House Democratic Caucus. Dingell is known as a fierce protector of the automobile industry and thus was often opposed to increased fuel efficiency standards and other environmental legislation that could harm automakers. Waxman was seen by some as having views more in line with Speaker Nancy Pelosi and incoming President Barack Obama. For his part, Dingell tried to reassure caucus members by pointing to his experience and ability to shepherd legislation though the House. The weeks-long campaign culminated in both Dingell and Waxman giving impassioned speeches to the caucus urging other members to support them. Democrat George Miller of California said, "It was like Zeus and Thor in there, hurling lightning bolts at each other. You just wanted to get out of the way." Despite his last-minute pleas, Dingell lost the vote by a count of 137–122.

Formal reforms have been reinforced by changes in practice. After the Republicans won a House majority in the 1994 elections, Speaker Newt Gingrich assumed responsibility for appointing committee chairs even before his conference had had an opportunity to meet. For three committees, Gingrich bypassed the most senior committee Republican and backed a more assertive or conservative member as chair. At the same time, House Democratic leader Dick Gephardt chose a close political ally to be ranking member on the House Oversight Committee (now House Administration), dumping the former chairman, who had challenged Gephardt for his leadership post. Speaker Dennis Hastert followed Gingrich's lead by considering member loyalty to be an important element in the selection of committee chairs when vacancies occurred. Speaker Nancy Pelosi made it quite clear prior to the Democratic victory in 2006 that seniority would be only one of the factors considered in determining committee assignments. In fact, the Democratic caucus rules drafted by the House Democratic leaders stated that the Steering committee "shall consider all relevant factors, including but not limited to merit, seniority, length of service on the committee, degree of commitment to Democratic principles and the Democratic agenda, and the diversity of the caucus."

Selecting Subcommittee Chairs

THE HOUSE. The means for selecting House subcommittee chairs have come full circle. Before the 1970s, full committee chairs appointed subcommittees and their chairs. That procedure was transformed into a more egalitarian one in the 1970s. Starting in the mid-1970s, House Democrats required that Democratic committee members bid for subcommittee leadership posts, chairs, or ranking minority member status in order of seniority and that appointments be ratified by a majority vote of the party members on the committee. Although seniority generally is observed, this procedure gives party members on a committee the right to reject the most senior member and elect someone else, as has happened more than a dozen times. House Democrats also bar full committee chairs or ranking members from serving as chair or ranking member of a subcommittee. To make the most important subcommittee leaders accountable to the party, House Democrats require subcommittee leaders of three committees – Appropriations, Energy and Commerce, and Ways and Means – to receive majority approval of the full House Democratic Caucus and, since early 2004, require those subcommittee leaders to first receive approval of the party's Steering and Policy Committee, which is chaired by the party leader.

In contrast, the House Republicans leave the appointment process to each committee's chair (or ranking minority member), although a majority of the Republican members on the full committee can override the chair's decisions. Like the House Democrats, the Republicans require that subcommittee leaders of the Appropriations Committee receive full approval of the party conference. In practice, nearly all of the Republican subcommittee leaders are selected on the basis of committee seniority. As a part of their late 1992 reforms, the House Republicans adopted a party rule prohibiting most chairs or ranking members of full committees from serving as chair or ranking member of any subcommittee. This party rule was made a rule of the House in 1995. These rules spread committee and subcommittee leadership posts among more members and limit the influence that any one member can enjoy by holding multiple leadership posts.

THE SENATE. Both Senate parties allow committee members to select their subcommittee chairs or ranking members in order of seniority. Less conflict over subcommittee chairs has arisen in the Senate than in the House, perhaps because nearly all senators can count on having at least one subcommittee leadership post. Senate rules merely prohibit any member from holding more than one chair on a single committee. With most senators serving on three standing committees, they may have up to three subcommittee chairs (or two if they hold a full committee chair on one of those standing committees). In the 110th Congress (2007–2008), roughly 80 percent of majority party members held at least one subcommittee chair, and more than one-half held two or three subcommittee leadership posts.

Limiting the Power of Full Committee Chairs

Compared with their predecessors of the 1950s and 1960s, today's full committee chairs face more effective competition for control over policy choices. Rank-and-file legislators are more likely to appeal to central party leaders and their party caucus to hold committee leaders accountable to them, and the parties have adopted changes in their rules to limit service of committee leaders and to force chairs to face party approval periodically. Moreover, as discussed earlier, rank-and-file legislators now have larger staffs and can turn to outside groups for assistance in challenging the handiwork and arguments of committees and their leaders.

House Committee Chairs

We have noted a few of the changes affecting the power of full committee chairs, but it is useful to review the two waves of reforms that altered the role of House committee chairs. First, the House Democratic majority of the early 1970s adopted rules to reduce the influence of full committee chairs over the decisions of their committees:

- Chairs were required to stand for election by the Democratic caucus at the start of each Congress,
- Committees with 15 or more members were required to form at least four subcommittees,
- Subcommittees were empowered with written jurisdictions and provided staffs,
- Proxy voting by chairs and ranking members was restricted (see box "Congressionally Speaking. . . ."),
- The minority party contingents on committees were guaranteed staff,
- Committees were required to open their meetings to the public unless a majority of committee members agreed to close them,
- Committee members were empowered to call meetings (on a majority vote) so that chairs could no longer refuse to hold meetings, and

■ Chairs were required to report legislation promptly after it was approved by their committees.

Furthermore, as discussed above, House Democrats adopted a new procedure for subcommittee assignments so that full committee chairs could no longer stack important subcommittees with their supporters. Thus, the ability of full committee chairs to block legislation favored by their committees was curtailed.

Second, following the Republican takeover in 1995, the House passed a series of reforms that would increase the power of the majority party at the expense of both committee and subcommittee chairs. First, and, perhaps most visible, House rules reduced the number of committees by three and the number of subcommittees by 28. The elimination of these committees and subcommittees resulted in a loss of 484 seats. Additional reforms were passed that placed the majority party leadership at the center of decision-making, and further constrained the behavior of committee chairs:

■ Six-year term limits on committee chairs (since repealed),
■ Committees were limited to forming five subcommittees (some exceptions granted),
■ Proxy voting was banned (see box "Congressionally Speaking... "),
■ TV and radio coverage had to be accommodated for all committee meetings that were open to the public,
■ Overall committee staff budgets were cut.

Senate Committee Chairs

The Senate also adopted rules to provide guidelines for the conduct of committee meetings, hearings, and voting and to require committees to publish additional rules governing committee procedures. But unlike in the House, Senate chamber and party rules have never specified internal committee organization in any detail and are silent on the functions of subcommittees; indeed, most Senate committees' rules are very brief. In the majority of cases, the full committee chair is assumed to have great discretion, although even that is left unstated. For nearly all Senate full committees, the referral of legislation to subcommittees and the discharge of legislation from subcommittees remain under the formal control of the committee chair.

Senate Republican party rules specify limitations on the number and type of committees Republicans can lead. In 1995, after the Senate Republicans

Congressionally Speaking...

Attendance at committee meetings has been a problem for many years. Members often have multiple committee meetings or hearings scheduled at the same time and must fulfill other obligations – meet with constituents, vote on the House floor – while their committees are meeting. Thus, members often grant their committee leaders authority to cast proxy votes in their absence.

To control abuses of proxy voting, the House and Senate have adopted rules on their use. An old House rule provided that a majority of committee members must actually be present at the meeting for a committee to report legislation to the floor. If a majority were not present, a point of order could be raised against a bill when it reached the floor, which would lead the Speaker to rule a bill out of order.

But getting a majority of committee members to show up at one time and circumventing points of order can be troublesome. House Democrats moved in 1993 to minimize the problem. Their rule allowed a "rolling quorum." House Rule 11 now counts as "present" members who voted in committee even if no majority was actually present at the same time. Moreover, no point of order could be raised on the House floor unless it was raised at the appropriate time in committee.

House Republicans banned proxy voting and rolling quorums after they gained a majority in the 1994 elections. Since that time, attendance has continued to be a problem for committee chairs, some of whom have suggested returning to some form of proxy voting. Despite persistent problems with committee attendance, the rules remained intact when Democrats took over in 2007.

Furthermore, party leaders have become more involved in committee chairmanship fights and creating task forces and other forums for writing legislation.

regained a majority, they joined their House counterparts in placing even stricter limitations on committee chairs in party rules. The Senate Republicans adopted a party rule prohibiting full committee chairs from chairing any subcommittees and further barring any Republican senator from chairing more than two subcommittees. Both rules were intended to spread chairmanships among as many senators as possible and to limit the special influence that any one senator might enjoy through multiple chairmanships. The rule soon proved to be a hardship for the party, however. On a few committees, the Republicans found themselves without a sufficient number of eligible senators to take another subcommittee chairmanship, so they began to grant waivers to the rule. Senate Democrats have not adopted similar rules.

Subcommittees

Subcommittees became more common after the Legislation Reorganization Act of 1946 consolidated committee jurisdictions and reduced the number of standing committees in both chambers. The number of subcommittees continued to grow into the 1970s, as individual committees responded to new policy problems and as members demanded their own subcommittees. Currently, of the committees with authority to report legislation, the only ones without subcommittees are the House Budget, House Administration, and Standards of Official Conduct Committees and the Senate Budget, Rules and Administration, Indian Affairs, Small Business and Entrepreneurship, Veterans' Affairs, and Intelligence committees.

THE HOUSE. In the House, the resistance of some full committee chairs to efforts to create legislative subcommittees was eventually overcome by a 1974 rule that provides that "each standing committee . . . except the Committee on the Budget . . . that has more than twenty members shall establish at least four subcommittees." As a result, subcommittees proliferated to the extent that over 125 subcommittees existed in 1980. Later, problems associated with the growth in the number of House subcommittees – jurisdictional squabbles between subcommittees, scheduling difficulties, and the burden of subcommittee hearings on executive officials – led the Democratic caucus in 1981 to limit the number of subcommittees. The 1981 rule was supplanted by a new House rule, adopted in 1993, limiting the number of subcommittees to five per committee, unless a committee maintains a subcommittee on oversight (in which case the committee may have six subcommittees). The 1993 rule permitted only two committees to exceed the subcommittee limit – Appropriations (which may have 13 subcommittees) and Government Reform (which may have seven). The rules changes adopted in 1993 required the abolition of 16 subcommittees, and additional changes introduced by the Republicans in 1995 further scaled back the number of subcommittees. Cumulatively, these changes brought the House back to the 1955 level of about 80 subcommittees. The number of subcommittees has crept up since then, reaching 101 in 2007. Contributing to this trend was a 2007 rules change granting additional exemptions to subcommittee limits to Armed Services (which may have seven), Foreign Affairs (which may have seven), and Transportation and Infrastructure (which may have six).

THE SENATE. The Senate and the Senate parties do not have formal rules on the number of subcommittees. Instead, the Senate's limits on the number of subcommittee assignments that individual senators may hold effectively

---

Congressionally Speaking...

The first great book about Congress was Woodrow Wilson's *Congressional Government*, written in 1883 and 1884 when Wilson was a graduate student at Johns Hopkins University. He penned two frequently quoted phrases – "Congressional government is *committee government*" (emphasis added) and "Congress in session is Congress on public exhibition, whilst Congress in its committee-rooms is Congress at work." Wilson later became president of the United States.

The power of subcommittees was enhanced during the early 1970s, leading observers to look for new ways to label Congress. Political scientists Roger Davidson and Walter Oleszek characterized the House as *subcommittee government* in their 1977 book *Congress Against Itself*. Neither Davidson nor Oleszek has exhibited ambitions for high public office.

---

restricts the number of subcommittees that can be created. In 1985, compliance with the limits on subcommittee assignments led to the elimination of 10 subcommittees. Republicans further reduced the number of subcommittees after taking majority control of the Senate in 1995. In 1997, the Senate had 68 subcommittees, down from nearly 90 ten years earlier. The number of Senate subcommittees has changed little since that time, increasing only to 71 in 2007.

Checking the Power of Subcommittees in the House

In the Democratic House of the 1970s, subcommittees became very important in committee decision making in the House. The House and the Democratic caucus adopted rules in the early 1970s that substantially weakened the ability of full committee chairs to control subcommittees. Consequently, decision-making processes within House committees became more decentralized than they had been in the 1950s and 1960s. Most legislation originated in subcommittees, the vast majority of hearings were held in subcommittees, about half of all committee staff was allocated to subcommittees, and subcommittee chairs usually served as the floor managers for legislation originating in their subcommittees. The House and Democratic party rules together created substantial uniformity across House committees in their reliance on subcommittees for initial action on legislation. The pattern in the House led some observers to label House decision making "subcommittee government."

Subcommittee government evaporated with the new Republican majority in 1995. House subcommittees were no longer guaranteed that legislation sent to their parent committees would be referred to them. In addition, as noted previously, the Republicans forced most House committees to reduce the number of their subcommittees from six to five (with exception to those committees maintaining an oversight subcommittee and those granted explicit exemptions), and they returned to full committee chairs control over subcommittee appointments and over all committee and subcommittee staff. When they cut committee budgets, a disproportionate share of the resulting staff cutbacks occurred in subcommittee staffs. Whereas subcommittee chairs once had the authority to hire one staffer, House rules now give full committee chairs the authority to determine the staff allotted to subcommittees. Subcommittee staff now constitutes less than 40 percent of all committee staff, down nearly 10 percent from the 1980s. The consequence of these changes has been the reemergence of variation across House committees in the way they use subcommittees.

It is too early to determine whether the Democratic majority elected to the House in 2006 will return to greater reliance on subcommittees for initial consideration of legislation. Early signs are that the Democratic full committee chairs are giving subcommittee chairs greater independence than did their Republican predecessors.

The Senate and its parties never adopted rules granting subcommittees the kind of independence that House subcommittees enjoyed under the Democrats in the 1970s and 1980s. The lack of formal rules empowering subcommittees in the Senate has produced great variation among committees in their reliance on subcommittees. Several Senate committees hold no or only a few hearings in subcommittee, and only a few Senate committees use subcommittees to write legislation. "Subcommittee government" never fit the decision-making processes in most Senate committees.

Committee Staff

Committees in the early nineteenth century worked without staff assistance, which meant that committee chairs personally managed the administrative details of committee business. However, the growing workload of the mid-1800s rendered this practice infeasible. In 1856, the House approved committee assistance for the Ways and Means committee, and the Senate did the same for the Finance committee. Expansion in committee assistance following this was slow; it was not until 1890 that the total number of committee employees in both chambers exceeded 100.

The Legislative Reorganization Act of 1946 was a significant turning point in the history of committee staffing as it established statutory provisions for the allocation of staff. Specifically, it granted standing committees in both chambers the authority to hire four professional staff assistants and six clerical aides. The number of professional assistants was raised to six (totaling 12 statutory positions) in 1970 by the second Legislative Reorganization Act. In addition, committees were extended the opportunity to make annual requests for committee staff beyond the statutory allotments. This gave way to a rapid expansion of committee staff, particularly in the non-statutory category (referred to as "investigative"). After the 1970 Legislative Reorganization Act, committee staffing has followed different courses in the two chambers.

THE HOUSE. In 1974, the House increased the personnel limit to 18 professional assistants and 12 clerical aides, where it remains today. The number of committee staff in the House exploded in the 1970s, primarily as a result of the growth in subcommittees. While growth leveled off in the House during the 1980s, the total number of committee staff employed continued to rise through the early 1990s. By 1990, only one House committee had a staff smaller than 40, while six committees had more than 100 assistants.

THE SENATE. Although growth in committee staff was more gradual in the Senate, Senate committees, like their House counterparts, took advantage of the 1970s procedures permitting investigative staff. However, the adoption of a 1980 Senate resolution eliminated the distinction between statutory and investigative staff, and moved to annual funding (changed to biennial funding in 1985) of committee staff. As is now the practice, committees were directed to draft budget requests to be packaged and voted on by the chamber.

REPUBLICAN CUTS RESTORED. As they promised, the Republicans elected in 1994 cut committee budgets and staff. House committee (full and subcommittee) staff dropped from just over 1,700 to under 1,100; Senate committee staff dropped from nearly 1,000 to under 800. Since the mid-1990s, House committee staff has risen to approximately 1,300, and Senate committee staff has grown back to over 900.

Both chambers guarantee the minority party a share of the staff. Senate rules state that the allocation of committee staff "should reflect the relative number of majority and minority members of committees." The standing rules of the House are less favorable to the minority than in the Senate. The

House guarantees to the minority only 10 staff members, or one-third of the committee staff, whichever is less.

Conclusions

Committees are a central but changing feature of legislative policy making. Changes in the role of committees are primarily the products of:

- the emergence of new and salient policy problems,
- fluctuations in the strength of congressional parties, and
- the character of the existing institutional arrangements.

When interest in an issue is narrow, the policy outcome satisfies most members, and the issue has little impact on party fortunes, autonomous committees are tolerated and even revered. However, when an issue is more complex and few members are indifferent to the outcome, as appeared to be the case more frequently in the 1970s, committees become constrained by their parent chambers and must rely on formal procedural safeguards to preserve their control over legislative details. When the parties' electoral fortunes are tied to the issue and the policy outcome, as happened on budget matters in the 1980s, party leaders and their functionaries assume decision-making responsibilities that otherwise would fan to committees.

The direction of change over the last three decades – toward less autonomous committees and a less committee-oriented process – must not be confused with the degree of change. The changes reported in this chapter, particularly those in the House, appear to be quite sweeping. Many of the procedural sources of committee power seem to have been weakened. Developments affecting committee assignments, bill referrals, floor debate, conferences, and the budget process have reduced committee autonomy. Additionally, the informal norm of deference to committee recommendations certainly is much weaker today than it was in the 1950s and 1960s.

But some care must be taken in drawing inferences about these changes. Most legislation comes from a single committee in each chamber, receives few or no floor amendments, and does not require a conference. Necessary conferences are managed by conferees chosen nearly exclusively from the committee of origin. Moreover, committees have devised a remarkable variety of legislative tricks to minimize the effect of budget constraints. With the creative use of special rules and large omnibus measures in the 1980s, committees have actually recovered some of the autonomy they lost in the 1970s.

Above: Sen. Robert Byrd (D-WV) speaks, Monday, during the Senate impeachment trial against President Clinton. Byrd introduced a motion to dismiss the trial. (KRT) PL,KD 1999 (Horiz)
Below: Sen. Christopher Dodd, D-CT, (L) and Sen. Richard Shelby, R-AL, listen to testimony during a Senate Banking, Housing and Urban Affairs Committee hearing on the crises facing investment banks and other financial institutions on Capitol Hill in Washington on September 23, 2008. (UPI Photo/Roger L. Wollenberg)

7

The Rules of the Legislative Game

C ONGRESSIONAL POLITICS OFTEN HAS THE FLAVOR OF A GAME – ALBEIT A very important game – as the contending factions vie for control over public policy. The game is characterized by bargaining, procedural maneuvers, and close votes. On many issues, the outcome is uncertain. When the interests and rights of large groups in society are at stake, the game is emotionally charged. And the game is made more compelling by the personalities of the players. Members of Congress, presidents, staff aides, lobbyists, and other participants in congressional politics are ambitious people with large egos. Many of the players hate to lose. Skilled players are masters of the rules; they are proficient in strategy and tactics and take pleasure in anticipating the moves of their opponents. Their knowledge of the rules and their aptitude for strategy do not guarantee success, but can give them an advantage. Even for spectators, mastering the rules and strategy is essential to appreciating and enjoying the game.

The rules of the game change – and legislators do the changing. Each chamber of Congress is empowered by the Constitution to enact its own rules. The rules of the House of Representatives extend to more than 60,000 words, while the Senate's rules are less than half that long at around 30,000 words. The differences in the length of the rules reflect not only the differences in the sizes of the two chambers, with the larger House requiring more formalities to keep order, but also the different paths that the two chambers took at critical junctures in their parliamentary histories. The Senate, at a very early point in its history, eliminated the means to limit debate, which created the possibility of preventing a vote on a measure by refusing to stop talking. As a result, controversial changes in the rules can be blocked by a minority in the Senate. The House, in contrast, adopted a means to limit debate by a simple majority vote, which allowed even small majorities to impose new rules on that chamber. The result is that the House gradually accumulated a much larger and more detailed set of rules.

Legislative Rules in Perspective

Perhaps the most remarkable feature of the legislative process is how much it is stacked against the enactment of new law. Typically, getting a major bill passed involves attracting majority support in successive stages – first in a subcommittee, then in the full committee, then on the floor, then in conference, and then on the floor again for the conference report. This must be done in both chambers and usually requires the cooperation of both the minority and majority party leadership in the Senate and, in the case of the House, the majority party leadership and the Rules Committee. Once congressional passage is acquired, presidential approval or the support of an extraordinary majority in both chambers must be obtained. Success, then, depends on finding support from multiple groups and subgroups that are not likely to have identical policy preferences. Proponents of a new program or project usually must successfully pilot the necessary legislation through the process twice – once for an authorization bill to create the program and once for the related appropriations bill to fund the program.

Often, the members of Congress and other players in this game take the rules as they are and adjust their strategies accordingly. However, the players also seek to shape and create rules that suit their political needs, which change over time. The existing rules are seldom reevaluated in their entirety. Rather, their weaknesses or biases are considered individually and solutions are adopted piecemeal. New options, limitations, and contingencies have been added incrementally, making the rules more elaborate and altering the strategic context within which legislative factions must compete for majority support. Over the more than two centuries that Congress has been making law, a remarkably complex set of rules, further elaborated by precedents and informal practices, have evolved to shape the legislative process.

It would be a serious mistake to infer that the rules are so detailed and biased that they dictate policy outcomes. They are not. Rules are typically created to facilitate action, not determine outcomes. With a few exceptions, rules do not stipulate the issues to be considered by Congress. National and international events shape those issues, and much of the legislative struggle involves getting new issues on the congressional agenda. Moreover, rules do not determine the policy preferences of the players. Who gets elected is the most important factor in determining what policies will be favored by Congress, although interest groups, presidents, and others influence members' policy choices as well. In addition, the rules do not determine which of the interest groups, local government officials, political commentators, and others exercise the most influence on policy decisions. Larger social forces are more important than the legislative rules in this regard. Generally, the rules are not so detailed and biased that they can compensate for a scarcity of support and votes.

Nevertheless, the rules of the legislative game do matter. Some rules restrict or expand the options available to members by placing certain bills in order on the floor at certain times or by regulating the amendments that may be offered. Other rules set the decision rule – requiring a majority or supermajority for certain kinds of motions or measures – while still others specify which members have the right to make a motion or to speak at certain times. Members know that Congress's rules matter and often regret that the general public does not appreciate their importance. Robert Michel (R-Illinois), the House Republican leader from 1981 to 1994, once lamented the difficulty of attracting public attention to the plight of the minority party under House rules:

> Nothing is so boring to the layman as a litany of complaints over the more obscure provisions of House procedures. It is all "inside baseball." Even among the media, none but the brave seek to attend to the howls of dismay from Republicans [then the minority party] over such esoterica as the kinds of rules under which we are forced to debate. But what is more important to a democracy than the method by which its laws are created?

> We Republicans are all too aware that when we laboriously compile data to demonstrate the abuse of legislative power by the Democrats, we are met by reporters and the public with that familiar symptom best summarized in the acronym "MEGO" – my eyes glaze over. We can't help it if the battles of Capitol Hill are won or lost before the issues get to the floor by the placement of an amendment or the timing of a vote. We have a voice and a vote to fight the disgraceful manipulation of the rules by the Democrats, and we make use of both. All we need now is media attention, properly directed to those boring, but all-important, House procedures.[1]

Representative Michel was well aware that misconceptions about congressional rules abound. Some believe that "if there's a will, there's a way" – legislators' effort, not rules, determine outcomes. Others see congressional procedures as arcane and deeply biased against action – "the outcome is rigged by the rules." Particular rules become critical factors in shaping policy choices only in combination with the preferences of the players. If all members of Congress support a particular bill, it doesn't matter whether only a simple majority or a supermajority is required to pass it. But as divisions emerge, the particular rules under which bills are crafted and brought to a vote may influence the outcomes. The ability to offer an amendment at a crucial moment, to delay action until more support can be attracted, or to gain enactment with a simple majority rather than a supermajority can be critical to the final policy outcome.

Knowledge of the rules can be an important resource. Former House Energy and Commerce Chairman John Dingell (D-Michigan) once said, "If I let you write the substance and you let me write the procedure. I'll screw you every time." In both chambers of Congress, the rules and precedents are sufficiently complex that most members do not master them in their entirety. Instead, they rely on knowledgeable colleagues, staffers, the parliamentarians, and others to advise them. But a member who masters the rules is valuable to other members, more likely to be consulted, and more likely to be viewed as fit for a leadership position.

The rules governing the legislative process have two main sources: the Constitution and Congress itself. The Constitution sets a few basic but critically important rules (see Chapter 2). However, the chambers themselves are a source of rules in three ways. First, the rules adopted by the House and Senate supplement the constitutional requirements. Second, several statutes or laws passed by Congress set procedural requirements for the two chambers of Congress (although most of these allow the House and Senate to supplement or supplant the statutory requirements with their own rules). Third, the two chambers of Congress have a large body of procedural precedents, built up over their more than 200-year history, that govern many aspects of congressional operations that are not addressed elsewhere. This chapter outlines the rules that are critical to understanding legislative politics.

Beyond the Constitution: House and Senate Rules

The Constitution outlines the fundamental rules of the legislative game but leaves out important details. How legislation is to be prepared for a vote in the House and Senate is left undefined, as are the means for resolving differences between the House and Senate. The Constitution makes the vice president the presiding officer of the Senate and specifies that an elected Speaker shall preside over the House, but it does not mention the specific powers of these presiding officers. The Constitution also does not mention how the president is to decide what to recommend to Congress or the degree to which the president will rely on departments and agencies to speak for the executive branch. Moreover, the means for resolving differences between Congress and the executive branch are not discussed.

The details of legislative procedure have been filled in by the evolution of informal practices and the accumulation of recognized precedents. But in both chambers of Congress, a sizable number of formal rules have been established as well. Such rules both reflect and shape the distribution of power within Congress and between Congress and the president.

The framers of the Constitution anticipated the need for rules of procedure. The Constitution's Article I, Section 5, provides that "each house may determine the rules of its proceedings." As a result, each chamber has devised a complex set of standing rules. They concern the committee systems, procedures for amending and voting on legislation, ethics regulations for members and staff, and many other matters. It is important to keep three things in mind: (1) each chamber has its own set of rules, (2) each chamber may change its rules whenever it desires, and (3) each chamber may waive its rules whenever it desires.

Formally, the House dissolves at the end of each two-year Congress and must reestablish its rules as one of its first items of business at the start of each new Congress. In nearly all cases, this is done with a few amendments sponsored by the majority party and approved on a party-line vote. The Senate, in contrast, considers itself to be a continuous body because at least two-thirds of its members continue to serve from one Congress to the next. For that reason, the Senate's rules remain in effect from Congress to Congress unless the Senate votes to change them.

In addition to their own standing rules, the House and Senate are guided by statutes and precedents established by rulings of their presiding officers. When Congress chooses to include certain procedures in new statutes, such as the Congressional Budget and Impoundment Control Act of 1974 (see Chapter 12), these have the force of standing rules. Party rules govern such things as the selection of party leaders and committee appointments. In some cases party rules dictate limits on the use of standing rules by party or committee leaders. Rulings of the presiding officers concern interpretations of statutory or standing rules.

The Standard Legislative Process

The standard legislative process in the modern Congress is outlined in Figure 7.1. It is called the standard process because it is patterned after the typical route legislation follows. The chambers are free to alter it for certain legislation, and they have done so with greater frequency in the last decade or two. Even the standard process involves many options that are used regularly. The standard process involves multiple stages in each chamber, followed by

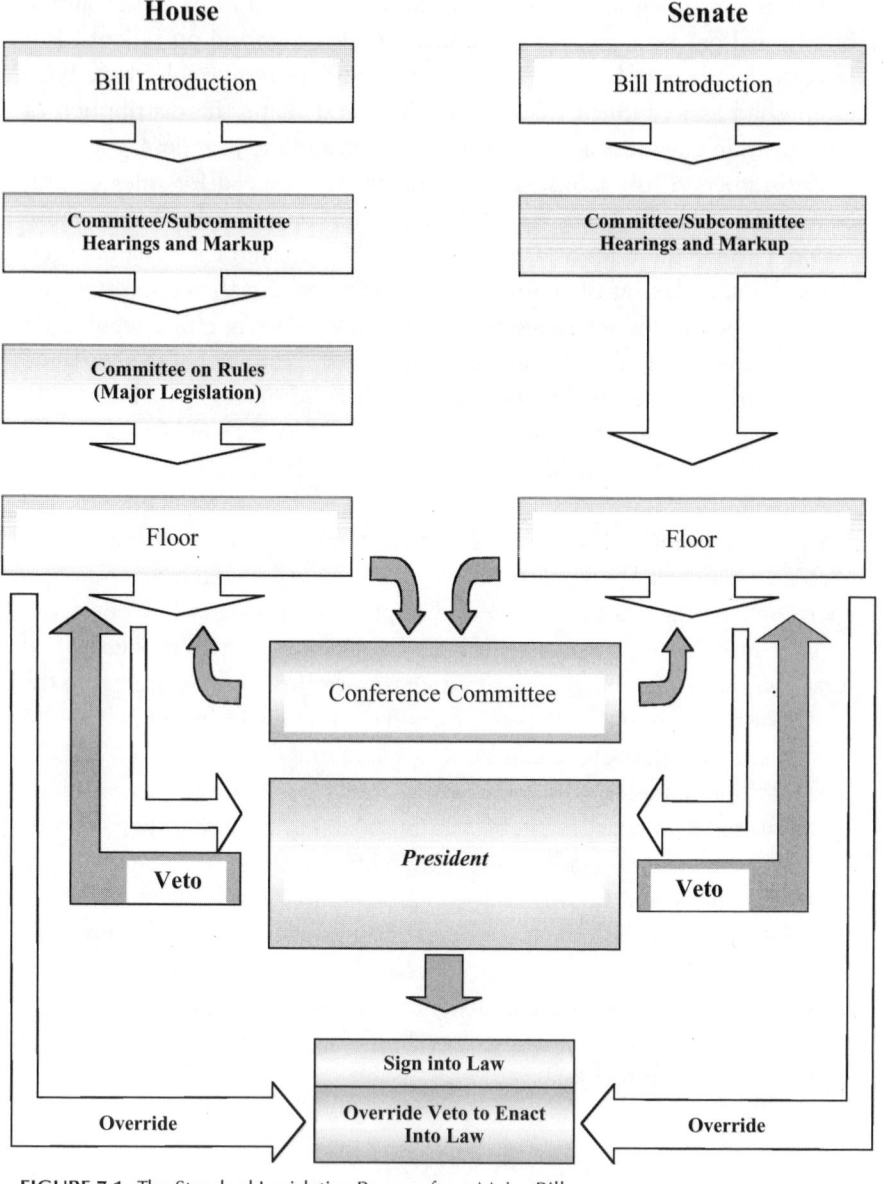

FIGURE 7.1. The Standard Legislative Process for a Major Bill.

steps for resolving House-Senate differences. The Constitution stipulates that after the House and Senate agree on legislation, the president must approve or veto it, and if it is vetoed, Congress may then attempt to override the veto. The standard process is like an obstacle course in which majorities must be created at several stages among different groups of legislators.

Introduction of Legislation

The modern legislative process gives a member who is interested in enacting a new law three basic procedural options. First, she could introduce her own bill and work to gain passage in each chamber. Second, she could seek to have her ideas incorporated into legislation drafted by a committee or by other members. And third, she could offer her proposal as an amendment to someone else's legislation. She might even pursue the three options simultaneously.

Legislation may be drafted by anyone – a member and his or her staff, a committee, lobbyists, executive branch officials, or any combination of insiders and outsiders – but it must be introduced by a member and while Congress is in session. In the House, a member simply places a copy of the draft legislation in a mahogany box, the "hopper," which is located at the front of the House chamber. In the Senate, members hand their draft legislation to a clerk or gain recognition to introduce it orally from the floor. In both chambers, the chief sponsor of a measure may seek cosponsors. Legislation is designated as a bill, a joint resolution, a concurrent resolution, or a resolution, and is numbered as it is introduced (see box, "Types of Legislation").

Although legislation is given a number, it may be known by several names. Each bill is required to have a formal title, which is often quite long. For example, the 2005 Energy Policy Act was "An act to ensure jobs for our future with secure, affordable, and reliable energy." But the bill is known by a more convenient, short title – 2005 Energy Policy Act. Most participants and observers simply called it the energy bill. In addition, bills often come to be known informally by the names of their chief sponsors. The Pell Act, which provided grants to college students, was named after Senator Claiborne Pell (D-Rhode Island), who fought hard for student financial aid.

Because lobbyists and other outsiders cannot introduce legislation, they search for members who are willing to champion their causes and introduce legislation they have drafted. Although they would prefer to have influential members introduce their proposals, they also seek members who have the time and interest to give their legislation some priority. The right mix is often found in a majority party member of mid-level seniority who sits on the committee with jurisdiction over the bill. Usually gaining the sponsorship of several members willing to work together on behalf of the legislation is advantageous. Better still is a group of cosponsors who are known as serious legislators and who represent a range of views in both parties. Of course, sponsors also are sought in both chambers so that companion bills can be introduced at about the same time.

TYPES OF LEGISLATION

There are four types of legislation. In each Congress, legislation of each type is generally numbered in the order it is introduced, although sometimes members request that specific numbers be reserved for their bills.

• **Bills** are designated H.R. (number) or S. (number). Public bills change public law. If enacted into law, public bills are published in a volume entitled *Statutes at Large* and given a public law number, such as P.L. 111. Private bills address matters affecting individuals, such as an immigration case and, if enacted into law, are not reported in *Statutes at Large*.

• **Joint Resolutions** are designated H. J. Res. (number) or S. J. Res. (number). Most joint resolutions are the same as bills for all purposes – they change public law and, if enacted into law, are published in *Statutes at Large* and given a public law number. By tradition, certain kinds of legislation, such as special appropriations measures, are labeled joint resolutions. A special class of joint resolution is proposed constitutional amendments, which if passed by Congress do not go to the president but rather go directly to the states for ratification.

• **Concurrent Resolutions** are designated H. Con. Res. (number) or S. Con. Res. (number) and do not change public law. They concern matters affecting both chambers, such as certain changes in congressional procedures, and so must be adopted by both chambers. They sometimes are used to express the "sense of Congress" about certain issues or events.

• **Resolutions** are designated H. Res. (number) or S. Res. (number) and do not change public law. They concern matters affecting only one chamber, such as most standing rules, and so are adopted only by that chamber. They sometimes are used to express the "sense of the House" or the "sense of the Senate" about certain issues or events.

Members sometimes introduce measures "on request," as a courtesy to the president or someone else. When this is done, it is indicated next to the sponsors' names at the top of the first page of the legislation, signifying that the sponsor does not endorse the provisions of the bill. Similarly, legislation is often introduced by a committee chair on behalf of his or her committee, usually after the committee has drafted and approved the details. The chair is the formal sponsor, but the bill is recognized as a "committee bill."

Referral to Committee

After draft legislation is introduced, the Speaker of the House or the Senate's presiding officer refers it to the appropriate committee(s). In practice, the House and Senate parliamentarians inspect the content of proposed legislation and recommend referral to the committee or committees with the appropriate jurisdiction. Careful drafting of legislation may favorably influence the referral decision.

Legislation may be referred to more than one committee, an action called multiple referral, because committees sometimes share jurisdiction over the content of legislation. Multiple referral has become quite common in the House. Since 1974, the Speaker of the House has been authorized to send legislation to multiple committees. The current rule requires that the Speaker identify a "primary" committee. The Speaker may send a bill, in whole or in part, reflecting the different jurisdictions of committees, to one or more additional committees either before or after consideration by the primary committee. The Speaker also may set time limits for committee action. In recent Congresses, about one in five House measures has been multiply referred, with a higher proportion of important measures, closer to one in four, being so referred.

Most referrals are routine, but occasionally referrals can become controversial. Committee members care about referrals – staking a claim and winning a dispute over jurisdiction may expand a committee's jurisdiction and influence for years to come. Large, complex bills – such as major health care reform and telecommunications bills – often generate competition among committees with jurisdictions relevant to the legislation. Bills dealing with issues not anticipated by the existing rules governing committee jurisdictions are especially likely to stimulate competing jurisdictional claims. On some matters, the composition of the committee that receives a bill may affect the nature of the legislation it eventually reports to the floor, so bill sponsors and outside interests care about which committee receives the referral. On occasion, protracted negotiations among bill sponsors, committee leaders, and party leaders will precede introduction and referral of draft legislation.

Committee Action

Formally, committees have many options concerning how to process most of the legislation referred to them. They may approve the legislation and report it back to the parent chamber, with or without amendments; reject the measure outright; simply not consider it; or set it aside and write a new bill on the same subject. In practice, most proposed legislation does not survive committee consideration. Inaction at the committee stage dooms most legislation. In the 109th Congress (2005–2006), a fairly typical Congress, 4,920 bills and resolutions were introduced in the Senate and 8,154 were introduced in the House. But only 518 and 679 measures were reported by committees of the Senate and House, respectively – 10.5 and 8.3 percent.

Committees may send a bill to a subcommittee for initial action or hold it for the full committee to consider. Although nearly all committees have sub-committees with well-understood jurisdictions, full committee chairs have substantial discretion in deciding whether to refer measures to subcommit-tees or hold them for full committee consideration. Full committee chairs can also control the scheduling of meetings to expedite or delay action on a bill.

Committees and subcommittees may hold hearings to receive testimony on proposed legislation from members, administration officials, interest-group representatives, outside experts, and others. Hearings may address a general issue related to the legislation or the specifics of the legisla-tion itself. Hearings are perhaps the most important formal information-gathering mechanism for Congress and its committees. Still, some hearings generate little but rhetoric and media coverage – members' questions turn into lengthy statements, celebrity witnesses offer scripted answers, and the television networks later replay a 20-second exchange between an antagonis-tic committee member and an acerbic witness. Other hearings are designed more to advertise a bill, raise issues, or draw public attention to a problem than to gather information.

If a committee or subcommittee intends to act on a bill, it normally conducts a "markup" on the legislation – a meeting at which the commit-tee or subcommittee reviews the measure line-by-line or section-by-section and considers amendments. Committees may write their own legislation and have it introduced by their chair. When this approach is taken, the chair often proposes a "chair's mark" as the starting point for the markup. Once the markup by the full committee is complete, the measure may be reported to the floor if a majority of the committee votes to do so. Committees are free to report legislation with or without amendments or even without a recommen-dation that the legislation pass. But most important legislation is amended or written as a "clean" committee bill and then recommended to pass.

In the House, a bill reported to the floor from a committee must be accompanied by a document called a committee report. Senate committees are not required to write these reports but usually do. Committee reports provide the committee's justification for the bill and are usually drafted by staff members as a routine matter. Committee reports may include a statement of minority views on the legislation. On occasion, committee reports are controversial because they provide further interpretations of the bill that might guide later actions on the part of executive agencies or the courts. Committee reports sometimes help non-committee members and their aides explain complicated legislation to constituents. In the House, the Ramseyer rule (named after Rep. John Ramseyer who proposed it years ago) requires that committee reports specify all changes to existing law that the proposed legislation would make.

Circumventing Committees

Proponents of legislation opposed by a committee have a variety of means for gaining floor action on the legislation without having it reported from the committee. These mechanisms are different in the two chambers. Circumventing committees is more difficult in the House.

Circumventing Committees in the House

In the House, the options are to move to suspend the rules, to employ a discharge petition, or to gain a discharge resolution from the Rules Committee. To successfully suspend the rules and pass a bill (one motion), a member must be recognized by the Speaker to make the motion to suspend, and then a two-thirds majority must approve the motion. Because the Speaker is usually supportive of committees dominated by members of his or her own party, this approach is seldom a feasible strategy. Also, a two-thirds majority is unlikely to be obtained for a measure opposed by a committee. In recent decades, committee leaders have used the suspension process to speed floor action or avoid amendments to committee bills.

The discharge procedure allows any member to introduce a motion to discharge or extract a measure from a committee once the measure has been before the committee for 30 legislative days (that is, days on which the House meets). After the motion is filed, a discharge petition is prepared and made available for members to sign. If 218 or more members sign the petition, the motion to discharge becomes privileged business on the second and fourth Mondays of the month (except during the last six days of a session). If the discharge motion is adopted by majority vote, a motion to call up the bill for immediate consideration is in order.

Until 1993, the identity of members signing a discharge petition was not made public until the 218th signature was added. The secrecy of the signatories made it difficult to hold members accountable and undermined lobbyists' efforts to pressure members to sign. Still, both before and after the 1993 rule change, the discharge process has seldom produced House action on a bill. In fact, only 19 bills have been discharged and passed by the House since 1931. Two factors may account for this. First, committees are probably more or less in line with the House majority most of the time.

UNORTHODOX LEGISLATING

The committee process is sometimes circumvented on important legislation in order to facilitate top-level negotiations between party leaders, committee chairs, the administration, and sometimes key representatives of outside groups. In 2008, for example, the $700 billion financial market bailout bill was drafted by the top leaders and administration officials in close consultation with the Federal Reserve chairman and outside financial system experts. The bailout provisions were added to a House bill pending in the Senate. The Senate approved the bill, with a variety of additional provisions on unrelated matters, without committee approval and only eleven hours after the Senate version was posted online. Quick Senate action was made possible by a unanimous consent agreement providing for the bill's consideration. The House approved the bill with the Senate amendments (which added the $700 bailout provisions). The House moved in this way by adopting a special rule for the consideration of the bill that provided for 90 minutes of debate, barred amendments, and waived points of order.

Second, members may prefer to discourage a practice that could be used to discharge legislation from their own committees.

The third approach involves the Rules Committee's authority to report a privileged resolution that, if adopted, brings a bill to the floor for immediate consideration. The majority party members of the Rules Committee are appointed by the Speaker, so the committee is unlikely to use this power without the support of the Speaker. Again, the Speaker usually works to support the actions of committee majorities.

Circumventing Committees in the Senate

In the Senate, committees can be circumvented by introducing nongermane amendments to bills under consideration on the floor, by placing bills directly on the calendar for floor action, by moving to suspend the rules, and by employing the discharge procedure. Unlike the House, which requires that amendments offered to a bill be germane to the content of the bill, Senate rules are silent on the content of amendments offered to most bills. Consequently, a senator is free to offer his or her bill as an amendment to another measure pending before the Senate, thus circumventing a committee that is refusing to report the bill to the floor. There is no guarantee that a majority will support the amendment, of course, but the mechanism is very easy to employ.

Another approach is to object to the standard procedure of referring a bill to committee. Under Senate Rule XIV, a single senator may object and have a bill placed on the calendar, thus avoiding delays that might be caused by an unfriendly committee. But this action may alienate senators who otherwise might support the bill. Senators also may seek to suspend the rules, but doing this requires a two-thirds vote under Senate precedents, which makes it more difficult to use successfully than a nongermane amendment. Alternatively, a senator can move to discharge a committee, but such motions are debatable and thus can be filibustered.

Floor Scheduling

Legislation is listed, in the order it is reported from committee, on one of four calendars in the House and one of two calendars in the Senate. Each chamber has multiple mechanisms for scheduling legislation for floor consideration so that priority legislation will not get backlogged behind less important legislation. Moreover, for certain types of "privileged" legislation – such as budget and appropriations bills – the House allows committee leaders to call up the legislation directly on the floor. In both chambers, the majority party leaders assume primary responsibility for scheduling, but the two chambers have developed very different methods for setting the floor agenda.

Scheduling in the House

Minor legislation and major legislation are treated differently in the House. In recent years, minor bills have been called up most frequently by unanimous consent requests or by motions to suspend the rules. When legislation is called up by unanimous consent, there typically is no discussion. Under a motion to suspend the rules and pass a bill, debate is limited to no more than 40 minutes, no amendments are allowed (unless specified in the motion), and a two-thirds majority is required for approval. Although legislation can only be brought up under suspension of the rules on specified days (typically Monday, Tuesday, and Wednesday only), this has become a very common means for disposing of bills on the House floor. In the 109th House (2005–06), more than 900 measures were passed under suspension of the rules.

Major or controversial legislation is more troublesome. Sponsors of a major or controversial bill usually cannot obtain unanimous or even two-thirds majority support, so they go to the Rules Committee to request a resolution known as a "special rule," or simply a "rule." The following box shows a recent rule adopted by the House for a 2008 bill dealing with wage disparities between men and women. The rule provides for priority consideration of the measure by allowing the Speaker to move the House into the Committee of the Whole, where the bill may be amended (see the section on Floor Consideration). The rule limits general debate on the bill to one hour and allows only those amendments to the committee version that are listed in an accompanying report from the Rules Committee. This rule also sets aside objections (waives points of order) that may be made to the provisions of the bill or to amendments that violate House rules.

Special rules are highly flexible tools for tailoring floor action to individual bills. Amendments may be limited or prohibited. The order of voting on amendments may be structured. For example, the House can adopt a special rule known as a king-of-the-hill rule. First used in 1982, a king-of-the-hill rule provides for a sequence of votes on alternative amendments, usually full substitutes for the bill. The last amendment to receive a majority wins, even if it receives fewer votes than some other amendment. This rule allows members to vote for more than one version of the legislation, which gives them the freedom both to support a version that is easy to defend at home and to vote for the version preferred by their party's leaders. Even more important, the procedure advantages the version voted on last, which is usually the proposal favored by the majority party leadership.

If the Rules Committee grants the rule and a majority of the House supports it, the way is paved for floor debate on the bill. Since the mid-1970s, the Rules Committee has been under the direction of the Speaker. In 1975, after years of struggle to get friendly, timely rules from a Rules Committee dominated by conservatives, the House Democratic Caucus granted the Speaker the power to appoint the committee's Democratic members, subject to its approval. Because the Democrats were the majority party and insisted on firm control of the rules, they reserved nine of the 13 seats on the committee for their part – a ratio that is still in place today. Since the late 1970s, Rules Committee Democrats, often at the direction of the Speaker, have become much more creative in structuring the amendment process on the House floor.

Finally, five House committees (Appropriations, Budget, House Administration, Rules, and Standards of Official Conduct) have direct access to the floor for certain kinds of legislation. Privileged measures – such as appropriations or tax bills – are considered critical to the House as an institution. When other legislation is not pending on the floor, a member authorized by one of these committees can move for immediate consideration of a privileged measure. Special rules from the Rules Committee are the single biggest group of privileged measures. Although privileged bills do not require a special rule from the Rules Committee, their sponsors often seek one anyway to limit or structure debate and amendments or to waive a House rule that might otherwise be used to raise a point of order against the bill.

Resolved. That at any time after the adoption of this resolution the Speaker may, pursuant to clause 2(b) of rule XVIII, declare the House resolved into the Committee of the Whole House on the state of the Union for consideration of the bill (H.R. 1338) to amend the Fair Labor Standards Act of 1938 to provide more effective remedies to victims of discrimination in the payment of wages on the basis of sex, and for other purposes. The first reading of the bill shall be dispensed with. All points of order against consideration of the bill are waived except those arising under clause 9 or 10 of rule XXI. General debate shall be confined to the bill and shall not exceed one hour equally divided and controlled by the chairman and ranking minority member of the Committee on Education and Labor. After general debate the bill shall be considered for amendment under the five-minute rule. It shall be in order to consider as an original bill for the purpose of amendment under the five-minute rule the amendment in the nature of a substitute recommended by the Committee on Education and Labor now printed in the bill. The committee amendment in the nature of a substitute shall be considered as read. All points of order against the committee amendment in the nature of a substitute are waived except those arising under clause 10 of rule XXI. Notwithstanding clause 11 of rule XVIII, no amendment to the committee amendment in the nature of a substitute shall be in order except those printed in the report of the Committee on Rules accompanying this resolution. Each such amendment may be offered only in the order printed in the report, may be offered only by a Member designated in the report, shall be considered as read, shall be debatable for the time specified in the report equally divided and controlled by the proponent and an opponent, shall not be subject to amendment, and shall not be subject to a demand for division of the question in the House or in the Committee of the Whole. All points of order against such amendments are waived except those arising under clause 9 or 10 of rule XXI. At the conclusion of consideration of the bill for amendment the Committee shall rise and report the bill to the House with such amendments as may have been adopted. Any Member may demand a separate vote in the House on any amendment adopted in the Committee of the Whole to the bill or to the committee amendment in the nature of a substitute. The previous question shall be considered as ordered on the bill and amendments thereto to final passage without intervening motion except one motion to recommit with or without instructions.

Scheduling in the Senate

Scheduling is one area, and certainly not the only one, in which the Senate is very different from the House. In some respects, floor scheduling is simple in the Senate. Bringing up a bill is a matter of making a motion to proceed to its consideration. This is done by the majority leader, and though the motion technically requires a majority vote, it usually is approved by unanimous consent. The Senate has no committee empowered to report special rules.

SPECIAL RULES OF THE HOUSE

Since 1979, the House Rules Committee, in partnership with the majority party leadership, has proven remarkably creative in designing special rules to govern floor debate and amendments on major legislation. Different styles of special rules have gained informal names that are widely recognized by the members of the House. All of these creative special rules waive many standing rules of the House governing floor debate and amendments.

• *Restrictive Rules.* Three kinds of rules restricting amending activity were known before the 1980s – modified open, modified closed, and closed rules. Closed rules simply barred all amendments. Modified open rules allowed amendments except for a specific title or section of a bill. Modified closed rules barred amendments except for a specific title or section of a bill. Since the early 1980s, restrictions have come in so many combinations that these traditional categories do not capture their diversity.

• *King-of-the-Hill Rules.* Invented by Democrats in the early 1980s and sometimes called king-of-the-mountain rules, these rules provide that the House will vote on a series of alternative versions of a bill (substitutes) in a specified order and that the last version to receive a majority vote (no matter how large the majority on other versions) wins.

• *Queen-of-the-Hill Rules.* Invented by Republicans in 1995, these rules provide that the House will vote on a series of alternative versions of a bill in a specified order and that the version with the most votes wins. If two versions receive the same number of votes, the last one voted on wins.

• *Time-Limit Rules.* Invented by Republicans in 1995, these rules provide that all debate and amending activity will be completed within a specified period of time.

What appears bizarre to many newcomers to Senate politics is that the motion to proceed is debatable and may be subject to a filibuster (see the accompanying box). That is, senators may refuse to allow the majority leader's motion to come to a vote by conducting extended debate. In fact, they may not even have to conduct the filibuster, because just the threat of doing so is usually enough to keep legislation of only moderate importance off the floor. The reason is that the majority leader usually cannot afford to create a logjam of legislation awaiting floor consideration by subjecting one measure to extended debate. Under Senate Rule XXII, breaking a filibuster is a time-consuming process that requires a three-fifths constitutional majority – if no seat is vacant, 60 senators – willing to invoke cloture. In 1994, a proposal to limit debate on motions to proceed was blocked by Republicans who threatened to filibuster the resolution providing for the change in the rules.

A good example of a bizarre filibuster was the one conducted by Senator Alfonse D'Amato (R-New York) in October 1992. D'Amato objected to the fact that a tax break for a Cortland, New York, typewriter manufacturer had been stricken from a bill in a conference committee, so he filibustered the entire bill. D'Amato held the floor for more than 15 hours, sometimes with the assistance of Senators Patrick Moynihan (D-New York) and John Seymour (R-California). Under the Senate's rules, D'Amato could not sit down or excuse himself to go to the bathroom without yielding the floor. The quality of this extended "debate," which prevented the Senate from completing its business and adjourning for the year, degenerated as time wore on. At one point, D'Amato reported:

> The young lady who works for me in my Syracuse office, Marina Twomey – her parents. She married a young boy who I ran track against in high school – went to Andrew Jackson, met Larry, he went up to Syracuse on a track scholarship, competed. And he married this lovely girl, Marina, who came from Cortland. This is how I came to know Cortland. I visited her and her family.

> Fate and life and what not, circumstances as we talk, Marina is now one of the two people – the other you know for many years, Gretchen Ralph, who used to be the leader of the symphony or the executive director- and a great community person. She and Marina Twomey run my Syracuse office. We talk about Cortland and knowing and having an affinity.[2]

By the time D'Amato gave up, the filibuster consumed a little more than 86 pages of the Congressional Record. This number was not enough to break the record established by Strom Thurmond (R-South Carolina), who spoke for more than 24 hours against a civil rights bill in 1957.

The ever-present threat of a filibuster requires that scheduling be a matter of consultation and negotiation among the majority leader, the minority leader, bill sponsors, and other interested senators. These discussions, conducted in private, often yield bargains about how to proceed and may include compromises about substantive policy matters. The agreement, which may include limitations on debate and amendments, is then presented to the Senate. It requires unanimous approval to take effect. The process contrasts sharply with the formal Rules Committee hearings and majority approval of special rules in the House.

Floor Consideration

For most minor and routine legislation that reaches the House or Senate floor, floor consideration is brief, no amendments are offered, and the

---

Congressionally Speaking . . . The Filibuster

The term filibuster is an anglicized version of the Dutch word for "free-booter." A "filibusterer" was a sixteenth- and seventeenth-century pirate. How it came to be the Senate term for talking a bill to death in the nineteenth century is not clear. Political lexicographer William Safire notes that one of the term's first appearances was in 1854, when the Kansas-Nebraska Act was filibustered.

The current Senate Rule XXII provides for cloture (closing of debate) with the approval of a three-fifths majority of all senators present. That is, if all senators are present, at least 60 senators must support a motion for cloture to stop a filibuster. An exception is made for measures changing the Senate rules, for which a vote of two-thirds of those senators present and voting is required.

---

legislation is approved by voice vote or by unanimous consent. On major legislation, many members usually want to speak and offer amendments, creating a need for procedures that will maintain order and expedite action. The two chambers have quite different floor procedures for major legislation.

Floor Action in the House

In the House, committee chairs write a letter to the Rules Committee chair, requesting a hearing and a special rule for major legislation they are about to report to the floor. Once a special rule for a measure is adopted, the House may resolve to convene "the Committee of the Whole House on the State of the Union" to conduct general debate and consider amendments. The Committee of the Whole, as it is usually abbreviated, consists of the full House meeting in the House chamber and operating under a special set of rules. For example, the quorum required to conduct business in the Committee of the Whole is smaller than it is for the House (100 versus 218), making it easier to conduct business while members are busy with other activities.

A chair appointed by the Speaker presides over the Committee of the Whole. The Committee of the Whole first conducts general debate on the bill and then moves to debate and votes on amendments. Legislation is considered section by section. An amendment must be relevant – germane – to the section under consideration, a requirement that is interpreted very restrictively. For example, an amendment to limit abortions cannot be considered when a bill on water treatment plants is being debated. Amendments sponsored by the committee originating the legislation are considered first for each section and are considered under the five-minute rule. That is, members are allowed to speak for five minutes each on an amendment. The special rule providing for the consideration of the measure may – and often does – alter these standard procedures.

Voting on amendments in the Committee of the Whole can take one of three forms: voice vote, standing division vote, or recorded vote. On a voice vote, members yell out "yea" or "nay," and the presiding officer determines whether there were more yeas or nays. On a standing division vote, members voting "yea" stand and are counted, followed by those voting "nay." Since 1971, it has been possible to get a recorded vote, for which each individual member's position is officially and publicly recorded. Under the current rule, a recorded vote in the Committee of the Whole must be demanded by 25 members. Since 1973, recorded voting has been done by a computerized system. Members insert an identification card into a small voting box and push a "yea," "nay," or "present" button. This system is used for recording other voting in the House as well.

Legislation cannot be passed in the Committee of the Whole, so once debate and amending actions are complete, the measure, along with any approved amendments, is reported back to the House. Special rules usually provide that the "previous question" be ordered, preventing additional debate by the House. The amendments approved in the Committee of the Whole may then be subject to separate votes; if no one demands separate votes, however, the amendments are voted on as a group. Next, a motion to recommit the legislation to committee, which by custom is made by a minority party member, is in order. If the motion to recommit is defeated, as it nearly always is, or simply not offered, the House moves to a vote on final passage.

Floor Action in the Senate

The Senate lacks detailed rules or a well-structured process for debating and amending legislation on the floor. What happens after the motion to proceed is adopted depends on whether or not unanimous consent has been obtained to limit or structure debate and amendments. In the absence of a unanimous consent agreement providing otherwise, Senate rules do not limit debate or amendments for most legislation. Debate and amending activity may go on for days. In contrast to the House, the Senate has no five-minute rule or general germaneness rule for amendments. The floor schedule becomes very unpredictable. Normally, the Senate muddles through controversial legislation with one or more unanimous consent agreements that limit debate, organize the consideration of amendments, and lend some predictability to its proceedings.

THE CHANGING CONGRESS: "GOING NUCLEAR"

Going nuclear is a term used in the Senate to describe a strategy for limiting debate on judicial nominations and other matters. In principle, presidential nominations and treaties can be filibustered. If they are, a two-thirds majority is required to invoke cloture in order to get a vote on them. It has been argued that this practice violates the spirit of the Constitution, which provides that the president may make appointments to top executive and judicial positions with "the advice and consent" of the Senate. If the Senate cannot vote on a presidential nomination, the argument goes, it is not meeting its constitutional obligation under the advice and consent clause.

One approach to addressing filibusters is to change the cloture rule, perhaps just for nominations and treaties. However, proposals to change the cloture rule may be filibustered and would themselves require a two-thirds majority to invoke cloture. So Senate majorities have looked for another approach, an approach that Democrats and the media have described as the "nuclear option."

The idea is to get a ruling from the presiding officer (the Vice President, in all likelihood) that would establish the precedent that the Senate must vote on nominations (and maybe treaties). The proposed tactic goes as follows

• A senator makes a point of order that the Constitution implies that a simple majority can bring a nomination to a vote and the presiding officer rules in favor of the point of order;

• the opposition appeals the ruling of the presiding officer to a vote of the Senate, but the senator making the point of order moves to table the appeal, a motion that is not debatable and so receives an immediate vote; and the majority votes to table the appeal and the presiding officer's ruling stands.

Why haven't Senate majorities used this tactic before to get new rules established as precedents? The primary reason is that a minority can retaliate by obstructing action on the majority's larger agenda. Partisanship would become red hot, other legislation would be filibustered, unanimous consent for routine actions would not be given, Senate action would slow to a crawl, and ultimately the majority might be blamed by the public for mismanaging the Senate. All out partisan war – going nuclear – is the likely result. In 2005, then-Senate Majority Leader Bill Frist (R-Tennessee) threatened to use the nuclear option to do away with filibusters of judicial nominations. A showdown was avoided when a group of seven Democrats and seven Republicans agreed to oppose the strategy, support votes on some of the nominations in dispute, and avoid filibusters on nominations during that Congress.

One reason consent may not be acquired for a time limitation on debate is that some senators may want to have the option of filibustering. A filibuster, and sometimes just the threat of one, will force a compromise. If a compromise is not possible, cloture must be invoked, or the majority leader will be compelled to withdraw the measure from the floor. Once cloture is invoked, 30 hours of debate are permitted (under the current rule), and germane amendments submitted before cloture was invoked can be considered. In fact, cloture is sometimes invoked to avoid the inclusion of nongermane amendments that may require embarrassing votes, complicate negotiations with the House, or risk a presidential veto.

To avoid an unanticipated filibuster, Senate floor leaders seek to learn of possible objections to their plans to bring up a bill on the floor. An informal practice has arisen in recent decades that allows senators to register their objections, usually in writing, to floor action on a bill. An objection is known as a "hold." A hold gains its bite when a majority leader refuses to bring up a measure or nomination on which a hold has been placed or when the minority leader indicates his or her objection to the consideration of a measure or nomination on the basis of a hold that has been registered. Since at least the 1970s, holds have been a source of frustration, particularly for majority leaders and bill managers, but rank-and-file senators of both majority and minority parties have voiced concerns about the practice with regularity. Making holds even more frustrating is the practice of keeping secret the identity of the senator placing a hold. While floor leaders do not always observe holds or confidentiality, the practice is difficult to avoid as long as the majority leader needs unanimous consent to take up measures and wants to avoid filibusters that would make the floor schedule unpredictable for all senators.

The Senate attempted to make holds a matter of public record in 2007. The new rule requires that a senator is require to disclose a hold "following the objection to a unanimous consent [sic] to proceeding to, and, or passage of, a measure or matter on their behalf" by the floor leader. This exceptionally poorly phrased rule goes on to say that the disclosure – a "Notice of Intent to Object" – must be published in the *Congressional Record* within six session days. In other words, a senator is required to have his objection to the consideration of a bill published *after* the objection is first exercised by the leader on the floor. This procedure does not force disclosure if a hold is observed by the majority leader without attempting to gain Senate action on the targeted bill. That is, the rule is not enforceable without the cooperation of the floor leaders, who continue to have an incentive to accommodate their colleagues. Only a few notices of holds have been published since the new rule was adopted.

The modern Senate does not use a committee of the whole. Floor voting can take one of three forms: voice vote, division vote, and roll-call vote. Voice and division votes are similar to those in the House, although the Senate very seldom uses division votes. The Senate does not have an electronic voting system, so recorded votes, which can be demanded by 11 senators, are conducted by a name-by-name call of the roll. The vote on final passage of a bill occurs as specified in the unanimous consent agreement or, in the absence of an agreement, whenever senators stop talking about and offering amendments.

Resolving Differences between the Chambers

The Constitution dictates that the two chambers must approve identical bills before legislation can be sent to the president. This can be accomplished in several ways. One chamber can accept a measure passed by the other. The chambers may exchange amendments until they agree on them, or they may agree to hold a conference to resolve matters in dispute and then send the bill back to each chamber for approval. For complex or controversial legislation, such a conference is the only practical approach.

Members of conference committees, known as conferees, are appointed by the presiding officers of the two chambers, usually according to the recommendations of standing committee leaders. Committee leaders take into account potential conference committee delegates' seniority, interest in the legislation, and other factors, and some committees have established traditions concerning who shall serve on conference committees, which the leaders observe. Conference committees may be of any size. Except for the large conferences held for budget measures, the average conference has roughly 24 representatives and 12 senators.

Agreements between House and Senate conferees are written up as conference reports, which must be approved by a majority of each chamber's conferees. Conference reports must then be approved by majority votes in the House and Senate. In the 109th Congress (2005–2006) only 29 conference reports were filed. Plainly, most legislation is routine and non-controversial and therefore does not require conference action.

House and Senate Rules Compared

The procedures of the House reflect a majoritarian impulse: A simple majority is allowed to take action expeditiously and can do so easily if it is led by the majority party leadership. The House carefully follows established rules

---

Congressionally Speaking . . .

The Constitution stipulates that the vice president serve as president of the Senate. The vice president retains an office in the Capitol, may preside over the Senate, and may cast a vote to break a tie. Because recent vice presidents have had a policy-making role in the administration and travel frequently, they have not used their Capitol office on a regular basis and have seldom presided over the Senate.

Eleven vice presidents never cast a vote in the Senate. In contrast, George Bush, when he was vice president between 1981 and 1989, cast seven votes, and Albert Gore, vice president under President Bill Clinton, cast two votes in 1993. The record belongs to John Adams, the first vice president, who cast 29 tie-breaking votes during the eight-year presidency of George Washington.

---

and practices, which are quite lengthy. The House makes exceptions to its most important floor procedures by granting and adopting special rules by simple majority vote. Procedures dictating internal committee procedures are elaborate. Debate is carefully limited, and the timing and content of amendments are restricted.

The rules of the Senate are relatively brief. They reflect an egalitarian, individualistic outlook. The right of individuals to debate at length and to offer amendments on any subject is generally protected. Only extraordinary majorities can limit debate or amendments. For reasons of practicality, most scheduling is done by unanimous consent. The majority party usually must negotiate with minority party members to schedule floor action and to bring important measures to a vote. Consequently, Senate decision making is more informal and less efficient than House decision making.

In part, these differences (which are highlighted in Table 7.1) are due to the different sizes of the chambers. The large size of the House requires that its rules more explicitly and stringently limit participation on the floor. Scheduling floor action to suit the needs of individuals is out of the question. In contrast, Senate leaders manipulate the floor schedule through unanimous consent agreements to meet the requests of individual senators. The Senate's smaller size allows peer pressure to keep obstructionism in check. A senator who objects frequently to unanimous consent requests risks objections to consideration of his or her own bills.

The differences also reflect the unique parliamentary history of each chamber. In their earliest days, the rules of both the House and Senate contained a previous question motion. In modern times, standard parliamentary rules

TABLE 7.1. Major House-Senate Differences in Rules of Practice.

House	Senate
Does not allow filibusters	Allows filibusters on most legislation
Has a general rule limiting debate	Has no general rule limiting debate
Bars non-germane amendments	Has no general rule barring non-germane amendments
Uses special rules from the Rules Committee to schedule major legislation for floor action	Relies on unanimous consent agreements to schedule major legislation for floor action
Frequently adopts restrictive special rules to limit the number of amendments and limit debate	Must rely on unanimous consent or cloture to restrict debate and amendments
Uses multiple referral frequently	Rarely uses multiple referral
Committees are not easily circumvented	Committees easily circumvented
Rules permit efficient action without minority party cooperation	Rules do not permit efficient action without minority party cooperation
Considers major legislation in the "Committee of the Whole" first	Has no Committee of the Whole
Speaker of the House empowered by House rules	Presiding officer given little power by Senate rules
Records votes by electronic device	No electronic voting system; roll calls are tabulated manually

Source: Collected by authors from House and Senate rules.

such as *Roberts Rules of Order* provide for a motion that, if passed, forces an immediate debate on the issue before the body. In this way, the previous question motion is a means to end debate, but in the early Congresses neither chamber used the previous question motion as a tool to end debate. The question took the form of "shall the main question be now put," which was the traditional parliamentary means of putting off discussion on a controversial measure. If the motion failed, discussion was put off; if it passed, discussion continued. The early Senate rarely invoked the motion and eliminated it from its rules in 1806. The House overturned a ruling of the Speaker in 1807 that a successful previous question motion ended debate on a bill, before reversing this precedent in the face of obstruction in 1811. Thus, from 1811 forward, the House had an effective means for a majority to end debate on a bill or proposed rule change, while the Senate, bound by its lack of a previous question motion, has never been able to develop an efficient means of ending debate.

The previous question played a pivotal role in the development of House and Senate rules. With the previous question motion, House majority parties could get a vote on new rules they wanted adopted. Senate majority parties faced minority filibusters when they proposed rules that advantaged the majority. Consequently House majority parties have regularly modified and elaborated on their chamber's rules, while Senate majority parties seldom seek, let alone achieve, a change in their chamber's rules. The result is that modern House rules are several times as long as Senate rules. When the House and Senate have determined that some limitation on debate is desirable, as for budget measures and trade agreements, special provisions have been written for the Senate to guarantee that debate could be closed. But this has happened only when supermajorities favor the change and often has happened as a part of a much larger legislative package.

Not until 1917, 111 years after the Senate dropped the previous question motion from its rules, did the Senate again adopt a rule that provided a means for closing debate. Rule XXII allowed an extraordinary majority to invoke cloture – that is, to force an end to debate. The 1917 rule provided for a two-thirds majority to invoke cloture. The 1975 reform of the rule reduced the required majority to three-fifths of all elected senators (60 votes with 100 elected senators), except for matters affecting the Senate's rules, which are still subject to a two-thirds majority cloture threshold. As a result, a fairly broad base of support is still required to bring a rules change to a vote in the Senate.

Authorizing and Appropriating

Under congressional rules, most federal government programs are subject to two types of legislation: authorization bills and appropriations bills. Theoretically, an authorization bill sets the program's organization, rules, and spending ceiling, and an appropriations bill provides the money. House and Senate rules require that an authorization bill creating a federal program or agency be passed before an appropriations bill providing spending authority can be adopted. The authorization bill and the appropriations bill for each program or set of programs both follow the standard legislative process. For most programs, a new appropriations bill must be approved each year.

For example, suppose proponents of a bill creating a new financial aid program for college students managed to get the measure enacted into law. They would have taken the bill through the House Committee on Education

Congressionally Speaking...

An **engrossed bill** is the final version of a bill passed by one house, including any amendments that may have been approved, as certified by the clerk of the House or the secretary of the Senate.

An **enrolled bill** is the final version of a bill as approved by both houses, printed on parchment, certified by either the clerk of the House or the secretary of the Senate (for the house that first passed it), and signed by the Speaker of the House and the president pro tempore of the Senate; it has a space for the signature of the president.

and the Workforce and the Senate Committee on Health, Education, Labor, and Pensions. The bill would specify how the program was to be organized, how financial aid decisions were to be made, and how much – say $400 million – could be spent, at most, on the program in any one year. It is likely that the bill would authorize the program for a specific period of time – say, four or five years. A separate appropriations bill, which would include spending authority for the new program, must be passed before the program could begin operations. The House and Senate appropriations committees might decide that only $250 million should be spent on the program. If the House and Senate went along with the lower figure, the program would be limited to a $250 million budget for the next year.

In the modern Congress, jurisdiction over authorization legislation is frag-mented among many standing committees. Jurisdiction over appropriations is consolidated in one appropriations committee in each chamber, although each of the appropriations committees has 13 subcommittees that do most of the work. Jurisdiction over taxes, the major source of federal revenue, falls to one tax-writing committee in each house: the House Committee on Ways and Means and the Senate Committee on Finance. Thus, power over fiscal policy is not only shared between the House, Senate, and president, it is shared among the various committees within House and Senate as well.

The system creates tensions between the congressional committees. Tax committees do not like to pass bills increasing taxes to cover spending other committees have authorized. Authorizing committees often dislike the handiwork of the appropriations committees. A small appropriation can defeat the purpose of the original authorization bill. In response, authorizing committees have pursued a number of tactics, such as including provisions for permanent appropriations for some programs (social security is one), to avoid the appropriations process.

A MAJOR GLITCH

In 2008, the House and Senate passed the conference report to an important farm bill in identical form. President George W. Bush vetoed the bill and returned it to the House, with everyone unaware that Title III concerning international trade had not been included in the papers sent to the president. The omission of the title from the 15-title bill was made by the enrolling clerk of the House in the rush to complete action on renewal of farm programs before they expired. No one in the administration reported the missing title when the bill was vetoed. The error was not discovered and reported to the House leadership until the day of the veto override vote. Minority party members complained, but the House and Senate proceeded to override the veto. To clarify the status of Title III, the two houses repassed the farm bill with all titles in their proper place, the president vetoed the new bill, and the House and Senate again overrode the veto.

Provisions limiting the length of authorizations are known as *sunset* provisions. In principle, sunset provisions force the authorizing committee and Congress to re-pass authorization legislation periodically, which compels the executive branch to justify the continuation of the programs and gives the authorizing committees additional influence over the executive agencies. In recent years, many authorizations have expired but the programs have not died – sometimes out of neglect but often because of conflict over the program. Welfare reform, college student financial aid, and federal highway programs are among the dozens of unauthorized programs in recent years. These programs can continue as long as Congress passes the separate appropriations bills for them. An appropriation is possible by use of a waiver of the House rule, which may be included in the special rule under which the appropriations bills are considered on the House floor. A consequence of this practice is that the authorizing committees do not realize the special influence over the direction of these programs that was expected when the sunset provisions were first enacted.

Evolution of the Legislative Process

For most of the twentieth century, nearly all major and minor legislative measures have followed the path of the standard processes described in this chapter. The House and Senate were always free to modify their processes and have sometimes handled a bill in a special way. In the last three decades of the twentieth century, nonstandard approaches to preparing legislation for a vote have been employed with increasing frequency. Bypassing committees, negotiating details in summits between congressional leaders and representatives of the president, having multiple committees consider bills, and drafting omnibus bills characterize the action on a large share of major legislation considered by recent Congresses. In fact, according to one survey of the processes used by the House and Senate on major legislation since the late 1980s, four out of five measures in the House and two out of three in the Senate were considered under some nonstandard procedure.

Unorthodox legislative procedures have been invented for many reasons. The sheer complexity of some new public policies and legislative measures forces action by many committees – and compels committee and party leaders to find new ways to piece together legislation, negotiating a bewildering array of technical provisions and working with the president to avoid a veto. The reforms of the 1970s – which strengthened the House Speaker's procedural options and reduced the power of full committee chairs – were discovered to have unanticipated uses. Perhaps most important, partisan maneuvering stimulated procedural innovations as first one party and then the other sought parliamentary advantages when pushing legislation.

Furthermore, both chambers of Congress often create new rules in response to new challenges. In some cases the House and Senate have tailored their procedures to particular kinds of legislation or specific issues. In the last two decades, for example, Congress has created "fast-track" procedures for considering trade agreements negotiated by the executive branch with foreign governments. These procedures limit debate and bar amendments to speed congressional approval and limit congressional second-guessing of executive branch decisions.

An even more important class of legislation that has inspired special procedures concerns fiscal policy: decisions about federal spending, taxing, and budget deficits and surpluses. The Congressional Budget and Impoundment Control Act of 1974, often known simply as the Budget Act of 1974, established a process to coordinate congressional decision making affecting fiscal policy. In the 1980s and early 1990s, skyrocketing federal deficits motivated Congress to set tight rules constraining fiscal choices and to adopt unique procedures for enforcing the new constraints.

In other cases, special procedures are invented for an individual bill. In the House, special rules governing floor debate have become more complex, as have the provisions of unanimous consent agreements in the Senate. Task forces, usually appointed by party leaders, have become an everyday part of decision making in the House. Inter-committee negotiations guided by party leaders sometimes occur after committees report but before legislation is taken to the floor. In these ways, the traditional committee-to-floor-to-conference process has become a less accurate description of the increasingly meandering route that major legislation takes through the modern Congress.

Conclusion

Rules matter. Legislative rules, whether they arise from the Constitution or elsewhere, determine procedural advantages among the players, factions, and parties that compete for control over public policy. The rules also are the foundation of Congress's major organizational features, such as its leadership positions and committees, which help the institution manage a large and diverse workload and are generally designed to serve the political needs of its members.

The House and Senate have evolved quite different rules. Compared with Senate rules, House rules make it more difficult to circumvent committees, more strictly limit participation on the floor, and give the majority a greater ability to act when confronted with an obstructionist minority. The House is more majoritarian; the Senate is more egalitarian. The House is more committee oriented; the Senate is more floor oriented.

But the rules do not determine the political and policy objectives of legislators. Those objectives are primarily the product of the electoral processes through which people are selected to serve in Congress. Campaigns and elections connect members to their constituencies and lead many members to take a local, sometimes quite parochial, outlook in legislative politics.

Above: Sen. Olympia Snowe, R-Me., is questioned by reporters on her way to vote on the economic stimulus bill, February 10, 2009.
Below: January 1999: The vote board in the House of Representatives. Rebecca Roth/Roll Call.

8

The Floor and Voting

T HE TALLY WAS STUCK AT 207 IN FAVOR, 226 AGAINST, BUT THE DOW JONES
industrial average continued to fall. First, it was 200 points, then 300
points, and finally close to 800 points before the gavel fell – more than 30
minutes after the vote began – with 205 in favor, 228 against. In a dramatic scene that seemed to catch the public, stock traders, and the leaders
of both congressional parties by surprise the House had failed to pass a
bill that would commit $700 billion to buy up troubled banking assets in
an attempt to calm credit markets. In the days that followed, Democratic
leaders blamed Republican leaders for not delivering promised votes, while
Republican leaders blamed Democrats for poisoning the atmosphere surrounding the vote with partisan rhetoric. A compromise bill passed without
drama a few days later, but the failed vote revealed a change in the way
congressional leaders manage some controversial bills.

Votes are occasionally held open to allow straggling members to vote or
in hopes of changing the outcome, but it is relatively rare to see a surprise
outcome on the floor. Both the House and Senate have developed elaborate committee and party systems that can take much of the policy-making
process off the chamber floors, but in recent Congresses, Democrats and
Republicans alike have not been as hesitant to bring a bill to the floor without having a firm majority in place before hand and then doing enough
"arm-twisting" to secure a majority.

During most of Congress's history, responsibility for the details of public policy rested with the standing committees. At times, power over the
details of important bills resided in the hands of central party leaders. Most
scholars have used this continuum – from decentralized, committee-oriented
decision making to centralized, party-oriented decision making – to characterize the decision-making processes and distribution of power within the

TABLE 8.1. Possible Patterns of Congressional Decision Making.

Number of units	Number of effective participants	
	Few	Many
Few	Centralized (party leadership)	Collegial (floor)
Many		Decentralized (committees)

two chambers. Everything that goes on within the House and Senate is, in principle, subject to the approval of the parent chambers in floor sessions. In principle, therefore, the details of all legislation could be written and reviewed on the chamber floors, but in modern practice, this rarely happens.

These alternatives are depicted in Table 8.1. If important decisions were made on the chamber floor, all members, in that one place, would have the opportunity to participate effectively in deliberations on all measures. In general, as we saw in Chapter 6, the modern House is more dependent on committees than is the Senate. But there have been times when central party leaders dominated the House. Thus, the House is often characterized as varying along the centralized-decentralized continuum. The Senate is more collegial – more likely to make detailed policy choices on the floor. Both committees and party leaders are important in the Senate, but relative to the House, the Senate has long been far more floor oriented. Neither committees nor party leaders have found the Senate floor predictable or controllable. These differences are obvious every day in the Capitol.

In this chapter, we report on a typical day on the House and Senate floors and explain how differences in floor procedure shape the distribution of power in the two chambers. In addition, the chapter reviews how members' records of floor voting are most commonly analyzed by political scientists, journalists, and interest groups, providing a "consumer's guide" to studies of floor voting. The chapter concludes with a review of the factors that influence the relationship between the parties, committees, and the floor.

A Typical Day on the House and Senate Floors

On a March day in 2007, a fairly typical day while Congress is in session, dozens of committees and subcommittees held morning meetings and hearings in the congressional office buildings while clerks and pages prepared for the opening of the House and Senate floor sessions. In the Senate, this meant distributing various documents to individual senators' desks, which are arranged by party (when facing the front, Democrats are on the left and Republicans are on the right) and seniority (junior members are in the back). In the House, members do not have desks or assigned seats, although, by tradition, the Democrats sit on the left and the Republicans on the right. As the clerks and pages went about their work, tourists went in and out of the galleries, some disappointed that they did not have a chance to see a debate before they hurried off to other sites in Washington. As usual, the Senate session opened before the House session – the Senate at 9:15 A.M. and the House at 10 A.M.

The Day in the House

The House session began when Speaker pro tempore Jan Schakowsky (D-Illinois) assumed the chair. The Speaker does not always preside over House proceedings. She frequently appoints other members (Speakers *pro tempore*) to take her place presiding over the House so that she can conduct business in her office or elsewhere. Typically, several members will preside during the course of the day.

The session opened with a prayer from the Reverend Thomas J. McCarthy of St. Paul Catholic Church in Salem, Ohio. The Speaker pro tempore then announced that she had examined the *Journal* of the House and announced her approval of it. Approval of the *Journal* used to require a vote of the House, but dilatory requests for votes led House Democrats to push through a rule allowing the Speaker to approve the *Journal*. A member may still demand a vote on the *Journal*, but that vote may be postponed until late in the day. Next came the Pledge of Allegiance, which has been recited since 1989. The practice was started the year the Supreme Court ruled that burning the American flag was constitutionally protected speech, and Congress responded with legislation to ban flag burning. House Republicans proposed – and the Democrats did not dare block – a House rule that required that the Pledge be recited after the prayer. After the Pledge, several members of the Ohio delegation welcomed Reverend McCarthy to the House and gave brief speeches on his life and accomplishments. The floor session was televised (see box, "The Changing Congress: Televising the House and Senate").

The Speaker pro tempore announced that members of each party would be recognized to give one-minute speeches. The reservation of time for one-minute speeches gives legislators a brief period to address the House and the nation on any matter they choose. Frequently, members use

THE CHANGING CONGRESS: TELEVISING THE HOUSE AND SENATE

The House began televising its floor sessions in 1979. After becoming somewhat jealous of the attention given to the House, the Senate began to televise its sessions in 1986. Congressional employees operate both television systems, and the signal is made available to television networks and individual stations via satellite.

Floor proceedings are carried live on C-SPAN, the Cable-Satellite Public Affairs Network. Most cable television systems carry C-SPAN I, on which House sessions are shown. Many cable systems also carry C-SPAN II, where Senate sessions are broadcast. Many committee hearings, press conferences, and other public affairs programs are shown on C-SPAN when the House and Senate are not in session.

In both chambers, the most obvious consequence of television coverage has been an increase in floor speeches. In the House, one-minute and special-order speeches have become more numerous. One-minute speeches are made at the beginning of the day for about half an hour. Special-order speeches are made after the House finishes its regular business for the day. In 1994, House Democratic and Republican leaders agreed that special-order speeches should be limited to four hours on most days. They also began to experiment with structured, Oxford-style debates. In 1995, "reaction shots" of members on the floor were limited after members complained about being caught in unflattering shots by the floor cameras.

The Senate created a new class of speeches, the aforementioned special-order speeches, which are limited to five minutes. In addition, representatives and senators have made increasing use of large poster charts and graphs to illustrate their points for the television audience. In addition, many senators now address their chamber from the back row, some distance from their personal desks, so that the camera angle will be less steep and, in the case of male senators, will not expose their bald spots to home viewers.

one-minute speeches to respond to the news of the day, and they often use the opportunity to compliment or criticize the president. Occasionally, a group of members will organize themselves to emphasize a particular theme – and being outrageous or flamboyant increases the chance of getting on the evening news. On this day, there was a mix of speeches, some concerned the bill to provide more funding for military operations in Iraq, others addressed the Democrats plans for the federal budget, while others concerned less controversial topics such as prevention of veteran suicides, and honoring U.S. Marshal award winners.

After about a half hour of one-minute speeches, the Speaker pro tempore declared that the House dissolve into the Committee of the Whole House on the state of the Union for further consideration of H.R. 1227, a bill to assist in the provision of affordable housing to low-income families affected by Hurricane Katrina. The Committee of the Whole (COW) is what it sounds like, a committee of which all members of the House are members. The House often dissolves into the COW to debate and vote on amendments to bills. The quorum requirement is reduced to 100 from 218, which makes it easier to transact business. Since 1971, the House has allowed recorded voting on amendments in the COW, but the rules stipulate than any member can request that a vote be taken by the House on any amendments that pass in the COW.

Under the previously adopted special rule governing consideration of the bill, Representative Randy Neugebauer (R-Texas) was recognized to offer an amendment to the bill striking the section of the bill that would allow families to continue receiving housing vouchers after the termination of the Disaster Voucher program. Under the provisions of the special rule (see box "The Special Rule for H.R. 1227"), the amendment was debated for 60 minutes, with the time divided between Rep. Neugebauer and a member opposed to the amendment, in this case Rep. Barney Frank (D-Massachusetts). The debate centered on whether allowing hurricane victims to continue receiving housing vouchers would undermine the Section 8 public housing program. Proponents of the amendment argued that extending the vouchers was too expensive and was the wrong way to solve the region's housing problem. Opponents argued that given the level of destruction of housing in the Gulf region, there was insufficient public housing available. It was, therefore, crucial that the government not disadvantage beneficiaries of this program by putting a time limit on the voucher program.

At the conclusion of debate on the amendment, a voice vote was taken and it was announced that the amendment had failed. Rep. Neugebauer asked for a recorded vote on the amendment. House rules allow the chairperson of the Committee of the Whole to delay requests for recorded votes. This is typically done as a time-saving measure so that debate can continue on amendments. It is common practice for votes to be "stacked," that is occur one after another, so that members who are not on the floor can vote on several items in succession. The COW then debated an amendment offered by Rep. Tom Price (R-Georgia). At the close of debate on the amendment offered by Rep. Price, recorded votes on both the Price amendment and

THE SPECIAL RULE FOR H.R. 1227 (ANNOTATIONS BY THE AUTHORS)

Resolved, That at any time after the adoption of this resolution the Speaker may, pursuant to clause 2(b) of rule XVIII, declare the House resolved into the Committee of the Whole House on the state of the Union for consideration of the bill (H.R. 1227) to assist in the provision of affordable housing to low-income families affected by Hurricane Katrina.

This provision gives the Speaker control over when the bill will be considered.

The first reading of the bill shall be dispensed with. All points of order against consideration of the bill are waived except those arising under clause 9 or 10 of rule X.

This provision bans points of order that might be raised against consideration of the bill on the grounds that its provisions violate some rule or precedent.

General debate shall be confined to the bill and shall not exceed one hour equally divided and controlled by the chairman and ranking minority member of the Committee on Financial Services. After general debate the bill shall be considered for amendment under the five-minute rule.

This provision sets time limits on debate. General debate – that is, debate not directed at a specific amendment – is divided so that the two bill managers control 30 minutes each. They may allocate some time to colleagues by yielding time to them. The five-minute rule refers to a standing rule of the House that governs debate in the Committee of the Whole. The Chair first recognizes the amendment's sponsor to speak for five minutes. Next a Member opposing the amendment can claim five minutes to speak in opposition. Other Members may secure five minutes for debate by offering pro forma amendments. This is done by asking the Chair "to strike the last word."

The amendment in the nature of a substitute recommended by the Committee on Financial Services now printed in the bill, modified by the amendment printed in part A of the report of the Committee on Rules accompanying this resolution, shall be considered as adopted in the House and in the Committee of the Whole. The bill, as amended, shall be considered as the original bill for the purpose of further amendment under the five-minute rule and shall be considered as read. All points of order against provisions in the bill, as amended, are waived.

These provisions provide that the Financial Services Committee's version of the bill, rather than the version originally introduced, will be the subject of floor amending activity. An amendment to the committee's version, which was considered by the Rules Committee, would be automatically adopted upon the adoption of the special rule.

Notwithstanding clause 11 of rule XVIII, no further amendment to the bill, as amended, shall be in order except those printed in part B of the report of the Committee on Rules. Each further amendment may be offered only in the order printed in the report, may be offered only by a Member designated in the report, shall be considered as read, shall be debatable for the time specified in the report equally divided and controlled by the proponent and an opponent, shall not be subject to amendment, and shall not be subject to a demand for division of the question in the House or in the Committee of the Whole. All points of order against such further amendments are waived except those arising under clause 9 or 10 of rule X.

These provisions allow consideration of amendments specified in the accompanying report, which also specifies the order of consideration and the time allowed for debate. Other amendments are prohibited. Points of order against the amendments for violating House rules or precedent are prohibited.

At the conclusion of consideration of the bill for amendment the Committee shall rise and report the bill, as amended, to the House with such further amendments as may have been adopted. The previous question shall be considered as ordered on the bill and amendments thereto to final passage without intervening motion except one motion to recommit with or without instructions.

This provision gives the minority party an opportunity to offer an amendment as "instructions." If the instructions are adopted as a part of a motion to recommit, the bill is amended and immediately considered for final passage.

Sec. 2. During consideration in the House of H.R. 1227 pursuant to this resolution, notwithstanding the operation of the previous question, the Chair may postpone further consideration of the bill to a time designated by the Speaker.

the Neugebauer amendment were taken in succession. The Neugebauer amendment was rejected by a vote of 185–247 and the Price amendment was rejected by a vote of 96–333.

With all amendments having been considered, the COW then "rose" and the Speaker pro tempore resumed presiding over the House. The House then moved into the final stages of consideration of the H.R. 1227. Rep. Price asked for a revote on an amendment that had been adopted in the COW, which subsequently passed by a vote of 242–184. Rep. Bobby Jindal (R-Louisiana) then offered a motion to recommit with instructions that would give priority in public housing to displaced returning residents who were both "law-abiding" and employed. The motion to recommit is reserved for the minority party or someone who is opposed to the bill "in its current form." A motion to recommit with instructions to report forthwith – the type offered by Jindal – is essentially a substantive amendment to the bill. If it is adopted, the bill does not leave the floor at all, the change is reported by

---

Congressionally Speaking . . .

On the House floor, members engage in a carefully scripted language when debating on the floor. When a bill manager wishes to speak about a bill on the floor they say, "I yield myself such time as I may consume." If another member wishes to interject into debate he or she will say "Will the gentleman [gentlewoman] yield?" If the member holding the floor wishes to yield he/she will say in return, "I yield two minutes [or another block of time] to the gentleman [gentlewoman] from New Hampshire." The interjecting member will then say, "I thank the gentleman [gentlewoman] for yielding. I rise in support/opposition . . . " Once they have concluded they may say, "I yield back to the balance of my time." The bill manager will then begin his/her speech again with "Reclaiming my time . . . " This back and forth between floor managers and other members continues until the time allotted for debate is consumed.[1]

---

the committee immediately. Rep. Jindal's motion passed by a vote of 249–176, with a majority of Democrats voting no, and a majority of Republicans voting yea. During the 12 years of Republican rule it was rare for a motion to recommit with instructions to pass against the will of the Republican Party, but in the early months of the 110th Congress, the Democrats have lost a handful of these votes. The vote on the motion to recommit is the last procedural step before the "final passage" vote on a bill. The House then passed H.R.1227 by a vote of 302–125, with all Democrats voting in favor of passage along with 72 Republicans.

Following passage of H.R. 1227, the House considered several bills under suspension of the rules. This is a procedure in which a member can ask to "suspend the rules and pass" a particular bill. Bills taken up under this procedure are allotted 40 minutes of debate and amendments are not allowed. If two-thirds of the House votes in favor, the bill is passed. This procedure is used for non-controversial bills that typically involve a cost of less than $100 million. On this day, the House considered numerous bills and resolutions under this procedure, including a resolution authorizing the use of the capitol rotunda for a Holocaust remembrance ceremony, a reauthorization of the Hawaiian Homeownership Opportunity Act, the Judicial Disclosure Responsibility Act, and a bill to change the cost of living adjustment for veterans – with six receiving recorded votes – all passing except for the Hawaiian Homeownership Opportunity.

The House then heard a number of special order speeches – most concerning the status of the War in Iraq and what, if any, policy changes the

THE CHANGING CONGRESS: *THE CONGRESSIONAL RECORD*

The proceedings of the House and Senate are published daily in the *Congressional Record*. The *Record* is printed overnight and distributed to Capitol Hill and to many other places, including most large libraries. Hardcover, permanent editions are published and distributed periodically.

The *Record* is much more than a report of the words spoken on the chamber floors. Introduced bills, committee meetings, and many other items are listed in the *Record* each day. The text of bills and conference reports considered on the floor is included, as are the many newspaper articles, scholarly studies, executive agency reports, and other items that members place in the *Record* by gaining unanimous consent of their house. As a general rule, the charts or graphs that members use on the floor cannot be printed in the *Record,* although tabular material may be inserted if the member receives unanimous consent.

The members' ability to alter prose reported in the *Record* after they have spoken has long been a controversial issue. Members are allowed to make non-substantive grammatical changes in their prose. As a result, some members appear far more articulate in the *Record* than they do on the floor. Statements and other insertions in the *Record* are supposed to be distinguished by a bullet (●). In the Senate, members frequently seek, and then always receive, unanimous consent to have their statements placed in the *Record* "as though read." This revision makes distinguishing what was said from what was inserted nearly impossible. Frequently, senators request that their statements be included "at the appropriate place," which is usually done so that the statement does not interrupt the discussion on a pending matter in the *Record*.

The *Congressional Record* tends to be a more faithful record of House proceedings than of Senate proceedings. Representatives frequently seek permission to "revise and extend" their remarks, so many statements reported in the *Record were* not actually read on the floor. But the House has more restrictive rules about including extraneous matter and speeches in the *Record* and requires that newspaper articles and other insertions be printed in a separate section, "Extensions of Remarks." The House also has long required that revisions or extensions that are not "a substantially verbatim" account be distinguished by a different typeface. The House adopted an even tighter rule in 1995 that limits changes to corrections of grammar and typographical errors.

House should adopt as part of the bill providing supplemental funding for the Iraq war. Special orders typically take place at the conclusion of other business that the House is considering that day. Members are allowed to give speeches on topics of their choice regardless of whether the speech concerns pending legislation. Members typically reserve time for special orders through the party leadership and may choose to insert the speech into the *Congressional Record* without actually delivering the speech – unde-livered speeches appear in the *Extension of Remarks* section of the *Congres-sional Record*. The House adjourned at 1:05 A.M. until 10:00 A.M. the same morning.

The Day in the Senate

The Senate convened at 9:15 A.M. when Senator Sheldon Whitehouse (D-Rhode Island) called the Senate to order. The vice president is the pres-ident of the Senate, but tends to preside only at ceremonial occasions (for example, when the oath of office is administered to newly elected senators at the start of a Congress) and when a tie-breaking vote might be needed. The Constitution provides for a president pro tempore to preside in the absence of the vice president. But the president pro tempore, who by tradition is the most senior member of the majority party, is not able to preside on a full-time basis because of other duties. Consequently, the president pro tempore's staff arranges for other majority party senators, usually the most junior ones, to take turns presiding over the Senate.

On this day, following the pledge of allegiance, Senator Whitehouse read a letter from the president pro tempore, Senator Robert Byrd (D-West Virginia), appointing Whitehouse as acting president pro tempore. After the prayer, Senator Kent Conrad (D-North Dakota), serving as acting major-ity leader in the absence of Majority Leader Harry Reid (D-Nevada), was recognized and indicated that the Senate immediately resume debate on the budget resolution for fiscal year 2008. Senator Conrad indicated that Senator John Ensign (R-Nevada) would be recognized to offer an amend-ment, followed by an amendment from the majority party. Senator Con-rad also informed senators that there would be no recorded votes taken before 5:00 P.M. Senator Conrad also urged his colleagues to speed up debate on the budget resolution, warning them that the session could run to midnight if necessary. Senator Ensign's amendment sought to "ensure that troops serving in harm's way remain America's top budget priority by: ensuring full funding for the Department of Defense within the reg-ular appropriations process, reducing reliance on supplemental appropri-ation bills, and by improving the integrity of the Congressional budget process." Debate on the Ensign amendment continued with several sen-ators expressing their support or opposition. Then Senator Barack Obama (D-Illinois) asked for and was granted 10 minutes to discuss the costs – both monetary and in terms of human life – of the Iraq war and to urge

---

Congressionally Speaking...

On the Senate floor, *quorum calls* are used to get a temporary break in the
action – a time out. A senator might say, "Mr. President, I suggest the absence
of a quorum," and the presiding officer will respond, "The clerk will call the
roll." Technically, if a quorum is not discovered, the Senate will have to adjourn.
Indeed, filibustering senators sometimes note the absence of a quorum to force
senators to appear on the floor. Most of the time, however, a quorum call is
used as a time out that gives absent senators time to come to the floor to offer an
amendment or speak. At other times, a quorum call is used to give leaders time to
work out agreements on issues or procedure.

---

senators to consider these costs. The speech by Senator Obama highlights the fact that the rules of debate in the Senate are much more
casual than in the House. Senators regularly ask for and receive unanimous
consent to give speeches that are not related to the bill currently under
consideration.

When debate on the Ensign amendment was concluded, the Senate
moved on to an amendment offered by Senator Jim Bunning (D-Kentucky)
concerning Social Security funding, along with several other amendments.
Debate on these amendments continued until late into the afternoon, at
which point the Senate moved into "morning business." Despite the name,
morning business does not necessarily occur in the morning. During morning business, the Senate conducts routine business such as receiving messages from the House and the president, as well as petitions and memorials,
committee reports, and bill introductions.

Following morning business the Senate moved into Executive session to
consider a nominee for the post of Assistant Secretary of Preparedness and
Response in the Department of Health and Human Services. The nominee
was confirmed by unanimous consent. The Senate then adjourned for the
day at 7:52 P.M.

House-Senate Differences

The events of this day illustrate many of the differences between the two
chambers of Congress. Most of the differences are the by-product of one
fact: Floor debate and amendments are governed by strict rules in the
House, but are generally limited only by unanimous consent agreements or

super-majority votes in the Senate. Representatives must worry that their floor amendments might not be put in order by a special rule from the Rules Committee. Once a bill is on the House floor, representatives are compelled to conform to the schedule laid out by the Speaker and the special rules. In sharp contrast, senators can introduce amendments freely, even on subjects unrelated to the bill at hand, and protect their ability to do so by objecting to requests for unanimous consent to limit amendments. Moving the Senate from amendment to amendment and from bill to bill is a constant struggle for the majority leader and bill managers. The House has a schedule that is followed in the main; scheduling in the Senate is often much like fortune telling.

Voting Procedure

By the end of that March day in 2007, the House had held 12 recorded votes, all using its computerized voting system. The Senate had held seven recorded votes, all on amendments to the budget resolution. When the Senate conducts a roll-call vote, the process is time consuming. It is an old-fashioned roll call for which a clerk calls out the individual names of the senators in alphabetical order ("Mr. Akaka... Mr. Alexander... Mr. Allard... Mr. Baucus," and so on) and waits for senators to arrive on the floor and respond. After calling all of the names, the roll-call clerk starts from the beginning to call the names of senators who have not voted. The clerk is then interrupted by senators appearing during the vote to recognize them and hear their votes. The Constitution provides that "the Yeas and Nays of the Members of either House on any question shall, at the desire of one-fifth of those present, be entered upon the Journal." This rule means that 20 senators or 87 representatives (if all members are present) may demand a vote in which each member's vote is recorded. In practice, with few members being present, usually only 11 senators or 44 representatives are required – one-fifth of a quorum, which is half of the membership of the chamber. Because the quorum requirement is not enforced unless a member makes a point of order that a quorum is not present, the presiding officer will assume that a quorum is present and order the yeas and nays based on the lower threshold. Under the rules of the House, 25 members may demand a recorded vote in the Committee of the Whole, where most votes on amendments to bills take place. The Constitution does not specify how the houses should vote in the absence of a demand for the yeas and nays.

House Voting Procedure

In today's Congress, the House votes by three means: voice vote, division vote, and recorded vote. On most motions, the presiding officer (the chair of the Committee of the Whole or the Speaker) first asks for a voice vote. He or she might say, "The question is on the amendment by the gentlewoman from Illinois. All in favor say 'aye,' all opposed say 'no.' The noes have it, and the amendment is rejected." In many cases, this is spoken so rapidly that it is obvious that the number voting each way had little to do with the announcement of the winning side. Sometimes, the issue is not controversial, and the presiding officer is merely reporting the obvious result. In other cases, the presiding officer knows that his or her announcement will make no difference because a member will demand a recorded vote on the issue.

The division, or standing, vote is used little and is virtually never decisive. Any member may demand such a vote, which is conducted by having members voting aye stand and be counted and then having members voting no stand and be counted. Only the vote tally – the number of ayes and noes – is recorded. Because few members are on the floor for debate on most matters, the result usually shows that less than a quorum of members is present (a quorum is 100 or more in the Committee of the Whole) which leads automatically to a recorded vote. Consequently, this method is seldom used any longer.

Recorded votes are conducted with the assistance of an electronic voting system and nearly always occur upon the demand of the necessary number of members after a voice vote. In the Committee of the Whole, 25 members must demand a recorded vote. (The Constitution's requirement that one-fifth of those present demand a recorded vote applies only to requests for recorded votes in the House, not in the Committee of the Whole.)

Each member is issued a voting card about the size of a credit card. To vote, a member uses his or her card in any one of the nearly 40 voting boxes scattered around the House chamber (most are attached to the back of the chamber's bench-like seats). With the card inserted, the member presses one of three buttons – yea, nay, or present – and his or her vote is recorded by the computer system. As the votes are cast, they are displayed on panels above the gallery at the front of the chamber, and the running totals can be viewed on computer terminals. Under the House rules, recorded votes take 15 minutes, although the presiding officer often holds the vote open a little longer to allow members to make it to the floor and cast their votes. On a few occasions, the Speaker has held open the vote for several minutes to find

THE CHANGING CONGRESS: LONG VOTES LEAD TO CONTROVERSY

On November 23, 2003, the House of Representatives passed a prescription drug benefit for senior citizens under the Medicare programs. Debate on the bill had continued until 3:00 A.M. at which time presiding officer Richard Hastings (R-Washington) announced that the House would have a 15-minute vote. At the end of 15 minutes the bill was losing by 15 votes, and after one hour, the tally stood at 216–218. By most accounts, then-Speaker Dennis Hastert (R-Illinois) was resolved to the fact that the bill would fail, but he, along with then-Majority Leader Tom DeLay (R-Texas) and others, continued to try to convince recalcitrant Republicans to vote for the bill. At 5:00 A.M., then President Bush was awakened to begin calling wayward members. The combination of his encouragement and other persuasive activities was enough to secure victory. Democrats cried foul and called for reform. Upon gaining a majority in House after the 2006 elections, Democrats enacted a rule banning holding a vote open for the "sole purpose of reversing the outcome."

The new rule did not prevent the Democrats from becoming ensnared in their own controversy over vote outcomes in August 2007 on a motion to recommit. Republicans charged that the vote count was reported incorrectly and that the vote had been closed while members were still trying to change their vote. A Select Committee on Voting Irregularities agreed and urged the House to repeal the apparently unenforceable rule on holding votes open.

the last vote or two his or her side needed to win. The rules do permit the Speaker to postpone votes – to "stack" votes is the jargon used – in some circumstances, such as votes on motions to suspend the rules and pass a measure. Stacked votes are cast in rapid succession in periods of five minutes each, usually near the end of a session, to allow members to vote on several matters without having to make multiple trips back-and-forth between their offices and the House floor. By the way, the record for the number of recorded votes cast without missing one belongs to Representative William Natcher (D-Kentucky), who cast 18,401 consecutive votes over 22 years before he became ill and died in 1994.

Senate Voting Procedure

The Senate, too, has voice, division, and recorded votes, but virtually no division votes are cast in the Senate because of its smaller size. On voice and recorded votes, Senate practice is quite different from House practice. On many, perhaps most, "votes," the Senate does not really vote at all. The presiding officer often brings a matter to a vote when debate appears to have ended by saying, "Hearing no further debate, and without objection, the amendment is agreed to." In this way, even the pretense of a voice vote is not observed in the Senate. Recorded roll-call votes often are ordered in advance, upon the successful demand of a senator, so no preliminary voice vote is held, as in the House.

Recorded votes in the Senate are properly called roll-call votes. The names of the senators are called out, one by one, by a clerk, and senators' responses are recorded by hand. Roll-call votes are supposed to take only 15 minutes, as stipulated by a unanimous consent agreement that the majority leader arranges at the beginning of each Congress. Many, if not most, Senate roll-call votes last longer than 15 minutes, however, to accommodate senators who need more time to make it to the floor. At times, these delays have become so burdensome that majority leaders have promised to insist that the 15-minute limit be observed, but the desire to accommodate colleagues seems so overwhelming that votes extending to 20 minutes or more remain common. Senator Robert Byrd (D-West Virginia) cast his 17,000th roll-call vote in April 2004 – a Senate record.

Changes in Floor Decision Making

On the surface, it might seem that the differences in voting procedures between the two chambers matter little. The record suggests otherwise. House voting procedures changed in the early 1970s – and with important consequences. As earlier chapters have discussed, the early 1970s was a period of remarkable change in House politics. Power devolved from full committee chairs to subcommittee chairs, many of whom were inexperienced as bill managers. Personal and subcommittee staffs were growing, which enabled more members to design and promote their own legislation. Also, a new breed of member – more media-oriented and more insistent on having a meaningful role – seemed to be flooding into Congress. In this context, the House changed the voting rules in such a way that encouraged members to pursue floor amendments more frequently and more actively.

The House voting reforms had two components. First, a new rule extended recorded voting to the Committee of the Whole. Before 1971, no recorded votes took place in the House's Committee of the Whole, where action on floor amendments takes place. That meant that members' positions on most floor amendments were not recorded. As is still the case, a roll-call vote could be demanded on amendments approved in the Committee of the Whole just before the vote on final passage of the bill, but rejected amendments could not be considered again.

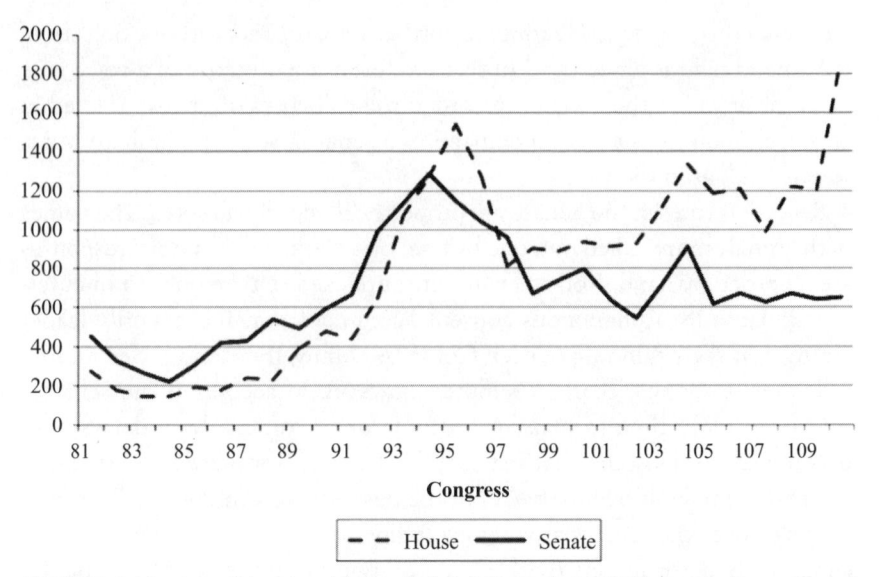

FIGURE 8.1. Number of House and Senate Roll-Call Votes, 1947–2008. *Source: Data collected by the authors.*

Second, the electronic voting system was used for the first time in 1973. Voting "by electronic device," as they call it in the House, nearly completely replaced the old system of teller voting in the Committee of the Whole and the traditional call of the roll in the House. Teller voting was done by having members pass by tellers (members appointed to do the counting), with the yes voters to one side and the no voters to the other. The 1971 reform allowed recorded teller voting, in which members signed green (yes) or red (no) cards, deposited them in a box, and then waited for tellers to count them and turn them over to clerks, who would record each member's individual vote. This cumbersome process discouraged recorded voting in the Committee of the Whole. Automated vote counting by the electronic system allowed the Committee of the Whole and the House to complete a vote and have the results in 15 minutes.

Electronic recorded voting produced a surge in amending activity. Being able to put one's position on a particular issue on the record (and forcing one's opponents to do the same) created new incentives to offer amendments, particularly for the minority party. Electronic voting also reduced the burden imposed on colleagues by demands for recorded votes. The result, as Figure 8.1 illustrates, was an increase in the number of floor votes, most on amendments, beginning in the first Congress (the 93rd, 1973–1974) that used both electronic and recorded voting in the Committee of the Whole. By the late 1970s, the House floor began to look much more like the Senate floor than it had for a century. Longer daily floor sessions, repetitive amendments, and scheduling uncertainty had become the norm. Worse yet for the Democratic leaders, more free-wheeling amending activity made it more difficult for them to enforce deals made in committee and to hold a majority coalition together on the floor.

House Democrats sought relief in new rules and practices. In 1979, after several aborted attempts, they finally increased from 20 to 25 the number of members required to support a request for a recorded vote in the Committee of the Whole. This change seemed to have little effect on amending activity, however. A more important reaction to the increase in amendment votes was an expansion of the number of days each month in which motions to suspend the rules were in order. A motion to suspend the rules simultaneously brings a measure to the floor and passes it. No amendments are allowed and debate is limited to 40 minutes, which makes suspending the rules an attractive procedure for bill managers. Although a successful motion to suspend the rules requires a two-thirds majority, Democrats managed to increase the use of suspension motions during the 1970s, a trend that has continued.

The most important response by the Democrats was to have the Rules Committee design more special rules to restrict floor amendments. The change in the content of special rules in the 1980s was quite dramatic. Most special rules continued to put in order at least some, and often many, amendments (open or modified open rules), but Republicans correctly complained that many special rules had been designed to prevent all or most amendments (closed or modified closed rules). Consequently, Republicans made procedural reforms a centerpiece of the 1994 congressional campaign. As Figure 8.2 reveals, after becoming the majority party following the 1994 elections, Republicans initially kept their campaign promise to offer more open/modified open rules than had the Democrats, although there was a slight increase in the use of restrictive rules under the new Republican majority. This policy has changed dramatically in recent congresses. In 2005–2006, more than half of the special rules (59 percent) were either closed or modified closed, while only 12 percent were open or modified – a complete reversal from the last democratically controlled Congress in 1993–1994. The trend toward more restrictive rules has only accelerated as the House has reached an all time high in the rule restrictiveness in the 109th and 110th Congresses – both with Democratic majorities.

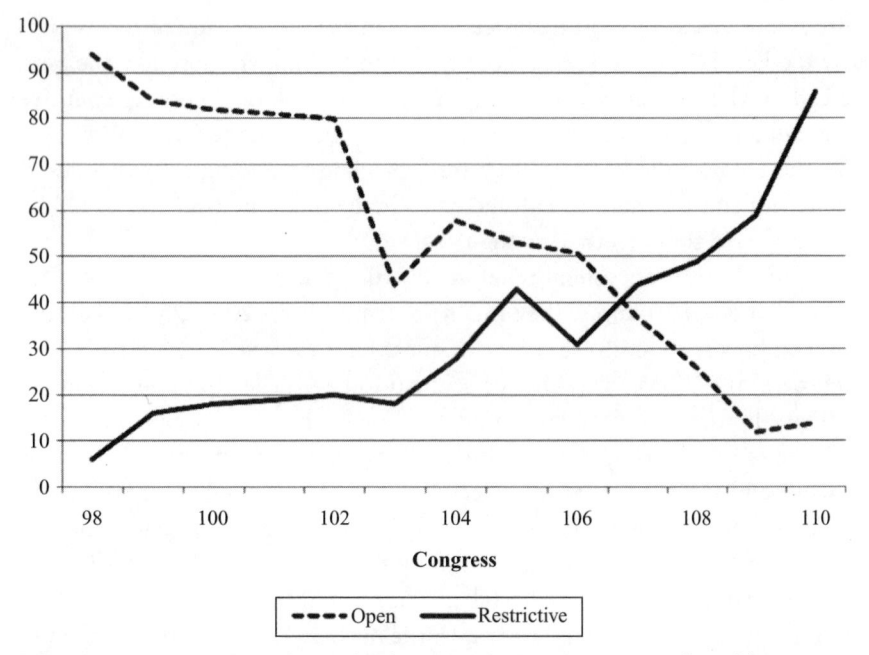

FIGURE 8.2. Restrictiveness of Special Rules, 1983–2008. *Source:* Data collected from reports of the House Committee on Rules.

The net result of the more than two decades of adjustments to the voting reforms of the early 1970s has been a more bifurcated process for managing legislation on the House floor. Legislation that is of little importance is not subject to amendments; it is considered under suspension of the rules or, if it is sufficiently non-controversial, it is brought up by unanimous consent and passed without a recorded vote. Legislation that is likely to attract even a few amendments is likely to be considered under a special rule that limits amending activity in some way, often to the disadvantage of the minority party.

These changes have renewed the distinctiveness of House floor decision-making. While the number of House floor votes has been similar to that of the Senate in recent Congresses, House floor action is more predictable and more carefully controlled to advantage committees' legislation.

Analyzing Votes

Nearly all members participate in recorded floor votes, so floor votes offer a natural basis for comparing members' policy positions. The voting record

is available in the *Congressional Record* and a variety of commercial publications. It can even be examined on personal computers through the use
of THOMAS, a service of the Library of Congress (http://thomas.loc.gov).
Political scientists, journalists, interest groups, challengers to incumbents,
and many others have long analyzed the roll-call record for scientific, educational, and political purposes. Consequently, the use – and misuse – of the
congressional voting record to make inferences about legislators is a subject
that recurs in nearly every congressional campaign.

The Problems of Interpreting the Roll-Call Vote

A legislator's roll-call vote can be thought of as an act based on (1) a policy
preference and (2) a decision about how to act on that preference. The policy
preference may be influenced by an array of political forces – constituents,
the president, interest groups, party and committee leaders, the legislator's
personal views, and so on. Thus, the personal view of a legislator is not easily
inferred from a roll-call vote. Moreover, whatever the basis for his or her
policy preference, the legislator may hold that preference intensely or only
weakly.

A member's decision about how to vote can be sincere or strategic. For
example, a member may strategically vote against a bill even if she prefers
the bill to no bill at all, if she believes that killing the bill will lead to action
on an alternative that she will like even more. Such "strategic voting" on the
first bill might lead an observer to conclude incorrectly that the member
prefers the status quo to the first bill. A member also might cast a deceptive
vote. An extreme example is a member who holds a strong policy preference
and works hard behind the scenes to push his point of view, yet votes the
other way on the floor to make the folks back home happy.

Plainly, the political and strategic character of members' policy preferences and voting choices is an obstacle to the use of roll-call votes as the
basis for making claims about legislators' intentions or objections in casting
a vote. But the situation is not as hopeless as it might seem. Most votes are
not strategic or deceptive. They reflect the political preference of the member fairly well, which makes political sense. Members know that their votes
on important issues may be used against them, so they have an incentive to
cast votes that are easily explained. Besides, the number of situations that
present an opportunity for strategic or deceptive voting is not nearly as large
as it could be. Nevertheless, caution is required when making inferences
from a particular vote.

The possibility of strategic or deceptive voting is less troublesome in ana-lyzing summary statistics on members' voting records than it is when consid-ering votes individually. Many voting indices summarize members' records over a large number of votes by counting the number of times that they vote in a certain way – for example, in favor of the president's position. Instances of strategic or deceptive voting are not likely to affect the scores assigned to the legislators, but skepticism is in order for scoring based on subsets of the larger voting record.

Common Voting Measures

Political scientists and journalists have relied on several indices to character-ize members' voting records. The most widely reported measures are those calculated by the research department of the Congressional Quarterly (CQ), which publishes *Congressional Quarterly Weekly Report*, a news magazine that provides in-depth coverage of Congress. CQ calculates objective indicators of members' support for and opposition to the president, support for and opposition to their party's positions, and support for and opposition to the conservative coalition.

Measures of the role that party plays in members' voting decisions are the most frequently used roll-call statistics. Many of these measures are based on the party vote, which CQ defines as a vote on which a majority of Democrats oppose a majority of Republicans. The percentage of all votes that are party votes is a common measure of the degree of partisanship in the House and Senate. The historical record for party votes – sometimes called party unity votes – is demonstrated in Figure 8.3. An individual member's overall level of support for his or her party is usually determined by the percentage of times he or she has supported the party's position on party votes. CQ calls these party unity scores.

CQ's label is a little misleading. Because a party vote occurs any time a majority of one party votes differently than a majority of the other party, a party vote might occur when the parties actually differ very little. For exam-ple, a vote on which 51 percent of Democrats and 49 percent of Republicans voted yea would be a party unity vote. This result would hardly be an indi-cation of unified parties, and party influences or differences might not have played much of a role in the outcome. Of course, any objective measure requires that some standard be used – if not a simple majority, then perhaps a two-thirds or a 90 percent majority. Thus, whereas some caution is required in using CQ's measure, it remains one of the best available for examining the frequency of party alignments in Congress over time.

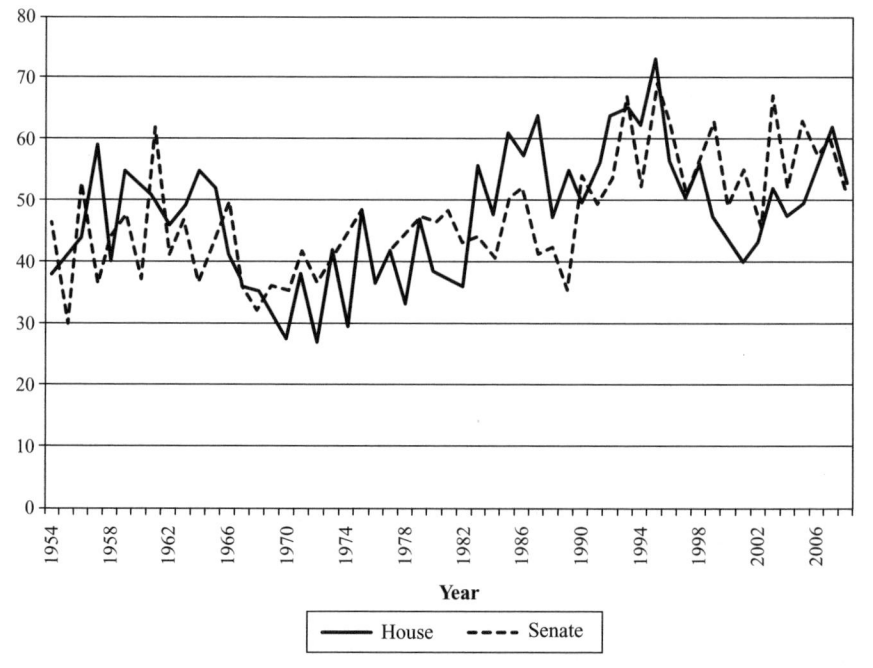

FIGURE 8.3. Percent of All Votes that Were Party Votes, 1954–2008.

CQ also analyzes congressional votes on bills for which the president has taken a position by examining the public statements of the president and administration officials. CQ calculates a success rate for the president, consisting of the percentage of such votes on which the president's position prevails. Analysts using CQ's scores must rely on the CQ staff's ability to accurately identify the votes and the president's position. They must also hope that CQ is consistent in applying its selection criteria over time. Perhaps because CQ says nothing beyond a single sentence about the president's public statements, no one has effectively challenged CQ's work on this score.

The most obvious weakness of the CQ scores is that they do not take into account the varying importance of the issues behind the votes. One way to handle this problem is to use only votes that are contested – those that show a close division. The argument is that lopsided votes – for example, 90 to 10 – are less likely to have been seen as decisive, controversial, or critical to the choices made on issues important to members. Besides, one-sided outcomes do not allow analysts to distinguish among members. Thus, analysts frequently limit their choice of votes to those with less than

75 percent, or perhaps even 60 percent, of the members voting in the majority.

CQ offers a corrective of its own by identifying 15–20 key votes every year for each chamber. The publication first identifies the year's major issues subjectively – identifying those that were highly controversial, a matter of presidential or political power, or had a great impact on the country – and then, for each issue identified, chooses the vote that was the most important in determining an outcome. CQ does not calculate scores based on these key votes, although political scientists have frequently used key votes for the construction of their own voting measures.

The Ratings Game

Dozens of interest groups regularly report ratings for members of Congress. The wide range of groups that do this includes ideological groups, farmers' organizations, environmental and consumer groups, and large labor and business associations. Not surprisingly, the ratings are used for political purposes. Most interest groups send press releases to the news media in members' home states and districts, praising their supporters in Congress and chastising their opponents. They also use their own ratings as a factor in decisions about campaign contributions. Nearly all groups use their scores to enlighten their memberships about their friends and enemies in Congress. Even incumbents and challengers advertise interest group ratings to substantiate their claims about the policy stances of the incumbents.

Interest groups' ratings of legislators are based on a limited number of votes selected by group officials. The processes by which groups select votes on which to base their ratings vary widely. Some groups do not complete their analyses until their board of directors or some other authoritative group approves the list of votes, whereas others allow low-level staff to identify the pertinent votes. Typically, groups have compiled and published their annual lists at the end of a congressional session. However, more recently some groups have begun choosing votes prior to their occurrence and sometimes even at the request of individual members or party leaders. In publicizing that a particular vote will be "scored," interest groups seek to influence wavering members to support the group's position. Upon preselecting a vote for scoring, groups will fax notices to members' offices or distribute cards prior to the vote that are imprinted with the group's logo and position on the vote. Some accounts suggest that the failure in the House to pass a comprehensive bankruptcy reform bill at the end of the

107th Congress was due in part to interest groups announcing that they would be "scoring" the vote on the special rule, which contained a provision concerning the ability of anti-abortion activists to avoid fines by filing for bankruptcy.

Groups vary in how narrowly or broadly they define their interests. The AFL-CIO, for example, includes votes in its ratings that concern issues that "affect working people who are not necessarily union members." The National Farmers Union has included votes on such issues as the MX missile, social security financing, and constitutional amendments requiring a balanced budget in its scales.

Moreover, the number of votes included in interest group scales varies widely as well. Sometimes as few as nine or 10 votes are included in an interest group's scale, which means that just one or two votes can produce great swings in the scores assigned to legislators. Groups sometimes include several votes on the same issue to give that issue greater weight in their calculations, whereas others carefully avoid doing so. And groups have been known to alter their selection of votes to get a certain scale that will benefit friends or make enemies look bad.

Further complicating the interpretation of interest groups' ratings of lawmakers is the type of votes these groups select. Quite naturally interest groups want to separate supporters and opponents, so they tend to choose important votes that show close divisions. Because legislators tend to be consistent in their policy positions, the tendency to pick votes with close divisions has the effect of repeatedly counting the same set of members as supporters and another set of members as opponents. As some critics of interest group ratings have noted, this process produces a polarized distribution of scores even when the real distribution of legislators' preferences more closely approximates a normal curve (a bell-shaped curve).

The lesson is that we should be quite skeptical of claims that legislators' interest group ratings are reliable indicators of their support for particular causes. Anyone seriously concerned about legislators' support for a cause should seek additional clues. Using the ratings of two or more groups with similar agendas is a good place to start. Sometimes, a better guide than a legislator's specific percentage rating is how that figure compares with other legislators' ratings. The legislator might have a rating of 85 percent support on a group's rating scale, but places in only the 50th percentile among all legislators on that scale. The latter often is a better indicator of where the member is positioned on the full spectrum of views on a given issue. Moreover, whenever a member's degree of commitment to a cause is at issue, we should look for corroborating evidence – bills sponsored, amendments offered, speeches made, and behind-the-scenes effort – that may be reported in the press or identified by knowledgeable observers.

Yet, interest group ratings retain their special appeal for analysts because collectively they provide a summary of legislators' policy views across a broad array of issue areas. Scholars often argue that the selection of the votes used in the ratings by knowledgeable interest group officials gives the ratings validity as measures of support for various causes. But convenience, rather than a careful judgment about the ratings' validity, seems to underlie many scholars' use of interest group ratings.

Dimensions, Alignments, and Coalitions

Given the limitations of interest group ratings, asking whether legislators' policy positions can be characterized in more objective ways is natural. They can. Political scientists have developed ways to determine the basic attitudes or dimensions that underlie voting patterns and the nature of the voting alignments in Congress (who votes with whom). Three basic concepts – dimensions, alignments, and coalitions – are important to understand.

Political scientists' techniques involve a search for consistency in the voting patterns across a set of roll-call votes. The idea is simple: If the legislators' voting behavior exhibits a discernable pattern for a set of votes, then we might assume that a particular mix of political forces were at work on members for that set of votes. A dimension of political conflict is said to be present when a certain alignment of members is visible throughout a set of votes.

For example, liberal and conservative members are often identified at opposite ends of an ideological dimension. The usual assumption is that each member holds a fairly stable ideological perspective and is guided by that perspective when deciding how to vote. Of course, members' voting behavior also may reflect the political outlook of their home state or district, the influence of party or faction leaders, and other political forces that produce an alignment of members that appears to have a liberal-to-conservative character. This is one reason politicians often resist being labeled liberals or conservatives. Some members may not even have personal views about the policies at issue on most votes and still demonstrate voting patterns that appear to fit neatly on a liberal-conservative continuum.

In principle, many dimensions of conflict may organize voting patterns, perhaps a different dimension for different sets of votes. Indeed, many scholars argue that we should expect many dimensions in congressional voting because Congress operates in a pluralistic political system, one in which a different set of interest groups and constituents wages the legislative battle on each issue. The issues may divide urban and rural Americans, producers and consumers, employers and employees, coastal- and middle-Americans, retired and not-yet-retired people, and, of course, Democrats and Republicans. The number of possible bases for conflict is large. The analyst's task is to find the important dimensions of conflict without arbitrarily limiting the search to a few of the possible alignments, such as party-based alignments.

Two schools of thought about the dimensions and alignments of congressional voting have emerged. The older school adopts the pluralistic view and emphasizes the multidimensionality of congressional voting. A newer school emphasizes the consistent presence and explanatory power of a liberal-conservative dimension. Some of the difference between the schools is due to differences in the statistical techniques they use. Part of the difference is due to differences in judgment or taste – just how much must a voting alignment vary from what is thought to be a liberal-conservative division before we count it as something else?

The difficulty of making a satisfactory interpretation is visible in an analysis of Senate votes during the 109th Congress (2005–2006). Senators' scores on two dimensions, calculated by political scientist Keith Poole, are arrayed in Figure 8.4. The horizontal dimension is related to the general liberal-conservative position on economic, tax, and spending issues; the vertical dimension separates senators according to their behavior on the very few issues that do not cleanly divide senators along liberal/conservative lines, such as free trade, immigration, and abortion. Senators with nearly identical scores on one of the dimensions often have a wide range of scores on the other dimension. However, in recent congresses the first dimension has explained more than 90 percent of the variance in roll-call voting. Party leaders, presidents, and lobbyists do not dare ignore such differences. They see important differences among members who operate in a complex world filled with conflicting pressures on legislators.

The alignment of legislators in Figure 8.4 is clearly partisan. Democratic senators are grouped in the upper left and Republicans are grouped in the lower right. We might be tempted to say that the two parties were strong coalitions on the issues confronting Congress. And yet, both parties show substantial internal variation, with some Democrats and Republicans falling closer to each other than they do to fellow partisans. Ben Nelson (D-Nebraska) and Lincoln Chafee (R-Rhode Island) are virtually indistinguishable on the liberal conservative dimension. Although the parties have

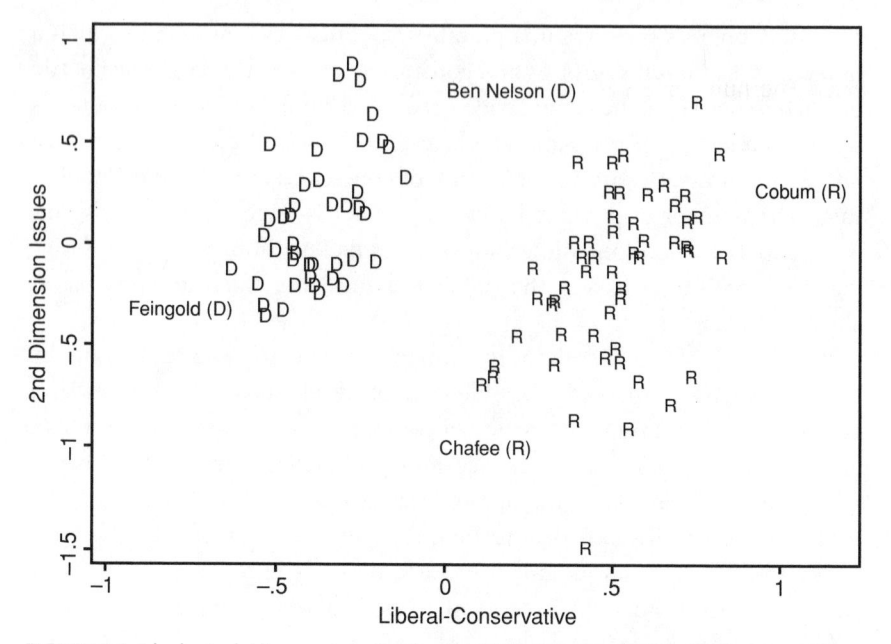

FIGURE 8.4. Ideological Alignments in the Senate, 109th Congress (2005–2006). *Source:* Data provided by Keith Poole and Howard Rosenthal, http://www.pooleandrosenthal.com.

quite different central tendencies, they simply are not tightly knit groups that keep their members from deviating from the position preferred by most party members. To be sure, party leaders and other factors tend to keep party members together, but many other forces lead party members to go their own way from time to time.

The distinction between alignments and coalitions is critical for under-standing legislative politics. An alignment merely shows the distribution of policy positions among members, based on their voting behavior. But a group of members may vote the same way for different reasons, and they may vote alike only because they have similar home constituencies. They can be called a coalition only if they consciously coordinate their voting. Thus, we simply cannot determine the presence of active coalitions from voting behavior alone.

During the middle decades of the twentieth century, southern Democrats often voted with Republicans, creating policy victories for what was known as the "conservative coalition." There has been some dispute about how much coordination actually took place between Republican leaders and southern Democratic leaders on these votes. That is, just how much of a coalition was the so-called conservative coalition? The answer seems to be that at times genuine coordination took place that affected members' voting behavior, but at most times the alignment of Republicans and southern Democrats against northern Democrats appeared without coordination as members made largely independent judgments about how to vote.

The Floor, Committees, and Parties

This chapter completes the examination of the three major features of congressional organization – the parties, the committees, and the floors. These three components combine to create the policy-making process in Congress. As we have seen, just how the components are combined varies between the two chambers and, within each chamber, over time. This is a good place to summarize the forces that lie behind those variations – the character of Congress's policy agenda, the distribution of policy preferences among members, and the institutional context.

Issue Agenda

The character of the legislative process is greatly affected by the nature of the issues that Congress confronts. As a general rule, Congress relies more heavily on committees to make policy choices when it must deal with a large number of issues and when the issues it considers are readily separable, recur frequently, or are less salient. Why? A large workload requires a division of labor so that many issues can be addressed simultaneously. A system of standing committees provides such a division of labor. If the issues are separable into distinct categories, then committees with distinct jurisdictions work well. Furthermore, if the same issues arise time and again, then fixing committee jurisdictions can be done without concern that some committees will become superfluous over time. Moreover, if most issues concern only a few members, committees are a natural place for those members to gather and make the detailed policy choices that do not interest other members.

Alignment of Policy Preferences

Because the process by which decisions are made may influence which choices are made, the contending parties and factions in Congress often seek to shape the decision-making process to their liking. Sometimes party divisions predominate; at other times, cross-party coalitions arise to make the important policy choices. When issues are salient to most members and the members of the majority party share similar policy views, the majority party may centralize policy making in the hands of its leaders. When most members care about the issues, but the majority party is not cohesive, neither committees nor majority party leaders may be trusted. Members then turn to the floor as the place where they can shape policy details.

Institutional Context

Differences in the institutional arrangements in the House and Senate are likely to cause different responses to similar changes in issue agendas and policy alignments. The Senate's rules and practices protect the rights of individual senators to offer amendments and conduct debate on the floor. Consequently, the Senate usually retains a more collegial, floor-oriented decision-making process. In contrast, the rules and practices of the House advantage the Speaker and standing committees. If the majority party is united, the Speaker tends to direct policy making with vigor; if not, the committees are more independent. As a result, House decision making is generally less collegial and less floor-oriented. Change in the House tends to come as movement along the centralized-decentralized continuum described previously.

Indeed, the constraints on floor amendments under House special rules are the product of cooperation between the traditional centers of power in the House – committees and majority party leaders. Rules Committee decisions about special rules often represent the terms of an agreement between committee and party leaders. Cohesiveness in the majority party enables agreements between committee and party leaders to gain the majority required to adopt restrictive special rules on the floor. In the Senate, the carefully preserved rights of individual members to debate and offer amendments to legislation stand in the way of committee and party leaders who might otherwise seek to structure floor action in a way that would disadvantage the minority party or individual member.

Conclusion

The floor is not only a place where the full House and Senate conduct business, it also is where the most vital stage in the policy-making process, when members exercise their equal voting rights, occurs. We have seen variations between the House and Senate in the degree to which the details of legislation are devised on the floor, but the possible reaction of the floor to the handiwork of committees and parties has always been a central consideration in legislative strategies. Despite similarities in the nature of floor activity in the two chambers, we see obvious inter-chamber differences – the details of legislation are far more likely to be determined on the Senate floor than on the House floor.

Above: President Barack Obama acknowledges applause before his address to a joint session of Congress in the House Chamber of the U.S. Capitol in Washington, D.C., Tuesday, February 24, 2009. (Pablo Martinez Monsivais/Pool/MCT)
Below: President-elect Barack Obama meets with Vice President-elect Joe Biden, Senate Majority Leader Harry Reid (D-NV), House Speaker Nancy Pelosi (D-CA), and Rep. John Boehner (R-OH) Monday, January 5, 2009, on Capitol Hill in Washington, D.C. (Chuck Kennedy/MCT)

9

Congress and the President

THE PRESIDENT IS AN INTEGRAL PART OF THE LEGISLATIVE PROCESS. THE basic rules of the legislative game specified by the Constitution provide for three institutional players – the House, the Senate, and the president. The president requires Congress to pass legislation for any policy that requires statutory authorization. In turn, the enactment of legislation necessitates presidential approval unless both chambers of Congress can muster a two-thirds majority to override a veto. Moreover, the Senate must ratify treaties negotiated by the president and must approve the president's choices for top executive and judicial posts. Congress must approve all funding for federal programs. Interdependency, based on shared as well as separate powers, characterizes the relationship among the three institutions.

Interdependency would not be important if the House, Senate, and president held similar policy preferences on important issues. Even when one party controls the House, Senate, and presidency, incumbents of the three institutions are not likely to have identical views. Representatives, senators, and presidents are elected on different cycles and they have diverse constituencies. They are likely to anticipate and react to somewhat different political demands and conditions.

To complicate matters, the framers left ambiguities in the Constitution about congressional and presidential functions and powers. For example, the president is instructed to appoint ambassadors and make treaties with the "advice and consent" of the Senate, but it is unclear how the president is to receive and account for senatorial advice. When the framers granted Congress the power to declare war, they did not anticipate the speed of modern military technology and the scope of the threats, which in some circumstances requires the president to make decisions about war without congressional involvement. In addition, when the framers allowed the president to kill a bill after a congressional adjournment by taking no action, they did not define adjournment. In each of these examples of constitutional ambiguity, and in many others, presidents have argued for interpretations that maximize their power at the expense of Congress.

The role of the president in policy making expanded during the twentieth and early twenty-first centuries. Congress has delegated more power to the president and executive agencies by delegating to the executive branch the authority to determine the details and methods of implementing a wide range of policies. Presidents have asserted their ability to make policy through executive orders and other means. In addition, the enhanced role of the United States in foreign affairs, and the increased importance of world events for American life, have given the president, who has important advantages over Congress in foreign affairs, a more powerful role.

While presidents have become more important relative to Congress in policy making over the last century, Congress has moved to reassert its own role, at least to some degree. An expanded staff, restrictions on appropriated funds, new approaches to designing programs, and other developments have helped Congress retain a meaningful role in policy making when faced with aggressive presidents.

The President as a Legislative Player

The president is central to the legislative process, although he does not always assert himself. Many pieces of legislation do not interest the president and are routinely signed into law at the recommendation of trusted administration officials. On some issues, the president chooses to remain silent and inactive for political reasons. Yet, when the president chooses to become involved, he usually can have some influence over the outcome by threatening to use his veto power, employing his unilateral powers, and mobilizing support for his position with his considerable political resources.

The President's Formal Role

The Constitution defines a formal role for the president at both the beginning and the end of the legislative process. With respect to the beginning of the process, the Constitution assigns the president responsibility to recommend a legislative agenda. The Constitution provides that the president "shall from time to time give to the Congress information of the state of the union and recommend to their consideration such measures as he shall judge necessary and expedient; he may, on extraordinary occasions, convene both houses, or either of them, and in case of disagreement between them, with respect to the time of adjournment, he may adjourn them to such time as he shall think proper." This provision is supplemented by various federal laws that require the president to recommend legislation to Congress.

With respect to the end of the legislative process, the Constitution provides that "every order, resolution, or vote to which the concurrence of the Senate and House of Representatives may be necessary (except on a question of adjournment) shall be presented to the President of the United States; and before the same shall take effect, shall be approved by him, or being disapproved by him, shall be repassed by two thirds of the Senate and House of Representatives, according to the rules and limitations prescribed in the Case of a Bill." This veto power is not unambiguous and has been a source of controversy between the branches.

AGENDA SETTING. By requiring the president to report to Congress on the state of the union and recommend legislation, the framers of the Constitution expected the president to energize and focus the legislative process. Of course, Congress is not required to consider matters the president brings to its attention. This is true even if the president calls a special session. Indeed, the president's powers and duties were designed to spur congressional action without giving the president coercive power over the activity of Congress or the ability to impose new laws unilaterally.

Presidents now address a joint session of Congress early in each calendar year with a speech known as the State of the Union Address. The speech is covered on live, prime-time television. It signals the president's priorities and is designed to generate support for his program. Some recent presidents have sent to Congress longer written versions of their addresses to provide more detail and rationale. Since the 1970s, a congressional leader of the opposite party has sought network television time after the speech to respond to the president. The major networks, however, have not always given opposition leaders the requested time.

Federal law requires the president to submit a variety of statements and proposed legislation to Congress. Of particular importance is the requirement that the president submit an annual budget message and an annual economic message to Congress. The budget message, required by the Budget and Accounting Act of 1921, specifies the president's taxation and spending proposals for the forthcoming fiscal year. The economic message, prescribed by the Employment Act of 1946, provides a presidential assessment of the state of the U.S. economy and details the chief executive's

---

Congressionally Speaking...

Executive orders are directives issued by the president to require or authorize some action of executive branch agencies. Some executive orders are authorized by law, but in most cases they are issued on the basis of the express or implied constitutional powers of the president. Executive orders can have a significant affect on the structure of the executive branch and public policy. For example, an executive order created the Office of Homeland Security following the 9–11 terrorist attack. Some executive orders establish important policy, particularly in areas, such as civil rights, where Congress did not enact relevant legislation. President Harry Truman desegregated the military by executive order, and President John Kennedy created the Presidential Committee on Equal Employment Opportunity by an executive order in which the term "affirmative action" was first used in federal policy. In recent decades, the use of executive orders has increased, often when an opposition Congress made legislative action impossible. In many cases, presidents justify the use of executive orders by citing previous executive orders as precedents for the assertion of unilateral presidential authority.

---

economic projections for the coming fiscal year. These messages sometimes stir controversy and often shape congressional debate over spending and tax policy each year.

Starting with President Truman in 1948, modern presidents have offered special messages providing additional detail – and often drafts of legislation – for the components of the administration's legislative program outlined by the State of the Union addresses and the budget and economic messages. The administration's legislation usually is introduced by members of the House and Senate as a courtesy to the president. Since Truman, presidents have devised formal processes within the executive branch for generating, synchronizing, and clearing legislative proposals from the administration.

The implied powers of the president under the Constitution also contribute to the president's role in agenda setting. In particular, the president's implied authority to issue regulations and executive orders to subordinates in the executive branch without the direct authorization of Congress boosts the president's ability to influence policy. This positive power becomes particularly controversial when the president seeks to interpret laws in a manner inconsistent with the expectations of members of Congress. Presidential actions often stimulate Congress to clarify its position in new legislation, if such legislation can survive a presidential veto.

In theory, the use of executive orders is constrained by the Constitution and law. Executive orders must be linked to executive authority and must not contradict provisions of the Constitution or a statute passed by Congress. In fact, during most of the eighteenth and nineteenth centuries, executive orders were principally used for routine administrative matters. In recent decades, however, executive orders have become more common, more important, and, at times, inconsistent with statute. In the 1980s, the Supreme Court upheld executive orders provided that they do not directly challenge explicit statutory provisions. Since it is unrealistic for statutes to address all contingencies, these decisions grant the president substantial flexibility in policy making. Furthermore, in a few cases, the courts have sided with the president when executive orders and statutes were directly at odds with each other and the Supreme Court even has found circumstances in which an executive order or proclamation invalidates a law. Thus, step by step over recent decades, the use of executive orders and judicial tolerance has expanded presidential power at the expense of Congress.

Formal constitutional rules also grant the president agenda-setting power in negotiating treaties and international agreements. Specifically, the Constitution authorizes the president to make treaties "by and with the Advice and Consent of the Senate." The executive branch customarily initiates treaties and international agreements, although the president does not have exclusive power over the treaty-making process. The president must submit treaties to the Senate and obtain ratification by a two-thirds majority vote. The Senate, however, is under no obligation to act on treaties presented by the president. Furthermore, the president is often dependent on the House for the appropriation of the necessary funds or to modify domestic law to comply with the terms of a treaty. Nevertheless, the power to determine the starting point for policy bargaining on treaties and international agreements gives the president considerable influence over the outcome. It is exceedingly unusual for the president's proposal to fail, and the Senate accepts a majority of treaties without change.

THE VETO POWER. The power to sign, veto, or take no action on legislation passed by Congress makes the president a critical actor in the legislative process. When the president vetoes a measure (a bill or joint resolution), he returns it to the chamber that first passed it along with a message indicating his objection to the legislation in its present form. If the chamber that first passed the measure is capable of obtaining the votes of two-thirds of the members to override the veto, the measure is then sent to the other chamber.

This chamber also must vote to override the veto by a two-thirds majority before the measure can become law.

The veto power gives the president both the ability to block legislation (subject to a possible override) and a source of leverage with legislators to gain policy concessions. Legislators must necessarily consider both a potential presidential veto and the likelihood of forming a two-thirds coalition to override a veto in their initial legislative decisions. For instance, members interested in passing some form of legislation may choose to make policy concessions to the president if they expect the president to veto their most preferred legislation and they lack sufficient numbers to orchestrate an override. It should be noted, however, that there are instances in which congressional majorities that lack enough support for an override will present the president with legislation they know the president will find unacceptable. Typically, this is a strategic maneuver with the purpose of intensifying partisan differences or forcing the president to expend valuable political capital to win a veto battle.

Congress seldom overrides a presidential veto – since 1789, Congress has overridden just 4 percent of all vetoes (Table 9.1). Recent presidents facing opposing majority parties in Congress have increasingly resorted to vetoes in confronting Congress. President George H.W. Bush (1989–1993) used vetoes rather successfully; only one of his 31 regular vetoes was overridden. Of the 36 regular vetoes issued by President Clinton, all during periods of divided government, only two were overridden. Presidents challenge the House and Senate with vetoes much less frequently when their parties have enjoyed majorities in both houses. While President Clinton issued a number of vetoes during Republican Congresses, he did not veto a single measure passed when Democrats had majorities in both chambers. Republican President George W. Bush (2001-2009) vetoed only one bill when dealing with Republican Congresses for nearly six years, but vetoed 11 bills in the last two years of his administration when dealing with a Democratic Congress. Four of those 11 vetoes were overridden by Congress.

In some circumstances, the veto is a sign of presidential weakness. Failing to persuade Congress to pass legislation to his liking, the president resorts to a veto. For example, President Reagan in 1988 – weakened by revelations of the Iran-Contra scandal – vetoed several bills that had broad congressional support, including measures to overhaul the nation's water pollution control and highway funding programs. The vetoes were swiftly overridden.

At other times, a veto is an interim step in a longer bargaining process as presidents use the veto in the hope of forcing additional concessions from Congress. An analysis of vetoed bills between 1946 and 1991 shows that

TABLE 9.1. Presidential Vetoes, 1947–2007.[1]

Year (Congress)	President (Party)	Total Vetoes	Regular Vetoes	Pocket Vetoes	Vetoes Overridden
1947–1948 (80th)	TRUMAN (D)	75	42	33	6
1949–1950 (81st)	**TRUMAN (D)**	**79**	**70**	**9**	**3**
1951–1952 (82d)	**TRUMAN (D)**	**22**	**14**	**8**	**3**
1953–1954 (83d)	*EISENHOWER (R)*	*52*	*21*	*31*	*0*
1955–1956 (84th)	EISENHOWER (R)	34	12	22	0
1957–1958 (85th)	EISENHOWER (R)	51	18	33	0
1959–1960 (86th)	EISENHOWER (R)	44	22	22	2
1961–1962 (87th)	**KENNEDY (D)**	**20**	**11**	**9**	**0**
1963 (88th)	**KENNEDY (D)**	**1**	**1**	**0**	**0**
1963–1964 (88th)	**JOHNSON (D)**	**8**	**4**	**4**	**0**
1965–1966 (89th)	**JOHNSON (D)**	**14**	**10**	**4**	**0**
1967–1968 (90th)	**JOHNSON (D)**	**8**	**2**	**6**	**0**
1969–1970 (91st)	NIXON (R)	11	7	4	2
1971–1972 (92d)	NIXON (R)	20	6	14	2
1973–1974 (93d)	NIXON (R)	12	11	1	1
1974 (93d)	FORD (R)	27	16	11	4
1975–1976 (94th)	FORD (R)	37	32	5	8
1977–1978 (95th)	**CARTER (D)**	**19**	**6**	**13**	**0**
1979–1980 (96th)	**CARTER (D)**	**12**	**7**	**5**	**2**
1981–1982 (97th)	REAGAN (R)	15	9	6	2
1983–1984 (98th)	REAGAN (R)	24	9	15	2
1985–1986 (99th)	REAGAN (R)	20	13	7	2
1987–1988 (100th)	REAGAN (R)	19	8	11	3
1989–1990 (101st)	GEORGE BUSH (R)	21	16	5	0
1991–1992 (102d)	GEORGE BUSH (R)	25	15	10	1
1993–1994 (103d)	**CLINTON (D)**	**0**	**0**	**0**	**0**
1995–1996 (104th)	CLINTON (D)	17	17	0	1
1997–1998 (105th)	CLINTON (D)	8	8	0	1
1999–2000 (106th)	CLINTON (D)	12	11	1	0
2001–2002 (107th)*	GEORGE W. BUSH (R)	0	0	0	0
2003–2004 (108th)	*GEORGE W. BUSH (R)*	*0*	*0*	*0*	*0*
2005–2006 (109th)	*GEORGE W. BUSH (R)*	*1*	*1*	*0*	*0*
2007–2008 (110th)	GEORGE W. BUSH (R)	11	11	0	4

Democratic presidents facing a unified Democratic Congress appear in **bold**
Republican presidents facing a unified Republican Congress appear in *italics*.
Presidents (D or R) under divided control of government appear in regular typeface.
* Congress was under unified Republican control from January 20, 2001, to June 6, 2001.
Source: http://www.senate.gov/reference/reference_index_subjects/Vetoes_vrd.htm.

Congress re-passed about 35 percent of them in a modified form. Of the re-passed bills, 83 percent became law, which reflects the success of the president in extracting policy concessions following a veto.[2]

The pocket veto deserves special mention. The Constitution allows the president to kill a bill by simply failing to sign it if Congress has adjourned within 10 days (Sundays excepted) of enacting a measure. If Congress has adjourned and therefore is not in session, its absence prevents the president from returning the bill to Congress with an official veto message. The informal name for such a veto is a pocket veto.

The pocket veto has been controversial. What counts as a congressional adjournment has been challenged in several court cases. In response to a lawsuit filed by Senator Edward Kennedy (D-Massachusetts), the Ford administration in 1976 declared that pocket vetoes would be used only after the adjournment at the end of a Congress's second session. This move limited the president's ability to use the pocket veto during vacation recesses and the adjournment period between the first and second sessions of a Congress, provided that Congress had made arrangements for receiving veto messages during the intervening periods. President Reagan maintained that such inter-session pocket vetoes were constitutional. A federal district judge upheld the president's position, but an appeals court reversed the decision. The appeals court ruling stands as the most definitive ruling to date. Fearing an unfavorable ruling from the Supreme Court, the Reagan administration did not appeal further. Since the Supreme Court has yet to rule directly on the issue, presidents continue to argue that mid-session pocket vetoes are valid.

The President's Informal Role

Formal institutions place the president firmly in the legislative game. So too do the expectations of the American public and the president's fellow partisans and presidents' own aspirations.

PARTISAN BONDS. The president's service as the recognized leader of his party positions him as a player in the legislative process. Parties often are a means for bridging the gap between the legislative and executive branches, and much of the responsibility of building this bridge is borne by the president. There are powerful incentives for a president and his Capitol Hill partisans to work together. Presidents usually need the support of fellow partisans in Congress for their legislative program and partisans in Congress know that their own political success is affected by the standing of the president. This mutual dependence means that a president and his congressional partisans can influence each other.

The relative weakness of American political parties makes it difficult for the president to merely command support from his party colleagues in Congress. The president does not determine who represents his party in Congress; legislators gain the ballot through primaries and are elected largely on the basis of their own efforts. The president does not select his party's leaders in the House and Senate; legislators elect their own leaders. Consequently, while the president is expected to and generally wants to take the lead in setting legislative strategy for his party, the president often must bargain with legislators of his own party over priorities and the direction of public policy.

PUBLIC EXPECTATIONS. The American people expect presidential leadership on matters of national importance. The emergence of the president as the focal point of an expanding federal government after the Great Depression and World War II was accompanied by heightened public expectations of the president. Increased media concentration on the chief executive, as well as the president's tendency to resort to public appeals for support, has contributed to the president's standing as the most visible elected official in the country. Since World War II, the American public has increasingly expected the president to be the nation's leading policy maker in both domestic and international affairs.

In response to public expectations, presidential candidates and sitting presidents make many public policy commitments. These pledges help attract political support, but, because violating a commitment is likely to alienate some supporters in the electorate and in Congress, policy pledges also may constrain a president while in office. The president's policy objectives are determined in part by the public commitments he makes during campaigns. Thus, as presidents have become more likely to try to mobilize public pressure on Congress, public policy commitments have become more of a double-edged sword for them.

The chief executive's role as a legislative player also is conditioned on public approval ratings. Members of Congress, primarily for electoral reasons, are more willing to pay heed to the legislative proposals and policy positions of a president who has the confidence of the public. A president with high approval ratings cannot, however, be expected to dominate all policy formation. High approval ratings do not translate to presidential influence on all types of legislation. Instead, scholars have found that approval ratings are related to a president's legislative influence on matters that are both salient and complex. When the public is paying little attention to an issue, legislators do not fear electoral repercussions from opposing a popular president.

PERSONAL ASPIRATIONS. Most presidents, and surely all presidents since the 1920s, have had aspirations that required they take an active role in the legislative process. Whether seeking to move the federal government into new endeavors or modify or repeal existing policy, presidents have had to work with, and often resist, Congress. Presidents' personal interests, political commitments, and circumstances beyond their control compel them to become engaged.

Presidents' Strategies

Presidential strategies for influencing legislative outcomes depend upon the political context. Although executed in a variety of ways, every recent president has confronted decisions about how to structure his legislative agenda, how to generate congressional support, how to employ the veto power, and how to control the bureaucracy in the face of competition from Capitol Hill.

Agenda Setting

Perhaps nothing affects presidential success in Congress as much as a president's decisions about what legislation to recommend to Congress, when to recommend it, and what priority to give each recommendation. Political scientist Paul Light observes that "control of the agenda becomes a primary tool for securing and extending power. Presidents certainly view the agenda as such."[3] The president's legislative choices send a signal to a wide audience – Congress, administration officials, interest groups, the media, and the public – about the president's view of the lessons of the last election, the president's policy preferences, and the president's likely priorities. The president's choices shape the strategies of other legislative players and help set expectations by which the president's own success or failure will be judged.

In most situations, the president cannot force Congress to address his proposals. Rather, he must convince members of Congress to give priority to his legislation. Members of Congress may see national problems differently, give precedence to other issues, or approach problems in a different way. The president must, therefore, motivate Congress by generating support among important members or groups of members, organized interest groups, and the general public. He may employ the full range of presidential resources available to encourage Congress to take his proposals seriously.

Except in times of national crisis, the president's ability to influence the legislative agenda is strongest at the beginning of his first term, followed, perhaps, by the beginning of the second term. At those times, public support, a claim to an electoral mandate, and core congressional support tend to be most in his favor. Opponents of the president's programs are likely to have fewer seats in Congress, be the most disorganized, and suffer low public esteem.

Even in the best of times, the president must carefully calculate which issues to pursue. He or she almost always wants more than Congress is willing to support. The president must not overload Congress and his own staff with too many proposals. Congress and its committees have a finite capacity to produce major legislation quickly. And the administration has a limited ability to formulate detailed proposals, lobby Congress, and negotiate compromises in its first few months in office. The president also is unable to generate media attention and public support for more than a few proposals at a time.

Among recent presidents, Ronald Reagan appears to have used the early months of his first term most effectively. Reagan moved quickly and set his priorities carefully by defining his agenda as two major bills, one for domestic budget cuts and one for tax cuts. Although both were complex, multifaceted proposals, Reagan was successful in leading the media and the public to focus on the broad effects of his proposals. The approach allowed the Reagan administration to concentrate its resources, stimulate public pressure on Congress for widely recognized proposals, and gain legislative action in its first year in office.

Attracting Congressional Support

On important legislation, modern presidents usually pursue a mixed strategy – both bargaining in Washington with members of Congress and lobbyists and soliciting public support to affect legislators' estimates of the public response to their treatment of the president's proposals. In deciding how to allocate resources to inside and outside strategies, the White House takes into account how many and which members of Congress must be persuaded, the strategies of the opposition, whether public opinion currently favors the president's position, the commitment of resources to other issues, and how much time the president has before Congress makes a decision. Daily, even hourly, tactical adjustments are common in the midst of a tough legislative fight.

A president's legislative strategy is often shaped by the demands of members of Congress. Congressional leaders of the president's party regularly consult with the White House and other administration officials about the substance of policy proposals and legislative tactics. In fact, recent presidents have met with their party's congressional leaders at least once a week while Congress is in session. Committee and faction leaders also press the administration to pursue certain strategies. Presidents are compelled to consider these demands so as not to jeopardize the reelection of their party's congressional membership. In addition, cooperating with important members of Congress, as well as with influential interest groups, bureaucrats, and others, may encourage these actors to employ their own resources on behalf of the administration's program.

INSIDE STRATEGIES. The inside strategy is one of bargaining. Although often seen as underhanded, presidents must frequently employ bargaining tactics to accomplish legislative objectives. This is particularly true when presidents are faced with an effective, committed opposition within Congress. Knowing when, where, and how to make a deal with the members and factions of Congress requires information and skill on the part of presidents and their legislative advisors. Successful bargaining also accounts for formal rules of the game, the composition of the Congress, public opinion, and other resources.

The cost to the president of doing business with Congress depends upon the political context. When the president is popular, legislators are more likely to be happy to be associated with the president and his program and fewer legislators will require special attention to get their votes. When the president is unpopular, the cost of attracting votes – whether by making concessions on the substance of policy proposals or in offering other incentives – will be higher.

Presidents may use the stick as well as the carrot. In 2006, Representative Peter King (R-New York) was the target of retribution after refusing to support President George W. Bush's proposal to allow a Dubai company to assume operations at six major U.S. ports. King, who was chair of the House Homeland Security committee, threatened to block Bush's port deal. In a matter of days after King issued the threat, the Pentagon notified him that it would no longer provide an aircraft and military support for his upcoming trip to Iraq – a trip that had been cleared months earlier.

OUTSIDE STRATEGIES. Observers of presidential strategies have noticed that presidents have become more reliant on outside strategies in recent decades. Twentieth-century presidents as early as Theodore Roosevelt sought public support to strengthen their hand against Congress, but only recent presidents have routinely done so. Through such activities as televised prime-time addresses, press conferences, domestic and foreign travel, exclusive interviews, timely leaks, and now television talk shows and call-in programs, presidents are increasingly cultivating external allies to strengthen their position within Washington.

"Going public," as the outside strategy is labeled by political scientist Samuel Kernell, is an attractive strategy for several reasons. First, technological advances, such as transcontinental jets and live satellite feeds, have increased the ease of reaching a wide audience. Second, campaign finance practices and declining presidential coattails have reduced legislators' dependence on support from the president and the parties. Third, the administration's advantage in information and expertise has weakened, as rank-and-file members have benefited from the diffusion of power and staff within Congress. Finally, budgetary constraints have reduced the president's supply of projects and other favors that he can use to trade with individual members.

Fundamentally, going public is about taking credit and issuing blame. With this strategy, the president seeks to increase the benefits to legislators of supporting him and to increase the electoral costs of opposing him. But every move produces counter-moves. Opposition leaders are encouraged to develop public relations strategies of their own, and, in doing so, they are motivated to propose alternatives to the president's program that the president and his supporters would be embarrassed to oppose. In this way, outside strategies encourage early public commitments by legislators, foster partisan maneuvering and grandstanding, and discourage bargaining and compromise that require a softening of positions and a sharing of credit and blame.

A high-profile appeal, such as a special televised address to the nation from the Oval Office, entails risks for a president. Members of Congress sometimes view this approach as an effort by the president to go over their heads, can cause problems of legislators in the home constituencies, and can create tension between Congress and the president. Since the president cannot make such appeals frequently, he must reserve this approach for only those issues of significant importance in which his appeal is likely to generate critical support. Failure to gain more public or congressional support may damage the president's reputation, reducing his effectiveness in future legislative battles and perhaps hurting his own reelection chances. Therefore, more cautious, less publicized, and more narrowly targeted approaches, such as speaking before certain groups and calling on small groups of newspaper editors, may be preferred at times.

President Barak Obama is adding a new direction to the outside strategy. His 2008 campaign organization developed a database of email addresses for about 13 million supporters. The database was given to a group overseen by the Democratic National Committee, which employed it to request that people work in their communities and contact legislators in support of the president's budget proposals. The group, called Organizing for America, was announced by Obama in a YouTube video, another outlet that administration backers exploit.

The Veto

The veto inserts the president into the legislative game. A threatened veto may lead congressional leaders to set aside certain legislation or to make concessions to the president before passing the legislation. Particularly when control of the Congress and presidency is divided between the parties, the veto gives the president a critical source of leverage with legislators. It has been argued that the increasing polarization of Congress has limited the president's ability to bargain directly with Congress, and therefore has elevated the relative importance of the veto within the president's arsenal.

Veto threats are relatively infrequent events, but tend to result in policy changes that are favorable to the president. Veto threats are most common when the legislation under consideration is important and the president is faced with a Congress dominated by the opposing party. One study estimates that presidents threaten to veto roughly 14 percent of important measures; this number increases to 23 percent under divided government.

Moreover, it appears that presidents are often quite successful in extracting policy concessions from Congress when veto threats are issued. In fact, by one approximation, roughly 90 percent of bills that encounter a veto threat are modified, to varying extents, to accommodate the preferences of the president.[4] Given the success of veto threats, why do we not see presidents issuing threats on *all* congressional proposals?

The answer to this question lies largely in the fact that successful veto threats require credibility. It would be neither feasible nor politically prudent for a president to veto all legislation, and therefore threatening to do so would result in the veto threat losing its credibility with members of

---

The Veto Process

To veto a bill, the president signs a veto message that is sent to Congress. The message may contain the president's reasoning. The house of Congress that first passed the legislation acts first on the veto. That house may attempt an override, pass new legislation without an override attempt, or take no further action. The bill dies if a two-thirds majority is not acquired to override the veto. If the first house does override the veto, the other house also may attempt an override, pass new legislation without an override attempt, or take no further action. The bill dies if a two-thirds majority is not also acquired in that house to override the veto. New legislation may reflect concessions to the president. It must be approved by both houses and sent to the president for signature or veto.

Congress. A president who fails to follow through on threats is likely to gain a reputation for bluffing.

Members of Congress are certainly not passive bystanders in the veto game. Members frequently solicit a veto threat from the administration to solidify their bargaining position on Capitol Hill. Sometimes a congressional party will bait the president with a bill that it knows he will find unacceptable in order to force a veto of a popular bill. A well-documented example of this was the 1995–96 legislative struggle in which a Republican-controlled Congress presented Democratic President Bill Clinton with a bill it knew to be unacceptable to him, received the expected veto, approved another virtually identical bill, and received another veto. Congressional Republicans hoped to portray Clinton as an opponent to welfare reform as the 1996 elections approached.

Statistically, attempts to override vetoes are associated with low presidential popularity, a strong opposition party in Congress, and bipartisan support for the legislation. Low presidential popularity and bipartisan support for the legislation also contribute to successful override attempts. Generally, highly partisan legislation, as vetoed legislation tends to be, is not overridden because a two-thirds majority is required. Parties seldom have close to the two-thirds of the seats in both chambers needed to override a veto.

Controlling the Executive Branch

Much of the competition between Congress and the president concerns control of the executive agencies whose responsibility it is to implement policy. Agencies become players in the legislative game once they are established and begin to perform functions that are valuable to others. They have resources of their own to bring to the legislative battle. Much of the information and expertise about federal programs resides in the agencies. That information and expertise can be shared selectively with Congress and the White House. Agencies also have friends within the interest group community and the general public to whom they can appeal for support.

An unfavorable agency policy is not always easy for Congress to change. The need for agreement among all three legislative institutions – House, Senate, and president – makes a formal legislative response difficult and perhaps impossible. Consequently, members of Congress, presidents, and the organized interests seek means other than the legislative process to control agencies. For presidents, the most direct means of control is to appoint department and agency heads who support administration policies. But appointment power is not the only presidential tool.

Presidents seek to control departments and agencies by several means. The primary means of presidential control is the appointment of agency heads who share the president's policy views and are willing to be responsive to directions and suggestions from the White House. In the Small Business Administration, for example, the president appoints the director, assistant directors, and regional administrators, none of whom must be confirmed by the Senate. In cabinet departments, confirmation is required for most top administrators – under 600 overall – but more than 3,000 are "at will" appointees who serve at the president's discretion without Senate confirmation.

The central organizational tool of the president for controlling the executive branch is the Office of Management and Budget (OMB). This agency, like its predecessor, the Bureau of the Budget, constructs the president's budget proposals for the federal government. Furthermore, central clearance – the job of coordinating and approving all executive branch proposals sent to Congress – is the responsibility of the OMB. OMB responsibilities also entail scrutinizing written proposals and even preparing the congressional testimony of executive branch officials to ensure consistency with the president's policy goals. In addition, the OMB reviews enacted legislation to provide the president with a recommendation to sign or veto it.

In recent decades, the OMB has become more politicized and has expanded its bureaucratic control functions. By appointing aides ideologically aligned with himself to run the OMB, and by centralizing the rulemaking process within the OMB, President Reagan turned the OMB into a major instrument in shaping national policy and managing relations between

Congressionally Speaking . . .

As Chief Executive, the constitution requires that the president "take care that the laws be faithfully executed." In recent years, the practice of issuing signing statements at the time the president signs legislation has raised questions about whether the president is fulfilling this constitutional obligation.

Signing statements are written declarations issued by the president that indicate to Congress how he intends to direct his administration in the implementation of the law and often to articulate constitutional limits on the implementation of certain provisions. In practice, the signing statement has become reminiscent of the line-item veto. While proponents of signing statements say that they communicate valuable information to Congress, opponents contend that they are used by presidents to pick and choose the provisions they wish to enforce or implement.

Some scholars credit President Ronald Reagan for developing the signing statement into a policy-making tool, but President George W. Bush used signing statements with unprecedented frequency. Through January 2007, one study found that Bush used signing statements to challenge 1,149 provisions in 150 bills.[5] Some observers speculated that the signing statement supplanted the veto in Bush's arsenal. The advantage of the signing statement is that it is far less visible than the veto, allowing the president greater flexibility in shaping policy out of the public eye and without creating a veto override showdown with Congress.

Early in his administration, President Barak Obama issued a memorandum requiring executive agencies to consult with the attorney general before enforcing provisions of his predecessors' signing statements. Obama said that he would use signing statements only to address "constitutional concerns." He soon used a signing statement to list five objections to provisions of a large economic stimulus bill. For example, he observed that Congress lacks power to demand that executive officials reallocate certain money only after gaining approval of congressional committees. Signing statements are likely to remain an important means for presidential objections to provisions of larger bills that a presidential considers unconstitutional.

the administration and Congress. By executive order, Reagan authorized the OMB's Office of Information and Regulatory Affairs (OIRA) to review the proposed rules and regulations of executive agencies and to evaluate them by a strict cost-benefit analysis. In practice, granting this authority to OIRA provided a means for the president to make certain that agency activity was in step with his preferences or policy objectives. On numerous occasions during the Reagan administration, OIRA intervened in agency rule making and stopped agencies from issuing congressionally mandated regulations.

This intervention was principally achieved through use of return letters – a letter from the administration that returns a rule for further consideration. These requirements undercut the independence of agency and department heads, delayed action on many regulations, and ultimately led to killing or substantially changing some regulations.

Under the George H.W. Bush administration, the OMB's regulatory review functions were supplanted to some extent by the efforts of the Council on Competitiveness, also created by executive order. The council was officially located in the office of, and headed by, Vice President Dan Quayle. This organizational arrangement protected under the umbrella of executive privilege the council's inner workings from the public and congressional scrutiny to which the OMB is subject. As the administration intended, members of Congress, lobbyists, and the media found it difficult to anticipate or react to unfriendly White House efforts to interpret law and mold regulations required by law (executive privilege is discussed in Chapter 10).

President Clinton did not reestablish the Council on Competitiveness, but instead returned authority to the OMB. Early in the administration, Clinton issued an executive order supplanting the executive order issued by Reagan that had governed regulatory review up to that time. Clinton's executive order preserved the use of cost-benefit analysis in evaluating regulatory rules and their alternatives, it also mandated "the primacy of Federal agencies in the regulatory decision-making process." Although OIRA under Clinton maintained powers of bureaucratic oversight, it reviewed only the most salient regulatory matters. Furthermore, Clinton restructured OIRA to allow for preferred interest groups to gain greater access to the decision-making process.

Under President George W. Bush, OIRA's role in regulatory oversight returned to a state similar to that seen under the Reagan administration. Much like Reagan, George W. Bush has used his broad appointment powers to place individuals with like ideologies in key agency and OIRA positions. The Bush OIRA issued many more return letters than the Clinton OIRA, reflecting Bush administration opposition to agency proposals. Morevoer, the Bush OIRA created a new tool of control over the regulatory process known as a "prompt letter." Whereas return letters require agencies to reevaluate proposed regulations, prompt letters request that agencies reconsider an existing regulation. The addition of the prompt letter gives the president greater ability to curtail regulations according to his preferences. In 2007, President Bush signed an executive order that mandated that all agencies put into place a regulatory policy office to supervise the development of agency rules. The regulatory policy offices were run by appointees of the president. The addition of these offices, imbedded in the agencies, effectively gives the White House another gatekeeper to monitor agency activity and to block, if not preempt, rules that are unfavorable to the administration.

At this writing, it is too early to outline the innovations in regulatory review of the Obama administration. Administration officials made clear that they want to streamline the review process to allow the executive branch to address global warming and other issues more rapidly. Interest in revising the use of cost-benefit analysis was expressed by many experts close to the administration. The result is likely to be a substantial revision of the executive orders that governed OMB's involvement in the rulemaking functions of executive agencies.

Foreign and Defense Policy

The legislative politics of foreign and defense policy are typically different from the politics of domestic affairs. Political scientist Aaron Wildavsky argues that the presidential activities associated with these policy arenas differ substantially. Moreover, the degrees of success that presidents have in foreign and domestic affairs are sufficiently different that the American presidency can be thought of as two distinct presidencies. Although the "two presidencies" thesis is not always useful, it is true that the rules of the game often advantage the president in foreign policy. Under the Constitution, the president more clearly takes initiative and has greater autonomy over action related to foreign and defense matters than he does in domestic affairs. He appoints ambassadors (with the advice and consent of the Senate), makes treaties (subject to the approval of a two-thirds majority in the Senate), receives the ambassadors of other countries, serves as the commander in chief of the armed forces and of state militias when they are called into federal service, and commissions the officers of the United States. Although senators have become increasingly involved in monitoring treaty negotiations, the president largely retains control over U.S. diplomacy.

Congress is not helpless, of course. In fact, the Constitution gives Congress many resources. Because funding is required for much international activity, control of appropriations inserts Congress as a critical factor in foreign and defense policy. The Constitution also gives Congress the power to declare war, create and organize armed forces, regulate foreign commerce, and define offenses against the law of nations. Yet in practice substantial ambiguity exists about the proper role of the two branches. How much discretion is granted to the president in using troops, making minor agreements with other governments, or conducting secret negotiations is not clearly defined in the Constitution. For the most part, the courts have left it to Congress and presidents to work out their differences.

Presidents who claim broad implicit powers argue that they are free to ignore Congress on some matters of foreign and defense policy. This position has been strengthened by the increasing importance of world affairs during the twentieth century. Scientific and technological advances have integrated economies and yielded weapons of mass destruction, increasing the importance of the president's ability to coordinate U.S. policy, act with secrecy, and respond quickly. Presidents often argue that the dangers of the modern world and the prominent role of the United States in international affairs, requires that the president be free to conduct diplomacy, launch secret operations, and even deploy armed forces as he sees fit. Several Supreme Court cases have endorsed an unfettered right of presidents to conduct foreign policy. Chief among these rulings was *United States v. Curtiss-Wright Export Corp.*, a 1936 ruling asserting that even if extensive powers over foreign affairs were not spelled out for the president in the Constitution, the president is best suited to assume those responsibilities.

As international affairs gained importance to the United States, control of national security was increasingly centralized and institutionalized in the White House. The 1947 National Security Act consolidated control of the military in a single Defense Department and created the Central Intelligence Agency and National Security Council. All three organizations are headed by individuals who are directly accountable to the president – the secretary of defense, the director of central intelligence, and the national security adviser. In 2004, new legislation created the position of Director of National Intelligence, appointed by the president, to supervise intelligence activities of the government and serve as the principal intelligence advisor to the president. These developments have enhanced the president's ability to collect and digest information and to act promptly without substantial congressional participation.

Public expectations of presidential leadership also give the president an advantage in the area of foreign policy. Because the electorate supports centralized leadership on national security matters, particularly in times of international crisis, congressional opposition to an assertive president is unpopular with the electorate. The public is especially supportive of the president if the lives of Americans are at stake.

In the decades after World War II, the liberties given to the president to fight world communism led some observers to believe that Congress was

THE CHANGING CONGRESS: EVOLVING WAR POWERS

The Constitution grants Congress the power to declare war (Article I, Section 8), but also makes the president the commander in chief of the armed forces (Article II, Section 2). Congress has formally declared war only five times – the War of 1812, the Mexican War (1846–1848), the Spanish-American War (1898), World War I (1917–1918), and World War II (1941–1945).

Presidents have used the commander-in-chief power, various treaty obligations, resolutions of the United Nations, and their implicit duty to provide for national security as grounds for committing U.S. forces abroad without a declaration of war. By one count, the United States had been involved in 192 military actions without a declaration of war by 1972. At least nine more have occurred since then, including the response to the Iraqi invasion of Kuwait in 1990 (the Persian Gulf War), the use of troops in Somalia beginning in 1992, the military efforts in Afghanistan following the events of September 11, 2001, and the conflict in Iraq beginning in 2003. Many of these commitments were very brief, and Congress had no time to respond. In other cases, such as the Vietnam War, Congress implicitly supported the president by approving the funding he requested for the effort.

The costly Vietnam War in the 1960s and early 1970s stimulated efforts in Congress to limit the war powers that presidents had assumed. In 1973, Congress enacted, over President Richard Nixon's veto, the War Powers Resolution. This law requires that the president notify Congress about any commitment of military forces within 48 hours and terminate the commitment within 60 days unless Congress approves an extension or is unable to meet. The commitment may be extended by the president for another 30 days. Congress may halt the action at any time by concurrent resolution (that is, by a resolution that does not require the president's signature).

No one seems particularly satisfied with the 1973 law. Supporters of broad presidential discretion argue that the act infringes on the president's con-stitutional powers; supporters of a literal interpretation of the Constitution claim that the act gives away Congress's constitutional powers by allowing the president to initiate wars. Since 1973, presidents have observed the reporting requirement, but have sought alternatives to formal congressional approval. In 1983, President Reagan and Speaker O'Neill negotiated a timetable for the involvement of U.S. Marines in Lebanon. In 1991, Congress approved a resolution that authorized President George H.W. Bush to use "all neces-sary means" to enforce the United Nations resolution calling for the removal of Iraqi forces from Kuwait. In 2002, Congress approved a resolution that authorized the use of force against Iraq to "defend the national security of the United States against the continuing threat posed by Iraq" and to "enforce all relevant United Nations Security Council resolutions regarding Iraq,"

(continued)

THE CHANGING CONGRESS: EVOLVING WAR POWERS (*continued*)

which concerned weapons of mass destruction. In all three cases, the president avoided endorsing the constitutionality of the War Powers Resolution. In none of the cases did Congress actually declare war, but in the latter two cases Congress indicated that the terms of the War Powers Resolution requirement for congressional authorization were met.

In 2008, a private commission headed by two former secretaries of state, a Democrat and a Republican, recommended new war powers legislation that would (a) require the president to consult with Congress before any military operation that is expected to last more than a week, (b) require discontinuation of the operation if Congress has not approved it by concurrent resolution within 30 days, and (c) allow Congress to approve a joint resolution of disapproval to force discontinuation of the operation, by overriding a presidential veto, if necessary. If the operation required secrecy, the president would have to consult a joint committee of top party and committee leaders within three days after the operation began.

acting as if it ought to defer to the president on matters of foreign affairs. By the early 1970s, as Congress was beginning to assert itself against presidential policies it opposed, views about congressional deference to the president began to change. However, the national consensus about Cold War policy generated a basic agreement between Congress and presidents about international affairs that effectively returned Congress to a state of greater passivity. When that consensus began to disintegrate, members of Congress looked for ways to recapture their influence. In the immediate aftermath of the terrorist attacks of September 11, 2001, however, the president was once again poised to forge the way in foreign and defense policy. With growing discontent over the war in Iraq, and an administration embroiled in controversy, the current shifting balance in power is reminiscent of the early 1970s.

The reassertion of congressional power in the early 1970s represented the beginning of a tug-of-war between congressional Democrats and White House Republicans that is still evident today. Between 1969 and 2006, there were only 10 years in which the president's party controlled both chambers of Congress. Conversely, for 20 years during that period presidents faced a unified Congress of the opposing party. Therefore, partisanship confounded matters by reinforcing institutional conflict between the branches. In addition, legislative action became increasingly central to the making of foreign policy as international economic relations, human rights, environmental problems, and other issues gained a more prominent role in this sphere of policy making. This, in conjunction with the ideological gap between Congress and the president that prevailed for the better part of this period, made deference to the president particularly costly for Congress.

Policies governing the intelligence agencies have been a prime source of conflict between Congress and the president. The tension between the branches increased significantly after the revelations of the Iran-Contra affair. In 1985 and 1986, the administration secretly sold arms to the Iranians in efforts to negotiate the release of American hostages in the Middle East. Furthermore, the administration used the profits from the arms sales to fund the Contras in Nicaragua, which violated congressional restrictions on funding and covert assistance to the Contras.

Presidents' Resources

The strategies adopted by presidents and members of Congress to influence policy outcomes are influenced by the quality and quantity of resources available to each. The president possesses numerous resources that serve to strengthen the role of the presidency in legislative politics. Some of these resources, such as constitutional powers, White House staff, information, and expertise, are relatively secure and may even expand during a president's term of office.

The president has a sizable staff operation to assist him in managing relations with Congress. The president controls the size of his White House staff, although it is subject to congressional appropriations. In recent decades, the White House staff has expanded, particularly in the offices for legislative affairs, communications, and domestic and foreign policy. In addition, presidents have expanded agencies within the larger Executive Office of the President, such as the Office of Management and Budget (OMB) and Council of Economic Advisers, to enhance their policy-making capability. These staffs help the president monitor developments on Capitol Hill, work with committees and leadership, and give the president adequate representation on legislative matters.

Congress has moved to curtail the president's discretion in managing executive office staff. In the 1970s, after the OMB had gained great importance in the development and implementation of policy, Congress required the president to receive Senate confirmation for the director of the agency as for cabinet secretaries. In the 1980s, when President Ronald Reagan was proposing cuts in domestic programs, congressional Democrats made sure that funding for White House staff was constrained as well. In 1992, House Democrats moved to eliminate funding for Vice President Dan Quayle's Council on Competitiveness to show their opposition to its role in disapproving regulations proposed by federal agencies. In general, however, presidents have been able to organize their staffs as they choose and have had adequate funding to do so.

Some resources, such as information and expertise, may increase during a presidency as experience is acquired. For example, a lack of Capitol Hill experience was a serious shortcoming of President Jimmy Carter and his top aides when he entered office in 1977. As time went on, the Carter team gained familiarity with the people and ways of doing business in Congress. But Carter also recognized the limitations of his White House staff and moved to hire more experienced people. An important element of the change was giving more responsibility to Vice President (and former senator) Walter Mondale in the planning of legislative strategies.

In contrast, the president can suffer losses of other resources while in office. One scholar called this the "cycle of decreasing influence." Party strength in Congress and public support often diminish during a president's term. Recent exceptions aside (see Chapter 3), the president's party typically loses congressional seats in midterm elections.

Public support for a president often declines during a presidential term, weakening support for the president in Congress. As President Johnson reportedly once told his staff:

> You've got to give it all you can that first year. Doesn't matter what kind of majority you come in with. You've got just one year when they treat you right and before they start worrying about themselves. The third year, you lose votes.... The fourth year's all politics.[6]

This advice, which most presidents take to heart, encourages presidents to try to move quickly on their legislative programs early in their terms.

Presidents eventually run out of time. The two four-year terms that a president may serve under the Twenty-second Amendment are a long time, to be sure, but they are shorter than the legislative careers of many members of Congress and far shorter than the time horizons of many lobbyists and most bureaucrats. In fact, the president often seems to be in more of a hurry than others in Washington. Beyond the diminishing political capital that results from typical patterns of decreasing public and congressional support associated with the natural progression of the presidency, members of Congress, lobbyists, and even bureaucrats tend to limit their relations with the incumbent president nearing the end of his term.

LEGISLATIVE RESOURCES OF PRESIDENTS

Partisan base in Congress. The size of the House and Senate caucuses of the president's party can boost presidential success in enacting their priorities. When a president's partisans in Congress are cohesive and ideologically in step with him, the advantages offered to the president increase.

Formal powers. Presidents gain leverage with legislators by using, or threatening to use, their formal powers. The most obvious power is the power to veto legislation. In addition, the president may issue executive orders that interpret laws or regulate the behavior and decisions of executive branch agencies.

Visibility and public approval. The national media concentrate on the president. Unlike Congress, which finds speaking with one voice difficult, the president can dominate the news and manipulate the types of information Americans receive about his activities. If presidents mobilize public support for their initiatives, members of Congress must weigh carefully the costs of opposing the president.

Expertise and information. Broad policy expertise is available to the president from the agencies of the executive branch.

White House staff. The president has a large personal staff in the White House that allows the president to monitor and communicate with Congress, lobbyists, the media, and others.

Patronage and projects. Presidents and top cabinet officials use personnel appointments to assert control of the bureaucracy and to do favors for members of Congress. Modern presidents make more than 6,000 executive and judicial branch appointments. Presidents and top administration officials can influence decisions about who wins federal contracts and the location of federal installations and buildings.

National party organizations. The president effectively controls the resources of his party's national committees, which can be used to do favors for members of Congress.

Campaign resources. The president may exploit his campaign apparatus to generate support for his program. President Obama did this in using the large email list he developed as a candidate.

Congressional Resources and Strategies

The tendency to see legislative-executive relations as a zero-sum game is strong. Observers tend to think that if the president is gaining power, then Congress must be losing power. That perspective is too simplistic. Both Congress and the president have gained power as the role of the federal government has expanded over the decades. Moreover, neither branch is monolithic. Within the executive branch, power has been distributed in a variety of ways between the White House, departments, and independent regulatory commissions. Within Congress, the somewhat different constitutional responsibilities of the House and Senate have meant that their power has not always shifted in the same direction. Moreover, developments that seem to affect the power of Congress adversely may enhance the power of certain members, factions, or parties within the institution. Since members of Congress and the president represent different audiences with different interests, it also may be the case the changes in the legislative-executive relationship benefit both branches even if one side appears to be gaining an advantage.

Thus, it is wise to keep in mind that Congress does not really use its resources – individual members, groups of members, and legislative parties use the institution's resources as they pursue their political goals. The exercise of congressional power is usually the by-product of the competition among members within the institution. In other words, congressional output is the result of (sometimes intense) competition between members with different preferences. Given the degree to which preferences in Congress diverge, seldom do all members consider themselves to be winners on important matters.

Congress's most fundamental resources are the formal powers granted to it by the Constitution. The ability to exercise those powers effectively depends on the human and technological resources of the institution. The membership's motivation, committee and party structures, parliamentary procedure, staffing arrangements, electronic information systems, relations with outside experts and information sources, and other factors affect Congress's performance. Congress has periodically attempted to better equip itself to compete with the expanding capabilities of the president. The legislative reorganization acts of 1946 and 1970, among many other less-extensive efforts, expanded staff, reorganized committees, and changed procedures. In sum, Congress has developed a battery of resources to support an expanding repertoire of strategies for responding to challenges from the executive branch.

Periodic Authorizations

Historically, most agencies and programs have continued indefinitely once they were created. Although they must receive annual appropriations from Congress, most of the basic laws creating and empowering agencies have been permanent. Delegating authority to an executive branch agency in such a manner increases the difficulty of retracting or altering the authority later.

MULTIPLE USES OF SUNSET PROVISIONS

Although the concept of a sunset provision – a provision in law that requires periodic reauthorization of a program – dates back to the writings of Thomas Jefferson, its use as a legislative tool is a recent phenomenon. Sunset provisions grew in popularity among reformers in the late 1960s and 1970s who argued that programs must be reexamined by Congress from time to time. When the Republicans, who opposed many federal programs, took control of Congress in 1995, the idea of imposing limits on the lifespan of programs.

A prominent example of the recent use of sunset provisions is the Patriot Act, first enacted in 2001. At the time, the Republican leadership added sunset provisions as a concession to Democrats and members within their party who were skeptical about the intelligence-gathering authority granted to law enforcement and national security agencies. The legislation was reauthorized in 2006 and included provisions scheduled to expire again in 2009. Senator Dianne Feinstein (D-California) declared that the sunset provisions were an "important element of the continued vigorous oversight necessary to ensure this law is carried out in an appropriate manner."[7]

Republican majorities used sunset provisions on tax cut bills for a different purpose. By making certain provisions to the bills temporary, they were able to minimize projected costs and present a more favorable long-term estimated budget. Republicans now face the reality that the tax cuts may be reversed if Congress fails to extend them when the expiration dates arrive in 2010.

After all, a new law requires the agreement of the House, Senate, and president, or, in the case of a presidential veto, a two-thirds majority in both houses of Congress.

In recent decades, Congress has moved away from permanent authorizations. When Congress enacts legislation creating a program or establishing a new policy, it may limit the length of the authorization. A "sunset" provision sets an end date for a program, thus requiring new authorizing legislation to continue a program or policy past that date. This approach requires administration officials to return to Congress to justify the continuation of the program and it ensures that Congress will periodically review the law underlying the program. An important case is the authorization for defense programs, which must be passed each year. Before the 1960s, defense programs were authorized for an indefinite period. During the 1960s and 1970s Congress added more defense programs – military personnel, weapons systems, research and development, and so on – to the annual defense authorization bill. The immediate effect was to give members of the armed services committees greater influence over the activities of the Department of

Defense. The long-term effect was to give all members of Congress a regular opportunity to influence the direction of defense policy.

Designing Agencies

In practice, much of the conflict over legislation is about the design of the agencies charged with implementing policy. The line of authority, decision-making and appeals procedures, decision-making criteria, rule-making deadlines, reporting requirements, job definitions, personnel appointment processes and restrictions, and salaries all may affect the ability of Congress, the president, the courts, and outside interests to gain favorable action by agencies. Legislators, responding to political pressures from organized interests and others, generally seek to insulate agencies from unfriendly influences, including future Congresses and presidents, and to guarantee that agencies are guided by their policy preferences. Presidents, on the other hand, generally seek to place new programs in the hierarchy of executive departments to which they can appoint politically loyal individuals to important administrative positions. Thus, congressional and presidential views about the organization and control of agencies are often in conflict.

The effort to elevate the Environmental Protection Agency (EPA) to department-level status – making the head of the EPA a member of the president's cabinet – is a good example of structural politics. Democrats in Congress sought to modify the EPA's status in 1990 to give environmental programs more priority and authority within the executive branch. The bill, passed by the House on a vote of 371 to 55, also called for the creation of a Bureau of Environmental Statistics, which was to be independent of the new department. In addition, the bill would have established a separate Commission on Improving Environmental Protection, with the purpose of coordinating the regulations of the new department and other federal agencies with environmental jurisdiction.

The independent department was designed to be insulated from political manipulation. In fact, the bill required the department to report its findings directly to Congress, without review by the OMB or the new secretary of the environment. Furthermore, the multimember commission would have added a policy-making unit outside of the president-department line of authority. The White House, which wanted a bill that would reinforce President George H.W. Bush's claim to be the "environment president," opposed the bureau and commission on the grounds that they undermined the president's line of authority over agency activities. The bill stalled in the

Senate because of credible threats of a filibuster by Republicans after the administration threatened a veto.

In the next Congress, the bill passed the Senate on a voice vote after its Senate sponsors met the Bush administration's demands by folding the statistics bureau into the new department and restricting the policy-making authority of the commission. House Democrats refused to act on the Senate bill. The bill died in the House Committee on Government Operations because House Democrats wanted to deny President Bush an opportunity to claim credit for pro-environmental legislation in an election year.

The EPA bill is typical of the conflict between Congress and the president over the structure of agencies. Agreement about the general policy was not enough to guarantee enactment because the conflict over presidential control of the agency proved to be too divisive. Conflict over the control of information and personnel in this case was at least as controversial as the policy. Specifically, the point of contention was whether the executive branch official controlling the information going to Congress would be responsible to the president or an independent bureau chief. The president's veto power ultimately forced concessions from Senate Democrats, but House Democrats were more concerned about the political sacrifices than about raising the EPA to cabinet status.

Structural politics is not limited to original authorizations and reauthorizations. The fight is continuous, as the issue of personnel ceilings demonstrates. In recent decades, Congress has become more specific in dictating the design of executive agencies. On occasion, administrations have undermined congressional efforts to bolster agency resources by refusing to hire or replace important personnel. The appropriations committees have responded in committee reports by specifying a minimum number of personnel for agencies, requiring reports on deviations, and insisting on a formal presidential request when an agency seeks to reduce spending with a personnel ceiling. Increasingly, Congress has imposed statutory restrictions on personnel ceilings, thus limiting the administration's control over agencies' personnel resources.

The structure of many executive agencies is the result of compromise. The give-and-take process can produce a variety of outcomes, ranging from agencies that are distant from the president and responsive to Congress to agencies that are firmly under the control of the executive administration. The decision of political actors to make concessions on some aspects of structural policy and not on others is principally a function of the impact that the given agency has upon preferred constituents. Members of Congress and the president are reluctant to relinquish power over an agency when the agency under consideration has a significant direct effect – either positive or negative – on constituents of interest.

The Power of the Purse

A major congressional strategy for controlling policy and its implementation involves Congress's "power of the purse" – the constitutional provision that "no money shall be drawn from the treasury, but in consequence of appropriations made by law." Since laws must originate in Congress, the legislative body can refuse to appropriate funds for certain purposes or condition the use of funds upon certain stipulations. Thus, the authority over appropriations gives Congress the ability to shape the actions of the executive branch in a manner consistent with congressional preferences. Certainly, conditioning appropriations upon specific activity explicitly mandates behavior consistent with the will of Congress. Even the threat that appropriations for an agency or program will be reduced or eliminated may achieve the same end.

In the field of foreign and military affairs, the power of the purse is often the only effective tool for Congress to influence policy. Congress's ability to restrict the uses of appropriated funds is well supported by court decisions, giving Congress a clear avenue of response to a president who asserts broad constitutional powers. By forbidding the executive branch from spending federal monies for certain purposes, Congress can prevent the president from pursuing a policy it opposes.

Committee Reports

Committees often make clear their expectations about the implementation of programs in the reports that are required by House and Senate rules to accompany legislation when it is sent to the floor. Reports usually indicate the objectives of the legislation and sometimes interpret the language used, both of which may guide rule-making decisions by agencies. At times, committee reports indicate that the committee "clearly intends," "expects," or even "anticipates" that an executive branch official or agency will or will not do something. Earmarks for specific projects are sometimes listed in committee reports. Although they are not legally binding, committee reports often guide courts when they seek to interpret ambiguous statutory language. More important, reports make explicit the expectations of important members of Congress who will influence future legislation affecting an agency.

Packaging Strategies

The Constitution requires that the president have an opportunity to sign or veto legislation passed by Congress, but it does not indicate the size or format of the legislation Congress presents to the president. For example, a variety of items are often included in one bill to facilitate bargains among members of Congress, the president, and other interested parties. By using their ability to package legislation, members of Congress may encourage or discourage a presidential veto.

Congress exercises considerable influence over policy outcomes from its ability to package multiple measures and present the president with a single take-it-or-leave-it offer. When several bills or aspects of bills are combined into one package that includes legislation both favored and opposed by the president, Congress reduces the president's capacity to control national policy. Because the president does not have the formal authority to strike from a bill those provisions that he finds unfavorable, he is forced to make a difficult decision. Issuing a veto means losing, at least temporarily, those provisions of the legislation that he does find satisfactory. Of course, a packaged proposal that does encounter a veto may result in Congress losing valued provisions as well.

The advantages and disadvantages of packaging can be seen in the use of omnibus continuing resolutions (called CRs), which combine two or more regular appropriations bills for the coming fiscal year into one giant package. CRs are required when Congress and the president fail to appropriate bills enacted before the beginning of a new fiscal year. If the president vetoes the bill that contains the funding for some executive agencies and no new bill is enacted, those agencies must shut down. Hence, the president needs to weigh carefully how effective a veto would be. Congress also risks losing measures packed into a CR that provoke the president's opposition. For example, Representative John Dingell's attempt in 1987 to codify in the CR the "fairness doctrine" governing broadcasters (a bill previously vetoed by President Reagan) was dropped from the bill after Reagan drew attention to its inclusion in the CR. The bundling strategy on these bills and other "must pass" legislation – such as bills to raise the federal government's debt ceiling – thus have the potential to help Congress reassert influence over the legislative game.

Recent presidents have promoted the line-item veto as a means to combat Congress's packaging strategies in appropriations bills. Adopting the line-item veto, an authority held by 43 state governors, would allow the president to strike out individual provisions nestled in individual or omnibus spending bills. However, creating a line-item veto would require a constitutional amendment. The Supreme Court ruled the line-item veto as passed by Congress in 1996 unconstitutional. Presidential signing statements have been used to register a president's objections to provisions in larger bills, particularly to provisions considered to be unconstitutional, even when the president chooses to sign the bill (see above).

Presidential Nominations

The Senate is given a special opportunity to influence the administration every time the president nominates someone for a top executive branch post. Beyond judges, ambassadors, and "other public ministers and consuls," the Constitution allows Congress to determine by law who must stand for confirmation by the Senate. Currently, the Constitution and public law subject about 3,000 civilian executive branch positions to confirmation by the Senate. Judicial nominations and confirmations are considered in Chapter 10. In addition, the promotions of all military officers are submitted to the Senate.

The Senate tends to defer to the president on executive branch appointments, particularly on positions below the cabinet level. This is not to say, however, that the president's appointments go unchecked. In fact, in 1989 President George H.W. Bush's first nominee for secretary of defense, former senator John Tower, was rejected by the Senate largely because of concerns about the senator's private behavior. The president swiftly moved to nominate House Republican Dick Cheney, a choice calculated to be far more acceptable to the Senate. In 1993, President Bill Clinton's first nomination for attorney general was withdrawn when it was discovered that the nominee, Zoe Baird, had hired illegal aliens as household help. In 2009, President Obama's choices for secretaries of Health and Human Services and a new position, Chief Performance Officer within the Office of Management and Budget, withdrew after irregularities in past tax payments were made public.

Occasionally Congress acts to require that certain executive officials be subject to Senate confirmation. In 1973, Congress required the president to receive Senate confirmation on appointments to director of the OMB. In 1986, Congress extended their authority by requiring that the president also receive Senate confirmation on appointments to head OIRA. When Congress approved legislation to create the Department of Homeland Security in 2002, the new secretary of the department automatically became subject to Senate confirmation.

Moreover, Congress may, and does, get involved in executive branch personnel matters beyond Senate action on presidential nominations. Congress

Congressionally Speaking . . .

The Constitution and many statutes require that the president submit the names of certain appointees to the Senate for confirmation. The Constitution also allows the president to make a *recess appointment* when the Senate is not in session. A recess appointment is good until the end of the next session of Congress, which could be more than a year in duration. Presidents have used recess appointments to avoid the regular confirmation process, but they usually announce their intention to forward a regular nomination to the Senate at the time appointments are made. Because recess appointments are a way for the president to circumvent, at least for a short while, the authority of the Senate, this practice can and does create animosity.

President George W. Bush employed the recess appointment with greater frequency than his two predecessors, but lagged slightly behind President Ronald Reagan and eventually was thwarted by a parliamentary maneuver. In his first six years as president, George W. Bush made 167 recess appointments, whereas President Bill Clinton made 140 over two terms and President George H.W. Bush made 77 in his single term. Reagan made 240 recess appointments during his eight years in office.[8] Senate Democrats blocked recess appointments in the last year of the Bush administration by avoiding long recesses. Rather than taking a recess, the Senate could remain officially in session by holding a *pro forma* session every three days. Why three days? The Constitution does not define a recess. A 1993 Justice Department opinion argued that the president may make a recess appointment during a recess of more than three days (that is, more than a long weekend).

In a *pro forma* session (an informal name), the Senate session opens, no business is conducted, and is immediately gaveled closed by the only senator in attendance.

is able to specify in law the qualifications required of presidential appointees, and it may even grant department heads, rather than the president, the authority to appoint certain officials. Congress also may limit the ability of the president or agency heads to dismiss employees. In these ways, Congress may seek to insulate certain executive branch officials from White House pressure.

Oversight

A member of Congress dissatisfied with agency performance or with presidential directives to an agency can choose from several oversight strategies to try to bring the bureaucracy into line. Oversight strategies centered on formal hearings include committee or subcommittee hearings, which regularly bring agency heads in front of legislators, special hearings designed to draw attention to a disputed policy or agency action, and more dramatic investigations, such as the Watergate hearings in 1973 and 1974 and the 1987 Iran-Contra hearings, usually conducted by special committees.

Less formal methods of monitoring and influencing agency behavior include written and telephone communications with agency officials, discussions with agency heads and other interested parties during informal office visits, public relations campaigns, and threats to pursue new legislation. Such approaches can be useful in congressional efforts to increase agency responsiveness to the interests of Congress. Although a considerable amount of bureaucratic oversight occurs within the committee forum, there are oversight mechanisms available to members that are independent of committees. Members seeking to influence agency actions in their districts also have recourse to informal visits and more formal inquiries conducted by staff. Often, members acting on behalf of communities in their district will pressure agency officials to respond to local concerns. For example, individual members frequently push the Environmental Protection Agency to investigate hazardous waste sites or to initiate cleanups in their districts. At other times, members will compel the administration not to act in their district when agencies have the potential to adversely affect preferred constituents.

Some observers have distinguished between "police-patrol" and "fire-alarm" oversight. Under police-patrol oversight, Congress pursues routine, systematic surveillance of executive branch agencies on its own initiative. In contrast, fire-alarm oversight is more decentralized. Instead of initiating and maintaining patrols, Congress develops a system that lets others "pull the alarms." Citizens, interest groups, or the media bring agency decisions to the attention of legislators and motivate them to act. Members may prefer fire-alarm oversight because it is more cost efficient and because it allows them to claim credit for acting when the alarm bells ring.

Yet police-patrol oversight appears to have become more common since the early 1970s. Fiscal constraints may have led members to turn away from legislation for new programs and instead to focus on overseeing the implementation of established programs. Expanded committee staffs and the independence of subcommittees, some devoted exclusively to oversight activities, have also facilitated more conventional oversight. Furthermore, the centralization of the executive branch's regulatory process in the OMB and the Council on Competitiveness motivated members to pursue formal oversight hearings more aggressively. Partisan rivalries when there is divided

THE IRAN-CONTRA AFFAIR

A Lebanese newspaper reported in early November 1986 that the Reagan administration had been engaged in trading arms to Iran for release of hostages held by Islamic extremists in Lebanon. When Attorney General Edwin Meese later that month uncovered a memo outlining the diversion of profits from the arms sales to the Nicaraguan Contras, a series of executive and congressional investigations ensued. Together, these events sparked the biggest scandal of President Reagan's two terms in office and helped precipitate Reagan's marked decline in popularity and influence.

An investigation by special House and Senate panels into the Iran-Contra affair uncovered a remarkable series of events, in which officials of the Reagan administration lied to Congress and helped subvert normal democratic decision-making processes. The Reagan administration essentially pursued secret policies that were in direct conflict with public policy objectives. On one hand, the administration's public policies were to ban arms shipments to Iran and to make no concessions for the release of hostages. On the other hand, the administration pursued secret policies of selling sophisticated missiles to Iran and trading weapons to get the hostages back. Although Reagan originally told a special investigatory commission that he approved the shipments, he later reversed this statement. In the end, he testified that he could not remember whether or not he had approved the shipments.

Reagan's advisors admitted to directing the covert arms transactions and the subsequent attempts to divert the profits to the Contras. They confessed to concealing and, at times, outwardly lying about the activities to Congress. The arms sales violated laws requiring that such transactions be reported to Congress. Even though law prohibited military or paramilitary assistance to the Contras, the National Security Council (NSC) staff sought illicit funding from foreign countries and private citizens, and turned over much of the operation to private arms merchants. The private enterprise accumulated approximately $10.6 million, carrying out covert U.S. policies with funds in a way that was entirely unaccountable to Congress.

Eventually, several senior administration officials were convicted of lying to Congress.

party control of Congress and the White House have motivated legislators to be more aggressive in their oversight activities.

Congress has increasingly turned to the Government Accountability Office (GAO) to assist with oversight. The GAO is an agency of Congress and is authorized to examine any federal agency. It gives members of Congress the option of having its expert, nonpartisan staff conduct an investigation of executive branch performance without a large commitment of time on the part of members or their staff. The duties of the GAO were expanded under the Legislative Reorganization Act of 1970, and since then the GAO has significantly increased the range and number of its audits and analyses of program effectiveness.

In recent decades, Congress has more frequently required the president and executive agencies to provide written reports on their actions and performance. In some cases, the requirement is designed to ensure the timely receipt of information – for example, just before Congress must reauthorize a program. In other situations, Congress demands that an agency conduct a special study of a problem and report the results. Executive branch officials often complain that they spend too much time writing reports that few members, if any, read. From Congress's perspective, however, the exercise is another aspect of police-patrol oversight that shifts the burden to agencies themselves.

Beginning in 1978, police-patrol oversight was extended by the creation of offices of inspectors general within major departments and agencies. Inspectors general are given substantial independence from political appointees and agency heads, are authorized to conduct wide-ranging audits and investigations, and are required to submit their reports directly to Congress. With few exceptions, Congress has looked favorably upon having a full-time, on-site bureaucratic oversight mechanism.

Police-patrol oversight also is reflected in Congress's intensified scrutiny of "reprogramming" by agencies. Congress usually appropriates funds for executive branch activities in large lump-sum categories, with the understanding that the funds will be spent in accordance with the more detailed budget justifications that agencies submit each year. Frequently, variation from the budget justifications – reprogramming – is deemed prudent or even necessary because of changing conditions, poor estimates, or new congressional requirements. Agencies and the White House, however, have occasionally taken advantage of reprogramming discretion to spend money for purposes not anticipated – or even opposed – by Congress. Congress has responded by establishing more and more requirements, such as demanding advanced notification of reprogramming actions and even requiring prior approval by the appropriate committees.

National security is an area in which Congress's ability to oversee the executive branch and publicize what it learns is somewhat limited. Several committees, including the appropriations, national security, and intelligence committees, receive classified information from executive agencies and hold hearings on classified matters in executive sessions. Committee reports from hearings or investigations are cleared with executive agencies and frequently must exclude materials that the agencies determine should remain classified. In 2004, as a part of a large intelligence reform package, Congress assigned the Public Interest Declassification Board (PIDB), comprised of members appointed by both Congress and the president, to resolve disputes between Congress and executive agencies about classified material that Congress wishes to publish.

Legislative Veto

A congressional strategy of disputed constitutionality is the use of the legislative veto. A legislative veto is a provision written into legislation that delegates authority for certain actions to the president or agencies, subject to the approval or disapproval of one or both houses of Congress, certain committees, or even designated committee leaders. The legislative veto gives Congress a way to check executive branch action without having to pass new legislation that would require presidential approval. Congress can, then, avoid writing detailed legislation by delegating rule-making power to the executive branch, and still retain the final say over executive decisions. Legislative vetoes may, at first glance, appear to be a strategy used exclusively by congressional players against the president. The origins of the legislative veto, however, convey a different story. In 1932, Congress and President Herbert Hoover reached an agreement on executive branch reorganization that included the first legislative veto. The compact delegated reorganization powers to the president, provided that Congress did not disapprove his plan within 60 days. The agreement effectively gave the president wide latitude in exercising powers delegated to him, but it also gave Congress a chance to control those actions without having to enact another law. The provision seemingly benefited both Congress and the president by expanding the powers of the president, but giving Congress an opportunity to nullify those decisions.

The Supreme Court eventually saw it differently and declared legislative vetoes unconstitutional in 1983 in *Immigration and Naturalization Service v. Chadha*. The majority of the Court noted that some legislative vetoes circumvent constitutional requirements that legislative actions be passed by both chambers. Perhaps more important, the Court said, legislative vetoes violate the constitutional requirement that all measures subject to congressional votes be presented to the president for signature or veto. The Court's position was evident: If Congress wants to limit executive branch use of delegated authority, it must pass new legislation by the traditional route.

Congress has devised no consistent strategy to replace the legislative veto. At times, Congress has written more detailed legislation or committee reports, added new procedural requirements for agencies, or turned to sunset provisions. At other times, it has turned toward informal agency-committee spending agreements, which require agencies to notify certain committees before they act. Although advance notification requirements have been upheld by the courts, committees actually retain an implicit form of veto under these arrangements. Specifically, agencies encountering opposition from the committees that fund them are not likely to proceed with their original plans out of fear of reprisal when their authorizing and appropriations legislation is next before Congress.

Despite the Court's 1983 ruling, Congress has continued to add legislative vetoes to new laws. In just over a year after the Chadha decision, an additional 53 legislative vetoes were enacted into law. By the completion of the 105th Congress (1997–1998), more than 400 new legislative vetoes had been enacted. New forms of legislative vetoes are still being attempted and, in some cases, enacted. These efforts reflect the desire of Congress, the president, and the executive agencies to find mutually acceptable ways to balance the delegation of power with checks on the use of that power. The president and agency officials know that courts would rule in their favor if they chose to challenge legislative vetoes, but they often agree to comply with them because legislative vetoes are a necessary condition for the latitude that accompanies them.

A convenient inference is that the Supreme Court's 1983 decision had little practical effect on inter-branch relations. Such an inference is premature and probably incorrect. A scholarly review of inter-branch relations in the foreign policy arena indicates that the 1983 decision eliminated an important means for resolving conflict. Where Congress and the executive branch are in serious disagreement, the executive branch appears unwilling to accept even symbolic legislative veto provisions, and Congress seems unwilling to delegate power that the executive branch seeks. Thus, changing the rules of the game seems to have affected the ability of the branches to identify cooperative strategies.

Conclusion

This review of congressional and presidential strategies suggests how dynamic and complex the relationship between the legislative and executive branches has become. As political conditions have evolved, senators, representatives, presidents, and bureaucrats have devised new and sometimes ingenious strategies to influence policy outcomes. Dissatisfaction with the likely or realized outcomes of the game has often yielded institutional innovations, such as expanding the responsibilities of the OMB, creating the line-item veto, expanding the use of executive orders, and creating legislative vetoes. Incrementally, the web of statutes, court rulings, and informal understandings produced by this process of innovation has made interbranch relations more complex. On the whole, the separation of powers between Congress and the president has become less clearly defined with the expansion of the president's legislative powers and Congress's administrative capabilities. What keeps the system operating is a minimal level of agreement among the House, Senate, and president, or at least an understanding that compromise is essential to prevent complete gridlock.

The three-institution legislative game of the House, Senate, and presidency generates cooperation and conflict as the policy preferences and political interests of officeholders vary across issues and over time. However, the requirement that the three institutional players agree before new law can be made, in the absence of sufficient congressional support to override a veto, leads to exploitation of extra-statutory tactics and often necessitates informal accommodation. Accommodation is frustrating to players set on gaining outright victories, and it often is possible only after a long struggle. Furthermore, accommodation produces unstable results. New Congresses and presidents seeking new strategies to meet their own political needs frequently alter the state of the institutions. Consequently, relations between the branches seldom remain in equilibrium for long.

Above: Supreme Court Justices arrive at the inauguration of Barack Obama as 44th U.S. President.
Below: Anti-abortion and pro-choice advocates rally in front of the U.S. Supreme Court on the 36th anniversary of the *Roe v. Wade* decision.

10

Congress and the Courts

S UPREME COURT NOMINATIONS WERE AT THE CENTER OF ATTENTION IN
the summer of 2005. Sandra Day O'Connor announced her intentions to resign on July 1, 2005 creating the first vacancy on the Supreme
Court in 11 years. Then, before O'Connor's seat could be filled, Chief Justice William Rehnquist lost his battle with thyroid cancer on September 3,
2005. Rehnquist's death created a second vacancy on the Supreme Court
and gave President George W. Bush an opportunity to shape the ideological
direction of the Court for a generation. Chief Justice Rehnquist was often
considered a reliably conservative vote, while O'Connor was considered the
"swing" justice who often cast the deciding vote in bitterly divided 5–4 decisions. President Bush first nominated John Roberts, a judge on the D.C.
Circuit Court of Appeals, to replace O'Connor, but following Rehnquist's
death, Bush nominated Roberts to become the new Chief Justice. Roberts
was considered a "home run" of a nominee with impeccable credentials
and qualifications. Conservatives were sure he would be a reliable vote on
their side, while liberals could find little in his record to warrant opposing
him. Roberts played his part well in his confirmation hearings as he repeatedly showed off his intellect all the while proclaiming judicial modesty, best
exemplified in his opening statement where he declared:

> Judges are like umpires. Umpires don't make the rules; they apply them. The
> role of an umpire and a judge is critical. They make sure everybody plays by the
> rules. But it is a limited role. Nobody ever went to a ball game to see the umpire.
> Judges have to have the humility to recognize that they operate within a system
> of precedent, shaped by other judges equally striving to live up to the judicial
> oath.

Roberts easily won Senate confirmation by a vote of 78–22, which then
focused the nation's attention on who President Bush would nominate to

replace Justice O'Connor – the first female justice to serve on the Supreme Court. Bush first nominated White House Counsel Harriet Miers, a long-time ally and loyal soldier in the Bush administration. Unlike Roberts, Miers immediately came under fire from politicians of all political stripes. Conservatives questioned whether or not she was conservative enough, given her apparent support for abortion rights in her earlier work as an attorney, while others questioned her qualifications given that she had never worked as a judge or served in any posts that would have appeared to prepare her for the job. Both sides questioned whether President Bush put cronyism above finding the best nominee for the post. Miers eventually asked to have her name withdrawn from consideration citing, among other factors, the growing opposition to her nomination.

Bush quickly named a new nominee – 3rd Circuit Court Judge Samuel Alito – who was cut from the same model as Chief Justice Roberts. Alito was eminently qualified, having spent 15 years as a judge, and was thought to be a judicial conservative – in fact, many compared him to current Justice Antonin Scalia. Alito found the Senate much less receptive to his nomination than it had been to Roberts. Alito endured grueling confirmation hearings – that once brought his wife to tears – and an attempted filibuster on the Senate floor before eventually winning confirmation by a vote of 58–42.

The battle over judicial nominees such as Roberts, Miers, Alito, and scores of lower court nominees has raged in the past two decades at least in part because the House, Senate, and president are not the only institutional players in the policy-making game. Federal judges serve, as Justice Roberts stated, as "umpires" in encounters between players in the legislative and executive arenas and help determine the boundaries of each institution's powers. In separation-of-powers cases, for example, judges often draw lines between the two branches and specify the constitutional powers on each side. Judges also consider the scope of legislative powers generally, including the scope of congressional power to investigate the executive branch and where the line between federal and state jurisdictions should be drawn.

The courts are not simply umpires in the legislative game, however. They are both political and legal institutions. In the past generation, judges have increasingly contributed to making policy – not merely interpreting statutes already enacted. The growth of judicial activism since the 1970s and the reactions to judicial activism are an important part of the story of relations between Congress and the courts.

Congress is not a quiet bystander to the decisions of the courts. Most important areas of law are the product of interaction between the legislative institutions (Congress and the president) and the courts. The legislative institutions have a number of ways to influence, at least indirectly, the decisions the courts make, as Congress and the president determine the composition of the courts. The president nominates judges and the Senate must confirm the nominees. Moreover, the size of the Supreme Court and lower courts, the organization and funding for the federal court system, and the Supreme Court's jurisdiction with respect to appeals from lower courts are determined by law, making them subject to the legislative process controlled by the House, Senate, and president. More directly, Congress and the president anticipate and react to court rulings. They sometimes comply with, ignore, or even reverse judicial decisions. They may speed, slow, or even exclude court consideration of certain matters in the way they write law. This chapter takes up each of these subjects – the courts as umpires, the courts as policy makers, and congressional resources and strategies.

Courts as Umpires

The Constitution implicitly grants to the Supreme Court the power to declare actions of state and federal legislatures and executives unconstitutional. This authority inserts the court into the dynamics of the legislative game. First exercised in *Marbury v. Madison* in 1803, the power of *judicial review* – the ability to declare laws unconstitutional – gives the courts a say in the enactment of new legislation.

Most cases come to the courts when a private party, sometimes an interest group, challenges the constitutionality of an act of Congress after an executive agency seeks to implement or enforce the act. Occasionally, members of Congress file suit against the executive branch for its failure to implement laws in a manner consistent with the members' expectations. In fact, members have been plaintiffs in suits filed against the executive branch in more cases during the past two decades than in all previous decades. Issues of great importance are appealed from lower courts to the Supreme Court, although this process might take years after the original enactment of the legislation.

As Figure 10.1 shows, the Supreme Court has overturned federal provisions at an uneven pace over its history. Before 1865, few provisions were overturned. Indeed, for much of its history the Supreme Court has exercised its review powers only intermittently. Intense legislative-judicial conflict is relatively infrequent, occurring in the decades around the New Deal and in more recent decades. Even then, historically the majority of laws and provisions overturned by the Court are actually minor or relatively unimportant, yet this tendency has changed in recent years as the Court has taken on

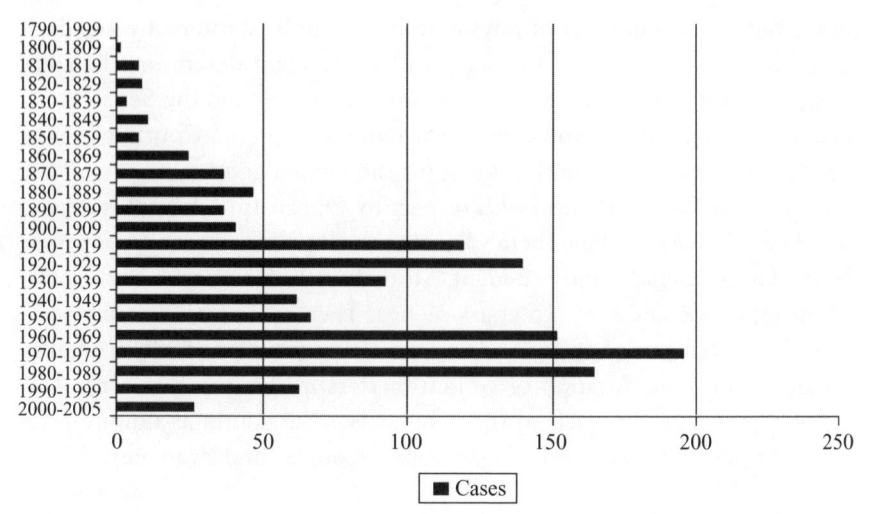

FIGURE 10.1. Number of Provisions Ruled Unconstitutional by the Supreme Court. *Source:* Lawrence Baum, *The Supreme Court,* 9th edition. Washington, D.C.: Congressional Quarterly Press.

high-profile legislation such as the Violence Against Women Act and the Religious Freedom and Restoration Act.

In this section, two types of cases involving the interpretation of the Constitution are discussed: cases involving the separation-of-powers between Congress and the executive branch and cases concerning the scope of congressional powers. The section concludes with a discussion of the role of courts as umpires in disputes about the meaning of statutes.

Separation-of-Powers Cases

In the decades before the 1970s, court involvement in separation-of-powers cases was uncommon. Because Congress was relatively deferential to the executive branch, fewer encounters were likely to provoke conflict over the powers of each branch. That situation changed dramatically during the Nixon administration (1969–1974) and in the following years when Congress moved to reassert itself.

President Richard Nixon asserted broad presidential powers in his conflict with a Congress controlled by the Democrats. The most conspicuous conflict was Nixon's battle with Congress over federal spending. Nixon claimed a right to withhold funds from executive agencies – a process called impoundment – even after the appropriations legislation was enacted into law. For example, Nixon impounded funds appropriated for sewage treatment plants administered by the Environmental Protection Agency. The impoundments were frequently challenged in the courts and Nixon usually lost. In 1973 and 1974 alone, only six of more than 50 cases upheld the president's position on impoundments in any way. Most of the decisions were made at the U.S. district court level and were not appealed by the administration to higher courts. In the sewage-treatment case, the Supreme Court ruled that the president was obligated to follow the law and allocate the funds.

In the 1980s, partisan dissension between the Republican White House and the Democratic House continued to drive each branch to the courts for redress against the perceived excesses of the other branch. For most of the Reagan and G. H. W. Bush presidencies, the Supreme Court followed a "doctrinal notion of separated powers" – the view that a sharp line can be drawn between executive and legislative powers. Two particularly revealing decisions in which the Court decided against Congress during this period were *Immigration and Naturalization Service v. Chadha* (1983) and *Bowsher v. Synar* (1986). These decisions merit attention in light of the ways in which the Court refereed contentious encounters between the branches. A later case, *Clinton v. City of New York* (1998), further demonstrates the Court's willingness to draw sharp distinction even in the absence of inter-branch contention.

In the *Chadha* decision, the Supreme Court ruled 7 to 2 that the legislative veto (see Chapter 9) was unconstitutional. According to the Court, Congress was to present bills to the president, who had the sole power to veto them. Arguments that the legislative veto was a workable means of extending authority to the executive short of formal enactment of a law were rejected. Still, the ban on legislative vetoes has largely been ignored by Congress, with more than 400 legislative vetoes enacted into law after *Chadha* – often with the agreement of the executive branch. Although the *Chadha* decision has forced Congress to be more creative in crafting provisions that give the legislature a potential veto, the response to the decision shows the weakness of the Court as an umpire when Congress and presidents agree on mutually beneficial ways to distribute power between themselves.

Building upon *Chadha*, the *Bowsher* decision advanced a stricter concept of separation of powers. *Bowsher* struck down a provision of the 1985 Gramm-Rudman-Hollings Act that required the President to implement spending reductions determined by the Comptroller General when the budget deficit exceeded a prescribed maximum. A majority of the Court concluded that such budget cuts were a power belonging to the Executive. Furthermore, the Court asserted that the Comptroller General, who can be removed from office by a joint resolution of Congress, was essentially an officer of the legislative branch. Therefore, this provision was deemed an unconstitutional infringement by the legislative branch on the powers of the Executive. While the *Bowsher* decision focused on a relatively narrow legal question, it ultimately forwarded a model of legislative-executive relations in which the legislative branch has a limited role in supervising the implementation of the laws it enacts. The Court wrote, "once Congress makes its choice in enacting legislation, its participation ends. Congress can thereafter control the execution of its enactment only indirectly – by passing new legislation." As discussed in chapter 9, the strict model forwarded by the Court in *Bowsher* has clearly not been practiced by the branches.

The Supreme Court's decision in *Clinton v. City of New York* (1998), striking down the line-item veto, demonstrated that the Court will enforce the separation of powers between Congress and the President even when the two branches are not in conflict. In 1996, Congress passed and President Clinton signed the line-item veto, which gave the President the power to remove or veto specific spending or tax breaks from bills while signing the underlying bill, with the law taking effect after the presidential election of 1996. Presidents had long sought this power to control federal spending, while many in Congress were eager to let the President help control it and take the blame for cutting popular programs. In striking down the line-item veto, the Court ruled that allowing the modification of a bill before signing it violated the constitutionally prescribed legislative process, specifically the "presentment" clause of Article I. During the presidency of G. W. Bush, he and many members of Congress expressed their desire to reenact a version of the line-item veto, but the Court's ruling has made it clear that it will guard the constitutionally prescribed separation-of-powers.

It has been noted by some observers that the modern Court has increasingly taken cases that pit the principle of separation of powers against that of checks and balances – related, yet not wholly compatible principles. While neither of these principles is spelled out in detail by the Constitution, they are nonetheless implicit. On the one hand, a strict view of separation of powers, as expressed in the *Bowsher* decision, confines the branches to their own designated arena, which may be inferred from the separate articles that outline the powers of the branches. Conversely, the principle of checks and balances, implied by the powers granted to the branches to prevent overreaching by other branches, requires that the branches occasionally engage in activities that extend beyond the strict definition of their role. Given that the Constitution offers little guidance regarding the details of these principles, it is silent as to when one principle should prevail over the other. In other words, the Constitution offers no roadmap as to when the branches should be confined to their own arena or granted shared powers for the sake of oversight.

Several actions of the G. W. Bush administration, many related to the War on Terror, have brought the tensions between these principles to the forefront, particularly regarding the limits of legislative oversight of the executive branch. And it appears that the Court will someday be the final arbiter on a number of these issues. Of particular interest in legislative-executive relations, is how the courts will rule on questions relating to executive privilege. G. W. Bush's broad claims of executive privilege on sensitive matters marked some of the most expansive use of the privilege in history, which enraged many in congress.

Perhaps the most controversial use of executive privilege came when Bush instructed former White House Counsel Harriet Miers and White House Chief of Staff Joshua Bolten to ignore congressional subpoenas relating to the investigation of the firing of nine U.S. attorneys, thought by some in congress to be politically motivated. On July 31, 2008, a U.S. District Court for the District of Columbia ruled in favor of Congress, holding that Miers and Bolten must comply with the subpoenas. However, the U.S. Court of Appeals for the District of Columbia later stayed that ruling, stating that the matter could not be resolved before the completion of the session of Congress. It was left to the next Congress to determine whether it would pursue the matter. The House rules package for the 111th Congress (2009–10) subsequently authorized the House to continue its lawsuit against Miers and Bolten, indicating that the Democratic-led Congress did not intend to put the issue to rest. However, members were increasingly concerned about letting judges determine the limitations of executive privilege, especially considering that a Democrat had recently entered the White House. Consequently, a deal was struck that required Miers (and former Deputy Chief of Staff, Karl Rove) to be interviewed under oath by the House Judiciary Committee in closed depositions. This agreement averted an almost certain path to the Supreme Court.

Should the rather delicate matter of executive privilege be resolved in the courts at some future date, the decision will have significant consequences for legislative-executive relations. A ruling against Congress would certainly enforce a vision that the branches are to operate in mutually exclusive spheres, thereby severely limiting congress's ability to check the executive branch. Conversely, a decision in Congress's favor would support the view that checks and balances are to be a central aspect in the relationship between Congress and the president.

Congressional Powers

The courts also referee the legislative game by their involvement in questions of congressional powers. Although Article I of the Constitution specifies in some detail the powers of Congress, the Supreme Court has often ruled on whether certain acts of Congress are permissible. In contrast, the Supreme Court has heard relatively few cases on Congress's authority over its internal affairs. On questions of membership qualifications, Congress's ability to punish its members, and speech privileges of members, the Court has generally given Congress a good deal of leeway. A few examples show how difficult the issues can be and how much the role of the courts as umpire can change in particular areas of the law.

THE COMMERCE CLAUSE. The most frequent way that the courts have refereed legislative politics is by interpreting the limits of congressional power under the Constitution. Perhaps the best examples are Supreme Court rulings that interpret the commerce clause of the Constitution (Article I, Section 8). The commerce clause allows Congress to enact legislation that regulates interstate commerce, and it has been used by Congress to regulate many aspects of American life that are related, however indirectly, to interstate commerce. Over the years, the Supreme Court has decided many cases that affect the limits of what activities are related to interstate commerce. As the national economy became more integrated and as Congress sought to establish more uniform policies for the nation in the late 1800s and early 1900s, congressional powers under the commerce clause became a controversial issue.

In the late 1800s and early 1900s, the Supreme Court took a narrow view of interstate commerce. If an activity concerned production or manufacturing, concerned only intrastate exchange, and did not directly affect interstate commerce, the Court tended to protect it from federal regulation. This interpretation greatly limited the ability of Congress and the president to respond to the rapidly changing national economy. In fact, the Court's narrow view of the commerce clause led it to strike down Franklin Roosevelt's New Deal legislation in the early 1930s, which was enacted in response to the Great Depression. After Roosevelt requested, but failed to get, congressional approval to enlarge the Court so that he could change the balance of opinion on the Court, two justices changed their views on the commerce clause, and the Court reversed itself on several major decisions.

Since the 1930s, step-by-step, the Court has allowed Congress to determine what activities are related to interstate commerce. In the 1960s, the Court affirmed the right of Congress to forbid owners of public accommodations with an interstate commerce connection (e.g., hotels, restaurants, etc.) from denying access on the basis of race or color. In the 1980s and early 1990s, the Court upheld laws that ban threats and extortion to collect on loans, set minimum wages for employees of state and local governments, and prohibited age discrimination by agencies of state government. Until recently, Court action appeared to erase the line between intrastate and interstate commerce and leave very broad powers for Congress under the commerce clause.

In 1995, led by conservative justices, the Supreme Court changed the direction of 70 years of rulings in favor of congressional discretion to determine the breadth of the commerce clause. In *United States v. Lopez*, the Court struck down a 1990 law that prohibited anyone from knowingly carrying a firearm in a school zone. The government argued that Congress had implicit authority, from its ability to interpret the commerce clause, to regulate firearms for such a public purpose. The Court ruled that nothing in the commerce clause or other constitutional provisions authorizes Congress to regulate such behavior, absent compelling evidence that the presence of firearms in school zones had an adverse effect on interstate commerce.

The Court continued its efforts to set limits on Congress's ability to stretch the commerce clause by striking down parts of the Violence Against Women Act in *U.S. v. Morrison* (2000). The 5–4 ruling invalidated a portion of the statute allowing women who were victims of sexual assault to sue their attackers in federal court. Congress had granted women this power citing numerous studies indicating that fear of violence had a chilling effect on the mobility of female students and employees. The majority opinion in *U.S. v. Morrison* held that Congress's attempt to regulate crimes against women in this manner could, "obliterate the Constitution's distinction between national and local authority" while the dissent held that Congress had adequately demonstrated the link between violence against women and interstate commerce.

The conservative majority that had seemed intent on limiting the power of Congress under the commerce clause splintered in *Gonzales v. Raich* (2005). The case dealt with whether or not the federal government could prohibit states from enacting laws sanctioning the use of medicinal marijuana. The government argued that the Controlled Substances Act – a law regulating the use of drugs such as marijuana – did not allow the use of the drug for medicinal purposes. The defendants argued that the Controlled Substances Act was unconstitutional because the drug was homegrown, did not cross state lines, and was not sold; hence did not involve interstate commerce. A 6–3 majority of the Supreme Court disagreed, finding that Congress did have the power to regulate medicinal marijuana under the commerce clause, signaling a reversal in the Court's tightening of Congress's powers under the commerce clause.

POWER TO INVESTIGATE. One area in which the courts have been more active in interpreting congressional powers has been Congress's power to investigate. Although the power to investigate is not mentioned explicitly in the Constitution, investigatory authority has traditionally been considered an implied power of Congress. In general, the authority to acquire information is usually seen as necessary for the proper functioning of a legislature. For example, the investigative and contempt powers of the English Parliament are exempt from judicial review. Although most investigations by the U.S. Congress are carried out without ending up in court, the Supreme Court has on occasion reached some rather controversial decisions about the scope of congressional investigatory authority. In particular, the Court has refereed cases contesting the subjects Congress can investigate and the rights that congressional witnesses retain. The Court originally took a narrow view of congressional investigative and contempt authority in *Kilbourn v. Thompson*, decided in 1881. In overturning the arrest of Hallet Kilbourn, who refused to provide information to the House about certain real estate deals, the Supreme Court limited Congress's ability to investigate private matters. The Court also delineated several principles concerning the proper scope of congressional powers to investigate. Specifically, the Court limited the scope of congressional authority to matters on which Congress could legitimately legislate and on which the chamber had indicated its intent to legislate.

Those standards stood for nearly 50 years, until the Supreme Court broadened congressional authority in *McGrain v. Daugherty* in 1927. The Court ruled that Congress had no general power to investigate private matters, but the Court extended the scope of congressional authority to any subject of *potential* legislation. The Court also affirmed Congress's power to compel private individuals to testify. Still, the Court did reserve for individuals the right to refuse to answer certain questions if they were not pertinent to the general investigation. Reserving a right for individuals to refuse to testify was to become central to Senator Joseph McCarthy's investigations of subversive activities in the 1950s.

In the 1950s and 1960s, the Warren Court moved to protect the right of private individuals to refuse to answer questions, based on their Fifth Amendment privilege against self-incrimination (*Watkins v. United States*, 1957; *Bernblatt v. United States*, 1959). *Watkins* concerned the rights of persons convicted of contempt of Congress for failing to answer questions about their association with the Communist Party that were posed by the House Un-American Activities Committee. In this case, the Court ruled that the committee did not have a sufficiently well-defined legislative purpose to justify requiring an individual to respond to questions. Chief Justice Earl Warren, writing for the Court, noted that "there is no congressional power to expose for the sake of exposure."

REGULATING CAMPAIGN SPENDING. In overturning parts of campaign finance legislation passed in 1974, the Supreme Court ruled in *Buckley* v. *Valeo* (1976) that Congress cannot limit individual or group expenditures in a political campaign when those expenditures are made independently of a particular candidate or party. The Court said that the First Amendment of the Constitution, which guarantees freedom of speech, prevents the government from regulating political speech – in this case, speech funded by an individual on her own behalf.

The Court said that limitations on campaign expenditures, as for any restraint on political speech, are constitutional only if some compelling government interest exists. The determination of what constitutes a compelling interest requires the courts to exercise discretion and judgment. In this case, the Supreme Court decided that the goal of limiting the electoral influence of wealthy individuals or groups was insufficient and ran directly counter to the intent of the First Amendment.

The Court reached a different conclusion in a case regarding the constitutionality of the 1974 law restricting the amount of money that political parties could spend directly on behalf of candidates. In reversing a previous decision by a circuit court, the Supreme Court held in *FEC v. Colorado Republican Federal Campaign Committee* (1996), that coordinated spending by political parties was not protected by the First Amendment and thus could be constitutionally regulated. Further, a majority of the Court found that there was a compelling government interest in regulating the spending activities of political parties. The Supreme Court upheld Congress's most recent attempt to regulate campaign finance, the 2002 Bipartisan Campaign Reform Act, in *McConnell v. FEC* (2003). As we describe in detail in Chapter 3, the Court allowed Congress to ban soft money and set restrictions on issue advocacy ads placed on television.

The Politics of Statutory Interpretation

When courts act as umpires in the legislative game, they often make judgments about the meaning of statutes. The imprecision of language, inconsistencies among various laws adopted at different times, and evolving circumstances to which a statute must be applied guarantee that the courts will face difficult decisions about the interpretation of laws. Compounding matters is that the legislators and presidents responsible for drafting legislation may have disagreed about the legislation's meaning or even deliberately left certain provisions vague to smooth over differences among themselves that would have been obstacles to enactment. Judges, when asked to resolve disputes about the interpretation of statutes, may affect the direction of public policy and sometimes alter the strategies of legislators, presidents, and others who care about policy.

Judges and legal scholars have developed several approaches to interpreting statutes, each reflecting a different view about how Congress functions, how legislative outcomes are reached, and how capable judges are of understanding congressional intent. The most traditional approach to interpreting statutes relies on the "canons of statutory construction." The canons outline for judges how to interpret the language of laws and are often stated in Latin. For example, one canon – *inclusio unius est exclusio alterius* – means that the inclusion of one thing indicates the exclusion of another. Other canons apply to specific subjects. For example, the "rule of lenity" stipulates that statutes that make certain conduct unlawful and impose penalties must be construed to apply narrowly to the conduct specified.

Unfortunately canons often conflict and there is no canon to help judges choose the appropriate canon. One school of legal scholars advocates that judges determine the objective or purpose of the statute and then deduce the outcome most consistent with the law's purpose. Another school insists that judges should determine how legislators, motivated by the special interests influencing them, would decide a question if asked to do so. Yet others contend that judges should be free to interpret and reinterpret statutes as the societal or legal context changes. Not surprisingly, some scholars argue that judges should refuse to resolve ambiguities and insist that they be resolved in the legislative process.

Perhaps the most important issue in statutory interpretation is being waged over the relevance and content of legislative histories. A few purists argue for strict construction of statutes. Rather than turning to committee reports and floor debates to interpret legislative intent, supporters of this approach urge courts to restrict themselves to the "plain meaning," or intrinsic meaning, of a statute's text. This view seems to be gaining support in the federal judiciary. Its most prominent proponent is Supreme Court Justice Antonin Scalia.

In practice, most judges still gladly accept guidance from committee reports, the record of floor debate, statements of bill or amendment sponsors, presidential messages, and other documented evidence of the intent of a bill's authors. Yet, because legislative histories often encapsulate conflicting views, they are not straightforward guides to statutory interpretation for judges. Further, members of Congress can try to add things to the legislative history to influence the decisions of judges. Most judges seem willing to exercise some judgment about which views should be considered most authoritative. Some effort has been made in recent years to improve communication between the federal judiciary and Congress so that problems of statutory interpretation can be minimized.

In recent years, a majority of justices on the Supreme Court have begun to look more carefully at legislative histories in the context of federalism cases. In striking down major provisions of the Americans with Disabilities Act, the Violence Against Women Act, and the Religious Freedom and Restoration Act, and upholding provisions of the Family and Medical Leave Act, the Court has cited legislative histories extensively in their opinions. The Court in these cases has used the content of legislative histories to determine whether or not Congress has generated a record of mistreatment of individuals by the States. The Court has reasoned that a substantial legislative record is necessary for Congress to abridge states' Eleventh Amendment protection against lawsuits in order to enforce the equal protection clause of the Fourteenth Amendment. This new line of reasoning by the Court has altered the balance of power between Congress and the States, and raised new questions about the quality and content of legislative deliberation, such as what standards of evidence Congress should be held to in demonstrating the need for new laws.

Members, lobbyists, and administrations often anticipate that legislative history may be important when issues are taken to the courts. Sometimes, the language of committee reports is the subject of as intense a fight as the bill language itself. For example, after the House Energy and Commerce Committee voted to approve a major overhaul of clean air laws in 1990, it took nearly a month for committee staff to hammer out report language that was acceptable to all sides. On most matters, carefully prepared statements by committee chairs and bill sponsors are made on the floors of the two chambers to give weight to a particular interpretation of major provisions of legislation and to set a record that judges cannot easily ignore.

Judges as Policy Makers

Although the courts' primary role is to serve as an umpire for disputes about legislative authority and procedure, the relationship between courts and the legislative institutions is more complex than that. In recent decades, federal

---

Congressionally Speaking...

Members frequently attempt to establish a clear record about how certain provisions of a bill should be interpreted. One way of doing this is to discuss the provisions in the *committee report* that accompanies the bill. Committee reports provide the background and justification for the bill and its provisions and often provide detailed sections on the meaning of key words or phrases. They are drafted by committee staffs and approved by committees, sometimes after long debate. Members also engage in *colloquies* – scripted exchanges on the floor among two or more members to clarify the interpretation of a bill or an amendment. Colloquies, of course, are transcribed in the *Congressional Record*, where judges, executive branch officials, and others can find floor statements.

In recent years, presidents have used *signing statements*, issued at the time they sign legislation, to offer their interpretation of controversial provisions. These statements send a message to administrative agencies about the interpretation of the law. Courts have not yet placed much weight on signing statements in their reading of legislative histories. They have tended to place greater weight on *veto statements* when the veto is not overridden by Congress and the legislation is modified in the direction suggested by the president.

---

judges have been seen as policy makers, that is, as players and not just umpires. At times, judges have even moved aggressively to place themselves at the center of political disputes. But in many areas, Congress and the president have encouraged courts' policy-making activities in the legislation they have enacted.

The assertiveness of the Warren Court in the 1950s in addressing racial desegregation marked a considerably more active and aggressive involvement of the courts in national policy making. Although the Burger Court impeded somewhat the extent of judicial involvement in policy making, the Rehnquist Court was the most "activist" ever (see Figure 10.1).

In the 1970s and 1980s, the mix of liberal, conservative, and moderate judges on the Supreme Court further fueled the expansion of court involvement in policy making. Reading statutes broadly and sometimes creatively enabled the two sides to sidestep controversial constitutional issues, which as a by-product expanded court involvement in the creation of national policy. In lower courts, judges often found that they were much less likely to evoke criticism from the Supreme Court if they misread statutes than if they misread the Constitution.

Judicial activism was reinforced by legislative activism on the part of Congress and the president. The wave of legislation between the mid-1960s and mid-1970s created new civil rights, broadened eligibility for welfare and health benefits, established new consumer rights, and set new public health, safety, and environmental standards. Much of the legislation required administrative agencies to design new regulations. Other legislation required agencies to account formally for additional factors in making their decisions. And some new laws were enacted that assigned the executive branch the duty to achieve certain policy goals. At the same time, new and often complex procedures were imposed on agencies by new legislation – the Freedom of Information Act, the Privacy Act, Government in the Sunshine Act, and other legislation. These procedural requirements were designed to open agency decision making to public scrutiny, protect individual rights, and ensure that agency officials heard all interests and views.

Although the role of the courts in the administrative process is, in part, the result of judges' assertiveness, it is much more than that. The creation of new substantive and procedural rights is often the direct product of interest group politics. Interest groups that lack confidence in decisions by regulatory agencies often view litigation as an alternative route for securing favorable policy outcomes. The type of agency decisions that are reviewable by courts, the actions courts may take, the parties who have standing to sue, and other issues are subject to the give-and-take of legislative politics.

The result is that courts are often left to enforce new rights and procedures, determine whether certain factors were given adequate weight in decisions, and evaluate the effectiveness of agency strategies for achieving specified goals. On the procedural side, judicial review sometimes encourages or even requires agencies to elaborate decision-making processes in ways unanticipated by Congress. Political scientist William Gormley[1] notes that

> by stressing the need for due process and by defining due process very broadly indeed, many federal courts have encouraged administrative agencies to adopt cumbersome procedures when handling individual cases, such as welfare or social security cases. A similar development in rule-making review has stimulated the growth of "hybrid ruling-making" procedures, including opportunities to cross-examine witnesses and other procedural guarantees. In practice, hybrid rule-making often benefits special interest groups, who need little additional protection. That is because such groups can afford the legal representation that hybrid rule-making requires.

The courts have often taken the step from procedural matters to the substance of agency decisions. In some cases, the law provides explicitly for the appeal of agency decisions to the courts. For example, the law requiring public schools to provide education for children with disabilities provides appeals to give local groups a chance to challenge federal, state, and local decisions affecting education in their communities. In such cases, courts are called on to judge what constitutes adequate education. In doing so, the courts are asked to direct public policy, even to influence the spending priorities of government.

In other cases, lawsuits pursued by affected parties or interest groups unhappy with agency decisions have led courts to make policy judgments. Gormley explains:

> Citing the "hard look doctrine" popularized by the late Judge Harold Leventhal, [courts] have insisted that agencies take a hard look at the available evidence, engage in reasoned decision-making, and give careful consideration to alternatives. All of this sounds rather innocuous. In practice, however, the hard-look doctrine enables judges to substitute their judgment for that of administrative officials who possess far greater technical expertise.

Thus, by applying judicially derived doctrine for situations in which agencies have been delegated substantial policy-making discretion, the courts sometimes have become policy makers themselves.

The question of why Congress has tended to devolve quasi-legislative powers to agencies and the courts remains. Plainly, institutional politics has become quite complex. Some commentators argue that members of Congress often use the agencies and the courts to avoid difficult choices and political blame. Members, according to this view, often are unable or unwilling to resolve their differences, so they give up and leave legislation ambiguous or include contradictory provisions, a practice which sometimes leaves interested parties no option but to take the matter to court. Other observers note that Congress and the courts have largely been willing allies in the expansion of the federal bench into the legislative arena. Unwilling to trust agency regulators under Republican administrations, Democratic majorities in Congress repeatedly turned to the courts to help put teeth into increasingly complex and detailed legislation in the 1970s and 1980s. Yet other analysts emphasize the influence of interest groups to whom Congress and the president are responding when they approve legislation.

Each of these interpretations seems to fit at least some major legislation. Members of Congress have certainly tried to use the courts when they have lacked the political support to secure policy goals through legislation. As just discussed, failed efforts by members to enforce the War Powers Resolution in the courts show the limits of enticing the courts to resolve political controversies. But Congress's tendency to draw the courts into the policy arena also reflects the cumbersome nature of legislating under divided government. Unable to procure favorable outcomes from regulators, members of Congress and organized groups have deliberately sought the assistance of the courts in battling administrators.

Congressional Resources and Strategies

Congress has formidable tools for dealing with an unfriendly federal judiciary. The framers of the Constitution left several tools for Congress and the president to check the actions of the courts. Lifetime tenure of federal judges is intended to provide some autonomy to the courts, as is the prohibition against reducing the compensation of judges. But neither Congress nor the president has been willing to give a free hand to the federal judiciary. Congress has used its constitutional authority to impeach federal judges, change the number of judges and courts, set the courts' budgets, and alter the appellate jurisdiction of the Supreme Court. Perhaps most familiar to even casual observers of American politics, the president and Congress frequently struggle over appointments to the federal bench.

In addition, Congress has responded legislatively to court decisions. Congress often enacts new legislation that is adapted to court rulings. For example, in 1993 Congress enacted the Religious Freedom and Restoration Act – a direct refutation of the Court's decision in *Oregon v. Smith* (1990), which dealt with religious practice and federal unemployment benefits. When Congress objects to a court's interpretation of a law, Congress sometimes passes a new bill that clarifies its intentions. In some cases, Congress adjusts the new legislation to take into account a court's ruling about the constitutionality of certain kinds of provisions. In recent years, several bills have been introduced in Congress to remove federal court jurisdiction from certain policy areas. And, of course, Congress may propose a constitutional amendment to overrule the courts' interpretation of an existing provision.

Congress and the Structure of the Federal Judiciary

The Constitution vests judicial power in the Supreme Court but grants to Congress the authority to establish inferior courts when it chooses. The size, budget, and appellate jurisdiction of the Supreme Court, as well as the structure, size, budget, and jurisdiction of lower courts, are determined by law and are therefore subject to the normal legislative process. In addition,

Congress is authorized by the Constitution to create what are known as Article I courts, or legislative courts – the military courts, tax court, customs courts, and bankruptcy courts. These courts are located in either the executive or judicial branches, the judges are appointed by the president with Senate confirmation, and the judges serve fixed, limited terms.

Partisan politics has been an ever-present condition in Congress's handling of the judiciary. The first major effort to structure the courts for political purposes occurred in 1801, when the defeated president John Adams and his Federalist supporters in Congress created new circuit court judgeships to be filled with Federalists. The effort to influence the character of the federal bench failed, however, when the new Republican Congress repealed the act and abolished the judgeships. Even though Congress postponed the next meeting of the Supreme Court to prevent it from hearing a challenge to its repeal, the Court upheld Congress's power to repeal the Federalists' Judiciary Act of 1801 a year later.

Congress has only once limited the jurisdiction of the Supreme Court. In 1868, striking down parts of Reconstruction legislation in 1866, the court was scheduled to hear another case on Reconstruction law – the Habeas Corpus Act, which concerned the rights of individuals held in detention. Anticipating that the Court would use the occasion to find all Reconstruction laws unconstitutional, Congress enacted a law to prevent the Court from hearing cases related to the Habeas Corpus Act. The Supreme Court, incidentally, backed down from any confrontation with Congress when it upheld the constitutionality of the repeal of its jurisdiction a year later.

With the exception of the Reconstruction-era episode, efforts to curb the Supreme Court's jurisdiction have failed. This result is not too surprising. After all, the House, Senate, and president, or two-thirds of both houses of Congress, must agree to legislation curbing Court jurisdiction before it is enacted. Nevertheless, members of Congress continue to introduce bills that would restrict the jurisdiction of the Supreme Court or all federal courts. Between 1975 and 2002, according to one count, 132 bills were introduced to limit the federal judiciary's jurisdiction in some way. While none of these efforts were successful, and none have been since then, many members see them as an opportunity to demonstrate to judges that Congress can limit jurisdiction, and these efforts are often popular with constituents.

Congress also has had a mixed record in efforts to control the Supreme Court by changing its size. In the nineteenth century, Congress used its power over the size of the Court several times to exert pressure on the Court and to help change its ideological shape. Although Presidents James Madison, James Monroe, and John Quincy Adams each claimed that a growing nation needed a larger Supreme Court (that started with just six members), Congress did not change the Court's size until 1837. Even then, it postponed the change to nine members until the last day of President Andrew Jackson's term that year. Later, by increasing the size of the Court to ten justices, Congress gave President Abraham Lincoln an opportunity to solidify a pro-Union majority on the Court. Soon thereafter, Congress reduced the number of justices from ten to eight to prevent President Andrew Johnson from filling any vacancies. When Johnson's successor, Ulysses S. Grant, took office, Congress changed the number of justices to nine, where it has remained.

The best-known attempt to influence Supreme Court decisions by altering its size was the "court-packing" plan of President Franklin Roosevelt. Roosevelt, disturbed by rulings that struck down important parts of his New Deal legislation, proposed in 1937 that the Supreme Court be expanded from nine to 15 justices so that he could appoint new justices and change the balance of opinion. Congressional resistance, as well as a series of Supreme Court decisions more favorable to Roosevelt's New Deal legislation, led Roosevelt to drop his plan. But the uproar over the Roosevelt plan has had a chilling effect on other presidents and Congresses that might have pushed legislation to alter the size of the Court for political purposes.

The Senate and Judicial Nominations

The shared power of appointment remains the primary means by which senators and presidents influence federal courts. Needless to say, the president and the Senate do not always agree on what course federal courts ought to take. Historically, this battle was largely fought over presidential nominations to the Supreme Court, with the nominations of Judge Robert H. Bork in 1987 and Judge Clarence Thomas in 1991 standing out as particularly controversial. As we explore in the following section, recent years have seen the controversies extend to appointments to the lower courts.

LOWER COURT NOMINATIONS. Senators of a president's party typically have had a great deal of influence over the president's appointments to federal district courts and the courts of appeal. These senators usually play an active role in the nominating process by suggesting acceptable candidates to the administration. But only a few senators usually play an active role in Senate deliberations considering judicial appointments at the district level. Unlike nominations to the Supreme Court, and more recently circuit courts, which elicit much broader interest, district court seats generally draw fairly localized interest from the Senate body. In most cases, the Senate's Judiciary Committee staff studies lower-court nominees, receives reports from the American Bar Association and the Federal Bureau of Investigation, and routinely recommends approval to the full Senate, which confirms the nominees with little or no discussion.

The record of judicial appointments during the Reagan and G. H. W. Bush presidencies continued the pattern of routine approval for most nominees, but with the addition of a few very controversial cases. During the course of the Reagan and G. H. W. Bush presidencies, more than 460 appointments were made to appeals and district courts, meaning that by the end of the Bush administration, more than 70 percent of sitting federal judges had been appointed during the Reagan and Bush years. These appointments have produced a much more conservative federal bench. Although the Democrats controlled the Senate for more than half the period, they largely acquiesced to presidential preferences for more conservative, younger, white federal judges. Not until the few months before the 1992 presidential election did Senator Joseph Biden (D-Delaware) and the Judiciary Committee take a more aggressive stance against the administration's nominees, apparently emboldened by the possibility that Democrat Bill Clinton would win the presidency. After suggesting that he would be more selective about which Bush nominees would receive hearings before the election, Biden and the Judiciary Committee slowed down the pace of confirmation hearings for appellate court appointments.

When Bill Clinton assumed the presidency, he had 99 seats on the federal bench to fill – seats that observers expected would be filled by a greater proportion of minorities and women than were those filled by Bush and Reagan. With a Democratic majority in the Senate during his first two years in office, Clinton was successful in getting rapid confirmations. But after the Republicans took majority control of the Senate in 1995, the speed of Senate confirmations declined markedly. In 1998, Chief Justice William Rehnquist complained about the slow pace, noting that 101 judicial nominees had been confirmed in 1994 but only 17 were confirmed in 1996 and 36 in 1997.

Many vacancies had gone unfilled for more than 18 months, with some going up to four years between nomination and confirmation. Senate Judiciary Committee Chairman Orrin Hatch (R-Utah) insisted that the Republican Senate had been just as responsive as the Democrats had been for President G. H. W. Bush, and the battle continued into the administration of G. W. Bush. In all, the confirmation rate for lower court judges has declined somewhat in the past two decades amidst increasing partisan polarization, yet remains quite high. Some variation has occurred in the

THE CHANGING CONGRESS: "REVERSE FILIBUSTER" HIGHLIGHTS INCREASED PARTISANSHIP ON JUDICIAL NOMINEES

Lacking a majority on the Senate Judiciary Committee, Senate Democrats in 2003 refused to allow a floor vote on some of President G. W. Bush's lower court nominees. Senate Republicans, who had the slimmest of majorities in the 108th Senate (51), were short of the 60 votes needed to invoke cloture, or end debate, on these nominees. Although they pursued several options to change Senate rules regarding filibusters on judicial nominees, Senate Republicans remained frustrated by their inability to gain up or down votes on some judicial nominations. In an attempt to raise public awareness of the impasse on these nominations, in November 2003 Senate Republicans staged a 39-hour continuous debate seeking to highlight Democratic obstruction. The marathon debate, labeled a "reverse filibuster" by its organizers, was ironic in that it used extended debate to highlight real or threatened obstruction by some members of the Democratic Party. Senate Republican leaders hoped that the event would attract enough publicity to increase public pressure on Senate Democrats to agree to vote on the stalled nominees and would increase public support for their efforts to reform the filibuster rule.

Instead, the event turned into political theatre, with lots of melodrama, but nothing of substance was accomplished. Republicans labeled the session a "Justice for Judges" marathon, complete with T-shirts and signs bearing the slogan, while Democrats countered with a large sign emblazoned "168–4"– representing the number of Bush's judges confirmed (168) and the number blocked (4). Cots were set up for tired senators, beer was provided for the reporters covering the event, Democrat Tom Harkin posted a sign reading, "I'll Be Home Watching 'The Bachelor'," and a filibuster bingo game was unveiled. At the end of the marathon session, it did not appear that much had changed; none of the judges in question received a vote in the Senate, and there was no noticeable public outcry. In fact, one of the police officers standing guard outside the Senate summed up the likely opinion of most of the public, stating: "I could see if it was something important like the budget or Iraq, but who cares about judicial appointments?"

confirmation rate for district court nominees, however there has been a more appreciable decline in circuit court confirmations. The confirmation rate for district court nominees has generally centered around 90 percent among recent presidents, with G. W. Bush having the lowest rate of approximately 79 percent. On the other hand, there has been a reasonably consistent drop in the circuit court confirmation rate over this period. The Carter administration enjoyed an approximately 92 percent confirmation rate for circuit court nominees, which fell to 71 and 73 percent for the Clinton and G. W. Bush administrations respectively.

Congressionally Speaking...

Senatorial courtesy is the practice of conferring with senators of the president's party whenever a vacancy in a position subject to presidential appointment is located within the senators' state. The practice applies to vacancies in federal district courts. For many years, senators could exercise a virtual veto over appointments affecting their states. The practice rests on the willingness of the Senate and its Judiciary Committee to refuse to act on nominees opposed by those senators. It gives senators a form of patronage with which to reward political friends.

Senatorial courtesy is institutionalized through the use of *blue slips* – blue sheets of paper sent out by the Judiciary Committee asking senators from a nominee's home state his or her opinion of the nominee. A home state senator who objects to a nominee will often write on the blue slip that the nominee is "personally offensive." This practice has existed since the early 1910s, with negative blue slips usually meaning that the Judiciary Committee will not act on a nominee. Although not always the case today, a negative blue slip usually makes confirmation of the nominee extremely difficult.

The influence of partisanship in appointment to the lower courts is clear. More than 90 percent of nominees to the lower courts are affiliated with the party of the president nominating them. Moreover, lower-court nominees in the fourth year of a four-year presidential term are much less likely to be confirmed than are nominees sent to the Senate in other years, and the confirmation process typically takes much longer when the Senate and presidency are controlled by different parties. At the end of a president's term, senators of the opposition party often prefer to leave judgeships vacant until they see which party wins the presidency. If their party wins the presidency, the new president can submit new names – presumably more to their liking.

SUPREME COURT NOMINATIONS. As the Miers/Alito spectacle described in the introduction points out, Supreme Court nominations are not routine. Unlike the appointment process for district court seats, presidential nominations to the Supreme Court garner a much broader spectrum of interest across the Senate. In fact, lower court nominees are often screened more carefully if they are thought to be potential Supreme Court nominees. After a president makes a nomination, the Senate Judiciary Committee has the nominee complete a lengthy questionnaire, orders its staff to conduct an extensive background investigation on the nominee, receives an evaluation from the American Bar Association, and then holds several days of hearings. Recently interest groups have actively lobbied senators and generated publicity for the groups' views. The administration, which sometimes discusses a list of possible nominees with senators in advance of the nomination, coaches the nominee in preparation for the hearings.

The outcomes of Supreme Court confirmation efforts hinge on numerous factors. First, the partisan makeup of the Senate matters. When the president's party has been in the majority, close to 90 percent of nominees have been confirmed. In contrast, during times of divided government, only 59 percent of nominees have been approved by the Senate. Second, the timing of the nomination also has implications. Not only does partisanship in Congress tend to increase in election years, but the president's influence in the legislative arena usually declines during the course of his term in office. Presidents also appear to be more successful when they make public statements on behalf of their nominees. Overall weakness of a president clearly affects his ability to get a nominee approved by the Senate. Reagan nominated Robert Bork in 1987 after the revelations of the Iran-Contra scandal had significantly weakened the president's standing in Congress and public approval. Bork was turned down by the Senate.

Timing is important from other perspectives as well. Many argue that senators up for reelection give greater weight to public opinion than do senators who do not face reelection in the near future. But most senators appear to take into account the qualifications and ideological outlook of nominees. The greater distance the nominee's positions are from the senator and the less qualified the nominee is, the lower the probability of the senator voting in favor of the president's choice. The appearance of one or more of these factors – partisan balance, presidential popularity, proximity to the end of the presidential term, ideological placement, or nominee qualifications – increases the likelihood of conflict in the Senate during the confirmation process. On many confirmation votes, individual senators are also likely to be influenced by constituency concerns. In the case of Thurgood Marshall and Clarence Thomas's nominations to the Court, state racial composition had a determinative effect on votes by senators representing states with large African American populations.

The Senate has failed to confirm only 26, or about 20 percent, of presidents' nominations to the Supreme Court. Twentieth-century presidents have had better luck than their predecessors, but even recent presidents have stumbled. President Lyndon Johnson was forced to withdraw two nominations, two nominees of President Richard Nixon were rejected, President Reagan withdrew one nomination and one nominee was rejected, and both Presidents G. H. W. and G. W. Bush withdrew one name. Two nominations deserve special mention: President Reagan's nomination of Robert Bork, which was rejected by the Senate, and President G. H. W. Bush's nomination of Clarence Thomas, which was approved by a narrow margin, 52 to 48.

In 1987, President Reagan faced a Democratic Senate when he nominated Judge Bork, then a judge on the U.S. Court of Appeals for the District of Columbia and a former solicitor general and law school professor. Bork's longstanding and well-published opposition to affirmative action and the established ruling on abortion, along with his judicial activism, stimulated an extraordinary and influential effort by civil rights groups and others to prevent his confirmation by the Senate. Interest in his nomination stimulated unprecedented scrutiny by the media – the media even reported Bork's videotape rentals. The Senate voted 58 to 42 against his confirmation.

Four years later, President Bush nominated Clarence Thomas, also a sitting judge on the U.S. Court of Appeals for the District of Columbia, and a former chair of the Equal Employment Opportunity Commission (EEOC). Thomas had relatively little judicial experience: He had been on the appeals court for only 18 months and had never argued a case before a court. The American Bar Association's review committee rated him "qualified" on their three-point scale (highly qualified, qualified, and not qualified), with two members of the committee voting "not qualified," making Thomas the only Supreme Court nominee rated by the Bar Association to receive such a weak evaluation. Thomas had a record of commitment to conservative views on many issues, leading liberal groups to mobilize against him and drawing tough questions from the liberal Democrats on the Judiciary Committee.

Nevertheless, Thomas's confirmation seemed likely until the eve of the scheduled vote by the full Senate. National Public Radio reported that a complaint of sexual misconduct against Thomas had been disclosed to Judiciary Committee staff and noted in an FBI report, although it had not been mentioned in the initial committee hearings. The committee reopened the hearings to listen to the testimony of Anita Hill, a University of Oklahoma law professor who had worked for Thomas at the EEOC. At the hearings, she repeated her charges against Thomas. He responded, and the committee heard character witnesses for both Thomas and Hill, all before a very large national television audience.

After Thomas was confirmed by the full Senate by a vote of 52–48, the committee and the Senate were criticized for the manner in which they had conducted the hearings. Senator Arlen Specter ran into difficulty in his 1992 reelection bid because of the way he had grilled Professor Hill. In response to the criticism, Senator Biden announced changes in Judiciary Committee practice guaranteeing that all information received by a committee and its staff would be placed in the nominee's FBI file to ensure all senators access to FBI reports and provide for closed briefings for all senators so that any charges against nominees, if there were any, could be reviewed. And, in a conspicuous move to make sure that any sexism on the committee would be held in check, two women – Senators Dianne Feinstein (D-California) and Carol Moseley-Braun (D-Illinois) – were appointed to the committee in 1993.

Congress and the Impeachment of Judges

Under the Constitution, judges "shall hold their offices during good behaviour," but the House is empowered to bring and vote on impeachment charges against judges. If a judge is impeached by the House, the Senate conducts a trial on the charges. A two-thirds vote of the senators present is required to convict and remove a judge – the same number required for removing a president from office. Removal of a judge by House impeachment and Senate conviction is rare. Over the course of the history of the federal bench, no Supreme Court justice has been removed from office by Congress. In 1804, Republicans tried to impeach justice Samuel Chase on several charges, but they failed to get a two-thirds vote to convict. Thirteen lower federal judges have been impeached by the House, and only seven have been convicted by the Senate. Of the seven judicial convictions, three have occurred since 1986.

Congress's impeachment power has not proven to be a source of leverage over the courts. Even the threat of impeachment has only once been credited with inducing a change in Supreme Court membership: Justice Abe Fortas resigned in 1969 after revelations of questionable financial practices. Impeachment trials do pose certain challenges for a Senate already having trouble managing its time and discharging its duties. Any trial procedure involving the full Senate inevitably distracts the Senate from its legislative agenda. To address this problem, the Senate moved in 1986 to form a special 12-member committee to gather and review evidence on behalf of the full Senate.

Legislative Responses to the Courts

Interaction between Congress and the courts does not necessarily end with judicial action. Congress can, of course, use its traditional legislative powers to respond to court decisions. For example, after the Supreme Court decided in 1988 that burning the U.S. flag in protest of government policy should be afforded First Amendment protection as a form of political speech,

Congress eventually enacted a statute designed to strip flag burning of its constitutional protection. In another case, Congress overrode a presidential veto to reverse a Supreme Court decision concerning sex discrimination in colleges and universities.

But successful reversals of unpopular Supreme Court decisions are not automatic. On some occasions, efforts to reverse decisions pass one chamber and get stalled in the other. Other efforts often get stymied at the committee level, after hearings are held on possible legislation to reverse the decision.

Studies show that Congress responds to about one-third of these Supreme Court moves to nullify a federal law. Why? The three-institution legislative game makes a response to the Court difficult. All three institutions must agree, or at least two-thirds of both chambers must agree, to any legislative response. If the committees with jurisdiction over the affected legislation recognize that gaining the approval of the House, Senate, and president is impossible, they may choose to take no action. Nevertheless, Congress sometimes does respond to court decisions. Several factors appear to motivate congressional efforts to respond to court decisions. One study emphasizes the important role of public opinion in motivating Congress to act. If the majority of public opinion is in favor of action by Congress, the probability of a congressional response increases dramatically. Salience of the issue to organized interest groups, sometimes indicated by the participation of groups in the case before the Supreme Court, also appears to influence congressional decisions to respond. In many cases, however, members seem to have been motivated to take preliminary steps to respond to demands, but they did not push the legislation to the point of passage.

Not surprisingly, Congress is also more likely to respond to Supreme Court decisions when invited to do so by judges on the bench. On occasion, the Court rules that although particular provisions are unconstitutional, Congress could remedy the problem by rewriting the provision. In effect, the Supreme Court outlines the boundaries of what changes would be considered constitutional. Such guidance by the courts markedly increases the chances that Congress will undertake efforts to respond to or reverse the nullifying decision. Judicial invitations to review give a different cast to relations between Congress and the courts. Far from the conflict that many normally assume exists when the Court overturns a federal law, these invitations to reverse reflect a more cooperative relationship between the branches.

Amending the Constitution

A frequent response of members to court decisions is to propose a constitutional amendment. Since the Supreme Court's decision in *Roe v. Wade*

(1973), for example, many members have supported a constitutional amendment that would reserve to the states the power to regulate abortions. The constitutional requirement that an amendment receive the support of two-thirds of both chambers before it is sent to the states for ratification sets a high threshold that has seldom been met. Only four amendments to the Constitution were adopted in direct response to Supreme Court decisions: the Eleventh Amendment, on the ability of citizens of one state to bring suit against another state; the Fourteenth Amendment, on the application of the first 10 amendments to the states; the Sixteenth Amendment, on the federal income tax; and the Twenty-sixth Amendment, on the right of 18-year-olds to vote.

Conclusion

The courts occupy a critical, but often overlooked, place in forming national policy. The roles played by the courts vary widely – from separation-of-powers umpire to congressional overseer and partner in policy making.

Relationships between the branches clearly depend on the rules of the game. But those rules, as we have seen, are themselves often the product of political battles. The rules of the policy-making process can be ambiguous, and this ambiguity gives the courts an opening into the legislative game. As a result, members of Congress have an incentive to watch over the actions of courts carefully and, on occasion, to enlist judges in their campaigns against a recalcitrant executive branch.

Judges, however, are not always willing to take the bait. Sometimes, the courts smell a political contest and send the dispute back to congressional players to resolve themselves. Other times, judges simply define respective powers of each contending actor and set boundaries for future interactions between the players. Although Congress and the president can shape the membership of the bench, other congressional tools rarely give members enough leverage over the courts to limit judicial independence and discretion. When the courts have chosen to enter the policy process, however, major changes in policy making have often occurred. Whether expanding procedural rights of individuals or forcing executive agencies to work more assiduously to follow congressional intent, federal courts in recent decades have made inroads into the legislative arena. Attention to the interactions of judges, legislators, and executives thus markedly affects our understanding of how separate branches are indeed sharing power to shape national policy.

Above: Senator Roger Wicker (R-Mississippi), right, walks with lobbyists on his way from a meeting to the Senate floor for a vote.
Below: Former-Senator Ted Stevens (R-Alaska) departs the Senate floor for the last time after being convicted on seven counts of corruption relating to false statements he made on Senate ethics forms to cover up hundreds of thousands of dollars he received in gifts. Stevens was defeated by Mark Begich, the former-mayor of Anchorage, in his bid for an eighth term.

11

Congress, Lobbyists, and Interest Groups

THE FIRST AMENDMENT TO THE CONSTITUTION PROVIDES THAT CONGRESS may make no law abridging the right of the people to petition the government for a redress of grievances. Court rulings interpret the Amendment broadly to include organized and paid representatives of the people, therefore limiting Congress's ability to regulate lobbying. In practice, interest groups and their lobbyists are a very important means by which the public conveys their expectations and demands to Congress. Nevertheless, Americans believe that members of Congress are beholden to special interests and lobbyists. A 2008 survey conducted by the Center on Congress at Indiana University found that 71 percent of Americans gave Congress a grade of D or F when asked to assess Congress's representation of the American people; over 76 percent of those surveyed gave Congress a D or F on its ability to control the influence of special interests.[1] A 2006 CBS/*New York Times* survey found that 75 percent of Americans agreed that most members of Congress are more interested in serving special interest groups than the people they represent.[2]

These contrasting views – that lobbyists are essential to democracy and yet reviled by the public – give interest groups and lobbyists an uneasy place in congressional politics. In earlier chapters, we have noted that representation of organized interests is a rapidly growing industry in Washington. In this chapter, we reemphasize this theme, discuss the evolving strategies of interest groups, and review the limited efforts of Congress to regulate lobbying. Congress, in accordance with the Constitution, has been able to put in place only minimal regulations on lobbying. As an alternative, Congress has placed more severe restrictions on legislators, as it is allowed to do, with respect to their relations with organized interests. Restrictions on campaign contributions from organized interests were detailed in Chapter 3. In this chapter, we concentrate on developments in the legislative strategies of groups and lobbyists.

The Expanding Community of Lobbyists and Interest Groups

Lobbyists have been present since the first congresses. The wide reach of federal policy and Congress's central role in shaping it motivates many citizens, organized groups, and lobbyists to converge on Washington (see box "Congressionally Speaking..."). Congress's internal decision-making processes are largely responsible for this. Reliance on committees and subcommittees for writing the details of most legislation gives outsiders many points of contact with legislators and staff. Even congressional parties are quite permeable. Many legislators influence party strategies through their participation in party caucuses, committees, and task forces. If legislators can be influenced, so too can party strategies. The vast institutional partitioning of Congress (i.e., bicameralism, parties, committees, subcommittees, etc.) gives lobbyists more opportunities for influence than they find in most other national legislatures. The more complex the legislative process and the more places that interests can be protected, the more valuable the experienced lobbyist is to the average citizen.

Generalizing about lobbyists is difficult. Some lobbyists are officials of organized interest groups such as the U.S. Chamber of Commerce, the Sierra Club, and the National Cable Television Association. Other lobbyists are lawyers, former members or staff of Congress, or public relations specialists who have their own lobbying firms that are hired by interest groups, corporations, or other organizations to represent their interests, sometimes on a specific bill or issue. Many lobbyists work for universities and colleges, state and local governments, and even foreign governments that seek to influence federal policy. Frequently, lobbyists are citizens who have made the trip to Washington to make their case in person. As discussed later in this chapter, important legal distinctions are made between those hired to lobby for a person or organization and concerned citizens that lobby on their own behalf.

Most interest groups represent occupational or organizational communities. Occupational groups include organizations representing doctors, teachers, accountants, and even association executives. Government employees have many specialized interest groups – the American Association of State Highway and Transportation Officials, for example. Many, perhaps most, interest groups are associations comprised of organizations. Most trade associations, such as the American Petroleum Institute, the Association of American Railroads, and the National Association of Wholesaler-Distributors, represent corporations in a particular sector of the economy. But associations representing member unions, universities, local governments, and other organizations are important as well. The Association of American Universities and the National League of Cities are prominent examples.

Congressionally Speaking . . .

Lobbyist is a term that referred originally to reporters waiting in the lobby of the British House of Commons to speak to members of Parliament. In the mid-nineteenth century, the term came to be used for people seeking to influence legislators and soon gained quite negative connotations because of the money and other resources with which lobbyists plied legislators.

Today, a lobbyist has a more technical meaning in federal law – someone who is paid to communicate with Congress on behalf of others. And lobbyists now see themselves as specialized professionals. They even have their own professional association, the American League of Lobbyists.

Citizens' groups compose about 20 percent of the interest group community. Their members generally are individuals rather than representatives of organizations or institutions. Political scientist Jack Walker observed that these groups usually arise in the wake of broad social movements concerned with such problems as the level of environmental pollution, threats to civil rights, or changes in the status of women. Citizens' groups include Citizens for Tax Justice, Common Cause, the National Association for the Advancement of Colored People, the National Organization for Women, and Ralph Nader's Public Citizen.

Citizens' groups often are created by political entrepreneurs operating with the support of wealthy individuals, private foundations, or elected political leaders who act as their protectors, financial supporters, and patrons. It is common to see a few individuals bearing much of the cost of group formation. Such an arrangement is often essential to overcoming the numerous obstacles associated with collective action.

The greatest dilemma that interest groups encounter in the formation process is that of free riders – individuals who consume the benefits of a public good without paying a fair share of the costs of its production. All groups seek to attract members by appealing to a sense of obligation to support a cause, but often that is not enough to attract and retain members. Some groups overcome this problem by offering selective benefits restricted to those who contribute. For example, members of the AARP (formerly the American Association of Retired Persons but now using just the initials) receive a variety of benefits including discounts on airfare, car rentals, hotels, and cruises, as well as reasonably priced legal services and health care. Others offer special events, club memberships, or other social benefits to attract members.

The size of the lobbying and interest group community has expanded tremendously in recent decades. The *Encyclopedia of Associations* listed more than 22,500 organizations in 2008, which marks a more than 50 percent increase in the number of interest groups since 1980 and an almost 400 percent increase since 1955. The most rapid documented growth in interest groups occurred between the 1960s and 1980s, during which many federal programs were created and expanded. During this period, the interest group community became significantly more diverse as well. Along with the rapid expansion and diversification of the interest group community came a proliferation of organizations settling in Washington. A 1982 survey of 2,800 organizations that had lobbying offices in Washington found that 40 percent had been created since 1960 and an additional 25 percent since 1970.[3] One analyst found that the number of Washington offices for trade associations – the National Association of Manufacturers and the National Independent Retail Jewelers, for example – nearly tripled from about 1,200 in 1960 to 3,500 in 1986. Even greater proportionate growth in the number of corporations with offices in Washington occurred in the same period.[4]

Since the 1990s, the size of the interest group community has remained relatively stable. Nevertheless, the number of groups with Washington representation continues to grow, which points to the significance of lobbying in modern-day politics. Today, nearly 5,000 organizations have some kind of representation in Washington. In 2009, the privately published directory *Washington Representatives* listed more than 18,000 "persons working to influence government policies and actions" – a number that has more than quadrupled since the early 1970s. Even with these soaring numbers, it appears that there is no shortage of demand for their services. Between 2000 and 2005, by one account, D.C. lobbyists increased their fees to new clients by as much as 100 percent.[5]

Many factors have contributed to the proliferation of the interest group community and lobbying activity. Among the most important factors is the rapid social and economic change characteristic of recent decades. The expanding role of federal programs and regulation motivated individuals, firms, and local governments to organize and lobby. A series of social movements, such as civil rights, women's rights, environmental protection, and consumer rights, swept the country, redefined the nation's policy agenda, and spawned lasting interest groups. And organization spurred counter-organization. For example, Planned Parenthood was challenged by the National Right to Life Committee. The consequence of organization and counter-organization was the proliferation of strongly issue-oriented citizens' groups and greater diversity in the kinds of groups found in Washington.

While citizens' groups have changed the contours of Washington lobbying, the interest group community remains dominated, at least numerically, by business groups. By one estimate, 70 percent of organized interests in

Washington are business groups. Nevertheless, the growth of citizens' group does mean that business interests are more likely to be challenged and challenged successfully.

An enlarged middle class and technological advances also contributed to the growth of the Washington interest group community. The middle class has become an important base of support for occupational and citizens' groups that depend on membership dues and other contributions for financial support. Technological advances in communications and computer-generated mailings have facilitated the growth of groups that require support from the general public. Also, advances in communication and transportation have made it more convenient and affordable for groups to headquarter in Washington, far from concentrations of their members.

Finally, the federal government is responsible for directly stimulating the creation of some groups and underwriting their costs of operations. Much of the domestic legislation of the 1960s and 1970s required some kind of citizen participation in executive agency rule making or provided for the creation of community-based groups. Many interest groups representing citizen, environmental action groups, and legal and health care organizations for the poor were stimulated by these public policies. Indeed, the activists running many of the new social programs vigorously promoted the creation of new organizations to represent their clients' interests. In other cases, federal agencies encouraged the formation of groups to facilitate communication between the agencies and the sector they served and to build a base of support for their own programs and budgets. Additionally, as federal domestic programs expanded, many more citizens' groups received grants or contracts from the federal government to conduct studies or perform services for executive agencies.

The enlarged community of lobbyists and interest groups has altered the political environment of members of Congress in important ways. The most obvious effect is that the expanded lobbying community has increased the diversity and intensity of demands placed on members of Congress. Issues of even modest importance are more likely to generate conflict among groups, and no one group is as likely to dominate policy making as was often the case at mid-twentieth century. There is now greater uncertainty about the mix of organized interests that will seek to influence congressional action and hold members accountable for their individual actions.

Developments in Interest Group Strategies

Influencing Congress involves much more than gaining the votes of individual members. Lobbyists work hard to find legislators who are willing to

...RS AS LOBBYISTS

...ong organized interest groups is to hire the relatives of key
...bers and their top aides as lobbyists on a variety of issues.
...ified 63 sitting members of Congress with relatives who had
...ed on government relations at the federal or the state level in
...number is likely a conservative estimate, considering that it fails
...for relatives of members who are corporate or nonprofit board members
or political consultants. Some estimates from political insiders put the number of
members with relatives in the lobbying community closer to 100.

At least a portion of these cases can be attributed to the fact that members are increasingly entering the lobbying profession following public service, and some of these members are being succeeded in office by a relative. In addition, some members meet their spouses, who are already lobbyists, through political circles. However, a substantial number of these cases result from lobbying firms actively pursuing the relatives of sitting members. Relatives, after all, have certain inside advantages, such as access, that can substitute for experience working on the Hill. GOP attorney, Randy Evans, commented, "It's about access, but equally important is the degree to which folks know each other. That can be a product of time: You can have been around 10 Congresses and gotten to know enough members to make a difference, or you can just have grown up in Congress and gotten to know it that way."

The obvious concern with such an arrangement is the possibility that relatives will have undue influence over legislative outcomes, and there is some evidence to suggest that this is a legitimate concern. For instance, a 2005 study of the 94 members of the House and Senate appropriations committees and their 250 top staffers found that spending bills reflected the lobbying efforts of family members. Specifically, the study found 30 instances in which a relative lobbied for money in an appropriations bill that his or her family member or family member's boss helped write. In 22 of these cases, the relative was successful in obtaining funds – a total of roughly $750 million in projects.

To curb the influence family members can have on legislative outcomes, the Honest Leadership and Open Government Act of 2007 placed greater restrictions on the interaction that can take place between a member's office and relatives of that member who are registered as lobbyists. The Senate rules were changed to prohibit all staff from having any official contact with the member's spouse or immediate family if the relative is a registered lobbyist. Moreover, Senate rules prohibit staff from officially contacting the spouse of any Senator who is a lobbyist. An exception is granted to the spouse of a Senator who served as a registered lobbyist at least one year prior to the member's election or at least one year prior to marrying the member. House rules changes were less extensive, and only require a member to instruct his or her staff to refrain from official contact with that member's spouse if the spouse is a registered lobbyist. While these rules changes do, indeed, limit the influence that family members can have in their capacity as lobbyists, critics of the legislation claim that loopholes prevent the rules changes from being truly effective.

Source: Based on information from Matt Kelley and Peter Eisler, "Relatives Have 'Inside Track' in Lobbying for Tax Dollars," *USA Today*, October 17, 2006; Marisa Katz, "Family Ties," *National Journal Magazine*, March 31, 2007.

champion their causes. Lobbyists need members to introduce their proposals as legislation, to offer amendments in committee and on the floor, and to help them get issues on, or keep issues off, the agendas of committees and subcommittees.

Moreover, lobbyists spend more time gathering, digesting, and reporting information to their clients than they do trying to influence Congress. They help their clients anticipate and track legislative developments that are difficult for people not experienced in congressional politics to follow. Because congressional politics and federal policy are so much more complex and important than they were a few decades ago, corporations and other organizations need the assistance of experienced insiders to observe and interpret congressional activity that might affect their interests. A good lobbyist seeks to develop access to well-placed members and staff on Capitol Hill to meet the demands of his or her clients for information.

Lobbyists employ a wide range of techniques, which have evolved as lobbyists have adapted to changes in technology, society, and Congress. The empowerment of House subcommittees in the 1970s, the greater individualism in the membership, and expansion of congressional staffs since the mid-twentieth century have forced lobbyists to develop relationships with more members and staff and follow the activity of more committees and subcommittees. At the same time, developments in electronic communications and computers have enabled lobbyists and interest groups to reach people throughout the country with ease.

These developments have stimulated important changes in the way lobbyists do their work. Many observers of Washington politics have noted the change from inside lobbying, or face-to-face efforts to influence a few important legislators, to outside strategies, or public relations efforts to generate public support for special interest causes. Perhaps more accurately, outside strategies have supplemented the old-style inside strategies that once dominated Washington lobbying.

Inside Lobbying

The more traditional form of lobbying – inside lobbying – involves personal contact between a lobbyist and members of Congress. Successful lobbyists use access to important decision makers, a network of contacts, mastery of the process, policy expertise, Washington experience, and money to develop strong ties to legislators and their staffs. Their success often depends on their being able to phone a prominent member of Congress, get the call returned promptly, and gather critical intelligence about when an issue will be raised or which member is wavering on an important provision. An aide to a former House Speaker characterized the work of the inside lobbyist this way:

> They know members of Congress are here three nights a week, alone, without their families. So they say, "Let's have dinner. Let's go see a ballgame." Shmooze with them. Make friends. And they don't lean on it all the time. Every once in a while, they call up – maybe once or twice a year – ask a few questions. Call you up and say, "Say, what's Danny [Rostenkowski, chair of the House Ways and Means Committee] going to do on this tax-reform bill?" Anne Wexler [a former official in the Carter White House, and now a lobbyist] will call up and spend half an hour talking about left-wing politics, and suddenly she'll pop a question, pick up something. They want that little bit of access. That's what does it. You can hear it. It clicks home. They'll call their chief executive officer, and they've delivered. That's how it works. It's not illegal. They work on a personal basis.[6]

Career Washingtonians – former members, former executive branch officials, and even some family members of prominent public officials who have developed personal friendships with members and their staffs – are greatly advantaged in direct lobbying. Former members are particularly advantaged because they retain special privileges of access on Capitol Hill – access to the House and Senate floors, gyms, and dining rooms. They also benefit from the political and policy expertise gained from service in Congress, a certain visibility in Washington and in the country, and their established contacts with people and organizations with money. In 2006, the Center for Responsive Politics identified 155 registered lobbyists as former members of Congress.

Former congressional staff aides and federal employees share many of the advantages and knowledge enjoyed by former members, so they also make ideal lobbyists. In 2008, for instance, more than one-third of the top congressional staffers who left their positions that year went on to work for lobbying firms or other groups seeking to influence the government.[7] Because staff aides and federal employees develop contacts and skills that make them attractive to law firms, corporations, and lobbying firms, many individuals enter jobs on the Hill with the intent of going to these other more lucrative positions (see box, "Limits on Lobbying after Leaving Capitol Hill").

Beyond personal relations, money and information are essential ingredients of successful inside strategies. Money, of course, can be used as an outright bribe, though it seldom is any longer. But money has been a vital asset to gaining access to legislators. In recent years, money has allowed lobbyists to arrange for members to take trips to exclusive resorts to attend conferences or charity functions that are also attended by lobbyists and corporate leaders, to host outings to golf courses, ball games, and

LIMITS ON LOBBYING AFTER LEAVING CAPITOL HILL

The exchange of personnel between high-level public and private sector positions is commonly referred to as the *revolving door*. Upon leaving their positions within government, former members of Congress as well as congressional staffers and employees of the federal government frequently enter private sector positions to serve as lobbyists. Furthermore, it is often the case that individuals in top positions within industries are called upon to fill key roles within the government, such as agency directors.

The heightened access that former members, congressional staffers, and federal employees have does not, however, go unchecked. As established by the Lobbying Disclosure Act of 1995 (LDA), exiting members of Congress are banned from lobbying in Congress for a duration of time, known as a "cooling off" period. The cooling off period for House members is currently one year, which is the duration originally set by the LDA. In 2007, the Senate changed its rules to extend the cooling off period for Senators to two years. Congressional staff whose salaries are at least 75 percent of members' salaries (or $130,500 in 2009) are also prohibited from lobbying in Congress immediately after leaving their positions. In the House, there is a one-year ban on senior staff lobbying the committee or member for whom they worked. The 2007 rules changes prohibit senior Senate staff from lobbying *any* Senator or employee of the Senate for a period of one year. In addition, former members and senior staff are prohibited from lobbying the executive branch on behalf of another party for one year as well.

concerts, and to sponsor lunches, dinners, and receptions in Washington. However, such behavior was severely curtailed after the House and Senate passed rules changes in 2007 in response to a series of high-profile scandals linking several members of congress to lobbyist Jack Abramoff (see box, "The DeLay-Abramoff Scandal"). Both chambers placed heavy restrictions on gifts from lobbyists and imposed more extensive oversight of member-lobbyist relations. Although gifts from lobbyists valued at less than $50 were permitted by the former rules, both chambers eliminated this exception to the gifts restriction. Moreover, the rules changes now require members to gain prior approval from the appropriate ethics committee before accepting travel paid for by an outside, private source. It is important to note, though, that money allows lobbyists to do more than simply dole out goodies. With adequate financial means, lobbyists are also able to acquire other resources, such as the assistance of policy experts, which are often critical in dealing with legislators and their staffs.

The most obvious, and perhaps most important, use of money is for campaign contributions. Some lobbyists are able to make considerable

THE DELAY-ABRAMOFF SCANDAL

In May 2000, then-House Majority Whip Tom DeLay (R-Texas) took a 10-day vacation to Great Britain coordinated by lobbyist Jack Abramoff. DeLay, his wife, and two aides, stayed at lavish hotels, ate at the best restaurants, went to the theater, and took a four-day side trip to play golf at the historic links at St. Andrews golf course. DeLay's financial disclosures reported that the $70,000 trip was paid for by a nonprofit conservative organization, the National Center for Public Policy Research. It was later discovered that a Native American tribe and a gambling services company that had hired Abramoff had each contributed $25,000 to the National Center for the purpose of the trip. Large portions of the trip were found to have been paid with a credit card under Abramoff's name. And this was not the only such trip. DeLay accepted a similarly extravagant trip from Abramoff to the Northern Mariana Islands as well.

House ethics rules permit members and their staff to have travel expenses paid for only when travel is connected to official business and only by organizations directly connected to the trip. House ethics rules also prohibit travel paid for by registered lobbyists. Finally, rules require that members accurately report the cost of a trip and the names of the people and organizations that paid for it. Given the facts that were uncovered, the trip was in violation of each of these rules. To make matters worse, email correspondences later confirmed that DeLay's office was aware of the infractions and was perhaps even concerned "if someone starts asking questions."

Although we cannot be certain what DeLay's motivations were in making policy decisions, we do know that following the trip DeLay helped kill legislation opposed by the tribe and the gambling services company that were represented by Abramoff. In addition, DeLay was a key player in blocking legislation that would have required the Northern Mariana Islands, a U.S. territory, to comply with U.S. labor laws. According to reports, Abramoff received $1.36 million from the Northern Mariana Islands to block this legislation, which would have ended the territory's ability to produce goods with the "Made in the USA" label in sweatshop conditions. A similar bill subsequently passed in 2008, after DeLay had vacated his seat.

Sources: Jeffrey Smith, "DeLay Airfare Was Charged to Lobbyist's Credit Card," *Washington Post*, April 24, 2005; James V. Grimaldi and Jeffrey Smith, "Gambling Interests Funded DeLay Trip," *Washington Post*, March 12, 2005; John Solomon, "E-mails: DeLay Staff Knew Lobbyist Paid for Golf Trip," *The Associated Press*, May 7, 2006; Mark Shields, "The Real Scandal of Tom DeLay," *CNN*, May 9, 2005.

contributions themselves. And many are in a position to orchestrate contributions from numerous political action committees and wealthy individuals to maximize their influence with a few legislators.

Just how much influence is exercised through campaign contributions is an open question. Most campaign contributions appear to flow to members who already support the positions of the contributors – the money follows the votes, the saying goes. But measuring the influence of campaign contributions is very difficult. Some contributions are intended to encourage members to remain inactive, or at least not to challenge policies favored by groups. Other contributions are designed to generate action at less visible stages of the legislative process – to offer an amendment in a subcommittee markup, to hold to a policy position in private negotiations in conference, and so on. Of course, members in key positions, such as party leaders or committee chairs, attract substantial contributions. In her first congress as House Speaker, contributions to Nancy Pelosi (D-California) increased by more than one million dollars compared to her previous two years of service ($1.68 million in 2005–06 and $2.86 million in 2007–08).

Despite the difficulties in gauging the influence of campaign contributions, few doubt that contributions are an important link between members and those lobbyists who can generate large sums for the members' campaigns. We can infer from interest group behavior that there are returns to making contributions (see box, "Fannie and Freddie Launch Targeted Attack"). In recent years, members have increasingly called upon lobbyists to organize fundraising activities on their behalf. Lobbyists often do not dare refuse, because they fear losing access that they have worked so hard to gain.

Information is a critical resource for the lobbyist engaged in inside lobbying. Legislators appear to have an insatiable desire for information about the policy and political consequences of their actions. Political scientists David Austen-Smith and John R. Wright contend that legislators are imperfectly informed about constituency preferences and, therefore, lobbyists provide an important source of information. Furthermore, they argue that competition among interests induces truthful behavior from the interest groups. Lobbyists who develop a reputation for having reliable information at hand are called on more frequently by legislators and are more likely to gain the access necessary for exercising influence. Of course, the amount of technical information a professional lobbyist is likely to have is limited, so success depends on having a network of contacts in research institutes, universities, executive agencies, corporations, or wherever expertise relevant to the lobbyist's interests is found. In fact, many lobbying firms and interest groups hire technical specialists such as lawyers and social and physical scientists

TABLE 11.1. Percent of Interest Groups that Reported Using a Lobbying Technique.

Testify at hearings	99
Contact government officials directly to present your point of view	98
Engage in informal contacts with officials – at conventions, over lunch, etc.	95
Present research results or technical information	92
Send letters to members of your organization to inform them about your activities	92
Enter into coalitions with other organizations	90
Attempt to shape the implementation of policies	89
Talk with people from the press and the media	86
Consult with government officials to plan legislative strategy	85
Help draft legislation	85
Inspire letter-writing or telegram campaigns	84
Mount grassroots lobbying efforts	80
Have influential constituents contact their congressman's office	80
Make financial contributions to electoral campaigns	58
Publicize candidates' voting records	44
Run advertisements in the media about your position on issues	31

Source: TABLE (Adapted) – "Percent of Interest Groups That..." from *Organized Interest and American Democracy* by Kay Lehman Schlozman and John T. Tierney 150. Copyright ©1986 by Kay Lehman Schlozman and John T. Tierney. Reprinted by permission of HarperCollins Publishers, Inc.

so that they can provide timely information to decision makers and even conduct original research of their own.

Outside Lobbying

The most dramatic change in the lobbying business in recent decades has been the increase in outside, or grassroots, lobbying. Rather than relying solely on Washington lobbyists to make appeals on behalf of a cause, groups often attempt to mobilize their membership or the general public to generate outside pressure on members of Congress. Successful mobilization of members' constituents increases the stakes for members by increasing the likelihood that their actions will have electoral consequences. The survey of lobbying groups reported in Table 11.1 shows that more than 80 percent of groups inspired letter-writing or telegram campaigns, 80 percent mounted grassroots lobbying efforts and prodded influential constituents to contact their congressional representatives, and about one-third ran advertisements

348

FANNIE AND FREDDIE LAUNCH TARGETED ATTACK

In September 2008, the U.S. federal government took over con
and Freddie Mac, the nation's two largest mortgage finance co
one of the largest corporate rescues in U.S. history, the federal gov
decision to bail out Fannie and Freddie came as a response to the impending
failure of the mortgage giants amidst the financial crisis. Together, Fannie and
Freddie hold about half of the nation's $9.5 trillion of mortgage debt, and the
collapse of the companies would have a catastrophic effect on the economy.

How did Fannie and Freddie end up in such a precarious situation? Some
economists argue that it was risky lending behavior backed by the federal
government that was responsible, while others point to the companies'
excessive borrowing to generate capital. In all likelihood both are partially to
blame. What we can be certain of is that both explanations are rooted in myopic
corporate strategies that pay dividends when economic times are good and can
prove disastrous when times are bad. For years, though, government officials
had been aware of these dangerous practices and their possible consequences
and did nothing.

Why, then, did the government not intervene? In part the answer to this
question is that Fannie and Freddie were able to stave off regulation through
well-orchestrated lobbying efforts. Senator Chuck Hagel's (R-Nebraska) attempt
to regulate the companies in 2005 was a particularly telling incident. Hagel
sponsored legislation that, among other things, would have instituted independent oversight of the companies, and would have required the companies to sell
off hundreds of billions of dollars of assets. Despite overwhelming Republican
support, at a time when the Republicans had a 10-seat advantage in the Senate,
the bill never made it to the floor for final consideration. The Democrats opposed
the legislation, citing concerns that the forced sale of portfolio assets would
make it difficult for low- and moderate-income families to buy houses, but the
Republicans remained only a few votes short of a majority. It was later discovered
that Freddie had spent $2 million on a stealth lobbying campaign that strategi-
cally targeted 17 Republican senators, many of whom were vulnerable in the
upcoming election. Nine of the targeted senators indicated that they would not
back the bill, and therefore the bill was never brought to the floor due to lack of
sufficient support.

Hagel's struggle to overcome the efforts of Freddie and Fannie is not an isolated
story. Freddie ranks in the top 20 lobbying spenders over the period of 1998 to
2008, having spent a total of more than $96.1 million on lobbying. Fannie was
close behind with a total of more than $80.4 million in lobbying expenditures
over the same period.

Sources: Yost, Pete, "AP IMPACT: How Freddie Mac Halted Regulatory Drive,"
Washington Post, December 7, 2008; Yost, Pete, "AP IMPACT: Mortgage Firm
Arranged Stealth Campaign," *Washington Post*, October 19, 2008; Center for
Responsive Politics at opensecrets.org.

., the media about their positions on the issues. And evidence suggests that grassroots campaigns do influence legislators' decisions, which we might expect considering the widespread use of this technique.

Technology and money have driven innovations in outside lobbying. Throughout the history of Congress, groups of people from around the country have converged on Washington to demand action on their programs. Improved means of transportation have increased the frequency with which groups mobilize their members or the general public for marches, special lobbying days, and other events in Washington that are designed to heighten congressional interest and support for their causes. Mass marches have always been the necessary strategy of large groups without the money and experienced Washington lobbyists essential to execute effective inside strategies. But today, many groups, even well-established groups, bring large numbers of people from around the country on special occasions to pressure members of Congress.

By the 1970s, computer-generated mailings allowed groups to send "legislative alert" letters to group members or targeted groups in the general public to stimulate an avalanche of mail and waves of phone calls to congressional offices. Members of Congress soon learned to identify and discount orchestrated letter-writing campaigns. Nevertheless, as lobbyist Bill Murphy observes, "The congressman has to care that *somebody* out there in his district has enough power to get hundreds of people to sit down and write a postcard or a letter – because if the guy can get them to do *that*, he might be able to influence them in other ways. So, a member has no choice but to pay attention."[8] At a minimum, a member must worry that those same constituents could be motivated, by the same means used to stimulate their letter writing, to contribute their money to or cast their votes for a member's opponent.

Today's lobbyists take outside strategies several steps further. For example, Washington-based firms have adapted telemarketing strategies to congressional politics. Working from computer-generated lists of Americans likely to support a particular point of view, telephone operators dial homes, ask a few questions, and then transfer the call to the appropriate congressional offices so that constituents' views can be registered with their representatives and senators. Particular geographic constituencies can be targeted to maximize the pressure on a few members of Congress.

The internet also serves as a valuable, low-cost resource for interest groups looking to engage the public. Large-scale email campaigns have become a common grassroots strategy among organized interests. And considering the minimal cost of the approach, the returns tend to be sizeable. In one instance, an email campaign organized by the National Education

Association (NEA) encouraged public education advocates to pressure members of Congress to back a class-size reduction and a 15 percent increase in education funding – an ambitious proposal. The effort prompted 20,000 emails and resulted in a 12 percent increase in the education budget.

Media advertising has become an increasingly integral part of lobbying strategies. Most advertising of this variety is intended to increase the visibility of an issue or cause and shape opinion in the general public. For the most part, the media ads are designed and produced by the same people who produce election campaign ads. One group, the U.S. Chamber of Commerce, produces its own television programs that are shown on local stations throughout the country. It uses its production and satellite facilities to link its Washington studios (which are just one block from the White House) with corporate sponsors.

A particular advantage of outside lobbying is that there are few registration and disclosure requirements. Under current law, organized interests and representatives of organized interests that engage exclusively in grassroots lobbying are not obligated to register as lobbyists or file any disclosure statements. Disclosure of grassroots lobbying is only triggered by participation in direct, or inside, lobbying. Groups that have limited lobbying ambitions may, therefore, adopt grassroots strategies to avoid undue reporting burdens. This loophole has, however, led to the emergence of massive grassroots lobbying organizations whose practices go largely unchecked. There have been a number of recent efforts by reformers to close this loophole by extending disclosure requirements to grassroots lobbyists. In fact, the Honest Leadership and Open Government Act of 2007 – the major lobbying and ethics reform legislation passed at the outset of the 110th Congress (2007–08) – contained such a provision, but the legislation was later amended to remove all disclosure requirements for grassroots lobbyists.

The growing importance of outside strategies has led to the proliferation of "full-service" lobbying firms. These large firms combine traditional insider lobbyists with policy experts, specialists in public relations, graphic arts, and electronic media, speechwriters, fundraisers, communications and computer technicians, and pollsters. The model is Hill & Knowlton Public Affairs, a firm with more than 180 employees that boasts its own broadcast studio. The firm includes former members of Congress, staff assistants, and executive officials from both parties. Firms, like Hill & Knowlton, with the capacity to effectively employ both inside and outside strategies must determine the mix of strategies that will position them to best meet their goals. According to political scientists Marie Hojnacki and David Kimball, organized interests are likely to use inside lobbying to target allies in committee, so as to influence the content of legislative proposals. Outside lobbying, on

GRASSROOTS VS. ASTROTURF

New technologies and strategies have greatly expanded efforts to influence members of Congress by generating an avalanche of phone calls and letters to Capitol Hill. A type of grassroots lobbying, astroturf lobbying refers to seemingly spontaneous citizen-based lobbying efforts that are in reality orchestrated by organized groups.

Sometimes these strategies are too obvious to succeed. For example, a group called the Health Care Coalition had operators call small business owners who were likely to be affected by an amendment pending in the House, tell them that the amendment would be bad for managed health care, and then offer to connect them to the office of the member from their district. Dozens of calls were targeted at critical members.

In another case, hundreds of telegrams were dumped onto the floor of the House Commerce Committee to show public opposition to a telecommunications bill. Perhaps thousands more were sent directly to members. Suspicious congressional aides discovered that many of the telegrams were sent without the signatories' permission by a group called the Seniors Coalition. The public relations firm in charge of the effort blamed shoddy work by a mass marketing subcontractor. Some of the signatories proved to be deceased.

Legislators are likely to discount communications that are so heavily coordinated, but they cannot ignore such communications altogether. It is possible that the citizens who acquiesced to the astroturf scheme could also be motivated to vote against the member in the future.

Source: Juliet Eilperin, "Dingell Takes on Bogus Mailgram," *Roll Call*, October 16, 1995, 1, 20. Reprinted by permission.

the other hand, has the broader goal of maintaining and expanding the base of legislative support, and, therefore, is used to influence members irrespective of their policy position. Outside lobbying, however, has less potential to affect meaningful policy change (also see box, "The Choice of Strategies").

Coalitions

Whatever an interest group's mix of inside and outside strategies, it seldom stands alone in major legislative battles. Many coalitions are created for specific issues and then disappear once congressional action on certain legislation is complete. Other coalitions are more enduring. Some coalitions have formal names; others do not. Coalitions are a means for pooling the resources of lobbyists and groups. They also are a means for lobbyists and groups to demonstrate a broad base of support for their cause and to make

THE CHOICE OF STRATEGIES

In an effort to learn more about interest group strategies, political scientist Jack Walker conducted a detailed survey of the top officers in 734 national interest groups. Walker found that:

most groups adopt a preferred style of political action early in their histories, and, when these early choices are made, group leaders naturally emulate the tactics being employed at that time by the most successful groups. Once either an inside or outside strategy becomes the association's dominant approach, it is very difficult to move in a new direction. Choices made early in the history of a group establish a strategic style that restricts innovation, largely because political strategies are so intertwined with other basic organizational decisions.

Not surprisingly, Walker discovered that groups facing organized opposition to their goals tend to more aggressively pursue both inside and outside strategies than do other groups. Outside strategies, however, are more frequently the choice of groups with many local chapters or subunits, citizens' groups, and groups from the nonprofit sector (local governments, universities, nonprofit professions, and so on). Inside strategies are more likely to be the choice of groups representing business and groups that have established large central office staffs, usually in Washington.

Source: Based on information from Jack L. Walker, Jr., *Mobilizing Interest Groups in America: Patrons, Professions, and Social Movements* (Ann Arbor: University of Michigan Press, 1991), 103–121; quote from 119–120.

their effort appear to be as public-spirited as possible. Some coalitions are the creation of lobbyists looking to manufacture a new client.

An impressive example of an interest group coalition was the Archer MSA (medical savings account) Coalition, which played a prominent role in shaping the 2003 Medicare Prescription Drug, Improvement, and Modernization Act. The coalition was comprised of 49 interest groups, including such notable organizations as the American Medical Association (AMA) and the Christian Coalition of America. It was a vocal proponent of tax-preferred health savings accounts (HSAs). Although there was some resistance to the inclusion of HSAs among Republicans, the coalition made its presence felt. The final version of the legislation included the HSAs and passed by narrow margins in both chambers, handing the Archer MSA Coalition a major victory.

Much remains unanswered about interest group coalitions. There is, for instance, no clear-cut answer for why coalitions emerge when they do. There is a tremendous amount of variation across issues in terms of the number e of coalitions that form. Scholars have suggested that the emergence of coalitions is systematically related to such factors as issue conflict and salience. There is, however, only tentative support for these hypotheses. Also it is somewhat unclear whether interest groups in coalitions are actually more successful than ones acting alone. While the Archer MSA Coalition appears to have been successful in 2003, not all coalitions are so fortunate. Moreover, there were interest groups that acted alone on the Medicare legislation, such as the AARP (formerly the American Association of Retired Persons), that also were successful in achieving their policy objectives. One study of coalition success found that a mere 58 percent of coalitions accomplished any of their goals.[9] This lackluster rate could reflect some of the disadvantages to coalition formation – namely, greater collective action problems to overcome. While the comparative advantages of belonging to a coalition are not entirely clear, there is some evidence that coalition formation leads to greater success when seeking to defend the status quo.

Legislators Influencing Organized Interests

The path of influence between lobbyists and members is a two-way street. Plainly, lobbyists seek to influence outcomes in the legislative process by persuading at least a few members to support or even champion their cause that would not have done so otherwise. But legislators often want something from lobbyists, too. And because lobbyists want to cultivate or maintain good relations with key legislators, they are often quite responsive to legislators' demands. Legislators frequently pressure interest groups to generate campaign contributions for them. They ask lobbyists for assistance in attracting support from other legislators, the public, or others on issues not directly of concern to the lobbyists. Legislators may enlist the support of lobbyists on matters before the executive branch or encourage lobbyists to take action in the courts. Lobbyists may resist these pressures. After all, the requests may not be compatible with other objectives the lobbyists pursue. But lobbyists must assess how important the legislator is, or will be in the future, to their groups' or their personal interests. Ignoring senior party and committee leaders can come at a significant cost.

When congressional Republicans gained majority party status in 1995, GOP leaders launched a project to pressure Washington lobbying firms to hire Republicans for top positions. Called the K Street Project, Republican leaders tracked the party affiliation of Washington lobbyists and rewarded those that were loyal. With like-minded individuals in key lobbying positions, congressional Republicans could limit the power of opposing interests. With unified control of Congress and the White House between 2000 and 2006, lobbying firms had to stay in the good graces of Republicans if they wished to exert influence over legislative outcomes. Whereas lobbying firms have historically hired lobbyists from both parties to accommodate changes in party control, there is reason to believe that lobbying firms predicted lasting Republican dominance. This, along with the strict oversight of the K Street Project, led many lobbying firms to pass up Democrats for important lobbying positions. In 2004, the Capitol Hill newspaper, *The Hill*, reported that "retiring House Democrats are feeling a cold draft from K Street as they seek post-congressional employment at lobbying firms, trade groups and corporations. By contrast, K Street is aggressively courting GOP lawmakers who have announced their retirements."[10]

[handwritten margin note: incentive to work w/ lobby if want to work true]

Things began to change in the months leading up to the 2006 elections, as lobbying firms sensed a Democratic takeover of one or both houses of Congress. The same firms that, months earlier, had shunned Democrats were now embracing them with open arms. The eventual Democratic victory led to a rush to hire Democratic lobbyists. One prominent lobbyist reported that the average annual salary for Republican lobbyists plummeted $50,000 upon the election returns. Shortly after taking control, House and Senate Democrats addressed the practices of the K Street Project that had burdened them for the past decade. Both chambers adopted rules in 2007 that expressly prohibit members from influencing "on the basis of partisan political affiliation, an employment decision or employment practice of any private entity."

Regulating Lobbying

Modern lobbying is remarkably clean and ethical, at least when compared with lobbying during most of American history. In the nineteenth century, lobbyists ran gambling establishments to put legislators in their debt and openly paid members for representing their interests on Capitol Hill. With few (recent) exceptions, the retainers and bribes are gone. In fact, lobbyists now have their own professional code of ethics.

At various points throughout history, congressional, journalistic, and criminal investigations have exposed remarkably corrupt lobbying practices, but on only a few occasions did Congress or either house impose any restrictions on lobbying. In 1876, for example, Congress for the first time required that lobbyists register, but the rule was in effect for only one Congress. Congress did not pass its first comprehensive lobbying regulations until 1946, when the Federal Regulation of Lobbying Act was adopted as a part of the Legislative Reorganization Act.

The central feature of the 1946 law was the requirement that people who solicit or receive money for the purpose of influencing legislation must register with the clerk of the House or the secretary of the Senate. Lobbyists were required to file quarterly reports on the money they received for and spent on lobbying. The authors of the 1946 act hoped that disclosure of lobbyists' clients and legislative purposes would put members, reporters, and the public in a better position to evaluate lobbyists' influence.

The law proved to be unenforceable. In 1954, the Supreme Court ruled in *United States v. Harriss* that the registration and reporting requirements applied only to those persons who are paid by others to lobby, who contact members directly, and whose "principal purpose" is to influence legislation. The Court argued that the First Amendment to the Constitution, which prohibits Congress from making a law that abridges the right "to petition the Government for a redress of grievances," limits Congress's ability to regulate an individual's right to represent him or herself before Congress and to organize others with the intent of influencing Congress. By confining the force of the 1946 act to those lobbyists whose principal purpose is to influence legislation, the Court created a large loophole for anyone who wanted to claim that influencing legislation was not his or her principal purpose.

Interest in creating meaningful registration and reporting requirements was renewed in the early 1990s. Ross Perot gave great emphasis to the influence of "special interests" in his 1992 presidential campaign. Perot's theme was reinforced by television reports about members' all-expenses-paid trips to vacation resorts where they fraternized with lobbyists. In response to the heightened public scrutiny of the relationship between lobbyists and members of Congress, a large number of members elected for the first time in the 1990s had promised to reduce the influence of special interests in Washington. The result was the consideration of significant lobbying reforms.

In late 1995, Congress enacted new legislation designed to close some of the loopholes in the 1946 law. The new law, titled the Lobbying Disclosure Act of 1995 (LDA), extended the 1946 law that covered only people who lobbied members of Congress, to also include those who seek to influence congressional staff and top executive branch officials. The LDA formally defines a lobbyist as:

> Any individual who is employed or retained by a client for financial or other compensation for services that include more than one lobbying contact [Defined as any oral or written communication (including an electronic communication) to a covered executive branch official or a covered legislative branch official that

is made on behalf of a client], other than an individual whose lobbying activitie constitute less than 20 percent of the time engaged in the services provided by such individual to the client over a six month period.

Anyone who is hired to lobby a covered public official and spends 20 percent or more of his or her time in paid lobbying, must register with the clerk of the House and the secretary of the Senate within 45 days of being hired or making the first contact, whichever is earlier. Under the LDA, individuals who received $5,000 or less in a six-month period and organizations that spent less than $20,000 in a six-month period were not required to register. This exception was included to allow average citizens to have their voices heard without needing to register. Lobbyists are required to file reports that disclose who their clients are, the general issue area they were hired to influence, and a good faith estimate of the total amount paid by clients. The LDA originally required these reports to be filed on a semiannual basis. Lobbyists for foreign governments or organizations must also register. The registration requirement excludes grassroots lobbying, such as efforts to persuade people to write members of Congress.

Due to the introduction of these registration requirements, the LDA had the effect of more than doubling the number of registered lobbyists. Among the newly registered were a variety of lobbying coalitions – organized groups of lobbyists, associations, and lobbying firms – that had not been registered under the old law. Even still, the law fell short of registering many individuals that acted as lobbyists.

Separately, the House and Senate also adopted rules limiting lobbyists' gifts to members and staff. The rules banned gifts valued at more than $50, including meals and entertainment. Gifts from any one source could not exceed $100 in value for a year, with gifts under $10 excluded from the calculation. Gifts from family members and gifts of token value (T-shirts, mugs) were also excluded. In addition, chamber rules permitted privately funded trips but banned travel paid for directly by a lobbyist.

In the months leading up to the 2006 elections, the public witnessed an inordinate number of lobbying scandals. In March 2006, former Representative Randall "Duke" Cunningham (R-California) was convicted of accepting $2.4 million in bribes primarily from defense contractors in return for securing contracts. In May 2006, the FBI raided the home of Representative William Jefferson (D-Louisiana) to find $90,000 in his freezer. The government claimed that Jefferson took in excess of $400,000 in bribes. He was later indicted on 16 charges of corruption. In October 2006, former Representative Bob Ney (R-Ohio) pled guilty to accepting gifts in exchange for favorable action on behalf of convicted lobbyist Jack Abramoff's clients.

nes were, at least in part, a reaction to the many scandals.
of voters in the 2006 congressional elections, corruption
cited by voters as "extremely important" than any other
rism, the economy, and Iraq.[11]

rities in the House and Senate in the 2006 elections,
...ucrats set out to fulfill promises of ethics and lobbying reform.
House Democrats did so immediately by including reforms in their chamber
rules. The Senate opted to pursue statutory reforms, and passed legislation
containing rules changes similar to those the House passed days earlier.
In August 2007, the House and Senate approved the Honest Leadership
and Open Government Act of 2007, and President Bush then signed the
legislation into law the following month. The newly passed Act amended
the LDA of 1995 in several important areas, including, but not limited to,
disclosure requirements, revolving door restrictions, and gift limitations.

The Act requires quarterly instead of semiannual filing of lobbying disclosure reports, and reduces the monetary thresholds by half to conform
to the new quarterly periods. Reports must identify if a client is a state or
local government, department, agency, or other instrumentality, and must
be filed electronically to facilitate transparency. For former senators, the Act
bans directly lobbying in Congress for two years after leaving office, rather
than one year under the LDA. The House retained the one-year "cooling
off" period specified by the LDA. The Act also prohibits senior Senate staff
from lobbying any Senator or employee of the Senate for a one-year period.
In addition, the Act prohibits Senate staff from having official contact with
the Senator's spouse or immediate family member, should the relative be
a registered lobbyist. Senate staff are also prohibited from contacting the
spouse of any Senator who is a lobbyist. Legislators are furthermore banned
from negotiating private employment until after their successor is elected,
unless they file a report disclosing the name(s) of the entity involved in the
negotiations.

Perhaps the most pertinent reforms, considering the events leading up to
the elections, related to restrictions on gifts from lobbyists to members and
their staff. The Act sharply limits gifts to Senators, striking the exception that
previously permitted Senators and their staff to receive gifts under $50. The
House passed the identical rule. According to the Act, Senators and their
staff are not permitted to accept privately financed travel from lobbyists
or entities that employ lobbyists. Moreover, Senators and their staff are
prohibited from traveling with lobbyists present on any segment of the trip.
The rules do allow travel for one day and one night to locations where
there is minimal lobbyist involvement. The House adopted substantially

similar rules. The Act requires Senators to receive advanced approval for all travel paid for by an outside, private source. To promote adherence to the lobbying laws, the Act increases the maximum civil penalty for violations of the provisions from $50,000 to $200,000, and provides for criminal penalties of imprisonment for deliberate noncompliance.

Members' Groups and Legislative Service Organizations

Groups of members frequently coalesce or even formally organize to pursue specific political interests. In fact, informal groups of members have been prominent features of Washington politics since the early Congresses. In the early nineteenth century, members tended to find lodging in boarding houses where they found like-minded colleagues. Informal but conspicuous intra-party factions, such as southern Democrats, have been quite important from time to time. And state delegations, particularly those of the larger states, have been the building blocks for coalitions throughout the history of Congress. Two developments of recent decades have altered the character of membership groups.

The first is that intra-party factions developed formal organizations with formal memberships, elected leaders, staff, offices, and even membership dues. The prototype, and still the largest such group, is the Democratic Study Group (DSG). The DSG was formed in 1959 by House Democratic liberals to counter the strength of the conservative coalition of Republicans and southern Democrats. The services of the DSG – especially issuing and scheduling reports – eventually became so highly valued that nearly all Democrats joined and contributed dues to take advantage of the group's work. Nevertheless, the DSG remains the organizational focal point for liberal activists in the House.

Since the 1970s there has been a remarkable increase in the number of single-issue caucuses. Today there are over 200 such caucuses, and many have bipartisan memberships. The Congressional Arts Caucus and the Congressional Sportsmen's Caucus formed to promote certain public funding for the arts and to oppose many proposed regulations on fire arms, respectively; regional interests are promoted by the Northeast-Midwest Congressional Coalition and the Congressional Western Caucus. Both constituency concerns and personal circumstances provide a foundation for the Congressional Black Caucus, the Congressional Hispanic Caucus, and the Congressional Caucus for Women's Issues. District economic interests are reflected in the Congressional Coastal Caucus, Congressional Steel Caucus, and the Congressional Tourism and Travel Caucus.

Caucuses, now officially called congressional members organizations in the House, are a way for members to become involved in and demonstrate a commitment to a particular cause or issue that falls outside of the scope of their regular committee duties. This is particularly true in the House, where most members are limited to two committee assignments. In fact, about 90 percent of caucuses are found in the House. In most cases, a caucus is a basis for publicizing a cause or an issue and building policy coalitions within Congress. Outside interest groups seeking to cultivate congressional support for their interests have stimulated the creation of many congressional caucuses.

Until recently, many caucuses were formally recognized in the House as "legislative service organizations," or LSOs, and were subject to audits and a few regulations. LSOs were controversial because they received dues from members' office accounts and gained office space in the House office buildings. Critics charged that this practice allowed money from office accounts to be spent indirectly for purposes, such as dinners, for which office account funds cannot be spent directly. Moreover, many LSOs bridged the gap between interest groups and congressional caucuses by creating foundations and institutes with close ties to both external groups and internal caucuses. In the view of some critics, the ability of lobbyists and interest groups to contribute money to these new foundations was just another way for special interests to support travel and social events for members and congressional staff participating in the work of the foundations. These critiques of LSOs paved the way for the second significant development in membership groups in recent decades.

The newly elected Republican majority of 1995 fundamentally changed the character of membership groups by banning LSOs. Membership groups lost several special privileges – the ability to receive dues paid from official budgets and office space in House buildings. Slowly, congressional member organizations, or CMOs, replaced LSOs and are granted more limited privileges. Members of CMOs may jointly pay for staff and other functions, but they do not pay dues for separate staff and activities. Dozens of member organizations have been created and, among other activities, serve to advertise legislators' interests in subjects important to key groups in their districts and states.

The Influence of Lobbyists and Interest Groups

Even experienced and insightful watchers of the lobbying and interest group community have mixed views about the influence of special interest lobbying. A popular view in the 1950s and 1960s was that policy making was dominated by "subgovernments" or "iron triangles" – tightly bound sets of interest groups, executive agencies, and committees. According to this view, cozy relationships among lobbyists, bureaucrats, and members prevented other interests from influencing policy choices and implementation. The subgovernments perspective was always recognized as an overly stylized view, but it captured an important feature of Washington politics: In many policy areas, only a few groups, agencies, and members took an interest in the issues, so they dominated the policy choices that were made.

The classic case of subgovernment policy making was mid-twentieth century agriculture policy politics. Generally, only those agriculture groups directly affected by certain federal commodities programs, the Agriculture Department bureaus that ran the programs, and a few members sitting on the agriculture committees of Congress took an active interest in farm policy. Those groups, bureaucrats, and members interested in the various farm commodities assisted each other in gaining congressional approval of the periodic legislation that supported federal programs. Although federal taxpayers paid for these programs, the costs were not so high as to breed resistance. And the lack of conflict among agriculture sector groups and decision makers helped keep others from paying attention.

Many political scientists responded to the subgovernments' perspective by noting the special conditions that allow a subgovernment to develop and dominate policy making. The most important feature is little conflict. Conflict among the interested groups and members would encourage the contending forces to recruit supporters from a broader range of groups, legislators, executive branch officials, and even the general public. Expanding the scope of the conflict in this way usually alters the balance of forces and the policy outcome. The low level of conflict, in turn, is the product of the concentrated benefits and widely distributed costs of some programs. The beneficiaries are motivated to organize and lobby to protect their interests, and the fairly small burden on taxpayers stimulates little opposition. But the number of people affected by policy choices, distribution of costs and benefits, and the scope and intensity of conflict varies greatly across policy areas. The result is significant variation in the role of groups in shaping policy choices.

Political scientist Hugh Heclo noticed that policy areas once dominated by subgovernments had lost their insular character by the 1970s. Heclo coined the term *issue networks* to capture the more diverse, mutually antagonistic, and fluid character of the lobbying and interest group community found in many policy areas. Many factors contributed to the change. In the 1960s and 1970s, new citizens' groups, many of which were by-products of broad-based social movements, challenged established groups. Groups representing economic interests proliferated, partly in response to new government policies and regulations, which led to a fragmentation of Washington representation in many policy areas that were once dominated by just one or two groups. In addition, congressional reforms made Congress more open, accessible, and democratic, which encouraged new groups to lobby and stimulated more members of Congress to champion the cause of once-neglected interests.

Analysts are divided over the political implications of the expansion of the interest group community and the breakdown of subgovernments. Tierney and Schlozman emphasize the continuing numerical advantage of business-oriented groups. They also observe that the explosion of interest group activity has

> introduced a potentially dysfunctional particularism into national politics. If policymakers in Congress are forced to find an appropriate balance between deference to the exigencies of the short run and the consideration of consequences for the long run, between acquiescence to the clearly expressed wishes of narrow groups that care intensely and respect for the frequently unexpressed needs of larger publics, the balance may have shifted too far in the direction of the near-term and the narrow.[12]

Political scientist Robert Salisbury disagrees. He insists that the large number of corporate lobbyists and the tremendous resources of business groups should not lead us to conclude

> that business interests or even self-serving groups invariably prevail. The total system of policy advocacy is far broader than the array, vast as it is, of organized interest groups. Every holder of public office – indeed, every candidate for public office – is or may be an advocate of some policy alternatives. Members of Congress do not wait passively for lobbyists to persuade them one way or the other; they too are advocates, as are the more prominent members of the administration, the editorialists and commentators in the mass media, the academic pundits and writers, and a host of other citizens who write letters, attend rallies, argue with each other, and generally make their views known on policy questions of the day.[13]

Besides, Salisbury contends, most business-group resources are devoted to monitoring government activity important to business decisions rather than to influencing policy choices.

It seems fair to say that Tierney and Schlozman's critical view is more widely shared among sophisticated observers of congressional politics than is Salisbury's more forgiving perspective. Nevertheless, Salisbury's note of caution is important. Lobbyists and interest groups are not the only source of pressure on members, nor are they the only important source of change in the nature of congressional politics. Communications and transportation technologies, electoral campaigns, the structure of the legislative process, the distribution of power within Congress, and other factors affect the balance of forces influencing congressional policy choices as well.

Conclusion

Lobbyists and interest groups are among the most controversial and least well-understood features of the legislative game. They appear to be both an essential part of the representation of interests before Congress and a potential source of bias in the policy choices made by Congress. Generally, they direct members' attention to narrow and parochial issues that might otherwise not be addressed. Whatever their consequences, the relationship that lobbyists and interest groups have with members of Congress has changed markedly over the years. In particular, transformations in Congress have caused lobbyists and interest groups to evolve. They are now:

- a much larger and more diverse community than just a few decades ago,
- more professional, with increasingly developed infrastructures,
- a more central player in congressional elections, both in terms of direct contributions and advocacy efforts, and
- better able to provide legislators with quick and accurate information.

These developments have sensitized the general public about the influence of special interests and produced new efforts to regulate lobbyists and lobbying.

Above: Representative Paul Ryan (R-Wisconsin), left, and Senator Judd Gregg (R-New Hampshire), right, the ranking House and Senate Budget Committee members, react to the fiscal 2010 budget proposed by President Obama.

Below: Senate Budget Chairman Kent Conrad (D-North Dakota), left, and House Budget Chairman John Spratt, Jr. (D-South Carolina), right, during a news conference on President Obama's fiscal 2010 budget request.

12

Congress and Budget Politics

THE FEDERAL BUDGET IS OFTEN THE CENTER OF CONGRESSIONAL politics. For fiscal year 2009, the federal government's spending will exceed $3 trillion, or approximately $10,000 for every American.[1] And estimates for fiscal year 2010 project an even larger number. Although many people are bored to tears when the details of spending and tax policy are discussed, the budget reflects fundamental choices about the role of government in American life. Action on the annual budget tends to generate the most partisan fights in Washington. The twists and turns of budget politics have strongly influenced winners and losers in elections, shaped the political careers of the most prominent politicians, reshaped congressional decision-making processes, and altered the distribution of power within Congress.

Federal budgeting since the 1970s has been a roller coaster ride. Beginning in the late 1970s and continuing for more than a decade, presidents and Congress struggled with annual deficits. In fiscal year 1992, the federal government spent about $290 billion more than it received from taxes and other revenues. To pay the interest on the debt that had accumulated over the years (nearly $4 trillion by that point), the federal government spent a little more than $200 billion – about 14 percent of its $1.5 trillion budget for fiscal year 1992. By 1998, the budget picture had improved markedly. Fiscal year 1998 ended with a small surplus, and annual surpluses were achieved in the three following years. Deficits returned by late 2001 during an economic recession. The fight against terrorism and the war in Iraq prompted increases in defense and homeland security spending, while tax cuts enacted in 2001 and 2003 cut into revenues. Deficits were looming again by 2002 and have continued through to the present. A deficit of nearly $1.2 trillion was projected for fiscal year 2009, a record high.

During the past four decades, political battles stimulated by budget deficits have produced a series of procedural innovations in the way

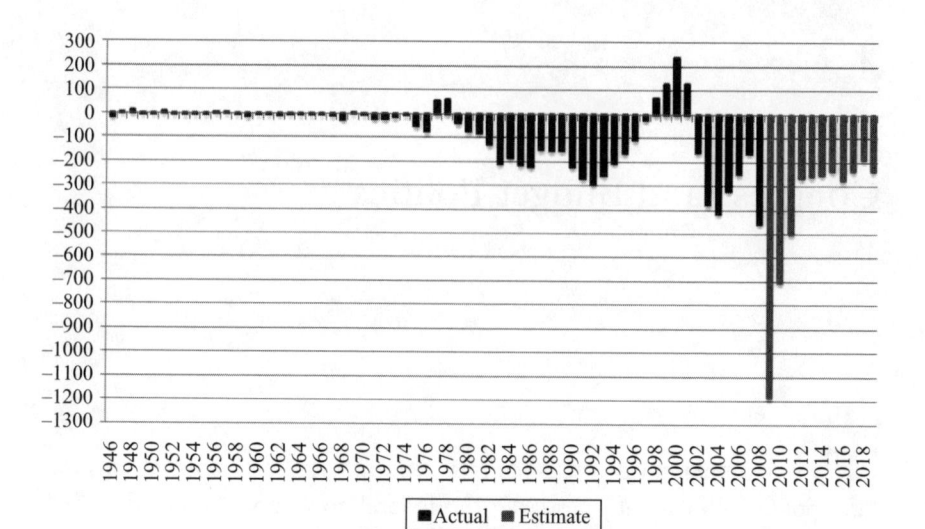

FIGURE 12.1. Annual Surplus (+) or Deficit (–) in Billions of Dollars, for Fiscal Years 1946–2019. *Source: Congressional Budget Office.*

Congress drafts the budget. In the 1970s and early 1980s, the process was modified to force congressional committees to write legislation that would either reduce spending or raise more revenue. Since then, the emphasis has been on enforcing multiyear budget plans. Each new effort to enforce deficit and spending agreements was a response to legislators, whose votes were often pivotal to passing budget legislation, to take credible action against deficits.

This is an important story. Step-by-step, the changes in rules reshaped the congressional decision-making process, contributed to heightened partisanship, and shifted the relative power of party and committee leaders. Cumulatively, these changes proved so important that they warrant special attention in this chapter.

Overview of the Federal Budget

Figure 12.1 shows the history of the federal deficit since the end of World War II. In the aftermath of the war, the federal government managed small annual budget surpluses about as often as it experienced budget deficits. In the 1960s, small deficits were the norm. Deficits crept upward during the 1970s and became a dominant issue in the 1980 presidential campaign, which ended with the election of the Republican candidate, Ronald Reagan, and a Republican majority in the Senate. During the 1980s and early 1990s,

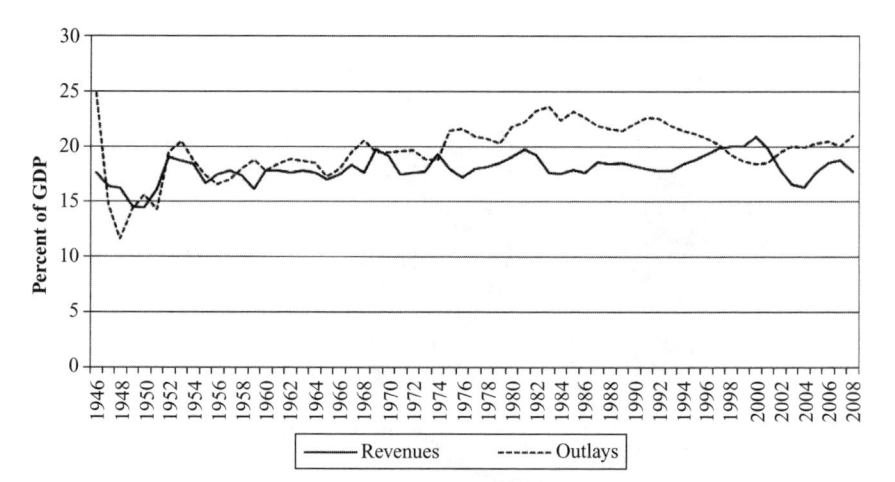

FIGURE 12.2. Federal Receipts and Outlays as a Percent of Gross Domestic Product, Fiscal Years 1946–2008. *Source: Congressional Budget Office.*

the deficit never approached the level experienced in 1980, Jimmy Carter's last year as president. The deficit contracted a little in the mid-1980s, but returned to a pattern of continued growth thereafter. President Clinton confronted this situation when he entered office in 1993. Clinton left office after surpluses had returned and his successor, George W. Bush, served while deficits expanded. Estimates from the Congressional Budget Office suggest that President Obama's first year in office will mark the largest deficit in history, followed by gradually receding levels.

The federal deficit must be seen in the context of the overall size of the U.S. economy, which has grown a great deal in the last half century. Figure 12.2 shows the size of federal expenditures and revenues as percentages of the gross domestic product (GDP), an annual measure of all of the goods and services produced in the United States. The figure demonstrates that federal revenues as a percentage of GDP have been fairly stable since World War II, seldom reaching 20 percent of GDP. It also shows that the deficit since 2002 is due to both higher spending and generally low revenues.

The increase in federal outlays that has put spending over 20 percent of GDP in most years since the early 1980s is due to both defense and domestic spending. Higher defense spending accounted for about half of the overall increase in expenditures between 1979 and 1983 and again after 2001. Most of the rest of the increase – and nearly all of it since the mid-1980s – is due to the rising cost of entitlement programs.

Entitlements are provisions in law that guarantee individuals certain benefits if they meet eligibility requirements. The spending is considered

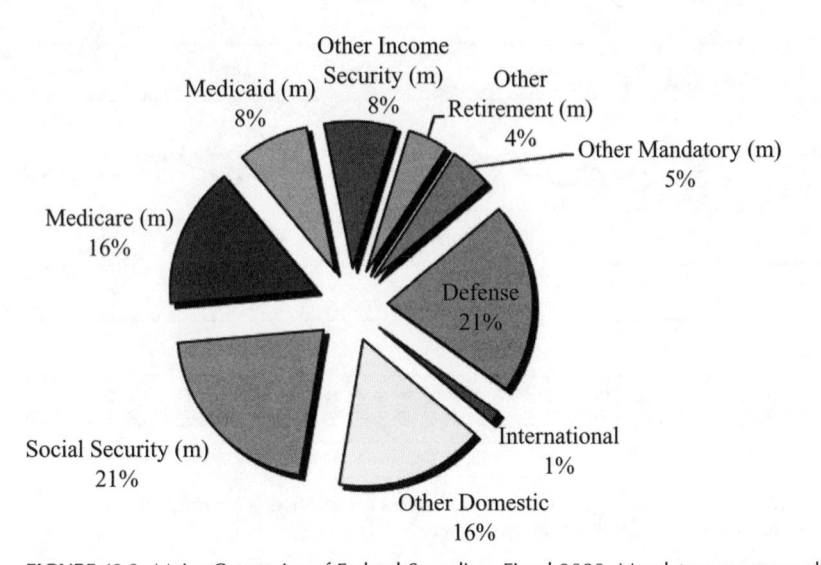

FIGURE 12.3. Major Categories of Federal Spending, Fiscal 2008. Mandatory programs designated with (*m*), others are discretionary. *Source: Congressional Budget Office.*

mandatory – unless Congress changes the law it must provide the required funding. In contrast, for *discretionary* programs, year-to-year spending is not dictated by eligibility requirements but rather is determined by Congress. Social security, Medicare (health care for the elderly), Medicaid (health care for the poor), veterans' benefits, and other income-security programs such as pensions are examples of entitlement programs with mandatory spending. Defense, education, environmental protection, medical research, and space programs are examples of discretionary spending. Entitlements have grown so much that they now account for over 60 percent of federal expenditures, as Figure 12.3 shows.

Creating a Congressional Budget Process: 1974

In the early 1970s, interest in budget reform was spurred by chronic deficits and political tensions between the Democratic Congress and a Republican president. In retrospect, the deficits of that period seem small, but they were unprecedented for a time without a declared war. The shortfall was largely the result of new and expensive domestic initiatives (President Lyndon Johnson's Great Society program) and the Vietnam War. Promising to gain control of the budget, Republican Richard Nixon won the 1968 presidential election and then proceeded to engage in intense battles with

---

Congressionally Speaking . . .

The *fiscal year* for the federal government begins on October 1 and runs through September of the following year. For example, fiscal year 2010 starts on October 1, 2009, and ends on September 30, 2010. Thus, Congress aims to have spending and tax bills for the next fiscal year enacted by October 1 of each year. The president proposes a budget in February, leaving Congress less than eight months to act on it. Failure to pass bills that approve spending for federal agencies, called *appropriations bills*, may force a shutdown of some government agencies. In most such cases, Congress passes *continuing resolutions*, which are joint resolutions of Congress that authorize temporary spending authority at the last year's level or at some percentage of that level.

---

the Democratic Congress over spending and taxes. These battles motivated Congress to strengthen its own budget-making capacities by adopting the Congressional Budget and Impoundment Control Act of 1974, usually called the Budget Act of 1974.[2]

The Budget Act created a process for coordinating the actions of the appropriations, authorizing, and tax committees. Each May, Congress would pass a preliminary budget resolution setting nonbinding targets for expenditures and revenues. During the summer, Congress would pass the individual bills authorizing and appropriating funds for federal programs, as well as any new tax legislation. Then, in September, Congress would adopt a second budget resolution, providing final spending ceilings. This resolution might require adjustments to some of the decisions made during the summer months. Those adjustments would be reflected in the second resolution, and additional legislation, written by the proper committees, would then be drafted to make the necessary changes. This process of adjustment was labeled "reconciliation," to reflect the need to reconcile the earlier decisions with the second budget resolution. The reconciliation legislation was to be enacted by October 1, the first day of the federal government's fiscal year.

The Budget Act provided for two new committees, the House and Senate Budget Committees. The budget committees write the budget resolutions and package reconciliation legislation from various committees ordered to adjust the programs under their jurisdiction. The Congressional Budget Office (CBO) was created by the act to provide Congress with nonpartisan, expert analyses of the economy and budget.

dget Act also modified Senate floor procedures in a critical way. The
.ct barred nongermane amendments and set a limit of 20 hours on debate
over budget resolutions and reconciliation legislation. These rules mean that
budget measures cannot be loaded with extraneous floor amendments or
killed by a Senate filibuster. However, the rules did not restrict the kinds
of provisions committees could write into budget measures. Consequently,
the door was left open for committees to include in reconciliation bills
legislation unrelated to spending cuts. This became a common practice once
reconciliation bills became a central feature of the budget-making process
in the 1980s.

Reducing the Discretion of Committees: 1980 and 1981

The new budget process worked smoothly during its first four years, primarily because congressional Democrats did not use budget resolutions to
constrain or compel action from appropriations, authorizing, or tax committees. But in 1979 and 1980, the last two years of the Carter administration,
escalating deficits spurred a search for new means to control spending. An
effort in 1979 to include reconciliation instructions to committees in the second budget resolution ended in failure, in part because of resistance from
some committees to reducing spending on programs under their jurisdiction.
Confronting projections of a rapidly rising deficit and a reelection campaign
in 1980, President Carter and Democratic congressional leaders agreed to
include reconciliation instructions in the first budget resolution, adopted in
May. That is, they decided to order some committees to report legislation
that would reduce spending at a point in the process before the usual authorization and appropriations legislation was considered. This switch meant
that the initiative would shift from the various authorizing committees to
the budget and party leaders, who together with administration officials
would devise the reconciliation instructions. The innovation worked. The
1980 reconciliation legislation reduced the deficit by $8.2 billion, through a
combination of spending cuts and tax increases. Strangely, the term reconciliation was and still is used, even though it ostensibly refers to the process
of reconciling the decisions of the summer months with the second budget
resolution.

Republicans learned from the experience of the Carter years and used
reconciliation instructions to force much deeper cuts in domestic programs
once they took over the White House and the Senate after the 1980 elections.
The Republicans managed to gain adoption of reconciliation instructions

IMPOUNDMENT

During the early 1970s, the Nixon administration began to cut off funds for programs opposed by the president. That is, the president unilaterally stopped spending for programs for which funds had been appropriated by law. The practice, known as *impoundment*, created a constitutional crisis. Many members of Congress charged the president with violating his constitutional responsibility to see that the laws are faithfully executed. The courts agreed, for the most part, although some programs had been irreparably harmed by the time a court had ruled on the issue.

Congress responded in its 1974 budget reforms by providing for two types of impoundments – rescissions and deferrals. To withhold funds permanently for a particular purpose (make a rescission), a president would have to gain prior approval from both houses of Congress. To temporarily delay spending (make a deferral), a president would only have to notify Congress, and the president could defer spending unless either house specifically disapproved.

In 1983, the Supreme Court ruled that the legislative veto was unconstitutional because it allowed Congress to check an executive action without passing a regular bill. The ruling implied that the deferral process of the 1974 reforms was unconstitutional. Congress responded in 1987 by formally limiting the deferral authority to routine administrative matters.

Rescission authority continues to be used but it has involved only a very small fraction of total federal spending. Between 1976 and 2005, presidents requested nearly $73 billion in rescissions but Congress approved only about $25 billion.

and pass a reconciliation bill that cut spending for fiscal year 1982 by about $37 billion.

Figure 12.4 illustrates how the inclusion of reconciliation instructions in the first budget resolution has altered the budget process. Reconciliation, authorization, and appropriations legislation now proceed simultaneously, so there is no need for a second budget resolution.

Sequestration: 1985 and 1987

The savings achieved by the 1981 reconciliation bill were more than offset by a large tax cut enacted in separate legislation that year, continued increases in entitlement spending, and the budget crisis which intensified in the early 1980s. A tax increase in 1982 – initiated by Senate Republicans and quietly accepted by President Reagan – helped reduce the deficit a little, but it was not enough to change its long-term upward trajectory.

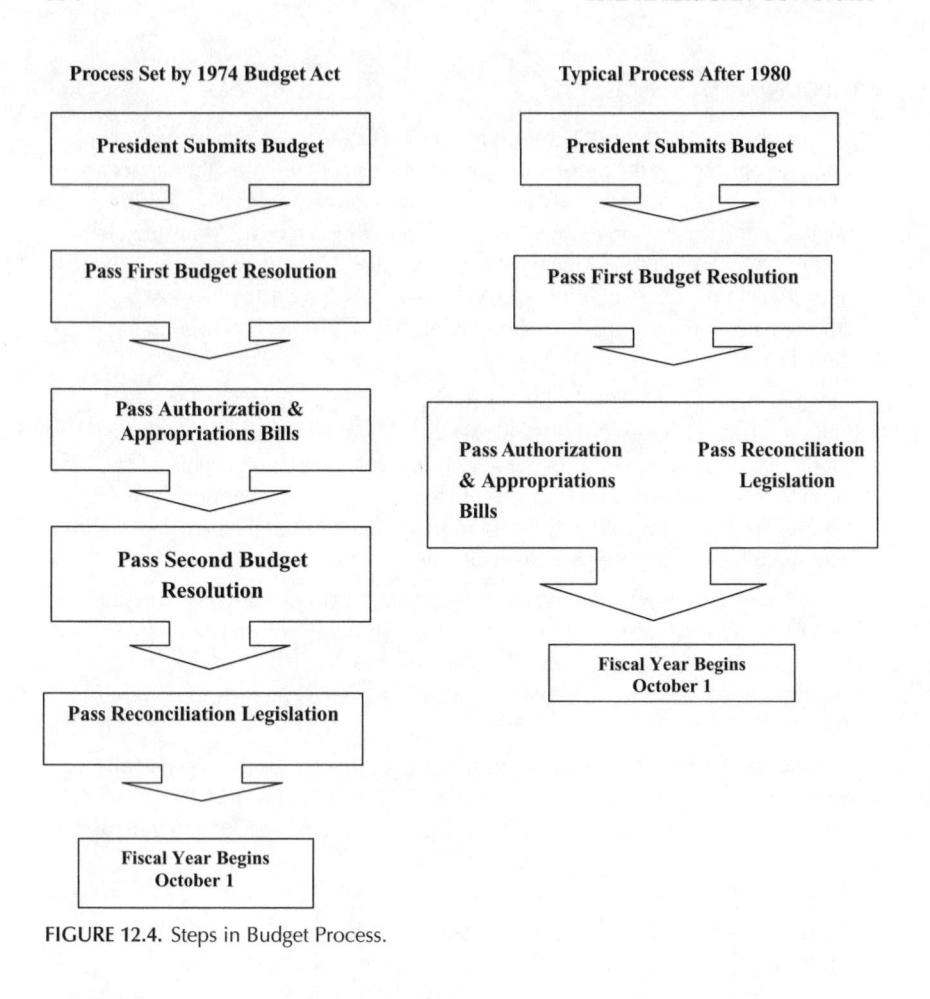

FIGURE 12.4. Steps in Budget Process.

In 1985, a trio of senators – Phil Gramm (R-Texas), Warren Rudman (R-New Hampshire), and Ernest Hollings (D-South Carolina) – pushed a seemingly irresistible amendment to a debt-ceiling bill, establishing the amount of outstanding debt the federal government is permitted to carry. The Gramm-Rudman-Hollings proposal was adopted as the Balanced Budget and Emergency Deficit Control Act of 1985. It provided for reducing the deficit by $36 billion in each of the following five years, so that the deficit would drop from about $172 billion in fiscal year 1986 to zero in fiscal year 1991. If Congress failed to meet any year's deficit target by more than $10 billion, as determined by the comptroller general (who headed the General Accounting Office, now called the Government Accountability Office), across-the-board cuts in spending would be ordered by an amount necessary to reduce the deficit to the specified level. This process of withholding a certain percentage of funding from programs was called "sequestration." Sequestration, it was argued, would be so distasteful to lawmakers that Congress and the president would be motivated to find a way to reduce the deficit without triggering the automatic cuts. If Congress and the president failed to do the job, sequestration would do it for them.

To reinforce this deficit-reduction scheme, the 1985 law barred floor amendments to budget resolutions and reconciliation measures that would raise the projected deficit beyond specified levels. A point of order could be made against any ineligible amendment. But the Senate had a history of overruling its presiding officer on points of order and dozens of popular nongermane amendments were proposed to the reconciliation bill considered in the fall of 1985. Senator Robert Byrd (D-West Virginia) therefore proposed, and the Senate approved, a new rule that provided that the presiding officer's ruling on the germaneness of an amendment to a reconciliation bill could not be overturned unless a three-fifths majority agreed. The "Byrd rule" reinforced the 1974 Budget Act's restrictions on floor amendments and debate and made Senate rules governing the content of budget measures and amendments to them even more restrictive than those in the House.

On paper, Congress and the president met the deficit targets in the next three fiscal years. But, in each case, this goal was accomplished through a remarkable combination of creative accounting and absurdly optimistic estimates about the economy, future demands on federal programs, and the next year's revenues. "Blue smoke and mirrors" became the catch phrase used to describe federal budgeting. As a result of this budgetary legerdemain, the actual deficit in fiscal 1988 turned out to be $155 billion rather than the targeted $108 billion.

In the fall of 1987, another debt-ceiling bill presented an opportunity to restart the Gramm-Rudman-Hollings process. Congress attached to the bill a new set of targets, this time moving the zero-deficit deadline back from 1991 to 1993. The measure also made it more difficult for the Senate to waive the deficit targets, by requiring a three-fifths rather than a simple majority vote. But many observers, including stock market investors, thought that merely restarting the Gramm-Rudman-Hollings process was woefully inadequate, a view that appeared to contribute to a crash in the stock market in October 1987.

The crisis of the stock market crash and the November 20 sequester deadline propelled Congress and President Reagan to reach a new agreement. The agreement was unique because it provided separate spending ceilings for defense and nondefense spending for a two-year period – fiscal 1987 and 1988. This compromise allowed the Reagan administration to end with a

Congressionally Speaking . . .

Only a few congressional rules are known by the name of their original author. One of them is the Byrd rule, named after Senator Robert C. Byrd (D-West Virginia), the former majority leader and former Appropriations Committee chair.

The *Byrd rule* bars extraneous matter from reconciliation bills. A provision is considered to be extraneous if it does not change spending or revenues, concerns issues that lie outside of the jurisdiction of the committee reporting it, or leads to a net increase in spending or decrease in revenues for the years beyond those covered by the bill. In addition, strangely, any change in social security, Washington's political sacred cow, is considered a violation of the Byrd rule.

The rule is enforced by points of order raised by senators from the floor and upheld by a ruling of the chair, who depends on the advice of the Senate parliamentarian. The Senate may overturn the ruling of the chair as long as 60 senators agree. If a point of order is successful, either through a ruling of the presiding officer or by a vote, the entire bill falls. The rule gives a sizable minority the ability to force certain kinds of provisions from reconciliation bills. It is one of the few places in which Senate rules are more restrictive than House rules.

truce with Congress on the budget. Neither party was eager to continue the battle into the election year of 1988.

PAYGO: 1990

The partisan war over the budget resumed in 1989, the first year of the Republican George H. W. Bush administration. By late 1989, it was clear that the Gramm-Rudman-Hollings procedure had been a failure. Instead of a $100 billion deficit, as targeted in the 1987 Gramm-Rudman-Hollings Act, the deficit turned out to be a record $221 billion because of a slumping economy. The Gramm-Rudman-Hollings procedure was shown to have a major weakness: the absence of a means for forcing further reductions during a fiscal year for which the original deficit estimates had been too optimistic.[3]

The 1990 budget package set a new direction for enforcing agreements, as indicated by its title – the Budget Enforcement Act (BEA). The 1990 BEA focused on spending limits rather than deficit reduction *per se*. For fiscal years 1991 to 1993, the BEA provided for three categories of non-entitlement spending (defense, international, and domestic) and established spending ceilings for each. These ceilings were to be adjusted for inflation each year so that economic conditions would not make them more or less onerous. If a category's ceiling was exceeded, sequestration would apply only to programs within that category – thus, this process is called categorical sequestration. "Firewalls" were established; that is, it became a violation of the rules to transfer funds between the three categories. In this way, Republicans would not fear a raid on defense funding to increase domestic spending, and Democrats did not have to worry about transfers in the opposite direction.

The 1990 BEA added teeth to the budget-making process by requiring that all tax and direct spending legislation be deficit-neutral. That is, if a bill cut taxes or increased spending, it also would have to provide fully offsetting tax increases or spending cuts. This pay-as-you-go mechanism – known as PAYGO – was enforced by a provision allowing any member to raise a point of order against a bill on the grounds that it was not deficit-neutral. If a bill that was not deficit-neutral were to sneak through, a sequester on spending in the appropriate category would be applied.

The PAYGO focus on spending ceilings rather than deficit-reduction targets meant that Congress and the president had given up on the Gramm-Rudman-Hollings approach. Of course, if the economy slumped and revenues declined, the deficit would go up even if the spending ceilings were obeyed. But if the economy performed better than expected, spending would be controlled as expected, revenues would flow into the Treasury faster than expected, and the increased revenues would reduce the deficit.

The 1990 budget deal made it more difficult for authorizing and tax committees to propose new policy initiatives. Legislation that would create a new program that entailed spending would have to provide for spending cuts somewhere else. Tax-writing committees could not propose legislation to grant tax breaks to some groups or industries unless they increased taxes or cut spending for other programs under their jurisdiction. The net winners under the 1990 rules seemed to be the appropriations committees. Although they had to operate under the spending ceilings, the ceilings were viewed as reasonably generous, given the programs that had to be funded, and would be adjusted for inflation. The appropriators also had substantial flexibility on how to set priorities within the broad categories.

Unfortunately for President G. H. W. Bush, deficits shot upward in 1991 and 1992, despite the fact that domestic discretionary spending was constrained. The economy did not perform well, which reduced revenues over those two years by nearly $90 billion from what had been predicted in 1990. The slow economy contributed to increased spending on entitlements – particularly Medicare, Medicaid, and farm price supports – outside of the discretionary spending ceilings. Unanticipated expenditures for the Persian

Gulf War and disaster aid to help Florida and Hawaii recover from hurricanes added to the deficit. The 1992 deficit of $290 billion was nearly $140 billion larger than the deficit in 1989, Bush's first year in office. Bush failed to win election to a second term.

Deficit-Reducing Trust Fund and Entitlement Review: 1993

Congress demonstrated remarkable creativity in devising new rules and processes for budgeting during the 1970s, 1980s, and early 1990s. But the impressive array of budgetary enforcement devices – reconciliation, sequestration, points of order, spending ceilings, PAYGO, and firewalls – did not seem to improve the bottom line. Deficits were never put on a downward path during the Reagan and G. H. W. Bush administrations, as the major deficit-reduction packages had promised. By the time Bill Clinton was sworn in as president in January 1993, the public was deeply cynical about federal budgetary politics, the annual deficit was at a record high, and the deficit was a major obstacle to the new president's other policy objectives.

Entitlement spending, particularly health care spending, spurred large annual increases in the budget. As Figure 12.5 demonstrates, the escalating costs of health care programs poses serious threats to deficit control. The major government health care programs, Medicare and Medicaid, are entitlement programs for the elderly and the poor. Cutting those programs entails either reducing the number of eligible people, which is an unpopular option, or cutting payments to hospitals, doctors, and state governments. Reducing payments, however, leads hospitals and doctors to shift their costs to people with private insurance, thereby increasing the cost of health care for everyone else.

Domestic programs that do not involve entitlements – most education, law enforcement, transportation, housing, energy, research, construction, and space programs – have declined as a percentage of GDP since 1980. Most federal programs were cut or frozen, in terms of constant dollars, during the 1980s. In most cases, further cuts would mean a basic change in the direction of public policies that are popular or have strong constituencies. Moreover, defense spending has been on a downward path for several years.

In 1993, President Clinton sought increases for some domestic programs, cuts in others and in defense, and some tax increases, all in the hope of reducing the deficit by $500 billion over five years. The Democrats decided to move budget measures at a more rapid pace and to incorporate Clinton's proposed tax increases in the reconciliation bill. Placing the tax increases in

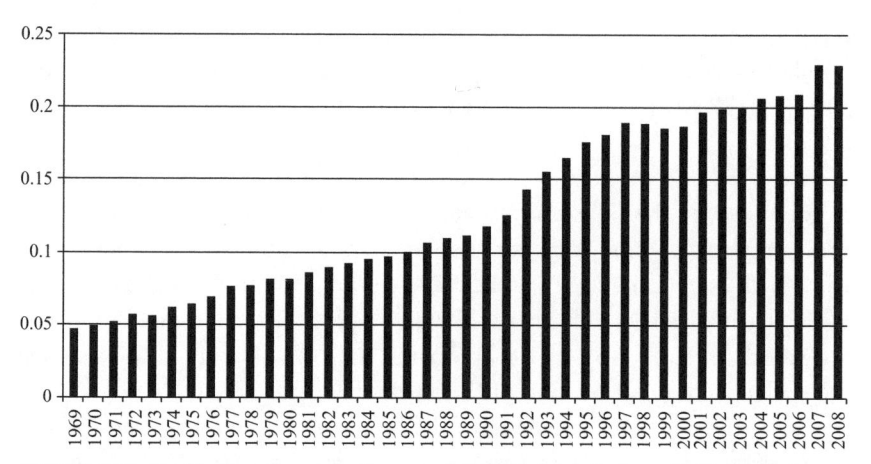

FIGURE 12.5. Health Spending as a Percent of Total Federal Outlays, 1962–2008. *Source: Congressional Budget Office.*

the reconciliation bill had important advantages for the Democrats. Selling never-popular tax increases might be easier as a part of a larger deficit-reduction package. Furthermore, reconciliation instructions to committees set deadlines on reporting legislation. This change meant that the two tax-writing committees, House Ways and Means and Senate Finance, could not indefinitely delay the tough decisions about taxes. And just as important, reconciliation bills are subject to a 20-hour limit on debate in the Senate, which protects them from filibusters and nongermane amendments. These special budget procedures meant that Republican opponents of the tax legislation could not delay Senate action.

The administration's plan ran into serious difficulty with conservative Democrats and, as had happened in previous years, the president's plan was adopted only once. New procedural devices – a deficit-reduction trust fund and a mandatory review of entitlement spending – were invented to satisfy legislators who lacked confidence in the legislation's goals. The trust fund plan provided that an amount equal to the projected deficit reduction from the bill be placed in a trust fund that could be used only to pay maturing public debt obligations, thereby reducing the national debt. The trust fund innovation proved insufficient to satisfy many conservative Democrats, however, so an agreement was reached between Democratic leaders and leading conservatives to make highly privileged legislation to address entitlement spending if such spending ultimately exceeded levels specified in the budget bill. In this way, the conservatives were assured that Congress would consider more serious entitlement reform if the budget plan proved too optimistic. With this agreement in place, a sufficient number of the Democrats supported the reconciliation bill for it to pass, 219 to 213. No Republicans voted for it, and 38 Democrats still voted against it.

After the Senate passed its version of the bill, the conference committee negotiations on the bill occurred almost entirely among Democrats. Their problem was a common one for the Democrats – how to keep liberals satisfied with commitments for domestic spending without raising taxes to the point that the party's conservatives would object. To make matters worse, a deadline of sorts loomed for approving the bill. The August recess was scheduled to begin at the end of the week of August 2. The Democrats did not want their internal divisions to delay the recess and give Republicans an opportunity to score political points by claiming that the Democrats had failed to end gridlock in Washington. Protecting the party's public image, as well as its policy objectives, appeared to motivate the Democratic leaders, and the conference's many staff assistants labored through several nights to produce the 1,800-page conference report.

As House and Senate leaders began to reveal the compromises they were making on various details of the conference report, some conservative Democrats who had supported the reconciliation bill indicated their intention to vote against the conference report. To appease at least some of them, President Clinton acted unilaterally to add credibility to the promise that the new tax revenues would be used to reduce the deficit rather than to increase spending. By executive order, he created the deficit trust fund and established an entitlement review process to measure whether legislators were abiding by the budget plan's requirements. Moreover, the House would adopt, as a part of a special rule for the conference report, a requirement that it act on new legislation to address any overages in entitlement spending when they occur. No provisions were made to bind the Senate to the same process, but House action on entitlement spending in future budget resolutions would force the Senate to confront the issue.

Even with these last-minute concessions, the outcome eventually turned on the vote of a freshman member, Marjorie Margolies-Mezvinsky, a Democrat from a Republican-leaning district just outside Philadelphia. She had voted against the president's position on the budget resolution and on passage of the House bill, but reportedly she had promised her support if her vote turned out to be pivotal – no doubt hoping it would not be. Early in the 15-minute period for the vote, Margolies-Mezvinsky cast a no vote. But with no time left in the vote, the Democrats had only 216 votes – two votes short of a majority – so the Speaker held the vote open. Ray Thorton (D-Arkansas), who had not yet voted, signed a red voting card to vote no. Only if both Margolies-Mezvinsky and Pat Williams (D-Montana) changed their votes to yes would the conference report pass. Williams was a 14-year veteran Democrat from Montana who had made the same promise as Margolies-Mezvinsky. Williams changed his vote first, and then all eyes fell on Margolies-Mezvinsky, who was being ushered to the front desk by a group of colleagues. The Republicans chanted, "Goodbye, Marjorie," referring to her reelection prospects if she voted against them. She signed a green card to vote yes, and the Speaker gaveled the vote closed.

Margolies-Mezvinsky spent the next few days explaining her vote. She appeared on local television and radio; was interviewed on National Public Radio, the MacNeil/Lehrer News Hour, and CNN's Moneyline; and immediately aired radio ads in her district to explain her vote. Her explanation was that she had extracted an important promise from the president. Minutes before the vote, she was called to the phone to talk to the president. Asked what it would take to get her vote, she told the president that she wanted a high-level conference for a serious discussion of cutting entitlement spending. Clinton agreed, so she agreed to vote yes. The next week, Secretary of Health and Human Services Donna Shalala traveled to Philadelphia to discuss plans for the conference. The full conference finally took place in December, with the president in attendance. Margolies-Mezvinsky lost her bid for reelection in 1994.

The Senate outcome came down to the decision of Senator Bob Kerrey, a Nebraska Democrat. Kerrey, who had acquired the nickname "Cosmic Bob" during his failed 1992 presidential bid, frustrated the White House because there were no particular provisions or promises of future action that he was looking for that could be used to get him to vote yes. Several talks with Clinton did not clarify Kerrey's position. Finally, hours before the Senate vote, Kerrey went to the Senate floor to announce his decision in favor of his party. He said, in part, "President Clinton, if you are watching now, as I suspect you are, I tell you this: I could not and should not cast a vote that brings down your Presidency. You have made mistakes and know it far better than I. But you do not deserve, and America cannot afford, to have you spend the next sixty days quibbling over whether or not we should have this cut or this tax increase." His Democratic colleagues rose in applause. The Republicans watched in silence. With Kerrey staying with his party, another tie vote was ensured. Once again Vice President Gore cast the deciding vote, and the conference report was approved, 51 to 50.

Tax Bill Certification: 1995–1996

Budget legislation became the central battleground for the new Republican majorities elected to the House and Senate in 1994. In 1995, the Republicans failed to gain congressional approval of a constitutional amendment to require an annually balanced budget, but in 1996 they gave the president the line-item veto for spending bills (although it was later struck down by the courts). In the interim, the Republicans pursued a strategy that they thought would compel the president to accept a budget reconciliation bill representing a far different mix of spending and taxing priorities than those contained in the 1993 bill. They failed miserably. The result contributed to the demise of Speaker Newt Gingrich's House career and bolstered President Clinton's chances for reelection in 1996. It also proved to be a lesson about political brinksmanship that congressional majority parties would carry into future Congresses.

In designing their budget resolution and reconciliation bill in 1995, the congressional Republican majorities largely ignored the proposals of the Clinton administration. They combined the goal of achieving a balanced budget by 2002 – which had been jettisoned in the fight over the 1993 bill – with a plan to cut taxes by $245 billion over seven years, which meant that federal spending had to be cut deeply. They sought to limit Medicaid spending and to give the states administrative responsibility for the program, stem the growth of Medicare, eliminate three executive departments (the Departments of Education, Commerce, and Energy), cut welfare spending, limit environmental regulations, and eliminate dozens of federal programs.

Procedural innovations were once again used to help bridge policy differences. Many senators were concerned that the deep tax cuts proposed would undermine the effort to balance the budget. To gain their support for the budget resolution, a provision was included that required the Finance Committee to wait to mark up tax cut provisions for the reconciliation bill until the Congressional Budget Office had officially certified that the bill would actually balance the federal budget by 2002. In this way, a nonpartisan staff arm of Congress, the CBO, had to approve estimates of the long-term effects of the budget package *before* a committee could act on the budget package.

By the time Congress approved the budget resolution, in the early summer of 1995, the House Republican leadership had devised a strategy that they hoped would gain the president's signature for their reconciliation bill, which would incorporate their spending and tax legislation. The Republicans would refuse to pass two critical sets of legislation – appropriations bills and a debt-ceiling increase – until the president agreed to approve their reconciliation bill. Failure to enact appropriations bills would force many departments to shut down at the end of the fiscal year (at midnight on September 30). Failure to increase the debt ceiling when needed would force the government to stop borrowing and possibly default on its debt obligations. The ceiling would be reached sometime in the fall. The strategy was predicated on the assumption that the Republican budget plan would be popular with the public. The Republicans' view, articulated by Speaker Gingrich, was that the president would not dare to shut down federal services or allow the government to default on its loans and would feel compelled to sign their legislation.

As the October 1 deadline approached, talk of the "train wreck" that would occur if the appropriations bills were not enacted began to dominate Washington. The reconciliation bill was due on September 22, but that date slipped by as Republicans struggled to resolve differences within their own ranks and finish writing the huge bill. Unfortunately for the Republicans, public enthusiasm for their budget plan had weakened. By November 13, Congress had failed to pass any appropriations bills or the reconciliation bill and the debt ceiling was about to be reached. The need for the debt-ceiling bill was eased when the administration found ways to juggle money in trust funds to create cash for the government to continue to pay its debt-service obligations.

The Republicans remained eager to force a showdown with the president. They passed an extension of appropriations authority through December 15 and a temporary debt-ceiling increase measure extending the government's borrowing authority to December 12. The debt-ceiling bill included provisions that prevented the president from juggling the trust funds and would revert the debt ceiling to its previous level on December 12. The continuing resolution was designed to be unpalatable to the president – it reduced spending in the affected agencies to just 60 percent of the previous year's level and canceled a scheduled reduction in Medicare premiums.

To the Republicans' surprise, Clinton vetoed both bills. As the administration knew, the Republicans lacked the two-thirds majority in each house required to override a presidential veto. The result was a shutdown of the unfunded federal agencies, forcing about 800,000 "nonessential" federal workers to be furloughed. Additional accounting moves made the veto of the debt-ceiling bill inconsequential, but the shutdown caused by the veto of the continuing resolution proved politically costly – for the Republicans. Although the Republicans blamed the shutdown on Clinton's unwillingness to bargain, the public blamed the Republicans over Clinton by a two-to-one margin. The fact that Republicans had made their strategy so conspicuous but still didn't have a reconciliation bill ready to pass hurt their cause. Worse yet for the Republicans, the president's willingness to take a stand enhanced his popularity with the public, giving the president a stronger bargaining position. The Republicans had misjudged Clinton's willingness to veto the bills and had badly miscalculated the general public's response.

Scrambling to determine what to do next, the Republicans adopted another continuing resolution – which ended a six-day shutdown – and soon approved a conference report on the reconciliation bill. It was expected that the reconciliation bill would be vetoed as well, so the issue was how to conduct negotiations to find a version acceptable to the president and to both houses of Congress. The second continuing resolution included a new feature: It stipulated that the president and Congress must agree to a plan to balance the federal budget within seven years – by 2002 – using economic estimates provided by the Congressional Budget Office. The Republicans viewed the commitment to a balanced budget as a large victory, but the details of a new budget plan were yet to be negotiated.

Partisan rhetoric sharpened. Differences between the parties over the reconciliation bill continued to concern the size of spending cuts in domestic programs and the size of tax cuts. A handful of regular appropriations bills passed and received presidential approval, but several others remained unfinished by December 15, again forcing a shutdown of many federal agencies, this time involving approximately 260,000 workers. House Speaker Gingrich and Senate Majority Leader Bob Dole appeared to be willing to pass another continuing resolution, but hard-line House Republicans made it plain that they would not support another resolution. Before they would agree to fund certain federal agencies, they wanted concessions from the president that the president was simply unwilling to grant. The result was that this shutdown lasted 21 days.

News stories of hardships suffered by government workers over the holidays worsened the standing of the congressional Republicans in the polls. By the first week of January, Clinton's poll ratings were heading up, and the Republicans were eager to pass continuing resolutions. In fact, they passed three measures – one narrow appropriations bill, to keep the most popular programs funded through September 1996; a second appropriations bill, to fund a couple of other programs through March 15; and a continuing resolution to keep the remaining programs and agencies open until January 26. Meanwhile, deep divisions among Republicans concerning the efficacy and political costs of their strategy began to emerge.

MAJOR DEVELOPMENTS IN THE BUDGET PROCESS, 1974–2007

1974 Congressional Budget and Impoundment Control Act

Created the modern budgeting process, established the budget committees, and provided for congressional review of presidential rescissions and deferrals.

1980 Reconciliation Bill

Provided that (for the first time) reconciliation be used at the start of the budget process. Committees were required to forward legislation drafted specifically to reduce spending as required by the first budget resolution.

1985 and 1987 Gramm-Rudman-Hollings Bill

Set fixed annual targets for deficit reduction and established a sequestration process to bring spending down to levels required to meet targets.

1990 Budget Enforcement Act

Dropped the fixed deficit targets of the Gramm-Rudman-Hollings approach and replaced them with caps on spending in domestic, defense, and international budgetary categories; pay-as-you-go rules for spending and revenues; and restrictions on loans and indirect spending.

1993 Omnibus Budget Reconciliation Act

Modified spending priorities and extended the enforcement provisions of the 1990 act through 1998.

1996 Balanced Budget Act

Modified spending priorities, extended the enforcement provisions of the 1993 act through 2002, and projected a balanced budget in fiscal year 2002.

2002

PAYGO enforcement provisions allowed to expire.

2007

PAYGO rule adopted; rules requiring sponsors of earmarks to be identified; House rule provides a "trigger" that establishes a point of order against tax-cut legislation that does not require that the OMB certify that the tax cuts cost less than $179.8 billion through fiscal 2012 or more than 80 percent of any surplus projected for 2012 at the time.

2009

PAYGO rule changed in the House to align it with the rule in the Senate so that both chambers use the same CBO baseline to assess compliance, to allow separate House-passed bills to be considered collectively deficit-neutral provided they are linked at engrossment, and to include an emergency exception to the PAYGO rule; rule providing a point of order against any earmark inserted in a general appropriations conference report.

The debt ceiling loomed on the horizon yet again. The financial adjustments that had allowed the administration to avoid defaulting on the country's debt obligations were just about exhausted. To avoid being blamed for playing games with the debt ceiling, Republican leaders wrote President Clinton that they intended to increase the debt ceiling when required. No progress had been made on the reconciliation bill by January 26, however, so another continuing resolution was enacted. It was now four months after the start of the fiscal year, and still no budget was in place. The process for drafting a budget for the next fiscal year began on February 5, when the president submitted his budget proposals to Congress. Plainly, those proposals meant little in the absence of a budget for the current fiscal year.

Just before March 15, for the fifth time since September of the previous year, a continuing resolution was passed to avoid a shutdown of federal agencies, this time for only a week. This practice of passing short-term continuing resolutions went on for several more weeks. Eventually, late in the evening of April 24, nearly seven months late and after a total of 14 limited spending bills and short-term continuing resolutions, the president and congressional Republican leaders agreed on a budget. The next day, Republican leaders rushed through to passage an appropriations bill to fund government agencies for the rest of the fiscal year. Compromise spending and tax cuts were quickly enacted.

Dropping and Reinstating PAYGO Rules: 1997–2009

With the 1996 budget plan in place, the Republicans did not challenge President Clinton on the budget again; instead, they turned to tactical fights on individual appropriations bills. They had no interest in repeating the political disaster of the 1995–1996 budget fight. Many Republican conservatives did not like Speaker Gingrich's willingness to compromise with Clinton, but, at least in the Speaker's view, there was little to be gained by laying down more ultimatums for the president. By the end of 1997, a strong economy, which yielded both reduced spending and increased tax revenues, had cut the deficit much faster than expected. In fact, a balanced budget was achieved in 1998, four years earlier than predicted in the 1996 budget. The large strategic moves of deficit politics were replaced with the less visible, tactical moves of surplus politics, with congressional Republicans and the Democratic president fighting over the details of appropriations bills.

Partisan differences caused four straight years of gamesmanship with appropriations bills. Sparring over spending details routinely led to delays in passing appropriations bills, which required that Congress pass numerous continuing resolutions. Moreover, when agreement was finally reached, compromises often extended over several appropriations bills and many extraneous measures that were packaged in large omnibus appropriations bills. In 1998, for example, eight of the 13 regular appropriations bills and over 30 non-appropriations measures were included in the omnibus appropriations bills for fiscal 1999. In 2000, 21 continuing resolutions were adopted before an omnibus appropriations bill was passed a few days before Christmas. That bill included the provisions of three regular appropriations bills, some new emergency spending, and non-appropriations legislation on Medicare, Medicaid, medical savings accounts and other tax provisions, immigration, and commodities regulation. This multidimensional bill represented many bargains and reflected members' realization that it was the last opportunity to address some issues before that Congress ended.

The political tables had turned in Washington after Republican President George W. Bush was elected in 2000. Bush was in office for less than a year when the 9–11 terrorist attack occurred. The subsequent airline and New York subsidies, homeland security, war on terrorism, and Afghan and Iraqi wars cost many hundreds of billions for the federal government, contributing to the creation of the first deficit after four years of surpluses. A prolonged recession and spending on national security contributed to the deficits, as did a tax cut enacted in 2001 when surpluses were still projected. Despite significant loss of revenue, the 2001 Bush tax cuts were passed without sequestration due to some shrewd maneuvering. Fearing that PAYGO may prevent the tax cuts from becoming permanent, congressional Republicans allowed it to expire in 2002. The Senate did, however, adopt its own PAYGO rule shortly after the statute expired.

In February 2003, President Bush proposed a budget deficit of over $300 billion for fiscal 2004. He proposed more tax cuts, some of which were opposed by at least a few Senate Republicans, and some spending increases. The administration argued that much of the tax proposal and some of the spending hikes were needed to boost the economy. The proposals, if adopted, would require Congress to adjust spending ceilings in the budget enforcement mechanisms.

The return of deficits was accompanied by failure to pass appropriations bills on time. From 2001 through 2004, most appropriations bills were not enacted until after the October 1 deadline and most were wrapped into

large omnibus bills. For example, in 2002, when the appropriations bills for
fiscal 2003 were considered, no appropriations bill was enacted by October 1 and eventually 10 continuing resolutions were adopted. Democrats
argued that Republicans deliberately delayed action on a few of the bills so
that Republicans would not have to cast potentially embarrassing votes just
before the 2002 election. Not until January 2003, more than four months
after the bills were due to be passed and after a new Congress was in place,
did the House and Senate pass an omnibus bill that incorporated 11 of the
13 regular appropriations bills. Conference committee negotiations over the
bill were not complete until February – six months late and halfway through
the fiscal year. The Republican Congress passed all appropriations bills in
2005 and 2006 before adjourning. Although many were passed long after
the October deadline, Republicans were confronted with difficult choices
in the 2006 election year, leaving work on nine of 11 appropriations bills
incomplete after they lost their House and Senate majorities.

The new House Democratic majority of 2007 reinstated the PAYGO rule,
having scored political points against Republicans in the 2006 campaign for
letting the deficit drift upward. House Democrats did not include a sequestration process, so the more recent adoption lacks the tough enforcement
mechanism that was included in the 1990, 1993, and 1996 versions. Instead,
they provided for only a point of order, which can be waived by approving
a special rule, to be raised against a bill or amendment that increases the
deficit. The Senate had implemented its own PAYGO rule in 2002 following the expiration of the statute, and extended the rule with some revisions
in 2007. The latest versions of the PAYGO rules in the House and Senate
closely resemble one another. Similar to the House rule, the Senate rule
likewise enforces PAYGO requirements by point of order. In the Senate,
points of order raised against a bill for PAYGO violations can be waived
with 60 votes. Since PAYGO now exists only in the form of chamber rules,
the houses have greater flexibility to set aside the rules when they prove to
be an obstacle. For this reason, President Obama has advocated statutory
PAYGO, but has received some resistance from within Congress. As of the
time of this writing, Congress has taken no such action.

In 2007, both houses also moved to put in place new rules governing earmarks, the term used to describe funding for specific projects. The rules do
not ban earmarks but rather require the disclosure of the name of the legislator sponsoring each project, publication of a justification for the project,
and certification that the project does not benefit the legislator or his or her
spouse. In addition to spending on construction projects, the rule applies to
tax and tariff provisions geared to individual firms or organizations.

THE BATTLE OVER EARMARKS

In early 2006, Republicans found themselves embarrassed by the volume of earmarks – totaling about $20 billion – included in a supplemental appropriations bill, which President George W. Bush threatened to veto. Earmarks are provisions to fund individual projects that are championed by individual members, often in collaboration with outside interests and lobbyists. Republican leaders passed the bill only after promising earmark reform. The promised reform included a requirement that the names of earmarks' sponsors be made public. Members of the Appropriations committees believed that they were being singled out for earmarks when members of the tax-writing committees used legislation to write into law narrow provisions for tax breaks or tariff protection. As a consequence of the bad publicity for the bill and other developments, particularly a lobbying scandal, Republicans started but never completed work on an ethics reform bill that addressed earmarks.

House Democrats, after gaining a majority in the 2006 elections, incorporated earmark reform, including provisions that Republicans invented but did not adopt in the previous Congress. In response to the reform, House committees must keep a record of requests for earmarks. Critics of the reform approved of the provision requiring publication of sponsors' names but preferred that floor votes be guaranteed on individual earmarks. The Senate adopted similar rules included in the passage of the Honest Leadership and Open Government Act of 2007.

The reforms appear to have limited the number of earmarks, but legislators and lobbyists have looked for ways to circumvent the new requirements. Lobbyists have increasingly turned their attention to persuading executive branch officials to include specific projects in the president's budget requests so that legislators do not have to file requests with committees. Executive officials are also lobbied to use their discretion to favor certain projects after receiving appropriations.

The House passed some changes to its PAYGO rule in 2009. One such change aligns the House rules with those of the Senate, so that both chambers use the same Congressional Budget Office baselines when estimating the costs of bills. Another change allows the House to pass one bill that offsets the spending in another bill, provided that both are linked at engrossment. Previous rules required all bills passed by the House to be independently deficit-neutral over a one- and five-year period. Finally, the House inserted an exception that permits the House to waive the PAYGO rule for provisions designated as emergency spending. In addition to the PAYGO rules, the 2009 rules changes also prohibit conference committees from inserting earmarks into general appropriations bills that did not appear in either of the chamber bills.

Conclusion

The history of budgetary politics discussed in this chapter illustrates several important features of congressional politics that have been recurrent themes throughout this book:

1. Legislative outcomes in the United States are the product of a three-player legislative process in which the House, the Senate, and the president must negotiate and reach compromises. In the budget battles described in this chapter, differences in policy preferences among the three institutional players, combined with the necessity of gaining the consent of all three, produced compromised efforts to reduce the deficit and procedural innovations designed to force other players to act.

2. The president is a central player in congressional politics. When the president proposes a change in direction in budget policy, it usually changes Congress's agenda. The president's proposals may be set aside by the majority party in Congress, as they were initially in 1995. Doing so entails great political risks, however. For the party controlling the White House, the president, not the party's congressional leaders, tends to be the chief strategist for the party.

3. Rules matter. The constitutional requirement of a two-thirds majority in each house to override a presidential veto prevented the majority party in Congress from imposing its budget priorities in 1995 and 1996. Statutory limits on appropriations authority and the debt ceiling proved vital. The Senate rule that prevents extraneous amendments from being attached to budget bills (the Byrd rule) limited the options of House and Senate committees. Also, enforcement provisions included in previous budget agreements were essential to crafting compromises that the players could trust would be honored. Except for the basic rules outlined in the Constitution, all of these rules were subject to change and became a part of the debate over budget policy.

4. The Budget Act, and how the different players made use of it, altered the traditional relationship between the parent houses and their committees. Historically, committees had taken the initiative in setting the policy agenda and designing legislation within their jurisdictions. The new budget process, however, allowed top party and budget leaders to present comprehensive budget resolutions to the parent houses and required committees to produce legislation, after the fact, that

they most certainly would not have drafted had they been left to their own discretion.

5. The rules of the legislative game are changed by the players. The players often turned to new procedural rules to guarantee that promises critical to achieving a compromise would be kept in the future. New enforcement mechanisms were invented on several occasions to convince key groups of legislators that uncertainties about the future would not work to their disadvantage.

6. Elections have clear and powerful effects on policy making. In the history described in this chapter, elections produced realignments in the preferences of key players – the president and members of Congress – concerning budgetary policy. Divided party control of the House, Senate, and White House was the direct product of elections and shaped the players' strategies in basic ways. Less significant, but clearly present, were the effects of election timing. On several occasions, approaching elections tended to dampen partisanship and encourage compromise on the part of the party with the greater public relations problem. In addition, public opinion polls, which are taken as a gauge of the potential electoral consequences of political events and policy positions, appeared to alter players' strategies on many occasions.

7. Parties are the primary building blocks for creating voting coalitions, but party discipline is far from perfect. Leaders of both the Democratic and the Republican parties, when in the majority in Congress, first attempted to satisfy enough fellow party members to create a majority before soliciting support from the other party. In the end, voting on the budget plans, which typically encapsulated the major policy priorities of the majority party, was very partisan. Those party members who voted against the position of their own party leaders were criticized but ultimately faced no formal punishment.

8. Party leaders are important players in Congress, but they are not all-powerful. In the budget negotiations described in this chapter, the distribution of power within Congress showed a fairly centralized pattern that was partly the result of the rules governing the budget process and partly a reflection of the need for high-level negotiations to work out differences of great importance to the parties and the two branches. The large differences in the two parties' budgetary policy preferences and each party's fairly great internal cohesiveness encouraged party leaders to be assertive strategists on behalf of their party. But party leaders, it appears, were more than mere agents of

their parties. They focused agendas, made good and poor tactical decisions, and shaped their parties' images with the general public in ways that had consequences for the eventual legislative outcome. Some reliance on party leaders is inevitable, given the difficulty of producing collective action among the dozens of members in each of the four congressional parties. Still, as was most obvious in the 1995–1996 budget battle, even the most aggressive leader is constrained by what his or her party colleagues are willing to accept in terms of strategy and policy.

9. Committees play a central role in the legislative process, but their influence is not constant. Budgetary politics since the late 1970s has tended to push key decisions up to central budget and party leaders, and to reduce the independence of committees and their chairs. And yet, it is important to qualify this important consequence of budgetary politics by observing that committees were still responsible for writing the details of most of the legislative provisions of budget packages, even if they were highly constrained by agreements negotiated elsewhere. Even when the top party leaders and administration officials were hammering out the overall shape of the budget deals, most of the language of the budget packages was written by committees, and hundreds of specific policy provisions were negotiated by committee representatives.

The importance of parties, leaders, and committees in congressional policy making will continue to be shaped by the alignment of members' policy preferences, the nature of the issues, and the inherited rules of the game. Perceptions and preferences about budgetary issues are particularly important because of the pervasive effect of the budget on policy initiatives throughout the government. If budget issues begin to lose salience as the deficit fades from memory, then more policy initiatives originating from interest groups and creative members may rejuvenate the committees.

Appendix

Introduction to the Spatial Theory of Legislating

Much of congressional politics has geometric characteristics. When we speak of most Democrats as liberals, most Republicans as conservatives, and some legislators as moderates, we have in mind an ideological or policy spectrum – a line or dimension – along which we can place legislators. In recent Congresses, the parties have been sharply divided, with very little overlap between the parties. Figure A-1 illustrates this for the 109th Congress (2005–2006) for senators. Using a statistical technique, senators were scored on the basis of their overall voting record in the Congress. Democrats and Republicans were concentrated on opposite sides of the spectrum, creating one of the most polarized Senates in history.

Legislators' policy positions also can be represented in two or more dimensions, when appropriate. In Figure A-2, senators' policy positions are identified in two dimensions for a debate on an immigration reform bill in 2006. Their locations are identified with the help of a statistical analysis of their votes on about three dozen amendments and other motions that were considered on the Senate floor. The most significant issue during the debate concerned the standards for allowing illegal immigrants to gain legal entry to the United States. Senators who opposed special arrangements for reentry lined up on the far right, while senators who favored standards that would ease reentry for work or citizenship were located on the left (the horizontal dimension). Other issues, such as the ceiling on the number of legal immigrants allowed, were debated, too, and sometimes divided senators differently than the votes related to the treatment of current illegal immigrants (the vertical dimension). Democrats tended to favor both standards that facilitated reentry and larger quotas, while Republicans were split on reentry standards and tended to favor smaller quotas.[1]

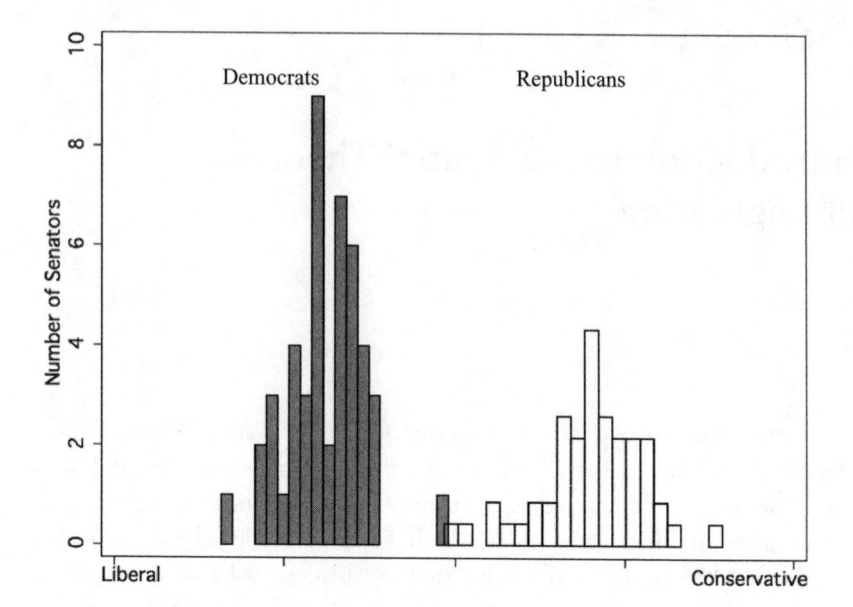

FIGURE A-1. Distribution of Senators on Liberal-Conservative Dimension, 2005–2006 (Democrats on left; Republicans on right). *Source:* Optimal Classification scores; www.voteview.com.

Basic Concepts for Analyzing a Legislative Body

Political scientists have taken advantage of geometric representations to develop spatial theories of legislative politics. The theories provide a way to conceptualize the location of legislators, policy alternatives, and policy outcomes. Like all scientific theories, spatial theories are based on assumptions that allow us to draw inferences about expected behavior. With a few assumptions about legislators, the policy space, and the rules governing

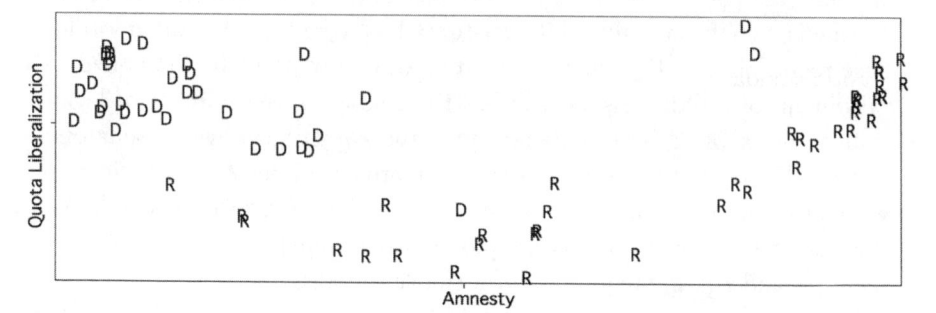

FIGURE A-2. Senators' Policy Positions on 2006 Immigration Bill in Two Dimensions (Democrats, D; Republicans, R). *Source:* Optimal Classification scores on Senate votes related to S2611, 109th Congress.

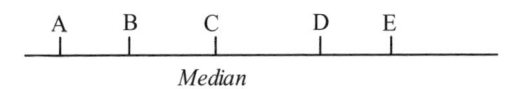

FIGURE A-3. Illustration of the Median Voter Theorem.

decisions, we can deduce remarkably useful and usually intuitive propositions about the location of legislative outcomes. Non-intuitive predictions
are particularly useful because they often yield insights that even the close
observer of legislative politics might overlook.

Preferences and the Policy Space

Spatial theories assume the legislators, presidents, and other players have
preferences about policy outcomes. Preferences may reflect personal beliefs
or political influences. The preferences are assumed to be consistent. For
example, if a legislator prefers policy *A* over policy *B* and also prefers *B*
over *C*, then she favors *A* over *C* (transitive preferences, we say). When
a legislator's preference is depicted geometrically, as in the figures, it is
usually assumed that alternatives that are closer to the legislator's ideal
point are preferred to more distant points (a Euclidean policy space, we
say). Furthermore, it is assumed that each legislator chooses a strategy that
she believes will yield the best possible outcome – that is, minimizes the
distance between her ideal point and the outcome.

Simple Majority Rule and the Median Voter Theorem

Spatial theorists define "institutions" as a set of rules that govern decision
making. Rules may concern who has the right to participate, the "weight"
that each participant has in determining the outcome, the way in which
policy proposals are constructed, the order in which policy proposals are
considered, the standard for a final decision, and so on. Here, we assume
that each legislator has the right to cast one vote and, to begin, that a simple
majority of legislators is required for a proposal to be adopted.

In Figure A-3, a small legislature with five legislators is illustrated. With a
simple majority decision rule, a winning majority will always include legislator C. As the median legislator, C can join two other legislators – to the left
with A and B, to the right with D and E, or in the middle with B and D – to
form a three-vote majority. Of course, larger majorities could form, but they
will always include C. A spatial theorist would say that C is pivotal – C must
be included in a majority and so can demand that the outcome be located
at her ideal point. The *median voter theorem*, which we will not formally prove

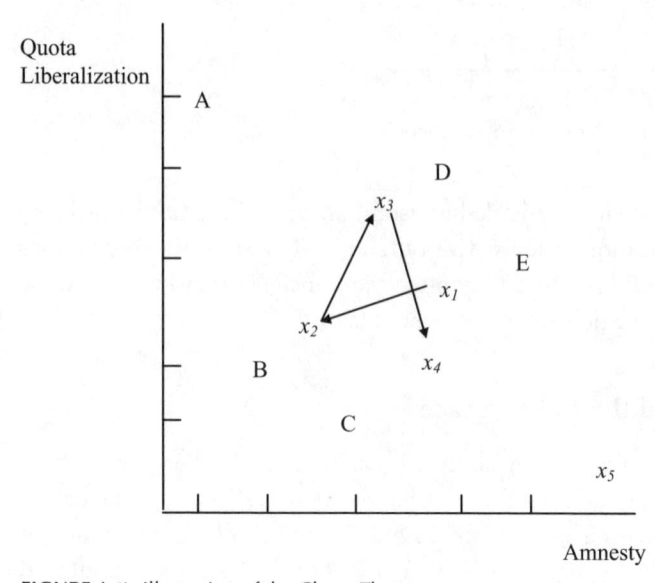

FIGURE A-4. Illustration of the Chaos Theorem.

here, provides that if C's position is adopted it cannot be defeated by another proposal. A corollary is that if two alternatives are presented, a majority will always prefer the alternative closer to the median legislator.

The median voter theorem means that when a median exists we can predict the outcome by knowing only the median legislator's ideal point. Spatial theorists refer to the stable prediction of the median outcome as an *equilibrium*. When a new legislature is elected, a new median location would lead us to predict a change in the outcome. That is, a new equilibrium is expected.

Multidimensional Spaces and the Chaos Theorem

A multidimensional policy space, such as the one in Figure A-4, creates important complications for predicting legislative outcomes. No legislator is the median on both dimensions. C is the median on the amnesty dimension but E is the median on the quota liberalization dimension. What is the expected outcome? In fact, political scientists have demonstrated mathematically that in most cases there is no single predicted outcome, no equilibrium, as there is in the unidimensional case.

A thought experiment will demonstrate an important point. Let us assume that current policy is located at x_1. Legislator B might propose a policy at x_2 and would win the support of A and C, both of whom are closer to x_1 than to x_2 and so would join B to form a majority to vote for x_2 and defeat x_1. But then D might offer x_3 and win the support of A and E. This process can continue indefinitely with a new majority of three forming at each step. If the rules allow a continuous flow of new proposals, there is no single outcome that cannot be defeated by some other proposal. This illustrates the *chaos theorem*. The theorem provides that, as a general rule, we cannot expect a stable outcome from simple majority rule in two (or more) dimensions.

Agenda Setting, Structure-Induced Equilibria, and Political Power

The chaos result – or majority rule cycling – may seem surprising. Legislatures regularly make final decisions without endless cycling through proposals. Why that is the case is the subject of a vast literature in political science. We do not want to review the complexities here, but three important points about legislative politics need to be understood.

First, legislative rules may not allow multidimensional proposals or may limit the number of proposals that may be considered. Such rules would limit the range of possible outcomes and make those outcomes more predictable. If only unidimensional proposals may be considered, the median voter theorem applies and majority rule chaos is avoided. Theorists use the label *structure-induced equilibria* for constraints on outcomes that are imposed by the rules. Thus, even if legislators' preferences are multidimensional, the rules may generate median outcomes by either limiting the range of proposals that are allowed or imposing unidimensionality on the proposals that may be considered.

Second, special influence over the agenda, either granted under the rules or gained through informal means, may control the alternatives subject to a vote and further limit the possible outcomes. A Speaker or presiding officer may be able to limit who is recognized to offer a motion. A coalition of legislators, such as members of the majority party, may agree to support only those proposals that a majority of the coalition endorses, thus limiting the set of proposals that can win majority support.

Three, introducing a proposal that creates a new dimension can transform a situation that would produce a median outcome into one with no predictable outcome. A legislator who dislikes the median outcome might be motivated to offer a proposal on an issue that divides his colleagues in a new way in order to avoid the certain, but undesirable outcome. The original median legislator would be motivated to create an agenda that prevents the proposal on the new issue from being considered.

In practice, then, rules and legislative strategies can contract or expand the range of possible outcomes. Real politics is often played in this way. Political scientists have studied many of the consequences of a variety of rules and

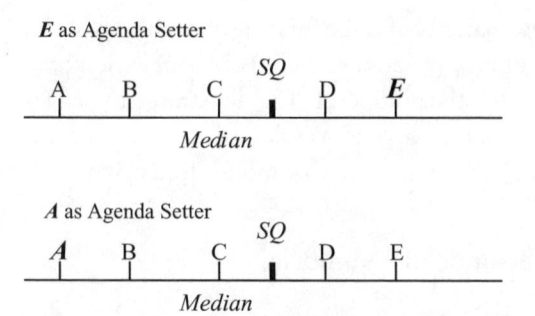

FIGURE A-5. Illustration of the Effect of the Status Quo and an Agenda Setter, the Unidimensional Case.

strategies, but continue to pursue research on the relationship between rules, strategies, and outcomes.

The Status Quo and Agenda Setting

A legislature often inherits policy from past legislatures. In most cases, the inherited policy, which we call the *status quo* (*SQ*), remains in place until a new policy is adopted. That is, the *SQ* is the default outcome if it is not defeated by a new proposal. The set of proposals that can defeat the *SQ* is called the *win set of SQ*. When there are no proposals that can defeat the *SQ*, we say that the win set is empty and predict that the outcome will remain at *SQ*.

The effect of the *SQ* on legislative strategies is important and intuitive. In Figure A-5, five legislators are arrayed on a single dimension. In the figure's top panel, let's assume that no proposal can be considered unless legislator E approves, but if a proposal is offered it can be amended. E, of course, wants the outcome at her own ideal point and might make a proposal there. However, A, B, or C might offer an amendment to move the outcome away from E and to the other side of *SQ*. Such an amendment would win a majority and E would be worse off than if he left the policy at *SQ*. Consequently, we would expect E to refuse to make an initial proposal. In this case, the agenda setter, E, protects the status quo. In contrast, in the lower panel in Figure A-5, legislator A is the agenda setter. Because A prefers the median's position over the *SQ*, A is willing to allow the legislature to consider a proposal and have it amended to C, the expected outcome.

Thus, the location of the status quo relative to the median determines the agenda setter's strategy. With the same agenda setter and median, different issues can generate different outcomes – the median or the *SQ*.

The same logic applies to the multidimensional case, as in Figure A-6. Legislators will support a proposal that improves on the status quo, *SQ*. In

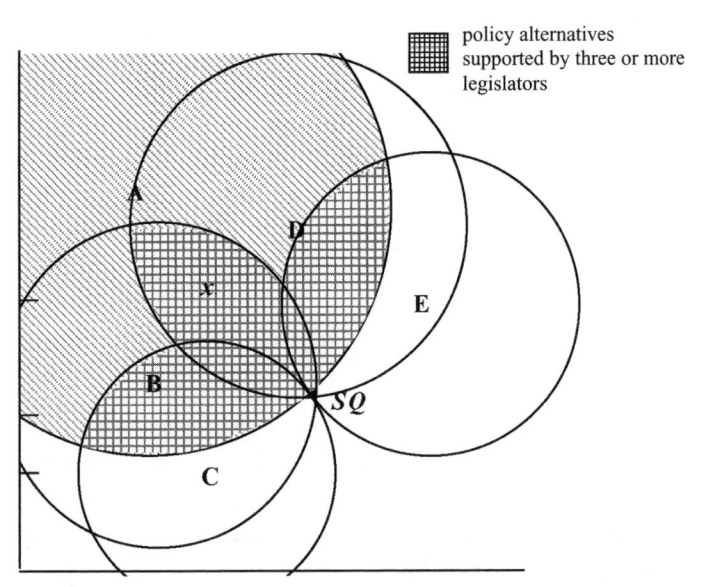

policy alternatives
supported by three or more
legislators

FIGURE A-6. Illustration of the Effect of the Status Quo and an Agenda Setter, the Multidimensional Case.

the figure, these *preferred-to* sets are denoted by the partial or full circles. For example, within the shaded circle centered on legislator A is the preferred-to set for A. The double shaded areas are the sets of locations preferred by at least three of the five legislators over SQ. Because points in the double shaded areas attract majority support for a proposal over the SQ, they define the win set of SQ. A large number of locations will not defeat SQ so majority rule narrowed the possible outcomes considerably. But, in this two-dimensional space, the win set includes a wide range of possibilities, many of which are less preferred to the SQ by one or two of the legislators. A, B, and D might agree to an outcome at x, which would make C and E worse off than leaving the policy at SQ.

Bicameralism, Separation of Powers, Agency Decisions, and Legislative Outcomes

Bicameralism

In the previous section, we considered a single legislative body. Congress and many other legislatures are bicameral, and usually require that a majority of each chamber approve legislation before it is sent to the president or chief executive. Spatially, this means that we must consider the relationship between the outcomes in the two chambers.

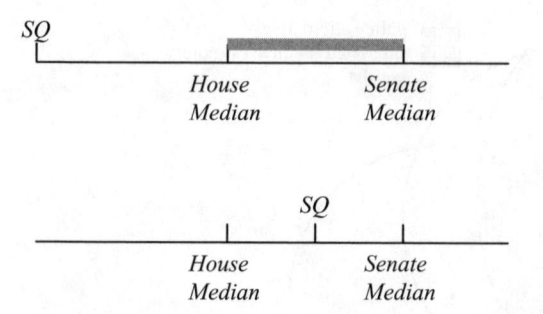

FIGURE A-7. Illustration of a Bicameral Outcome in One Dimension.

In unidimensional space, shown in Figure A-7, the outcome would be negotiated between the House and Senate medians. If both medians favor some of the same proposals over *SQ*, as they do in the top panel, they will negotiate an outcome among the range of proposals that they both prefer to *SQ*. If *SQ* falls between the two medians so that each house median prefers *SQ* to anything the other house would prefer to *SQ*, as in the figure's lower panel, the houses will not agree to a new policy and the outcome will be *SQ*.

In multidimensional space, as depicted in Figure A-6, we would define the bicameral win set as the intersection of the win sets in the two houses. We do not show that situation here. The overlap in the win sets for the two houses can be very small or very large. Little overlap greatly narrows the range of possible outcomes. Large overlap creates the possibility that a conference committee charged with finding compromise legislation will be able to exercise great discretion in determining the location of the final bill and still be able to attract majority support in both houses for the final version.

The President and the Veto

Under the Constitution, the president may veto legislation and a veto can be overridden only with the support of a two-thirds majority in each house of Congress. The threshold of a two-thirds majority in each house makes it necessary to appeal to more legislators than the requirement of a simple majority for initial approval of legislation. In our five-legislators illustrations, this means attracting the support of four of the five legislators (three of five would be less than the two-thirds required).

The president will veto any legislation that makes him worse off than *SQ*. In one dimension, several possibilities arise. In Figure A-8, the president's ideal point is *P* and the House and Senate medians are M_H and M_S, respectively. The two houses of Congress negotiate a bill at *B* somewhere between their medians. The president prefers *SQ* to *B* so he vetoes the bill. Both

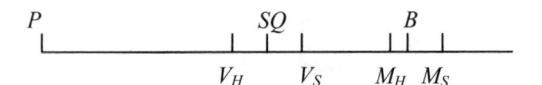

FIGURE A-8. Illustration of Upholding a Presidential Veto, in One Dimension.

House and Senate medians would like to override the veto but they must gain the support of two thirds of their colleagues. V_H and V_S are the *veto pivots*. That is, they are the legislators who are the leftmost members of the two-thirds majority that is required to override a veto. Without their support for the bill over the SQ, the veto cannot be overridden. In this case, V_H prefers SQ to B and so votes against the override. SQ is the outcome. Thus, the general rule is that a presidential veto will kill a bill whenever at least one of the veto pivots is on the same side of SQ as the president.

Other scenarios are easy to understand without illustration. Whenever the chamber medians are on the same side of SQ as the president, the president will sign the bill with a veto. Whenever V_H and V_S are on the same side of SQ opposite the president (not shown), the two houses of Congress can override the veto of the president.

As always, the multidimensional case is more complicated but it is still easy to visualize. In Figure A-9, there are two regions in which four of the five legislators of one house would favor the bill over the SQ. Consequently, a veto would be overridden any time the president vetoes a bill that is located in those regions. The bill also would have to be located in similar regions in the other house for both houses to override a president's veto. A bill that is located in the *veto win set of SQ* is one for which a veto can be overridden in both houses.

Plainly, the two-thirds majority requirement for a veto override shrinks the region of bill locations that can survive a veto to one that is smaller than the region of bill locations that can receive simple majority support in both houses. The implication is that the threat of a veto requires more careful negotiations within Congress and may have implications for legislators who win and lose. In Figure A-9, for example, the bill at x_2 survives a veto but a bill at x_1 does not, although both would receive simple majority support. But the outcome at x_2 is less favorable to legislators A and D and more favorable to B and C.

Agency Decisions

Political scientists often think of executive branch agencies as having policy preferences of their own. Staffed by people who have personal or

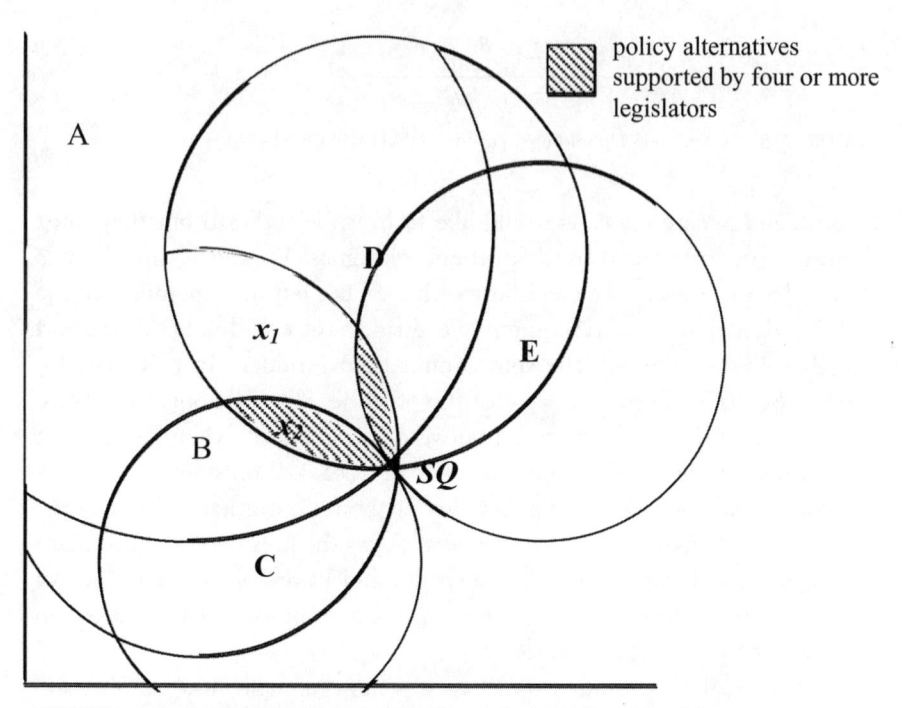

FIGURE A-9. Location of Veto Override Coalitions, the Multidimensional Case.

professional experience in a policy field, agencies are likely to devise rules and regulations that implement law in a manner that reflects their own preferences. Congress and presidents may seek to control the independence of agencies, but agency officials know that it may not be easy for Congress and the president to enact new legislation to place additional constraints on them. After all, new legislation requires the approval of the House, Senate, and president, or, in the case of a veto, a two-thirds majority in both houses. This is a high threshold. If a House majority, Senate majority, or president favors the direction an agency is taking, it can block legislation that would place new constraints in statute. (We have reported on other congressional strategies in Chapter 9.)

The strategic setting of agency decision making can be treated spatially, as we do in Figure A-10. To simplify, we characterize the House and Senate as having specific locations in multidimensional space just as the president does. If an agency took action to move a policy from a_1 (the current policy) to a_2, the Senate would like the move and block any effort by the House to enact legislation to require that the policy be returned to a_1. In this case, the agency, knowing that the Senate will protect its move, is free to shift policy without fear that the law will be changed. In contrast, if the agency

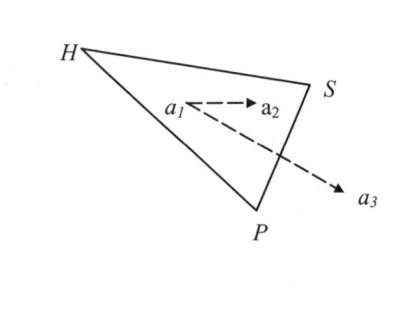

FIGURE A-10. Illustration of Agency Discretion, in Multidimensional Space.

sought to move policy as far as a_3, all three of the policy-making institutions would be better off by enacting legislation located on the line between S and P.

These scenarios demonstrate that the autonomy of an agency is limited to the range of policy moves that will not generate a new law. The farther apart the House, Senate, and president, the greater the discretion the agency enjoys. In fact, the triangle formed by the House, Senate, and president defines the limits of agency discretion. Any move that yields policy inside or to the edge of the triangle will be defended by at least one of the House, Senate, or president. Any move outside of the triangle will stimulate new legislation.

Advanced Theory and the Limits of Spatial Theory

We have presented a rudimentary introduction to the spatial theory of legislative politics. Political scientists have extended the theory in many directions. They have developed additional theory on the conditions that limit the range of possible outcomes under majority rule, explored the effect of agenda control rules that advantage parties or committees, and considered the effects of different assumptions about legislators' preferences and decision rules. We encourage our readers to pursue these important subjects elsewhere.

Spatial theory is not the ultimate theory of legislative politics. The spatial theorist assumes that legislators' policy preferences are known and invariant and theorizes only about how they motivate strategies. The determinants of legislators' policy preferences are beyond the scope of spatial theory.

The effects of nonpolicy motivations, such as the desire for reelection or to serve in the majority party, also are beyond the scope of spatial theory. Such motivations may be the overriding consideration in some circumstances. A legislator whose bill is rejected by the House of Representatives might be seen as a loser by some observers, but she may benefit from favorable press coverage and an appreciative home constituency for putting up a good fight. A legislative majority that fails to override a presidential veto may use the issue in a campaign to get more fellow partisans elected in the next Congress. Winning and losing in politics is sometimes hard to judge, at least in the short term.

Nevertheless, spatial theory is a powerful tool for predicting behavior and legislative outcomes. It often establishes a baseline expectation for outcomes against which the effects of other considerations can be measured. We can better judge the effects of persuasion by party leaders or presidents once we have a prediction for the outcome expected on the basis of legislators' prior policy preferences. It also shows that policy preferences and parliamentary rules often do not yield very specific predictions and define sometimes large ranges of possible outcomes that can be influenced by other political forces at work. Most important, spatial theory yields important insights about the effects of institutions – the rules of the game – that are so transparent in legislative decision making.

Notes

1. The American Congress

1. Paul Boller, *Congressional Anecdotes* (New York: Oxford University Press, 1991), 18.
2. Norman J. Ornstein, "Congress Inside Out: Here's Why Life on the Hill Is Meaner Than Ever," *Roll Call*, September 20, 1993, 27.
3. Robert A. Dahl, "Americans Struggle to Cope with a New Political Order That Works in Opaque and Mysterious Ways," *Public Affairs Report* (Institute of Governmental Studies, University of California, Berkeley, September 1993), 1, 4–6.
4. Robert H. Salisbury, "The Paradox of Interest Groups in Washington–More Groups, Less Clout," in *The New American Political System*, 2nd ed., ed. Anthony King, 203–229 (Washington, D.C.: American Enterprise Institute, 1990). For an analysis of the effects of these developments on Congress, see Barbara Sinclair, *The Transformation of the U.S. Senate* (Baltimore: Johns Hopkins University Press, 1989), 57–64.
5. See Theodore J. Lowi, "Toward a Legislature of the First Kind," in *Knowledge, Power, and the Congress*, ed. William H. Robinson and Clay H. Wellborn, 9–36 (Washington, D.C.: Congressional Quarterly Press, 1991).
6. Lawrence C. Dodd, "Congress and the Politics of Renewal: Redressing the Crisis of Legitimation," in *Congress Reconsidered*, 5th ed., ed. Lawrence C. Dodd and Bruce I. Oppenheimer, 426 (Washington, D.C.: Congressional Quarterly Press, 1993).
7. David E. Price, "Comment," in *Knowledge, Power, and the Congress*, 128.
8. Richard F. Fenno, Jr. *Learning to Govern: An Institutional View of the 104th Congress* (Washington, D.C.: Brookings Institution, 1997). On the consequences of alternating party control of Congress, also see Lawrence C. Dodd and Bruce I. Oppenheimer, "Congress and the Emerging Order: Conditional Party Government or Constructive Partisanship?" in *Congress Reconsidered*, 6th ed., 390–413.
9. "Capitol Hill's Uncertainty Principle," *National Journal*, November 2, 1996: 2365.

2. Representation and Lawmaking in Congress

1. Robert S. Weissberg, "Collective vs. Dyadic Representation in Congress," *American Political Science Review* 72 (1978): 535–547.

2. Jane J. Mansbridge, *Beyond Adversarial Democracy* (Chicago: University of Chicago Press, 1983).

4. Members, Goals, Resources, and Strategies

1. David E. Price, *The Congressional Experience: A View from the Hill* (Boston: Little, Brown, 1973), 146.
2. Quoted in Craig Winneker, "That Was The Year That Was...Whew!" *Roll Call*, December 21, 1992, 15.
3. As quoted in Deering and Smith, *Committees in Congress*, 67.
4. Richard F. Fenno, Jr., *The Making of a Senator: Dan Quayle* (Washington, D.C.: Congressional Quarterly Press, 1989), 29.
5. From Neil MacNeil, *Forge of Democracy: The House of Representatives* (NewYork: D. McKay, 1963), 141.
6. Adapted from Richard F. Fenno, Jr., *Home Style: House Members in Their Districts* (Boston: Little, Brown, 1978), 1–30.
7. Michael J. Malbin, *Unelected Representatives: Congressional Staff and the Future of Representative Government* (New York: Basic Books, 1980), 5.
8. Lori Montgomery and Paul Kane, "Sweeping Bailout Bill Unveiled," *Washington Post*, September 29, 2008.
9. John W. Kingdon, *Congressmen's Voting Decisions*, 2nd ed. (New York: Harper & Row, 1981), 96.
10. Richard F. Fenno, Jr., *The Emergence of a Senate Leader: Pete Domenici and the Reagan Budget* (Washington, D.C.: Congressional Quarterly Press, 1991), 134.
11. A report on the Senate aides' responses can be found in Steven S. Smith, "Informal Leadership in the Senate," in *Leading Congress*, ed. John Kornacki (Washington, D.C.: Congressional Quarterly Press, 1990), 71–83. Most respondents were members' legislative directors or administrative assistants.
12. Press release, "U.S. Senator Dan Quayle: Effective Leadership for Indiana," November 3, 1986.

5. Parties and Leaders

1. *Majority and Minority Leaders of the Senate*. U.S. Senate No. 91–20 (Washington, D.C.: Government Printing Office, 1969), 13.

6. The Standing Committees

1. Joel D. Aberbach, "What Has Happened to the Watchful Eye?" *Congress and the Presidency* 29 (2002): 3–23.

7. The Rules of the Legislative Game

1. Robert H. Michel, "The Minority Leader Replies," *Washington Post*, December 29, 1987, A14.
2. *Congressional Record*, October 5, 1992, S16894.

8. The Floor and Voting

1. Information taken from "Pocket Guide to Common Parliamentary Phrases in the House of Representatives." Congressional Research Service.
2. Some rules do not affect amending activity, so percentages do not sum to 100.

9. Congress and the President

1. Charles M. Cameron, *Veto Bargaining: Presidents and the Politics of Negative Power* (New York: Cambridge University Press, 2000), 188.
2. Paul Light, *The President's Agenda*, revised edition (Baltimore: Johns Hopkins University Press, 1991), 2.
3. Citing a study by Christopher Kelley, Charlie Savage, "House Panel Probing Bush's Record on Signing Statements," *The Boston Globe*, February 1, 2007.
4. Quoted in Light, *President's Agenda*, 13.
5. *Congressional Record*, February 16, 2006: S1402.
6. Henry B. Hogue, "Recess Appointments: Frequently Asked Questions," CRS Report, Congressional Research Services, September 10, 2002; Henry B. Hogue, "Recess Appointments: Frequently Asked Questions," CRS Report, Congressional Research Services, January 16, 2007.

10. Congress and the Courts

1. William T. Gormley, Jr. "The Bureaucracy and its Masters: The New Madisonian System in the U.S." *Governance*, January 1991, 10–11.

11. Congress, Lobbyists, and Interest Groups

1. Survey conducted by The Center on Congress at Indiana University in March 2008. Available at http://www.centeroncongress.org/learn_about/feature/survey_public_attitudes_detail_march_2008.php.
2. CBS New/*New York Times Poll* conducted September 15–19, 2006. Available at http://www. pollingreport. com/congress.htm#misc.

3. Kay Lehman Schlozman and John T. Tierney, *Organized Interests and American Democracy* (New York: Harper & Row, 1986), 74–82.

4. Jeffrey M. Berry, *The Interest Group Society*, 2nd ed. (Glenview, IL: Scott, Foresman, 1989), 20–21.

5. Jeffrey H. Birnbaum, "The Road to Riches is Called K Street," *The Washington Post*, June 22, 2005.

6. Hedrick Smith, *The Power Game* (New York: Ballantine Books, 1988), 232.

7. Matt Kelley, "Third of Top Aides Become Lobbyists," *USA Today*, December 26, 2008.

8. Quoted in John T. Tierney and Kay Lehman Schlozman, "Congress and Organized Interests," in *Congressional Politics*, ed. Christopher J. Deering (Chicago: Dorsey Press, 1989), 212.

9. Christine Mahoney and Frank Baumgartner, "When To Go It Alone: The Determinants and Effects of Interest-Group Coalitions," Working Paper.

10. Hans Nichols, "K Street Freezes out Dems," *The Hill*, September 15, 2004.

11. "Corruption Named as Key Issue by Voters in Exit Polls." Available at CNN.com http://www.cnn.com/2006/POLITICS/11/07/election.exitpolls/index.html.

12. Tierney and Schlozman, "Congress and Organized Interests," 216.

13. Robert H. Salisbury, "Putting Interests Back into Interest Groups," in *Interest Group Politics*, 3rd ed., ed. Allan J. Cigler and Burdett A. Loomis (Washington, D.C.: Congressional Quarterly Press, 1991), 382–383.

12. Congress and Budget Politics

1. The most current budget figures and estimates are available in the current budget projections section of the Congressional Budget Office's website, http://www.cbo.gov.

2. On the developments leading up to the enactment of budget reform in 1974, see Allen Schick, *Congress and Money: Budgeting, Spending and Taxing* (Washington, D.C.: The Urban Institute, 1980), 17–81.

3. On the 1989 budget battle, see Lawrence J. Hass, *Running on Empty: Bush, Congress, and the Politics of a Bankrupt Government* (Homewood, IL: Business One-Irwin, 1990).

Appendix. Introduction to the Spatial Theory of Legislating

1. Figure A-2 is drawn to show greater variance on the first dimension, which explains far more the variance in voting behavior than the second dimension.

Suggested Readings

1. The American Congress: Modern Trends

Burrell, Barbara C. *A Woman's Place Is in the House*. Ann Arbor: University of Michigan Press, 1994.

Carroll, Susan J. *The Impact of Women in Public Office*. Bloomington: Indiana University Press, 2001.

Cook, Elizabeth Adell, Sue Thomas, and Clyde Wilcox, eds. *The Year of the Woman: Myths and Reality*. Boulder: Westview, 1994.

Cooper, Joseph, ed. *Congress and the Decline of Public Trust: Why Can't the Government Do What's Right*. Boulder: Westview Press, 1999.

Dodson, Debra L. 2006. *The Impact of Women in Congress*. Oxford; New York: Oxford University Press.

Gamble, Katrina L. "Black Political Representation: An Examination of Legislative Activity Within U.S. House Committees." *Legislative Studies Quarterly* 32, no. 3 (2007): 421–443.

Gertzog, Irwin N. *Women and Power on Capitol Hill: Reconstructing the Congressional Women's Caucus*. Boulder: Lynne Reinner Publishers, 2004.

Hibbing, John R., and Elizabeth Theiss-Morse *Congress as Public Enemy*. Cambridge: Cambridge University Press, 1995.

Hibbing, John R. *Congressional Careers: Contours of Life in the U.S. House of Representatives*. Chapel Hill: University of North Carolina Press, 1991.

Kean, Thomas H., Lee Hamilton, and Benjamin Rhodes. *Without Precedent: The Inside Story of the 9/11 Commission*. 1st ed. New York: Alfred A. Knopf, 2006.

Lawless, Jennifer L., and Richard Logan Fox. *It Takes a Candidate: Why Women Don't Run for Office*. Cambridge; New York: Cambridge University Press, 2005.

Loomis, Burdett A. *The New American Politician: Ambition, Entrepreneurship, and the Changing Face of Political Life*. New York: Basic Books, 1988.

Mann, Thomas E., and Norman J. Ornstein. *The Broken Branch: How Congress is Failing America and How to Get It Back on Track*. Oxford; New York: Oxford University Press, 2006.

Mayhew, David R. *America's Congress: Actions in the Public Sphere-James Madison through Newt Gingrich*. New Haven: Yale University Press, 2000.

Mikulski, Barbara. et al. *Nine and Counting: The Women of the Senate*. William Morris and Company, 2000.

Mondak, Jeffery J., Edward G. Carmines, Robert Huckfeldt, Dona-Gene Mitchell, and Scot Schraufnagel. "Does Familiarity Breed Contempt? The Impact of Information on Mass Attitudes toward Congress." *American Journal of Political Science* 51, no. 1 (2007): 34–48.

Ornstein, Norman J., Thomas E. Mann, and Michael Malbin. *Vital Statistics on Congress, 2001–2002*. Washington, D.C.: AEI Press, 2002.

Povich, Elaine S. *Nancy Pelosi: a biography. Greenwood biographies*. Westport, Conn.: Greenwood Press, 2008.

Rosenthal, Cindy S., ed. *Women Transforming Congress*. Norman: University of Oklahoma Press, 2002.

Schaffner, Brian F, Wendy J. Schiller, and Patrick J. Sellers. "Tactical and Contextual Determinants of U.S. Senators' Approval Ratings." *Legislative Studies Quarterly* 28, no. 2 (2003): 203–223.

Schwindt-Bayer, Leslie A., and Renatto Corbetta. "Gender Turnover and Roll-Call Voting in the U.S. House of Representatives." *Legislative Studies Quarterly* 29, no. 2 (2004): 215–229.

Shepsle, Kenneth. *"The Changing Textbook Congress,"* In *Can the Government Govern?*, John E. Chubb and Paul E. Peterson, eds. Washington, D.C.: Brookings Institution Press, 1989.

Sinclair, Barbara. *The Transformation of the U.S. Senate*. Baltimore: Johns Hopkins University Press, 1989.

Swain, Carol. *Black Faces, Black Interests: The Representation of African Americans in Congress*. Cambridge: Harvard University Press, 1993.

Swers, Michele L. *The Difference Women Make: The Policy Impact of Women in Congress*. Chicago: University of Chicago Press, 2002.

Thomas, Sue. *How Women Legislate*. New York: Oxford University Press, 1994.

Tolchin, Susan, and Martin Tolchin. *Glass Houses: Congressional Ethics and the Politics of Venom*. Boulder: Westview Press, 2003.

United States. Congress. House. Committee on House Administration., and United States. Congress. House. Office of History and Preservation. 2008. *Black Americans in Congress, 1870–2007*. Washington, D.C.: U.S. G.P.O.

Whitby, Kenny J. *The Color of Representation: Congressional Behavior and Black Interests*. Ann Arbor: University of Michigan Press, 1998.

2. Representation and Lawmaking in Congress: The Constitutional and Historical Context

Anderson, Thorton. *Creating the Constitution: The Convention of 1787 and the First Congress*. University Park: Pennsylvania State University Press, 1993.

Baker, Richard A., Nancy Erickson, and United States. *Congress. Senate. 2007. Traditions of the United States Senate.* Washington, D.C.: U.S. Senate, 2007.

Barclay, John M. *Constitution of the United States of America with the Amendments thereto: To Which are Added Jefferson's Manual of Parliamentary Practice, The Standing Rules and Orders for Conducting Business in The House of Representatives and Senate of the United States and Barclay's Digest of the Rules of Proceeding in the House of Representatives of the United States.* Washington, D.C.: Government Printing Office. 1860, 1863, 1867, 1868, 1872.

Bates, Ernest S. *The Story of Congress: 1789–1935.* New York: Harper and Brothers, 1936.

Bessette, Joseph M. *The Mild Voice of Reason: Deliberative Democracy and American National Government.* Chicago: University of Chicago Press, 1994.

Binder, Sarah. "Dynamics of Legislative Gridlock, 1947–96." *American Political Science Review* 93 (1999): 519–534.

Byrd, Robert C. The Senate, 1789–1989. Vol. 4. Historical Statistics, 1789–1992. 100th Congress, 1st session.S. Doc. 100–20. Washington, D.C.: Government Printing Office, 1993.

Cooper, Joseph. *Congress and its Committees: A Historical Approach to the Role of Committees in the Legislative Process.* New York: Garland Publishing, Inc., 1988.

Cooper, Joseph. *The Origins of the Standing Committees and the Development of the Modern House.* Houston: William Marsh Rice University, 1970.

Currie, David P. *The Constitution Congress: The Federalist Period, 1789–1801.* Chicago: University of Chicago Press, 1997.

Davidson, Roger, and Walter Oleszek. *Congress Against Itself.* Bloomington: Indiana University Press, 1977.

Devins, Neal, and Keith E. Whittington. *Congress and the Constitution.* Durham: Duke University Press, 2005.

Fenno, Richard, Jr. *The United States Senate: A Bicameral Perspective.* Washington, D.C.: American Enterprise Institute, 1982.

Grant, J. Tobin, and Thomas J. Rudolph. "The Job of Representation in Congress: Public Expectations and Representative Approval." *Legislative Studies Quarterly* 29, no. 3 (2004): 431–445.

Haynes, George H. *The Election of Senators.* New York: Henry Holt and Company, 1906.

Haynes, George H. *The Senate of the United States: Its History and Practice.* 2 vols. Boston: Houghton Mifflin, 1938.

Hoffer, William James. 2007. *To Enlarge the Machinery of Government: Congressional Debates and the Growth of the American State, 1858–1891, Reconfiguring American Political History.* Baltimore: Johns Hopkins University Press.

Jefferson, Thomas. *A Manual of Parliamentary Practice for the Use of the Senate of the United States.* First Edition 1801 With Annotations by the Author. Washington, D.C.: Samuel Harrison Smith, 1801. Reprint, Washington, D.C.: Government Printing Office (page references are to the reprint edition), 1993.

Jillson, Calvin, and Rick Wilson. *Congressional Dynamics: Structure, Coordination, and Choice in the First American Congress, 1774–1789.* Stanford: Stanford University Press, 1994.

Lapinski, John S. "Policy Substance and Performance in American Lawmaking, 1877–1994." *American Journal of Political Science* 52, no. 2 (2008): 235–251.

Morgan, Donald. *Congress and the Constitution*. Cambridge: Harvard University Press, 1966.

Polsby, Nelson W. *How Congress Evolves: Social Bases of Institutional Change*. Oxford; New York: Oxford University Press, 2004.

Rakove, Jack N. *Original Meanings: Politics and Ideas in the Making of the Constitution*. New York: Vintage, 1997.

Remini, Robert V. and the Library of Congress. *The House: The History of the House of Representatives*. New York: Harper Collins, 2006.

Riker, William H. "The Senate and American Federalism." *American Political Science Review* 49, no. 2 (1955): 452–469.

Rothman, David J. *Politics and Power: The United States Senate, 1869–1901*. Cambridge: Harvard University Press, 1966.

Schickler, Eric. *Disjointed Pluralism*. Princeton: Princeton University Press, 2001.

Schiller, Wendy. *Partners and Rivals: Representation in U.S. Senate Delegations*. Princeton: Princeton University Press, 2000.

Swift, Elaine K. *The Making of an American Senate: Reconstitutive Change in Congress, 1787–1841*. Ann Arbor: University of Michigan Press, 1996.

Wilson, Woodrow. *Congressional Government: A Study in American Politics*. Boston: Houghton Mifflin Company, 1885 [1985].

Wilson, Woodrow, and Walter Lippmann. *Congressional Government: A Study in American Politics*. Mineola, NY: Dover Publication, 2006.

Wirls, Daniel, and Stephen Wirls. *The Invention of the United States Senate*. Baltimore: Johns Hopkins University Press, 2004.

Young, James S. *The Washington Community, 1800–1828*. New York: Columbia University Press, 1966.

Zelizer, Julian E. 2006. *On Capitol Hill: The Struggle to Reform Congress and Its Consequences, 1948–2000*. 1st pbk. ed. Cambridge; New York: Cambridge University Press.
Websites:
U.S. Senate History. http://www.senate.gov/pagelayout/history/g three sections with teasers/origins.htm

3. Congressional Elections and Policy Alignments

Abramowitz, Alan I., and Jeffrey Segal. *Senate Elections*. Ann Arbor: University of Michigan Press, 1992.

Baretto, Matt A., Gary M. Segura, and Nathan D. Woods. "The Mobilizing Effect of Majority-Minority Districts on Latino Turnout." *American Political Science Review* 98, no. 1 (2004): 65–76.

Benoit, Kenneth, and Michael Marsh. "The Campaign Value of Incumbency: A New Solution to the Puzzle of Less Effective Incumbent Spending." *American Journal of Political Science* 52, no. 4 (2008): 874–890.

Bickerstaff, Steve. 2007. *Lines in the sand: congressional redistricting in Texas and the downfall of Tom DeLay.* 1st ed. Austin, Tex.: University of Texas Press.

Biersack, Robert, John Green, Paul Herrnson, Lynda Powell and Clyde Wilcox. *The Financiers of Congressional Elections: Investors, Ideologues, and Intimates.* New York: Columbia University Press, 2003.

Brady, David W. *Critical Elections and Congressional Policy Making.* Stanford: Stanford University Press, 1988.

Brady, David W., Hahrie Han, and Jeremy C. Pope. "Primary Elections and Candidate Ideology: Out of Step with the Primary Electorate?" *Legislative Studies Quarterly* 32, no. 1 (2007): 79–105.

Burden, Barry, and David Kimball. *Why Americans Split Their Tickets: Campaigns, Competition, and Divided Government.* Ann Arbor: The University of Michigan Press, 2002.

Campbell, James E. *The Presidential Pulse of Congressional Elections.* Lexington, KY: University of Kentucky Press, 1993.

Canon, David T. *Race, Redistricting, and Representation.* Chicago: University of Chicago Press, 1991.

Canon, David. *Race, Redistricting, and Representation: The Unintended Consequences of Black Majority Districts.* Chicago: University of Chicago Press, 1999.

Carson, Jamie L., Erik J. Engstrom, and Jason M. Roberts. "Candidate Quality, the Personal Vote, and the Incumbency Advantage in Congress." *American Political Science Review* 101, no. 2 (2007): 289–301.

Citrin, J, Eric Schickler, and John Sides. "What if Everyone Voted? Simulating the Impact of Increased Turnout in Senate Elections." *American Journal of Political Science* 47, no. 1 (2003): 75–90.

Corrado, Anthony, Thomas E. Mann, and Trevor Potter, eds. *Inside the Campaign Finance Battle: Court Testimony on the New Reforms.* Washington, D.C.: Brookings Institution Press, 2003.

Currinder, Marian L. "Leadership PAC Contributions Strategies and House Member Ambitions." *Legislative Studies Quarterly* 28, no. 4 (2003): 551–577.

Currinder, Marian. *Money in the House: Campaign Funds and Congressional Party Politics.* 1st ed. Boulder, CO: Westview Press, 2008.

Dion, Douglas. *Turning the Legislative Thumbscrew.* Ann Arbor: University of Michigan Press, 1997.

Dwyer, Diane, and Victoria Farrar-Meyers. *Legislative Labyrinth: Congress and Campaign Finance Reform.* Washington, D.C.: Congressional Quarterly Press, 2000.

Fenno, Richard, Jr. *Congress at the Grassroots: Representational Change in the South, 1970–1998.* Chapel Hill: University of North Carolina Press, 2000.

Fenno, Richard, Jr. *Senators on the Campaign Trail: The Politics of Representation.* Norman: University of Oklahoma Press, 1996.

Fiorina, Morris P. *Congress: Keystone of the Washington Establishment,* 2nd ed. New Haven: Yale University Press, 1989.

Fowler, Linda, and Robert McClure. *Political Ambition: Who Decides to Run for Congress.* New Haven: Yale University Press, 1989.

Glazer, Amihai, and Bernard Grofman. "Two Plus Two Plus Two Equals Six: Tenure of Office of Senators and Representatives, 1953–1983." *Legislative Studies Quarterly* 12, no. 4 (1987): 555–63.

Gronke, Paul. *The Electorate, the Campaign, and the Office: A Unified Approach to Senate and House Elections.* Ann Arbor: University of Michigan Press, 2000.

Gross, Christian, and Antoine Yoshinaka. "The Electoral Consequences of Party Switching by Incumbent Members of Congress, 1947–2000." *Legislative Studies Quarterly* 28, no. 1 (2003): 55–76.

Herrnson, Paul S. *Congressional Elections: Campaigning at Home and in Washington,* 3rd ed. Washington, D.C.: Congressional Quarterly Press, 2000.

Jacobson, Gary C. *The Politics of Congressional Elections.* 6th ed. New York: Longman, 2004.

Jacobson, G. and S. Kernell. *Strategy and Choice in Congressional Elections.* New Haven: Yale University Press, 1983.

Jacobson, Gary, Samuel Kernell, and Jeffrey Lazarus. "Assessing the President's Role as Party Agent in Congressional Elections: The Case of Bill Clinton in 2000." *Legislative Studies Quarterly* 29, no. 2 (2004): 159–184.

Jones, David R., and Monika L. McDermott. "The Responsible Party Government Model in House and Senate Elections." *American Journal of Political Science* 48, no. 1 (2004): 1–12.

Kahn, Kim F., and Patrick J. Kenney. *The Spectacle of U.S. Senate Campaigns.* Princeton: Princeton University Press, 1999.

Kazee, Thomas, ed. *Who Runs for Congress? Ambition, Context, and Candidate Emergence.* Washington, D.C.: Congressional Quarterly Press, 1994.

Lewis-Beck, Michael, and Tom Rice. *Forecasting Elections.* Washington, D.C.: Congressional Quarterly Press, 1992.

Lipinski, Daniel L., William T. Bianco, and Ryan Work. "What Happens When House Members 'Run with Congress'? Consequences of Institutional Loyalty." *Legislative Studies Quarterly* 28, no. 3 (2003): 413–429.

Maestas, Cherie, Sarah Fulton, L. Sandy Maisel, and Walter Stone. "When to Risk It? Institutions, Ambitions, and the Decision to Run for the U.S. House." *American Political Science Review* 100 (2) (2006): 195–208.

Maestas, Cherie D., and Cynthia R. Rugeley. "Assessing the 'Experience Bonus' Through Examining Strategic Entry, Candidate Quality, and Campaign Receipts in U.S. House Elections." *American Journal of Political Science* 52, no. 3 (2008): 520–535.

Magleby, David B., J. Quin Monson, and Kelly D. Patterson. *Electing Congress: New Rules for an Old Game: Real Politics in America.* Upper Saddle River, NJ: Pearson Prentice Hall, 2007.

Maisel, L. Sandy. *From Obscurity to Oblivion: Running in the Congressional Primary.* Knoxville: University of Tennessee Press, 1982.

Mann, Thomas E. *Unsafe at Any Margin: Interpreting Congressional Elections.* Washington, D.C.: American Enterprise Institute Press, 1978.

Nelson, Candice J., David A. Dulio, and Stephen K. Medvic. *Shades of Gray: Perspectives on Campaign Ethics.* Washington, D.C.: Brookings Institution Press, 2002.

Peterson, David, et al. "Congressional Response to Mandate Elections." *American Journal of Political Science* 47, no. 3 (2003): 411–426.

Stone, Walter, L. Sandy Maisel, and Cherie Maestas. "Quality Counts: Extending the Strategic Politician Model of Incumbent Deterrence." *American Journal of Political Science* 48, no. 3 (2004): 479–495.

Sulkin, Tracy. *Issue Politics in Congress*. Cambridge; New York: Cambridge University Press, 2005.

Tate, Katherine. "Black Opinion on the Legitimacy of Racial Redistricting and Minority-Majority Districts." *American Political Science Review* 97, no. 1 (2003): 45–56.

Thurber, James. ed. *The Battle for Congress: Consultants, Candidates, and Voters*. Washington, D.C.: Brookings Institution Press, 2000.

West, Darrell M. *Air Wars: Television Advertising in Election Campaigns 1952–1996*. Washington, D.C.: Congressional Quarterly Press, 1997.

Wolfensberger, Donald. *Congress and the People: Deliberative Democracy on Trial*. Baltimore: Johns Hopkins University Press, 1999.

Websites:

Federal Election Commission. http://www.fec.gov/

Census Bureau (Districts and Apportionment). http://fastfacts.census.gov/home/cws/main.html

4. Members, Goals, Resources, and Strategies

Abramson, Paul, John Aldrich, and David Rohde. "Progressive Ambition Among United States Senators: 1972–1988." *Journal of Politics* 49, no. 1 (1987): 3–55.

Baker, Ross K. *Friend and Foe in the U.S. Senate*. New York: Free Press, 1980.

Bianco, William. *Trust: Representatives and Constituents*. Ann Arbor: University of Michigan Press, 1994.

Burden, Barry C. *Personal Roots of Representation*. Princeton: Princeton University Press, 2007.

Cain, Bruce, John Ferejohn, and Morris Fiorina. *The Personal Vote: Constituency Service and Electoral Independence*. Cambridge: Harvard University Press, 1987.

Canon, David. *Actors, Athletes, and Astronauts: Political Amateurs in the United States Congress*. Chicago: University of Chicago Press, 1990.

Cook, Timothy E. *Making Laws and Making News: Media Strategies in the U.S. House of Representatives*. Washington, D.C.: Brookings Institution Press, 1989.

Davidson, Roger H. *The Role of the Congressman*. Indianapolis: Bobbs-Merrill, 1969.

Dodd, Lawrence C. 1977. "Congress and the Quest for Power." In *Congress Reconsidered*, L.C. Dodd and B. Oppenheimer, eds. New York: Praeger.

Fenno, Richard, Jr. *Going Home: Black Representatives and Their Constituents*. Chicago: University of Chicago Press, 2003.

Fenno, Richard, Jr. *Home Style: House Members in Their Districts*. Boston: Little, Brown, 1978.

Fowler, Linda, and Robert McClure. *Political Ambition: Who Decides to Run for Congress?* New Haven: Yale University Press, 1989.

Fox, Harrison, Jr., and Susan W. Hammond. *Congressional Staffs: The Invisible Force in American Lawmaking*. New York: Free Press, 1977.

Lee, Frances E., *and Brice I. Oppenheimer. Sizing Up the Senate: The Unequal Consequences of Equal Representation*. Chicago: University of Chicago Press, 1999.

Lee, Frances E. "Bicameralism and Geographic Politics: Allocating Funds in the House and Senate." *Legislative Studies Quarterly* 29, no. 2 (2004): 185–213.

Loomis, Burdett. The New American Politician. New York: Basic Books, 1988.

Matthews, Donald. *U.S. Senators and their World*. Chapel Hill: University of North Carolina Press, 1960.

Miller, Warren E., and Donald E. Stokes. "Constituency Influence in Congress." *American Political Science Review* 57, no. 1 (1963): 45–56.

Parker, Glenn R. *Homeward Bound: Explaining Changes in Congressional Behavior*. Pittsburgh: University of Pittsburgh Press, 1986.

Price, David E. *The Congressional Experience: A View from the Hill*, 2nd ed. Boulder: Westview Press, 2000.

Rocca, Michael S. "Military Base Closures and the 1996 Congressional Elections." *Legislative Studies Quarterly* 28, no. 4 (2003): 529–550.

Sidlow, Ed. *Freshman Orientation: House Style and Home Style*. Washington, D.C.: CQ Press, 2006.

Wawro, Gregory. *Legislative Entrepreneurship in the U.S. House of Representatives*. Ann Arbor: University of Michigan Press, 2000.

Websites:

Current Representatives. http://www.house.gov/house/MemberWWW.shtml

Current Senators. http://www.senate.gov/general/contact information/senators cfm.cfm

Congressional Budget Office. http://www.cbo.gov/

Government Accountability Office. http://www.gao.gov/

5. Parties and Leaders

Aldrich, John, and David Rohde. "The Transition to Republican Rule in the House: Implications for Theories of Congressional Politics." *Political Science Quarterly* 112, no. 4 (1997): 541–567.

Aldrich, John, Mark Berger, and David Rohde. "*The Historical Variability in Conditional Party Government, 1877–1994*." In *Parties, Procedure and Policy: Essays on the History of Congress*, D. Brady and M. McCubbins, eds. Stanford: Stanford University Press, 2002.

Aldrich, John H. *Why Parties? The Origin and Transformation of Political Parties in America*. Chicago: University of Chicago Press, 1995.

Ansolabehere, Stephen, James Snyder, Jr., and Charles Stewart III. "The Effects of Party and Preferences on Congressional Roll Call Voting." *Legislative Studies Quarterly* 26, no. 4 (2001): 533–572.

Bawn, Kathleen. "Congressional Party Leadership: Utilitarian versus Majoritarian Incentives." *Legislative Studies Quarterly* 23, no. 2 (1998): 219–243.

Brady, David, David Epstein, and Mathew McCubbins, eds. *Party, Process, and Political Change in Congress*. Stanford: Stanford University Press, 2002.

Brady, David W., and Mathew D. McCubbins. Party, Process, and Political Change in Congress. v. 2: *Further New Perspectives on the History of Congress, Social Science History.* Stanford, Calif.: Stanford University Press, 2007.

Burden, Barry C., and Tammy N, Frisby. "Preferences, Partisanship, and Whip Activity in the U.S. House of Representatives." *Legislative Studies Quarterly* 29, no. 4 (2004): 569–590.

Caro, Robert A. *The Years of Lyndon Johnson: Master of the Senate*. New York: Alfred A. Knopf, 2002.

Connelly, William, Jr. and John Pitney. *Congress' Permanent Minority? Republicans in the U.S. House*. Lanham, MD: Rowman and Littlefield, 1994.

Cox, Gary, and Mathew McCubbins. *Legislative Leviathan: Party Government in the House*. Berkeley: University of California Press, 1993.

Cox, Gary W., and Mathew D. McCubbins. *Setting the Agenda: Responsible Party Government in the U.S. House of Representatives*. Cambridge: Cambridge University Press, 2005.

Cox, Gary W., and Mathew D. McCubbins. *Legislative Leviathan : Party Government in the House*. 2nd ed. Cambridge; New York: Cambridge University Press, 2007.

Currinder, Marian. *Money in the House: Campaign Funds and Congressional Party Politics*. 1st ed. Boulder, CO: Westview Press, 2008.

Finocchiaro, Charles J., and David W. Rohde. "War for the Floor: Partisan Theory and Agenda Control in the U.S. House of Representatives." *Legislative Studies Quarterly* 33, no. 1 (2008): 35–61.

Forgette, Richard. "Party Caucuses and Coordination: Assessing Caucus Activity and Party Effects." *Legislative Studies Quarterly* 29, no. 3 (2004): 407–430.

Frohman, Lewis, Jr., and Randall Ripley. "Conditions for Party Leadership: The Case of the House Democrats." *American Political Science Review* 59, no. 1 (1965): 52–63.

Gamm, Gerald, and Steven S. Smith. "*The Dynamics of Party Government in Congress*." In *Congress Reconsidered*, 7th ed., edited by Lawrence C. Dodd and Bruce I. Oppenheimer. Washington, D.C.: Congressional Quarterly Press, 2001.

Gamm, Gerald, and Steven S. Smith. The Emergence of Senate Party Leadership, in *Senate Exceptionalism*, edited by Bruce I. Oppenheimer. Columbus: Ohio State University Press, 2002.

Hasbrouck, Paul D. *Party Government in the House of Representatives*. New York: Macmillan, 1927.

Hess, Stephen. *The Ultimate Insiders*. Washington, D.C.: Brookings Institution Press, 1986.

Jacobson, Gary C. "Party Polarization in National Politics: The Electoral Connection," in *Polarized Politics: Congress and the President in a Partisan Era*, edited by J. Bond and R. Fleischer. Washington, D.C.: Congressional Quarterly Press, 2000.

Jenkins, Jeffrey, and Charles Stewart III. "Out in the Open: The Emergence of Viva Voce Voting in House Speakership Elections." *Legislative Studies Quarterly* 28, no. 4 (2003): 481–508.

Jenkins, Jeffrey A., Michael H. Crespin, and Jamie L. Carson. "Parties as Procedural Coalitions in Congress: An Examination of Differing Career Tracks." *Legislative Studies Quarterly* 30, no. 3 (2005): 365–389.

Jones, Charles O. *The Minority Party in Congress*. Boston: Little, Brown, 1970.

Kolodny, Robin. *Pursuing Majorities: Congress Campaign Committees in American Politics*. Norman: University of Oklahoma Press, 1998.

Lawrence, Eric, Forrest Maltzman, and Steven S. Smith. "Who Wins? Party Effects in Legislative Voting." *Legislative Studies Quarterly* 31, no. 1 (2006): 33–69.

Lebo, Matthew J., Adam J. McGlynn, and Gregory Koger. "Strategic Party Government: Party Influence in Congress, 1789–2000." *American Journal of Political Science* 51, no. 3 (2007): 464–481.

Lee, Frances E. "Agreeing to Disagree: Agenda Content and Senate Partisanship, 1981–2004." *Legislative Studies Quarterly* 33, no. 2 (2008): 199–222.

Maltzman, Forrest. *Competing Principals: Committees, Parties, and the Organization of Congress*. Ann Arbor: University of Michigan Press, 1997.

Manley, John F. The Politics of Finance. Boston: Little, Brown, 1970. Nokken, Timothy, and Keith Poole. "Congressional Party Defection in American History." *Legislative Studies Quarterly* 29, no. 4 (2004): 545–568.

Peabody, Robert. *Leadership in Congress: Stability, Succession, and Change*. Boston: Little, Brown, 1976.

Peters, Ronald M. *The American Speakership: The Office in Historical Perspective*, 2nd ed. Baltimore: Johns Hopkins University Press, 1997.

Ripley, Randall B. *Majority Party Leadership in Congress*. Boston: Little, Brown, 1969.

Rohde, David W. *Parties and Leaders in the Postreform House*. Chicago: University of Chicago Press, 1991.

Sinclair, Barbara. *Legislators, Leaders, and Lawmaking: The U.S. House of Representatives in the Postreform Era*. Baltimore: Johns Hopkins University Press, 1995.

Sinclair, Barbara. *Majority Leadership in the U.S. House*. Baltimore: Johns Hopkins University Press, 1983.

Sinclair, Barbara. *Party wars: Polarization and the Politics of National Policy Making*, The Julian J. Rothbaum *distinguished lecture series; v.* 10. Norman: University of Oklahoma Press, 2006.

Smith, Steven S. Parties and Leadership in the Senate. In The Legislative Branch, P. J. Quirk and S. A. Binder, eds. New York: Oxford University Press, 2005.

Smith, Steven S. *Party Influence in Congress*. New York: Cambridge University Press, 2007.

Smith, Steven S., and Gerald Gamm. 2001. *The Dynamics of Party Government in Congress*. In *Congress Reconsidered*, Lawrence C. Dodd and Bruce I. Oppenheimer, eds. Washington, D.C.: Congressional Quarterly Press.

Strahan, Randall. 2007. *Leading Representatives: The Agency of Leaders in the U.S. House*. Baltimore: Johns Hopkins University Press.

Taylor, Andrew J., and Norman J. Ornstein. *Elephant's Edge: The Republicans as a Ruling Party*. Westport, CT: Praeger Publishers, 2005.

Theriault, Sean M. *Party Polarization in Congress*. Cambridge; New York: Cambridge University Press, 2008.

Websites:

House Party Leaders & Organizations.

http://www.house.gov/house/orgs pub hse ldr www.shtml

Senate Party Leaders & Organizations.

http://www.senate.gov/pagelayout/senators/a three sections with teasers/leadership.htm

6. The Standing Committees

Adler, E. Scott, and John D. Wilkerson. "Intended Consequences: Jurisdictional Reform and Issue Control in the U.S. House of Representatives." *Legislative Studies Quarterly* 33, no. 1 (2008): 85–114.

Aldrich, John, and David W. Rohde. "The Republican Revolution and the House Appropriations Committee." *Journal of Politics* 62, no. 1 (2000): 1–33.

Baumgartner, Frank., Brad. Jones, and Michael. MacLeod. "The Evolution of Legislative Jurisdictions." *Journal of Politics* 62, no. 2 (2000): 321–349.

Crombez, Christophe, Keith Krehbiel, and Tim Groseclose. "Gatekeeping." *Journal of Politics* 68, no. 2 (2006): 322–334.

Davidson, Roger H. *Subcommittee Government: New Channels for Policy Making.* In The New Congress, Thomas Mann and Norman Ornstein, eds. Washington, D.C.: American Enterprise Institute Press, 1981.

Deering, Christopher J., and Steven S. Smith. *Committees in Congress*, 3rd ed. Washington, D.C.: Congressional Quarterly Press, 1997.

Evans, C. Lawrence, and Walter Olezsek. *Congress under Fire: Reform Politics and the Republican Majority.* Boston: Houghton Mifflin, 1997.

Evans, C. Lawrence. *Leadership in Committee: A Comparative Analysis of Leadership Behavior in the U.S. Senate.* Ann Arbor: University of Michigan Press, 1991.

Fenno, Richard, Jr. *Congressmen in Committees.* Boston: Little, Brown, 1973.

Fenno, Richard, Jr. *The Power of the Purse.* Boston: Little, Brown, 1966.

Fowler, Linda L., and R. Brian Law. "Seen but Not Heard: Committee Visibility and Institutional Change in the Senate National Security Committees, 1947–2006." *Legislative Studies Quarterly* 33, no. 3 (2008): 357–385.

Frisch, Scott A., and Sean Q. Kelly. *Committee Assignment Politics in the U.S. House of Representatives.* Norman: University of Oklahoma Press, 2006.

Goodwin, George. *The Little Legislatures: Committees of Congress.* Amherst: University of Massachusetts Press. 1970.

Hall, Richard I. *Participation in Congress.* New Haven: Yale University Press, 1996.

Kiewiet, D. Roderick, and Mathew McCubbins. *The Logic of Delegation: Congressional Parties and the Appropriations Process.* Chicago: University of Chicago Press, 1991.

King, David. *Turf Wars: How Congressional Committees Claim Jurisdiction.* Chicago: University of Chicago Press, 1997.

Krehbiel, Keith. *Information and Legislative Organization.* Ann Arbor: University of Michigan Press, 1991.

Kriner, Douglas, and Liam Schwartz. "Divided Government and Congressional Investigations." *Legislative Studies Quarterly* 33, no. 2 (2008): 295–321.

Longley, Lawrence, and Walter Oleszek. *Bicameral Politics: Conference Committees in Congress*. New Haven: Yale University Press, 1989.

Mayhew, David R. *Congress: The Electoral Connection*. New Haven: Yale University Press, 1974.

McConachie, Lauros G. *Congressional Committees: A Study of the Origins and Development of Our National and Local Legislative Methods*. New York: Thomas Y. Crowell, 1898.

Schickler, Eric, Eric McGhee, and John Sides. "Remaking the House and Senate: Personal Power, Ideology, and the 1970s Reforms." *Legislative Studies Quarterly* 28, no. 3 (2003): 297–331.

Shepsle, Kenneth. *The Giant Jigsaw Puzzle*. Chicago: University of Chicago Press, 1978.

Smith, Steven S. *Call to Order: Floor Politics in the House and Senate*. Washington, D.C.: Brookings Institution Press, 1989.

Strahan, Randall. *New Ways and Means: Reform and Change in a Congressional Committee*. Chapel Hill: University of North Carolina Press, 1990.

Vander Wielen, Ryan. "Conference Committees and Bias in Legislative Outcomes." Ph.D. Dissertation, Political Science, Washington University, St. Louis, 2006.

Websites:

House Committees. http://www.house.gov/house/CommitteeWWW.shtml

Senate Committees. http://www.senate.gov/pagelayout/committees/d three sections with teasers/committees home.htm

Historical Committees. http://web.mit.edu/17.251/www/data page.html#1

7. The Rules of the Legislative Game

Adler, E. Scott. *Why Congressional Reforms Fail*. Chicago: Chicago University Press, 2002.

Alexander, DeAlva S. *History and Procedure of the House of Representatives*. Boston: Houghton Mifflin, 1916.

Bach, Stanley, and Steven S. Smith. *Managing Uncertainty in the House of Representatives: Adaptation and Innovation in Special Rules*. Washington, D.C.: Brookings Institution Press, 1988.

Beeman, Richard R. "Unlimited Debate in the Senate: The First Phase." *Political Science Quarterly* 83, no. 3 (1968): 419–34.

Binder, Sarah. "Partisanship and Procedural Choice: Institutional Change in the Early Congress, 1789–1823." *Journal of Politics* 57, no. 4 (1995): 1093–1118.

Binder, Sarah. *Minority Rights, Majority Rule: Partisanship and the Development of Congress*. Cambridge, U.K.; New York: Cambridge University Press, 1997.

Binder, Sarah. "Parties and Institutional Choice Revisited." *Legislative Studies Quarterly* 31, no. 4 (2006): 413–532.

Binder, Sarah, and Steven S. Smith. *Politics or Principle? Filibustering in the United States Senate*. Washington, D.C.: Brookings Institution Press, 1997.

Burdette, Franklin L. *Filibustering in the Senate*. Princeton: Princeton University Press, 1940.

Foley, Michael. *The New Senate: Liberal Influence on a Conservative Institution, 1959–1972*. New Haven: Yale University Press, 1980.

Lawrence, Eric D. Essays on Procedural Development in the U.S. Congress. Ph.D. Dissertation, *University of Minnesota*, 2004.

Oleszek, Walter J. *Congressional Procedures and the Policy Process*. 7th ed. Washington, D.C.: CQ Press, 2007.

Roberts, Jason M. Minority Rights and Majority Power: Conditional Party Government and the Motion to Recommit in the House. *Legislative Studies Quarterly* 30, no. 2 (2005): 219–234.

Shepsle, Kenneth, and Barry Weingast. "When Do Rules of Procedure Matter?" *Journal of Politics* 46, no. 1 (1984): 206–221.

Sinclair, Barbara. *Unorthodox Lawmaking: New Legislative Processes in the U.S. Congress*, 2nd ed. Washington, D.C.: Congressional Quarterly Press, 2000.

Tiefer, Charles. *Congressional Practice and Procedure*. Westport, CT: Greenwood Press, 1989.

Wawro, Gregory, and Eric Schickler. *Filibuster: Obstruction and Lawmaking in the U.S. Senate, Princeton Studies in American Politics*. Princeton, NJ: Princeton University Press, 2006.

Wolfensberger, Donald. *Congress and the People: Deliberative Democracy on Trial*. Washington, D.C.: Woodrow Wilson Center Press, 2000.

Websites:

House Rules. http://www.house.gov/rules Senate Rules.

http://www.senate.gov/reference/reference index subjects/Rules and Procedure vrd. htm

Library of Congress (Thomas). http://thomas.loc.gov/

Bill Process (brief). http://www.house.gov/house/Tying it all.shtml

Bill Process (long). http://thomas.loc.gov/home/holam.txt

8. The Floor and Voting

Anderson, William, Janet Box-Steffensmeier, and Valeria Sinclair-Chapman. "The Keys to Legislative Success in the U.S. House of Representatives." *Legislative Studies Quarterly* 28, no. 3 (2003): 357–386.

Arnold, R. Douglas. *The Logic of Congressional Action*. New Haven: Yale University Press, 1990.

Bach, Stanley, and Steven S. Smith. *Managing Uncertainty in the House of Representatives: Adaptation and Innovation in Special Rules*. Washington, D.C.: Brookings Institution Press, 1988.

Binder, Sarah, and Steven S. Smith. *Politics or Principle? Filibustering in the United States Senate*. Washington, D.C.: Brookings Institution Press, 1997.

Calvert, Randall, and Richard F. Fenno, Jr. "Strategy and Sophisticated Voting in the Senate." *Journal of Politics* 56, no. 2 (1994): 349–376.

Clausen, Aage. *How Congressmen Decide*. New York: St. Martin's Press, 1973.

Clinton, Joshua, Simon Jackman, and Douglas Rivers. "The Statistical Analysis of Roll Call Data." *American Political Science Review* 98, no. 2 (2004): 355–370.

Frantzich, Stephen, and John Sullivan. *The C-SPAN Revolution*. Norman: University of Oklahoma Press, 1999.

Gamm, Gerald, and Steven S. Smith. *Last Among Equals: The Presiding Officer of the Senate*. In *Esteemed Colleagues: Civility and Deliberation in the United States Senate*, edited by B. Loomis. Washington, D.C.: Brookings Institution Press, 2000.

Jackson, John, and John Kingdon. "Ideology, Interest Group Score, and Legislative Votes." *American Journal of Political Science* 36, no. 3 (1992): 805–823.

King, David C., and Richard L. Zeckhauser. "Congressional Vote Options." *Legislative Studies Quarterly* 28, no. 3 (2003): 387–411.

Kingdon, John W. *Congressmen's Voting Decisions*, 3rd ed. Ann Arbor: University Of Michigan Press, 1989.

Krehbiel, Keith. *Pivotal Politics: A Theory of U.S. Lawmaking*. Chicago: University of Chicago Press, 1998.

Loomis, Burdette, ed. *Esteemed Colleagues: Civility and Deliberation in the U.S. Senate*. Washington, D.C.: Congressional Quarterly Press, 2001.

Poole, Keith T. *Spatial Models of Parliamentary Voting, Analytical methods for social research*. Cambridge; New York: Cambridge University Press, 2005.

Poole, Keith, and Howard Rosenthal. *Congress: A Political-Economic History of Roll Call Voting*. New York: Oxford University Press, 1996.

Poole, Keith T., Howard Rosenthal, and Keith T. Poole. *Ideology and Congress*. New Brunswick, NJ: Transaction Publishers, 2007.

Roberts, Jason M., and Seven S. Smith. "Procedural Contexts, Party Strategy, and Conditional Party Voting in the U.S. House of Representatives: 1971–2000." *American Journal of Political Science* 47, no. 2 (2003): 305–317.

Smith, Steven S. *Call to Order: Floor Politics in the House and Senate*. Washington, D.C.: Brookings Institution Press, 1989.

Young, Garry, and Vicky Wilkins. "Vote Switchers and Party Influence in the U.S. House." *Legislative Studies Quarterly* 32, no. 1 (2007): 59–77.

Websites:

Library of Congress (Thomas). http://thomas.loc.gov

Roll-Call Voting Data, NOMINATE Scores. http://www.voteview.com

Recent Roll-Call Voting Data, Raw Voting Files. http://web.mit.edu/17.251/www/data page.html#3

House Committee on Rules. http://www.house.gov/rules/

9. Congress and the President

Aberbach, Joel D. *Keeping a Watchful Eye: The Politics of Congressional Oversight*. Washington, D.C.: Brookings Institution Press, 1990.

Barrett, David M. The CIA and Congress: The Untold Story from Truman to Kennedy. Lawrence, Kan.: University Press of Kansas, 2005.

Binder, Sarah. "The Dynamics of Legislative Gridlock, 1947–1996." *American Political Science Review* 93, no. 3 (1999): 519–533.

Binder, Sarah. *Stalemate: Causes and Consequences of Legislative Gridlock*. Washington, D.C.: Brookings Institution Press, 2003.

Binkley, Wilfred. *President and Congress*. New York: Knopf, 1947.

Bond, Jon R., and Richard Fleisher. *The President and the Congress in a Partisan Era*. Washington, D.C.: Congressional Quarterly Press, 2000.

Bond, Jon R., and Richard Fleisher. *The President in the Legislative Arena*. Chicago: University of Chicago Press, 1990.

Brady, David W., and Craig Volden. *Revolving Gridlock: Politics and Policy from Jimmy Carter to George W. Bush (Transforming American Politics)*, 2nd ed. Boulder, CO: Westview Press, 2005.

Cameron, Charles. *Veto Bargaining: Presidents and the Politics of Negative Power*. Cambridge: Cambridge University Press, 2000.

Collier, Kenneth E. *Between the Branches: The White House Office of Legislative Affairs*. Pittsburgh: University of Pittsburgh Press, 1997.

Dodd, Lawrence C., and Richard Schott. *Congress and the Administrative State*, 2nd ed. Boulder: Westview, 1994.

Edwards, George C. *At the Margins: Presidential Leadership of Congress*. New Haven: Yale University Press, 1989.

Epstein, David, and Sharon O'Halloran. *Delegating Powers: A Transaction Cost Politics Approach to Policy Making Under Separate Powers*. Cambridge: Cambridge University Press, 1999.

Fenno, Richard F., Jr. *Divided Government*. New York: Allyn & Bacon, 1995.

Fiorina, Morris P. *Divided Government*, 2nd ed. Needham Heights: Allyn & Bacon, 1996.

Fisher, Louis. *Congressional Abdication on War and Spending*. College Station: Texas A&M University Press, 2000.

Fisher, Louis. *Constitutional Conflicts Between Congress and the President*, 4th ed. Lawrence: University Press of Kansas, 1997

Fisher, Louis. *The Constitution Between Friends: Congress, the President, and the Law*. New York: St. Martin's, 1978.

Fisher, Louis. *The Politics of Shared Power: Congress and the Executive*. College Station: Texas A&M Press, 1998.

Foreman, Christopher J., Jr. *Signals from the Hill: Congressional Oversight and the Challenge of Social Regulation*. New Haven: Yale University Press, 1988.

Gilmour, John B. *Strategic Disagreement: Stalemate in American Politics*. Pittsburgh: University of Pittsburgh Press, 1995.

Hersman, Rebecca K.C. *Friends and Foes: How Congress and the President Really Make Foreign Policy*. Washington, D.C.: Brookings Institution Press, 2000.

Hinckley, Barbara. *Less Than Meets the Eye: Foreign Policy Making and the Myth of the Assertive Congress*. Chicago: University of Chicago Press, 1994.

Howell, William G., and Jon. C. Pevehouse. *While Dangers Gather: Congressional Checks on Presidential War Powers*. Princeton: Princeton University Press, 2007.

Jones, Charles O. *Separate but Equal Branches: Congress and the Presidency*, 2nd ed. New York: Chatham House, 1999.

Kernell, Samuel. *Going Public: New Strategies of Presidential Leadership*. Washington, D.C.: Congressional Quarterly Press, 1986.

Krehbiel, Keith. *Pivotal Politics: A Theory of U.S. Lawmaking*. Chicago: University of Chicago Press, 1998.

Larocca, Roger T. *The Presidential Agenda: Sources of Executive Influence in Congress*. Columbus: Ohio State University Press, 2006.

Lindsay, James. *Congress and the Politics of U.S. Foreign Policy*. Baltimore: Johns Hopkins University Press, 1994.

Light, Paul. *The President's Agenda*. Rev. ed. Baltimore: Johns Hopkins University Press, 1991.

Lowenthal, Mark M. *Intelligence: From Secrets to Policy*. Washington, D.C.: Congressional Quarterly Press, 1999.

MacDonald, Jason A. "The U.S. Congress and the Institutional Design of Agencies." *Legislative Studies Quarterly* 32, no. 3 (2007): 395–420.

Mann, Thomas, ed. *A Question of Balance: The President, the Congress, and Foreign Policy*. Washington, D.C.: Brookings Institution, 1990.

Marshall, Bryan W., and Brandon C. Prins. "Strategic Position Taking and Presidential Influence in Congress." *Legislative Studies Quarterly* 32, no. 2 (2007): 257–284.

Mayer, Kenneth R. *With the Stroke of a Pen: Executive Orders and Presidential Power*. Princeton: Princeton University Press, 2001.

Mayhew, David. *Divided We Govern: Party Control, Lawmaking, and Investigating: 1946–1990*. New Haven: Yale University Press, 1992.

McCarty, Nolan. "The Appointments Dilemma." *American Journal of Political Science* 48, no. 3 (2004): 413–428.

Mezey, Michael L. *Congress, the President, and Public Policy*. Boulder: Westview, 1989.

Miller, Russell A., ed. *U.S. National Security, Intelligence and Democracy: From the Church Committee and the War on Terror*. Milton Park, Abingdon, Oxon; New York: Routledge.

Moe, Terry. "An Assessment of the Positive Theory of 'Congressional Dominance.'" *Legislative Studies Quarterly* 12, no. 4 (1987): 475–520.

Moe, Terry. The Presidency and the Bureaucracy: The Presidential Advantage. In *The Presidency and the Political System*, M. Nelson, ed. Washington, D.C.: Congressional Quarterly Press, 2003.

Neustadt, Richard E. *Presidential Power*. New York: John Wiley and Sons, 1980.

Peterson, Mark A. *Legislating Together: The White House and Capitol Hill from Eisenhower to Reagan*. Cambridge: Harvard University Press, 1990.

Ripley, Randall, and James Lindsay, eds. *Congress Resurgent: Foreign and Defense Policy on Capitol Hill*. Ann Arbor: University of Michigan Press, 1993.

Sollenberger, Michael A. *The President Shall Nominate: How Congress Trumps Executive Power*. Lawrence, Kan.: University Press of Kansas, 2008.

Spitzer, Robert J. *President and Congress: Executive Hegemony at the Crossroads of American Government*. New York: McGraw Hill, 1993.

Stevenson, Charles A. *Congress at War: The Politics of Conflict Since 1789*. Dulles, VA: Potomac Books, 2007.

Thurber, James, ed. *Rivals for Power: Presidential-Congressional Relations*. Washington, D.C.: Congressional Quarterly Press, 1996.

Wayne, Stephen J. *The Legislative Presidency*. New York: Harper, 1978.

Wildavsky, Aaron. "*The Two Presidencies*." In Perspectives on the Presidency, edited by A. Wildavsky. Boston: Little, Brown, 1975.

Websites:

White House and Executive Agencies. http://www.whitehouse.gov/government/

10. Congress and the Courts

Abraham, Henry J. *Justices, Presidents, and Senators: A History of the U.S. Supreme Court Appointments from Washington to Clinton*. Lanham: Rowman and Littlefield, 1999.

Barnes, Jeb. *Overruled?: Legislative Overrides, Pluralism, and Contemporary Court-Congress Relations*. Stanford: Stanford University Press, 2004.

Berger, Raoul. *Congress v. The Supreme Court*. Cambridge: Harvard University Press, 1969.

Binder, Sarah, and Forrest Maltzman. "The Limits of Senatorial Courtesy." *Legislative Studies Quarterly* 29, no. 1 (2004): 5–22.

Cameron, Charles, Albert Cover, and Jeffrey Segal. "Senate Voting on Supreme Court Nominees: A Neoinstitutional Model." *American Political Science Review* 84, no. 2 (1990): 525–534.

Carson, Jamie L, and Benjamin A. Kleinerman. "A Switch in Time Saves Nine: Institutions, Strategic Actors, and FDR's Court-Packing Plan." *Public Choice* 113 (2002): 301–324.

Cohen Bell, Lauren. *Warring Factions: Interest Groups, Money, and the New Politics of Senate Confirmation*. Columbus: Ohio State University Press, 2002.

Frickey, Philip, and Seven S. Smith. "Judicial Review, the Congressional Process, and the Federalism Cases: An Interdisciplinary Critique." *The Yale Law Journal* 111, no. 7 (2002): 1707–1756.

Geyh, Charles Gardner. *When Courts and Congress Collide: The Struggle for Control of America's Judicial System*. Ann Arbor: University of Michigan Press, 2006.

Hoekstra, Valerie J. *Public Reaction to Supreme Court Decisions*. New York: Cambridge University Press, 2003.

Katzmann, Robert A. *Courts and Congress*. Washington, D.C.: Brookings Institution, 1997.

Lovell, George I. *Legislative Deferrals: Statutory Ambiguity, Judicial Power, and American Democracy*. New York: Cambridge University Press, 2003.

Maltzman, Forrest, James F. Spriggs, and Paul J. Wahlbeck. *Crafting Law on the Supreme Court: The Collegial Game*. New York: Cambridge University Press, 2000.

Moraski, Byron J., and Charles R. Shipan. "The Politics of Supreme Court Nominations: A Theory of Institutional Constraints and Choices." *American Journal of Political Science* 43, no. 4 (1999): 1069–1095.

Shipan, Charles R. *Designing Judicial Review: Interest Groups, Congress, and Communications Policy*. Ann Arbor: University of Michigan Press, 1997.

Solberg, Rorie L. Spill and Eric S. Heberlig. "Communicating to the Courts and Beyond: Why Members of Congress Participate in *Amici Curiae*." *Legislative Studies Quarterly* 29, no. 4 (2004): 591–610.

Urofsky, Melvin I. *Money and Free Speech: Campaign Finance Reform and the Courts*. Lawrence, KS: University Press of Kansas, 2005.

Wittes, Benjamin. *Confirmation Wars: Preserving Independent Courts in Angry Times*. Lanham, MD: Rowman & Littlefield, 2006.

Yalof, David. *Pursuit of Justices: Presidential Politics and the Selection of Supreme Court Nominees*. Chicago: University of Chicago Press, 1999.

Websites:

Supreme Court. http://www.supremecourtus.gov

Federal Court System. http://www.uscourts.gov/

Supreme Court Opinions. http://www.findlaw.com/casecode/supreme.html

11. Congress, Lobbyists, and Interest Groups

Austen-Smith, David, and John R. Wright. "Counteractive Lobbying." *American Journal of Political Science* 38, no. 1 (1994): 25–44.

Austen-Smith, David, "Campaign Contributions and Access." *American Political Science Review* 89, no. 3 (1995): 566–581.

Balla, Steven J., and John R. Wright. "Interest Groups, Advisory Committees, and Congressional Control of the Bureaucracy," *American Journal of Political Science* 45, no. 4 (2001): 799–812.

Baumgartner, Frank, and Beth Leech, "The Multiple Ambiguities of 'Counteractive Lobbying.'" *American Journal of Political Science* 40, no. 2 (1996): 521–542.

Biersack, Robert, Paul Herrnson, and Clyde Wilcox, eds. *After the Revolution: PACs, Lobbies, and the Republican Congress*. Boston: Allyn & Bacon, 1999.

Birnbaum, Jeffrey, and Alan S. Murray. *Showdown at Gucci Gulch: Lawmakers, Lobbyists, and the Unlikely Triumph of Tax Reform*. New York: Random House, 1987.

Caldeira, Greg, and John R. Wright, "Lobbying for Justice: Organized Interests, Supreme Court Nominations, and United States Senate." *American Journal of Political Science* 42, no. 2 (1998): 499–523.

Campbell, Colton, and John S, Stack, Jr., eds. *Congress Confronts the Court: The Struggle for Legitimacy and Authority in Lawmaking*. Lanham, MD: Rowman and Littlefield, 2001.

Cater, Douglas. *Power in Washington*. New York: Random House, 1964.

Cigler, Alan J., and Burdette A. Loomis. Always Involved, Rarely Central: Organized Interests in American Politics. In *Interest Group Politics*, 6th ed., Alan Cigler and Burdette Loomis, eds. Washington, D.C.: Congressional Quarterly Press, 2002.

Dexter, Lewis A. *How Organizations Are Represented in Washington*. Indianapolis: Bobbs-Merrill, 1969.

Hall, Richard L. and F.W. Wayman. "Buying Time: Moneyed Interests and the Mobilization of Bias in Congressional Committees." *American Political Science Review* 84, no. 3 (1990): 797–820.

Hammond, Susan W. *Congressional Caucuses in National Policymaking*. Baltimore: Johns Hopkins University Press, 1997.

Hansen, John Mark. *Gaining Access: Congress and the Farm Lobby, 1919–1981*. Chicago: University of Chicago Press, 1991.

Heclo, Hugh. *Issue Networks and the Executive Establishment*. In *The New American Political System*, Anthony King, ed. Washington, D.C.: American Enterprise Institute Press, 1978.

Hojnacki, Marie, and David C. Kimball. "Organized Interests and the Decision of Whom to Lobby in Congress." *American Political Science Review* 92, no. 4 (1998): 775–790.

Cigler, Allan, and Burdette Loomis, eds. *Interest Group Politics*, 6th ed. Washington, D.C.: Congressional Quarterly Press, 2002.

Loomis, B. and A. Cigler. The Changing Nature of Interest Groups. In *Interest Group Politics*, 6th ed. Washington, D.C.: Congressional Quarterly Press, 2002.

Lowi, Theodore J. *The End of Liberalism*. New York: Norton, 1979.

Lupia, Arthur and Mathew McCubbins. "Who Controls? Information and the Structure of Legislative Decision Making." *Legislative Studies Quarterly* 19, no. 3 (1994): 361–384.

Mackenzie, G.C., with Michael Hafken. *Scandal Proof: Do Ethics Laws Make Government Ethical?* Washington, D.C.: Brookings Institution Press, 2002.

McCubbins, Mathew, and Thomas Schwartz. "Congressional Oversight Overlooked: Police Patrols versus Fire Alarms." *American Journal of Political Science* 28, no. 1 (1984): 59–82.

McCubbins, Mathew, Roger Noll and Barry Weingast. "Administrative Procedures as Instruments of Political Control." *Journal of Law, Economics and Organization* 10, no. 2 (1987): 243–277.

McCune, Wesley. *The Farm Bloc*. New York: Doubleday, Doran, and Company, 1943.

Moe, Terry M. "Control and Feedback in Economic Regulation: The Case of the NLRB." *American Political Science Review* 79, no. 4 (1985): 1094–1116.

Olson, Mancur. *The Logic of Collective Action: Public Goods and the Theory of Groups*. Cambridge: Harvard University Press, 1965.

Ornstein, Norman, and Shirley Elder. *Interest Groups, Lobbying, and Policymaking*. Washington, D.C.: Congressional Quarterly Press, 1978.

Salisbury, Robert H., et al. "Who You Know Versus What You Know: The Uses of Government Experience for Washington Lobbyists." *American Journal of Political Science* 33, no. 1 (1989): 175–195.

Salisbury, Robert H. "An Exchange Theory of Interest Groups." *Midwest Journal of Political Science* 13, no. 1 (1969): 1–32.

Schlozman, Kay, and John Tierney. *Organized Interests and American Democracy*. New York: Harper & Row, 1986.

Shipan, Charles R. *Designing Judicial Review: Interest Groups, Congress, and Communications Policy*. Ann Arbor: University of Michigan Press, 2000.

Truman, David. *The Governmental Process*, 2nd ed. New York: Knopf, 1971.

United States. Congress. Senate. Committee on Homeland Security and Governmental Affairs. 2006. *Lobbying Reform: Proposals and Issues: Hearing Before the Committee on Homeland Security and Governmental Affairs, United States Senate, One Hundred Ninth Congress, Second Session, January 25, 2006*. Washington, D.C.: Government Printing Office.

Walker, Jack L., Jr. *Mobilizing Interest Groups in America*. Ann Arbor: University of Michigan Press, 1991.

Wright, John R. *Interest Groups and Congress: Lobbying, Contributions, and Influence*. Boston: Allyn & Bacon, 1996.
Websites:
Federal Election Commission. http://www.fec.gov/
House Lobbying Disclosure. http://clerk.house.gov/pd/index.html
Senate Lobbying Disclosure. http://www.senate.gov/pagelayout/legislative/g_three_sections_with_teasers/lobbyingdisc.htm

12. Congress and Budget Politics

Farrier, Jasmine. *Passing the Buck: Congress, the Budget, and Deficits*. Lexington: University Press of Kentucky, 2004.
Keith, Robert, and Allen Schick. *The Federal Budget Process*. New York: Nova Science Publishers, 2003.
Krutz, Glen S. *Hitching a Ride: Omnibus Legislating in the U.S. Congress*. Columbus: Ohio State University Press, 2001.
LeLoup, Lance T. *Parties, Rules, and the Evolution of Congressional Budgeting*. Pullman, WA: Washington State University, 2005.
Primo, David M. *Rules and Restraint: Government Spending and the Design of Institutions*. Chicago: University of Chicago Press, 2007.
Rubin, Irene S. *Balancing the Federal Budget*. New York: Chatham House, 2003.
Schick, Allen. *Congress and Money*. Washington, D.C.: Urban Institute Press, 1980.
Schick, Allen. *The Federal Budget: Politics, Policy Process*. Rev. ed. Washington, D.C.: Brookings Institution Press, 2000.
Sinclair, Barbara. *Unorthodox Lawmaking: New Legislative Processes in the U.S. Congress*, 2nd ed. Washington, D.C.: Congressional Quarterly Press, 2000.
United States. Congress. House. Committee on the Budget. 2007. Perspective on Renewing Statutory PAYGO: Hearing Before the Committee on the Budget, House of Representatives, One Hundred Tenth Congress, First Session July 25, 2007. Washington, D.C.: Government Printing Office.

Index

Note to the Index: An *f* following a page number denotes a figure on that page; a *t* following a page number denotes a table on that page.

AARP, 337, 352
abortion, 258–259, 330, 332–333
Abramoff, Jack, 4, 344–346, 355–356
"A" Committee, 188–189
Adams, John Q., 324–325
ad hoc committees, 149, 166–167
administrative assistant (AA), 111
adversarial democracy, 31
affirmative action, 270, 330
Afghanistan, 287
agencies
    Congress role in designing, 294–296
    executive (*see* executive agencies)
    president influence on, 110
    support, 71, 105, 186
agenda, congressional
    issue agenda, 263
    parties and, 162–163
    standing committees and, 172, 181–182
agenda setting, presidential, 269–271
agriculture policy, 359
Albert, Carl, 149, 160
Aldrich, Nelson, 45
Alexander, Rodney, 150
alignment, of policy preference. *See* elections/policy alignments, congressional
Alioto, Sam, 308
amendments
    Constitutional (*see individual amendment*)
    floor amendments, 158, 177, 184–185, 205, 247–248, 251
    Millionaires' Amendment, 61–62
American Bar Association, 326, 328

American Coming Together, 61
Americans with Disabilities Act, 319
appointments
    executive, 298–299
    judicial, 326–327, 329–331
    recess appointment, 299
    Senate confirmation of, 299
    by Speaker of the House, 150
apportionment
    changes in seats, by region, 14*t*
    defining,
    federal law on, 57
appropriation bills
    defining, 231–232
    omnibus, 156, 297, 383–384
    privileged, 220
    subcommittees, 232–233
    waiver of special rule, 233
appropriations
    agency funding, 292, 295
    annual approval of, 231
    Congress control of, 35, 285, 296
    federal agency shutdown and, 380, 382
    for foreign affairs, 39, 271, 296
    impoundment and, 310–311
    line-item veto and, 297–298
    lobbyists and, 340
    for military spending, 246–247
    special, 214
    spending ceilings and, 373
    staff funding, 130, 289
Appropriations Committee, House, 189–192, 194, 197, 201

approval ratings
    of Congress, 5
    of presidents, 275–276
Archer MSA (medical savings account)
        Coalition, 351–352
Arnold, R. Douglas, 90
Austen-Smith, David, 345–346
authorization
    defining, 231–232
    expired, 232–233
    jurisdiction over, 232–233
    legislative rules, 231–232
    periodic, 292–294

Baird, Zoë, 298
Balanced Budget Act, 1996, 381
Balanced Budget and Emergency Deficit
        Control Act of 1985. See
        Gramm-Rudman-Hollings Act
bankruptcy reform, 258–259
"B" Committee, 188
Bernblatt v. United States, 316
bicameral legislature, 33–34
Biden, Joseph, 55, 326, 330–331
Bill of Rights, 38, 333
bills
    appropriation (see appropriation bills)
    authorization (see authorization)
    debt-ceiling, 378–382
    engrossed, 232
    enrolled, 232
    length/complexity of, 11–12
    numbers introduced, 215
    reconciliation, 381
    referral rules in House, 185–186
Bipartisan Campaign Reform Act (BCRA) of
        2002, 59, 317
Black Caucus, 16, 126
Blagojevich, Rod, 56
Blount, Roy, 125
Blue Dog Coalition, 126
blue slips, 328
Boehner, John, 113t
Bork, Robert H., 325, 329–330
Bowsher v. Synar, 311–312
Boxer, Barbara, 16
Brooks, Preston, 26f
Brownback, Sam, 179
Buckley v. Valeo, 59–62, 317–319
Budget Act of 1974, 156, 234, 366–368, 381,
        386–387
Budget and Accounting Act of 1921,
        269

Budget Enforcement Act (BEA), 372–373,
        381
budget policy
    annual surplus/deficit, 1946–2009, 364f
    budget overview, 364–366
    budget process, steps in, 370f
    budget reform, 366–367
    Byrd rule, 371–372
    committees and, 388
    compromise and, 386
    conclusions, 386–388
    congressional budget process, 1974,
        366–368
    congressional constraints on, 22–24
    debt ceiling, 378–382
    deficit-reducing trust fund, 374–377
    deficits, 22–23, 158, 182, 234, 363–364,
        364f, 374–377
    earmarks, 91, 296, 385
    elections role in, 387
    entitlement spending, 365–366, 373–374,
        377–378
    federal agency shutdown, 380, 382
    firewalls, 373
    health spending as percent of total federal
        outlay, 1962–2008, 375f
    impoundment, 310–311, 369
    introduction to, 363–364
    legislation, 156, 366–368, 381, 386–387
    major developments in process,
        1974-2005, 381–382
        Balanced Budget Act, 1996, 381
        Budget Act, 1974, 156, 366–368, 381
        Budget Enforcement Act, 1990, 381
        Gramm-Rudman-Hollings Act, 1985
            and 1987, 311–312, 369–371, 373,
            381
        Omnibus Budget Reconciliation Act,
            1993, 381
        PAYGO, 372–374, 381–385
        Reconciliation Bill, 381
    parties and, 387
    parties leaders and, 387–388
    points of order, 200, 220–221, 242
    president role, 386
    receipts and outlays, 1946–2008, 365f
    recissions, 369
    reconciliation instructions, 367–369
    rules/rule changes, 182, 386–387
    sequestration, 369–373, 381, 383
    spending categories, 366f
    spending ceilings, 367, 371–374
    spending control, 368–369

spending deferrals, 369
tax bill certification, 1995–1996, 378–380
Burris, Roland, 16, 56
Bush, George H. W.
    budget policy under, 372–374
    control over regulatory process, 284–285
    executive appointments, 298–299
    ideological alignment, 82
    judicial appointments, 326–327, 329–331
    OMB under, 284
    use of veto by, 272
    war powers and, 287–288
Bush, George W., 261
    budget policy under, 383–384
    control over regulatory process, 284
    executive appointments, 299
    ideological alignment and, 82
    judicial appointments, 329
    OIRA under, 284–285
    tax cuts and, 383
    use of signing statements by, 283
    use of veto by, 261
Byrd, Robert, 157, 195, 251, 371–372
Byrd rule, 371–372, 386

Calhoun, John C., 44
campaign contributions
    bundling of, 58
    soft money, 58–59
campaign finance
    incumbency advantage, 73–74
    reform legislation, 57–59, 60t, 61–62
    spending limits, 59
campaigning
    costs of reelection, 8
    by party leaders, 135
    spending regulation, 317–319
    vs. governing, 7–8
Campbell, Ben Nighthorse, 15
Cannon, Joe, 45
canons of statutory construction, 318
Cantwell, Maria, 61
Carter, Jimmy, 290, 327, 368
caseworker, congressional, 71
caucus
    election of leaders, 138, 197
    King Caucus, 129
    party, 129
    single-issue, 357
    vs. conference, 129
"C" Committee, 188
Central Intelligence Agency, 286
Chafee, Lincoln, 261

Cheney, Dick, 261
circuit court judgeships, 324
citizens' groups, 337. *See also*
        lobbyists/interest groups
classified information oversight. *See*
        intelligence oversight
Clay, Henry, 44, 47
clean air laws, 319
Clinton, Bill
    budget policy under, 22, 374–382
    control over regulatory process, 284
    executive appointments and, 298–299
    ideological alignment and, 82
    judicial nominations, 326–327
    line-item veto and, 312
    OMB under, 284
    tax increases and, 374–375, 377
    use of veto by, 272, 281
Clinton v. City of New York, 311
cloture, 148–149, 224, 227, 231
Clyburn, James, 17
coattail effect, 78–79
    incumbents and, 79
Cole, Tom, 16
colloquies, 320
Colorado, redistricting in, 65
Committee of the Whole (COW), 224–225,
        241, 251
Committee on Committees, 44, 49, 130t,
        131t
committee reports, 296, 320
committees
    ad hoc committee, 149, 166–167
    apprenticeship period, 50
    autonomous, 170
    chairs, 50
    circumventing, 179
    committee reports, 296, 320
    conference committee, 167
    Constitution and, 27, 42
    distributive theory on, 170–171
    early foundations, 46–48
    elimination of, 49
    increase in numbers of, 48
    incremental change in, 166
    joint committees, 167–169
    less autonomous, 24
    modern system, 49–51
    nomenclature issues, 169
    party control of, 48–49
    removal of members, 137, 150
    select/special committee, 169
    specialization of members, 50

committees (*cont.*)
  steering, 130*t*, 131*t*
    early, 44
    House Democratic, 49
    House Republican, 126, 192
    House Steering and Policy Committee,
      154, 197
    subcommittee choice, 171
  types of, 166, 166*t*, 167*t*, 169. *See also*
    committees, standing; *individual*
    committee
committees, standing, 166
  attendance issues, 200
  bias in, 192
  changing party strength, 182–183
  changing policy agenda, 181–182
  committee leaders, 193–198
    election of, 195
    seniority system and, 194–196
    subcommittee chair selection in House,
      197
    subcommittee chair selection in Senate,
      197–198
  conclusions, 205
  declining autonomy, 181
  declining influence, 175–176
  disciplining members, 188
  full committee chair power, 198–199
    in House, 198–199
    House committee chair reform
    in Senate, 199–200
  gatekeeping, 176–177
  governed by majority party, 171–172
  information perspective on, 170
  institutional context, 183–186
    bill referral rules in House, 184
    conference rules, 185
    rank-and-file resources, 185–186
    sunshine rules, 183–184
    voting rules, 184–185
  legislative power, 173–174
  list of House and Senate, 168*t*
  median conservative score, 2007–2008,
    193*f*
  nature of
    institutional context, 172–173
    issue agenda, 263
    overview, 169–170
  negative power, 176–178
  origins of, 47–48
  oversight/investigative power of, 179–181
  overview, 165–166
  partisan perspective on, 171–172

pecking order, 190–192
positive power, 174
  domination of conference committees,
    174, 176
  information advantage, 174–175
  leverage, 174–175
  strategic packaging, 174–176
power of modern committees, 173–174
relationship with multiple principals,
  172–173
  institutional context, 172–173
  party strength, 172
  policy agenda, 172
staff, 203–205
  House, 204
  Republican cuts, 204–205
  Senate, 204
term limits, 194–195. *See also* committees,
  standing committee membership;
  individual committee
committees, standing committee
  membership, 186–187
assignments, 187
  Committees on Committees, 44, 49,
    130*t*, 131*t*
  in House, 187
  influences on, 189
  leadership prerogatives, 190
  rank of value of, 1979–2006, 191*t*
  in Senate, 188
  size/party ratios, 186
Common Cause, 108
compromise, 28
Comptroller General, 311–312
concurrent resolutions, 214
conference committee, 167
conference reports, 228
Congress, U.S.
  approval ratings, 5
  changing membership, 13–19
    previous occupations, 17
    regional shifts, 13–14
    women/minorities, 14, 15*t*, 17
  changing party control, 17–19
  information technology use by, 6–8
  life-span of each Congress, 9
  media coverage of, 4–5
  modern trends in
    low public confidence, 2–6
    new interest groups, 8–10
    plebiscitary politics, 6–7
    weakening governing/campaigning
      distinction, 7–8

new policy challenges, 10–13
overview, 1–2
partitioning of, 336
percent of seats held by Democrats, 18*f*
performance approval, 6*f*
post-reform era, 21
    budgets constraints, 22–24
    less autonomous committees, 24
    revitalized parties, 23
    tempered decentralization in, 20–22
    tempered individualism, 21–22
president and (*see* executive-legislative
    relations)
public ethics, 4
recent scandals in, 2–4
size of
term limits, 5
terrorist attacks and, 1, 5, 36–37, 288
war against terrorism. 20. *See also*
    members of Congress
Congress Against Itself (Davidson & Oleszek),
    202
Congressional Black Caucus, 16, 126
Congressional Budget and Impoundment
    Control Act of 1974. *See* Budget Act
    of 1974
Congressional Budget Office (CBO), 22,
    105, 367, 378
Congressional Caucus for Women's Issues,
    16
Congressional Government (Wilson), 202
Congressional Hispanic Caucus, 16, 126
congressional members organizations,
    357–358
Congressional Quarterly (CQ), 256–258
Congressional Quarterly Weekly Report, 256
Congressional Record, 245–246
Congressional Research Service (CRS),
    104–105
conservative coalition, 262–263
constituent services caseworker, 111
constituent services representative, 111
Consumers' Union, 108
Continental Congress, 32–33
continuing resolutions (CRs), 297
Contract with America, 134, 139
Controlled Substances Act, 315–316
Cooper, Christopher, 94
corruption, 355–356
Corzine, Jon, 61
Council of Economic Advisors, 289
Council on Competitiveness, 290, 300–301
court packing, 325

courts
    Article 1 courts, 323–324
    congressional resources/strategies,
        323–326
        amending Constitution, 332–333
        Congress/impeachment of judges, 331
        legislative responses to courts, 331–332
        structure of federal judiciary, 323–325
    court packing, 325
    courts as umpires, 309–319
        canons of statutory construction, 318
        conclusions, 333
        congressional powers cases, 314–319
            commerce clause, 314–316
            power to investigate, 316–317
            regulating campaign spending,
                317–319
        legislative histories, 318–319
        overview of, 309–310
        rule of lenity, 318
        separation-of-powers cases, 310–313
        statutory interpretation, 317–319
    district, 326–327
    federal district, 328
    introduction, 307–309
    judges as policy makers, 319–323
    provisions proved unconstitutional, 310*f*
    Senate/judicial nominations, 325–326
        lower court nominations, 325–326
        senatorial courtesy and, 328
        Supreme Court nominations, 328–331
    swing justice, 307
Cox, Gary, 72–73
C-SPAN, 240
Culberson, John, 108
Cunningham, Dick, 3
Cunningham, Randall "Duke", 355
customs courts, 323–324
cycle of decreasing influence, 290

Dahl, Robert, 6
D'Amato, Alfonse, 222–223
Davidson, Roger, 202
Dayton, Mark, 61
"D" Committee, 188
Dear Colleague letters, 114
debt ceiling bills, 378–382
defense policy, 285–289, 293–294
defense spending, 117–118, 365, 374
deferral, spending, 369
deficits, budget, 22–23, 158, 182, 234,
    363–364, 364*f*, 374–377
DeGette, Diana, 261

DeLay, Tom, 3, 65, 73–74, 141, 250
Delay-Abramoff scandal, 344–346
democracy
    adversarial, 31
    unitary, 31
Democratic Congressional Campaign
        Committee, 130t, 131t
Democratic Senatorial Campaign
        Committee, 130t, 131t
Democratic Study Group (DSG), 126, 357
Democrats, percent of House/Senate seats
        held by, 18f
Department of Defense, 118, 246, 293–294
Department of Homeland Security, 298
desegregation
    of military, 270
    racial, 320
Dicks, Norm, 93
Dingell, John, 196, 210, 297
Director of National Intelligence, 286
Dirksen, Everett, 133
discharge, of legislation, 177–178, 199,
        217–218
Discharge Calendar, 177
discharge petition, 177–178
district courts, 326–327
districting, 13
divided-government debate, 83–85
    Mayhew thesis on, 83
    other evidence on, 83–85
division vote. See standing/division vote
Dodd, Lawrence, 12
Dole, Bob, 380
Dole, Elizabeth, 55
Domenici, Pete, 115–116
Dreier, David, 195
Durenburger, David, 3

earmarks, 91, 296
education, for child with disabilities, 322
elastic clause, 35
elections, 2008, 53
elections/policy alignments, congressional
    average spending by winning challenger,
        76f
    candidates, 67–69
    conclusions, 85
    divided-government debate, 83–85
        Mayhew thesis on, 83
        other evidence on, 83–85
        rates of success on roll-call votes, 84t
    election spending, 1974-2008, 76f
    federal law

        concerning apportionment, 57
        concerning campaign finance, 57, 60t,
            61–62
        election reform, 65–66
    House/Senate rules/office
            accounts/staff/frank, 66–67
    ideological outlook, 81, 81f, 83
    incumbency advantage, 69–77
        biased campaign funding, 73–74
        candidate quality, 74–76
        contact with voters, 76–77
        expanded constituency service, 71
        expanded perquisites of office, 70–71
        party identification decline, 70
        percentage of major party vote, 69f
        redistricting, 62, 72–73
    introduction to, 53–55
    national patterns in congressional
            elections, 77–81
        congressional elections/policy
            alignments, 80–81
        midterm elections, 79–80
        presidential election years/coattail effect,
            78–79
    replacing candidates on ballot, state law
            on, 56
    rules governing elections, 55
        chamber size, 57
        eligibility, 55
        voting rights, 55–56
    state law
        primaries, 64
        redistricting, 62–65
    swing ratio, 72
elective despotism, 33
electoral college, 40
electronic voting, 249–253
Eleventh Amendment, 333
email, 108, 348–349
Emergency Economic Stabilization Act of
        2008, 112
Emmanuel, Rahm, 73
Employment Act of 1946
engrossed bill, 232
enrolled bill, 232
Ensign, John, 113t
entitlement spending, 365–366, 373–374,
        377–378
Environmental Protection Agency (EPA),
        294–295, 300
Evans, Randy, 340
executive agencies
    appointments to, 282

authority of, 268
classified information and, 302–303
impoundment of funds and, 310–311
lobbyists and, 358–360
oversight of, 20
reports, 302
structure of, 295–296
sunset provisions and influence on,
    232–233
veto power and, 304
executive-legislative relations
agenda setting by president, 270
annual budget message, 269
annual economic message, 269–270
approval ratings of presidents, 275–276
conclusions, 304–305
congressional resources/strategies
    agency design/structure, 294–296
    appropriations, 296
    committee reports, 296
    legislative veto, 303–304
    oversight, 299–303
    overview of, 291–292
    packaging legislation, 297–298
    periodic authorizations, 292–294
    presidential nominations, 298–299
executive orders, 270–271
legislative resources of president, 268–276
    agenda setting, 269–271
    expertise and information, 291
    formal powers, 291
    formal role, 268–269
    informal role, 274–276
    national party organizations, 291
    partison bonds, 274–275, 291
    patronage and projects, 291
    veto power, 271–274
    visibility and public approval, 291
    White House staff, 291
overview of, 267–268
personal aspirations, 276
presidential strategies
    agenda setting, 276–277
    executive branch agency control,
        281–285
    foreign/defense policy, 285–289
    inside strategies, 278
    mixed strategies, 277–280
    outside strategies, 279–280
    overview of, 276
    veto, 273t, 280–281
    veto process, 37, 281
public expectations, 275–276

public policy commitments of president,
    275
resources for president, 289–291
State of the Union Address, 269
treaty making powers, 271
waning support of president, 290
war powers, 287–288
executive orders, 270
executive privilege, 313
expenditures, federal
categories of, 365–366, 366f
as percentage of GDP, 365, 365f

factionalism, in congressional parties, 126
fairness doctrine, 297
Family and Medical Leave Act, 319
Fannie Mae/Freddie Mac takeover, 347
fast-track procedures, 234
FEC v. Colorado Republican Federal
    Campaign Committee, 59–61
Federal Bureau of Investigation (FBI), 326,
    330–331
federal district courts, 328
Federal Election Campaign Act (FECA),
    57–59
Federal Election Commission (FEC), 57–58
Federal Regulation of Lobbying Act,
    353–354
Feinstein, Dianne, 293, 331
Fenno, Ricard F. Jr., 17–18, 90–91, 105–106,
    115–116
Fifth Amendment, 316
filibuster, 45, 224
    reverse filibuster, 326, 327
Financial Services Committee, 242
fire-alarm oversight, 300
firearm control, 92, 315
First Amendment, 59–61, 317, 319,
    331–332, 335
First Congress, 32
fiscal policy, 234
fiscal year, 367
Fitzgerald, Peter, 61
five 501(c)3 groups, 61
five 527 groups, 61
flag burning, 331–332
floating voters, 70
floor scheduling, 219–223
    in House, 219–220
    in Senate, 221–222
floor/voting
    conclusions, 264–265
    Congress, differences in

floor/voting (*cont.*)
    H.R. 1227, 242–244
    ideological alignments in Senate, 262*f*
    institutional context, 264
    issue agenda differences, 263
    overview, 237–238
    party votes, as percent of all votes, 257*f*
    policy preference alignment, 263–264
    possible decision-making patterns, 238*t*
    roll call votes, 1947–2008, 252*f*
    scripted language of, 244, 320
    social rules restrictiveness, 1983–2008,
        252*f*
    televised floor sessions, 153, 240, 243
    typical day on House/Senate floors
        House, 239
        House–Senate differences, 247–248
        overview of, 238–239
        Senate, 246–247
    votes, analyzing
        common voting measures, 256–258
        dimensions/alignments/coalitions,
            260–263
        interest group ratings reports, 258–260
        overview, 254–255
        roll-call votes, problems interpreting,
            255–256
    voting procedure
        changes in floor decision making,
            251–254
        in House, 249–250
        overview of, 248
        in Senate, 250–251
focus groups, on public opinion, 6
Foley, Mark, 4
Foley, Thomas, 139
Ford, Gerald, 274
foreign affairs, appropriations for, 39,
    296
foreign policy
    president and, 285–286, 289
    treaties, 39
Fortas, Abe, 331
Fourteenth Amendment, 56, 333
Frank, Barney, 91
franking privilege, 66–67, 77,
    102–103
    incumbents and, 66–67, 77
free speech, 59–61, 317
Frisa, Dan, 92
Frist, Bill, 121, 226
Frontline, 74
full-service lobbying firms, 349–350

Gephardt, Dick, 125, 196
germaneness rule, 177–178
gerrymandering, 63
Gingrich, Newt
    brings charges against Wright, 140
    budget policy and, 378–380, 382
    committee reform and, 196
    Contract with America, 134, 139
    media visibility of, 153–154
    resignation as Speaker of the House, 125,
        136, 140
    scandal concerning, 3
    as Speaker of the House, 23
going nuclear, 226
going public, 279
Gonzales v. Raich, 315–316
Gore, Albert, 377
Gorman, Arthur P., 45–46
Gormley, William, 321–322
governing *vs.* campaigning, 7–8
Government Accountability Office (GAO),
    105, 301–302
Gramm, Phil, 369–371
Gramm-Rudman-Hollings Act, 311–312,
    369–371, 373, 381
Grant, Ulysses S., 325
grassroots lobbying, 346–350
    vs. Astroturf lobbying, 350
Gregg, Judd, 112, 179
Griswold, Roger, 26*f*
gross domestic product (GDP), 365, 374
gun control, 92, 315

Habeas Corpus Act, 324
Hagel, Chuck, 347
Hamilton, Alexander, 43
hard look doctrine, 322
hard money, 59
Hastert, Dennis, 23, 121, 125, 136, 140–141,
    196
Hastings, Richard, 250
Hatch, Orrin, 179, 326
Hatfield, Mark, 195
Hays, Wayne, 103
Health Care Coalition, 350
health care spending, 374, 375*f*
health savings accounts (HSAs), 351
hearings committee, 216
Heclo, Hugh, 359–360
Help America Vote Act (HAVA), 65–66
Hill, Anita, 330
Hill & Knowlton Public Affairs, 349
Hispanic Caucus, 16, 126

Hojnacki, Marie, 349
hold, in Senate, 146–147, 227
Hollings, Ernest, 369–371
Honest Leadership and Open Government
    Act of 2007, 340, 349, 356
Hoover, Herbert, 303
House Administration Committee, 190, 192,
    196
House Agriculture Committee, 192
House Appropriations Committee, 190–192,
    194
House Armed Services Committee, 192
House Budget Committee, 192, 367
House Commerce Committee, 190–191
House Committee on Oversight and
    Government Reform, 180
House Democratic Caucus, 16–17
House Democratic Steering Committee, 49,
    196–197
House Energy and Commerce Committee,
    319
House Finance Committee, 378
House Government Reform Committee, 201
House of Representatives
    leadership in early, 44
    overdrawn disbursements, 3
    percent of seats held by Democrats, 18f
    redistricting and, 62–64
    tax bill origination in, 22–23, 37
    term length. 40. (See also Congress, U.S.)
House Oversight Committee, 196
House party leaders
    floor leader, 141–142
    Speaker (see Speaker of the House)
    whips/whip organizations, 142–144
House Republican Steering Committee, 192
House Rule 10, 176
House Rule 11, 200
House Speaker. See Speaker of the House
House Steering and Policy Committee, 154,
    197
House Un-American Activities Committee,
    316
House Ways and Means Committee,
    190–192, 194, 375
Hull, Blair, 61
hybrid rule-making, 321

ideological alignment
    congressional elections and, 81, 81f,
        83
    president and, 82
    in Senate floor/voting, 262f

Immigration and Naturalization Service v.
    Chadha, 303, 311
impoundment, 310–311, 369
incumbents, advantages of, 5, 69–77
    biased campaign funding, 73–74
    candidate quality, 74–76
    coattail effect, 79
    expanded constituency service, 71
    expanded perquisites of office, 70–71
    franking privilege, 66–67, 77
    party identification decline, 70
    redistricting, 62, 72–73
    reelection, 67–69, 69f
    spending ratios, 74
    voter contact, 76–77
Indian Affairs Committee, 188
information technology
    Congress use of, 6–8
    Internet, 107–108, 348–349
instrumental behavior, 89
intelligence oversight, 19–20, 302–303
interest groups. See lobbyists/interest groups
Internet, 107–108, 348–349
Iran-Contra affair, 289, 301, 329
Iraq War (2003), 287–288
iron triangle. See subgovernment perspective,
        on policy making
issue ads, 59–61
issue advocacy
    by independent group, 59
    TV ad restrictions, 317
issue network, 359–360

Jackson, Andrew, 325
Jefferson, Thomas, 33, 43
Jefferson, William, 4, 355
Jeffords, James, 135
Jindal, Bobby, 243–244
Johnson, Andrew, 325
Johnson, Lyndon B., 133, 144–145, 329,
        366
Johnson rule, 188
Joint Committee on Printing, 167–169
Joint Committee on Taxation, 167
Joint Committee on the Library, 169
joint committees, 167–169
Joint Economic Committee, 167
joint resolutions, 214
judges, federal
    impeachment of, 323, 331
    nomination/appointment of
    as policy makers, 319–323
    protections for, 41–42

judges, federal (*cont.*)
  statutory interpretation by, 41. *See also*
    courts
judicial activism, 308, 320, 330
judicial review, 41–42, 309, 316, 321
Judiciary Act of 1801, 324
Judiciary branch. *See* courts; judges, federal;
  Supreme Court

Katz, Jonathan, 72–73
"Keating Five" affair, 3
Kennedy, Edward, 274
Kern, John, 46
Kernell, Samuel, 279
Kerrey, Bob, 377
Kilbourn v. Thompson, 316
Kim, Jay, 3
Kimball, David, 349
King, Peter, 278
King Caucus, 129
Kingdon, John, 112–114
king-of-the-hill rules, 222
Klobuchar, Amy, 171
K Street Project, 352–353
Kuwait, 287

Larson, John, 187
lawmaking. *See* representation/lawmaking
leaders, party. *See* Party leaders
Lebanon, 287
legislative activism, 320
legislative assistant (LA), 111
legislative correspondent (LC), 111
legislative counsel, 111
legislative director (LD), 111
legislative histories, 318–319
Legislative Reorganization Act of 1946,
  49–50, 180–181, 203–204, 353–354
Legislative Reorganization Act of 1970,
  50–51, 180, 204, 302
legislative service organization (LSO), 358
legislative veto, 311
less autonomous committees, 24
Library of Congress, 169
Lieberman, Joseph, 151–152
Light, Paul, 276
Lincoln, Abraham, 325
line-item veto, 297–298, 312
Lipinski, Daniel, 94
Livingston, Bob, 136
Lobbying Disclosure Act (LDA) of 1995,
  343, 354–355
lobbyists/interest groups

Astroturf lobbying, 350
conclusions, 361
disclosure and, 349
examples of interest groups, 336
examples of lobbyists, 336
expansion of, 336–339
  overview of citizens groups, 337
  overview of interest groups
  overview of lobbyists, 337–339
family members as lobbyist, 340–341
free riders, 337
full-service lobbying firms, 349–350
gifts to members and staff, 355–357
health/medical research caucuses,
  108
increase in activity, 360
influence of, 114, 358–361
interest group strategy development,
  339–341
  coalitions, 350–351
  inside lobbying, 341–343
  outside lobbying, 346–350
  percent using lobbying technique, 346*t*
introduction to, 335
legislative leverage with interest groups,
  352–353
legislative service organizations, 358
limits on lobbying after leaving Capitol
  Hill, 343–345
meaning of *lobbyist,* 337
media relations, 349
members' groups, 357–358
proliferation/diversity of, 8–9, 337–339
public opinion on, 335
ratings of interest groups, 258–260
regulating lobbying, 353–357
revolving door and, 343
scandals, 355–356
strategy choice, 351–353
technology use by, 10, 341, 348–349
logroll, 170–171
long votes, 250
Lott, Trent, 125
Lyon, Matthew, 26*f*

Madison, James, 29–31, 43, 324–325
Mahoney, Tim, 4
Main Street Partnership, 126
Malbin, Michael, 110
Marbury v. Madison, 41, 309
Margolies-Mezvinsky, Marjorie, 376–377
markup on legislation, 216
Marshall, Thurgood, 329

Mayhew, David, 54, 83, 115
Mayhew thesis, 83
McCaffrey, Jeff, 261
McCain, John, 59
McCarthy, Carolyn, 92
McConnell, Mitch, 113*t*
McConnell v. FEC, 59, 317
McGrain v. Daugherty, 316
media
 managing relations with, 133–135
 party leaders and, 153–154
 television, 134–135. *See also* Internet
Media Fund, 61
media relations, and lobbyists/interest
   groups, 349
Medicaid, 373–374, 378
medical savings account, 351
Medicare, 352, 373–374, 378–379
medicinal marijuana, 315–316
Meese, Edwin, 301
members of Congress, 98
 assumptions about, 87
 casework, 71
 choosing strategies, 111–119
  coalition leadership, 115–119
  roll-call voting on floor, 111, 113*t*, 114
 conclusions, 119
 cost of reelection, 8
 goals of, 89–97
  good public policy, 92
  higher office, 94, 95*t*, 96
  legislating, 96
  multiple goals, 96–97
  political influence, 93
  reelection, 89–92
  serving constituents, 93–94
 individualism of, 158
 influences on, 104–105
  constituencies, 104–105
  interest groups/lobbyists, 107–109
  party leaders, 109
  president, 109–110
  staff, 111
 Internet use by, 108
 member resources, 97–103
  allocation of, 88
  congressional mail, 102–103
  party organizations/support agencies,
    71, 105, 186
  personal office/staff allowances, 97, 99*t*,
    101
  travel/recess, 101–102
 nasty constituent letters, 103–104

perceived constituencies, 106–107
protection from personal intimidation, 35
setting personal priorities, 88
Menendez, Robert, 17, 261
Michel, Robert, 209
midterm elections
 party of president, 79–80
 2006, 53
 voter turnout, 79
Miers, Harriet, 308
military affairs appropriations, 296
military courts, 323–324
Miller, George, 196
Millionaires' Amendment, 61–62
minorities, in Congress, *t* 14, 15*t*, 17, 30,
    92
Mitchell, George, 157
modified closed rules, 222
modified open rules, 222
Mondale, Walter F., 290
Monroe, James, 324–325
mortgage company bailout, 347
Moseley-Braun, Carol, 15, 331
MoveOn.org, 61
Moynihan, Patrick, 223
Murkowsli, Frank, 56
Murkowsli, Lisa, 56
Murphy, Bill, 348
Murray, Patty, 16

Natcher, William, 250
National Center for Public Policy Research,
    344
National Republican Congressional
    Committee, 130*t*, 131*t*
National Republican Senatorial Campaign,
    130*t*, 131*t*
national security
 classified information oversight, 302–303
 Patriot Act, 293
 policy, 19–20
 terrorist attacks and, 1, 5, 36–37, 288
 war powers, 287–288, 322–323
National Security Act (1947), 286
National Security Council (NSC), 286, 301
Nebraska, unicameral legislature in, 34
Nelson, Ben, 261
new breed of lawmaker, 158
New Deal, 49, 325
New Democratic Coalition, 126
New Partnership for America's Future, 134
Ney, Bob, 4, 355–356
Nicaraguan Contras. *See* Iran-Contra affair

Nineteenth Amendment, 56
Nixon, Richard, 310–311, 329, 366–367, 369

Obama, Barack, 16, 22–23
  budget issues, 23
  resigns Senate seat, 56
O'Connor, Sandra D., 307
Office of Homeland Security, 270
Office of Information and Regulatory Affairs
    (OIRA), 283–285, 298
Office of Management and Budget (OMB),
    282–285, 289, 300–301, 381
Office of Technology Assessment (OTA), 105
Oleszek, Walter, 202
omnibus appropriation bills, 156, 297,
    383–384
Omnibus Budget Reconciliation Act, 1993,
    381
O'Neill, Tip, 139, 149, 160, 287–288
opposition research, 8
Oregon v. Smith, 323
Organization, Study, and Review Committee,
    130t, 131t
Ornstein, Norman, 4–5
outside lobbying, 346–350
oversight
  classified information, 302–303
  congressional, 299–300, 303
  regulatory, 283–285, 298

packaging, of legislation, 297–298
Packwood, Robert, 3
PAC. See political action committee
parties
  caucus vs. conference, 129
  conclusions, 130t, 163
  Constitution and, 43
  coordination among House/Senate, 154
  in House and Senate, 1937–2008, 182f
  identification with party, 127
  intra-party factionalism, 126
  nature of
    common electoral interests, 123
    most common coalitions, 127–129
    overview, 122–123
    party identification, 129–130
    party organizations, 129
    shared policy preferences, 124–127
    stable but loose coalitions, 128–129
  number of Democrats/Republicans in
      House, 1955-2009, 148f
  number of Democrats/Republicans in
      Senate, 1955-2009, 146, 148f

party caucuses, 129
party committees, 111th Congress, 130t,
    131t
party organizations, 129, 143–144
percent of all votes as party votes,
    1954-2008, 124f
polarization of, 160
reinvigorated parties, 155–159
  demands of members, 157–158
  extension of rules for formal powers of
      Speaker, 160–161
  issues to encourage, 156–157
  overview of, 155
  policy alignments, 158–160
reinvigorated parties, adaptation
    strategies, 161–163
  expanded services, 161
  inclusion strategy, 161–162
  procedural strategies, 162
  public relations, 162–163
switching parties, 135, 150. See also party
    leaders
party leaders
  electoral trouble for, 125
  of House, 137–143
    House floor leader, 141–142
    House whips/whip organizations,
        142–144
    majority leader, 141–142
    minority leader, 141–142
    Speaker of the House (see Speaker of the
        House)
  leadership in other era, 159–160
  major responsibilities of, 132–137
    building coalitions on legislation, 132
    campaigning, 135
    enhancing public reputation of party,
        133–135
    managing floor, 132–133
    managing party and chamber, 136
    serving as intermediary with president,
        133
  overview of, 121–122, 131–132
  resources for, 147–155
    formal rules, 147–150
    information, 152–153
    leadership staffs, 154–155
    media access, 153–154
    party strength, 147, 148f
    tangible rewards, 151
  selection of leaders, 136–137
  of Senate, 144–147
    majority leader, 144–145, 148–149

minority leader, 145, 148–149
  Senate floor leaders, 144–146
  Senate whips/whip organization, 146
seniority system, 194–196
term limits, 138, 145
top leaders, January 2008, 131*t*
Patriot Act, 293
PAYGO, 381
Pell Act, 213
Pelosi, Nancy, 16, 23, 113*t*, 134, 261
  committees and, 175, 187, 196
  election to Speaker of the House, 136
  increase in contributions to, 345
Permanent Select Committee on
    Intelligence, 142, 145
Perot, Ross, 354
Persian Gulf War, 287
plebiscitary politics, 6–7
plurality voting, 64
pocket veto, 37, 39, 274
points of order, 200, 220–221, 242
police patrol oversight, 300
policy. *See* budget policy; elections/policy
    alignments, congressional
Policy Committee, 130*t*, 131*t*, 155
political action committee (PAC), 8, 58, 73
politico, Congress member as, 28
poll tax, 56
Poole, Keith, 261
pork barrel, 91–92
power of the purse,
powers, of Congress, 34–35
  campaign spending regulation, 317–319
  commerce clause, 314
  constraints on, 38–42
    direct/indirect representation, 40–41
    explicit restrictions, 38
    judicial review/statuary interpretation,
        41–42
    separate institutions sharing power,
        38–40
  franking privilege, 66–67, 77, 102–103
  power to investigate, 316–317
  war powers, 287–288
president
  agenda setting, 269–271, 276–277
  term length, 40. *See also*
      executive-legislative relations)
Presidential Committee on Equal
    Employment Opportunity, 270
president *pro tempore*, 131, 145
Price, David, 12, 90
procurement reform, 117–118

pro forma sessions, in Senate, 299
Progressive Caucus, 126
prompt letter, 284
provisional ballots, 66
proxy voting, 200
Public Interest Declassification Board
    (PIDB), 303
public laws enacted, numbers, 1947-2006,
    11*f*
public opinion, 332
  on lobbyists/interest groups, 335
public opinion polls, 6
public relations, 133–135

Quayle, Dan, 96, 117–118, 284, 290
queen-of-the-hill rules, 222
quorum, 36–37, 247–248
  rolling, 200

racial desegregation, 320
racial gerrymandering, 63
radio
  communicating with constituents via, 6–7
  congressional facilities, 71
  coverage of political scandals, 4–5
Ramseyer rule, 216–217
Randolph, Jennings, 159
Rayburn, Sam, 159–160
Reagan, Ronald
  budget policy under, 369–372, 374
  control over executive agencies, 289–290
  control over regulatory process, 283–284
  Iran-Contra affair and, 301
  judicial appointments, 326, 329–330
  OMB under, 282–284
  priority setting by, 277
  tax increase under, 369
  use of veto by, 272, 274
  war powers and, 287–288
reapportionment. *See* apportionment
recess appointment, 299
recissions, 369
Reconciliation Bill, 381
Reconstruction law, 324
recorded vote. *See* voice vote
redistricting
  as incumbent advantage, 62, 72–73
  state law, 62–65
Reed, Thomas B., 45
reelection
  costs of campaigns, 8
  as goal, 89–92
  incumbents and, 67–69

Rehnquist, William, 307, 326
Reid, Harry, 113*t*, 121, 143, 261
Religious Freedom and Restoration Act, 310,
    319
Reno, Janet, 298
reports
    committee, 296, 320
    conference, 228
    executive agency, 302
representation/lawmaking
    committees, 27, 46–51
        early foundations, 46–48
        modern system, 49–51
        party control, 48–49
    conclusions, 51
    congressional development, 42
    constitutional rules on, 27, 34–35
        congressional power constraints, 38–42
            direct/indirect representation, 40–41
            explicit restrictions, 38
            judicial review/statuary interpretation,
                41–42
            separate institutions sharing power,
                38–40
        congressional powers, 34–35
        legislative procedures, 35–37
        making of public law, 34
        presidential approval/disapproval of
            legislation, 39
    introduction to, 27–28
    lawmaking, 31–32
        adversarial democracy model, 31
        tradeoffs of, 31–32
        unitary democracy (deliberative), 31
    parties, 43–46
        early foundations of, 43–44
        party government, 44–45
        twentieth-century pattern, 45–46
    predecessors of Congress, 32–34
    representation, 28–31
        collective *vs.* dyadic, 29, 29*t*, 30
        by Congress, 28–29
        by individual lawmaker, 28
        party/group, 30
        tradeoffs of, 30–31
    republican government, 31
Republican Study Committee, 126
resolutions
    concurrent, 214
    continuing, 297
    joint, 214
    numbers introduced, 215
restrictive rules, 222

return letters, 284
reverse filibuster, 326, 327
revolving door, 343
Riddick, Floyd, 157
Roberts, John, 307
Roe v. Wade, 332–333
Rogers, Cathy McMorris, 16
roll-call votes
    nine 1947–2008, 252*f*
    party-line, 131–132
    problems interpreting, 255–256
    rates of success, 84*t*
    in Senate, 227–228, 248, 251
rolling quorum, 200
ROMP (Retain Our Majority Program),
    73–74
Roosevelt, Franklin D., 325
Rostenkowski, Dan, 3
Rudman, Warren, 369–371
rule of lenity, 318
rules, legislative
    authorization/appropriation bills, 231–233
    bill referral rules in House
    cloture, 148–149, 224, 227, 231
    committee, circumventing, 217–219
        in House, 217–218
        in Senate, 218–219
        unorthodox legislation, 218
    committee action, 215–217
        full committee chair role, 183, 193–194
        hearings, 216
        "markup," 216
        reports, 216–217
    committee referral, 214–215
    comparison between chambers, 228–229,
        230*t*, 231
    complex nature of, 43
    conclusions, 235
    conference rules,
    discharge petition, 217–218
    evolution of legislative progress, 233–235
    filibuster, Senate, 45, 224, 326, 327
    floor consideration, 223–224
        in House, 224–225
        in Senate, 225–228
    floor scheduling, 219–223
        in House, 219–220
        in Senate, 221–222
    House/Senate rules, 210–211
    introduction, 207–208
    introduction of legislation, 213
    naming of legislation, 213
    in perspective, 208–210

procedural rules, 211
reestablishing House rules, 211
resolving differences between chambers,
214, 228
special rules
of House, 222
king-of-the-hill rules, 222
queen-of-the-hill rules, 222
restrictive rules, 222
time-limit rules, 222
standard legislative process, 211, 212f, 213
sunshine rules, 183–184, 232–233, 293
suspension of, 217, 219, 244
type of legislation, 214
bills, 214
concurrent resolutions, 214
joint resolutions, 214
Rules Committee, House, 49, 137, 150, 160,
177, 190–192
running against Congress tactic, 5

Safire, William, 224
Salisbury, Robert, 360
Sanders, Bernard, 168t
scandals, 2–5
Delay-Abramoff scandal, 344–346
Gingrich and, 3
media coverage of, 4–5, 354
Schlozman, Kay L., 360
Schumer, Charles, 73, 113t, 121, 143, 261
scoring the vote in the special rule, 258–259
Select Committee on Ethics, 169
Select Committee on Voting Irregularities,
250
select/special committee, 169
self-financed candidate, 61–62
Senate
Committee on Committees, 44, 49, 130t,
131t
confirmation of presidential appointees,
299
congressional powers of, 35
courts and, 188
lower court nominations, 308, 325–326
senatorial courtesy and, 328
Supreme Court nominations, 307–308
direct election of Senators, 40–41, 56
leadership changes in 20th century, 46
leadership in early, 44–45
percent of seats held by Democrats, 18f
pro forma sessions, 299
replacing deceased member, 36
term length, 40

whips/whip organization, 146
Senate Budget Committee, 201, 367
Senate Centrist Coalition, 126
Senate Committee on Homeland Security
and Governmental Affairs, 180
Senate Committee on Indian Affairs, 188
Senate Democratic Communication Center,
163
Senate Finance Committee, 375, 378
Senate Health, Education, Labor, and
Pension Committee (HELP), 308
Senate Intelligence Committee, 201
Senate Joint Committee on Taxation, 188
Senate Judiciary Committee, 326, 328, 330
Senate Rules and Administration, 201
Senate Rule XIV, 218–219, 222
Senate Rule XXII, 231
Senate Select Committee on Ethics, 169, 188
Senate Small Business and Entrepreneurship
Committee, 201
Senate Special Committee on Aging, 169
Senate Veterans' Affairs Committee, 201
senatorial courtesy, 328
Senators' Official Personnel and Office
Expense Account (SOPOEA), 98
seniority system, in congressional
committees, 194–196
Seniors Coalition, 350
separation-of-powers cases, 310–313
September 11th attacks on U.S., 1, 5, 36–37,
288
sequestration, 381, 383
categorical, 373
nine 1985 and 1987, 369–372
Seventeenth Amendment, 40–41, 56
sexual harassment, 3–4
Seymour, Patrick, 223
Shalala, Donna, 377
Sierra Club, 108
signing statements, 283, 320
single-issue caucus, 357
Six for '06, 134
Sixteenth Amendment, 333
Smith, Nick, 3
soft money, 58–59, 61, 317
Somalia, 287
South, party polarization in, 160
Speaker of the House, 137–141
activist, 48–49, 139–140
appointment power of, 150
election of, 136
first woman, 141
media visibility of, 153–154

Speaker of the House (*cont.*)
  new powers of, 160–161
  powers of, 44–45, 137–139, 147
  procedural power of, 160, 162
  reduced power of, 45–46
  referral powers of, 149, 160–161
  term limits, 140–141
Speaker *pro tempore*, 36, 239
special appropriations, 214
Special Committee on Aging, 169
special rules, legislative
  king-of-the-hill, 222
  queen-of-the-hill, 222
  restrictive, 222
  time-limit, 222
Spector, Arlen, 195, 330
spending ceilings, 367, 371–374
Stabenow, Debbie, 16
staffs
  committee, 203–205
    House, 204
    Republican cuts, 204–205
    Senate, 204
  funding, 130, 289
  gifts to, 355–357
  influences on members, 111
  party leader, 154–155
  staff allowances, 97, 99*t*, 101
  types of congressional, 111
  White House, 291
Standards of Official Conduct Committees, 201
standing committees. *See* committees, standing
standing/division vote
  in House, 249
  in Senate, 227–228
state legislatures, power of, 33
State of the Union Address, 269
statutory interpretation, 41
steering committees, 130*t*, 131*t*
  early, 44
  House Democratic, 49
  House Republican, 126, 192
  House Steering and Policy Committee, 154, 197
  subcommittee choice, 171
Stem Cell Research Enhancement Act, 261
Stevens, Ted, 4
strategy of inclusion, 143, 161–162
structural politics, 294–295
Stupack, Bart, 175
subcommittees

appropriation bills, 232–233
  choice of, 171
  House, 201
    chair selection, 197
    checking power of, 202–203
    overview, 201
  Senate, 201–202
    chair selection, 197–198
    checking power of, 203
subgovernment perspective, on policy making, 358–360
subpoenas, 180
Sumner, Charles, 26*f*
sunset rules, 183–184, 232–233, 293
support agencies, 71, 105, 186
Supreme Court
  constitutional powers of, 309
  efforts to alter size of, 324–325
  nominations to, 307–308. *See also* specific decisions
swing justice, 307
swing ratio, 72
switching parties, 135, 150

tabling motion, 178–179
task force
  early, 44
  increased numbers of, 161–162
  influence of, 162
  as information source, 152–153
  leader use of, 142–144, 151–152, 155, 234
  media, 135, 154
  on procurement, 117
  public relations, 8
  role in legislation, 155, 177, 183, 200
tax
  income, 333
  poll, 56
  tax committees, 232
  tax cuts, 22–23, 363, 369
  tax increases, 363, 368–369
tax bills
  origination in House, 22–23
  sunset provisions on, 293
tax courts, 323–324
tax evasion, 3–4
technology
  Congress use of, 6–8
  lobbyist/interest group use of, 10, 341, 348–349. *See also* radio; television
televised floor sessions, 153, 240, 243
television

congressional facilities, 71, 103–104, 130, 161
constituent communication via, 6–7
importance for political communication, 134–135
lobbyist use of, 10, 349
president use of, 279–280
scandal coverage, 4–5, 354
teller voting, 251–252
tempered decentralization, 20–22
tempered individualism, 21–22
term limits
  committee chairs, 194–195
  Congress members, 5
  party leaders, 138, 145
  Speaker of the House, 140–141
terrorism, war against, 20, 22–23, 313, 363
terrorist attacks on U.S., and Congress, 1, 5, 36–37, 288
Texas, redistricting in, 65
think tanks, 104
THOMAS, 255
Thomas, Clarence, 325, 329–331
Thorton, Ray, 377
Thurmond, Strom, 125
Tierney, John T., 360
time-limit rules, 222
Title III, 233
Tower, John, 298
tradeoffs
  of lawmaking, 31–32
  of representation, 30–31
Traficant, James A. Jr., 3
travel allowance, 71, 101
trust, constituent, 90–91
trustee, Congress member as, 28
Tuesday Group, 126
Tuesday-Thursday club, 102
Twenty-fourth Amendment, 56
Twenty-sixth Amendment, 56, 333
two presidencies thesis, 285

uncertainty principle, 19
unemployment benefits, 163, 323
unicameral legislature, 34
unitary democracy, 31
United States v. Curtiss-Wright Export Corp., 286
United States v. Harriss, 354
United States v. Lopez, 315
U.S. Chamber of Commerce, 349
U.S. v. Morrison, 315

veto
  legislative, 303–304, 311
  line-item, 297–298, 312
  overriding presidential, 34
  pocket, 37, 39, 274
  presidential, 273t, 280–281
veto process, 37, 281
veto statement, 320
vice president, as president of Senate, 229
Vieth v. Jubelirer, 63
Vietnam War, 287, 366
Violence Against Women Act, 310, 315, 319
voice vote
  in House, 249
  in Senate, 227–228, 250–251
voter turnout, midterm elections, 79
voting age, 56, 333
Voting Rights Act, 63, 65
voting rules/procedures. See floor/voting

Waldholtze, Enid, 3
Walker, Jack, 337, 351
war against terrorism, 20, 22–23, 313, 363
war powers, 287–288
War Powers Resolution, 287, 322–323
Warren, Earl, 317
war room, 163
Washington administration, parties under, 43
Watkins v. United States, 316
Watts, J. C., 16–17
Waxman, Henry, 196
Ways and Means Committee, 190–192, 194, 375
Webster, Daniel, 44
Wesberry v. Sanders, 65, 72
whip/whip organizations
  growth in organizations, 161–162
  House, 142–144
  as information source, 152–153
  origin of whip, 142
  Senate, 46, 146
Wildavsky, Aaron, 285
Williams, Pat, 377
Wilson, Woodrow, 46, 202
women
  in Congress, 14, 15t, 17
  violence against, 310, 315, 319
Wright, James, 3, 139–140, 156
Wright, John R., 345–346